# The Wiley-Blackwell Handbook of Mood Disorders

# The Wiley-Blackwell Handbook of Mood Disorders

## Second Edition

### Edited by Mick Power

A John Wiley & Sons, Ltd., Publication

This edition first published 2013
© 2013 John Wiley & Sons, Ltd

Wiley-Blackwell is an imprint of John Wiley & Sons, formed by the merger of Wiley's global Scientific, Technical and Medical business with Blackwell Publishing.

*Registered Office*
John Wiley & Sons Ltd, The Atrium, Southern Gate, Chichester, West Sussex, PO19 8SQ, UK

*Editorial Offices*
350 Main Street, Malden, MA 02148-5020, USA
9600 Garsington Road, Oxford, OX4 2DQ, UK
The Atrium, Southern Gate, Chichester, West Sussex, PO19 8SQ, UK

For details of our global editorial offices, for customer services, and for information about how to apply for permission to reuse the copyright material in this book please see our website at www.wiley.com/wiley-blackwell.

The right of Mick Power to be identified as the author of the editorial material in this work has been asserted in accordance with the UK Copyright, Designs and Patents Act 1988.

Wiley also publishes its books in a variety of electronic formats. Some content that appears in print may not be available in electronic books.

Designations used by companies to distinguish their products are often claimed as trademarks. All brand names and product names used in this book are trade names, service marks, trademarks or registered trademarks of their respective owners. The publisher is not associated with any product or vendor mentioned in this book. This publication is designed to provide accurate and authoritative information in regard to the subject matter covered. It is sold on the understanding that the publisher is not engaged in rendering professional services. If professional advice or other expert assistance is required, the services of a competent professional should be sought.

*Library of Congress Cataloging-in-Publication Data*

The Wiley-Blackwell handbook of mood disorders / edited by Mick Power. – Second edition.
        pages cm
    Includes bibliographical references and index.
    ISBN 978-1-119-97892-3 (cloth)
    1. Affective disorders–Handbooks, manuals, etc.    2. Depression, Mental–Handbooks, manuals, etc.    I. Power, Michael J., editor of compilation.    II. Title: Handbook of mood disorders.
    RC537.W529 2013
    616.85′27–dc23

                                                                                            2013004483

A catalogue record for this book is available from the British Library.

Cover image: © Bruno Buongiorno Nardelli / iStockphoto
Cover design by Cyan Design

Set in 10/12.5pt Galliard by Aptara Inc., New Delhi, India
Printed in Malaysia by Ho Printing (M) Sdn Bhd

1    2013

# Contents

# About the Editor

Mick Power is currently Professor of Clinical Psychology at the Universities of Edinburgh and Tromsø in Norway. For many years he has worked with the World Health Organization to develop a measure of quality of life, the WHOQOL, which is now in widespread use throughout the world. He has written academic books that focus on emotion and the emotional disorders, such as *Cognition and Emotion: From Order to Disorder* written with his colleague Tim Dalgleish for which the second edition was published in 2008. In 2012 he published a book on psychology and religion, *Adieu to God—Why Psychology Leads to Atheism*. He is a founding editor of the journal *Clinical Psychology and Psychotherapy*.

# List of Contributors

Charlotte L Allan, Oxford, UK
Paul Bebbington, London, UK
Nicole Bergen, Geneva, Switzerland
Peter J. Bieling, Toronto, Canada
Antonia Bifulco, London, UK
Douglas Blackwood, Edinburgh, UK
Guy Bodenmann, Zurich, Switzerland
Jonathan Cavanagh, Glasgow, UK
Somnath Chatterji, Geneva, Switzerland
Yulia E. Chentsova-Dutton, Washington, USA
Melanie Cochrane, Toronto, Canada
Anthony J. Cleare, London, UK
Klaus Ebmeier, Oxford, UK
David A. Grant, Toronto, Canada
Paul Gilbert, Derby, UK
Kate L. Herts, Boston, USA
Kay Jamison, Columbia, USA
Sameer Jauhar, London, UK
Sidney H. Kennedy, Toronto, Canada
Ken Laidlaw, Edinburgh, UK
Andrew K. MacLeod, London, UK
Karine Macritchie, Edinburgh, UK
John C. Markowitz, New York, USA
Katie McLaughlin, Boston, USA
Louisa C. Michl, Boston, USA
Anne Palmer, Norwich, UK
Sagar Parikh, Toronto, Canada
Dave Peck, Edinburgh, UK
Mick Power, Edinburgh, UK
Ashley Randall, Arizona, USA
Lena J. Rane, London, UK

**Andrew Ryder**, Concordia, Canada
**Matthias Schwannauer**, Edinburgh, UK
**Zindel V. Segal**, Toronto, Canada
**David Semple**, Edinburgh, UK
**Douglas Steele**, Edinburgh, UK
**Anya Topiwalla**, Oxford, UK
**Kim Wright**, Exeter, UK

# Foreword to First Edition
## *Mood Disorders: A Handbook of Science and Practice*

Moods are so essential to our navigating the world that when they go awry, it is only a matter of time until distress and disaster hit. Moods allow us to gauge people and circumstance, alert us to danger or opportunity, and provide us with the means to convey our emotional and physical states to others. If we act rashly when we ought to be prudent or hang back when we could move forward to advantage, difficulties accrue. Problems compound if, in addition to disruptions in mood, energy, sleep, and thinking also are affected. Disorders of mood which result from this combined disturbance are common, painful, and too often lethal. Fortunately, they are usually treatable.

Scientists and clinicians have learned a remarkable amount about depression and manic depression, or bipolar disorder, during the past decade. These advances in our understanding of diagnosis, pathophysiology, epidemiology, comorbidity, and treatment are lucidly presented in this excellent handbook. There is a strong emphasis upon a complex approach to mood disorders, with the authors providing important coverage of both psychological and biological perspectives on the causes and treatment of depression and mania. The thorny issues of diagnostic categories, the ever-expanding spectrum of pathological into normal affective states, and the unsettled relation of major depression to bipolar disorder, are well addressed, as are the topics of evolutionary psychology, suicide, and pharmacological and psychotherapeutic treatments.

There remain many important questions: ethical and clinical considerations which will arise after the first genes for mood disorders are located; the intriguing psychological issues raised by mania—its relation to violence and creativity, its addictive qualities, and its place in the field of positive emotions; cross-species comparisons which will be possible as a result of mapping the human and other mammalian genomes and the increased understanding of normal moods which will follow from research into more pathological ones. Neuroscientists, clinicians, psychologists, and molecular biologists make a powerful alliance. This handbook gives an outstanding overview of their accomplishments to date and a sense of the excitement to come.

*Kay Redfield Jamison, Ph.D.*
*Professor of Psychiatry*
*The Johns Hopkins School of Medicine*

# Part I
# Unipolar Depression

# 1

# The Classification and Epidemiology of Unipolar Depression

## Paul Bebbington
UCL Mental Health Sciences Unit, UK

## Introduction

In the revised version of this chapter, the original structure has largely been maintained. After all, the principles of classification and the problems it poses for the
epidemiology of depression remain the same. However, I have summarized the slow
progress toward revision of the ICD and DSM classificatory systems. In the original
chapter, I provided illustrative examples of the epidemiology of depression in terms
of age, gender, life stress, and childhood antecedents of depression. In the current
version, I have, somewhat selectively, updated the account of research in these topics,
but have changed the emphasis away from well-established issues such as the effect
of gender, and toward the epidemiology of depression in the workplace. This seems
particularly relevant in a world where inexorable economic advancement is no longer
guaranteed and retrenchment has major effects on work and workers.

## Classification and Unipolar Depression

Psychiatric classification is quintessentially a medical procedure. The study of medicine
is based on the establishment of separate categories of disorder (illnesses, diseases).[1]
These are distinguished in terms of particular types of attributes of the people held
to be suffering from them. These attributes comprise *symptoms* (based on self-report)
and *signs* (based on observation). Individual disorders are conceived in terms of con-
catenations of symptoms and signs, which are termed syndromes. Such syndromes are
provisional constructs, whose validity (or otherwise) is then established by using them
as the basis of different sorts of theory: etiological theories, and theories of course and

---

[1] The terms illness and disease in ordinary usage strongly suggest a biological basis, while disorder is more
neutral, and in psychiatry is generally preferred.

---

*The Wiley-Blackwell Handbook of Mood Disorders*, Second Edition. Edited by Mick Power.
© 2013 John Wiley & Sons, Ltd. Published 2013 by John Wiley & Sons, Ltd.

outcome, of treatment, and of pathology (Bebbington, 2011; Wing, Mann, Leff, & Nixon, 1978). There is no doubt that the medical approach to malfunction has been a very effective one, generating new knowledge quickly and efficiently by testing out theories of this type (Bebbington, 1997).

Psychiatric disorders are classified in the hope that the classification can provide mutually exclusive categories to which cases can be allocated unambiguously (the process of case identification). The medical discipline of *epidemiology* is the study of the distribution of diseases (i.e., medical classes) in the population, and is based on categories of this type. It has been a very powerful method for identifying candidate causal factors, and is thus of great interest to psychiatrists and psychologists, as well as to clinicians from other specialties.

The idea of unipolar depression involves the application of this syndromal approach to psychological disturbance, and is therefore primarily a medical concept. However, the distinctiveness of psychiatric syndromes is both variable and limited. Unipolar depression, in particular, resembles, overlaps, and needs distinguishing from other disorders characterized by mood disturbance: anxiety disorders, other depressive conditions, and bipolar mood disorder. The particular problem with bipolar disorder is that its identification depends on the presence of two sorts of episode in which the associated mood is either depressed or predominantly elated. It is distinct from unipolar disorder in a variety of ways (e.g., inheritance, course, and outcome), and the distinction is therefore almost certainly a useful one. However, depressive episodes in bipolar disorder cannot be distinguished symptomatically from those of unipolar depression. As perhaps half of all cases of bipolar disorder start with a depressive episode, this means that unipolar depression is a provisional category—the disorder will be reclassified as bipolar in 5% of cases (Ramana & Bebbington, 1995).

## Symptoms and Syndromes

The first stage in the establishment of syndromes is the conceptualization of individual symptoms. Symptoms in psychiatry are formulations of aspects of human experience that are held to indicate abnormality. Examples include abnormally depressed mood, impaired concentration, loss of sexual interest, and persistent wakefulness early in the morning. They sometimes conflate what is abnormal for the individual with what is abnormal for the population, but they can generally be defined in terms that are reliable. Signs (which are unreliable and rarely discriminating in psychiatry, and thus tend to be discounted in diagnosis) are the observable concomitants of such experiences, such as observed depressed mood, or behavior that could be interpreted as a response to hallucinations. Particular symptoms (and signs) often coexist in people who are psychologically disturbed, and this encourages the idea that they go together to form recognizable syndromes. The formulation of syndromes is the first stage in the disease approach to medical phenomena, as syndromes can be subjected to investigations that test out the various types of theories described above.

It is often said, in both medical and lay discourse, that psychiatric disorders are like (or just the same as) disorders in physical medicine. This is not strictly true. Self-reports in general medicine relate to bodily sensation and malfunction in a way that can be linked to pathological processes. Thus the classical progression of symptoms in appendicitis is related straightforwardly to the progression of inflammation from the appendix to the peritoneal lining. Symptoms in psychiatry, in contrast, are essentially based on idiosyncratic mental experiences, with meanings that relate to the social world. Reformulating psychiatric disorders in terms of a supposed biological substrate would therefore result in the conceptualization of a different condition, which would map imperfectly onto the original disorder.

While syndromes are essentially lists of qualifying symptoms and signs, individuals may be classed as having a syndrome while exhibiting only some of the constituent symptoms. Moreover, within a syndrome there may be theoretical and empirical reasons for regarding particular symptoms as having special significance. Other symptoms, however, may be relatively nonspecific, occurring in several syndromes. Even so, clusters of such symptoms may achieve a joint significance. This inequality between symptoms is seen in the syndrome of unipolar depression: depressed mood and anhedonia are usually taken as central, while other symptoms (e.g., fatigue or insomnia) have little significance on their own. This reflects a serious problem with the raw material of human mental experience: it does not lend itself to the establishment of the desired mutually exclusive and jointly exhaustive categories that underpin medical classification.

In an ideal world, all the symptoms making up a syndrome would be discriminating, but this is far from true, and decisions about whether a given subject's symptom pattern can be classed as lying within a syndrome usually show an element of arbitrariness. The result is that two individuals may both be taken to suffer from unipolar depression despite exhibiting considerable symptomatic differences.

This is tied in with the idea of symptom severity: disorders may be regarded as symptomatically severe either from the sheer number of symptoms or because several symptoms are present in severe degree. In practice, disorders with large numbers of symptoms also tend to have a greater severity of individual symptoms. In classifications that rely on relatively few symptoms to establish diagnoses of depressive conditions, the issue of severity may need to be dealt with by including other markers, particularly impairment of social engagement and activity, and disabilities in self-care.

## The Limits of Classification

As classification aspires to "carve nature at the joints," the empirical relationships between psychiatric symptoms create special difficulties of their own. In particular, symptoms are related nonreflexively: thus, some symptoms are common and others are rare, and in general they are hierarchically related, rather than being associated in a random manner. Rare symptoms often predict the presence of common symptoms, but common symptoms do not predict rare symptoms. Deeply (i.e., "pathologically") depressed mood is commonly associated with more prevalent symptoms such as tension or worry, while in most instances tension and worry are *not* associated with depressed mood (Sturt, 1981). Likewise, depressive delusions are almost invariably associated with depressed mood, whereas most people with depressed mood do not have delusions of any kind. The consequence is that the presence of the rarer, more "powerful" symptoms indicates a case with many other symptoms as well, and therefore a case that is more symptomatically severe. It is because of this set of empirical relationships between symptoms that psychiatric syndromes are themselves quite largely hierarchically arranged. Thus, schizophrenia is very often accompanied by affective symptoms, although these are not officially part of the syndrome. Likewise, psychotic depression is not distinguished from nonpsychotic depression by having a completely different set of symptoms, but by having extra, discriminating symptoms such as depressive delusions and hallucinations.

## Leaky Classes and Comorbidity

The operational criteria set up to identify and distinguish so-called common mental disorders cut across the natural hierarchies existing between symptoms. The consequence is that many people who have one of these disorders also meet the criteria for one or more of the others. This *comorbidity* has generated much interest, and was even incorporated into the titles of recent major US epidemiological surveys (the National Comorbidity Survey and its replication Kessler, McGonagle, Zhoa, et al., 1994, Kessler et al., 2003). Researchers then divide into two camps: those who think the comorbidity represents important relationships between well-validated disorders, and those who think it arises as an artifact of a classificatory system that is conceptually flawed and fails adequately to capture the nature of affective disturbance.

## Depression and the Threshold Problem

The final difficulty with the classification of depression is that it involves imposing a categorical distinction on a set of phenomena that look more like the expression of a continuum. The empirical distribution of affective symptoms in the general population is characteristic: many people have a few symptoms, while few people have many.

For some authorities, this pattern of distribution calls into question the utility of a medical classification. It certainly makes case definition and case finding contentious, as decisions have to be made about the threshold below which no disorder should be identified. People who have few symptoms may still be above this threshold if some of their symptoms are particularly discriminating, but in general the threshold is defined by the number of symptoms. There has always been a tendency in medicine to move thresholds down, particularly as many people who may be regarded by primary care physicians as meriting treatment fall below the thresholds of DSM-IV or ICD-10.

The threshold problem has encouraged a considerable literature relating to subthreshold, subclinical, minor, and brief recurrent affective disorders (Schotte & Cooper, 1999). The tendency to extend the threshold downward is apparent in the establishment of the category of *dysthymia*, a depressive condition characterized only by its mildness (i.e., a *lack* of symptoms) and its chronicity. It has, nevertheless, become a study in its own right: it has clear links with major depression presumably because it is relatively easy for someone who already has some depressive symptoms to acquire some more and thereby meet criteria for the more severe disorder.

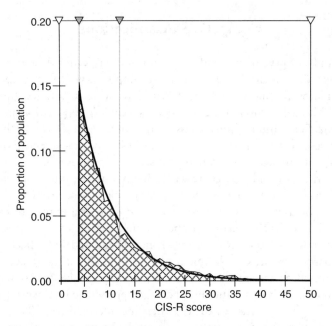

**Figure 1.1.**    Proportion of Population by Truncated Range of CIS-R Scores, and Fitted Exponential Curve. Reproduced with permission from Melzer et al. (2002)

The imposition of a threshold on an apparent continuum would be less arbitrary if it were possible to demonstrate a naturally occurring "step-change" in the distribution. Thus, while the distribution of IQ is largely continuous, Penrose (1963) noted a clear excess of subjects at the bottom of the continuum who are characterized by a distinct and identifiable pathology. Many have argued that no such distinction exists in affective symptoms (Goldberg, 2000; Tyrer, 1985). While it might be possible to create a threshold that represented a step-change in social disability (Hurry, Sturt, Bebbington, & Tennant, 1983), the evidence does, overall, suggest that affective symptoms are distributed more like blood pressure than IQ. Melzer, Tom, Brugha, Fryers, and Meltzer (2002) used symptom data from the British National Survey of Psychiatric Morbidity to test out the smoothness of the distribution. A single exponential curve provided the best fit for the whole population, but there were floor effects that produced deviations at symptom counts from zero to three. Truncation of the data to take account of this provided an excellent fit (Figure 1.1). This was not affected by selecting subgroups characterized by especially high or low prevalence for analysis.

It can be concluded from this discussion that the epidemiological literature on depressive disorder will need to be interpreted cautiously. We have disorders that are identified as classes imposed on what is empirically a continuum, and which in any event overlap each other. This is made worse because the classificatory schemes are changed at regular intervals. Moreover, two major schemes exist side-by-side. Added to this is the issue of how the symptoms of common mental disorders can be elicited, identified, and used in order to decide if together they can be said to constitute a case.

## Competing Classifications

The indistinctness of psychiatric syndromes and of the rules for deciding if individual disorders meet symptomatic criteria has major implications for attempts to operationalize psychiatric classifications. Two systems have wide acceptance: the Diagnostic and Statistical Manual (DSM) of the American Psychiatric Association and the World Health Organization's International Classification of Disease (ICD). In the early days, revision of classificatory schemata relied almost wholly on clinical reflection. However, since the classifications are set up primarily for scientific purposes, they should properly be modified in the light of empirical research that permits definitive statements about their utility. The standardized and operationalized classifications now available offer an opportunity for using research in this way, and current attempts to modify them are being based on extensive reviews of the evidence.

In the past, much of the pressure for change originated in clinical and political demands. In particular, the establishment of a diagnosis is central to accessing health care in the United States, in distinction to the more problem-based approach in Europe. Moreover, revisions sometimes had the appearance of tinkering in order to capture some imagined essence of the disorders included (Birley, 1990). What looks like fine-tuning can nevertheless make considerable differences to whether individual cases meet criteria or not, and thus disproportionately affects the putative frequency of disorders. We should only jettison classifications on grounds of inadequate scientific utility and as seldom as possible, since too rapid revision defeats the objective of comparison.

Like all such classifications, DSM and ICD are created by committees. It can be argued that the natural tendency for horse trading between experts selected precisely because they are powerful and opinionated has led to an overelaborate structure, an excess of allowable classes and subclasses, and complicated defining criteria. Thus, in DSM-IV (American Psychiatric Association [APA], 1994) there are potentially 14 categories to consider before allocating someone with depressed mood, and in ICD-10 (World Health Organization [WHO], 1992b) there are 22. Greater utility would probably accrue from limiting the primary categories to three (bipolar disorder, unipolar depressive psychosis, and unipolar nonpsychotic depression), and epidemiological research often uses these categories in any case.

Box 1.1 provides a comparison of the definitions of depressive disorder under DSM-IV (APA, 1994) and ICD-10 (WHO, 1992b), slightly simplified. Over the years there has been considerable convergence between the systems. Nevertheless, the differences remain important. The categories are too close together for empirical studies to establish their relative validity, as this would demand enormous samples. However, they are far enough apart to cause discrepancies in identification. Relatively severe cases are likely to be classified as a depressive disorder under both systems. However, milder disorders may be cases under one system and not the other. This becomes important in epidemiological studies of depressive disorder in the general population because such studies usually report their results under one system or the other, and the degree of comparability is hard to quantify. Thus, the use of different classificatory systems is one barrier to comparison between studies; there are others.

**Box 1.1** Criteria for depressive episode

| *DSM-IIIR/DSM-IV* | *ICD-10* |
|---|---|
| **Symptoms present nearly every day in the same 2-week period** | **Episode must have lasted at least 2 weeks with symptoms nearly every day** |
| **Change from normal functioning** | **Change from normal functioning** |
| **Key symptoms (n = 2)** | **Key symptoms (n = 3)** |
| Depressed mood | Depressed mood |
| Anhedonia | Anhedonia |
| | Fatigue/loss of energy |
| **Ancillary symptoms (n = 7)** | **Ancillary symptoms (n = 7)** |
| Fatigue/loss of energy | Weight and appetite change |
| Weight/appetite loss/gain | Sleep disturbance |
| Insomnia/hypersomnia | Subjective or objective |
| Observed agitation/retardation | Agitation/retardation |
| Low self-esteem/guilt | Low self-esteem/confidence |
| Impaired thinking/concentration | Self-reproach/guilt |
| Suicidal thoughts | Impaired thinking/concentration |
| | Suicidal thoughts |
| **Criteria: 1 key, 5 symptoms in total** | **Criteria** |
| **Plus** | Mild episode: 2 key, 4 symptoms in total |
| Significant distress | Moderate episode: 2 key, 6 symptoms in total |
| **Or** | |
| Social impairment | Severe episode: 3 key, 8 symptoms in total |
| **Exclusions** | **Exclusions** |
| Not mixed episode | No history (ever) of manic symptoms |
| Not substance related | Not substance related |
| Not organic | Not organic |
| Not bereavement | |
| Not psychotic | |

It is interesting to see the effect of applying algorithms for the diagnostic categories defined by different systems to a common set of symptom data. The Schedules for Clinical Assessment in Neuropsychiatry (SCAN; WHO, 1992a) allow diagnosis under both DSM and ICD. Table 1.1 shows the effect of applying ICD-10 and DSM-IV criteria to the dataset from a community survey (McConnell, McClelland, Gillespie, Bebbington, & Houghton, 2002) on the identification of cases of depressive episode (ICD) and depressive disorder (DSM). Of the 18 participants diagnosed with a depressive condition by either classification, two-thirds were diagnosed by both. Five cases of depressive episode were not diagnosed as DSM depressive disorder, whereas only one case of depressive disorder was not diagnosed as an ICD depressive episode. In contrast, DSM recognized many more cases of anxiety disorder. Fifteen of the cases defined by DSM were not classed as anxiety disorders by ICD, while only two classified

**Table 1.1.**
DSM-III-R and ICD-10 Classification Based on the Same Symptom Data: The Derry Survey

|                             | No depressive diagnosis |      | Depressive disorder DSM |
| --------------------------- | ----------------------- | ---- | ----------------------- |
| No depressive diagnosis     | 289 (94%)               |      | 1 (0.3%)                |
| Depressive episode ICD-10   | 5 (1.6%)                |      | 12 (3.9%)               |
| Kappa                       |                         | 0.79 |                         |
|                             | No anxiety diagnosis    |      | Anxiety disorder DSM    |
| No anxiety diagnosis        | 269 (87%)               |      | 15 (4.9%)               |
| Anxiety disorder ICD        | 2 (0.7%)                |      | 21 (6.8%)               |
| Kappa                       |                         | 0.68 |                         |

by ICD were not so classed by DSM. Thus, the ICD criteria appear to be less stringent for depressive episode, while the reverse is true of anxiety. The results suggest that the difference between the two systems arises because of differing thresholds rather than because of wide differences in the symptom contents of the classes.

## Revising the Classifications

It has been planned to publish new versions of both dominant classificatory systems: DSM-V in 2013, and ICD-11 in 2015. Around 20 years will then have passed since the previous revision of each system (Sartorius, 2010). This is a much longer gap than between previous editions, and represents an improvement: science is not well served by too frequent revision, which needlessly obstructs the possibility of comparison between studies. Some of the delay was inevitable, given the increasing complexity of the process of revision. It involves very many stakeholders, and the establishment by WHO and APA, respectively, of taskforces, advisory groups, and subgroups. The obligation to consult widely involves enormous amounts of work and demands complex processes of integration.

Three very appropriate criteria have been set out for the removal or introduction of categories. These relate to public health, practical utility, and empirical evidence (Sartorius, 2010). However, the precise application of the criteria is likely to lead to disagreement. The gathering and evaluation of the relevant empirical evidence is extremely time-consuming. Moreover, despite the rigor of the procedures involved, political considerations may sometimes trump these three criteria. This is not surprising: classification can have consequences for the way particular university departments and disciplines are funded, the licensed use of drugs is related to diagnostic entities, and, in the United States particularly, so is insurance cover for specific treatments.

A harmonization group has been set up, tasked with the work of ensuring that DSM-V and ICD-11 are as closely compatible as possible in their classificatory procedures. First (2009) has provided an impressively exhaustive article (particularly in its online version) on the potential for harmonization. Of the 176 sets of criteria that correspond in the ICD-10 and DSM-IV systems, only one was identical. Twenty-one percent of sets had conceptually based differences, while 78% had deficiencies that appeared unintentional. Thus, in the case of major depressive episode, eight items are in common, three are not. There are also algorithmic differences, and DSM-IV has a bereavement exclusion. In this context, there are proposals to include a formal category of mixed anxiety/depression in DSM-V. This category already exists in the appendix of DSM-IV, and is an acknowledged (albeit undefined) disorder in ICD-10.

There have been intense arguments about whether categories should actually be replaced by dimensions (bipolar or unipolar). As we have seen, dimensional considerations clearly apply not only to affective disorders, but also to personality disturbance, and even to psychotic disorder. Combinations of categories and dimensions are in any case feasible. In fact, some dimensions are expressed in the form of categories: for example, ICD-10 has three severity categories of depressive disorder, wherein the dimensional element is captured. Categories are probably more practicable for clinical purposes, but not necessarily for scientific ones.

## Case Identification in Research

The basis of epidemiology is case identification. The process of diagnosis involves allocating symptom patterns to a diagnostic class according to given rules. In recent years, these rules have been set out explicitly in diagnostic criteria for research (DCRs) serving the dominant classifications of ICD and DSM. These are so precise that they can be incorporated into computer algorithms like CATEGO (Wing et al., 1990) and OPCRIT (McGuffin, Farmer, & Harvey, 1991).

Once the presence of symptoms has been established, the information can be entered into one of these computer programs in order to provide a diagnostic classification. Human idiosyncrasy is reduced to an absolute minimum in this process. However, researchers must still decide how carefully the underlying symptoms should be identified. The choices include unstructured clinical assessment, responses to questionnaires, and semi-structured research interviews.

The first option, unstructured clinical judgment, introduces variability into the process of case allocation, since researchers are relying for consistency merely on their devotion to a common educational tradition. This situation is made worse when the judgments of an unspecified number of others (e.g., the treating physician) are used, as with the diagnostic information recorded in case registers or in national statistics.

In order to be practicable, questionnaires should seek simple responses to unelaborated questions. However, symptoms are traditionally recognized through an assessment of mental experiences, the subtlety of whose formulation demands quite elaborate inquiry (Brugha, Bebbington, & Jenkins, 1999). They are usually established by a process of clinical cross-examination. This is rather complicated, since it requires the questioner to frame further questions in a flexible way in the light of the answers given by the subject. While it might be possible to encapsulate this procedure in a standard questionnaire by using a branching algorithm, it would be exhaustive and exhausting—it might require paths comprising over a dozen questions just to establish, say, the presence of pathologically depressed mood. In these circumstances there are clearly practical limits to the process of standardization, and it is probably better to rely on the shortcuts available from using the skills of trained clinicians. Since diagnosis is built around symptoms defined and elicited in this manner, redefinition in terms of answers to much more limited questions would involve changing the concept of the diagnosis itself. No one has seriously suggested that the way psychiatric symptoms are conceptualized should be changed, so if a questionnaire is used, phenomena may be recorded as present or absent when subsequent clinical inquiry might reveal otherwise. Nevertheless, structured questionnaires do allow lay interviewers to be used, with considerable cost savings. The Diagnostic Interview Schedule (DIS; Robins, Helzer, Croughan, & Ratcliff, 1981) and the Composite International Diagnostic Interview (CIDI; Robins et al., 1988) are examples of fully structured questionnaires that have been widely used and have good reliability.

Semi-structured research interviews are costly in clinical time, and the way in which symptoms are established makes it impossible to standardize the procedure entirely (Robins, 1995). Because of the reliance on clinical judgment and the effect this has on the choice of follow-up questions, some variability will remain. This is the price paid for greater validity, that is, the closer approximation to the clinical consensus about the nature of given symptoms. The SCAN (Wing et al., 1990) are based on a semi-structured interview, and have been quite widely used in epidemiological research studies (Ayuso-Mateos et al., 2001; Bebbington, Marsden, & Brewin, 1997; McConnell et al., 2002; McManus, Meltzer, Brugha, Bebbington, & Jenkins, 2009; Meltzer, Gill, Petticrew, & Hinds, 1995; Singleton, Bumpstead, O'Brien, Lee, & Meltzer, 2001). SCAN has good inter-rater reliability despite its semi-structured format.

## Questionnaires and Interviews

If, as I have argued, there are doubts in principle about the validity of structured questionnaires, it is worth knowing how their performance compares with semi-standardized interviews. One head-to-head comparison has been made between SCAN and CIDI (Brugha, Jenkins, Taub, Meltzer, & Bebbington, 2001). This permits two separate questions: does the questionnaire provide a similar frequency of disorder to that established by the semi-structured interview? And to what extent are the same cases identified by the two instruments? Differences in frequencies would, at the very least, indicate some systematic biases separating the instruments. However, even if, for example, CIDI recognized more cases than SCAN, it could still be the case that CIDI picked up most or all of the cases identified by SCAN. This would imply that the constraints of a rigid questionnaire tended to lower the threshold of case identification, as might be the case if the rigidity, and the paucity of elaborative questions, led to over-recognition of specific symptoms. If on the other hand, in addition to over-recognition of cases, there were little overlap between the cases found by the two systems, it would indicate a more general failure of rigid questioning to establish symptoms properly.

Brugha et al. (2001) found that the coefficients of concordance for the various ICD-10 diagnoses varied between poor and fair. They calculated that using CIDI would give prevalences about 50% greater than those obtained from SCAN. The index of agreement for any depressive episode was poor (0.14). As expected, the discrepancies arose particularly from cases around the threshold for recognition.

However, we must also take into account the fact that the criteria for depressive disorder (DSM-IV) are more restrictive than those of ICD-10 major depressive episode. This should result in lower prevalence, perhaps 20% lower. There are therefore two influences on prevalence, of opposite effect, whose interaction will be responsible for a methodologically based discrepancy in prevalence. Thus, epidemiological studies reporting DSM-IV major depressive disorder often use CIDI, and this combination probably results in prevalences of depression around 20% above the output from a SCAN/ICD-10 combination. The short form of the CIDI, as used in the Finnish study (Lindeman et al., 2000), may result in particularly high prevalence (Patten, 1997, 2000).

The good news is that as most cases in dispute will lie around the threshold, their attributes are likely to be similar and hence the demographic and social characteristics of the disorder in question are likely to be identified with a fair degree of consistency and accuracy.

## Bottom-Up and Top-Down Case Identification

The other way in which instruments differ is whether they are diagnosis driven or symptom driven. Instruments that are diagnosis driven do not require eliciting the same set of symptoms in each case in order to establish the appropriate diagnostic category. All they have to do is to confirm that the required diagnostic criteria are met. The DIS and CIDI are examples of such instruments. The advantage is that they can cut corners by not having to check out all symptoms once a diagnosis has been made: this is often the way clinicians work in their ordinary practice.

Symptom-driven instruments however are exhaustive in their coverage of symptoms, and only then do they use the symptomatic information to check if diagnostic criteria have been met (e.g., SCAN, CIS-R). This has several advantages. The first is that in theory it should be possible to use the symptom information to serve a new algorithm if the diagnostic criteria were changed. This might be extremely arduous in practice, although attempts of this sort have been made. A further advantage is of particular relevance to the study of the common affective disorders. Establishing whether or not a set range of symptoms is present allows an overall symptom count to be made, and this is useful when it is appropriate to study the distributions of symptoms in the general population, as in the study by Melzer et al. (2002) mentioned above. In principle, it could also be used to identify more severe disorder, without invoking extrinsic attributes like social performance. Finally, the establishment of individual symptoms in epidemiological samples allows them to be studied in their own right as reflections of psychological processes.

## The Frequency of Depressive Disorder

In their seminal report on the Global Burden of Disease, Murray and Lopez (1996) projected that by 2020 depression would rank as the second leading cause of disability worldwide. This prediction however relies on the assumption that reasonably accurate statistics are available, and that they can be integrated across jurisdictions. At the time the estimates were made, these requirements had been met only in the most tenuous way. While things have definitely improved, particularly in the past 10 years, it does remain difficult to calculate the burden of depressive illness in different countries. Differences in the frequency of depression between countries may in part be substantive, but will inevitably be clouded by measurement issues. These include local constraints on the conceptualization and acknowledgement of depression, and variation in the performance of instruments in local hands. Effective quality control will reduce, but not eliminate, such methodological "noise."

In epidemiological studies, frequency can be measured in a variety of ways: incidence; point, period, and lifetime prevalence; and morbid risk. Box 1.2 defines commonly used rates in epidemiology. General population surveys usually report period or lifetime prevalence rates, while investigations of clinical series often use first contact or admission as a proxy for incidence. In this chapter, I shall rely largely on community studies of prevalence, as the characteristics of clinical series are distorted by *nosocomial* factors, such as the determinants of, and barriers to, referral to services.

The earliest community psychiatric surveys date back a century, but standardized methods of assessment allowing the comparison of research from different locations have been used only in the past 30 years. The earlier studies have been reviewed elsewhere (Bebbington, 1997, 2004; Weissman et al., 1996). The range of values for prevalence was appreciable, and somewhat greater than in more recent surveys. Moreover, the detailed results did not lend themselves to simple explanation, and there were considerable differences in the information gathered, and in the way it was gathered and combined.

Community psychiatric surveys based on standardized instruments were initially carried out in small areas, as this was relatively easy to organize, even when there were large numbers of subjects. The Epidemiologic Catchment Area surveys used the DIS to interview nearly 20,000 subjects, but were restricted to five localities in the United States (Robins & Regier, 1991). The overall lifetime prevalence of major depression was 4.9%, ranging from 3% to 5.9% in the different centers.

However, it is quite difficult to make sense of differences in prevalence in different locations in psychiatric community surveys, unless the geographical coverage is large.

---

### Box 1.2  Epidemiological rates

**Incidence rate:** the number of new cases in a given period as a proportion of a population at risk.

**Point prevalence rate:** the number of cases identified at a point in time as a proportion of a total population.

**Period prevalence rate:** the number of cases identified as in existence during a specified period as a proportion of a total population.

**Lifetime prevalence rate:** a variant of period prevalence where the period for case identification comprises the entire lifetime of each subject at the point of ascertainment.

This is one argument for having surveys of representative national populations. The first of these occurred in Britain (Jenkins et al., 1997), and there have now been three British National Surveys of Psychiatry Morbidity (Jenkins et al., 1997; McManus et al., 2009; Singleton et al., 2001), and two in Australia (Andrews, Hall, Teesson, & Henderson, 1999; Henderson, Andrews, & Hall, 2000; Slade, Johnston, Oakley Browne, Andrews, & Whiteford, 2009). They each involved interviews carried out by nonclinical interviewers with several thousand subjects selected at random from the whole national population. The British surveys were all based on the revised version of the Clinical Interview Schedule (CIS-R; Lewis, Pelosi, Araya, & Dunn, 1992), an interview that provides ICD-10 diagnoses (WHO, 1992a), while the Australian surveys used variants of CIDI (Robins et al., 1988). CIDI allows both DSM-IV and ICD-10 diagnoses, and the Australian series reported the latter.

The last decade has seen an ambitious attempt to improve the validity of international comparison. The WHO World Mental Health Initiative sought to minimize methodological noise by adopting a common instrument and common methods. The initiative is enormous: at the last count, surveys were being carried out in 28 countries. Some of these surveys were truly national, while others were of specific regions within a given country. The expectation is that over 154,000 people will eventually have been interviewed. The six European national ESEMeD samples are included in the World Mental Health Survey reports (Alonso et al., 2002).

The sheer number of the constituent surveys leads to inherent problems of interpretation. Frequencies may vary because of differential success in engaging participants, different population structures, and the lexical consequences of differences in the transcultural interpretation of emotion (Bebbington & Cooper, 2007). International variations in the ecological context of the population may be important: economic performance, the level of inequality, the degree of urbanization, and the extent of democratic freedoms. Some jurisdictions will be subject, intermittently or persistently, to the effects of war. These influences, identifiable at the national level, will have idiosyncratic impacts on individuals. Ideally, the analysis of international differences in social and other environmental influences should inform our understanding of the nature of psychiatric disorder, but complex results will often elude easy interpretation. However, if associations are observed consistently across different jurisdictions, this does add strength to any conclusions we might draw.

Bromet et al. (2011) provide a relevant example of an attempt to derive synthetic conclusions from the mass of data that has emerged from the World Mental Health Survey Initiative (see Table 1.2). They integrated the findings regarding the prevalence of major depressive episode in 10 high-income and 8 low- to middle-income countries. (The authors did not include participating surveys from Nigeria and Ethiopia because they were suspicious that the low rates of depression in those countries may have resulted from particular difficulties with the interview.) While some response rates were lower than would be regarded as necessary for a representative sample (46% in France), response rates were unrelated to the reported prevalence of depressive disorder.

*Lifetime prevalence* was significantly greater in the high-income countries, averaging 14.6%, compared to 11.1% in the low- to middle-income countries. In contrast, the range of values seen for *12-month prevalence* was much less, and very similar in the

**Table 1.2.**
Twelve-month and Lifetime Prevalence Percentage of Major Depressive Episode in 18
Countries: World Mental Health Survey

| | 12-month prevalence (%) | Lifetime prevalence (%) | 12-month/ lifetime (%) | Age of onset (years) |
|---|---|---|---|---|
| High-income countries | | | | |
| Belgium | 5.0 | 14.1 | 35.2 | 29.4 |
| France | 5.9 | 21.0 | 27.9 | 28.4 |
| Germany | 3.0 | 9.9 | 30.1 | 27.6 |
| Israel | 6.1 | 10.2 | 59.6 | 25.5 |
| Italy | 3.0 | 9.9 | 30.2 | 27.7 |
| Japan | 2.2 | 6.6 | 33.3 | 30.1 |
| Netherlands | 4.9 | 17.9 | 27.3 | 27.2 |
| New Zealand | 6.6 | 17.8 | 37.0 | 24.2 |
| Spain | 4.0 | 10.6 | 37.5 | 30.0 |
| US | 8.3 | 19.2 | 43.1 | 22.7 |
| Average | 5.5 | 14.6 | 37.7 | 25.7 |
| Low- to middle-income countries | | | | |
| Brazil | 10.4 | 18.4 | 56.7 | 24.3 |
| Colombia | 6.2 | 13.3 | 46.7 | 23.5 |
| India | 4.5 | 9.0 | 50.0 | 31.9 |
| Lebanon | 5.5 | 10.9 | 50.0 | 23.8 |
| Mexico | 4.0 | 8.0 | 50.0 | 23.5 |
| China | 3.8 | 6.5 | 58.0 | 18.8 |
| South Africa | 4.9 | 9.8 | 49.6 | 22.3 |
| Ukraine | 8.4 | 14.6 | 57.8 | 27.8 |
| Average | 5.9 | 11.1 | 53.3 | 24.0 |

*Source:* Data tabulated by the author from Bromet et al. (2011).

high-income and low- to middle-income countries (5.5% cf. 5.9%, respectively). The ratio of 12-month to lifetime prevalence can be taken as an indication of persistence, and therefore suggests less persistence in high-income countries. However, this result could also be due to reduced recall in low- and middle-income countries. The findings are probably not due to differential international usage of the standardized instruments, and are therefore likely to be substantive. However, interpretation in relation to local contexts is difficult.

The age of onset was really quite similar in high- and in low- to middle-income countries. However, there was an interesting and probably substantive finding in relation to age. Generally, people over 65 had the lowest rates of major depressive episode in high-income countries, but not in low- to middle-income countries, where the rates are uniform across the age groups. Kessler, Birnbaum, et al. (2010b) have shown convincingly that the decline in major depressive disorder with age cannot be due to the misattribution of affective symptoms to concomitant physical disorder. However, differential survivor bias is likely to effect comparisons between high-income countries and low- to middle-income countries. The relationship of age with prevalence is discussed further below.

Women had uniformly higher prevalences of major depressive episode, a difference that was significant in the large majority of countries. The mean ratio was around two (range 1.6 to 2.7). This finding is consistent with earlier surveys, and a detailed interpretation was included in the first edition of this chapter (Bebbington, 2004). Single, divorced, and widowed people had increased rates of major depressive episode, although variably so, probably dependent on the local status of people in these categories. The frequency of depression in single people was only increased in high-income countries.

The effect of educational level was very variable, and probably reflects the different social context in individual countries. Personal income seemed more important in high-income countries than in low- to middle-income countries, possibly the effect of a wider spread of income inequality.

The level of impairment associated with depression was substantial everywhere, but was particularly high in high-income countries (where impairment may have more apparent impact). The impairment reported by those with major depressive episodes was greater in countries with higher prevalence, suggesting that high prevalence does not merely reflect a relative readiness to acknowledge affective symptoms. Finally, impairment was greater in more recent onset conditions, implying progressive adaptation to persistent disorder.

These results from the World Mental Health Initiative clearly emphasize the serious and universal nature of the problem of depression.

## Depression and Age

There are clear general statements that can be made about the relationship between age and depression. First, the propensity for depression is rare before adolescence (Birmaher et al., 1996). Secondly, as we have seen from the World Mental Health (WMH) surveys described above, in developed countries the prevalence of depression declines in late middle age or early old age. This is also clearly apparent in the data on depressive episode from the three British national surveys of psychiatric morbidity (see Figure 1.2).

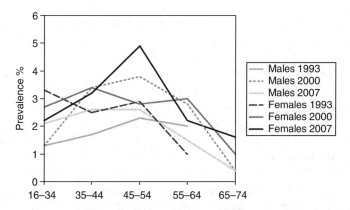

**Figure 1.2.**   Prevalence Percentage by Age of Major Depressive Episode in British National Surveys of Residents in England

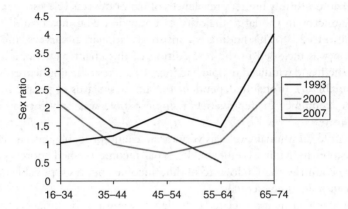

**Figure 1.3.** Sex Ratio of Prevalence Percentage by Age of Major Depressive Episode in British National Surveys of Residents in England

It has been said that the female-to-male sex ratio for depression is not constant over the life span, being around unity in childhood, rising during adulthood, and declining once again in elderly groups (Jorm, 1987). This reduction of the sex ratio in late middle age has been attributed to a reduction in female rates following the menopause (Bebbington et al., 1998). However, the change in the sex ratio with age shown in Figure 1.3 indicates a considerable degree of inconsistency, such that an impact of the menopause cannot be discerned.

The analysis of depression by age in different surveys makes explicit the temporal element in studies of prevalence, and therefore leads on to an issue that has been engaging epidemiologists since the 1970s. This is whether the prevalence of depression has been increasing (Compton, Conway, Stinson, & Grant, 2006; Klerman, 1988; Marcus & Olfson, 2010; Murphy, 1986).

## Is the Prevalence of Depression Increasing?

Three separate mechanisms may influence the apparent variation over time of rates of depression: age, period, and cohort effects. (A cohort is a group of people with birth dates occurring within a specified period.) People may be exposed to risk of disorder because they are passing through an *age of risk* (an age effect). They may also be exposed to disorder because they are passing through a *time of risk* (for instance, a period of economic turmoil). Different cohorts will then suffer the disorder at different ages, corresponding to their age at that time (a period effect). Finally, individual cohorts may have a differing overall propensity to develop the disorder. This arises because of a conflation of date and age, and the cohort's relative vulnerability or resilience results from some shared biological or social experience. In consequence, their contribution to total prevalence will then be independent of age and period, and there is a true cohort effect. The effect on prevalence is like the surge of water down a river after a storm, an effect on overall flow removed only by arrival at the sea. It is however extremely difficult to distinguish statistically between age, period, and cohort effects, and, as a result, changes in the prevalence of disorders are hard to interpret.

One of the strands of evidence used to argue for increasing rates of depression involves the use of cross-sectional data relating to lifetime prevalence and the date of onset of the first episode of depression. Survey participants can be divided by age group. It is generally found that younger age groups display a steeper curve in the rate of onset, leading to the inference that rates of depression are increasing (Kessler, McLaughlin, et al., 1994; Klerman & Weissman, 1989; Lewinsohn, Rohde, Seeley, & Fischer, 1993). However, it is possible that the age group effect is not one of increasing depression, but one of greater forgetfulness in older groups (Giuffra & Risch, 1994; Hasin & Link, 1988). Recall bias of this sort is supported by a 40-year study of a Canadian community (Murphy, Laird, Monson, Sobol, & Leighton, 2000).

Another way of deriving evidence for changing rates of depression is to compare national surveys repeated after an interval, using the same or similar methods of assessment. A number of these are listed in Table 1.3. It will be seen that there is appreciable variation in the recorded prevalence of major depressive disorder and depressive episode. The US National Comorbidity Surveys (Kessler et al., 2003; Kessler, McGonagle, Swartz, Blazer, & Nelson, 1993) actually show a decline, although this may be due to the fact that the earlier sample only extended to age 54, together with other methodological changes, particularly the shift from DSM-IIIR to DSM-IV criteria. However, there was also a decline in the Australian national surveys, in which case finding was more consistent. This contrasts with the sizable increase seen in the two US National Longitudinal Alcohol Epidemiologic Surveys, which used identical case findings. The three British national surveys are characterized by lower prevalences of depressive episode, but there is little variation over time. Taken together, these surveys do not provide evidence for increasing rates of depression.

Recently, the technique of pseudo-cohort analysis[2] has been used with the British National Surveys of Psychiatric Morbidity (Spiers et al., 2012). This involves the identification in each survey of groups of people defined by the same range of birth dates. This was done in order to investigate the age effect rather than the possibility of increasing rates, in other words whether the apparent age effect was best explained through a lasting association of depression with middle adult life, or by the effect of higher rates in certain cohorts.

Successive cohorts of men born since 1950 had experienced a similar prevalence of depression as they aged through adulthood. However, men born between 1950 and 1956 had a higher prevalence than those born between 1943 and 1949. The results for women were less consistent, with some significant increases and decreases in depression between pairs of earlier cohorts, but with stability or a decline in rates in those born since 1963.

Women born between 1957 and 1963 had a very high prevalence of depression when surveyed aged 44–50 years in 2007. This single-age sex group had unremarkable levels of depression when sampled in 1993 and 2000, so the high prevalence in 2007 was clearly unusual. This increase in a single group seems very unlikely to be due to improved recognition or a lower diagnostic threshold. While a change in

---

[2] *Pseudo*-cohort because given cohorts are made up of different individuals in successive surveys.

**Table 1.3.**

Period Prevalence of Depression in Repeated Surveys

| Survey | Number of participants | Prevalence (%) All | Male | Female | Notes |
|---|---|---|---|---|---|
| National Comorbidity Survey (Kessler et al., 1993) | 8,098 | | | | Age 15–54. 1-year prevalence. University of Michigan version of CIDI DSM-IIIR major depressive disorder |
| National Comorbidity Survey Replication (Kessler et al., 2003) | 9,282 | 6.8 | 4.9 | 8.6 | 1-year prevalence DSM-IV depressive disorder. WMH-CIDI |
| First Australian National Survey (Andrews et al., 1999) | 10,600 | 5.1 | 3.4 | 6.8 | 1-year prevalence ICD-10 depressive episode. Automated presentation of CIDI |
| Second Australian National Survey (Slade et al., 2009) | 8,841 | 4.1 | 3.1 | 5.1 | 1-year prevalence ICD-10 depressive episode. WMH-CIDI |
| National Longitudinal Alcohol Epidemiologic Survey 1991–1992 | 42,862 | 3.3 | 2.7 | 3.9 | As reported by Compton et al. (2006). Alcohol Use Disorder and Associated Disabilities Interview Schedule for DSM-IV (AUDADIS-IV). Major depressive episode. |
| National Longitudinal Alcohol Epidemiologic Survey and Related Conditions 2001–2002 | 43,093 | 7.1 | 4.9 | 9.1 | |
| First British National Survey (Meltzer et al., 1995) | 8,903 | 2.2 | 1.7 | 2.7 | 1-week prevalence – CIS-R. ICD-10 depressive disorder. Analysis presented here restricted to residents of England aged 16–64 |
| Second British National Survey (Singleton et al., 2001) | 6,175 | 2.8 | 2.6 | 2.9 | |
| Third British National Survey (McManus et al., 2009) | 5,425 | 2.2 | 2.2 | 3.0 | |

prevalence of this magnitude within 7 years is surprising, it is impossible to determine the extent to which it is a quirk of sampling, or represents some unique experience of this female birth cohort as they reached middle age. Overall, however, the analyses in this study are incompatible with an increasing overall trend toward depressive disorder.

It is clearly possible for rates of depression to vary with time, just as they may vary geographically. Like investments, prevalences may fall as well as rise, and fluctuation in both directions is likely to be the norm. For instance, general statements that say prevalence is continually and uniformly increasing, are almost certainly false. Sometimes the changes will be due to methodological vagaries, and in other cases due to small alterations in the risk and duration of recurrent or relapsing disease. Substantive changes over periods commensurate with human lifetimes are almost certain to be environmental, whether biological or social. Finally, differences in prevalence between studies are more likely to be the result of short-lived fluctuations picked up by chance than major trends. By the same token, they will mainly represent responses to short-lived contextual change. Paid employment is a frequent source of these fluctuations.

## Employment and Depression

Structured employment is a feature of developed societies, and many of us spend a sizable portion of our waking lives at work. Employment generally has beneficial effects on psychological health: it brings interest, income, fulfillment, social contacts, and status, and provides structure and a sense of control (Jahoda, 1982; Krause & Geyer-Pestello, 1985). The strong and persistent link between unemployment and mental ill-health, particularly depressive disorder, is long-established (Meltzer et al., 1995; Talala, Huurre, Aro, Martelin, & Prattala, 2009). Thus, in longitudinal studies, losing employment is associated with a deterioration in mental health, just as reestablishing it leads to improvement (Murphy & Athanasou, 1999).

The benefits of employment are likely to differ, both between men and women, and among women. In developed economies, the advantages of employment may be weaker in married women (Roberts, Roberts, & Stevenson, 1982; Roberts & O'Keefe, 1981; Warr & Parry, 1982), more so if they have children (McGee, Williams, Kashani, & Silva, 1983; Parry, 1986), most so when the children are of preschool age (Haw, 1995). Not surprisingly, full-time employment seems to be particularly demanding (Cleary & Mechanic, 1983; Elliott & Huppert, 1991). The most likely explanation for these findings is role conflict and overload. Thus, part of the excess of depressive disorders in women may be related both to their reduced involvement in employment and to the particular strains they are exposed to if they do work.

## Depression and the Characteristics of Work

The circumstances of employment are not always beneficial. Researchers have accordingly linked the specific attributes of employment to mental health outcomes. For example, in a recent longitudinal study, work with poor psychosocial characteristics (adverse levels of control, demands and complexity, job insecurity, and unfair pay) was as strongly associated with mental ill-health as unemployment (Butterworth et al., 2011). Moreover, moving from unemployment to poor quality work actually led to a decrease in mental health. The consequences of adverse work conditions appear to be relatively nonspecific, covering common mental disorders in general, but including depressive disorders. This has been established in prospective research over the past decade (Siegrist, 2008; Stansfeld & Candy, 2006).

Two main models have been developed to evaluate this putative link. They postulate effects that operate through the experience of strains and imbalances. Although these might be mediated through biological, psychological, or behavioral pathways (Melchior, Berkman, Niedhammer, Zins, & Goldberg, 2007), both models can be seen as primarily cognitive. Under the Job Demand–Control model (JDC; Karasek, 1979), job strain ensues when high job demands are combined with low job control. The model has been augmented by incorporating the beneficial effect of the social support obtainable through work (thus the Job Demand–Control–Support model, or JDCS; Johnson & Hall, 1988). The second model is the Effort–Reward Imbalance model (ERI; Siegrist, 2008). This asserts that adverse health is the consequence of circumstances in which the efforts of the work are high and the rewards are low, with a resulting sense of inequity. This in turn leads to poor health. The situation is exacerbated if the individual becomes overcommitted in the process of dealing with the situation (Siegrist, 1996).

Both models have been used to guide research, and both have been substantiated, although they have rarely been tested head to head. Thus, the adverse features postulated as important in each model have been linked to anxiety, and mood disorders (de Lange, Taris, Kompier, Houtman, & Bongers, 2003; Netterstrom et al., 2008; Siegrist, 2008; Stansfeld & Candy, 2006). Clark et al. (2012) analyzed data from a large population survey in England (the Adult Psychiatric Morbidity Survey of 2007): their results suggested that the characteristics of work associated with depression and other common mental disorders were actually broader, and revealed more complex interactions, than would have been predicted from the models. Disorder was, as expected, associated with high-demand/low-control jobs and low social support at work (JDCS) and with ERI. However, it was also associated with high-demand/high-control and low-reward/low-effort jobs. Interestingly, the impact of the work environment seemed insulated from the rest of people's lives: nonwork stressors did not appear to increase susceptibility to work-related stressors. The authors also found no support for a hypothesized moderating effect of nonwork social support, debt, and overcommitment on the impact of work stressors on common mental disorders.

## Job Security and Depression

Another attribute of employment is the degree of job security. Many industrialized economies have increasingly adopted policies of labor flexibility, the obverse of which is increased job insecurity. A considerable number of studies have now investigated the relationship between job insecurity and mental health. A meta-analysis of 37 surveys in the years to 1999, covering around 15,000 respondents confirmed that job insecurity was strongly associated with poor mental health (Sverke, Hellgren, & Näswall, 2002). Stansfeld and Candy (2006), in a meta-analysis of longitudinal studies from 1994 to 2005, found that job insecurity was one of several occupational stressors predictive of common mental disorders. Bonde (2008) reviewed 16 studies covering 63,000 employees, and concluded that the perception of adverse psychosocial conditions in the work place was linked to an increased risk of depressive symptoms and major depressive episode. The fear of job loss itself seems to be more important than the loss of specific features of the job (Hellgren, Sverke, & Isaksson, 1999).

Job insecurity is likely to have differing effects on different sorts of employee. Simmons and Swanberg (2009) showed that, for poor employees in the United States, job insecurity was the single, significant correlate of depressive symptoms even after controlling for other demographic and work environment characteristics. In contrast, in more affluent employees, depressive symptoms were associated with high psychological demands and low supervisor and coworker support.

When the current economic situation of an organization is perceived as poor, job insecurity is high (Mauno & Kinnunen, 2002). Future reorganization plans contribute to the rise in job insecurity (Ashford, Lee, & Bobko, 1989), as do nonpermanent job contracts (Mauno & Kinnunen, 2002). The stress of uncertainty may be more a cause of anxiety and depression than coming to terms with redundancy.

## Financial Strain and Depression

Unemployment, underemployment, and poorly rewarded employment create financial strain, and easily lead people into debt, with direct mental health consequences (Theodossiou, 1998). Problems with financial indebtedness and the impact that financial stress has on family well-being have been well documented in the media (Bridges & Disney, 2010). Moreover, at the time of writing, many developed economies are witnessing increasing rates of unemployment, cuts in pensions and benefits, and price inflation. These will inevitably contribute to the financial stress faced by individuals and families, and there is already evidence at the population level of increasing rates of depression (Lee et al., 2010; Madianos, Economou, Alexiou, & Stefanis, 2011).

Research at the individual level on the relationship between debt and mental disorder has been limited by the difficulties of measuring debt in large epidemiological surveys. It has rarely been possible to include questions about specific amounts of money relating to individual items of expenditure (housing costs, heating costs, weekly shopping bills). The topic is sensitive, and the information is time-consuming to collect, increasing both cost and respondent burden. In many cases, respondents are merely asked whether they can make ends meet or details of their budgeting strategies. These subjective assessments are then used as proxies for actual indebtedness and for underlying household budgetary problems. Moreover, many studies have relied on limited questionnaire measures, and few have used structured interviews and standardized diagnostic criteria (Hintikka et al., 1998; Roberts, Golding, Towell, & Weinreb, 1999). Hence very few population-based epidemiological studies have been able to conduct persuasive studies of debt and mental disorder (Eaton, Muntaner, Bovasso, & Smith, 2001; Muntaner, Eaton, Miech, & O'Campo, 2004).

Recent studies have used improved methods and report interesting findings. So, financial stress may be central to the association between lower socioeconomic status and depression (Butterworth, Olesen, & Leach, 2012). Jenkins et al. (2008) found that, although people with low income were more likely to have mental disorder, this relationship was attenuated after adjustment for debt. Conversely, even after adjustment for confounders, people in debt remained more than twice as likely to have depressive disorder than those who were not (Meltzer, Bebbington, Brugha, Farrell, & Jenkins, 2012). Although the source of debt had little effect, the *number* of debts were associated with an increasing likelihood of depressive disorder.

It should be acknowledged that the problem of causal direction is particularly acute in this field. Thus people may get into debt for a variety of reasons (gambling, substance abuse, compulsive shopping, marital or relationship breakdown, and redundancy), and these factors, alone or in combination, then increase the risk of anxiety and depression. Individual behavioral responses come in to play. When faced with a worsening financial situation, some people will cope by looking for opportunities to reduce its impact, while others may fall (or fall further) into debt. Moreover, people with mental disorders are less likely than others to obtain or maintain employment, and may also find it difficult to deal with indebtedness by budgeting effectively and applying for benefits. Their debt may also be exacerbated by a failure to appreciate its degree. Both these mechanisms probably apply—people with debts are more likely to have mental health problems and people with mental health problems are more likely to be in debt (Fitch et al., 2009).

Clark et al. (2012) found in a national sample of employed people that job insecurity and debt were independent correlates of depression. Job insecurity, being in debt, and working at the bottom of the occupation hierarchy were all independently associated with depression.

As with most life stresses, the effect of job strain and financial strain remains very nonspecific. Thus, debtors have high rates of all common mental disorders, including depressive episode (Meltzer et al., 2012).

## The Childhood Antecedents of Later Depression

There is a long history of research into the childhood antecedents of depressive disorder. Early studies looked at the effects of separation from, and loss of, parents (Brown & Harris, 1978; Tennant, Bebbington, & Hurry, 1980; Tennant, Hurry, & Bebbington, 1980). More recently, the focus has moved to specific unpleasant events and circumstances, such as bullying, witnessing marital violence, and exposure to sexual and physical abuse.

Childhood adversity may take the form of a repetition of minor upsets and constraints, or of major dramatic events, also sometimes repeated. The traumatic nature of some of these experiences is immediately obvious, and long-term effects are exceedingly plausible. However, damaging effects following the extended experience of parental child-rearing behavior are less self-evident. There has therefore been some debate about whether parenting style in itself is sufficient to account for much of the variance in adult depression. One school of thought is that children have a built-in plasticity in the face of quite considerable disparities in levels of care.

However, it is now established that parenting style does have an appreciable impact on later mental health. The Parental Bonding Instrument (PBI; Parker, 1990; Parker, Wilhelm, & Asghari, 1979) is a self-report inventory designed to measure perceived parental care. It divides parenting style into the aspects of *care* and *overprotection*.

Optimal parenting is reflected in high scores on care and low scores on overprotection (Parker, 1990). While adult depression is consistently (if not very strongly) related to lack of care, the association with overprotection is less consistent (Enns, Cox, & Clara, 2002; Parker, Hadzi-Pavlovic, Greenwald, & Weissman, 1995). These relationships have been found in a number of countries (Heider et al., 2006).

Clearly, the PBI is a self-report measure, and might merely represent a querulous response set in people whose mood is depressed. In fact there is little evidence of this. Parker (1981) demonstrated the validity of the PBI by examining the correspondence between sibling ratings of the subject's parenting with the subject's own. Moreover these ratings appear reasonably stable over a 20-year follow-up period (Wilhelm, Niven, Parker, & Hadzi-Pavlovic, 2005). It is quite possible that the apparent relationship between parenting and depression might be revealed as spurious by a third variable (neuroticism, for instance). It is equally possible that neuroticism mediates between the experience of poor parenting and depression (Kendler, Kessler, Neale, Heath, & Eaves, 1993). However, Duggan, Sham, Minne, Lee, and Murray (1998) found that the effects of poor parenting and neuroticism on later depression were independent of each other.

Childhood abuse, whether physical, emotional, or sexual, is associated with later psychopathology (Bifulco, Brown, & Adler, 1991; Fergusson, Horwood, & Lynskey, 1996; Mullen, Martin, Anderson, Romans, & Herbison, 1996). Adult depressive episodes are associated with a variety of childhood traumas (De Marco, 2000). One of these is bullying, in which there has been a persistent media interest. It can be defined as vicious, aggressive behavior directed toward people who cannot defend themselves effectively. While bullying used to be thought of as a school-related experience, it is now acknowledged to be prevalent in other settings, including the electronic media (Smith & Monks, 2008). It is a phenomenon in which victim characteristics are fairly consistent. These include certain personality traits—being shy, silent, fearful, anxious, physically weak, insecure, crying easily, having low self-esteem (Egan & Perry, 1998; Kumpulainen et al., 1998; Olweus, 1994) and being different from other children in some way—stuttering (Blood & Blood, 2007), being overweight (Robinson, 2006), or having learning difficulties (Reiter & Lapido-Lefler, 2007).

The persistent effects of bullying are abundantly clear. Sourander et al. (2009) reported that boys who had been bullied at the age of 8 were, 15 years later, considerably more likely than their nonbullied peers to suffer a variety of mental health consequences. These included depressive and anxiety disorders. This finding was confirmed by Kumpulainen (2008), who reported bullying was such a continuously distressing experience that it predicts both concurrent and future psychiatric symptoms and disorders. Being bullied in childhood and adolescence has sufficient effect on mood to increase appreciably the risk of suicidal ideation and behavior (Kim & Leventhal, 2008).

The mental health consequences of child sexual abuse have recently been subject to considerable scrutiny, in reaction to a long period in which reports of its occurrence were often discounted. It is now well established that sexual abuse in childhood (CSA) is common (Bebbington et al., 2011, Dinwiddie et al., 2000; Friedman et al., 2002; May-Chahal & Cawson, 2005; Pereda, Guilera, Forns, & Gomez-Benito, 2009). Rates of CSA do not differ in relation to most sociodemographic attributes, although it is commoner in women and in those who have not been brought up by both biological parents until the age of 16 (Bebbington et al., 2011). It may also be related to suboptimal parenting style. Low care appears to be associated with sexual abuse, not only by relatives, but also by nonrelatives (Hill et al., 2001).

There is consistent evidence of deleterious psychiatric sequelae in adulthood, and there are certainly enhanced risks of depression (Weiss, Longhurst, & Mazure, 1999). However, the mental health consequences are relatively nonspecific, as they include a whole range of other disorders (Bebbington et al., 2004, 2009; Coxell, King, Mezey, & Gordon, 1999; Dinwiddie et al., 2000; Janssen et al., 2004; Jonas et al., 2011; Kendler et al., 2000; King, Coxell, & Mezey, 2002; Nelson et al., 2006; Putnam, 2003; Read, van Os, Morrison, & Ross, 2005). The effects seem to be proportionate to the severity and persistence of the abuse (Anda et al., 2006; Bulik, Prescott, & Kendler, 2001; Kendler et al., 2000; Kendler, Kuhn, & Prescott, 2004; Molnar, Buka, & Kessler, 2001; Mullen, Martin, Anderson, Romans, & Herbison, 1993), and *may* be greater in women (MacMillan et al., ?; Molnar et al., 2001; Weiss et al., 1999; but see below).

Jonas et al. (2011) report data from the English Adult Psychiatric Morbidity Survey of 2007, in which detailed information on sexual abuse was elicited. Sexual abuse in childhood (before the age of 16) was strongly associated with a wide range of psychiatric disorders. However, their published analyses relate to the amalgamated category of *common mental disorders* (a mixed bag of six anxiety and depressive disorders). I therefore provide the equivalent results for major depressive episode, in relation to nonconsensual sexual intercourse, to all forms of abuse involving contact, and finally to all forms of abuse including uncomfortable sexual talk (see Table 1.4). The odds ratios are roughly equal in males and females, and tend to be higher for the more severe forms of abuse. However, because severe forms of abuse are relatively rare, the population attributable fraction (PAF) is greater for the category covering the whole range of abuse. PAFs provide an upper bound limit of the amount of disorder that can be attributed to the given factor. They do involve an assumption of causality and the presumption that the results are not confounded. Both assumptions are unlikely to be

**Table 1.4.**
Sexual Abuse and Depressive Episode

| Abuse type | Statistics | Males | Females |
|---|---|---|---|
| Nonconsensual sexual intercourse | Odds ratio (95% CI) | 4.1 (0.9–17.6) | 4.4 (2.4–7.8) |
| | Adjusted odds ratio | 2.4 | 4.3 |
| | Population attributable fraction | 2.1% | 7.8% |
| Contact abuse | Odds ratio (95% CI) | 3.9 (2.1–7.3) | 3.0 (2.0–4.5) |
| | Adjusted odds ratio | 4.6 | 2.7 |
| | Population attributable fraction | 13.2% | 17.3% |
| All forms of abuse | Odds ratio (95% CI) | 2.9 (1.6–5.3) | 2.7 (1.9–3.9) |
| | Adjusted odds ratio | 3.2 | 2.6 |
| | Population attributable fraction | 13.5% | 20.8% |

*Source:* Data from the Adult Psychiatric Morbidity Survey of England (2007).

more than partially true, but PAFs do give a rough idea of public health impact. In relation to all forms of sexual abuse, the PAF for depression in females was over 20%, and in males 13%. The lower value in males was largely due to the relative infrequency of their experience of abuse, rather than to reduced sensitivity.

The various forms of childhood disadvantage show an understandable but unfortunate tendency to cluster in the lives of given individuals (Bebbington et al., 2004). Green et al. (2010) and McLaughlin et al. (2010) used data from the National Comorbidity Survey Replication in the United States to provide analyses of 12 types of childhood disadvantage. Seven of these types formed a maladaptive family functioning cluster, within which were three forms of abuse: physical abuse, sexual abuse, and exposure to family violence. They examined childhood disadvantage in relation to the onset and persistence of a range of different disorders. Sizable relationships were apparent with all the disorders tested, with relatively little specificity. Links were generally stronger with onset than with persistence. One of the categories they examined was mood disorders, a catch-all in which the majority of cases were very probably of major depressive episode. Childhood adversities were associated with a quarter of cases of mood disorder. Family violence, physical abuse, and sexual abuse were significantly associated with the onset of mood disorder, and also with its persistence, albeit less strongly. Kessler, McLaughlin, et al. (2010) reported similar results from 21 high-, middle- and low-income countries in the World Mental Health Initiative. The impact of childhood adversity was apparent in each of these national groupings, and overall it was associated with onset in 23% of cases of mood disorders, very similar indeed to the US studies described above.

It is of interest to speculate how childhood traumas have their effects on the emergence of depression in adulthood. It is generally not because they cause childhood depressive disorder, as this is a rare condition. The links must therefore usually be indirect—the causal connection appears to operate over a gap of years. This suggests some enduring change that mediates the later propensity to depression. Candidates include mentally intrusive reminders of the abusive experience, psychological processes involving attitudes and beliefs, propensities toward mood disturbance in the face of subsequent experience, and styles of coping that may impair the processing of the original abuse. CSA certainly has extreme adverse effects on self-esteem, self-blame, and psychological well-being (Banyard, Williams, & Siegel, 2001; Kamsner & McCabe, 2000; Mannarino & Cohen, 1996; Murthi & Espelage, 2005). People who have been sexually abused often display avoidant coping, which is also seen in the various psychiatric disorders that have been linked to abuse (Cortes & Justicia, 2008; O'Leary, 2009). Abuse may also modulate the physiological stress response in deleterious ways (Driessen et al., 2000; Heim, Newport, Miller, & Nemeroff, 2000; Read et al., 2005; Spauwen, Krabbendam, Lieb, Wittchen, & van Os, 2006). Finally, it may create a vulnerability to later damaging exploitation. Thus, CSA seems to be followed by a significant increase in the risk of adult sexual abuse: in one study, 50% of those who had experienced abuse under 16 also reported an episode over the age of 16 (Jonas et al., 2011).

We must also ask ourselves why so many different disorders are associated with the same putative etiological agent? The explanation may merely reflect the nonexclusive nature of psychiatric classification, which results in the frequent comorbidity seen in

*Paul Bebbington*

practice. If not, the specific psychiatric consequences may arise from the particular context and attributes of the abuse, or a tendency in the individual, inhering from other causes, of responding in particular ways.

## Conclusions

In this chapter, I have considered the practical difficulties facing the epidemiological study of depression. Epidemiology is a medical approach that relies initially on the conceptualization of impaired functions as disorders, followed by a requirement to identify these disorders in a reliable way. So conceived, depression shades both into normal experience and into other affective disorders. Distinguishing it in a way at once useful and consistent is thus difficult, as I have argued in some detail. In particular, the comparability of studies is jeopardized by differences between classifications and instruments and in the way these are applied. The consequence is that no two research teams are likely to identify the same sets of respondents as cases; indeed, the overlap is in practice small and there may be systematic over- or under-identification, resulting in different prevalence rates. To a degree, these obstacles to precise case identification are probably insuperable, although the arguments remain strong for doing the best we can.

Two things alleviate this rather miserable conclusion. Because in general populations most cases identified are around the threshold that distinguishes them from noncases, different studies are likely to end up with case groups that have similar characteristics. Robust associations, for example, the association of depression with life events or with poverty, will therefore survive the inadequacies of our instrumentation. The second way around these inadequacies is to supplement the medical case approach with studies that look at the correlates of total symptom score. In this way, important findings can be triangulated, as they are in the study of blood pressure.

Finally, epidemiology provides more interpretable results when it is theory driven, with firm a priori hypotheses about how results might be mediated by social, psychological, and biological factors.

## References

Alonso, J., Ferrer, M., Romera, B., Vilagut, G., Angermeyer, M., Bernert, S., . . . Bruffaerts, R. (2002). The European Study of the Epidemiology of Mental Disorders (ESEMeD/MHEDEA 2000) Project: Rationale and methods. *International Journal of Methods in Psychiatric Research, 11*, 55–67.

American Psychiatric Association. (1994). *Diagnostic and statistical manual of mental disorders* (4th ed., revised). Washington, DC: American Psychiatric Association.

Anda, R. F., Felitti, V. J., Bremner, J. D., Walker, J. D., Whitfield, C., Perry, B. D., . . . Giles, W. H. (2006). The enduring effects of abuse and related adverse experiences in childhood. A convergence of evidence from neurobiology and epidemiology. *European Archives of Psychiatry and Clinical Neuroscience, 256*, 174–186.

Andrews, G., Hall, W., Teesson, M., & Henderson, S. (1999). *The mental health of Australians.* Canberra: Mental Health Branch, Commonwealth Department of Health and Aged Care.

Ashford, S., Lee, C., & Bobko, P. (1989). Content, causes, and consequences of job insecurity: A theory-based measure and substantive test. *Academy of Management Journal*, *32*, 803–829.

Ayuso-Mateos, J. L., Vazquez-Barquero, J. L., Dowrick, C., Lehtinen, V., Dalgard, O. S., Casey, P., … ODIN Group (2001). Depressive disorders in Europe: Prevalence figures from the ODIN study. *British Journal of Psychiatry*, *179*, 308–316.

Banyard, V. L., Williams, L. M., & Siegel, J. A. (2001). The long-term mental health consequences of child sexual abuse: An exploratory study of the impact of multiple traumas in a sample of women. *Journal of Traumatic Stress*, *14*, 697–715.

Bebbington, P. E. (1997). Diagnostic issues and epidemiology. In S. Checkley (Ed.), *The management of depression*. Oxford, UK: Blackwell.

Bebbington, P. E. (2004). The classification and epidemiology of unipolar depression. In M. Power (Ed.), *Mood disorders: A handbook of science and practice* (pp. 3–27). Chichester, UK: Wiley.

Bebbington, P. E. (2011). John Wing and the perils of nosolatry. *Social Psychiatry and Psychiatric Epidemiology*, *46*, 443–446.

Bebbington, P. E., Bhugra, D., Brugha, T., Singleton, N., Farrell, M., Jenkins, R., … Meltzer, H. (2004). Psychosis, victimisation and childhood disadvantage: Evidence from the Second British National Survey of Psychiatric Epidemiology. *British Journal of Psychiatry*, *185*, 220–226.

Bebbington, P. E., & Cooper, C. (2007). Affective disorders. In D. Bhugra, & K. Bhui (Eds.), *Textbook of cultural psychiatry* (pp. 224–241). Cambridge, MA: Cambridge University Press.

Bebbington, P. E., Cooper, C., Minot, S., Brugha, T. S., Jenkins, R., Meltzer, H., Dennis, M. (2009). Suicide attempts, gender, and sexual abuse: Data from the 2000 British Psychiatric Morbidity survey. *American Journal of Psychiatry*, *166*, 1135–1140.

Bebbington, P. E., Dunn, G., Jenkins, R., Lewis, G., Brugha, T., Farrell, M., Meltzer, H. (1998). The influence of age and sex on the prevalence of depressive conditions: Report from the National Survey of Psychiatric Morbidity. *Psychological Medicine*, *28*, 9–19.

Bebbington, P. E., Jonas, S., Kuipers, E., King, M., Cooper, C., Brugha, T., … Jenkins, R. (2011). Sexual abuse and psychosis: Data from a cross-sectional national psychiatric survey in England. *British Journal of Psychiatry*, *199*, 29–37.

Bebbington, P. E., Marsden, L., & Brewin, C. R. (1997). The need for psychiatric treatment in the general population: The Camberwell Needs for Care survey. *Psychological Medicine*, *27*, 821–834.

Bifulco, A., Brown, G. W., & Adler, Z. (1991). Early sexual abuse and clinical depression in adult life. *British Journal of Psychiatry*, *159*, 115–122.

Birley, J. L. (1990). DSM-III: From left to right or from right to left? *British Journal of Psychiatry*, *157*, 116–118.

Birmaher, B., Ryan, N. D., Williamson, D. E., Brent, D. A., Kaufman, J., Dahl, R., … Nelson, B. (1996). Childhood and adolescent depression: A review of the past 10 years. Part 1. *Journal of the American Academy of Child and Adolescent Psychiatry*, *35*, 1427–1439.

Blood, G. W., & Blood, I. M. (2007). Preliminary study of self-reported experience of physical aggression and bullying of boys who stutter: Relation to increased anxiety. *Perceptual and Motor Skills*, *104*, 1060–1066.

Bonde, J. P. (2008). Psychological factors at work and risk of depression: A systematic review of the epidemiological evidence. *Occupational and Environmental Medicine*, *65*, 438–445.

Bridges, S., & Disney, R. (2010). Debt and depression. *Journal of Health Economics*, *29*, 388–403.

Bromet, E., Andrade, L. A., Hwang, I., Sampson, N. A., Alonso, J., de Girolamo, G., . . . Kessler, R. C. (2011). Cross-national epidemiology of DSM-IV major depressive episode. *BMC Medicine, 9,* 90.

Brown, G. W., & Harris, T. (1978). *Social origins of depression.* London: Tavistock.

Brugha, T. S., Bebbington, P. E., & Jenkins, R. (1999). A difference that matters: Comparisons of structured and semi-structured psychiatric diagnostic interviews in the general population. *Psychological Medicine, 5,* 1013–1020.

Brugha, T. S., Jenkins, R., Taub, N., Meltzer, H., & Bebbington, P. (2001). A general population comparison of the Composite International Diagnostic Interview (CIDI) and the Schedules for Clinical Assessment in Neuropsychiatry (SCAN). *Psychological Medicine, 31,* 1001–1013.

Bulik, C. M., Prescott, C. A., & Kendler, K. S. (2001). Features of childhood sexual abuse and the development of psychiatric and substance use disorder. *British Journal of Psychiatry, 179,* 444–449.

Butterworth, P., Leach, L. S., Strazdins, L., Olesen, S. C., Rodgers, B., & Broom, D. H. (2011). The psychosocial quality of work determines whether employment has benefits for mental health: Results from a longitudinal national household panel survey. *Occupational and Environmental Medicine, 68,* 806–812.

Butterworth, P., Olesen, S. C., & Leach, L. S. (2012). The role of hardship in the association between socio-economic position and depression. *Australian and New Zealand Journal of Psychiatry, 46,* 364–373.

Clark, C., Pike, C., McManus, S., Harris, J., Bebbington, P., Brugha, T., . . . Stansfeld, S. (2012). The contribution of work and non-work stressors to common mental disorders in the 2007 Adult Psychiatric Morbidity Survey. *Psychological Medicine, 42,* 829–842.

Cleary, P. D., & Mechanic, D. (1983). Sex differences in psychological distress among married people. *Journal of Health and Social Behaviour, 6,* 64–78.

Compton, W. M., Conway, K. P., Stinson, F. S., & Grant, B. F. (2006). Changes in the prevalence of major depression and comorbid substance use disorders in the United States between 1991–1992 and 2001–2002. *American Journal of Psychiatry, 163,* 2141–2147.

Cortes, D. C., & Justicia, F. J. (2008). Child sexual abuse coping and long term psychological adjustment. *Psicothema, 20,* 509–515.

Coxell, A., King, M., Mezey, G., & Gordon, D. (1999). Lifetime prevalence, characteristics and associated problems of non-consensual sex in men: A cross sectional survey. *British Medical Journal, 318,* 846–850.

de Lange, A. H., Taris, T. W., Kompier, M. A., Houtman, I. L., & Bongers, P. M. (2003). "The very best of the millennium": Longitudinal research and the demand-control-(support) model. *Journal of Occupational and Health Psychology, 8,* 282–305.

De Marco, R. R. (2000). The epidemiology of major depression: Implications of occurrence, recurrence, and stress in a Canadian community sample. *Canadian Journal of Psychiatry, 45,* 67–74.

Dinwiddie, S., Heath, A. C., Dunne, M. P., Bucholz, K. K., Madden, P. A., Slutske, W. S., . . . Martin, N. G. (2000). Early sexual abuse and lifetime psychopathology: A co-twin-control study. *Psychological Medicine, 30,* 41–52.

Driessen, M., Herrmann, J., Stahl, K., Zwaan, M., Meier, S., Hill, A., . . . Petersen, D. (2000). Magnetic resonance imaging volumes of the hippocampus and the amygdala in women with borderline personality disorder and early traumatization. *Archives of General Psychiatry, 57,* 1115–1122.

Duggan, C., Sham, P., Minne, C., Lee, A., & Murray, R. (1998). Quality of parenting and vulnerability to depression: Results from a family study. *Psychological Medicine, 28,* 185–191.

Eaton, W., Muntaner, C., Bovasso, G., & Smith, C. (2001). Socioeconomic status and depression: The role of inter- and intra-generational mobility, government assistance, and work environment. *Journal of Health and Social Behaviour, 42,* 277–294.

Egan, S. K., & Perry, D. G. (1998). Does low self regard invite victimisation? *Developmental Psychology, 34,* 299–309.

Elliott, J., & Huppert, F. A. (1991). In sickness and in health: Associations between physical and mental wellbeing, employment and parental status in a British nation-wide sample of married women. *Psychological Medicine, 21,* 515–524.

Enns, M. W., Cox, B. J., & Clara, I. (2002). Parental bonding and adult psychopathology: Results from the US National Comorbidity Survey. *Psychological Medicine, 32,* 997–1008.

Fergusson, D. M., Horwood, J., & Lynskey, M. T. (1996). Childhood sexual abuse and psychiatric disorder in young adulthood: II. Psychiatric outcomes of childhood sexual abuse. *Journal of the American Academy of Child and Adolescent Psychiatry, 34,* 1365–1374.

First, M. B. (2009). Harmonisation of ICD-11 and DSM-V: Opportunities and challenges. *British Journal of Psychiatry, 195,* 382–390.

Fitch, C., Jenkins, R., Hurlston, M., Hamilton, S., Davey, R., & Walker, F. (2009). Debt and mental health: An overview of selected evidence, key challenges and available tools. *Mental Health Today, 23,* 26–31.

Friedman, S., Smith, L., Fogel, D., Paradis, C., Viswanathan, R., Ackerman, R., & Trappler, B. (2002). The incidence and influence of early traumatic life events in patients with panic disorder: A comparison with other psychiatric outpatients. *Journal of Anxiety Disorders, 16,* 259–272.

Giuffra, L. A., & Risch, N. (1994). Diminished recall and the cohort effect of major depression: A simulation study. *Psychological Medicine, 24,* 375–383.

Goldberg, D. (2000). Plato versus Aristotle: Categorical and dimensional models for common mental disorders. *Comprehensive Psychiatry, 41,* 8–13.

Green, J. G., McLaughlin, K. A., Berglund, P. A., Gruber, M. J., Sampson, N. A., Zaslavsky, A. M., & Kessler, R. C. (2010). Childhood adversities and adult psychopathology in the National Comorbidity Survey Replication (NCS-R) I Associations with First Onset of DSM-IV Disorders. *Archives of General Psychiatry, 67,* 113–123.

Hasin, D., & Link, B. (1988). Age and recognition of depression: Implications for a cohort effect in major depression. *Psychological Medicine, 18,* 683–688.

Haw, C. E. (1995). The family-life cycle—a forgotten variable in the study of women's employment and well-being. *Psychological Medicine, 25,* 727–738.

Heider, D., Matschinger, H., Bernert, S., Alonso, J., Angermeyer, M. C., & ESEMeD/MHEDEA 2000 investigators (2006). Relationship between parental bonding and mood disorder in six European countries. *Psychiatry Research, 143,* 89–98.

Heim, C., Newport, D. J., Miller, A. H., & Nemeroff, C. B. (2000). Long-term neuroendocrine effects of childhood maltreatment. *Journal of American Medical Association, 284,* 2321.

Hellgren, J. M., Sverke, M., & Isaksson, K. (1999). A two-dimensional approach to job insecurity: Consequences for employee attitudes and well-being. *European Journal of Work and Organizational Psychology, 8,* 179–195.

Henderson, S., Andrews, G., & Hall, W. (2000). Australia's mental health: An overview of the general population survey. *Australian and New Zealand Journal of Psychiatry, 34,* 197–205.

Hill, J., Pickles, A., Burnside, E., Byatt, M., Rollinson, L., Davis, R., & Harvey, K. (2001). Child sexual abuse, poor parental care and adult depression: Evidence for different mechanisms. *British Journal of Psychiatry, 179,* 104–109.

Hintikka, J., Kontula, O., Saarinen, P., Tanskanen, A., Koskela, K., & Viinamaki, H. (1998). Debt and suicidal behaviour in the Finnish general population. *Acta Psychiatrica Scandinavica, 98*, 493–496.

Hurry, J., Sturt, E., Bebbington, P. E., & Tennant, C. (1983). Sociodemographic associations with social disablement in a community sample. *Social Psychiatry, 18*, 113–122.

Jahoda, M. (1982). *Employment and unemployment.* Cambridge, MA: Cambridge University Press.

Janssen, I., Krabbendam, L., Bak, M., Hanssen, M., Vollebergh, W., de Graaf, R., & van Os, J. (2004). Childhood abuse as a risk factor for psychotic experiences. *Acta Psychiatrica Scandinavica, 109*, 38–45.

Jenkins, R., Bebbington, P. E., Brugha, T., Farrell, M., Gill, B., Lewis, G., ... Petticrew, M. (1997). The National Psychiatric Morbidity Surveys of Great Britain—Strategy and methods. *Psychological Medicine, 27*, 765–774.

Jenkins, R., Bhugra, D., Bebbington, P., Brugha, T., Farrell, M., Coid, J., ... Meltzer, H. (2008). Debt, income and mental disorder in the general population. *Psychological Medicine, 38*, 1485–1493.

Johnson, J. V., & Hall, E. M. (1988). Job strain, work place social support, and cardiovascular disease: A cross-sectional study of a random sample of the Swedish working population. *American Journal of Public Health, 78*, 1336–1342.

Jonas, S., Bebbington, P. E., McManus, S., Meltzer, H., Jenkins, R., Kuipers, E., ... Brugha, T. (2011). Sexual abuse and psychiatric disorder in England: Results from the 2007 Adult Psychiatric Morbidity Survey. *Psychological Medicine, 41*, 709–719.

Jorm, A. F. (1987). Sex and age differences in depression: A quantitative synthesis of published research. *Australian and New Zealand Journal of Psychiatry, 21*, 46–53.

Kamsner, S., & McCabe, M. P. (2000). The relationship between adult psychological adjustment and childhood sexual abuse, childhood physical abuse, and family-of-origin characteristics. *Journal of Interpersonal Violence, 15*, 1243–1261.

Karasek, R. A. (1979). Job demands, job decision latitude, and mental strain—Implications for job redesign. *Administrative Science Quarterly, 24*, 285–308.

Kendler, K. S., Bulik, C. M., Silberg, J., Hettema, J. M., Myers, J., & Prescott, C. A. (2000). Childhood sexual abuse and adult psychiatric and substance use disorders in women: An epidemiological and co-twin control analysis. *Archives of General Psychiatry, 57*, 953–959.

Kendler, K. S., Kessler, R. C., Neale, M. C., Heath, A. C., & Eaves, L. J. (1993). The prediction of major depression in women: Toward an integrated etiologic model. *American Journal of Psychiatry, 150*, 1139–1148.

Kendler, K. S., Kuhn, J. W., & Prescott, C. A. (2004). Childhood sexual abuse, stressful life events and risk for major depression in women. *Psychological Medicine, 34*, 1475–1482.

Kessler, R. C., Berglund, P., Demler, O., Jin, R., Koretz, D., Merikangas, K. R., ... National Comorbidity Survey Replication. (2003). The epidemiology of major depressive disorder: Results from the National Comorbidity Survey Replication (NCS-R). *Journal of the American Medical Association, 289*, 3095–3105.

Kessler, R. C., Birnbaum, H., Bromet, E., Hwang, I., Sampson, N., & Shahly, V. (2010b). Age differences in major depression: Results from the National Comorbidity Survey Replication (NCS-R). *Psychological Medicine, 40*, 225–237.

Kessler, R. C., McGonagle, K. A., Nelson, C. B., Hughes, M., Swartz, M., & Blazer, D. G. (1994). Sex and depression in the National Comorbidity Survey, II: Cohort effects. *Journal of Affective Disorders, 30*, 15–26.

Kessler, R. C., McGonagle, K. A., Swartz, M., Blazer, D. G., & Nelson, C. B. (1993). Sex and depression in the National Comorbidity Survey, I: Lifetime prevalence, chronicity and recurrence. *Journal of Affective Disorders, 29*, 85–96.

Kessler, R. C., McGonagle, K. A., Zhao, S. Y., Nelson, C. B., Hughes, M., Eshleman, S., ... Kendler, K. S. (1994). Lifetime and 12-month prevalence of DSM-III-R psychiatric disorders in the United States. Results from the National Comorbidity Survey. *Archives of General Psychiatry, 51,* 8–19.

Kessler, R. C., McLaughlin, K. A., Green, J. G., Gruber, M. J., Sampson, N. A., Zaslavsky, A. M., ... Williams, D. R. (2010). Childhood adversities and adult psychopathology in the WHO World Mental Health Surveys. *British Journal of Psychiatry, 197,* 378–385.

Kim, Y. S., & Leventhal, B. (2008). Bullying and suicide: A review. *International Journal of Adolescent Medicine and Health, 20,* 133–154.

King, M., Coxell, A., & Mezey, G. (2002). Sexual molestation of males: Associations with psychological disturbance. *British Journal of Psychiatry, 181,* 153–157.

Klerman, G. L. (1988). The current age of youthful melancholia: Evidence for increase in depression among adolescents and young adults. *British Journal of Psychiatry, 152,* 4–14.

Klerman, G. L., & Weismann, M. M. (1989). Increasing rates of depression. *Journal of the American Medical Association, 261,* 2229—2235.

Krause, N., & Geyer-Pestello, H. F. (1985). Depressive symptoms among women employed outside the home. *American Journal of Community Psychology, 13,* 49–67.

Kumpulainen, K. (2008). Psychiatric conditions associated with bullying. *International Journal of Adolescent Medicine and Health, 20,* 121–132.

Kumpulainen, K., Räsänen, E., Hentonen, I., Almqvist, F., Kresaniv, K., Linna, S.-L., ... Tamminen, T. (1998). Bullying and psychiatric symptoms among elementary school-age children. *Child Abuse and Neglect, 22,* 705–717.

Lee, S., Guo, W.-J., Tsang, A., Mak, A. D. P., Wu, J., Ng, K. L., & Kwok, K. (2010). Evidence for the 2008 economic crisis exacerbating depression in Hong Kong. *Journal of Affective Disorders, 126,* 125–133.

Lewinsohn, P. M., Rohde, P., Seeley, J. R., & Fischer, S. A. (1993). Age-cohort changes in the lifetime occurrence of depression and other mental disorders. *Journal of Abnormal Psychology, 102,* 110–120.

Lewis, G., Pelosi, A., Araya, R. C., & Dunn, G. (1992). Measuring psychiatric disorder in the community: A standardized assessment for use by lay interviewers. *Psychological Medicine, 22,* 465–486.

Lindeman, S., Hamalainen, J., Isometsa, E., Kaprio, J., Poikolainen, K., Heikkinen, M., & Aro, H. (2000). The 12-month prevalence and risk factors for major depressive episode in Finland: Representative sample of 5993 adults. *Acta Psychiatrica Scandinavica, 102,* 178–184.

MacMillan, H. L., Fleming, J. E., Streiner, D. L., Lin, E., Boyle, M. H., Jamieson, E., ... Beardslee, W. R. (2001). Childhood abuse and lifetime psychopathology in a community sample. *American Journal of Psychiatry, 158,* 1878–1883.

Madianos, M., Economou, M., Alexiou, T., & Stefanis, C. (2011). Depression and economic hardship across Greece in 2008 and 2009: Two cross-sectional surveys nationwide. *Social Psychiatry and Psychiatric Epidemiology, 46,* 943–952.

Mannarino, A. P., & Cohen, J. A. (1996). Abuse-related attributions and perceptions, general attributions, and locus of control in sexually abused girls. *Journal of Interpersonal Violence, 11,* 162–180.

Marcus, S. C., & Olfson, M. (2010). National trends in the treatment for depression from 1998 to 2007. *Archives of General Psychiatry, 67,* 1265–1273.

Mauno, S., & Kinnunen, U. (2002). Perceived job insecurity among dual-earner couples: Do its antecedents vary according to gender, economic sector and the measure used? *Journal of Occupational and Organizational Psychology, 75,* 295–314.

May-Chahal, C., & Cawson, P. (2005). Measuring child maltreatment in the United Kingdom: A study of the prevalence of child abuse and neglect. *Child Abuse and Neglect, 29*, 943–1070.

McConnell, P., McClelland, R., Gillespie, K., Bebbington, P., & Houghton, S. (2002). Prevalence of psychiatric disorder and the need for psychiatric care in Northern Ireland. Population study in the District of Derry. *British Journal of Psychiatry, 181*, 214–219.

McGee, R., Williams, S., Kashani, J. H., & Silva, P. A. (1983). Prevalence of self reported depressive symptoms and associated factors in mothers in Dunedin. *British Journal of Psychiatry, 143*, 473–479.

McGuffin, P., Farmer, A., & Harvey, I. (1991). A polydiagnostic application criteria in studies of psychotic illness. Development and reliability of the OPCRIT system. *Archives of General Psychiatry, 48*, 764–770.

McLaughlin, K. A., Green, J. G., Gruber, M. J., Sampson, N. A., Zaslavsky, A. M., & Kessler, R. C. (2010). Childhood adversities and adult psychopathology in the National Comorbidity Survey Replication (NCS-R) II Associations with Persistence of DSM-IV Disorders. *Archives of General Psychiatry, 67*, 124–132.

McManus, S., Meltzer, H., Brugha, T., Bebbington, P., & Jenkins, R. (2009). *Adult psychiatric morbidity in England, 2007: Results of a household survey.* London: National Health Service Information Centre for Health and Social Care.

Melchior, M., Berkman, L. F., Niedhammer, I., Zins, M., & Goldberg, M. (2007). The mental health effects of multiple work and family demands—A prospective study of psychiatric sickness absence in the French GAZEL study. *Social Psychiatry and Psychiatric Epidemiology, 42*, 573–582.

Meltzer, H., Bebbington, P., Brugha, T., Farrell, M., & Jenkins, R. (2012). The relationship between personal debt and specific common mental disorders. *European Journal of Public Health,* doi:10.1093/eurpub/cks021

Meltzer, H., Gill, B., Petticrew, M., & Hinds, K. (1995). *The prevalence of psychiatric morbidity among adults living in private households. OPCS Survey of Psychiatric Morbidity in Great Britain.* (Report 1). London: HMSO.

Melzer, D., Tom, B. D. M., Brugha, T. S., Fryers, T., & Meltzer, H. (2002). Common mental disorder symptom counts in populations: Are there distinct case groups above epidemiological cut-offs? *Psychological Medicine, 32*, 1195–1201.

Molnar, B. E., Buka, S. L., & Kessler, R. C. (2001). Child sexual abuse and subsequent psychopathology: Results from the National Comorbidity Survey. *American Journal of Public Health, 91*, 753–760.

Mullen, P. E., Martin, J. L., Anderson, J. C., Romans, S. E., & Herbison, G. P. (1993). Childhood sexual abuse and mental health in adult life. *British Journal of Psychiatry, 163*, 721–732.

Mullen, P. E., Martin, J. L., Anderson, J. C., Romans, S. E., & Herbison, G. P. (1996). The long-term impact of the physical, emotional, and sexual abuse of children: A community study. *Child Abuse and Neglect, 20*, 7–21.

Muntaner, C., Eaton, W., Miech, R., & O'Campo, P. (2004). Socioeconomic position and major mental disorders. *Epidemiologic Reviews, 26*, 53–62.

Murphy, J. (1986). Trends in depression and anxiety: Men and women. *Acta Psychiatrica Scandinavica, 73*, 113–127.

Murphy, G. C., & Athanasou, J. A. (1999). The effect of unemployment on mental health. *Journal of Occupational and Organizational Psychology, 72*, 83–99.

Murphy, J. M., Laird, N. M., Monson, R. R., Sobol, A. M., & Leighton, A. H. (2000). A 40-year perspective on the prevalence of depression—The Stirling County study. *Archives of General Psychiatry, 57*, 209–215.

Murray, C. J. L., & Lopez, A. D. (1996). *The global burden of disease.* Geneva: World Health Organization, Harvard School of Public Health, World Bank.

Murthi, M., & Espelage, D. L. (2005). Childhood sexual abuse, social support, and psychological outcomes: A loss framework. *Child Abuse and Neglect, 29,* 1215–1231.

Nelson, E. C., Heath, A. C., Lynskey, M. T., Bucholz, K. K., Madden, P. A. F., Statham, D. J., & Martin, N. G. (2006). Childhood sexual abuse and risks for licit and illicit drug-related outcomes: A twin study. *Psychological Medicine, 36,* 1473–1483.

Netterstrom, B., Conrad, N., Bech, P., Fink, P., Olsen, O., Rugulies, R., & Stansfeld, S. (2008). The relation between work-related psychosocial factors and the development of depression. *Epidemiologic Reviews, 30,* 118–132.

O'Leary, P. J. (2009). Men who were sexually abused in childhood: Coping strategies and comparisons in psychological functioning. *Child Abuse and Neglect, 33,* 471–479.

Olweus, D. (1994). Annotation: Bullying at school: Basic facts and effects of a school based intervention program. *Journal of Child Psychology and Psychiatry, 35,* 1171–1190.

Parker, G. (1981). Parental reports of depressives: An investigation of several explanations. *Journal of Affective Disorders, 3,* 131–140.

Parker, G. (1990). Parental rearing style: Examining for links with personality vulnerability factors for depression. *Social Psychiatry and Psychiatric Epidemiology, 28,* 97–100.

Parker, G., Hadzi-Pavlovic, D., Greenwald, S., & Weissman, M. (1995). Low parental care as a risk factor to lifetime depression in a community sample. *Journal of Affective Disorders, 33,* 173–180.

Parker, G., Wilhelm, K., & Asghari, A. (1979). Early onset depression: The relevance of anxiety. *Social Psychiatry and Psychiatric Epidemiology, 32,* 30–37.

Parry, G. (1986). Paid employment, life events, social support and mental health in working class mothers. *Journal of Health and Social Behaviour, 27,* 193–208.

Patten, S. B. (1997). Performance of the Composite International Diagnostic Interview Short Form for major depression in community and clinical samples. *Chronic Diseases in Canada, 18,* 109–112.

Patten, S. B. (2000). Major depression prevalence in Calgary. *Canadian Journal of Psychiatry, 45,* 923–926.

Penrose, L. S. (1963). *The biology of mental defect.* London: Sidgwick & Jackson.

Pereda, N., Guilera, G., Forns, M., & Gomez-Benito, J. (2009). The prevalence of child sexual abuse in community and student samples: A meta-analysis. *Clinical Psychology Review, 29,* 328–338.

Putnam, F. W. (2003). Ten-year research update review: Child sexual abuse. *Journal of the American Academy of Child and Adolescent Psychiatry, 42,* 269–278.

Ramana, R., & Bebbington, P. E. (1995). Social influences on bipolar affective disorder. *Social Psychiatry and Psychiatric Epidemiology, 30,* 152–160.

Read, J., van Os, J., Morrison, A. P., & Ross, C. A. (2005). Childhood trauma, psychosis and schizophrenia: A literature review with theoretical and clinical implications. *Acta Psychiatrica Scandinavica, 112,* 330–350.

Reiter, S., & Lapido-Lefler, N. (2007). Bullying among special education students with intellectual disabilities: Differences in social adjustment and social skills. *Intellectual and Developmental Disabilities, 45,* 174–181.

Roberts, C. R., Roberts, R. E., & Stevenson, J. M. (1982). Women, work, social support and psychiatric morbidity. *Social Psychiatry, 17,* 167–173.

Roberts, R., Golding, J., Towell, T., & Weinreb, I. (1999). The effects of economic circumstances on British students' mental and physical health. *Journal of American College Health, 48,* 103–109.

Roberts, R. E., & O'Keefe, S. J. (1981). Sex differences in depression re-examined. *Journal of Health and Social Behaviour, 22,* 394–400.

Robins, L. N. (1995). How to choose among the riches: Selecting a diagnostic instrument. In M. T. Tsuang, M. Tohen, & G. E. P. Zahner (Eds.), *Textbook in psychiatric epidemiology.* New York: Wiley-Liss.

Robins, L. N., Helzer, J. E., Croughan, J., & Ratcliff, K. S. (1981). National Institute of Mental Health Diagnostic Interview Schedule: Its history, characteristics and validity. *Archives of General Psychiatry, 38,* 381–389.

Robins, L. N., & Regier, D. A. (1991). *Psychiatric disorders in America: The epidemiological catchment area study.* New York: Free Press.

Robins, L. N., Wing, J. K., Wittchen, H. U., Helzer, J. E., Babor, T. F., Burke, J. D., … Towle, L. H. (1988). The composite international diagnostic interview. *Archives of General Psychiatry, 45,* 1069–1077.

Robinson, S. (2006). Victimization of obese children. *Journal of School Nursing, 22,* 201–206.

Sartorius, N. (2010). Revision of the classification of mental disorders in ICD-11 and DSM-V: Work in progress. *Advances in Psychiatric Treatment, 16,* 2–9.

Schotte, K., & Cooper, B. (1999). Subthreshold affective disorders: A useful concept in psychiatric epidemiology? *Epidemiologia e Psichiatria Sociale, 8,* 255–261.

Siegrist, J. (1996). Adverse health effects of high-effort/low-reward conditions. *Journal of Occupational Health Psychology, 1,* 27–41.

Siegrist, J. (2008). Chronic psychosocial stress at work and risk of depression: Evidence from prospective studies. *European Archives of Psychiatry and Clinical Neuroscience, 258,* 115–119.

Simmons, L. A., & Swanberg, J. E. (2009). Psychosocial work environment and depressive symptoms among US workers: Comparing working poor and working non-poor. *Social Psychiatry and Psychiatric Epidemiology, 44,* 628–635.

Singleton, N., Bumpstead, R., O'Brien, M., Lee, A., & Meltzer, H. (2001). *Psychiatric morbidity among adults living in private households, 2000.* London: The Stationery Office.

Slade, T., Johnston, A., Oakley Browne, M. A., Andrews, G., & Whiteford, H. (2009). 2007 National Survey of Mental Health and Wellbeing: Methods and key findings. *Australian and New Zealand Journal of Psychiatry, 43,* 594–605.

Smith, P. K., & Monks, C. P. (2008). Concepts of bullying: Developmental and cultural aspects. *International Journal of Adolescent Medicine and Health, 20,* 101–112.

Sourander, A., Ronning, J., Brunstein-Klomek, A., Gyllenberg, D., Kumpulainen, K., Niemela, S., … Almqvist, F. (2009). Childhood bullying behaviour and later psychiatric hospital and psychopharmacologic treatment. *Archives of General Psychiatry, 66,* 1005–1012.

Spauwen, J., Krabbendam, L., Lieb, R., Wittchen, H. U., & van Os, J. (2006). Impact of psychological trauma on the development of psychotic symptoms: Relationship with psychosis proneness. *British Journal of Psychiatry, 188,* 527–533.

Spiers, N., Brugha, T., Bebbington, P. E., McManus, S., Jenkins, R., & Meltzer, H. (2012). Age and birth cohort differences in depression in repeated cross-sectional surveys in England: The National Psychiatric Morbidity Surveys, 1993 to 2007. *Psychological Medicine, 42,* 2047–2055.

Stansfeld, S., & Candy, B. (2006). Psychosocial work environment and mental health—A meta-analytic review. *Scandinavian Journal of Work Environment and Health, 32,* 443–462.

Sturt, E. (1981). Hierarchical patterns in the incidence of psychiatric symptoms. *Psychological Medicine, 11,* 783–794.

Sverke, M., Hellgren, J., & Näswall, K. (2002). No security: A meta-analysis and review of job insecurity and its consequences. *Journal of Occupational Health Psychology, 7,* 242–264.

Talala, K., Huurre, T., Aro, H., Martelin, T., & Prattala, R. (2009). Trends in socio-economic differences in self-reported depression during the years 1979–2002 in Finland. *Social Psychiatry and Psychiatric Epidemiology, 44,* 871–879.

Tennant, C., Bebbington, P. E., & Hurry, J. (1980). Parental death in childhood and risk of adult depressive disorders: A review. *Psychological Medicine, 10,* 289–299.

Tennant, C., Hurry, J., & Bebbington, P. E. (1980). Parent–child separation during childhood: Their relation to adult psychiatric morbidity and to psychiatric referral. *Acta Psychiatrica, 285,* 324–331.

Theodossiou, I. (1998). The effects of low pay and unemployment on psychological well-being: A logistical regression approach. *Journal of Health Economics, 17,* 85–104.

Tyrer, P. (1985). Neurosis divisible? *Lancet, 1,* 685–688.

Warr, P., & Parry, G. (1982). Paid employment and women's psychological well-being. *Psychological Bulletin, 91,* 498–516.

Weiss, E. L., Longhurst, J. G., & Mazure, C. M. (1999). Childhood sexual abuse as a risk factor for depression in women: Psychosocial and neurobiological correlates. *American Journal of Psychiatry, 156,* 816–828.

Weissman, M. M., Bland, R. D., Canino, G. J., Faravelli, C., Greenwald, S., Hwu, H. G., . . . Yeh, E. K. (1996). Cross-national epidemiology of major depression and bipolar disorder. *Journal of the American Medical Association, 276,* 292–299.

Wilhelm, K., Niven, H., Parker, G., & Hadzi-Pavlovic, D. (2005). The stability of the Parental Bonding Instrument over a 20-year period. *Psychological Medicine, 35,* 387–393.

Wing, J., Wing, J. K., Babor, T., Brugha, T., Burke, J., & Cooper, J. E. (1990). SCAN: Schedules for Clinical Assessment in Neuropsychiatry. *Archives of General Psychiatry, 47,* 589–593.

Wing, J. K., Mann, S. A., Leff, J. P., & Nixon, J. N. (1978). The concept of a case in psychiatric population surveys. *Psychological Medicine, 8,* 203–219.

World Health Organization. (1992a). *SCAN: Schedules for clinical assessment in neuropsychiatry.* Geneva: WHO.

World Health Organization. (1992b). *Tenth revision of the international classification of diseases.* Geneva: WHO.

# 2

# Biological Models of Unipolar Depression

## Anthony J. Cleare and Lena J. Rane

King's College London, UK

## Introduction

In this chapter, the focus will be on reviewing what is currently known about biological dysfunction in depression, and attempting to develop coherent models of the relevance of these changes. The parallels, and interactions, of the biology of depression with other features will be referred to throughout.

## Genetic Models of Depression

It has been clear for decades that there is a significant genetic predisposition to depression. Family studies show increased familial risk—the earlier the age of onset the higher the familial risk—and twin and adoption studies confirm a clear genetic component, though less for community sampled or "neurotic" depression suggesting a lesser biological component (Hirschfield & Weissman, 2002). What is less clear is how this genetic risk translates into the expression of depressive illness. No evidence exists for true Mendelian inheritance. Family and twin studies also show a clear genetic component to life events themselves (Kendler & Karkowski-Shuman, 1997). Thus, both the tendency to suffer adversity and to respond to it by becoming depressed have genetic components.

There are a number of theories as to what mediates the genetic risk. Suggestions include

- other biological changes (such as genetic polymorphisms);
- the response to stress;
- the tendency to have life events;
- other factors and/or behaviors within the syndrome.

Several attempts have been made to look for polymorphic variation in gene alleles that might be linked to depression (Cravchik & Goldman, 2000). This candidate gene approach initially identified a number of positive findings; however, none were consistently replicated. Recent genome-wide association studies (GWAS), including

*The Wiley-Blackwell Handbook of Mood Disorders*, Second Edition. Edited by Mick Power.
© 2013 John Wiley & Sons, Ltd. Published 2013 by John Wiley & Sons, Ltd.

a meta-analysis of 6,000 cases, have also yet to provide consistent findings (Wray et al., 2010). Rather than genes increasing the risk of depression in isolation, it is the tendency to become depressed in response to stressful life events that seems to be inherited (Hirschfield & Weissman, 2002). It is perhaps not surprising then that studies of gene–environment interactions (G×E) have yielded more consistent results. These show that allelic polymorphisms of certain candidate genes interact with life stressors to increase the risk of depression.

The first G×E study of depression focused on the 5-HTTLPR (serotonin trans-porter promoter region) polymorphism and found that the short allele, associated with lower expression of the gene, was also associated with a higher risk of depression following stressful life events or childhood maltreatment (Caspi et al., 2003). This finding links genetic risk with the 5-HT hypothesis of depression. Although the find-ing was replicated in more than 20 studies, two subsequent meta-analyses (Munafo, Durrant, Lewis, & Flint, 2009; Risch et al., 2009) were negative. It has been sug-gested that these analyzed a biased subset of the literature and used an unreliable subjective measure of stress. The most recent meta-analysis, the largest undertaken thus far of 56 studies, has confirmed the association between 5-HTTLPR, stress, and the development of depression (Karg, Burmeister, Shedden, & Sen, 2011).

Similar replicated G×E effects have been identified in studies (Tyrka et al., 2009) of a gene encoding the corticotropin-releasing hormone receptor 1 (CRHR1), which modulates the activity of the hypothalamic–pituitary–adrenal (HPA) axis, a system thought to play a key role in the etiology of depression (see section on HPA-axis activity). G×E effects have also been found for a polymorphism of the gene encoding brain-derived neurotrophic factor (BDNF), where the val/met allele results in reduced expression of BDNF and confers increased risk for depression after childhood adversity (Juhasz et al., 2011); functionally, BDNF promotes neurogenesis in the hippocampus and may protect against glucocorticoid-induced reduction of neurogenesis.

One interesting question relates to the observation that depression tends to be recurrent, and that there is a tendency for each recurrence to be less dependent on precipitating stress, a process likened to kindling. Kendler, Thornton, and Gardner (2001) investigated the genetic contribution to this phenomenon in their large twin pair sample; they found that genetic risk tended to place people in a "prekindled" state rather than speeding up the process of kindling.

Future genetic research may investigate epigenetic modifications to the genome, such as DNA methylation, which is potentially a means of controlling the expression of genetic risk and may link early adverse environment to later psychopathology (for critical review see Miller, 2010).

## Endocrine Models of Depression

### Hypothalamic–pituitary–adrenal axis

*Research findings*   The HPA axis mediates the response of the body to stress; as such, it has been a natural focus of biological research into a disorder with a close link to stress. A schematic representation of the HPA axis is shown in Figure 2.1. The HPA axis has been extensively studied in depression; about 50% of depressed patients show a picture of hypercortisolemia. However, this varies with the symptomatic picture: rates

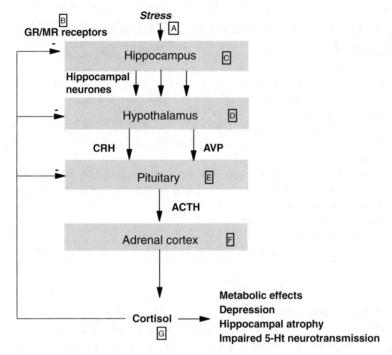

**Figure 2.1.** Schematic Representation of the Control of the Hypothalamic–pituitary–adrenal (HPA) axis. Abnormalities in this Axis in Depression are Shown in Box 2.1. CRH, corticotropin-releasing hormone; ACTH, pituitary corticotropin; AVP, arginine vasopressin; MR, mineralocorticoid receptors; GR, glucocorticoid receptors

are higher in those with features of DSM-IV melancholic depression, strong somatic symptoms, or psychosis (Schatzberg, Garlow, & Nemeroff, 2002).

Assessing the HPA axis can be problematic. Cortisol is a pulsatile hormone, has a strong diurnal rhythm, and it is released in stressful circumstances, such as in blood sampling. For this reason, more detailed methods of endocrinological assessment are needed. A widely used method in depression has been the dexamethasone suppression test (DST). Dexamethasone is a synthetic glucocorticoid which suppresses hypothalamic corticotropin-releasing hormone (CRH) and pituitary corticotropin (ACTH) via glucocorticoid receptors (Figure 2.1). In a proportion of depressed individuals such suppression fails to occur, averaging around 60–70% in melancholic depression and 30–40% in "neurotic" depression. The test is not specific to depression, as nonsuppression can be seen in other conditions. A further refinement of this test is the combined dexamethasone–CRH test. Dexamethasone preadministration usually attenuates the cortisol response to CRH; in depression, this effect is less pronounced due to downregulated glucocorticoid receptors. This test has proved more able to distinguish depressed subjects from normal ones than the simple DST (Heuser et al., 1994).

Recent approaches have tried to use naturalistic and noninvasive measures, such as the cortisol rise that occurs after waking, as an index of HPA activity. There is evidence that this is raised in depression (Bhagwagar, Hafizi, & Cowen, 2005), as well as in

---

**Box 2.1**   HPA axis abnormalities in depression (non-atypical) relating to Figure 2.1

---

A   Increased incidence of childhood adversity, life events, and chronic stress
B   Impaired hippocampal fast (rate-sensitive) feedback; GR resistance
C   Hippocampal atrophy
D   Raised CRH levels in the cerebrospinal fluid; impaired negative feedback by
      dexamethasone; impaired negative feedback by prednisolone in a subset of
      highly treatment-resistant patients
E   Impaired pituitary ACTH response to CRH administration; this may represent
      downregulated CRH receptors or negative feedback from high cortisol levels;
      pituitary hypertrophy
F   Hypertrophied adrenal cortices
G   Hypercortisolism

---

those in remission from depression (Bhagwagar, Hafizi, & Cowen, 2003) and those at high familial risk of depression (Mannie, Harmer, & Cowen, 2007).

Box 2.1 outlines the specific findings of the various tests applied to components of the HPA axis.

*Conceptual models*   Thus, in a substantial proportion of depressed patients, there is oversecretion of cortisol and reduced negative feedback at the hypothalamus and pituitary. Can cortisol hypersecretion be considered a plausible biological mechanism for depression? First, since cortisol is the main stress hormone, it is easy to see how it might mediate between life events and biological changes in depression. Evidence that raised cortisol levels may be driving depression rather than vice versa comes from studies showing that lowering cortisol levels, for example, by administering cortisol synthesis inhibitor drugs such as metyrapone or ketoconazole can alleviate depression (Murphy, 1997). Furthermore, successful antidepressant treatment is associated with resolution of the impairment in the negative feedback on the HPA axis by glucocorticoids (Pariante, 2006). On the other hand, raised cortisol secretion in endogenous Cushing's is associated with depression in between 50% and 85% of cases. Furthermore, abnormally high cortisol levels have been shown to be associated with other biological changes, such as inhibitory effects on neuronal 5-HT neurotransmission; given the links between 5-HT neurotransmission and mood changes, this is a feasible mechanism for the dysregulation of 5-HT neurotransmission. There are also suggestions that prolonged periods of high cortisol can lead to hippocampal atrophy—indeed, in Cushing's disease, the decreased hippocampus size can be correlated with plasma cortisol levels and cognitive impairment. Recent studies also show hippocampal atrophy in depression (Sheline & Minyun, 2002). Hippocampal volume loss is hypothesized to be a result of neurotoxicity, reduced neurogenesis or dendritic atrophy (see the section on *Neuroimaging* for further discussion on mechanisms of hippocampal atrophy). Antidepressants may exert their action via enhancement of hippocampal neurogenesis through activation of the glucocorticoid receptor (Anacker et al., 2011).

However, the role of the HPA may also be seen in other ways. Adverse circumstances in childhood, such as losing parents or suffering abuse, are well known to predispose an individual to depression. Recent work suggests that the HPA axis may provide some further understanding of the mechanism of this link. Experiencing childhood abuse leads to a long-term alteration of the stress response (Heim et al., 2000). Thus, it is also possible to use the HPA axis changes as a biological link between early life stresses and an increased vulnerability to stress and depression.

Others have noted that changes elsewhere in the HPA axis may mediate symptoms. For example, CRH may also act as a neurotransmitter, and produces symptoms of agitation, insomnia, and reduced feeding in animals. The amount of CRH expressed in cells, and the co-occurrence of CRH with its synergistic ACTH releaser vasopressin, is increased in depressed suicide victims. CRH levels in the CSF are increased. Furthermore, CRH receptors are found in the cortex, and show a reduced density in suicide victims, consistent with high levels of CRH release. Thus, increased CRH in depression could contribute to some symptoms (Nemeroff, 1996).

The importance of the HPA axis changes in depression go beyond the apparent ability to provide a neat mediator between stressful events and symptoms, but also into prognostic indicators. There are suggestions that DST nonsuppression is associated with a poorer response to placebo (though not a superior response to medication) and a poorer response to cognitive therapy (Thase et al., 1996). More strikingly, if clinical response to treatment is associated with continued nonsuppression, there is a four-fold increase in the risk of short-term relapse or suicide attempt. The long-term risk of suicide was also found to be more closely linked to DST nonsuppression than any other factor, more so even than past suicide attempts (Coryell & Sehlesser, 2001).

While dexamethasone acts predominantly on glucocorticoid receptors outside of the blood brain barrier, prednisolone has a more naturalistic effect on both glucocorticoid and mineralocorticoid receptors more akin to that of cortisol, and penetrates the blood–brain barrier. Recent work suggests that mineralocorticoid receptor function remains intact in depression (Juruena et al., 2010), and is able to compensate for the reduced glucocorticoid receptor function such that patients who are dexamethasone nonsuppressors are able to suppress to prednisolone (Juruena et al., 2006). Importantly, in severe cases of depression, the presence of a normal suppressive response to prednisolone predicts a good response to treatment, whereas prednisolone nonsuppression is associated with failure to respond even to the most intensive treatment (Juruena et al., 2009).

In summary, there is no doubt that HPA axis dysfunction is present in a large proportion of depressed patients, particularly those with more melancholic, psychotic, or treatment-resistant symptom patterns. The HPA axis is able to provide a plausible biological mechanism for some of the most replicated causal theories of depression. Thus, the links between depressive symptoms and stressful life events, chronic social adversity, and/or traumatic or abusive childhoods could all be explained through the mediating role of the HPA axis.

## Hypothalamic–pituitary–thyroid axis

Clinical disorders of thyroid function are known to cause alteration in mood. Classically, patients with hypothyroidism frequently report features similar to depression,

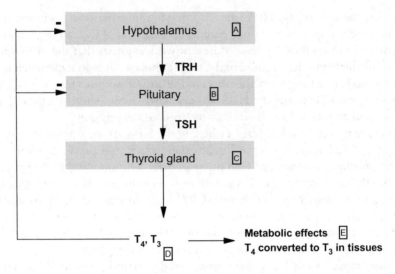

**Figure 2.2.** Schematic Representation of the Control of the Hypothalamic–pituitary–thyroid (HPT) axis. Abnormalities in this Axis in Depression are Shown in Box 2.2. TRH, thyrotropin-releasing hormone; TSH, thyroid-stimulating hormone; T$_3$, triiodothyronine; T$_4$, thyroxine

and while usually more closely linked to feelings of anxiety, depressive reactions are sometimes seen in hyperthyroid patients.

In depression, several abnormalities in thyroid function have been described. Figure 2.2 shows the axis and Box 2.2 lists the same abnormalities described. While not entirely consistent, the blunted TSH response to TRH could be due to hypersecretion of TRH, causing downregulation of pituitary TRH receptors.

Given the suggestions of subclinical hypothyroidism in depression, albeit in a minority, it is natural to ask about the effects of thyroid hormone treatment. There is evidence from older randomized controlled trials of tricyclic antidepressants that thyroid hormone may potentiate both speed and efficacy of antidepressant medication (Altshuler et al., 2001), and more recent evidence that triiodothyronine (T$_3$) augmentation of SSRIs is effective, and possibly linked to pretreatment subclinical thyroid dysfunction (Cooper-Kazaz et al., 2007). Furthermore, there is also evidence that patients resistant

---

**Box 2.2  Thyroid axis abnormalities in depression relating to Figure 2.2**

| | |
|---|---|
| A | Increased TRH in cerebrospinal fluid |
| B | Reduced TSH response to TRH administration (30%) |
| C | Anti-thyroid antibodies (9–20%) |
| D | Subclinical hypothyroidism |
| E | Treatment response to T$_3$ or T$_4$ augmentation strategies |

to other treatments may respond to such treatment. There is also some evidence that low $T_3$ levels are prospectively associated with a higher rate of relapse in the long term (Joffe & Marriott, 2000) and that antithyroid antibodies predict postpartum depression (Harris et al., 1992). Other theories of how $T_3$ might work include an effect on serotonergic receptors (Lifschytz et al., 2006) and increased hippocampus neurogenesis (Eitan et al., 2009).

## DHEA

There has been much recent interest in the role of dehydroepiandrosterone (DHEA), both in healthy aging and depression. Although not entirely clear what has emerged is that DHEA may exert an anticortisol effect. It has been argued, therefore, that increased "net" effects of cortisol may occur if there is low DHEA, and that high levels of cortisol may not be biologically damaging if they are accompanied by high DHEA levels. Thus, many have started to measure the cortisol/DHEA ratio as an index more likely to be relevant to the causation of depression. Work to date suggests that this ratio may be higher in patients with depression (Markopoulou et al., 2009; Young, Gallagher, & Porter, 2002). Also, in a large cross-sectional study, DHEA and dehydroepiandrosterone sulfate (DHEA-S) were found to be inversely correlated with depression scores (Barrett-Connor, von Muhlen, Laughlin, & Kripke, 1999). Finally, some studies do suggest that DHEA treatment may be an effective antidepressant, presumably acting by reducing the biological effects of cortisol (Wolkowitz et al., 1999). However, this work remains in its early stages.

# Neurochemical Models of Depression

Brain neurochemistry was one of the first suspects in the search for the biological basis of depression. The original monoamine hypothesis of depression derived from the findings that monoamine depletion from the drug reserpine caused depression, while antidepressants inhibited monoamine reuptake. Subsequent reports that there were reduced monoamine breakdown products in the CSF led to the theory that there is a deficiency of noradrenaline, dopamine and/or 5-HT at monoaminergic synapses. From this original hypothesis, several proposed biological models of depression are worthy of discussion.

## Serotonin hypothesis of depression

Classically, several pieces of evidence are cited to support this theory (see Maes & Meltzer, 1995, for review). First, there is evidence of a reduced availability of the 5-HT precursor tryptophan. Studies suggest reduced plasma levels of tryptophan and also enhanced non-CNS pathways for tryptophan catabolism, such as the kynurenine pathway in the liver.

Second, there is evidence of changes in the normal physiology of serotonin metabolism. For example, there is reduced uptake of 5-HT into the platelets (a model of the neuronal 5-HT transporter system).

Third, there are several ways of demonstrating 5-HT receptor changes in depression. Early work relied on the use of brains from postmortem studies of depressed suicides. Some studies reported increased 5-HT$_2$ receptors, although results are inconsistent and the link may be specifically with those who die by violent suicide (Horton, 1992). There is also evidence for reduced 5-HT$_{1A}$ receptor binding and/or affinity in the hippocampus and amygdala (Maes & Meltzer, 1995). A further approach has been to use neuropharmacological challenge tests. These tests are used to test the integrity of neurotransmitter systems. Standardized serotonergic drug challenges are given, and a physiological response is measured, such as hormone release or temperature change. The magnitude of the response is taken as an index of the activity of the system challenged. Many of these studies, although by no means all, have reported impairments in depression. One example is of a blunted prolactin response to fenfluramine, a 5-HT-releasing drug. Other positive examples include a blunted prolactin response to the 5-HT precursor L-tryptophan, and a blunted response to the serotonin reuptake inhibitor, clomipramine.

Fourth, the technique of tryptophan depletion (TD) suggests that there may be a casual relationship between 5-HT changes and depression. The TD paradigm involves administration of a mixture of amino acids without tryptophan. This leads to a large and rapid fall in plasma tryptophan, reduced brain tryptophan entry, and reduced 5-HT synthesis. TD in depressed subjects has not revealed consistent results, perhaps because the system is maximally dysregulated. On the other hand, TD depletion temporarily induces depressive symptoms in vulnerable groups such as remitted depressed patients, those with a family history of depression and females (Reilly, McTavish, & Young, 1997). This research provides powerful evidence that serotonergic function is causally related to mood states rather than merely showing a cross-sectional association. This technique may also have a predictive value, in that depressed patients in remission who show a mood reducing effect of TD have higher rates of true relapse in the following 12 months (Moreno, Heninger, McGahuey, & Delgado, 2000). This suggests that certain individuals may have a biological vulnerability to short-term depressogenic effects of reduced brain 5-HT availability, which places them at increased risk of future major depression, possibly as a response to other biological or environmental causes of reduced 5-HT availability.

One anomaly is the observation that the mood lowering effect of TD does not occur to a significant degree in remitted depressed patients receiving continuation treatment with desipramine, a noradrenergic specific tricyclic (Delgado et al., 1999). They do however experience the effect if noradrenaline synthesis is inhibited; however, this procedure does not affect patients taking SSRIs (Delgado et al., 1999).

More recently, neuroimaging techniques have increased our knowledge about 5-HT changes in depression; these will be described later in the chapter.

One argument against the significance of serotonergic changes in depression comes from observations that several enduring character traits may be closely related to 5-HT function. Thus, while early studies of CSF concentrations of the 5-HT breakdown product 5-HIAA reported reduced levels in depression, more recent studies suggest that low CSF 5-HIAA and other indices of reduced serotonergic function are linked more specifically to suicide, impulsivity, aggression, or other personality variables (Cleare & Bond, 1997; Mann, 1995). Thus, 5-HT changes in depression may reflect these factors.

**Table 2.1.**

Summary of Serotonergic Abnormalities in Depressed Patients

| Index of 5-HT function | Abnormality in depression (relative to controls) | Reliability of finding (consistency and/or replication) |
| --- | --- | --- |
| Platelets | | |
| Platelet 5-HT uptake | Lowered | Good |
| Platelet imipramine binding | Lowered | Modest |
| Platelet 5-HT2A receptor binding | Increased | Poor |
| Plasma | | |
| Plasma tryptophan | Lowered | Good |
| Cerebrospinal fluid | | |
| CSF-5HIAA | Lowered | Poor (but more consistent in suicidal patients) |
| Neuroendocrine challenges | | |
| Prolactin response to serotonergic challenges | Lowered | Good |
| Brain receptors/neuroimaging | | |
| 5-HT2A receptor binding (postmortem) | Increased—predominantly in violent suicide victims | Modest |
| 5-HT1A receptor binding (PET) | Lowered acutely; remains low in remission | Good |
| 5-HT2A receptor binding (PET/SPET) | Lowered/increased/normal | Poor |
| 5-HT transporter binding (PET/SPET) | Lowered/increased/normal | Poor |

*Source:* Adapted from Cowen and Harmer (2009).

A further issue is whether the serotonergic changes are state or trait related. Many of the neuroendocrine challenge tests such as fenfluramine normalize with treatment of the depression (Maes & Meltzer, 1995). However, the prolactin response to intravenous citalopram remains blunted even after patients have recovered (Bhagwagar, Whale, & Cowen, 2002) and the reduced $5\text{-HT}_{1A}$ receptor binding seen with PET does not normalize after treatment with SSRI medication (Sargent et al., 2000). This suggests that some of the observed changes in depression may indeed be trait markers, and could therefore be linked to vulnerability or personality rather than the depressive state.

Cowen and Harmer (2009) have recently reviewed the consistency of the evidence for various serotonergic abnormalities in depression; their conclusions are summarized in Table 2.1. They are further discussed under *Neurochemical imaging*.

## Noradrenergic theories

There is evidence of noradrenergic dysfunction in depression. Many antidepressants are potent inhibitors of the reuptake of noradrenaline, with little effect on serotonin reuptake. Neuroendocrine challenge studies have found evidence of reduced nora-drenergic function. For example, there is a reduced growth hormone (GH) response to the $\alpha_2$ agonist clonidine and desipramine, both of which suggest impaired $\alpha_2$ receptor function. This abnormality remains blunted when off medication and non-depressed, suggesting it could be a trait marker. Postmortem and platelet studies also provide some support for changes in $\alpha$ and $\beta$ adrenergic receptors. Several studies have shown that low urinary levels of the noradrenaline metabolite MHPG predict a favorable response to tricyclics (Schatzberg et al., 2002).

A novel method, though highly invasive, has more recently been described that provides further evidence of reduced catecholamine availability in the brain in depression (Lambert, Johansson, Agren, & Friberg, 2000). Patients with treatment-resistant depression underwent catheterization in the brachial artery for arterial blood and in the internal jugular vein for venous blood draining from the brain. The main findings were that there was a reduced concentration gradient in depression for noradrenaline and its metabolites and for the dopamine metabolite, homovanillic acid (HVA); this suggests reduced amounts of these neurotransmitters stemming from the brain.

## Dopaminergic theories

There is some evidence of a reduced GH response to apomorphine, a dopamine receptor agonist, in depression, but results are inconsistent with this challenge (Schatzberg et al., 2002). Interest in the dopaminergic system has been rekindled by the introduction of bupropion, an antidepressant that works largely through effects on dopamine reuptake.

## Cholinergic theories

Studies have shown an enhanced GH response to the anticholinesterase drug pyridostigmine, a measure of acetylcholine receptor function. Further evidence comes from the observation of reduced REM latency and increased REM sleep in depression, effects that may represent increased cholinergic activity. Furthermore, depressed patients show supersensitivity to the REM sleep effects of cholinergics. Janowsky and Overstreet (1995) proposed the cholinergic–adrenergic balance theory of depression, hypothesizing that increased cholinergic function and reduced noradrenergic function were both important in generating symptoms in depression.

## GABA-ergic theories

There is a reduced GH response to baclofen, a GABA-B receptor agonist, suggesting reduced GABA receptor activity in depression (O'Flynn & Dinan, 1993). Plasma GABA may also be low (Schatzberg et al., 2002).

## Interactions of monoamines

There is now increasing evidence that drugs that affect one neurotransmitter system can also affect another through downstream effects. If one looks simply at serotonin, there are innumerable examples. Thus, serotonergic heteroceptors are found on neurons primarily involved in the release of other neurotransmitters; there is evidence that 5-HT$_{1D}$ receptors may act in an inhibitory manner in this way. Noradrenergic receptors may be present on serotonergic nerve cell bodies and terminals: $\alpha_1$ receptors on serotonergic cell bodies act to increase cell firing and 5-HT release, while $\alpha_2$ receptors are present on serotonergic nerve terminals and are inhibitory to 5-HT release. Projections of serotonergic neurons to other areas of the brain are known to inhibit dopaminergic function in the cortex and elsewhere. The serotonin transporter protein is thought to interact with the ability of $\alpha_2$ receptors to inhibit 5-HT cell firing. Finally, noradrenaline reuptake inhibition is potentiated in the presence of simultaneous 5-HT reuptake inhibition.

It is likely that a number of neurotransmitter alterations are present in depression. Clinically, it is of relevance that drugs that act on both serotonin and noradrenaline, such as amitriptyline (Barbui & Hotopf, 2001) and venlafaxine (Smith, Dempster, Glanville, Freemantle, & Anderson, 2002), may have slightly enhanced efficacy in the treatment of depression.

It has also been suggested, although with little direct empirical evidence to date, that within the depressive syndrome, different clusters of symptoms may relate differentially to different monoamine dysfunction; for example, noradrenergic dysfunction being related to symptoms such as poor motivation, apathy and anergia, and serotonergic dysfunction to appetite and sleep disruption.

## Neuroimaging Models of Depression

Recent rapid advances in neuroimaging methodology have heralded attempts to relate the phenomenological abnormalities seen in depression to changes in brain structure and function (Fu, Walsh, & Drevets, 2003). Neuroimaging can broadly be broken up into structural and functional techniques.

### Structural

There is increasing evidence that depression may be associated with structural brain pathology. Magnetic resonance imaging has revealed decreased volume in cortical and subcortical regions. These findings are supported by postmortem studies. A recent meta-analysis has shown that unipolar depression is associated with reductions in frontal, hippocampal, thalamic, and basal ganglia volumes (Kempton et al., 2011). Amygdala volumes have been found to be increased or decreased compared with healthy controls according to whether subjects are taking antidepressants (Hamilton, Siemer, & Gotlib, 2008); some have postulated that this is due to the neurotrophic effects of psychotropics (see section on HPA axis). Similarly, there is evidence that hippocampal volumes are increased by lithium treatment, based on studies of patients with bipolar disorder. Gray matter volume loss is also affected by whether patients are in episode; hippocampal volume reduction is greater in acutely depressed compared with remitted patients (Kempton et al., 2011). In summary, then, the brain volumetric studies in depression generally demonstrate a reduction in gray matter volume; inconsistencies may be due to differences in scan resolution, delineation of anatomical parameters, stage of illness, duration of illness, inclusion of bipolar subjects, and use of psychotropic medication.

The mechanism of gray matter volume reduction has been attributed to elevated HPA-axis activity, which is often present in depressed patients; this is supported by studies of patients with Cushing's disease and those receiving corticosteroid therapy which show general cerebral volume reduction (Bourdeau et al., 2002) and smaller hippocampi (Starkman, Gebarski, Berent, & Schteingart, 1992). These structural changes are reversible on normalization of HPA-axis activity. Hippocampal volume reduction in depression, however, persists beyond the remission of depression. The hippocampus provides negative modulation of the HPA axis and therefore, hippocampal volume loss may lead to a vicious cycle that serves to maintain HPA-axis hyperactivity. A small hippocampus may be a marker of vulnerability for depression; there is evidence that it is smaller in the unaffected relatives of those with depression (Amico et al., 2010), and in subjects who have experienced early life trauma (Vythilingam et al., 2002, 2004). Furthermore, higher resolution scanning techniques also allow subregional changes in hippocampus morphology to be identified; whether these may have specificity to depression is not yet clear (Cole et al., 2010).

The postulated mechanisms of glucocorticoid-induced hippocampal loss include neurotoxicity and decreased neurogenesis. However, postmortem studies in patients with depression have only shown loss of dendrites and neuropil without frank cell loss (Stockmeier et al., 2004), casting doubt over the neurotoxicity hypothesis of depression. There is more compelling evidence from transgenic mice that glucocorticoids depress hippocampal neurogenesis, resulting in a depressive phenotype (Snyder, Soumier, Brewer, Pickel, & Cameron, 2011), although it is unlikely that reduced neurogenesis alone is responsible for the degree of hippocampal volume loss seen in neuroimaging studies of depressed subjects (up to 10–15%). Neurotrophic factors such as BDNF may also play a role in hippocampal neurogenesis and volume; subjects carrying the met allele of the BDNF gene polymorphism have smaller hippocampi than those with the val/val genotype (Bueller et al., 2006), and furthermore, various antidepressants have been shown to enhance expression of BDNF expression in the hippocampus.

It has been known for some time that elderly depressives have features of cerebral atrophy (sulcal widening and ventricular enlargement) midway between that in depression and dementia. Patients with pseudodementia have more abnormalities than those without. More recently, a model of "vascular depression" (Alexopoulos, 2005) occurring later in life has emerged, suggesting that some individuals with depression in old age have underlying cerebrovascular disease affecting areas of the brain important in the control of mood. While perhaps more obvious in the case of poststroke depression, microvascular disease seems also to be associated with depression. For example, MRI scans and measures of depression were taken in 1077, nondemented, elderly adults (Cees de Groot et al., 2000). Virtually all subjects had white matter lesions; the 5% of patients without them had lower depression scores than the rest. When adjusted for other relevant variables, those with more severe white matter lesions were up to five times more likely to have depressive symptoms compared to those with only mild white matter lesions. Of those with a depressive disorder, those with an onset after age 60 had more severe white matter lesions than those with an onset before age 60.

Postmortem studies show that these white matter lesions seen in depressed subjects are usually ischemic in origin, but may be due to other causes, such as dilated periventricular spaces, in nondepressed individuals (Thomas et al., 2002). Some have argued that the relationship between white matter lesions and depression may be confounded by physical disability, educational level, or cognitive impairment, but there is evidence that the association with depression remains even after controlling these factors (Teodorczuk et al., 2007). White matter lesion load may be the basis for the executive dysfunction and memory deficits (Kohler et al., 2010) often seen in late-onset and elderly depression, but it is less clear whether these deficits persist after remission.

Further support for the vascular depression hypothesis is given by the finding that the localization of white matter lesions, as well as overall white matter lesion volume, is important; thus, higher white matter lesion burden has been found in the frontal lobes (Simpson, Baldwin, Jackson, & Burns, 1998; Thomas et al., 2002), basal ganglia, and specific white matter tracts (Dalby et al., 2009; Sheline et al., 2008) of depressed subjects compared with nondepressed controls. These areas form part of frontostriatal tracts thought to be important in the regulation of mood. However, a comprehensive meta-analysis undertaken recently (Kempton et al., 2011) demonstrated that only basal ganglia lesions are significantly associated with unipolar depression, and that other white matter lesions are more important in bipolar disorder.

The implications of such vascular contributions to depression include the possibility of whether it can be prevented by early monitoring and intervention of cardiovascular risk factors thought to underlie white matter lesions. Clinically, depression associated with vascular disease appears to be more resistant to treatment (Heiden et al., 2005; Hickie et al., 1995; Taylor et al., 2003).

## Functional imaging

Functional neuroimaging assesses neural function in different brain regions by measuring metabolism (e.g., glucose utilization) or blood flow, both of which are thought to be closely coupled to neural activation. Most studies of resting activity have described hypofrontality, particularly in the dorsolateral prefrontal and anterior cingulate cortices, and several groups have also described decreased activity in the basal ganglia (Fu et al., 2003). However, criticisms of these studies include the difficulty in standardizing what the brain is actually doing in the resting state (Sheline & Minyun, 2002).

This has led to the use of functional neuroimaging while subjects undertake neuropsychological tasks. As well as standardizing what the brain is doing, this allows particular areas of the brain, or particular psychological functions, relevant to depression to be probed. In depression, this approach has uncovered impaired activation in, among other areas, the left anterior cingulate, right prefrontal cortex, and left caudate (Fu et al., 2003). Induction of low mood in normal subjects can induce similar changes to depressed subjects.

Several groups have studied emotional processing in depressed patients. Elliot, Rubinsztein, Sahakian, and Dolan (2002) used a cognitive task with emotional valence (happy, neutral, or sad). They found that depressed subjects demonstrated an attenuated response to neutral or happy objects, but an enhanced one to sad objects, again focused in anterior cingulate and prefrontal cortical regions. Facial expressions of differing emotional valences have also been used as the fMRI paradigm, and demonstrated abnormally increased amygdala activity in response to negative emotional faces, but decreased activity to positive emotional faces (Fu et al., 2004, 2007). It was notable that effective antidepressant treatment reversed these changes, thus enhancing the neural response to happy faces and reducing the response to sad faces. The concept of dynamic range was also considered by the authors, who measured the neural responses to differing intensities of emotional stimuli. In addition to the overall negative bias, there was a more constricted variation in neural responses to the varying emotional intensities in the depressed state than in the treated euthymic state (Fu et al., 2004). There is evidence that those at high familial risk of depression show similar abnormal neural responses to emotional stimuli (Mannie et al., 2008). It is also possible to present depressed subjects with emotional stimuli for too short a duration for conscious processing; the brain response to negative stimuli is enhanced and to positive stimuli is reduced even at these subliminal levels of perception (Suslow et al., 2009), suggesting a fundamental biological shift in emotional processing has occurred in the depressed brain. Genetics also influences neural responses to emotion; for example, polymorphisms and the 5-HT transporter modify the amygdala response to emotion (Frodl, Moller, & Meisenzahl, 2008).

A number of other studies have investigated the response to treatment in depression. Many show that pretreatment abnormalities reverse with treatment. The most consistent finding has been seen in the subgenual prefrontal cortex: activity is *increased* activation during an acute depressive state, which *decreases* following effective antidepressant treatment. It can also be shown that the negative biases characteristic of depression reverse early in the course of antidepressant treatment, before subsequent mood changes are observable (Harmer et al., 2009). The degree to which the brain shows enhanced emotional responses even after remission of depression also predicts relapse (Farb, Anderson, Bloch, & Segal, 2011).

Finally, rather than simply looking at one part of the brain in isolation, it may be most important to look at the various networks of the brain and how they are interlinked. These functional connections may be disrupted in the depressed state. Thus, one study revealed a complex picture of cortical and subcortical changes associated with treatment response to fluoxetine, with increases in the dorsal prefrontal cortex but decreases in the hippocampus (Mayberg et al., 2000). The analysis of changes in brain connectivity using path analysis and other statistical methodology may also yield more understanding of the clearly complex pathways in brain neurocircuitry. Thus, in the aforementioned studies of emotional processing, there was found to be a decoupling of the usual neural pathways involved in emotional processing, in this case between the amygdala and other corticolimbic regions; once again, this was found to reverse with treatment (Chen et al., 2008).

### Neurochemical imaging

Neuroimaging has also helped in the further investigation of the neurochemical deficits in depression. Positron emission tomography (PET) and single photon emission tomography (SPET) imaging can use radiolabeled ligands to measure receptor binding (a product of receptor density and receptor sensitivity) for specific neurochemical targets in the different brain regions. Please see Table 2.1 for a summary of the findings reported below.

The status of brain 5-HT$_2$ receptors in depression, and the effect of antidepressant treatment, remains unclear and varies depending on the method used to assess them: studies have found receptor binding to be increased, normal, or decreased. While the largest study to date using PET found a marked global reduction in receptor binding (between 22% and 27% in various regions), there remains difficulty reconciling the accumulating findings of reduced binding with the fact that effective antidepressant treatments lead to further downregulation of 5-HT2 receptors (Sheline & Minyun, 2002).

Using a different radioligand, Sargent et al. (2000) found a generalized reduction in 5HT$_{1A}$ receptor binding throughout the cortex. However, this was not altered by treatment with an SSRI. The authors note that receptor numbers may not represent receptor function, but hypothesize a trait reduction in 5HT$_{1A}$ receptors that is unaffected by treatment. Reduced 5-HT$_{1A}$ binding has been replicated elsewhere (Fu et al., 2003).

Some studies of depressed patients show decreased binding potential of the serotonin transporter or 5HTT in the midbrain and brainstem (Parsey et al., 2006); however, there are many inconsistencies (Reivich, Amsterdam, Brunswick, & Shiue, 2004), which may be due to the use of different ligands, comorbidity, or differences in medication status. PET studies in recovered unmedicated depressed patients have shown no change in 5HTT binding potential (Bhagwagar et al., 2007).

One of the pieces of evidence making up the serotonin hypothesis of depression is the impaired endocrine response to challenge with serotonergic drugs such as fenfluramine. This same approach has now been transferred to neuroimaging: challenge with the serotonin releaser fenfluramine leads to marked changes in neural activity. These serotonergically mediated changes were found to be markedly attenuated in depression, suggesting impaired central 5-HT neurotransmission. However, a study using the more specific d-isomer of fenfluramine could not replicate this finding (Fu et al., 2003).

As described earlier, a proportion of subjects show a depressive relapse after TD. When undertaken in the PET scanner, this depressive relapse correlated with reduced activity in the orbitofrontal cortex, anterior cingulate, left caudate nucleus, and superior parietal cortex, similar to those seen in unmedicated depressed subjects (Smith, Morris, Friston, Cowen, & Dolan, 1999). Furthermore, while performing a verbal fluency task, there was a significant attenuation of usual task-induced activation in the anterior cingulate. More recent studies have also shown that TD can induce alterations in emotional processing, for example of emotion-laden faces (Fusar-Poli et al., 2007). These results help link changes in serotonin function with changes in activity in specific brain areas during depressive relapse. Furthermore, they also provide a possible neurobiological link between 5-HT changes and the cognitive effects of depression.

Finally, support for dysfunction in other neurochemical systems is also emerging. For example, the use of the challenge drug clonidine reveals evidence of noradrenergic dysfunction in depression, postulated to arise from functionally impaired presynaptic alpha2-adrenoceptors as well as regionally supersensitive cortical alpha2-adrenoceptors (Fu et al., 2001). In relation to the neurotransmitter GABA, a PET study using radiolabeled flumazenil found reduced binding in depressed subjects (Klumpers et al., 2009), in line with earlier proton magnetic resonance spectroscopy (MRS) studies

(Hasler et al., 2007), but in contrast to a SPET study which found no differences in GABA binding between depressed patients and controls (Kugaya et al., 2003).

## Cellular Models of Depression

### Kindling model

Neurons that are repeatedly subjected to convulsions or electrical stimuli show a process of *kindling*, whereby the fit threshold is gradually lowered, and the cells eventually become autonomously firing. It has been suggested that this phenomenon might underlie the tendency for some patients with affective disorder to suffer increasingly severe or refractory episodes of depression, or to require fewer provoking life events, with passing time. Strong support was provided by a study from Virginia (Kendler, Thorton, & Gardner, 2000), which followed up over 2,000 community-based female twin pairs over 9 years, measuring depression and life event severity in this period. They found a clear tendency for each episode of depression to be followed by an increased subsequent risk of a further episode of depression. There was also a general tendency for each successive episode of depression to be less strongly related to preceding life stress. The mechanisms underlying this effect remain unclear, although suggestions are now being made that relate to the effects of gene expression, neural growth factors, and gene transcription changes; further work on these intriguing possibilities is needed.

### Intracellular signaling models

There is evidence that antidepressants are able to modify intracellular signaling, for example by enhancing the cyclic adenosine monophosphate (AMP) pathway activation occurring after serotonergic receptor stimulation. It has been hypothesized that G proteins, important signal transducers in the phosphoinositol system, are overactive in depression; they are also potentially important in the mechanism of action of lithium. Several growth factors and neurotrophins are altered in depression, and may be important in neuronal changes seen in depression. Antidepressants also have effects on the expression of these factors. A new cellular model of depression is evolving, in which there are felt to be impairments in signaling pathways that regulate neuroplasticity and cell survival (Manji, Drevets, & Charney, 2001).

Other models of depression have been developed based on observations in animals of the effects of certain cytokines on behavior, and of the effects of some of these cytokines in humans (Kronfol & Remick, 2000).

## Inflammatory Models of Depression

There are several strands of evidence suggesting that patients with depression have increased inflammation (Anacker et al., 2011; Miller, Maletic, & Raison, 2009). Briefly, there are raised levels of the acute phase response product, C-reactive protein (CRP), suggesting a general increase in inflammation as well as higher levels of specific inflammatory biomarkers, including proinflammatory cytokines such as inter-leukin (IL)-1, IL-6 and tumor necrosis factor alpha (TNF-$\alpha$). Some of these markers, such as CRP, are linked to other risk factors for depression, such as childhood maltreat-ment (Danese et al., 2008) and interpersonal stress (Fuligni et al., 2009). Notably, the administration of pro-inflammatory stimuli, such as interferon alpha, can induce marked depressive symptoms (Capuron & Miller, 2004). Of relevance to treatment is the presence of higher levels of inflammatory biomarkers in patients who fail to respond to conventional antidepressant treatment. This has led to trials of anti-inflammatory medication in depression. To date, there have been three placebo-controlled RCTs with Celecoxib, an inhibitor of the cyclooxygenase-2 (COX2) enzyme; all have found beneficial effects (Mendlewicz et al., 2006; Muller et al., 2006; Nery et al., 2008; Proper, van den Heuvel, De Vroome, Hildebrandt, & Van der Beek, 2006).

It is unclear whether the inflammation seen is a response to depression, or to other risk factors for depression, or both; indeed, while nondepressed adults with a history of childhood trauma have increased markers for inflammation, in depressed adults it is even higher (Danese et al., 2008; Danese, Pariante, Caspi, Taylor, & Poulton, 2007). Interactions with other biological aspects of depression, such as the HPA axis, also seem likely given the physiological interplay between the endocrine and immune systems. Increased inflammation is also likely to be relevant in the poorer general physical health seen in depression.

## Is Some Depression More Biological than Others?

### The concept of core depression

While most agree that depression is a heterogeneous condition, there have been innu-merable attempts to subdivide depression according to symptom patterns. Relevant to this chapter, most studies of depression have identified a group of patients character-ized by certain symptoms: early morning waking, weight loss, poor appetite, anhedo-nia, and agitation. This symptom grouping has been variously labeled as *endogenous*, *nuclear*, and *melancholic* depression. Early conceptualizations of this category noted that they were said to show a preferential response to physical treatments, and to show more dysfunction of biological correlates of depression such as the DST. Few good studies have made direct comparisons between melancholic depression and other types, preventing firm conclusions from being drawn. However, many of the studies referred to in this chapter have tended to select patients with more melancholic fea-tures, and how applicable the findings are to the more common but less severe cases remains unknown.

### Psychotic depression

The clinical importance of separating out psychotic depression relates to the prefer-ential response of this group to antidepressant–antipsychotic combinations or elec-troconvulsive therapy (ECT). In terms of neurobiology, some authors have argued that psychotic depression represents a separate and distinct category, based on clinical, genetic, treatment response, and biological features. There is some evidence that there may be biological differences between psychotic depression and nonpsychotic depression in terms of a more disturbed HPA axis, increased dopamine turnover (i.e., higher HVA levels in the CSF) and different patterns of disturbance of serotonin pathways (Wheeler Vega, Mortimer, & Tyson, 2000). Overall, however, a separation on the basis of neurobiology remains premature.

## Atypical depression

Atypical depression has been used in the past to mean a number of different conditions, including nonendogenous depression, depression secondary to another condition, depression associated with anxiety or panic, and depression with reversed biological features. However, as the concept has evolved, atypicality has been more tightly defined, and is now included within DSM-IV.

*Validity of atypical depression as a subtype*    Atypical depression does appear to be a valid concept. Sullivan, Kessler, and Kendler (1998) used data from the large US National Comorbidity Survey, and identified six syndromes, two of which corresponded to mild atypical depression and severe atypical depression, respectively. A study of 1,000 female twin pairs also found an atypical depression syndrome; furthermore, individuals tended to have the same syndrome on each recurrence and the concordance of syndrome type was greater in monozygotic than in dizygotic pairs (Kendler et al., 1996).

*Neurobiology of atypical depression*    In view of the relatively recent addition of atypical depression to the psychiatric nosology, little data exists on the similarities and differences between typical and atypical depression. One of the most frequently observed differences related to the HPA axis. While hypercortisolemia is characteristic of melancholic major depression, several studies have now suggested that atypical depression is associated with hypocortisolemia (Juruena & Cleare, 2007). Gold and colleagues have suggested that, while typical major depression can be characterized by an excessive activation of both the physiological stress systems, the locus ceruleus–noradrenergic system, and the HPA axis, the opposite changes are present in atypical depression (Gold, Licinio, Wong, & Chrousos, 1995). Some support for this is provided by studies showing that the control of noradrenergic function is relatively preserved in atypical depression compared to typical depression (Asnis, McGinn, & Sanderson, 1995). Gold et al. (1995) suggest that it is diminished central CRH activity that is specifically related to the symptoms of hypoarousal of the syndrome. Support that it is low CRH rather than low cortisol that is related to the atypicality syndrome comes from one detailed study of Cushing's syndrome, in which cortisol is high and CRH low, where atypical depression was the predominant depressive syndrome (Dorn et al., 1995). Studies of serotonergic function are lacking, though one study suggested that platelet serotonin function is unaltered in atypical depression (Owens & Nemeroff, 1994).

**Box 2.3** Organic causes of a depressive syndrome

| | |
|---|---|
| Endocrine | Disorders of cortisol, thyroxin or parathormone production; hypopituitarism; hypoglycemia |
| Infections | Glandular fever, syphilis, AIDS, encephalitis |
| Neurological | Stroke, Parkinson's disease, multiple sclerosis, brain tumors (classically meningioma), trauma, cerebral lupus |
| Carcinoma | Common non-metastatic manifestation, especially pancreatic carcinoma which may otherwise remain occult, and lung carcinoma |
| Nutritional | Deficiencies of folate, nicotinamide (pellagra), vitamins $B_{12}$, $B_1$ (thiamine), $B_6$ |
| Other | Cerebral ischemia, myocardial infarction |

## Postpartum and seasonal depression

Postpartum depression and seasonal depression represent other specifiers used in the DSM-IV classification. There are some suggestions of particular biological therapeutic modalities for seasonal depression (light therapy) and postpartum depression (estradiol). However, there are few indications that postpartum and seasonal depression represent biologically distinct subtypes.

## Depression as a result of organic illness

There are a number of systemic diseases in which depression may be a presenting feature or a common accompaniment (over and above the "normal" rate of depression). These are shown in Box 2.3. Drugs that may cause or exacerbate depression are shown in Box 2.4.

## Integrating the Neurobiology of Depression

We can attempt to integrate the neurobiological findings in depression to the "whole" in several ways. These include integrating neurobiological with other levels of understanding or research modalities, linking neurobiology to treatment, and attempting to relate the neurobiological changes to each other.

**Box 2.4** Drugs associated with depressive syndromes

| | |
|---|---|
| Cardiovascular | Methyl-dopa, reserpine, beta-blockers, clonidine, diuretics, digoxin |
| Endocrine | Steroids, combined oral contraceptive (high dose) |
| Neurological | L-Dopa, bromocriptine |
| Others | Pentazocine, indomethacin, chloroquine, mefloquine, interferon-alpha |
| On withdrawal | Psychostimulants (e.g., amphetamines, cocaine), benzodiazepines |
| Alcohol | Cause and consequence |

This chapter has already given some examples of how the biological models of depression can be tied in with other characteristics of depression from other disciplines such as epidemiology. The predisposition to suffer depression conferred by childhood experiences can be paralleled by the presence of "endocrine scars", or through a persistent abnormal amygdala response to emotion (Grant, Cannistraci, Hollon, Gore, & Shelton, 2011). Acute and chronic stress from the environment can be shown to have profound neurobiological correlates, for example, in the form of disruption to the HPA axis, and high cortisol levels are associated with cognitive dysfunction (Van London et al., 1998). Recent neuroimaging studies reveal a brain that is over responsive to unhappy stimuli and under responsive to happy ones (Elliot, Rubinsztein, Sahakian, & Dolan, 2002; Fu et al., 2007). It is easy to see how such brain dysfunction can be linked to the perceptual biases in depression, and to cognitive theories of depression, in which such cognitive distortions are felt to be a primary disturbance in depression.

Neurobiology may have relevance to the choice of different treatments available. For example, certain neurobiological disruption such as a disrupted HPA axis or shortened REM latency may be associated with a preferential response to physical rather than psychological treatments (Thase et al., 1996; Thase, Simons, & Reynolds, 1993). Exciting strides are now being made into whether neuroimaging can inform the response to therapy. For example, Brody et al. (2001) took 24 subjects with unipolar major depression and obtained resting PET scans of glucose metabolism at baseline and after 12 weeks of treatment with either interpersonal therapy (IPT) or paroxetine. With treatment, both groups showed a similar tendency for baseline PET abnormalities to normalize, despite the paroxetine-treated subjects having a greater decrease in depression scores. However, the lack of randomization at baseline means that there may be explanations other than the different treatments for these changes. Another paper measured brain blood-flow, using SPET, in 28 patients with major depression (Martin, Martin, Rai, Richardson, & Royall, 2001). In this case, subjects were randomized—receiving venlafaxine or interpersonal therapy—with scans being repeated at 6 weeks. Once again, the antidepressant group had a larger fall in depression scores. On this occasion, the two treatments produced a differential change, with the venlafaxine-treated group showing posterior temporal and right basal ganglia activation, whereas the IPT group had limbic, right posterior cingulate and right basal ganglia activation. Thus, both treatments caused basal ganglia activation, whereas only interpersonal therapy showed limbic blood-flow increase. Problems with this trial include the short duration of treatment, probably before the main effects of psychological therapy would have been detectable. Finally, structural neuroanatomical changes in depression have been shown to predict response to antidepressant medication, but not to cognitive behavioral therapy (Costafreda, Chu, Ashburner, & Fu, 2009).

It is likely several functional and structural abnormalities are relevant in the etiology of depression. Attempts to combine patterns of abnormalities to aid diagnosis, and as a prognostic aid, have utilized "machine learning" statistical methods (Nouretdinov et al., 2010). For example, using such methods on fMRI during emotional processing was able to give an 86% diagnostic accuracy in distinguishing depressed from control subjects (Fu et al., 2008). It is also notable that few studies have tried to utilize potential markers for major adverse outcomes in depression such as suicide. Reference to endocrine markers was made earlier in the chapter, but there is great scope to utilize functional imaging to understand more about the precursors of suicide. One recent study (Marchand et al., 2011) implicates a striatal–anterior cortical midline structures circuit as linked to the generation of suicidal ideation.

Certain treatments have a more fundamental basis in neurobiology. One of the more controversial treatments in psychiatry is psychosurgery. This is now only very rarely used as a last resort, but can be performed for cases of severe intractable depression under strict controls. Stereotactic techniques are used for more specific ablation, and a variety of operations have been developed focusing on limbic areas and their cortical connections. Clinically, approximately one-third of patients are reported to gain marked benefit, though side effects can include frontal lobe syndromes and epilepsy. There has been recent interest in deep brain stimulation in neurology and psychiatry: implanted electrodes can induce functional lesions, but have the advantage over psychosurgery of being reversible if not successful. Recent trials have suggested effectiveness but thus far lack a control group (Holtzheimer et al., 2012); furthermore the anatomical location and frequency stimulation parameters require refinement. The advances in the understanding of the neural basis of depression outlined in this chapter may allow an informed refinement of these techniques for those unfortunate cases of severe and resistant depression.

Another issue in relation to treatment is whether treatment, or lack of treatment, can itself influence the neurobiological basis of depression. We have already reviewed the extent to which treatments can potentially modify biological aspects of depression, such as brain structure. It is also of note that *lack* of treatment may also play a crucial role. For example, it has been shown in patients remitted from depression that the longer their depression had remained untreated prior to effective treatment was instigated the more hippocampal atrophy that was present (Sheline, Gado, & Kraemer, 2003). It is not known whether this in turn influences the long-term course of an individual's depression but, clearly, such avoidable consequences of undertreatment are best minimized.

Finally, it is worth reminding ourselves that separate biological systems do not act independently. Neurochemical systems modulate the activity of each other; endocrine systems act on neurochemical systems; neurochemical activation leads to intracellular activation; and so on. A recent study linked structural and functional neural systems and showed that the presence of white matter hyperintensities in the elderly was related to the degree of dysfunction present (seen using fMRI) in the anterior cingulate in response to emotional face recognition (Aizenstein et al., 2011). However, understanding the different changes in parallel and on several levels is rarely undertaken, and remains a huge obstacle at present to a full understanding of the neurobiology of mood disorders.

# References

Aizenstein, H. J., Andreescu, C., Edelman, K. L., Cochran, J. L., Price, J., Butters, M. A., . . . Reynolds, C. F., III. (2011). fMRI correlates of white matter hyperintensities in late-life depression. *American Journal of Psychiatry, 168,* 1075–1082.

Alexopoulos, G. S. (2005). Depression in the elderly. *Lancet, 365,* 1961–1970.

Altshuler, L. L., Bauer, M., Frye, M. A., Gitlin, M. J., Mintz, J., Szuba, M. P., . . . Whybrow, P. C. (2001). Does thyroid supplementation accelerate tricyclic antidepressant response? A review and meta-analysis of the literature. *American Journal of Psychiatry, 158,* 1617–1622.

Amico, F., Meisenzahl, E., Koutsouleris, N., Reiser, M., Moller, H. J., & Frodl, T. (2010). Structural MRI correlates for vulnerability and resilience to major depressive disorder. *Journal of Psychiatry and Neurosciences, 36,* 15–22.

Anacker, C., Zunszain, P. A., Cattaneo, A., Carvalho, L. A., Garabedian, M. J., Thuret, S., . . . Pariante, C. M. (2011). Antidepressants increase human hippocampal neurogenesis by activating the glucocorticoid receptor. *Molecular Psychiatry, 16,* 738–750.

Asnis, G. M., McGinn, L. K., & Sanderson, W. C. (1995). Atypical depression: Clinical aspects and noradrenergic function. *American Journal of Psychiatry, 152,* 31–36.

Barbui, C., & Hotopf, M. (2001). Amitriptyline v. the rest: Still the leading antidepressant after 40 years of randomised controlled trials. *British Journal of Psychiatry, 178,* 129–144.

Barrett-Connor, E., von Muhlen, D., Laughlin, G. A., & Kripke, A. (1999). Endogenous levels of dehydroepiandrosterone sulfate, but not other sex hormones, are associated with depressed mood in older women: The Rancho Bernardo Study. *Journal of the American Geriatrics Society, 47,* 685–691.

Bhagwagar, Z., Hafizi, S., & Cowen, P. J. (2003). Increase in concentration of waking salivary cortisol in recovered patients with depression. *American Journal of Psychiatry, 160,* 1890–1891.

Bhagwagar, Z., Hafizi, S., & Cowen, P. J. (2005). Increased salivary cortisol after waking in depression. *Psychopharmacology (Berl), 182,* 54–57.

Bhagwagar, Z., Murthy, N., Selvaraj, S., Hinz, R., Taylor, M., Fancy, S., . . . Cowen, P. (2007). 5-HTT binding in recovered depressed patients and healthy volunteers: A positron emission tomography study with [$^{11}$C]DASB. *American Journal of Psychiatry, 164,* 1858–1865.

Bhagwagar, Z., Whale, R., & Cowen, P. J. (2002). State and trait abnormalities in serotonin function in major depression. *British Journal of Psychiatry, 180,* 24–28.

Bourdeau, I., Bard, C., Noël, B., Leclerc, I., Cordeau, M. P., Bélair, M., . . . Lacroix, A. (2002). Loss of brain volume in endogenous Cushing's syndrome and its reversibility after correction of hypercortisolism. *Journal of Clinical Endocrinology & Metabolism, 87,* 1949–1954.

Brody, A. L., Saxena, S., Stoessel, P., Gillies, L. A., Fairbanks, L. A., Alborzian, S., . . . Baxter, L. R., Jr. (2001). Regional brain metabolic changes in patients with major depression treated with either paroxetine or interpersonal therapy: Preliminary findings. *Archives of General Psychiatry, 58,* 631–640.

Bueller, J. A., Aftab, M., Sen, S., Gomez-Hassan, D., Burmeister, M., & Zubieta, J. K. (2006). BDNF Val66Met allele is associated with reduced hippocampal volume in healthy subjects. *Biological Psychiatry, 59,* 812–815.

Capuron, L., & Miller, A. H. (2004). Cytokines and psychopathology: Lessons from interferon-alpha. *Biological Psychiatry 56,* 819–824.

Caspi, A., Sugden, K., Moffitt, T. E., Taylor, A., Craig, I. W., Harrington, H., . . . Poulton, R. (2003). Influence of life stress on depression: Moderation by a polymorphism in the 5-HTT gene. *Science, 301,* 386–389.

Cees de Groot, J., de Leeuw, F- E., Oudkerk, M., Cees Hofman, A., Jolles, J., & Breteler, M. M. B. (2000). Cerebral white matter lesions and depressive symptoms in elderly adults. *Archives of General Psychiatry, 57,* 1071–1076.

Chen, C. H., Suckling, J., Ooi, C., Fu, C. H., Williams, S. C., Walsh, N. D., . . . Bullmore, E. (2008). Functional coupling of the amygdala in depressed patients treated with antidepressant medication. *Neuropsychopharmacology, 33,* 1909–1918.

Cleare, A. J., & Bond, A. J. (1997). Does central serotonergic function correlate inversely with aggression? A study using d-fenfluramine in healthy subjects. *Psychiatry Research, 69,* 89–95.

Cole, J., Toga, A. W., Hojatkashani, C., Thompson, P., Costafreda, S. G., Cleare, A. J., . . . Fu, C. H. (2010). Subregional hippocampal deformations in major depressive disorder. *Journal of Affective Disorders, 126,* 272–277.

Cooper-Kazaz, R., Apter, J. T., Cohen, R., Karagichev, L., Muhammed-Moussa, S., Grupper, D., . . . Lerer, B. (2007). Combined treatment with sertraline and liothyronine in major depression: A randomized, double-blind, placebo-controlled trial. *Archives of General Psychiatry, 64,* 679–688.

Coryell, W., & Sehlesser, M. (2001). The dexamethasone suppression test in suicide prediction. *American Journal of Psychiatry, 158,* 748–753.

Costafreda, S. G., Chu, C., Ashburner, J., & Fu, C. H. (2009). Prognostic and diagnostic potential of the structural neuroanatomy of depression. *PLoS One, 4,* e6353.

Cowen, P. J., & Harmer, C. (2009). Is it all monoamines? In C. M. Pariante, R. M. Nesse, D. Nutt, & L. Wolpert (Eds.), *Understanding depression: A translational approach* (pp. 171–178). New York: Oxford University Press.

Cravchik, A., & Goldman, D. (2000). Genetic diversity among human dopamine and serotonin receptors and transporters. *Archives of General Psychiatry, 57,* 1105–1114.

Dalby, R. B., Chakravarty, M. M., Ahdidan, J., Sorensen, L., Frandsen, J., Jonsdottir, K. Y., . . . Videbech, P. (2009). Localization of white-matter lesions and effect of vascular risk factors in late-onset major depression. *Psychological Medicine, 40,* 1389–1399.

Danese, A., Moffitt, T. E., Pariante, C. M., Ambler, A., Poulton, R., & Caspi, A. (2008). Elevated inflammation levels in depressed adults with a history of childhood maltreatment. *Archives of General Psychiatry, 65,* 409–415.

Danese, A., Pariante, C. M., Caspi, A., Taylor, A., & Poulton, R. (2007). Childhood maltreatment predicts adult inflammation in a life-course study. *Proceedings of the National Academy of Sciences of USA, 104,* 1319–1324.

Delgado, P. L., Miller, H. L., Salomon, R. M., Licinio, J., Krystal, J. H., Moreno, F. A., . . . Charney, D. S. (1999). Tryptophan depletion challenge in depressed patients treated with desipramine or fluoxetine: Implications for the role of serotonin in the mechanism of antidepressant action. *Biological Psychiatry, 46,* 212–220.

Dorn, L. D., Burgess, E. S., Dubbert, B., Simpson, S. E., Friedman, T., Kling, M., . . . Chrousos, G. P. (1995). Psychopathology in patients with endogenous Cushing's syndrome: 'Atypical' or melancholic features. *Clinical Endocrinology, 43,* 433–442.

Eitan, R., Landshut, G., Lifschytz, T., Einstein, O., Ben-Hur, T., & Lerer, B. (2009). The thyroid hormone, triiodothyronine, enhances fluoxetine-induced neurogenesis in rats: Possible role in antidepressant-augmenting properties. *International Journal of Neuropsychopharmacology, 13,* 553–561.

Elliott, R., Rubinsztein, J. S., Sahakian, B. J., & Dolan, R. J. (2002). The neural basis of mood-congruent processing biases in depression. *Archives of General Psychiatry, 59,* 597–604.

Farb, N. A., Anderson, A. K., Bloch, R. T., & Segal, Z. V. (2011). Mood-linked responses in medial prefrontal cortex predict relapse in patients with recurrent unipolar depression. *Biological Psychiatry, 70,* 366–372.

Frodl, T., Moller, H. J., & Meisenzahl, E. (2008). Neuroimaging genetics: New perspectives in research on major depression? *Acta Psychiatrica Scandinavica, 118,* 363–372.

Fu, C. H., Mourao-Miranda, J., Costafreda, S. G., Khanna, A., Marquand, A. F., Williams, S. C., & Brammer, M. J. (2008). Pattern classification of sad facial processing: Toward the development of neurobiological markers in depression. *Biological Psychiatry, 63,* 656–662.

Fu, C. H., Reed, L. J., Meyer, J. H., Kennedy, S., Houle, S., Eisfeld, B. S., & Brown, G. M. (2001). Noradrenergic dysfunction in the prefrontal cortex in depression: An [$^{15}$O]H$_2$O PET study of the neuromodulatory effects of clonidine. *Biological Psychiatry, 49*, 317–325.

Fu, C. H. Y., Walsh, N. D., & Drevets, W. C. (2003). Neuroimaging studies of mood disorders. In C. H. Y. Fu, T. Russell, C. Senior, D. R. Weinberger, & R. M. Murray (Eds.), *A guide to neuroimaging in psychiatry* (pp. 131–169). London: Martin Dunitz.

Fu, C. H., Williams, S. C., Brammer, M. J., Suckling, J., Kim, J., Cleare, A. J., . . . Bullmore, E. T. (2007). Neural responses to happy facial expressions in major depression following antidepressant treatment. *American Journal of Psychiatry, 164*, 599–607.

Fu, C. H., Williams, S. C., Cleare, A. J., Brammer, M. J., Walsh, N. D., Kim, J., . . . Bullmore, E. T. (2004). Attenuation of the neural response to sad faces in major depression by antidepressant treatment: A prospective, event-related functional magnetic resonance imaging study. *Archives of General Psychiatry, 61*, 877–889.

Fuligni, A. J., Telzer, E. H., Bower, J., Cole, S. W., Kiang, L., & Irwin, M. R. (2009). A preliminary study of daily interpersonal stress and C-reactive protein levels among adolescents from Latin American and European backgrounds. *Psychosomatic Medicine, 71*, 329–333.

Fusar-Poli, P., Allen, P., Lee, F., Surguladze, S., Tunstall, N., Fu, C. H., . . . McGuire, P. K. (2007). Modulation of neural response to happy and sad faces by acute tryptophan depletion. *Psychopharmacology (Berl), 193*, 31–44.

Gold, P. W., Licinio, J., Wong, M. L., & Chrousos, G. P. (1995). Corticotropin releasing hormone in the pathophysiology of melancholic and atypical depression and in the mechanism of action of antidepressant drugs. *Annals of the New York Academy of Sciences, 771*, 716–729.

Grant, M. M., Cannistraci, C., Hollon, S. D., Gore, J., & Shelton, R. (2011). Childhood trauma history differentiates amygdala response to sad faces within MDD. *Journal of Psychiatric Research, 45*, 886–895.

Hamilton, J. P., Siemer, M., & Gotlib, I. H. (2008). Amygdala volume in major depressive disorder: A meta-analysis of magnetic resonance imaging studies. *Molecular Psychiatry, 13*, 993–1000.

Harmer, C. J., O'Sullivan, U., Favaron, E., Massey-Chase, R., Ayres, R., Reinecke, A., . . . Cowen, P. J. (2009). Effect of acute antidepressant administration on negative affective bias in depressed patients. *American Journal of Psychiatry, 166*, 1178–1184.

Harris, B., Othman, S., Davies, J. A., Weppner, G. J., Richards, C. J., Newcombe, R. G., . . . Phillips, D. I. (1992). Association between postpartum thyroid dysfunction and thyroid antibodies and depression. *British Medical Journal, 305*, 152–156.

Hasler, G., van der Veen, J. W., Tumonis, T., Meyers, N., Shen, J., & Drevets, W. C. (2007). Reduced prefrontal glutamate/glutamine and gamma-aminobutyric acid levels in major depression determined using proton magnetic resonance spectroscopy. *Archives of General Psychiatry, 64*, 193–200.

Heiden, A., Kettenbach, J., Fischer, P., Schein, B., Ba-Ssalamah, A., Frey, R., . . . Kasper, S. (2005). White matter hyperintensities and chronicity of depression. *Journal of Psychiatric Research, 39*, 285–293.

Heim, C., Newport, D. J., Heit, S., Graham, Y. P., Wilcox, M., Bonsall, R., . . . Nemeroff, C. B. (2000). Pituitary-adrenal and autonomic responses to stress in women after sexual and physical abuse in childhood. *Journal of the American Medical Association, 284*, 592–527.

Heuser, I., Yassouridis, A., & Holsboer, F. (1994). The combined dexamethasone/CRH test: A refined laboratory test for psychiatric disorders. *Journal of Psychiatric Research, 28*, 341–356.

Hickie, I., Scott, E., Mitchell, P., Wilhelm, K., Austin, M. P., & Bennett, B. (1995). Subcortical hyperintensities on magnetic resonance imaging: Clinical correlates and prognostic significance in patients with severe depression. *Biological Psychiatry, 37*, 151–160.

Hirschfield, R. M. A., & Weissman, M. M. (2002). Risk factors for major depression and bipolar disorder. In K. L. Davis, D. Charney, J. T. Coyle, & C. Nemeroff (Eds.), *Neuropsychopharmacology: The fifth generation of progress* (pp. 1017–1025). Philadelphia, PA: Lippincott, Williams & Wilkins.

Holtzheimer, P. E., Kelley, M. E., Gross, R. E., Filkowski, M. M., Garlow, S. J., Barrocas, A., . . . Mayberg, H. S. (2012). Subcallosal cingulate deep brain stimulation for treatment-resistant unipolar and bipolar depression. *Archives of General Psychiatry, 69*, 150–158.

Horton, R. W. (1992). The neurochemistry of depression: Evidence derived from studies of post-mortem brain tissue. *Molecular Aspects of Medicine, 13*, 191–203.

Janowsky, D. S., & Overstreet, D. H. (1995). The role of acetylcholine mechanisms in mood disorders. In D. J. Kupfer & F. E. Bloom (Eds.), *Psychopharmacology: The fourth generation of progress* (pp. 945–956). New York: Raven Press.

Joffe, R., & Marriott, M. (2000). Thyroid hormone levels in recurrence of major depression. *American Journal of Psychiatry, 157*, 1689–1691.

Juhasz, G., Dunham, J. S., McKie, S., Thomas, E., Downey, D., Chase, D., . . . Deakin, J. F. (2011). The CREB1-BDNF-NTRK2 pathway in depression: Multiple gene-cognition-environment interactions. *Biological Psychiatry, 69*, 762–771.

Juruena, M. F., & Cleare, A. J. (2007). Overlap between atypical depression, seasonal affective disorder and chronic fatigue syndrome. *Revista Brasileira de Psiquiatria, 29* (Suppl. 1), S19–S26.

Juruena, M. F., Cleare, A. J., Papadopoulos, A. S., Poon, L., Lightman, S., & Pariante, C. M. (2006). Different responses to dexamethasone and prednisolone in the same depressed patients. *Psychopharmacology (Berl), 189*, 225–235.

Juruena, M. F., Cleare, A. J., Papadopoulos, A. S., Poon, L., Lightman, S., & Pariante, C. M. (2010). The prednisolone suppression test in depression: Dose–response and changes with antidepressant treatment. *Psychoneuroendocrinology, 35*, 1486–1491.

Juruena, M. F., Pariante, C. M., Papadopoulos, A. S., Poon, L., Lightman, S., & Cleare, A. J. (2009). Prednisolone suppression test in depression: Prospective study of the role of HPA axis dysfunction in treatment resistance. *The British Journal of Psychiatry, 194*, 342–349.

Karg, K., Burmeister, M., Shedden, K., & Sen, S. (2011). The serotonin transporter promoter variant (5-HTTLPR), stress, and depression meta-analysis revisited: Evidence of genetic moderation. *Archives of General Psychiatry, 68*, 444–454.

Kempton, M. J., Salvador, Z., Munafo, M. R., Geddes, J. R., Simmons, A., Frangou, S., & Williams, S. C. (2011). Structural neuroimaging studies in major depressive disorder. Meta-analysis and comparison with bipolar disorder. *Archives of General Psychiatry, 68*, 675–690.

Kendler, K. S., Eaves, L. J., Walters, E. E., Neale, M. C., Heath, A. C., & Kessler, R. C. (1996). The identification and validation of distinct depressive syndromes in a population-based sample of female twins. *Archives of General Psychiatry, 53*, 391–399.

Kendler, K. S., & Karkowski-Shuman, L. (1997). Stressful life events and genetic liability to major depression: Genetic control of exposure to the environment? *Psychological Medicine, 27*, 539–547.

Kendler, K. S., Thornton, L. M., & Gardner, C. O. (2000). Stressful life events and previous episodes in the etiology of major depression in women: An evaluation of the "kindling" hypothesis. *American Journal of Psychiatry, 157*, 1243–1251.

Kendler, K. S., Thornton, L. M., & Gardner, C. O. (2001). Genetic risk, number of previous depressive episodes, and stressful life events in predicting onset of major depression. *American Journal of Psychiatry, 158*, 582–586.

Klumpers, U. M., Veltman, D. J., Drent, M. L., Boellaard, R., Comans, E. F., Meynen, G., … Hoogendijk, W. J. (2009). Reduced parahippocampal and lateral temporal GABAA-[$^{11}$C]flumazenil binding in major depression: Preliminary results. *European Journal of Nuclear Medicine and Molecular Imaging, 37*, 565–574.

Kohler, S., Thomas, A. J., Lloyd, A., Barber, R., Almeida, O. P., & O'Brien, J. T. (2010). White matter hyperintensities, cortisol levels, brain atrophy and continuing cognitive deficits in late-life depression. *British Journal of Psychiatry, 196*, 143–149.

Kronfol, Z., & Remick, D. G. (2000). Cytokines and the brain: Implications for clinical psychiatry. *American Journal of Psychiatry, 157*, 683–94.

Kugaya, A., Sanacora, G., Verhoeff, N. P., Fujita, M., Mason, G. F., Seneca, N. M., … Innis, R. B. (2003). Cerebral benzodiazepine receptors in depressed patients measured with [$^{123}$I]iomazenil SPECT. *Biological Psychiatry, 54*, 792–799.

Lambert, G., Johansson, G., Agren, H., & Friberg, P. (2000). Reduced brain norepinephrine and dopamine release in treatment-refractory depressive illness: Evidence in support of the catecholamine hypothesis of mood disorders. *Archives of General Psychiatry, 57*, 787–793.

Lifschytz, T., Segman, R., Shalom, G., Lerer, B., Gur, E., Golzer, T., & Newman, M. E. (2006). Basic mechanisms of augmentation of antidepressant effects with thyroid hormone. *Current Drug Targets, 7*, 203–210.

Maes, M., & Meltzer, H. (1995). The serotonin hypothesis of major depression. In F. E. Bloom, & D. J. Kupfer (Eds.), *Psychopharmacology: The fourth generation of progress* (pp. 933–944). New York: Raven Press.

Manji, H. K., Drevets, W. C., & Charney, D. S. (2001). The cellular neurobiology of depression. *Nature Medicine, 7*, 541–547.

Mann, J. J. (1995). Violence and aggression. In F. E. Bloom, & D. J. Kupfer (Eds.), *Psychopharmacology: The fourth generation of progress* (pp. 1919–1928). New York: Raven Press.

Mannie, Z. N., Harmer, C. J., & Cowen, P. J. (2007). Increased waking salivary cortisol levels in young people at familial risk of depression. *American Journal of Psychiatry, 164*, 617–21.

Mannie, Z. N., Norbury, R., Murphy, S. E., Inkster, B., Harmer, C. J., & Cowen, P. J. (2008). Affective modulation of anterior cingulate cortex in young people at increased familial risk of depression. *British Journal of Psychiatry, 192*, 356–361.

Marchand, W. R., Lee, J. N., Johnson, S., Thatcher, J., Gale, P., Wood, N., & Jeong, E. K. (2011). Striatal and cortical midline circuits in major depression: Implications for suicide and symptom expression. *Progress in Neuro-psychopharmacology and Biological Psychiatry, 36*, 290–209.

Markopoulou, K., Papadopoulos, A., Juruena, M. F., Poon, L., Pariante, C. M., & Cleare, A. J. (2009). The ratio of cortisol/DHEA in treatment resistant depression. *Psychoneuroendocrinology, 34*, 19–26.

Martin, S. D., Martin, E., Rai, S. S., Richardson, M. A., & Royall, R. (2001). Brain blood flow changes in depressed patients treated with interpersonal psychotherapy or venlafaxine hydrochloride: Preliminary findings. *Archives of General Psychiatry, 58*, 641–648.

Mayberg, H. S., Brannan, S. K., Tekell, J. L., Silva, J. A., Mahurin, R. K., McGinnis, S., & Jerabek, P. A. (2000). Regional metabolic effects of fluoxetine in major depression: Serial changes and relationship to clinical response. *Biological Psychiatry, 48*, 830–843.

Mendlewicz, J., Kriwin, P., Oswald, P., Souery, D., Alboni, S., & Brunello, N. (2006). Shortened onset of action of antidepressants in major depression using acetylsalicylic acid augmentation: A pilot open-label study. *International Clinical Psychopharmacology, 21*, 227–231.

Miller, A. H., Maletic, V., & Raison, C. L. (2009). Inflammation and its discontents: The role of cytokines in the pathophysiology of major depression. *Biological Psychiatry, 65*, 732–741.

Miller, G. (2010). Epigenetics. The seductive allure of behavioral epigenetics. *Science, 329*, 24–27.

Moreno, F. A., Heninger, G. R., McGahuey, C. A., & Delgado, P. L. (2000). Tryptophan depletion and risk of depression relapse: A prospective study of tryptophan depletion as a potential predictor of depressive episodes. *Biological Psychiatry, 48*, 327–329.

Muller, N., Schwarz, M. J., Dehning, S., Douhe, A., Cerovecki, A., Goldstein-Muller, B., . . . Riedel, M. (2006). The cyclooxygenase-2 inhibitor celecoxib has therapeutic effects in major depression: Results of a double-blind, randomized, placebo controlled, add-on pilot study to reboxetine. *Molecular Psychiatry, 11*, 680–684.

Munafo, M. R., Durrant, C., Lewis, G., & Flint, J. (2009). Gene X environment interactions at the serotonin transporter locus. *Biological Psychiatry 65*, 211–219.

Murphy, B. E. (1997). Antiglucocorticoid therapies in major depression: A review. *Psychoneuroendocrinology, 22*, S125–S132.

Nemeroff, C. (1996). The corticotropin-releasing factor (CRF) hypothesis of depression: New findings and new directions. *Molecular Psychiatry, 1*, 336–342.

Nery, F. G., Monkul, E. S., Hatch, J. P., Fonseca, M., Zunta-Soares, G. B., Frey, B. N., . . . Soares, J. C. (2008). Celecoxib as an adjunct in the treatment of depressive or mixed episodes of bipolar disorder: A double-blind, randomized, placebo-controlled study. *Human Psychopharmacology, 23*, 87–94.

Nouretdinov, I., Costafreda, S. G., Gammerman, A., Chervonenkis, A., Vovk, V., Vapnik, V., & Fu, C. H. (2010). Machine learning classification with confidence: Application of transductive conformal predictors to MRI-based diagnostic and prognostic markers in depression. *NeuroImage, 56*, 809–813.

O'Flynn, K., & Dinan, T. G. (1993). Baclofen-induced growth hormone release in major depression: Relationship to dexamethasone suppression test result. *American Journal of Psychiatry, 150*, 1728–1730.

Owens, M. J., & Nemeroff, C. B. (1994). Role of serotonin in the pathophysiology of depression: Focus on the serotonin transporter. *Clinical Chemistry, 40*, 288–295.

Pariante, C. M. (2006). The glucocorticoid receptor: Part of the solution or part of the problem? *Journal of Psychopharmacology, 20*, 79–84.

Parsey, R. V., Hastings, R. S., Oquendo, M. A., Huang, Y. Y., Simpson, N., Arcement, J., . . . Mann, J. J. (2006). Lower serotonin transporter binding potential in the human brain during major depressive episodes. *American Journal of Psychiatry, 163*, 52–58.

Proper, K. I., van den Heuvel, S. G., De Vroome, E. M., Hildebrandt, V. H., & Van der Beek, A. J. (2006). Dose–response relation between physical activity and sick leave. *British Journal of Sports Medicine, 40*, 173–178.

Reilly, J. G., McTavish, S. F. B., & Young, A. H. (1997). Rapid depletion of plasma tryptophan: A review of studies and experimental methodology. *Journal of Psychopharmacology, 11*, 381–392.

Reivich, M., Amsterdam, J. D., Brunswick, D. J., & Shiue, C. Y. (2004). PET brain imaging with [$^{11}$C](+)McN5652 shows increased serotonin transporter availability in major depression. *Journal of Affective Disorders, 82*, 321–327.

Risch, N., Herrell, R., Lehner, T., Liang, K. Y., Eaves, L., Hoh, J., . . . Merikangas, K. R. (2009). Interaction between the serotonin transporter gene (5-HTTLPR), stressful life events, and risk of depression: A meta-analysis. *Journal of The American Medical Association, 301,* 2462–2471.

Sargent, P. A., Kjaer, K. H., Bench, C. J., Rabiner, E. A., Messa, C., Meyer, J., . . . Cowen, P. J. (2000). Brain serotonin1A receptor binding measured by positron emission tomography with [$^{11}$C]WAY-100635: Effects of depression and antidepressant treatment. *Archives of General Psychiatry, 57,* 174–180.

Schatzberg, A. F., Garlow, S. J., & Nemeroff, C. B. (2002). Molecular and cellular mechanisms in depression. In K. L. Davis, D. Charney, J. T. Coyle, & C. Nemeroff (Eds.), *Neuropsychopharmacology: The fifth generation of progress* (pp. 1039–1050). Philadelphia, PA: Lippincott, Williams & Wilkins.

Sheline, Y. I., Gado, M. H., & Kraemer, H. C. (2003). Untreated depression and hippocampal volume loss. *American Journal of Psychiatry, 160,* 1516–1518.

Sheline, Y. I., & Minyun, M. A. (2002). Structural and functional imaging of affective disorders. In K. L. Davis, D. Charney, J. T. Coyle, & C. Nemeroff (Eds.), *Neuropsychopharmacology: The fifth generation of progress* (pp. 1065–1080). Philadelphia, PA: Lippincott, Williams & Wilkins.

Sheline, Y. I., Price, J. L., Vaishnavi, S. N., Mintun, M. A., Barch, D. M., Epstein, A. A., . . . McKinstry, R. C. (2008). Regional white matter hyperintensity burden in automated segmentation distinguishes late-life depressed subjects from comparison subjects matched for vascular risk factors. *American Journal of Psychiatry, 165,* 524–532.

Simpson, S., Baldwin, R. C., Jackson, A., & Burns, A. S. (1998). Is subcortical disease associated with a poor response to antidepressants? Neurological, neuropsychological and neuroradiological findings in late-life depression. *Psychological Medicine, 28,* 1015–1026.

Smith, D., Dempster, C., Glanville, J., Freemantle, N., & Anderson, I. (2002). Efficacy and tolerability of venlafaxine compared with selective serotonin reuptake inhibitors and other antidepressants: A meta-analysis. *British Journal of Psychiatry, 180,* 396–404.

Smith, K. A., Morris, J. S., Friston, K. J., Cowen, P. J., & Dolan, R. J. (1999). Brain mechanisms associated with depressive relapse and associated cognitive impairment following acute tryptophan depletion. *British Journal of Psychiatry, 174,* 525–529.

Snyder, J. S., Soumier, A., Brewer, M., Pickel, J., & Cameron, H. A. (2011). Adult hippocampal neurogenesis buffers stress responses and depressive behaviour. *Nature, 476,* 458–461.

Starkman, M. N., Gebarski, S. S., Berent, S., & Schteingart, D. E. (1992). Hippocampal formation volume, memory dysfunction, and cortisol levels in patients with Cushing's syndrome. *Biological Psychiatry, 32,* 756–765.

Stockmeier, C. A., Mahajan, G. J., Konick, L. C., Overholser, J. C., Jurjus, G. J., Meltzer, H. Y., . . . Rajkowska, G. (2004). Cellular changes in the postmortem hippocampus in major depression. *Biological Psychiatry, 56,* 640–650.

Sullivan, P. F., Kessler, R. C., & Kendler, K. S. (1998). Latent class analysis of lifetime depressive symptoms in the national comorbidity survey. *American Journal of Psychiatry, 155,* 1398–1406.

Suslow, T., Konrad, C., Kugel, H., Rumstadt, D., Zwitserlood, P., Schoning, S., . . . Dannlowski, U. (2009). Automatic mood-congruent amygdala responses to masked facial expressions in major depression. *Biological Psychiatry, 67,* 155–160.

Taylor, W. D., Steffens, D. C., MacFall, J. R., McQuoid, D. R., Payne, M. E., Provenzale, J. M., & Krishnan, K. R. (2003). White matter hyperintensity progression and late-life depression outcomes. *Archives of General Psychiatry, 60,* 1090–1096.

Teodorczuk, A., O'Brien, J. T., Firbank, M. J., Pantoni, L., Poggesi, A., Erkinjuntti, T., . . . Inzitari, D. (2007). White matter changes and late-life depressive symptoms: Longitudinal study. *British Journal of Psychiatry, 191,* 212–217.

Thase, M. E., Dube, S., Bowler, K., Howland, R. H., Myers, J. E., Friedman, E., & Jarrett, D. B. (1996). Hypothalamic-pituitary-adrenocortical activity and response to cognitive behavior therapy in unmedicated, hospitalized depressed patients. *American Journal of Psychiatry, 153*, 886–891.

Thase, M. E., Simons, A. D., & Reynolds, C. F., III. (1993). Psychobiological correlates of poor response to cognitive behavior therapy: Potential indications for antidepressant pharmacotherapy. *Psychopharmacological Bulletin, 29*, 293–301.

Thomas, A. J., O'Brien, J. T., Davis, S., Ballard, C., Barber, R., Kalaria, R. N., & Perry, R. H. (2002). Ischemic basis for deep white matter hyperintensities in major depression: A neuropathological study. *Archives of General Psychiatry, 59*, 785–792.

Tyrka, A. R., Price, L. H., Gelernter, J., Schepker, C., Anderson, G. M., & Carpenter, L. L. (2009). Interaction of childhood maltreatment with the corticotropin-releasing hormone receptor gene: Effects on hypothalamic-pituitary-adrenal axis reactivity. *Biological Psychiatry, 66*, 681–685.

Van Londen, L., Goekoop, J. G., Zwinderman, A. H., Lanser, J. B. K., Wiegant, V. M., & De Wied, D. (1998). Neuropsychological performance and plasma cortisol, arginine vasopressin and oxytocin in patients with major depression. *Psychological Medicine, 28*, 275–284.

Vythilingam, M., Heim, C., Newport, J., Miller, A. H., Anderson, E., Bronen, R., ... Bremner, J. D. (2002). Childhood trauma associated with smaller hippocampal volume in women with major depression. *American Journal of Psychiatry, 159*, 2072–2080.

Vythilingam, M., Vermetten, E., Anderson, G. M., Luckenbaugh, D., Anderson, E. R., Snow, J., ... Bremner, J. D. (2004). Hippocampal volume, memory, and cortisol status in major depressive disorder: Effects of treatment. *Biological Psychiatry, 56*, 101–112.

Wheeler Vega, J., Mortimer, A., & Tyson, P. J. (2000). Somatic treatment of psychotic depression: Review and recommendations for practice. *Journal of Clinical Psychopharmacology, 20*, 504–519.

Wolkowitz, O. M., Reus, V. I., Keebler, A., Nelson, N., Friedland, M., Brizendine, L., & Roberts, E. (1999). Double-blind treatment of major depression with dehydroepiandrosterone. *American Journal of Psychiatry, 156*, 646–649.

Wray, N. R., Pergadia, M. L., Blackwood, D. H., Penninx, B. W., Gordon, S. D., Nyholt, D. R., ... Sullivan, P. F. (2010). Genome-wide association study of major depressive disorder: New results, meta-analysis, and lessons learned. *Molecular Psychiatry, 17*, 36–48.

Young, A. H., Gallagher, P., & Porter, R. J. (2002). Elevation of the cortisol-dehydroepiandrosterone ratio in drug-free depressed patients. *American Journal of Psychiatry, 159*, 1237–1239.

# 3

# Cognitive Models and Issues

David A. Grant,[1,2] Peter J. Bieling,[3,4]
Zindel V. Segal,[1,5] and Melanie M. Cochrane[6]

[1]Centre for Addiction and Mental Health, Canada
[2]Temple University, USA
[3]McMaster University, Canada
[4]St. Joseph's Healthcare, Canada
[5]University of Toronto, Canada
[6]University of Victoria, Canada

## Overview

Among the various psychological theories of depression, cognitive models continue to be informed by empirical tests of both the theoretical framework and the clinical outcomes associated with this approach (Clark & Beck, 1999). Several scholarly reviews (Clark & Beck, 1999; Coyne & Gotlib, 1983; Disner, Beevers, Haigh, & Beck, 2011; Haaga, Dyck, & Ernst, 1991; Kwon & Oei, 1994; Teasdale, 1983) suggest consistent support for important aspects of the model and there is general agreement that cognitive therapy is an effective treatment for depression, with efficacy that equals antidepressant pharmacotherapy (Clark & Beck, 1999; DeRubeis & Crits-Christoph, 1998; DeRubeis et al., 2005; Dobson, 1989; Robinson, Berman, & Neimeyer, 1990). Our aim in this chapter is to describe the current cognitive model of depression and the evidence that supports this theoretical framework. We will focus on a number of important research questions within the cognitive model as well as point to patterns of evidence identified in previous reviews (Clark & Beck, 1999; Haaga et al., 1991). Beyond examining the evidence, we will also point out areas where evidence is weak or contradictory. Thus, our aim is not only to capture the current state of the field but also to suggest important future directions and unresolved issues.

## The Cognitive Model

At its most general, the cognitive model of depression suggests that there is a strong connection between an individual's construal of events, their behavior, and their emotional state. The model postulates that incoming information from the environment is processed via meaning making structures that result in particular interpretations for each individual and that in depression such cognitive structures are negatively oriented in their processing and tone, generating negative emotions and problematic behaviors (Beck, 1967). The cognitive model sees the processing of information as a primary, though not necessarily causal, factor in depression.

The cognitive model has its roots in two of the dominant currents of contemporary psychological thought, behaviorism and cognitivism. The developer of the cognitive model, Beck, was influenced considerably by behaviorism and learning theory which suggested that psychopathology could be learned and did not necessarily result from repressed psychosexual conflicts, the prevailing view into the 1960s (Clark & Beck, 1999). At the same time, theorists and researchers began to turn their attention away from straightforward associationist connections between a stimulus and a response to information processing that connected the external environment and behavior through meaning construction. Beck's critical clinical observation was that patients who are depressed construe many of their circumstances as negative, and that while this ran counter to the objective reality of the situation, it was the negative processing that kept problematic emotions and behaviors in place (Beck, 1967). Consistent with learning theory, he postulated that this negative information processing was the result of early learning and he began to pursue the idea that this kind of information processing was intimately connected with the signs and symptoms of depression. Since the 1960s, the cognitive model has evolved (Beck, 1967; Beck, Rush, Shaw, & Emery, 1979; Clark & Beck, 1999) and has been elaborated by others (Teasdale & Barnard, 1993).

Cognitive theory posits that the processing of information is crucial for the survival of any organism. Because the number of external stimuli in the environment is practically infinite, an organism needs to be able to filter out irrelevant inputs while selecting only the most relevant information for further attention. In psychopathology, these filters, or schemas, are thought to be rigid, absolute, and automatic as a result of early learning. The content of schemas is thought to be different across various disorders including depression, anxiety, and personality disorders. For example, depression schemas are thought to center on unlovability and inadequacy (Beck, 1995) and during an episode of depression negative schemas are believed to dominate the meanings that patients assign to events, while between episodes these schemas are less pronounced.

Schemas do not operate in a vacuum, quite the opposite, these systems of beliefs are brought to bear on everyday life events encountered by the person. The major avenue through which these schemas are thought to operate is by the production of automatic thoughts—specific, observable cognitions that occur in response to a situation and whose themes are often consistent with the schemas' content. Such automatic thoughts play a central role in negative emotions and behavioral decisions (Clark & Beck, 1999).

## Evidence for the Cognitive Model

The predictions of the cognitive model have been investigated in a variety of research areas including information processing, assessment of emotions and change in emotions, coping behaviors, treatment process and outcome, and developmental psychopathology. Researchers have tended to focus on a set of very specific predictions the models make and develop a paradigm to test those ideas. Conclusions about the cognitive model's integrity, therefore, rely on examination and review of numerous studies of specific predictions, which can be assembled into similar themes in order to draw inferences about the overall value of the model.

Other reviewers have used several organizing principles to assemble their review of the literature. For instance, the first comprehensive review of the area by Haaga et al. (1991) specified nine specific hypotheses that could be derived from the cognitive model. Similarly, Clark and Beck (1999) derived nine hypotheses from the cognitive model although these nine hypotheses differed considerably from the nine hypotheses created by Haaga et al. (1991). The approach of listing very narrow hypotheses has the benefit of being straightforward, especially when the task at hand is the review of studies numbering in the hundreds. Our approach was to use many of these hypotheses as a point of departure, but we will also use another level of organization that is partly derived from the cognitive conceptualization of clinical disorders (Beck, 1995). Our purpose in using this different approach is to offer a somewhat simpler, but still meaningful, heuristic to help the reader organize the large amount of information and number of studies. The questions we pose concern core predictions of the model of psychopathology and are relatively less focused on treatment issues such as the efficacy of cognitive therapy or mechanisms of action. The following questions will guide our examination of the evidence for cognitive models:

1.  What is the evidence regarding the existence of negative distortions in thoughts of depressed individuals?
2.  Are these cognitive distortions related to environmental stimuli and do these distortions have an impact on emotion and behavior?
3.  What is the evidence that there are different levels of cognition and that the presence of the different types of cognitions is important to the experience of depression?
4.  What is the evidence that early life experiences influence the development of negative cognitive structures?

For each question, we will review the weight of evidence and describe seminal studies in that area. We will also describe any issues that remain unresolved within each of those areas.

## What is the evidence regarding the existence of negative distortions in thoughts of depressed individuals?

The cognitive model of depression takes as its starting point the notion that it is the depressed person's moment-to-moment negative misinterpretation of an event, rather than the event itself, that leads to emotional distress (Beck et al., 1979; Clark & Beck, 1999). What is the empirical status of the assertion that depressed people are more likely to have negative thoughts? As reviewers have done previously, we frame the questions about negative cognitions in terms of central tenets. To examine the issue of cognitive distortions, we focus on two specific hypotheses:

(1) Negativity—depression is characterized by the presence of self-referent negative thinking; (2) Specificity—depression has a distinct cognitive profile in terms of both content and process. With regard to the first hypothesis, the large majority of studies and reviews support this notion of negativity. Since Beck's original research comparing the level of negative cognitions expressed by depressed patients during interviews to nondepressed psychiatric patients (Beck, 1967), the large majority of studies have supported this hypothesis. Later studies focused on objective "checklists" of depressotypic thoughts such as the Cognitions Checklist (Beck, Brown, Steer, Eidelson, & Riskind, 1987) or the Automatic Thoughts Questionnaire (Hollon & Kendall, 1980) where participants use Likert scales to assess the frequency of negative thoughts. These studies suggest that cognitions can be reliably measured and are associated with depression; that is, a higher frequency of negative thoughts characterizes depressed individuals when compared to a variety of control groups including nondepressed normals and nondepressed patients (Dobson & Shaw, 1986; Hollon, Kendall, & Lumry, 1986; Ingram, Kendall, Smith, Donnell, & Ronan, 1987; Whisman, Diaz, & Luboski, 1993). Further, recent studies suggest that this elevated frequency of negative thoughts may be related to, and compounded by, impairments in depressed individuals' ability to disengage their attention from negative self-referent information and to inhibit negative cognitions more generally (Eugène, Joormann, Cooney, Atlas, & Gotlib, 2010; Koster, De Lissnyder, Derakshan, & De Raedt, 2011).

Related to negativity is the notion of specificity, which is the idea that psychological disorders can be distinguished from one another based on distinct cognitive profiles. In other words, when contrasted with other disorders, depression is predicted to be more associated with thoughts concerning loss or deprivation (Clark & Beck, 1999). This hypothesis has been tested using group comparisons (contrasting those who have a diagnosis of depression with other diagnostic categories on self-report measures of a variety of cognitions) and examining correlations between continuous measures of psychiatric symptoms and different kinds of cognition. Most studies in this area have suggested specificity of depression and negative cognition when compared to individuals with generalized anxiety, social phobia, or test anxiety (Beck, Steer, & Epstein, 1992; Clark, Beck, & Stewart, 1990; Sanz & Avia, 1994; Steer, Beck, Clark, & Beck, 1994; Victor, Furey, Fromm, Öhman, & Drevets, 2010). Specificity has also been examined using information processing paradigms, such as having participants recall previously endorsed self-referent adjectives. Here too, depressed individuals appear to recall more negative-content adjectives when compared to anxious individuals (Greenberg & Beck, 1989; Ingram et al., 1987). Similarly, correlational studies examining the pattern of relations between symptom measures and measures of cognition suggest that depression is specifically associated with negative thoughts, even when controlling for the presence of anxiety or threat cognitions (Alford, Lester, Patel, Buchanan, & Giunta, 1995; Jolly & Dykman, 1994). These studies generally converge on the conclusion that, indeed, depressed states are typically associated with negative thoughts that do not characterize normal emotional states or anxiety. In fact, depressed states are typically associated with thoughts of loss, failure, and pessimism (Clark & Beck, 1999; Gotlib, Krasnoperova, Yue, & Joormann, 2004; Greenberg & Beck, 1989; Haaga et al., 1991; Ingram, Atchley, & Segal, 2011; Sanz & Avia, 1994; Steer et al., 1994).

Finally, early formulations of the cognitive model argued for exclusivity of negative thinking, that is, depression should be characterized by an absence of positive thoughts. However, researchers have found that depressed people do report some positive cognitions and self-views, which challenge the notion of exclusivity of negative thoughts (Derry & Kuiper, 1981; Segal & Muran, 1993). However, later writing on the cognitive model of depression emphasizes not an absolute lack of positive cognition, but rather a preponderance of negative thoughts (Clark & Beck, 1999). Indeed, the research literature does support the notion that depressed individuals have a relatively higher ratio of negative to positive thoughts, with a general consensus that in depression negative thoughts outnumber positive thoughts approximately by 2 to 1 (Schwartz, 1986, 1997). Taken together, evidences for the negativity and specificity hypotheses lend good support to the notion that depressive thinking is characterized by numerous negative biases.

## Are cognitive distortions related to environmental stimuli and do these distortions have an impact on emotion and behavior?

This question is equally important because the cognitive model specifies that negative thoughts will not occur randomly, but in response to specific events that are misinterpreted by the individual. Moreover, this misinterpretation is said to fuel a cycle of negative emotions and influence the behavior of the depressed individual. Phrased in more technical terms, these ideas have been termed selective processing and primacy. The selective processing hypothesis states that depression is characterized by a processing bias for negative self-referent information from the environment. The primacy hypothesis predicts that negative cognition influences both behavior and emotion (Clark & Beck, 1999; Haaga, Dyck, & Ernst, 1991).

It is important to note that the cognitive theory of depression does not suggest that depressed persons are always biased in their information processing (Segal, 1988), rather such biases are most likely to emerge in situations that are personally relevant and offer a degree of ambiguity (Beck, 1967; Clark & Beck, 1999). Unlike the research on negativity and specificity, which often involves simple self-report, evaluation of the selective processing hypothesis involves more laboratory-based studies. Participants in such studies are placed in a variety of specifically constructed situations, ranging from imagined scenarios in which an outcome is predicted, to performing a task and receiving feedback from others. Indeed, these studies do suggest that depressed individuals find negative and positive interpretations of ambiguous stimuli equally acceptable, whereas nondepressed individuals prefer positive interpretations (Crowson & Cromwell, 1995; Moretti et al., 1996). Depressed individuals are more likely to perceive their own performance in an experimental task as less positive and more negative (Dykman, Abramson, Alloy, & Hartlage, 1989; Weary & Williams, 1990), though some studies have suggested that depressed individuals see their performance only less positively (DeMonbreun & Craighead, 1977). Similarly, depressed individuals judge their social performances to be more negative than nondepressed individuals (Dow & Craighead, 1987; Gotlib & Meltzer, 1987). Depressed individuals selectively recall more negative self-referent adjectives in memory-based tasks, though in some studies depressed individuals recall fewer positive adjectives and not necessarily more negative adjectives (Kuiper & Derry, 1982). When compared to nondepressed controls in a recall task, depressed participants were also found to display poorer overall recall of previously presented cue words, but a greater likelihood to falsely recall negative "lure" words that had not been presented previously (Joormann, Teachman, & Gotlib, 2009). Also, responses of depressed individuals to standardized open-ended vignettes of typical achievements and interpersonal experiences often contain negative distortions (Krantz & Hammen, 1979; Krantz & Liu, 1987; Watkins & Rush, 1983), especially when the vignette is itself negative (Krantz & Gallagher-Thompson, 1990). This is true whether the comparison group is nondistressed controls or mixed psychiatric controls (Haaga et al., 1991). Similarly, an examination of thought records of depressed patients in treatment has revealed cognitive errors in response to situations that patients had recorded themselves (Blackburn & Eunson, 1989). Moreover, whether responses are gathered in the context of a lab or in the clinic, the types of cognitive errors made by depressed individuals appear to be similar. Arbitrary inference (e.g., attributing a cause in the absence of evidence), magnification (e.g., making a small mistake and seeing this out of all proportion), overgeneralization (e.g., taking a single case and seeing that as a general, negative rule), and personalization (e.g., attributing a negative outcome to the self) are the most common cognitive errors reported in these studies (Clark & Beck, 1999). Such studies certainly support the notion of selective, negative processing of information in depression.

However, there are also several issues in the area of selective processing that have been controversial. First, in some studies of information processing, depressed individuals have actually been found to be more accurate than nondepressed individuals. This effect has been termed "depressive realism" or the "sadder but wiser" phenomenon (Abramson & Alloy, 1981). Obviously, if the perceptions of depressed people are sometimes more accurate than those of nondepressed people, the notion of selective processing and the cognitive model itself are open to challenge. However, a closer examination of the experimental findings has suggested that there are specific conditions under which depressed individuals are more accurate, and that the depressive realism notion does not hold uniformly (Clark & Beck, 1999). Specifically, it seems that depressed individuals may be more accurate when asked to judge the probability of abstract outcomes, but not when judging personally relevant, everyday situations, which are much more central in the experience of depression (Clark & Beck, 1999; Haaga & Beck, 1995). Furthermore, research using clinical samples has demonstrated that what initially appears to be more accurate judgments by depressed individuals may instead be largely attributable to characteristically negatively biased thinking, as well as the misapplication of logical heuristics (Carson, Hollon, & Shelton, 2010). Another issue, and one that remains unresolved despite its prominence in the cognitive model, is the empirical status of the cognitive distortions. Depending on which source reference is used, the cognitive model sets out variable numbers and types of cognitive distortions. It has been relatively straightforward to demonstrate that depressed individuals have biases that are negative in tone. It has been more difficult to construct a comprehensive empirical taxonomy of the kinds of distortions depressed individuals make.

The next hypothesis to be explored in this section, that of primacy, predicts that there is a link between negative distortions and the individual's emotions and behavior. One program of research has illustrated that ruminative, self-focused negative thoughts are systematically related to enduring negative moods, particularly among depressed women (Nolen-Hoeksema, 1991; Nolen-Hoeksema, Morrow, & Fredrickson, 1993). Other studies attempt to reduce negative thought content to examine the impact of such cognitive change on affect (Persons & Burns, 1985; Teasdale & Fennell, 1982). Overall, both types of studies demonstrate a reciprocal link between negative moods and negative thoughts. There is also evidence that negative cognition is associated with both peripheral physiological changes and changes in cortical activity. Negative cognition has been linked to increased heart rate (Schwartz, Weinberger, & Singer, 1981) and respiration rate (Schuele & Wiesenfeld, 1983), as well as cerebral blood flow through the limbic, paralimbic, and brainstem structures in PET studies (George et al., 1995). The difficulty with such physiologic studies is teasing apart the nature of relationships between cognition and emotion. The design of these studies has typically been correlational rather than experimental and the degrees of association are sometimes modest. To establish causality better, some studies induce a negative mood and then examine the impact of the mood on cognitive networks, and these studies also support the primacy hypothesis (Ingram, Miranda, & Segal, 1998). Emerging research and recent advances in cognitive neuroscience have also begun to provide a conceptual framework for understanding the underlying anatomical and neurobiological correlates of cognition in depression (Disner et al., 2011; Ingram et al., 2011).

Unfortunately, less research is available that examines the connection between depressive thinking, mood, and overt behavior. Nonetheless, numerous authors have argued that depression is associated with actions that precipitate stress in the longer term (Hammen, 1991; Monroe & Peterman, 1988; Monroe & Simons, 1991; Rutter, 1986). Indeed, in one study, depressed women were found to generate more stress in a 1-year period, particularly in an interpersonal context (Hammen, 1991). In that study, depressed women had more life stressors that could be seen as random, but the behavioral choices of the women also contributed to the creation of more difficult circumstances. There is also recent evidence from a very large population-based twin registry that supports the notion that self-generated stress contributes to the onset of depression (Kendler, Karkowski, & Prescott, 1999; Kendler, Thornton, & Gardner, 2000). What is not well understood is whether the correlation between depression and problematic, potentially stress-generating, behaviors is cognitively mediated. That is, do the distortions of depressed individuals lead them to select behavioral strategies that are not optimal, and do these strategies eventually lead to increased stressors or other self-defeating behaviors? These ideas could be tested within presently available experimental paradigms and would be further evidence in positing cognition as a central feature in the experience of depression.

## What is the evidence that there are different levels of cognition, and that the presence of the different types of cognitions is important to the experience of depression?

The cognitive model makes it clear that negative cognition exists at different levels or layers. Some of these layers or levels are accessible to the person and can be spontaneously described; other levels are under less effortful control and cannot be reported by the individual directly without training. At the most observable level—negative thinking—we have seen that there is good evidence to support the notion that depressed individuals are likely to have more negative thoughts. Is there also evidence that there are other levels of cognition, and that these have a negative tone in depression? Moreover, are these other levels of cognition important in initiating or maintaining depression? These questions, though they seem simple, are complex to answer and pose several dilemmas for researchers. First, how does one ascertain the existence of cognitive processes that cannot be described by the individual or be observed directly? Second, if evidence for more implicit cognition exists, how might explanations drawing on these constructs demonstrate their incremental utility compared to accounts based on negative thoughts alone?

As in other areas of the model, one of the critical questions is whether one can measure the phenomenon of interest reliably and validly. These more implicit types of cognition are termed either "beliefs" or "schemas," and there have been attempts to measure these through self-report. The earliest and most established measure of these more deeply held beliefs is the Dysfunctional Attitudes Scale (DAS; Weissman & Beck, 1978). The DAS consists of three forms, a 100-item version and two more commonly used 40-item versions (Forms A and B). The DAS and its different forms have been found to display adequate psychometric properties (Beck, Brown, Steer, & Weissman, 1991; Oliver & Baumgart, 1985), and many of the DAS items are explicitly written as "if... then" statements to differentiate them from measures of automatic thoughts. The latter have strong self-relevant negative content, while beliefs are expressed mainly as rules or conditional assumptions.

Clearly, implicit beliefs need to be sufficiently differentiated from automatic negative thoughts in order to be useful concepts or to have explanatory power that goes beyond negative thoughts. The conditional nature of beliefs and their contents (e.g., "if... then" rules) is one factor that differentiates them. However, beliefs also need to meet additional criteria if they are to be useful in cognitive models. First, beliefs should be correlated moderately, but significantly, with negative thoughts; a correlation that is too high would suggest redundancy of concepts, whereas no correlation would suggest that beliefs and thoughts are independent of each another. Second, one would hypothesize that beliefs would be more stable than negative thoughts since the former are less tied to specific mood states or situations. Finally, the presence of these maladaptive beliefs should increase vulnerability to the onset or relapse of depression. These hypotheses have received positive support from research to date (Clark & Beck, 1999; Rude, Durham-Fowler, Baum, Rooney, & Maestas, 2010). For example, the DAS has been found to be correlated moderately, but significantly, with negative thoughts and depressive symptoms in many studies (Clark & Beck, 1999). Second, there is evidence that markers of these beliefs are evident even between episodes of depression (Gemar, Segal, Sagrati, & Kennedy, 2001; Ingram et al., 1998; Segal et al., 2006). Finally, a large body of research supports the notion that these kinds of beliefs, especially when coupled with stressors, lead to the emergence of depressive symptoms (Hammen, Marks, Mayol, & deMayo, 1985; Hammen et al., 1995; Segal et al., 2006; Segal, Shaw, Vella, & Katz, 1992). DAS scores have also been shown to prospectively predict episodes of depression in an initially nondepressed community sample (Rude et al., 2010).

Another interesting issue in the literature on beliefs is the question of content of these beliefs. Research has shown that the underlying factor structure of the DAS is determined by which version is at issue, and that the two forms (A and B) appear to have different factor structures. Form A consists of a need for approval, perfectionism, and avoidance of risk. Form B factors are need for success, need to impress others, need for approval, and need to control feelings (Oliver & Baumgart, 1985). The most comprehensive analysis of the DAS items, using the entire 100-item pool as a starting point, suggests that nine types of conditional assumptions are reliably measured by the DAS (Beck et al., 1991). The nine types of conditional assumptions are: vulnerability, need for approval, success perfectionism, need to please others, imperatives, need to impress, avoidance of appearing weak, control over emotions, and disapproval dependence. Two studies have also addressed the issue of DAS and coping, that is the connection between beliefs and behavior. In one study, there was no relationship between DAS scores and perceived social support (Kuiper, Olinger, & Swallow, 1987). However, in a study of depressed inpatients, elevated DAS scores were associated with perceiving one's support as inadequate and having lower social adjustment (Norman, Miller, & Dow, 1988). This research represents a promising line of inquiry, but it is too early to draw any conclusions about the link between conditional beliefs and coping strategies.

According to the cognitive model, beliefs contain meaning (or content), but are also processing constructs (Clark & Beck, 1999; Williams, Watts, MacLeod, & Matthews, 1997). There are numerous inherent difficulties in measuring the products of "implicit cognitive processing." Indeed, a self-report measure in which the respondent essentially endorses the content of an item cannot, in and of itself, support the notion of belief-based information processing (Gotlib & McCabe, 1992; Segal & Swallow, 1994). To study the information processing functions of beliefs, researchers have used a variety of experimental paradigms including sentence completion, trait adjective ratings, and autobiographical memory recall. These studies suggest that depression increases accessibility to negative self-referent schema content (Clark & Beck, 1999). Studies in this area share an underlying conceptual and methodological framework. Researchers compare individuals at risk for depression (e.g., patients who are formerly depressed, but currently remitted or recovered) with never-depressed or nondepressed psychiatric control groups. The two groups are exposed to an experimental stimulus, usually a "mood prime" designed to activate temporary negative emotions and thereby a negative set of beliefs. By comparing the beliefs of groups before and after mood prime, the presence of activated negative beliefs can be demonstrated. Using this paradigm, numerous studies demonstrate that remitted depressed individuals are likely to have more negative content in their thoughts, more negative recall and encoding of information, and problems with focusing their attention as a result of mood priming, when compared to controls (Ingram et al., 1998, 2011; Scher, Ingram, & Segal, 2005). Thus, the induced negative mood may be seen to be an analogue to negative environmental events, and the activation in cognitive structures, a vulnerability or risk factor for depression. Studies have also demonstrated a link between degree of activation of negative beliefs and vulnerability to depressive relapse, suggesting an important link between latent negative beliefs and the onset of full depression (Segal, Gemar, & Williams, 1999; Segal et al., 2006). These lines of research support the idea that deep cognition is a powerful explanatory construct in depression and that deep cognitive processes are distinct from negative automatic thoughts.

An elaboration of this approach to "deep" cognitive structures in depression has been provided by the Interacting Cognitive Subsystems (ICS) approach of Teasdale and Barnard (1993). This approach suggests that depression does not increase activation of negative core beliefs, but rather results in the application of a different set of mental models. Further, these mental models encode more globally negative views of self and views that are more closely allied with notions of lack of social approval and lack of success. Lending support to this model, Teasdale and colleagues were able to show that depressed patients completed sentence stems with positive words, when doing so changed the overall meaning of the belief to be dysfunctional. For example, in the sentence, "Always seeking the approval of other people is the road to _____," the depressed individuals were more likely to use the word "success" whereas nondepressed individuals were more likely to use a word such as "unhappiness." This finding suggests that depressed individuals process information, not in a monolithic or simplistic negative manner, but that they apply a template of beliefs that set them up to experience negative consequences (Teasdale, Taylor, Cooper, Hayhurst, & Paykel, 1995).

On the whole, the investigation of beliefs has proven to be one of the most important challenges for researchers investigating the cognitive model. To date, the literature is largely divided into information processing paradigms and self-report content categories. Each has its limitations. Investigations that focus on content tell us little about the operation of these beliefs. Likewise, studies examining the processing associated with these beliefs tell us little about the content of the beliefs that have been activated. Future approaches could be helpful if they are able to combine these two approaches. For example, can situation-specific "mood prime" paradigms demonstrate the activation of specific types of beliefs? Second, do these specific beliefs then influence the subsequent processing of information? This research will require considerable rigor, and a comprehensive integration of these approaches likely awaits the creation of new experimental paradigms that can test such complex questions. As a promising step toward addressing this line of inquiry, recent research has demonstrated an increasing ability to speak to both the content of beliefs as well as their structure and organization, in addition to an ability to examine the issue of stability versus change in organization of beliefs over time (Dozois, 2007; Dozois et al., 2009; Seeds & Dozois, 2010).

## What is the evidence that early life experiences influence the development of negative cognitive structures?

We have now reviewed the evidence that supports the idea that specific cognitive processes are associated with depression. We have seen that these processes operate on both the overt level and at deeper levels that can be detected indirectly but reliably. A logical question is: where do these beliefs and thoughts come from? The cognitive model suggests that a "child learns to construe reality through his or her early experiences with the environment, especially with significant others. Sometimes, these early experiences lead children to accept attitudes and beliefs that will later prove maladaptive" (Beck & Young, 1985, p. 207). Based on this assumption, the cognitive mediation hypothesis states that cognitive processes and maladaptive beliefs mediate between developmental risk factors and subsequent onset of depression (Ingram et al., 1998). Next, we address the scientific basis of the cognitive mediation hypothesis.

Certainly, children of depressed parents are at an increased risk of psychiatric problems, particularly major depression in adolescence and adulthood (Cohn, Matias, Tronick, Connell, & Lyons-Ruth, 1986; Field, 1984; Tronick & Gianino, 1986). Furthermore, depressed adults do tend to report having been parented in problematic ways in childhood (Brewin, Firth-Cozens, Furnham, & McManus, 1992; Koestner, Zuroff, & Powers, 1991; Zemore & Rinholm, 1989). A recent meta-analysis suggests that childhood maltreatment, conceptualized broadly, represents a significant risk factor for recurrent and persistent depressive episodes, and is also associated with a lack of response to treatment for depression (Nanni, Uher, & Danese, 2012). However, such findings could be due to a number of factors. What is more important to determine, from the perspective of the cognitive model, is whether early experiences influence the formation of cognitive systems that make an individual vulnerable to depression. Unfortunately, this mediation hypothesis has not been studied sufficiently to draw a conclusion. In one study using an undergraduate sample, very limited support was found for a mediating relationship of cognitive variables between reports of maladaptive parenting and subsequent depression (Whisman & McGarvey, 1995). Also, among depressed patients, a history of developmental adversity, most notably sexual abuse, is associated with more dysfunctional cognitive styles (Rose, Abramson, Hodulik, Halberstadt, & Leff, 1994). In another study using a young adolescent sample, self-worth was found to mediate between reports of maternal parenting and depressive symptoms (Garber & Robinson, 1997; Garber, Robinson, & Valentiner, 1997). To date, only limited innovative work is beginning to address cognitive mechanisms directly. This work tentatively suggests that maladaptive beliefs about the self and others may emerge early in the development of at-risk children (Bartholomew & Horowitz, 1991).

In summary, the research suggests guarded evidence for the cognitive mediation hypothesis in several circumscribed areas. Childhood loss coupled with inadequate post-bereavement care, poor parenting (particularly, lack of care, rejection/criticism, and overcontrolling disciplinary practices), insecure attachments, and childhood sexual abuse appear to set the stage for subsequent depression. However, the available evidence suggests that these factors are neither necessary nor sufficient causal factors, but instead may represent risk factors for subsequent problems that predate depression.

## Conclusion

The cognitive model, originally proposed over 40 years ago, continues to be refined and modified on the basis of empirical feedback and conceptual challenges. This theoretical approach has responded to numerous challenges through the development of more refined research strategies and paradigms that have addressed many of its critics' concerns. Paradigms have shifted from relatively simple experiments like recall of negative thoughts to sophisticated experiments that rule out a variety of alternative hypotheses and integrate neuroscience. In the future, the model is also likely to benefit from the convergence of cognitive psychology, clinical psychology, and neurosciences informed by imaging technologies. Exciting integrational research of this nature is presently underway and promises to inform a more thorough, multifaceted understanding of cognitive factors in depression in the future (Disner et al., 2011; Ingram et al., 2011). In sum, the model offers significant explanatory power and theoretical coherence to support the continued reliance on cognitive interventions as a front-line psychological treatment for unipolar depression.

# References

Abramson, L. Y., & Alloy, L. B. (1981). Depression, nondepression, and cognitive illusions: A reply to Schwartz. *Journal of Experimental Psychology: General, 110*, 436–447.

Alford, B. A., Lester, J. M., Patel, R. J., Buchanan, J. P., & Giunta, L. C. (1995). Hopelessness predicts future depressive symptoms: A prospective analysis of cognitive vulnerability and cognitive content specificity. *Journal of Clinical Psychology, 51*, 331–339.

Bartholomew, K., & Horowitz, L. M. (1991). Attachment styles among young adults: A test of a four category model. *Journal of Personality and Social Psychology, 61*, 226–244.

Beck, A. T. (1967). *Depression: Causes and treatment.* Philadelphia, PA: University of Pennsylvania Press.

Beck, A. T., Brown, G., Steer, R. A., Eidelson, J. I., & Riskind, J. H. (1987). Differentiating anxiety and depression: A test of the cognitive content-specificity hypothesis. *Journal of Abnormal Psychology, 96*, 179–183.

Beck, A. T., Brown, G., Steer, A. N., & Weissman, A. N. (1991). Factor analysis of the Dysfunctional Attitude Scale in a clinical population. *Psychological Assessment, 3*, 478–483.

Beck, A. T., Rush, A. J., Shaw, B. F., & Emery, G. (1979). *Cognitive therapy of depression.* New York: Guilford Press.

Beck, A. T., Steer, R. A., & Epstein, N. (1992). Self-concept dimensions of clinically depressed and anxious outpatients. *Journal of Clinical Psychology, 48*, 423–432.

Beck, A. T., & Young, J. E. (1985). Cognitive therapy of depression. In D. Barlow (Ed.), *Clinical handbook of psychological disorders: A step-by-step treatment manual* (pp. 200–237). New York: Guilford Press.

Beck, J. S. (1995). *Cognitive therapy: Basics and beyond.* New York: Guilford Press.

Blackburn, I. M., & Eunson, K. M. (1989). A content analysis of thoughts and emotions elicited from depressed patients during cognitive therapy. *British Journal of Medical Psychology, 62*, 23–33.

Brewin, C. R., Firth-Cozens, J., Furnham, A., & McManus, C. (1992). Self-criticism in adulthood and recalled childhood experience. *Journal of Abnormal Psychology, 101*, 561–566.

Carson, R. C., Hollon, S. D., & Shelton, R. C. (2010). Depressive realism and clinical depression. *Behaviour Research and Therapy, 48*, 257–265.

Clark, D. A., & Beck, A. T. (with Alford, B. A.) (1999). *Scientific foundations of cognitive theory and therapy of depression.* Chichester, UK: John Wiley & Sons.

Clark, D. A., Beck, A. T., & Stewart, B. (1990). Cognitive specificity and positive-negative affectivity: Complementary or contradictory views on anxiety and depression? *Journal of Abnormal Psychology, 99*, 148–155.

Cohn, J. F., Matias, R., Tronick, E. Z., Connell, D., & Lyons-Ruth, K. (1986). Face to face interactions of depressed mothers and their infants. In E. Z. Tronick, & T. Field (Eds.),

*Maternal depression and infant disturbance (New directions for child development, No. 34)* (pp. 31–45). San Francisco, CA: Jossey-Bass.

Coyne, J. C., & Gotlib, I. H. (1983). The role of cognition in depression: A critical appraisal. *Psychological Bulletin, 94*, 472–505.

Crowson, J. J., & Cromwell, R. L. (1995). Depressed and normal individuals differ both in selection and in perceived tonal quality of positive–negative messages. *Journal of Abnormal Psychology, 104*, 305–311.

DeMonbreun, B. G., & Craighead, W. E. (1977). Distortion of perception and recall of positive and neutral feedback in depression. *Cognitive Therapy and Research, 1*, 311–329.

Derry, P. A., & Kuiper, N. A. (1981). Schematic processing and self reference in clinical depression. *Journal of Abnormal Psychology, 90*, 286–297.

DeRubeis, R. J., & Crits-Christoph, P. (1998). Empirically supported individual and group psychological treatments for adult mental disorders. *Journal of Consulting and Clinical Psychology, 66*, 37–52.

DeRubeis, R. J., Hollon, S. D., Amsterdam, J. D., Shelton, R. C., Young, P. R., Salomon, R. M., & Gallop, R. (2005). Cognitive therapy vs medications in the treatment of moderate to severe depression. *Archives of General Psychiatry, 62*, 409–416.

Disner, S. G., Beevers, C. G., Haigh, E. A. P., & Beck, A. T. (2011). Neural mechanisms of the cognitive model of depression. *Neuroscience, 12*, 467–477.

Dobson, K. S. (1989). A meta-analysis of the efficacy of cognitive therapy for depression. *Journal of Consulting and Clinical Psychology, 57*, 414–419.

Dobson, K. S., & Shaw, B. F. (1986). Cognitive assessment with major depressive disorders. *Cognitive Therapy and Research, 10*, 13–29.

Dow, M. G., & Craighead, W. E. (1987). Social inadequacy and depression: Overt behavior and self-evaluation processes. *Journal of Social and Clinical Psychology, 5*, 99–113.

Dozois, D. J. A. (2007). Stability of negative self-structures: A longitudinal comparison of depressed, remitted, and nonpsychiatric controls. *Journal of Clinical Psychology, 63*, 319–338.

Dozois, D. J. A., Bieling, P. J., Patelis-Siotis, I., Hoar, L., Chudzik, S., McCabe, K., & Westra, H. A. (2009). Changes in self-schema structure in cognitive therapy for major depressive disorder: A randomized clinical trial. *Journal of Consulting and Clinical Psychology, 77*, 1078–1088.

Dykman, B. M., Abramson, L. Y., Alloy, L. B., & Hartlage, S. (1989). Processing of ambiguous and unambiguous feedback by depressed and nondepressed college students: Schematic biases and their implications for depressive realism. *Journal of Personality and Social Psychology, 56*, 431–445.

Eugène, F., Joormann, J., Cooney, R. E., Atlas, L. Y., & Gotlib, I. H. (2010). Neural correlates of inhibitory deficits in depression. *Psychiatry Research: Neuroimaging, 181*, 30–35.

Field, T. M. (1984). Early interactions between infants and their post-partum mothers. *Infants Behavior and Development, 7*, 527–532.

Garber, J., & Robinson, N. S. (1997). Cognitive vulnerability in children at risk for depression. *Cognition and Emotion, 11*, 619–635.

Garber, J., Robinson, N. S., & Valentiner, D. (1997). The relation between parenting and adolescent depression: Self-worth as a mediator. *Journal of Adolescent Research, 12*, 12–33.

Gemar, M., Segal, Z., Sagrati, S., & Kennedy, S. (2001). Mood-induced changes on the Implicit Association Test in recovered depressed patients. *Journal of Abnormal Psychology, 110*, 282–289.

George, M. S., Ketter, T. A., Parekh, P. I., Horwitz, B., Herscovitch, P., & Post, R. M. (1995). Brain activity during transient sadness and happiness in healthy women. *American Journal of Psychiatry, 152,* 341–351.

Gotlib, I. H., Krasnoperova, E., Yue, D. N., & Joormann, J. (2004). Attentional biases for negative interpersonal stimuli in clinical depression. *Journal of Abnormal Psychology, 113,* 127–135.

Gotlib, I. H., & McCabe, S. B. (1992). An information processing approach to the study of cognitive functioning in depression. In E. F. Walker, B. A. Cornblatt, & R. H. Dworkin (Eds.), *Progress in experimental personality and psychopathology research* (Vol. 15, pp. 131–161). New York: Springer.

Gotlib, I. H., & Meltzer, S. J. (1987). Depression and the perception of social skills in dyadic interaction. *Cognitive Therapy and Research, 11,* 41–54.

Greenberg, M. S., & Beck, A. T. (1989). Depression versus anxiety: A test of the content-specificity hypothesis. *Journal of Abnormal Psychology, 98,* 9–13.

Haaga, D. A. F., & Beck, A. T. (1995). Perspectives on depressive realism: Implications for cognitive therapy of depression. *Behaviour Research and Therapy, 19,* 121–142.

Haaga, D. A. F., Dyck, M. J., & Ernst, D. (1991). Empirical status of cognitive theory of depression. *Psychological Bulletin, 110,* 215–236.

Hammen, C. (1991). Generation of stress in the course of unipolar depression. *Journal of Abnormal Psychology, 100,* 555–561.

Hammen, C. L., Burge, D, Daley, S. E., Davila, J., Paley, B., & Rudolph, K. D. (1995). Inter-personal attachment cognitions and prediction of symptomatic responses to interpersonal stress. *Journal of Abnormal Psychology, 104,* 436–443.

Hammen, C., Marks, T., Mayol, A., & deMayo, R. (1985). Depressive self-schemas, life stress, and vulnerability to depression. *Journal of Abnormal Psychology, 94,* 308–319.

Hollon, S. D., & Kendall, P. C. (1980). Cognitive self-statements in depression: Development of an Automatic Thoughts Questionnaire. *Cognitive Therapy and Research, 4,* 383–395.

Hollon, S. D., Kendall, P. C., & Lumry, A. (1986). Specificity of depressotypic cognitions in clinical depression. *Journal of Abnormal Psychology, 95,* 52–59.

Ingram, R. E., Atchley, R. A., & Segal, Z. V. (2011). *Vulnerability to depression: From cognitive neuroscience to prevention and treatment.* New York: Guilford Press.

Ingram, R. E., Kendall, P. C., Smith, T. W., Donnell, C., & Ronan, K. (1987). Cognitive specificity in emotional disorders. *Journal of Personality and Social Psychology, 53,* 734–742.

Ingram, R. E., Miranda, J., & Segal, Z. V. (1998). *Cognitive vulnerability to depression.* New York: Guilford Press.

Jolly, J. B., & Dykman, R. A. (1994). Using self-report data to differentiate anxious and depressive symptoms in adolescents: Cognitive content specificity and global distress? *Cognitive Therapy and Research, 18,* 25–37.

Joormann, J., Teachman, B. A., & Gotlib, I. H. (2009). Sadder and less accurate? False memory for negative material in depression. *Journal of Abnormal Psychology, 118,* 412–417.

Kendler, K. S., Karkowski, L. M., & Prescott, C. A. (1999). Causal relationship between stressful life events and the onset of major depression. *American Journal of Psychiatry, 156,* 837–841.

Kendler, K. S., Thornton, L. M., & Gardner, C. O. (2000). Stressful life events and previous episodes in the etiology of major depression in women: An evaluation of the kindling hypothesis. *American Journal of Psychiatry, 157,* 1243–1251.

Koestner, R., Zuroff, D. C., & Powers, T. A. (1991). Family origins of adolescent self-criticism and its continuity into adulthood. *Journal of Abnormal Psychology, 100,* 191–197.

Koster, E. H. W., De Lissnyder, E., Derakshan, N., & De Raedt, R. (2011). Understanding depressive rumination from a cognitive science perspective: The impaired disengagement hypothesis. *Clinical Psychology Review, 31,* 138–145.

Krantz, S. E., & Gallagher-Thompson, D. (1990). Depression and information valence influence depressive cognition. *Cognitive Therapy and Research, 14,* 95–108.

Krantz, S. E., & Hammen, C. (1979). Assessment of cognitive bias in depression. *Journal of Abnormal Psychology, 88,* 611–619.

Krantz, S. E., & Liu, C. (1987). The effect of mood and information valence on depressive cognition. *Cognitive Therapy and Research, 11,* 185–196.

Kuiper, N. A., & Derry, P. A. (1982). Depressed and nondepressed content self-reference in mild depressives. *Journal of Personality, 50,* 67–80.

Kuiper, N. A., Olinger, L. J., & Swallow, S. R. (1987). Dysfunctional attitudes, mild depression, views of self, self-consciousness, and social perceptions. *Motivation and Emotion, 11,* 379–401.

Kwon, S., & Oei, T. P. S. (1994). The roles of two levels of cognitions in the development, maintenance, and treatment of depression. *Clinical Psychology Review, 14,* 331–358.

Monroe, S. M., & Peterman, A. M. (1988). Life stress and psychopathology. In L. Cohen (Ed.), *Research on stressful life events: Theoretical and methodological issues* (pp. 31–63). Newbury Park, CA: Sage.

Monroe, S. M., & Simons, A. D. (1991). Diathesis-stress in the context of life stress research: Implications for the depressive disorders. *Psychological Bulletin, 111,* 406–425.

Moretti, M. M., Segal, Z. V., McCann, C. D., Shaw, B. F., Miller, D. T., & Vella, D. (1996). Self-referent versus other-referent information processing in dysphoric, clinically depressed, and remitted depressed subjects. *Personality and Social Psychology Bulletin, 22,* 68-80.

Nanni, V., Uher, R., & Danese, A. (2012). Childhood maltreatment predicts unfavorable course of illness and treatment outcome in depression: A meta-analysis. *American Journal of Psychiatry, 169,* 141–151.

Nolen-Hoeksema, S. (1991). Responses to depression and their effects on the duration of depressive episodes. *Journal of Abnormal Psychology, 100,* 569–582.

Nolen-Hoeksema, S., Morrow, J., & Fredrickson, B. L. (1993). Response styles and the duration of episodes of depression. *Journal of Abnormal Psychology, 102,* 20–28.

Norman, W. H., Miller, I. W., & Dow, M. G. (1988). Characteristics of depressed patients with elevated levels of dysfunctional cognitions. *Cognitive Therapy and Research, 12,* 39–52.

Oliver, J. M., & Baumgart, E. P. (1985). The Dysfunctional Attitude Scale: Psychometric properties and relation to depression in an unselected adult population. *Cognitive Therapy and Research, 9,* 161–167.

Persons, J. B., & Burns, D. D. (1985). Mechanisms of action of cognitive therapy: The relative contributions of technical and interpersonal interventions. *Cognitive Therapy and Research, 9,* 539–551.

Robinson, L. A., Berman, J. S., & Neimeyer, R. A. (1990). Psychotherapy for the treatment of depression: A comprehensive review of controlled outcome research. *Psychological Bulletin, 108,* 1–20.

Rose, D. T., Abramson, L. Y., Hodulik, C. J., Halberstadt, L., & Leff, G. (1994). Heterogeneity of cognitive style among depressed inpatients. *Journal of Abnormal Psychology, 103,* 419–429.

Rude, S. S., Durham-Fowler, J. A., Baum, E. S., Rooney, S. B., & Maestas, K. L. (2010). Self-report and cognitive processing measures of depressive thinking predict subsequent major depressive disorder. *Cognitive Therapy and Research, 34,* 107–115.

Rutter, M. (1986). Meyerian psychobiology, personality development, and the role of life experiences. *American Journal of Psychiatry, 143,* 1077–1087.

Sanz, J., & Avia, M. D. (1994). Cognitive specificity in social anxiety and depression: Self-statements, self-focused attention, and dysfunctional attitudes. *Journal of Social and Cognitive Psychology, 13,* 105–137.

Scher, C. D., Ingram, R. E., & Segal, Z. V. (2005). Cognitive reactivity and vulnerability: Empirical evaluation of construct activation and cognitive diathesis in unipolar depression. *Clinical Psychology Review, 25,* 487–510.

Schuele, J. G., & Wiesenfeld, A. R. (1983). Autonomic response to self-critical thought. *Cognitive Therapy and Research, 7,* 189–194.

Schwartz, G. E., Weinberger, D. A., & Singer, J. A. (1981). Cardiovascular differentiation of happiness, sadness, anger and fear following imagery and exercise. *Psychosomatic Medicine, 43,* 343–364.

Schwartz, R. M. (1986). The internal dialogue: On the asymmetry between positive and negative coping thoughts. *Cognitive Therapy and Research, 10,* 591–605.

Schwartz, R. M. (1997). Consider the simple screw: Cognitive science, quality improvements, and psychotherapy. *Journal of Consulting and Clinical Psychology, 65,* 970–983.

Seeds, P. M., & Dozois, D. J. A. (2010). Prospective evaluation of a cognitive vulnerability-stress model for depression: The interaction of schema self-structures and negative life events. *Journal of Clinical Psychology, 66,* 1307–1323.

Segal, Z. V. (1988). Appraisal of the self-schema construct in cognitive models of depression. *Psychological Bulletin, 103,* 147–162.

Segal, Z. V., Gemar, M., & Williams, S. (1999). Differential cognitive response to a mood challenge following successful cognitive therapy or pharmacotherapy for unipolar depression. *Journal of Abnormal Psychology, 108,* 3–10.

Segal, Z. V., Kennedy, S., Gemar, M., Hood, K., Pedersen, R., & Buis, T. (2006). Cognitive reactivity to sad mood provocation and the prediction of depressive relapse. *Archives of General Psychiatry, 63,* 749–755.

Segal, Z. V., & Muran, J. C. (1993). A cognitive perspective on self-representation in depression. In Z. V. Segal, & S. J. Blatt (Eds.), *The self in emotional distress: Cognitive and psychodynamic perspectives* (pp. 131–170). New York: Guilford Press.

Segal, Z. V., Shaw, B., Vella, D., & Katz, R. (1992). Cognitive and life stress predictors of relapse in remitted unipolar depressed patients: Test of the congruency hypothesis. *Journal of Abnormal Psychology, 101,* 26–36.

Segal, Z. V., & Swallow, S. R. (1994). Cognitive assessment of unipolar depression: Measuring products, processes, and structures. *Behaviour Research and Therapy, 32,* 147–158.

Steer, R. A., Beck, A. T., Clark, D. A., & Beck, J. S. (1994). Psychometric properties of the Cognition Checklist with psychiatric outpatients and university students. *Psychological Assessment, 6,* 67–70.

Teasdale, J. D. (1983). Negative thinking in depression: Cause, effect or reciprocal relationship? *Advances in Behaviour Research and Therapy, 5,* 3–25.

Teasdale, J. D., & Barnard, P. J. (1993). *Affect, cognition, and change: Remodeling depressive thought.* Hove, UK: Erlbaum.

Teasdale, J. D., & Fennell, M. J. V. (1982). Immediate effects on depression of cognitive therapy interventions. *Cognitive Therapy and Research, 6,* 343–352.

Teasdale, J. D., Taylor, M. J., Cooper, Z., Hayhurst, H., & Paykel, E. S. (1995). Depressive thinking: Shifts in construct accessibility or in schematic mental models? *Journal of Abnormal Psychology, 104,* 500–507.

Tronick, E. Z., & Gianino, A. (1986). The transmission of maternal disturbance to the infant. In E. Z. Tronick, & T. Field (Eds.), Maternal depression and infant disturbance (New directions for child development, No. 34) (pp. 5–12). San Francisco, CA: Jossey-Bass.

Victor, T. A., Furey, M. L., Fromm, S. J., Öhman, A., & Drevets, W. C. (2010). Relationship between amygdala responses to masked faces and mood state and treatment in major depressive disorder. *Archives of General Psychiatry, 67,* 1128–1138.

Watkins, J. T., & Rush, A. J. (1983). Cognitive response test. *Cognitive Therapy and Research, 7,* 425–436.

Weary, G., & Williams, J. P. (1990). Depressive self-presentation: Beyond self-handicapping. *Journal of Personality and Social Psychology, 58,* 892–898.

Weissman, A. N., & Beck, A. T. (1978). *Development and validation of the Dysfunctional Attitudes Scale: A preliminary investigation.* Paper presented at the meeting of the Association for the Advancement of Behavior Therapy, Chicago, IL.

Whisman, M. A., Diaz, M. L., & Luboski, J. A. (1993). *Cognitive specificity of major depression and generalized anxiety disorder.* Paper presented at the annual meeting of the Association for Advancement of Behaviour Therapy, Atlanta, GA.

Whisman, M. A., & McGarvey, A. L. (1995). Attachment, depressotypic cognitions, and dysphoria. *Cognitive Therapy and Research, 19,* 633–650.

Williams, J. M. G., Watts, F. N., MacLeod, C., & Matthews, A. (1997). *Cognitive psychology and the emotional disorders* (2nd ed.). Chichester, UK: John Wiley & Sons.

Zemore, R., & Rinholm, J. (1989). Vulnerability to depression as a function of parental rejection and control. *Canadian Journal of Behavioural Science, 21,* 364–376.

# 4

# Psychosocial Models and Issues in Major Depression

Antonia Bifulco

Kingston University, UK

## Background

The history of investigating psychosocial risk for depression involves input from a range of psychological subdisciplines (e.g., cognitive, social, and psychodynamic) as well as sociological (epidemiology and medical sociology) and has also encompassed methodological innovation in measurement. This has brought together a rich seam of investigation of current and lifelong factors which lead to increased risk of adult depression. In addition, most recent approaches aim to include the biological substrata to determine truly biopsychosocial approaches (Caspi, Hariri, Holmes, Uher, & Moffitt, 2010; Kendler et al., 1995; Monroe & Reid, 2008). The modern challenge has been to measure the different psychosocial factors in sufficient depth to ascertain the timing and sequence and reflect the complex context and meaning of experience to uncover the mechanisms involved in onsets of major depressive disorder. While there are many parallels in the findings with both bipolar disorder (Hosang et al., 2010) and postnatal depression (Murray, Cooper, & Hipwell, 2003), the focus in this chapter will be on major depression in community rather than patient samples and on the contribution of Brown, Harris, and colleagues at the University of London.

George Brown and Tirril Harris proved to be pioneers in championing an approach to clinical depression in the community, particularly in women, which emphasized social inequality as a main theme. With Medical Research Council funding over nearly three decades from the 1970s, their combined expertise in anthropology/medical sociology (Brown) and psychology/psychoanalysis (Harris) provided a rich source for synthesizing narrative accounts of hardship in day-to-day life. This has been extended in recent years by the work of Bifulco and colleagues in the Lifespan Research Team, now at Kingston University, to further develop the lifespan and attachment aspects (Bifulco & Moran, 1998; Bifulco & Thomas, 2012). While their London community studies have had a significant impact on the understanding of social risk factors in depression, the distinctive measurement approach has been underutilized in recent years for the maximum benefit of new gene–environment models and for therapeutic intervention. A key element to the psychosocial approach used by Brown and Harris was the formalization of narrative interviews, which provided rich and contextualized

*The Wiley-Blackwell Handbook of Mood Disorders*, Second Edition. Edited by Mick Power.
© 2013 John Wiley & Sons, Ltd. Published 2013 by John Wiley & Sons, Ltd.

accounts of both stress (in terms of life events and difficulties) as well as vulnerability (problematic relationships, self-esteem, and childhood adversity). This was in stark contrast to the brief questionnaires used at the time, particularly of life events (Homes & Rahe, 1967). With such intensive methods allowing the greater specification of life events, it became possible to uncover likely mechanisms in depression onset and tease out the elements that made the experience stressful in relation to the individuals' context, thus exploring its likely meaning. But the accounts also provided a great deal of insight into the links between prior psychosocial vulnerability, stress, and the onset of disorder, illustrating the interplay of different aspects of social disadvantage in the lives of women and families in the community.

The aim of this chapter in outlining models and issues is to summarize the psychosocial models developed, particularly: (i) the vulnerability-provoking agent model for onset of depression covering a 12-month period, (ii) the lifespan model examining childhood developmental history and depressive vulnerability, and (iii) newer developments incorporating attachment style and resilience. Finally, remaining issues for further developing the models in relation to genetic investigations as well as translating the research into practice and policy will be outlined.

## Life Events, Vulnerability, and Depression

### Life events and difficulties

The importance of investigating life events and difficulties in relation to depression is to emphasize the role of externally based stressors, to provide an explanation of the timing of disorder onset and to enable a closer analysis of person–environment linkage in terms of coping with events.

Acute stressors, or life events, are considered severe in the Brown and Harris model, if high on objective indicators of threat or unpleasantness, that is, an investigator judgment of threat for the average person in that situation, aided by manualized examples. Importantly, it is not based on respondent reports of stressfulness, which can be influenced either by the incipient depression or by vulnerability characteristics. Such events need to remain threatening at 10 days after the inception of the event to be focused fully or partly on the individual, and not attributable to psychiatric symptoms (Brown & Harris, 1978). In analyses, those in a 6-week period before onset are typically analyzed compared to the longer study period for those without depression. Difficulties are chronic stressors lasting a minimum of 4 weeks, again objectively determined by factual details and judged stressful for the average person, with "major difficulties" having high severity and lasting 2 years or more. Both are assessed by means of the life events and difficulties schedule (LEDS) and in the vulnerability–stress model constitute provoking agents for depression (Brown & Harris). Studies using the LEDS and a clinical measure of depression on community women, either the Present State Examination (Wing, Cooper, & Sartorius, 1974) or latterly the SCID for DSM-IV (First, Gibbon, Spitzer, & Williams, 1996) in both the Camberwell (1970s) and two Islington studies of onset of disorder (1980s and 1990s). Results showed that severe events were common, with half of the London community women studied experiencing at least one per year. However, rates in those who developed depression were substantially higher and nearly all those with an onset of depression (94%) had a severe episode in the 6 weeks prior to onset (Brown, 1993). This was confirmed in a later study when women were interviewed every 3 months over the year to confirm the timing of events prior to depression (Bifulco, Brown, Moran, Ball, & Campbell, 1998). When categorization of severe events by domain was examined, those who developed depression experienced more bereavements, partner events, and pregnancy/birth events, but no more events concerning children, close others finance, housing, or health than the rest (Brown, Bifulco, & Harris, 1987). Further investigation showed that the domain or category of event was not the most crucial component. Instead, it was qualities of events, examined in terms of their matching to prior circumstances or motivation (the "Achilles heel") or characteristics particularly damaging to the self (such as loss, entrapment, or humiliation) and could occur in varied domains loss (Brown, Harris, & Hepworth, 1995). These will now be described.

The three types of "matching" events include "D-events," matching pre-existing severe difficulties of at least 6 months' duration; "C-events," matching areas of prior high commitment; and "R events," matching areas of prior role conflict (Brown et al., 1986). The presence of any one of these substantially raises the risk of depression three to four times more than other severe events. "D events" represent a potential exhaustion of coping and likely helplessness resulting from events that confirm the further progression of difficulties. An example would be finding out about one's husband's infidelity in the context of a long-term problematic partner interaction involving arguments and rows, so that the event signals the end of the relationship. Such an event may represent the "final straw". "C-events" match prior behaviorally assessed high commitments that can be seen as a great disappointment in terms of life plans and sense of a competent self. An example would be learning of failing an important exam following a period of extensive study involving sacrifice of time and resources. Finally, an "R-event" matches a pre-existing area of role conflict between commitments; for example, between motherhood and employment, and infer failure in key roles coupled with the strain involved in being overstretched. An example would be a child excluded from school with a parent who had long been struggling with childcare and full-time work. Thus these events, while happening as acute occurrences on a specific date, all have a longer inception in terms of prior difficult or demanding conditions and are therefore more than the sum of the event alone in terms of stressful experience (Brown et al., 1986).

These distinctions, which can be measured objectively in terms of behavioral indicators, begin to uncover the personalized aspects of context which make some life events more destructive for certain individuals and begin to indicate their underlying meaning. Some personalization is gender based. For example, replication with a sample of cohabiting couples selected for having a shared severe life event, found those involving children more often led to depression in women and those involving employment to depression among men, argued to reflect role investment (Nazroo, Edwards, & Brown, 1997). Other investigations of life events using the same model and measures have shown the importance of work events for men (Eales, 1988). Other aspects of events found most damaging and which had implications for self-worth and social status those involving humiliation (hostile and/or public rejections or put-downs) or entrapment (events which reinforce difficulty of escape from punitive relationships or circumstance) (Brown et al., 1995). This interpretation owes much to the cognitive approaches involving learned helplessness (Seligman, 1975), self-esteem, and hopelessness in relation to depression (Beck, 1967). It also fits with more recent evolutionary approaches to depression concerning defeat and lowered social ranking (Gilbert, 1992). Brown differentiates three types of meaning for the individual threatened by such events: role-based meaning derived from concerns, plans, and social roles; specific meaning linked to evolutionary-derived special purpose appraisal systems; and memory-linked emotional schemas including low self-esteem and helplessness (Brown, 2002).

In further understanding the linking mechanisms between severe life events and depression, the appraisal and coping with such events were also examined. The Crisis Coping Interview (Bifulco & Brown, 1996) was an adjunct to the LEDS, with questions about the aspects of problem solving, cognitive avoidance, attributions for the event, emotional response, and view of the likely outcome in relation to actual events and difficulties described. It was found that high levels of self-blame, pessimism, or inferred denial were the most highly related to onset of disorder. This was again linked with self-esteem and helplessness/hopelessness themes, although the denial finding was potentially linked to more dissociative mechanisms in disorder (Liotti, 2004). Other questions about support at the time of the crisis showed that lack of crisis support from close others again raised likelihood of an onset of depression occurring (Brown, Andrews, Harris, Adler, & Bridge, 1986). Further details are given below.

## Vulnerability

However, the presence of severe life events represents only half of the psychosocial model developed. The other element includes pre-existing vulnerability to depression. Thus, although depression frequently occurs shortly after the experience of a severe life event, the majority of individuals who suffer severe life events do not succumb; so severe life events are a *necessary* but not *sufficient* cause of depression. The other element in the model includes the individuals' prior susceptibility. The model argues for an interaction of vulnerability with severe events in leading to onset. The relationship of vulnerability and life events was first investigated in the cross-sectional study in Camberwell in the 1970s and identified social and demographic factors that included lack of intimacy with partner in terms of confiding, lack of other close confidants, presence of three or more children under age 15 at home, lack of employment, and the loss of one's mother in childhood as factors that increased the risk of depression among the women studied. These were argued to reflect the underlying loss of self-esteem, which was hypothesized as generalizing into hopelessness in the face of a severe life event and thus into depressive illness (Brown & Harris, 1978). These are the same mechanisms as those later developed in the more refined life event analysis.

Further, prospective investigation in the prospective Islington studies had the benefit of a long purpose-designed vulnerability interview—the Self Esteem and Social Support interview (SESS) (O'Connor & Brown, 1984). This explored the role domains identified as important and showed which attributes of each role were critical for vulnerability and predictive of disorder. Various qualities of relationships were measured, including confiding, negative interaction, felt attachment, and showed that negative interaction with partner, negative interaction with children in the household, and lack of a close confidant all increased risk. These were analyzed as an index of Negative Elements in Close Relationships (NECR) including any one of these elements. These were all highly related to a parallel index of Negative Evaluation of Self (involving negative evaluation of personal attributes, role competence, or lack of self-acceptance). Taken together, the social elements of poor interactions in close relationships, and the psychological element of low self-esteem, formed a "joint vulnerability index," which together with severe life events, provided the best model for depression (Brown, Bifulco, & Andrews, 1990; Brown, Bifulco, Veiel, & Andrews, 1990). Of the 303 representative Islington women studied prospectively, either NES or NECR occurred for 50% at first interview, but was present for 97% of those who developed depression. For joint vulnerability, there was a higher odds ratio at 17% versus 74% respectively. The model was replicated in a second prospective Islington study (Bifulco et al., 1998).

The vulnerability-provoking agent findings are summarized in Figure 4.1a. This shows that the joint vulnerability index created a 10-fold higher relative risk of depression occurring, with severe life events a 13-fold higher risk but the two together producing a relative risk of 46 illustrating the interaction effect. Figure 4.1b shows the elaborated model with crisis coping and support. Logistic regression showed vulnerability, coping, and crisis support all contributed to the model of onset among those with a provoking event: joint vulnerability (OR = 3.91, Wald = 9.12, 1 $df$, $p < 0.002$), poor cognitive coping (OR = 4.83, Wald = 8.18, 1 $df$, $p < 0.004$), and lack of crisis support (OR = 11.53, Wald = 12.24, 1 $df$, $p < 0.0005$) (Bifulco & Brown, 1996).

## Lifespan Models and Depression

Theorists from the psychodynamic, developmental, and cognitive psychology traditions have all agreed that the origins of vulnerability for adult depression lie in childhood experience. The advent of "developmental psychopathology" has developed this lifespan approach by looking at the impact of childhood development on adult behavior and disorder (Cicchetti & Cohen, 2006; Hetherington, Lerner, & Perlmutter, 1988). In terms of the vulnerability models developed, the original Camberwell findings in the 1970s identified that the early loss of mother (by death, or separation for 12 months or more before age 11) was subsequently examined more fully to determine the role of related experiences that might point to mechanisms in both problematic development and perpetuation of hostile environments (Bifulco, Brown, & Harris, 1987; Bifulco, Harris, & Brown, 1992; Harris, Brown, & Bifulco, 1990). For these investigations, the purpose-designed interview, the Childhood Experience of Care and Abuse (CECA[1]) was developed (Bifulco, Brown, & Harris, 1994; Bifulco & Moran, 1998), one of the only standardized interview measures of the range of

[1]www.cecainterview.com

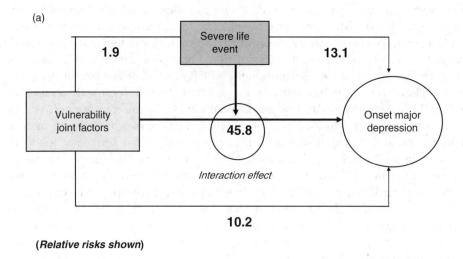

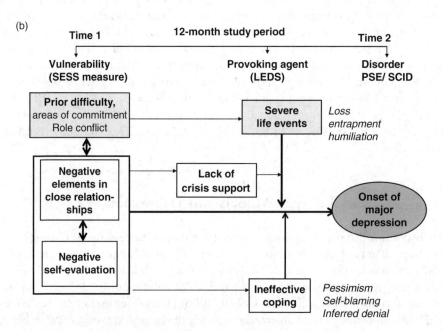

**Figure 4.1.** (a) Vulnerability/provoking Agent Model for Onset of Depression.
(b) Detailed Vulnerability/provoking Agent Model for Onset of Depression

childhood adversity required for the development of depression which gives a time-based scoring of childhood adversities with high levels of reliability and validity (Bifulco, Brown, Lillie, & Jarvis, 1997). The studies confirmed that while child-hood loss of the mother did increase risk of adult depression, it was associated factors involving neglect, parental antipathy, physical and sexual abuse that provided the best model of later disorder in regression analyses. Each of these experiences at severe levels

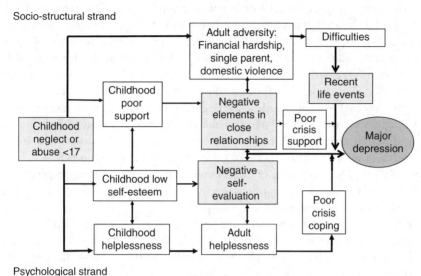

**Figure 4.2.**  Lifespan Psychosocial Model for Depression

increased the risk of lifetime depression (odds ratio of 2:5). An index of any one of these experiences tripled the risk in adult women studied, but in adolescent/young adults increased the risk of depression fivefold, with similar results holding for males and females (Bifulco et al., 2002). A lifespan model (see Figure 4.2) was developed looking at longer term impact of neglect or abuse experiences before age 17 on adult depression, including chronic and recurrent disorder (Bifulco & Moran, 1998). The two-stranded model showed influence through social adversity. Intervening variables proved to be both social (teenage pregnancy, single parent status, domestic violence, chronic adversity) and psychological (childhood low self-esteem and helplessness related to the adult factors and poor coping).

# New Developments

There have been three major developments that add to these models of depression. These include research findings on attachment style, resilience, and incorporation into genetic models. All three serve to create new dimensions for the lifespan model in particular, and for biopsychosocial approaches in general.

## Adult attachment style

Much of the lifespan model is highly consistent with attachment theory approaches as originally formulated by John Bowlby and Mary Ainsworth (Ainsworth, Blehar, Waters, & Wall, 1978; Bowlby, 1980) and now the focus of extensive research as evidenced by the second edition of the Handbook of Attachment (Cassidy & Shaver,

2008). The nature of the early relationship with parents is posited as creating developmental disturbances that extend into adulthood, influencing later ability to form relationships and develop high self-esteem. This occurs through the presence of insecure
attachment styles (anxious, avoidant, or disorganized) which disrupt relationships,
form barriers to accessing support, and create difficulties with parenting (Cassidy &
Shaver, 1999). The mechanism for extending childhood developmental disturbance
is through "internal working models" or cognitive templates, which dictate the type
of attachment style developing. Whereas the secure style is adaptive, insecure styles
relate to different types of difficulty in becoming involved with others and are associated with a range of psychological disorders including depression (Dozier, Stovall,
& Albus, 1999). The advantage of combining attachment and lifespan psychosocial
models involves the development of greater specificity in vulnerability profiling as well
as elaborating on developmental mechanisms.

In order to measure attachment style in a manner consistent with other measures used in the model, the Attachment Style Interview (ASI[2]) was developed as a
support-based assessment of adult attachment style (Bifulco, Moran, Ball, & Bernazzani, 2002). This was built on existing support scales reflecting confiding, negative
interaction, and felt attachment in close relationships. The measure examines the quality of the relationship with the partner and with up to two close confidants, together
with assessing the ability to make and maintain relationships as the basis of insecurity and then uses seven attitudinal scales to assess aspects of avoidance (mistrust,
constraints on closeness, self-reliance, and anger) and anxious attachment (fear of
rejection, fear of separation, high desire for closeness). On the basis of both behavi-
or in relationships and attitudes around closeness and autonomy, an overall profile
of secure or varieties of insecure (enmeshed, fearful, angry-dismissive, withdrawn, or
dual/disorganized) style were developed. An additional rating of dual or disorganized
style was also rated for those with evidence of two different styles (Bifulco et al.,
2002). In prospective measurement, women with marked or moderate levels of insecure styles (enmeshed, fearful or angry-dismissive) were more at risk of depression.
These styles were highly associated with negative evaluation of self and poor support,
as well as with childhood experience of neglect or abuse (Bifulco, Moran, Ball, &
Lillie, 2002). Such insecure attachment style was shown to mediate neglect or abuse
in childhood and new onset of depression (Bifulco et al., 2006). An abbreviated
lifespan model encompassing attachment style is shown in Figure 4.3 with coefficients from path analysis. It incorporates teenage depression to show independent
contribution of adverse experience over and above early psychiatric symptoms. Differentiating the different attachment styles provided greater specificity in the model. For
example, antipathy and loss of father related to enmeshed style and childhood abuse
(physical and psychological) related to angry-dismissive style, with both lack of care
(neglect, antipathy, or role reversal) and abuse relating to fearful or dual/disorganized
styles (Bifulco & Thomas, 2012). Similarly, there were patterns in differential partner
relating (fearful, the most likely to be single parents; enmeshed, most likely to be
married and have a previous partnership; enmeshed and disorganized, more likely

[2]www.attachmentstyleinterview.com

(a)                          Abbreviated Lifespan/attachment model

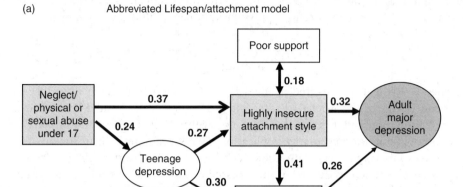

**(path analysis showing significant path coefficients)**

(b)                          **Elaborated lifespan/attachment model**

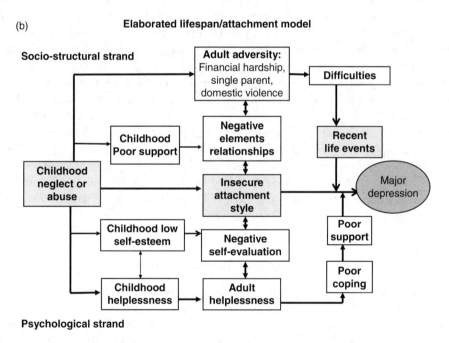

**Figure 4.3.** Psychosocial Models Incorporating Attachment Style

to have experienced domestic violence) (Bifulco & Thomas). Also in terms of coping style, those with fearful styles were the most helpless and pessimistic, those with angry-dismissive the most blaming, and enmeshed individuals used denial the most (Bifulco & Thomas, 2012). Differentiating such profiles potentially aids both clinicians in treating those vulnerable to depression, as well as pointing to different biological underpinnings of vulnerability. For example, the affect-regulation models (Mikulincer & Shaver, 2008) or mentalization approaches (Fonagy, 2003) in attachment.

## Resilience

Resilience was first investigated in the 1980s, with seminal research undertaken by Norman Garmezy and Michael Rutter and colleagues in the United States and the United Kingdom, and it is now taking a more central role in mental health research because of important preventative implications. Thus it requires an explanation of why individuals suffering adversity do not succumb to disorder (Rutter, 2007). Examples of resilience experiences quoted in the research include social support, secure attachment style, high IQ, religious belief, and benign economic environments (Fonagy, Steele, Steele, Higgitt, & Target, 1994). When investigating depression in community samples, it is evident that most individuals survive adversity in psychiatric terms. For example, two-thirds of those with childhood neglect or abuse do not develop adult depression (Bifulco & Moran, 1998). Examples of resilience in childhood or adolescence investigated in the lifespan model include support in childhood, being close to at least one parent, high self-acceptance in teenage years, and secure attachment style (Bifulco & Moran, 1998; Bifulco & Thomas, 2012). Interestingly, withdrawn style confers resilience against depression as do mild levels of the different insecure styles. In terms of the onset model, positive coping strategies (e.g., downplaying and optimism) and positive crisis support also serve to decrease onset (Bifulco & Brown, 1996). More complex models therefore need developing to show the impact of these factors. Lifespan models showing experiences related to resilience need to be developed; for example, in terms of pathways diverging from risk to resilient trajectories, in order to explain how individuals arrive at different risk points at different life stages (Elder, 1985; Rutter, 1989). This can usefully be tested in terms of key transition experiences, for example, involving school or home leaving, first pregnancy, starting and ending partner relationships (Bifulco, Bernazzani, Moran, & Ball, 2000). This can have important implications for preventative services.

## Gene–environment interaction

Psychosocial factors are playing an increasing role in the understanding of genetic bases of human behavior in relation to disorders such as depression. The main line of investigation is around the monoamine axis, with low serotonin, an MOAO neurotransmitter which promotes low levels of norepinephrine responsible for features of depression such as alertness and energy, attention, interest in life, and motivation and reward (McCrory, de Brito, & Viding, 2010). Pioneering studies in the last decade have found causal mechanisms involving interactions between the length polymorphism of the serotonin transporter gene (5-HTTPLR) and environmental adversity in the form of severe life events (Kim-Cohen et al., 2006). However, the evidence for this interaction has proved contradictory (Caspi et al., 2010; Risch et al., 2009; Uher & McGuffin, 2010) with inconsistent results even when multiple depression episodes have been examined (Fisher et al., 2012). Inconsistency and lack of replicability of findings has been attributed to paucity in the measurement of environmental stressors (Monroe & Reid, 2008; Uher & McGuffin, 2010). Thus, a self-report checklist of life events (RLEQ) (Brugha & Cragg, 1990) has often been utilized to represent the role of the environment in studies failing to show an interaction with issues of possible bias, under detection of severe events, and inaccuracies in timing in relation to disorder distorted.

Stressful experiences in childhood have also been shown to interact with a functional insertion/deletion polymorphism in the promoter region of the serotonin transporter gene (5-HTTTLR) to predict the presence of depression (Karg, Shedden, Burnmeister, & Sen, 2011). The childhood approach has also included investigating resilience with studies examining genetic differences that may constrain the stress response and increase the likelihood of resilience following maltreatment (Moffitt, Caspi, & Rutter, 2005). So gene–environment models need to encompass both vulnerability and resilience constructs (McCrory et al., 2010). Very recent work on epigenetics has argued that the environment can actually shape genetic expression. Thus, DNA methylation is an epigenetic event that affects cell function by altering gene expression. Animal studies in Canada have shown that early-life maternal separation can lead to different genetically mediated expression of traits and behavior, with some indication of possible reversibility (Meaney, 2001; Suomi, 2008). While the latter has not yet been tested in humans, the direction of investigation is to emphasize socio-environmental factors as a driver for subsequent biological change with implications for disease and disorder. For this, more careful timing and specification of adversity is likely to be needed. Thus, cumulative evidence suggests that accurate assessment of the social environment over time will be crucial for the future of psychiatric genetic psychiatry.

## Issues Arising

There are a number of issues raised by this brief review, to progress the further development and confirmation of the biopsychosocial and lifespan model of depression: the issue of measurement, the issue of vulnerability, and differential susceptibility models in genetics and finally the issue of using detailed psychosocial approaches for treatment and psychoeducational purposes. These will be outlined in turn.

### Intensive versus brief measurement

The intensive measures used by Brown and colleagues have tended to give way to brief self-report instruments in genetic research of depression, which in some instances have reduced the power of such variables in the models investigated. While there is a clear role for self-report measures for screening purposes and for use in very large samples, it would be a mistake to believe these are as effective as their interview counterparts, particularly for the development of very specific and time-based models. This principle is well established for clinical diagnoses, where symptom checklists are never accorded the same status as diagnostic interviews, but is not routinely applied to psychosocial measurement. In fact self-report questionnaires have been developed by the lifespan team to reflect vulnerability. For example, the Vulnerability to Depression Question-naire (VDQ) (Moran, Bifulco, Ball, & Campbell, 2001) validated against the SESS interview predicts depression, and this has been replicated cross-culturally (Abdul Kadir & Bifulco, 2011). The Childhood Experience of Care and Abuse Questionnaire (CECA.Q) is validated against the interview (Bifulco, Bernazzani, Moran, & Jacobs, 2005), similarly relates to depression and performs well against other childhood ques-tionnaires (Fisher, Barber, & Morgan, under review 1996) and has been utilized in a number of genetic investigations (Fisher, Morgan, & Fearon, 2006). Additionally, the Vulnerable Attachment Style Questionnaire (VASQ) (Bifulco, Mahon, Kwon, Moran, & Jacobs, 2003) is validated against the interview and differentiates those with high levels of insecure anxious and avoidant style. Its association to depression has been independently confirmed (Abdul Kadir, 2009).

However, brief self-reported life events measures have limited use and are far more likely to underrepresent the stressfulness of experience in terms of the number, sever-ity, and timing of critical life events. They also provide no measure at all of long-term difficulties. Their sole use in representing the environment in some genetic studies may have jeopardized the scientific gene–environment enterprise by oversimplifying the environmental factors, ignoring the psychological vulnerability factors and los-ing the life-course perspective which would allow proper empirical examination of timed gene–environment interaction. For example, the widely researched interaction between the length polymorphism of the serotonin transporter gene (5-HTTPLR) and environmental adversity is more consistently replicated in studies that use detailed interviews or objective independent information to record exposure to adversity rather than self-reports (Uher & McGuffin, 2008). Similar principles apply to childhood adversity measures, which need to be more consistently built into gene–environment models. For example, it is proposed that findings reported for recent life events are actually shaped by stress-generating effects of adversity early in life (Brown, Craig, & Harris, 2008; Brown & Harris, 2008). Given the assessment of childhood abuse and neglect is almost always required to be retrospective measures such as the CECA, assessment which can minimize biases in retrospective recall and use investigator expert scoring of material is required.

However, despite the benefits of using such in-depth investigator-based measures, there are barriers to use these in their present form for the needs of large genetic and epidemiological studies because of time and cost implications. Therefore, new modes of administration, which incorporate narrative and interactive elements and the critical investigator-based judgments but do not require face-to-face administration or audio-recording and slow transcription methods, need to be developed. While telephone interviews have been utilized successfully (Hosang et al., 2010), another approach is to use online methods whereby respondents access a personalized protocol using their home computers in a staged approach, incorporating both quantified and qualitative responses in an iterative process, finally scored by a trained researcher. Once devised, this approach would be of low cost, would cause little inconvenience to the respondent who can respond from home in his or her own time, would allow for wide geographic spread of respondents, and all responses generated would have a saved electronic record with no transcribing requirement. Such methods are currently being explored for research funding.

New methods for enabling such measures to be utilized in large genetic-sensitive research designs are required to allow for progress in developing sophisticated biopsychosocial models of a range of psychiatric disorders, including major depression and psychosis.

## Genetic models

There is currently a paucity of research undertaken on constructs of psychological vulnerability such as attachment style in genetic studies (Minnis, Reekie, Young, O'Connor, & Ronald, 2007). Individual differences in attachment style develop over time and significantly impact upon adult coping strategies with evidence of a neurobiological substrate to these differences beginning to accumulate (Fonagy & Target, 2008). As with life events, however, the assessment of attachment in most genetic studies relies on oversimplified instrumentation, with genetic studies of attachment changes over time failing to acknowledge social perspectives and gene–environment analysis. Adult attachment style may be conceptualized as an intermediate phenotype mediating the relationship between the early factors (genetic disposition and childhood experiences care and abuse) and adult outcomes including depression. The Attachment Style Interview (ASI) has not yet been used to explore qualities of relationships and support as well as psychological barriers to effective attachment in genetic models. By encompassing detailed support assessment, it can also be used as a moderating factor for disorder and enable better understanding of the relationship of genetic predisposition to both stressors and vulnerability to extend the theoretical interpretation of findings and the prediction of depression (Dozier, Stevenson, Lee, & Velligan, 1991; Read & Gumley, 2008). Again new modes of administering such interviews need exploring for large-scale genetic designs.

One intriguing development to have emerged from gene–environment interaction studies is the model of differential susceptibility (Belsky & Pluess, 2009). This constitutes an alternative to the vulnerability-provoking agent model (Bakermans-Kranenburg & van Ijzendoorn, 2007). It states that individuals vary in their developmental plasticity, with more plastic or malleable individuals being more susceptible than others to environmental influences in a "for better or worse" manner. That is, they are more sensitized to both negative and supportive environments with either adverse or positive developmental sequelae (Belsky, Bakermans-Kranenburg, & van Ijzendoorn, 2007). Thus a proportion of individuals (those less malleable) may be less affected by adversity in childhood. Another subset (those more malleable) will be more sensitive to their environment and suffer more from inadequacies of care and problem parenting, but flourish to a greater degree in benign circumstances. In other words, the genetic component which makes them do poorly under harsh conditions can also make them flourish under benign conditions. This model needs further investigation; for example, to show that given a very high level of childhood adversity involving neglect and abuse, the less malleable group do indeed remain impervious to its impact. Given direct impact of high levels of adversity on brain development and the HPA axis (McCrory et al., 2010) this model may not hold under all conditions. It does, however, provide an interesting variant on the vulnerability model and has enormous implications for intervention for those with more malleable genetic inheritance.

## Impact on treatment and intervention

The final issue concerns the use of psychosocial models for depression in the implementation of interventions and treatments for those vulnerable to depression. There is no doubt that the basic message concerning stressful events, coping, and support, as well as vulnerability to depression have influenced the cognitive behavioral therapy, interpersonal therapy, and other treatment models currently popular (Parry, 1995). In addition, those psychodynamically orientated therapies include both childhood adversity and attachment style into their treatment models for disorders including depression (Fonagy, 2006). In addition, befriending as a means of increasing support for depressed women has been initiated with some success as an intervention (Harris, Brown, & Robinson, 1999). There is also evidence that the lifespan model can effectively inform psychoeducational approaches (Allen, 2006).

However, not all the details of the model have penetrated into clinical practice to inform timing of intervention and specificity in vulnerability profiling. For example, the detailed matching that can be determined between individuals' vulnerability characteristics, the severe life events which will cause them the most damage, and their characteristic different modes of coping which follow from vulnerability are not utilized to their fullest potential. Similarly, the details of insecure attachment and how different adult styles which can differentiate between the type of childhood maltreatment experienced, coping styles, and susceptibility to depression can be exploited further in therapeutic contexts (Bifulco & Thomas, 2012). The fact that depression can be predicted from vulnerability status, even by brief questionnaire assessments, means that targeted preventative work could be undertaken with individuals at risk but prior to an episode of disorder (Moran et al., 2001). Thus far, these elements have not been incorporated into practice.

Challenges for future investigation include improved measurement adapted for use in the large samples required for investigating multiple factors in different disorders, identification of causes of time trends in changes in psychosocial risks and their effects, delineation of lifetime liability to poorer health outcomes, and understanding individual susceptibility to depression, which includes genetic influences. This needs to be incorporated into interdisciplinary approaches that acknowledge the importance of socioeconomic status, real-life adversity, and hostile and dangerous relationships, and how these impact on lifestyle. Thus, there is still important research that needs to be done on the role of psychosocial factors in depression. These also need to incorporate protective mechanisms to increase resilience and promote healthier lifestyles and choices to decrease depression rates, and these investigated together with risks acknowledged to be a function of disadvantage in people's context and circumstances.

# References

Abdul Kadir, N. (2009). *A psychosocial study of depression in a community-based sample of single and married mothers in Malaysia.* London: University of London.

Abdul Kadir, N., & Bifulco, A. (2011). Vulnerability, life events and depression among Moslem Malaysian women: Comparing those married and those divorced or separated. *Social Psychiatry and Psychiatric Epidemiology, 46,* 853–862.

Ainsworth, M. D. S., Blehar, M., Waters, E., & Wall, S. (1978). *Patterns of attachment: A psychological study of the strange situation.* Hillsdale, NJ: Lawrence Erlbaum Associates.

Allen, J. G. (2006). *Coping with depression: From catch-22 to hope.* Washington DC, London: American Psychiatric Publishing.

Bakermans-Kranenburg, M. J., & van Ijzendoorn, M. H. (2007). Genetic vulnerability or differential susceptibility in child development: The case of attachment [Research review]. *Journal of Child Psychology and Psychiatry, 48*(12), 1160–1173.

Beck, A. T. (1967). *Depression: Clinical, experimental and theoretical perspectives.* New York: Hoeber.

Belsky, J., Bakermans-Kranenburg, M. J., & van Ijzendoorn, M.H. (2007). For better and for worse: Differential susceptibility to environmental influences. *Current Directions in Psychological Science, 16*(6), 300–304.

Belsky, J., & Pluess, M. (2009). Beyond diathesis stress: Differential susceptibility to environmental influences. *Psychological Bulletin, 135*(6), 885–908.

Bifulco, A., Bernazzani, O., Moran, P. M., & Ball, C. (2000). Lifetime stressors and recurrent depression: Preliminary findings of the Adult Life Phase Interview (ALPHI). *Social Psychiatry and Psychiatric Epidemiology, 35,* 264–275.

Bifulco, A., Bernazzani, O., Moran, P. M., & Jacobs, C. (2005). The Childhood Experience of Care and Abuse Questionnaire (CECA.Q): Validation in a community series. *British Journal of Clinical Psychology, 44,* 1–20.

Bifulco, A., & Brown, G. W. (1996). Cognitive coping response to crises and onset of depression. *Social Psychiatry and Psychiatric Epidemiology, 31,* 163–172.

Bifulco, A. T., Brown, G. W., & Harris, T. O. (1987). Childhood loss of parent, lack of adequate parental care and adult depression: A replication. *Journal of Affective Disorders, 12,* 115–128.

Bifulco, A., Brown, G. W., & Harris, T. O. (1994). Childhood Experience of Care and Abuse (CECA): A retrospective interview measure. *Journal of Child Psychology and Psychiatry, 35,* 1419–1435.

Bifulco, A., Brown, G. W., Lillie, A., & Jarvis, J. (1997). Memories of childhood neglect and abuse: Corroboration in a series of sisters. *Journal of Child Psychology and Psychiatry, 38,* 365–374.

Bifulco, A., Brown, G. W., Moran, P., Ball, C., & Campbell, C. (1998). Predicting depression in women: The role of past and present vulnerability. *Psychological Medicine, 28*(1), 39–50.

Bifulco, A., Harris, T., & Brown, G. W. (1992). Mourning or early inadequate care? Reexamining the relationship of maternal loss in childhood with adult depression and anxiety. *Development and Psychopathology, 4,* 433–449.

Bifulco, A., Kwon, J. H., Moran, P. M., Jacobs, C., Bunn, A., & Beer, N. (2006). Adult attachment style as mediator between childhood neglect/abuse and adult depression and anxiety. *Social Psychiatry and Psychiatric Epidemiology, 41*(10), 796–805.

Bifulco, A., Mahon, J., Kwon, J. H., Moran, P., & Jacobs, C. (2003). The Vulnerable Attachment Style Questionnaire (VASQ): An interview-based measure of attachment styles that predict depressive disorder. *Psychological Medicine, 33,* 1099–1110.

Bifulco, A., & Moran, P. (1998). *Wednesday's child: Research into women's experience of neglect and abuse in childhood and adult depression.* London, New York: Routledge.

Bifulco, A., Moran, P. M., Ball, C., & Bernazzani, O. (2002). Adult attachment style. I: Its relationship to clinical depression. *Social Psychiatry and Psychiatric Epidemiology, 37,* 50–59.

Bifulco, A., Moran, P. M., Ball, C., Jacobs, C., Baines, R., Bunn, A., & Cavagin, J. (2002). Childhood adversity, parental vulnerability and disorder: Examining inter-generational transmission of risk. *Journal of Child Psychology and Psychiatry, 43,* 1075–1086.

Bifulco, A., Moran, P. M., Ball, C., & Lillie, A. (2002). Adult attachment style. II: Its relationship to psychosocial depressive-vulnerability. *Social Psychiatry and Psychiatric Epidemiology, 37,* 60–67.

Bifulco, A., & Thomas, G. (2012). *Understanding adult attachment in families. Research, assessment and intervention.* London: Routledge.

Bowlby, J. (1980). *Attachment and loss: Vol 3. Loss: Sadness and depression.* New York: Basic Books.

Brown, G. W. (1993). Life events and affective disorder: Replications and limitations. *Psychosomatic Medicine, 55,* 248–259.

Brown, G. W. (2002). Social roles, context and evolution in the origins of depression. *Journal of Health and Social Behavior, 43,* 225–276.

Brown, G. W., Andrews, B., Harris, T. O., Adler, Z., & Bridge, L. (1986). Social support, self-esteem and depression. *Psychological Medicine, 16,* 813–831.

Brown, G. W., Bifulco, A. T., & Andrews, B. (1990). Self-esteem and depression: III. Aetiological issues. *Social Psychiatry and Psychiatric Epidemiology, 25,* 235–243.

Brown, G. W., Bifulco, A., & Harris, T. O. (1987). Life events, vulnerability and onset of depression: Some refinements. *British Journal of Psychiatry, 150,* 30–42.

Brown, G. W., Bifulco, A. T., Veiel, H. O., & Andrews, B. (1990). Self-esteem and depression. II. Social correlates of self-esteem. *Social Psychiatry and Psychiatric Epidemiology, 25,* 225–234.

Brown, G. W., Craig, T. K., & Harris, T. O. (2008). Parental maltreatment and proximal risk factors using the Childhood Experience of Care & Abuse (CECA) instrument: A life-course study of adult chronic depression—5. *Journal of Affective Disorders, 110*(3), 222–233.

Brown, G. W., & Harris, T. O. (1978). *Social origins of depression: A study of psychiatric disorder in women.* London, New York: Tavistock.

Brown, G. W., & Harris, T. O. (2008). Depression and the serotonin transporter 5-HTTLPR polymorphism: A review and a hypothesis concerning gene-environment interaction. *Journal of Affective Disorders, 111*(1), 1–12.

Brown, G. W., Harris, T. O., & Hepworth, C. (1995). Loss, humiliation and entrapment among women developing depression: A patient and non-patient comparison. *Psychological Medicine, 25,* 7–21.

Brugha, T. S., & Cragg, D. (1990). The list of threatening experiences: The reliability and validity of a brief life events questionnaire. *Acta Psyciatrica Scandinavica, 82,* 77–81.

Caspi, A., Hariri, A. R., Holmes, A., Uher, R., & Moffitt, T. E. (2010). Genetic sensitivity to the environment: The case of serotonin transporter gene and its implications for studying complex diseases and traits. *American Journal of Psychiatry, 167*(5), 509–527.

Cassidy, J., & Shaver, P. R. (Eds.). (1999). *Handbook of attachment: Theory, research, and clinical applications.* New York: Guilford Press.

Cassidy, J., & Shaver, P. (2008). *Handbook of attachment. Theory, research and clinical applications* (2nd ed.). New York, London: Guilford Press.

Cicchetti, D., & Cohen, D. J. (2006). *Developmental psychopathology: Theory and method* (2nd ed.). New York: Wiley.

Dozier, M., Stevenson, A. L., Lee, S. W., & Velligan, D. I. (1991). Attachment organisation and familial overinvolvement for adults with serious psychopathology disorders. *Development and Psychopathology, 3,* 475–489.

Dozier, M., Stovall, K. C., & Albus, K. E. (1999). Attachment and psychopathology in adulthood. In J. Cassidy, & P. R. Shaver (Eds.), *Handbook of attachment: Theory, research, and clinical applications* (pp. 497–519). New York: Guilford Press.

Eales, M. J. (1988). Depression and anxiety in unemployed men. *Psychological Medicine, 18,* 935–945

Elder, G. H. (1985). *Life course dynamics: Trajectories and transitions.* Ithaca, NY: Cornell University Press.

First, M., Gibbon, M., Spitzer, R., & Williams, G. (1996). *Users guide for SCID.* Biometrics Research Division.

Fisher, H. L., Barber, R., & Morgan, C. (under review). Concurrent validity of the Childhood Experience of Care and Abuse Questionnaire (CECA.Q) and the Childhood Trauma Questionnaire (CTQ). *British Journal of Clinical Psychology.*

Fisher, H. L., Cohen-Woods, S., Hosang, G. M., Uher, R., Powell-Smith, G., Keers, R., & McGuffin, P. (2012). Stressful life events and serotonin-transporter gene (5-HTT) in recurrent clinical depression. *Journal of Affective Disorders, 136,* 189–193.

Fisher, H., Morgan, C., & Fearon, P. (2006). Child maltreatment as a risk factor for psychosis. *Schizophrenia Research, 81*(Suppl. 1), 235.

Fonagy, P. (2003). The interpersonal interpretive mechanism: The confluence of genetics and attachment theory in development. In V. Green (Ed.), *Emotional development in psychoanalysis, attachment, theory and neuroscience: Making connections* (pp. 107–126). London: Brunner-Routledge.

Fonagy, P. (2006). The mentalization-focused approach to social development. In J. G. Allen & P. Fonagy (Eds.), *Handbook of mentalization-based treatment.* Chichester, UK: John Wiley & Sons.

Fonagy, P., Steele, M., Steele, H., Higgitt, A., & Target, M. (1994). The Emanuel Miller Memorial Lecture 1992. The theory and practice of resilience. *Journal of Child Psychology and Psychiatry and Allied Disciplines, 35*(2), 231–257.

Fonagy, P., & Target, M. (2008). Attachment, trauma and psychoanalysis: Where psychoanalysis meets neuroscience. In A. Slade & E. Jurist (Eds.), *Mind to mind: Infant research, neuroscience and psychoanalysis* (pp. 15–49). New York: Other Press.

Gilbert, P. (1992 ). *Depression: The evolution of powerlessness.* Hove, UK: Lawrence Erlbaum Associates.

Harris, T., Brown, G. W., & Bifulco, A. T. (1990). Loss of parent in childhood and adult psychiatric disorder: A tentative overall model. *Development and Psychopathology, 2,* 311–328.

Harris, T. O., Brown, G. W., & Robinson, R. (1999). Befriending as an intervention for chronic depression among women in an inner city. 1: Randomised controlled trial. *British Journal of Psychiatry, 174,* 219–224.

Hetherington, E. M., Lerner, R. M., & Perlmutter, M. (1988). *Child development in life-span perspective.* Hillsdale, NJ: Lawrence Erlbaum Associates.

Homes, T. H., & Rahe, R. H. (1967). The social readjustment rating scale. *Journal of Psychosomatic Research, 11,* 213–218.

Hosang, G. M., Korszun, A., Jones, L., Gray, G. M., Gunasinghe, C. M., Mcguffin, P., & Farmer, A. E. (2010). Adverse life event reporting and worst illness episodes in unipolar and bipolar affective disorders: Measuring environmental risk for genetic research. *Psychological Medicine.*, *40*, 1829–1837

Karg, K., Shedden, K., Burnmeister, M., & Sen, S. (2011). The serotonin transporter promoter variant (5-HTTTLPR), stress and depression meta-analysis revisited: Evidence of genetic moderation. *Archives of General Psychiatry*, *68*(5), 444–454.

Kendler, K. S., Kessler, R. C., Walters, E. E., MacLean, C., Neale, M. C., Heath, A. C., & Eaves, L. J. (1995). Stressful life events, genetic liability, and onset of an episode of major depression in women. *American Journal of Psychiatry*, *152*(6), 833–842.

Kim-Cohen, J., Caspi, A., Taylor, A., Williams, B., Newcombe, R., Craig, I. W., & Moffitt, T. E. (2006). MAOA, maltreatment, and gene-environment interaction predicting children's mental health: New evidence and a meta-analysis. *Molecular Psychiatry*, *11*(10), 903–913.

Liotti, G. (2004). Trauma, dissociation, and disorganized attachment: Three strands of a single braid. *Psychotherapy: Theory, Research, Practice, Training*, *41*, 472–486.

McCrory, E., de Brito, S., & Viding, E. (2010). Research review: The neurobiology and genetics of maltreatment and adversity. *Journal of Child Psychology and Psychiatry*, *5*(10), 1079–1095.

Meaney, M. (2001). Maternal care, gene expression and the transmission of individual differences in stress reactivity across generations. *Annual Review of Neuroscience*, *24*, 1161–1192.

Mikulincer, M., & Shaver, P. R. (2008). Adult attachment and affect regulation. In J. Cassidy & P. R. Shaver (Eds.), *Handbook of attachment. Theory, research and clinical applications* (pp. 503–531). New York, London: Guilford Press.

Minnis, H., Reekie, J., Young, D., O'Connor, T., & Ronald, A. (2007). Genetic, environmental and gender influences on attachment disorder behaviours. *British Journal of Psychiatry*, *190*, 490–495.

Moffitt, T. E., Caspi, A., & Rutter, M. (2005). Strategy for investigating interactions between measured genes and measured environments. *Archives of General Psychiatry*, *62*, 473–481.

Monroe, S. M., & Reid, M. (2008). Gene-environment interactions in depression research: Genetic polymorphisms and life-stress procedures. *Psychological Science*, *19*(10), 947–956.

Moran, P. M., Bifulco, A., Ball, C., & Campbell, C. (2001). Predicting onset of depression: The vulnerability to depression questionnaire. *British Journal of Clinical Psychology*, *40*, 411–427.

Murray, L., Cooper, P., & Hipwell, A. (2003). Mental health of parents caring for infants. *Archives of Women's Mental Health*, *6*(2), 71–77.

Nazroo, J. Y., Edwards, A. C., & Brown, G. W. (1997). Gender differences in the onset of depression following a shared life event: A study of couples. *Psychological Medicine*, *27*, 9–19.

O'Connor, P., & Brown, G. (1984). Supportive relationships: Fact or fancy? *Journal of Social and Personal Relationships*, *1*, 159–175.

Parry, G. (1995). Social support processes and cognitive therapy. In T. S. Brugha (Ed.), *Social support and psychiatric disorder: Research findings and guidelines for clinical practice*. Cambridge, UK: Cambridge University Press.

Read, J., & Gumley, A. (2008). Can attachment theory help explain the relationship between childhood adversity and psychosis? *Attachment: New Directions in Psychotherapy and Relational Psychoanalysis*, *2*, 1–35.

Risch, N., Herrell, R., Lehner, T., Liang, K. Y., Eaves, L., Hoh, J., & Merikangas, K. R. (2009). Interaction between the serotonin transporter gene (5-HTTLPR), stressful life events, and risk of depression: A meta-analysis. *Journal of American Medical Association*, *301*(23), 2462–2471.

Rutter, M. (1989). Pathways from childhood to adult life. *Journal of Child Psychology and Psychiatry and Allied Disciplines, 30*(1), 23–52.

Rutter, M. (2007). Resilience, competence, coping. *Child Abuse and Neglect, 31*(3), 205–209.

Seligman, M. E. P. (1975). *Helplessness: On depression, development and death.* San Francisco, CA: W.H. Freeman.

Suomi, S. J. (2008). Attachment in rhesus monkeys. In J. Cassidy & P. Shaver (Eds.), *Handbook of attachment: Theory, research and clinical applications* (Vol. 2, pp. 173–191). New York, London: Guilford Press.

Uher, R., & McGuffin, P. (2008). The moderation by the serotonin transporter gene of environmental adversity in the aetiology of mental illness: Review and methodological analysis. *Molecular Psychiatry, 13*(2), 131–146.

Uher, R., & McGuffin, P. (2010). The moderation by the serotonin transporter gene of environmental adversity in the etiology of depression: 2009 update. *Molecular Psychiatry, 15*(1), 18–22.

Wing, J. K., Cooper, J. E., & Sartorius, N. (1974). *The measurement and classification of psychiatric symptoms: An instruction manual for the Present State Examination and CATEGO programme.* Cambridge, UK: Cambridge University Press.

# 5

# The Developmental Psychopathology of Depression

Katie A. McLaughlin,[1] Louisa C. Michl,[1] and Kate L. Herts[2]

[1] Boston Children's Hospital, USA
[2] Harvard School of Public Health, USA

The prevalence of major depression varies substantially across the life course. A meta-analysis of depression in youth reported that the prevalence of depression is only 2.8% in children under the age of 13 and increases to 5.6% in adolescents aged 13–18 (Costello, Erkanli, & Angold, 2006). By adulthood, the lifetime prevalence of depression is 16.2% with 6.6% of adults experiencing a major depressive episode in the past year (Kessler et al., 2003). The incidence of depression remains relatively low until about 11 years of age and rises most dramatically between ages 15 and 18 (Hankin et al., 1998; Kessler et al., 2003). Although the prevalence of childhood depression is similar for boys and girls, females are more likely than males to develop depression beginning at age 13 (Hankin et al., 1998; Nolen-Hoeksema & Girgus, 1994; Nolen-Hoeksema & Twenge, 2002). Risk for depression remains elevated among females relative to males throughout adolescence and adulthood (Kessler et al., 2003; Kim-Cohen et al., 2003; Newman et al., 1996).

This chapter presents a developmental psychopathology perspective on the emergence of major depression across the life course. We build on previous reviews that first articulated a developmental psychopathology perspective in regard to child and adolescent depression (Cicchetti & Toth, 1998, 2009a). Specifically, this chapter explores the impact of developmental processes on risk for depression in children and adolescents and examines the role of developmental factors in shaping risk for depression in adulthood. Application of a developmental psychopathology perspective to depression begins with the assumption that neurobiological, psychological, and social systems are organized across development (Cicchetti, 1993). The development of these systems is shaped by numerous contexts in which children are embedded and that interact with one another and with children's developing neurobiological, psychological, and social systems across time. We focus here on factors that can alter the developmental trajectories of these systems in ways that increase risk of depression during three specific developmental stages: early childhood, middle childhood, and adolescence.

*The Wiley-Blackwell Handbook of Mood Disorders*, Second Edition. Edited by Mick Power.
© 2013 John Wiley & Sons, Ltd. Published 2013 by John Wiley & Sons, Ltd.

# The Developmental Psychopathology Framework

Developmental psychopathology seeks to characterize patterns of adaptation and mal-adaptation across the life course by examining the dynamic interplay of social context and individual patterns of neurobiological, psychological, and social development over time. The core principles of this discipline provide an organizing framework for the chapter. First, a developmental psychopathology perspective emphasizes the reciprocal and integrated nature of our understanding of normal and abnormal development; normal developmental patterns must be characterized to identify developmental devia-tions, and abnormal developmental outcomes shed light on the normal developmental processes that lead to maladaptation when disrupted (Cicchetti, 1993; Sroufe, 1990). Critically, maladaptive outcomes—including psychopathology—are considered to be the product of development rather than diseases or disabilities (Sroufe, 1997, 2009). We incorporate this principle by highlighting the primary developmental tasks occur-ring within each stage of childhood and adolescence and reviewing the factors that can result in deviations from typical developmental trajectories that ultimately confer risk for depression. Although there are a variety of ways in which cognitive development influences major depression, our focus here is primarily on social and emotional devel-opment. Second, development is cumulative and hierarchical (Gottlieb, 1991a, 1991b; Sroufe & Rutter, 1984; Werner & Kaplan, 1963). This means that development is influenced not only by genetics and the environment, but also by previous develop-ment (Sroufe, 2009; Sroufe, Egeland, & Kreutzer, 1990). Acquisition of competencies at one point in development provides the scaffolding upon which subsequent skills and competencies are built, such that capabilities from previous periods are consolidated and reorganized in a dynamic, unfolding process across time. Developmental devi-ations from earlier periods are carried forward and have consequences for children's ability to successfully accomplish developmental tasks in a later period (Cicchetti & Toth, 1998). Here, we highlight how disruptions in developmental processes earlier in the life course may prevent the acquisition of competencies in later developmental peri-ods. Third, developmental psychopathology emphasizes the importance of individual differences in both developmental process and outcome (Cicchetti, 1993). Central in this conceptualization of development are the principles of equifinality and multi-finality. Equifinality refers to the notion that multiple developmental pathways may lead to the same outcome, whether adaptive or maladaptive (Cicchetti & Rogosch, 1996, 1997). In this chapter, we focus on the multitude of developmental pathways that may ultimately culminate in major depression. Conversely, the same risk and/or resilience factors may ultimately lead to different developmental outcomes, a process known as multifinality (Cicchetti & Rogosch, 1996). Finally, a developmental psy-chopathology perspective considers the dynamic interplay between risk and resilience factors operating at multiple levels to influence developmental outcomes (Cicchetti & Toth, 2009b). This includes a focus on neurobiological, psychological, and social development and, in particular, the importance of social context and social ecology in shaping each of these aspects of development (Cicchetti, 1996; Cicchetti & Lynch, 1993; Lynch & Cicchetti, 1998). Throughout the chapter, we refer to the numerous social contexts in which children are embedded and the mechanisms through which

**Figure 5.1.** Developmental Psychopathology Framework for Examining the Developmental Psychopathology of Depression. Children are Nested within Numerous Contexts that Influence Neurobiological, Psychological, and Social Development Across Time in Ways that Increase or Decrease Risk for Major Depression

these environments confer risk for depression (see Figure 5.1). The remainder of this chapter uses these guiding principles to explore the developmental origins of major depression.

## Early Childhood

The first developmental period examined here is early childhood. The bounds of this developmental period in terms of age vary across studies. Here, we focus on the time period from birth until formal school entry, which typically occurs at the age of five in the United States and Europe.

### Salient developmental tasks

Remarkable developmental changes occur during early childhood. In the first year of life, infants must learn to regulate physiological states to maintain homeostatic equilibrium and develop basic skills to manage arousal (Sroufe & Rutter, 1984). Infants typically rely on several types of behaviors to modulate arousal, including approach-withdrawal, attentional shifting, and self-soothing (Rothbart & Derryberry, 1981; Stifter & Braungart, 1995). However, the infant has a limited repertoire of behaviors to draw upon to regulate arousal independently, and the infant–caregiver relationship provides the primary means through which the young child modulates arousal (Kopp, 1989). Indeed, the development of a primary attachment relationship represents a central developmental task of infancy and early childhood (Bowlby, 1969; Sroufe,

1979). The attachment relationship involves an emotional bond between the child and caregiver that serves to organize infant behavior and arousal, particularly during exploration and periods of distress (Ainsworth, Blehar, Waters, & Wall, 1978; Sroufe, 1979). Patterns of interaction between the infant and caregiver consolidate into stable representational models of the self in relation to others (Bowlby, 1969, 1973; Bretherton & Waters, 1985). When children enter the toddler period, the development of skills to modulate and tolerate arousal lays the foundation for emotional and behavioral regulation, as children begin to explore the environment and develop autonomy from caregivers. During the toddler and preschool period the development of effortful control and self-regulation skills is paramount. These skills are related to intentional and voluntary control over attention and behavior and include effortful attention, delay of gratification, inhibition of action upon a desired goal/object, compliance, and goal-directed actions (Kochanska, Murray, & Harlan, 2000; Kopp, 1982; Rothbart, Ahadi, & Evans, 2000). Self-regulation skills play a crucial role in shaping both social and academic competence and psychopathology in subsequent developmental periods.

## Early childhood social environment and depressogenic deviations

What sorts of environmental conditions promote the successful accomplishment of these central developmental tasks of early childhood? We draw here on the notion of the "average expectable environment," which argues that for a given species there are a range of environments that can promote normal development (Cicchetti & Lynch, 1995; Hartmann, 1958). Specifically, we focus on deviations from the expectable environment that may disrupt developmental processes in ways that increase risk for depression. At the most basic level, normal development in early childhood requires safety and security from threats to physical integrity. The development of a secure attachment to a primary caregiver is contingent upon the child's ability to use the caregiver as a "secure base" from which to explore and to return to for protection in novel and potentially threatening situations (Ainsworth et al., 1978; Bowlby, 1969). Moving beyond the basic need for safety, the presence of caregivers who are responsive to the child's needs and provide sensitive and appropriate caregiving is an important component of the expectable environment that fosters adaptive development (Sroufe, 1979). Finally, caregiving that is predictable and regular provides the structure to promote successful development in early childhood. This type of caregiving environment facilitates the development of a secure attachment to a caregiver as well as the child's ability to adaptively regulate arousal, emotions, and behavior (Sroufe, 1979, 1983).

Because the expectable environment in early childhood is determined primarily by the child's caregivers, we examine how deviations from sensitive, responsive, and consistent parenting influence developmental processes in early childhood that have relevance for depression. First, we explore the influence of insensitive and inconsistent parenting behaviors on early child development. Second, we examine the impact of maternal depression on developmental processes in early childhood. Maternal depression poses numerous risks to the developing child including inherited biological vulnerability to depression, insensitive and inconsistent parenting, and exposure to marital conflict and other stressful, unpredictable, or unstable family environments (Goodman

& Gotlib, 1999). A substantial literature has established the increased risk of depression among the offspring of depressed mothers (Beardslee, Versage, & Gladstone, 1998; Downey & Coyne, 1990; Goodman & Gotlib, 1999). Exposure to maternal depression during infancy and early childhood is argued to be particularly detrimental to adaptive development (Bureau, Easterbrooks, & Lyons-Ruth, 2009), although empirical studies examining the impact of maternal depression in early versus later childhood are largely lacking (Goodman & Gotlib, 1999). Finally, a more marked departure from the expectable environment in early childhood involves exposure to maltreatment. Early childhood is a developmental period of high risk for maltreatment, particularly, for physical abuse and neglect (Finkelhor, Ormrod, Turner, & Hamby, 2005; Sedlak & Broadhurst, 1996). Child maltreatment is associated with elevated risk for major depression in childhood, adolescence, and adulthood (Brown, Cohen, Johnson, & Smailes, 1999; Green et al., 2010; Kaplan, Pelcovitz, & Labruna, 1999; Keiley, Howe, Dodge, Bates, & Pettit, 2001).

## Mechanisms linking the early childhood environment to depression risk

How do disruptions in caregiver behaviors influence development and risk of depression? A primary psychological mechanism linking parenting behaviors in early childhood to depression is attachment security. Attachment theory posits that children develop a secure emotional bond with caregivers who are sensitive, responsive, and predictable; securely attached children will readily explore new environments and return to the caregiver for safety (Ainsworth, et al., 1978; Bowlby, 1969). In contrast, inconsistent and insensitive parenting is argued to result in an insecure attachment style, in which children are unable to use their caregiver as the foundation for exploration and safety. Several classifications of insecure attachment styles have been characterized, including anxious/avoidant, ambivalent, and disorganized/disoriented (Ainsworth et al., 1978; Main & Soloman, 1986). Insensitive and nonresponsive parenting behaviors are robustly associated with the development of an insecure attachment style in infants (Egeland & Farber, 1984). Evidence also consistently suggests that children of depressed mothers are less likely to develop a secure attachment style than children of mothers without depression (Coyl, Roggman, & Newland, 2002; Martins & Gaffan, 2000; Teti, Gelfand, Messinger, & Isabella, 1995). Insecure attachment in children of depressed mothers is thought to emerge in response to a variety of insensitive and inconsistent parenting behaviors. Maternal behavior in depressed women has been characterized as unresponsive, inattentive, intrusive, punitive, hostile, and ineffective at resolving conflict (Gelfand & Teti, 1990; Goodman & Gotlib, 1999; Gotlib & Goodman, 1999). More extreme departures from the expected environment, including maltreatment and institutional rearing, have been shown to dramatically interfere with the development of a secure attachment style. Children exposed to maltreatment and institutional rearing are particularly likely to develop insecure attachment, and many children in these adverse environments display features of a disorganized/disoriented attachment style (Carlson, Cicchetti, Barnett, & Braunwald, 1989; Zeanah, Smyke, Koga, & Carlson, 2005). Disorganized/disoriented attachment is a particularly severe departure from a secure attachment style that is characterized by a lack of coherence in responses to caregiver separation and reunification, a blending of contradictory strategies, and bizarre behaviors that are not easily classified (Main & Soloman, 1986).

Insecure attachment has been consistently identified as a risk factor for major depression in children and adolescents (Allen, Porter, McFarland, McElhaney, & Marsh, 2007; Brumariu & Kerns, 2010; Moss et al., 2006), suggesting that attachment security is a mechanism underlying the association between adverse caregiving environments in early childhood and risk for depression. Perhaps, the strongest evidence for the role of attachment security as a mechanism linking the early rearing environment to risk for depression comes from a recent study documenting that changes in attachment security were a mechanism underlying the ameliorative effects of a foster care intervention on internalizing disorders in previously institutionalized children (McLaughlin, Zeanah, Fox, & Nelson, 2012). This study suggests that randomization to an improved rearing environment prevented the onset of internalizing disorders by improving attachment security. Attachment insecurity, therefore, appears to have a direct effect on risk for major depression. However, disruptions in the formation of a secure attachment relationship may also lead to depression at later points in development through indirect pathways related to emotion regulation and social competence. These pathways are described in the section on middle childhood.

Deviations from sensitive, responsive caregiving in early childhood can also set the stage for the onset of depression by disrupting the development of self-regulation. Maternal responsiveness, warmth, and consistency are associated with greater effortful control in the preschool period (Eisenberg et al., 2003; Kochanska et al., 2000; Lengua, Honorado, & Bush, 2007), whereas maternal negativity is associated with poor attentional and behavior regulation, including delay ability (Silverman & Ragusa, 1992). Although difficulties with effortful control have been linked most consistently to externalizing behavior problems in children (Eisenberg et al., 2000), poor effortful control—particularly poor attentional regulation—is also associated with depressive symptoms in children and adolescents (Eisenberg et al., 2001; Lemery, Essex, & Smider, 2002; Muris, Meesters, & Blijlevens, 2007; Zalewski, Lengua, Wilson, Trancik, & Bazinet, 2011).

Adverse rearing environments may also increase risk of depression by increasing children's emotional and physiological reactivity to the environment. As early as the neonatal period, offspring of depressed mothers exhibit both behavioral and physiological dysregulation, which is thought to result from either a heritable biological predisposition or atypical prenatal exposure to neurochemicals associated with depression (Field, 1998). Both maternal depression and poor quality parenting in infancy can disrupt brain development in ways that increase children's risk for depression. Specifically, these environments have been shown to influence the development of frontal electroencephalogram (EEG) asymmetry. Frontal regions of the cerebral cortex are differentially lateralized to process positive and negative stimuli and underlie both behavioral and expressive responses to emotional information. The left frontal region is activated by positive emotional stimuli and promotes approach behavior, whereas the right frontal region is activated by negative stimuli and underlies withdrawal or avoidance behavior (Davidson, 1992; Davidson, Ekman, Saron, Senulis,

& Friesen, 1990; Davidson & Fox, 1982; Fox, 1991). Asymmetrical resting activation in these frontal regions can be assessed using EEG. Both poor quality maternal caregiving and maternal depression are associated with greater activation in the right relative to the left frontal cortex in infants (Field, Fox, Pickens, & Nawrocki, 1995; Hane & Fox, 2006; Hane, Henderson, Reeb-Sutherland, & Fox, 2010; Jones, Field, Davalos, & Pickens, 1997; Jones, Field, Fox, Lundy, & Davalos, 1997). Frontal EEG asymmetry has also been observed among children exposed to more extreme environments in early childhood, including institutionalization (McLaughlin, Fox, Zeanah, & Nelson, 2011). Children with this pattern of hemispheric activation are more behaviorally inhibited, socially reticent, exhibit low positive emotionality, and experience greater negative affect in response to maternal separation than those without this pattern of neural activation (Davidson & Fox, 1989; Fox, 1991; Fox et al., 1995; Fox & Davidson, 1987; Shankman et al., 2005). Moreover, frontal EEG asymmetry is associated prospectively with internalizing psychopathology in children (McLaughlin et al., 2011) and with major depression in adults (Gotlib, Ranganathand, & Rosenfeld, 1998).

Maternal depression and insensitive caregiving can also disrupt the functioning of the hypothalamic–pituitary–adrenal (HPA) axis. Alterations in this physiological system may ultimately result in heightened risk for depression. The typical circadian rhythm of cortisol—characterized by high values in the morning, a relatively steady decline across the day, and lowest values in the evening—is evident in children as early as 12 months, although a smaller decline from morning to afternoon has been observed in early childhood as compared to later developmental periods (Watamura, Donzella, Kertes, & Gunnar, 2004). In early childhood, the transition to preschool is associated with changes in physiological stress response systems. Toddlers exhibit increases in cortisol during the period of the day when they leave home and are taken to preschool, but this increase in cortisol is less substantial for children who have secure attachments to their primary caregivers (Ahnert, Gunnar, Lamb, & Barthel, 2004). Toddlers with a secure attachment to their caregiver also exhibit a reduced cortisol response to novel situations than insecurely attached children; this effect is particularly pronounced for children with high levels of behavioral inhibition (Nachmias, Gunnar, Mangelsdorf, Parritz, & Buss, 1996). Early-life maternal stress, maternal depression, and a lack of sensitive, responsive caregiving are related to elevated cortisol during periods of stress in early childhood (Essex, Klein, Cho, & Kalin, 2002). Children with higher levels of cortisol and greater increases in cortisol across the day at child care engage in less play with peers and lower levels of play complexity, suggesting a link between cortisol regulation and social behavior in early childhood (Watamura, Donzella, Alwin, & Gunnar, 2003). Indeed, children who exhibit high levels of cortisol within play groups at preschool are rated as lower in social competence and effortful control than children whose cortisol levels are less reactive to social group interaction (Gunnar, Tout, de Haan, Pierce, & Stanbury, 1997). Elevated morning cortisol in early childhood is also associated concurrently with behavioral inhibition and shyness (Schmidt et al., 1997). Although depression is not a disorder observed in young children, neuroendocrine changes related to poor rearing environments may set the stage for depression through their associations with risk factors for the disorder at later developmental periods, including behavioral inhibition and poor social competence.

Social ecological factors

Economic disadvantage has been shown to play a more important role in cognitive development than emotional development during early childhood (Duncan, Brooks-Gunn, & Kato Klebanov, 1994; McLoyd, 1998). However, the effects of early-life economic deprivation on children's cognitive development influence school readiness and may carry over into middle childhood and adolescence to influence risk for depression through pathways related to academic competence and school performance. Parents who live in economically disadvantaged circumstances are more likely to be depressed (Lorant et al., 2003) and engage in harsh or inconsistent parenting practices (McLeod & Shanahan, 1993; McLoyd, 1998), which in turn can disrupt a variety of developmental processes in early childhood that culminate in risk for offspring depression. These factors may be particularly exacerbated in families who live in concentrated poverty neighborhoods that lack social and economic resources to support families with young children. Such factors can be structural (e.g., availability of low cost day care) or social (e.g., social norms around parenting and discipline and informal social controls regarding the use of corporal punishment) (Leventhal & Brooks-Gunn, 2000; Lynch & Cicchetti, 1998). Community level factors may also buffer against the effects of poverty on children's development. Access to early intervention programs provides essential support for at-risk families and can dramatically lower the risk of adverse developmental outcomes for young children (Anderson et al., 2003; Love et al., 2005).

# Middle to Late Childhood

We next examine factors that influence the development of depression during the period beginning with children's first entry into school and lasting until the pubertal transition. Although depression remains relatively rare in middle childhood, some children experience a first episode of major depression during this time period. We explore both the developmental factors that increase risk of depression in middle childhood and those factors that contribute to elevated risk for depression in adolescence and adulthood.

## Salient developmental tasks

The transition to school presents a variety of challenges for the developing child to navigate as more time is spent outside the home interacting with peers and with adults other than primary caregivers. Regular attendance at school introduces a novel set of competencies that the child must acquire to succeed in the school environment. Children are introduced for the first time to the domain of academic achievement. Achievement is shaped by a variety of dispositional characteristics, including cognitive ability, motivation, and attitudes about school and one's abilities (Dweck, 1986; Masten & Coatsworth, 1998). As children enter school, they quickly develop beliefs about their abilities and achievement-related goals that shape both academic motivation and school performance (Dweck, 1986; Elliott & Dweck, 1988; Greene & Miller, 1996; Harter, 1982). Academic achievement also requires a solid foundation of self-regulation skills. The development of self-regulation continues into middle childhood, as children must develop increased ability to sustain attention, inhibit behaviors, delay gratification, and engage in task switching in the school environment. Self-regulation skills also play an important role in the development of socially appropriate behavior. Specifically, children must learn to abide by social norms and rules of conduct (Masten & Coatsworth, 1998; Masten, Coatsworth, Neeman, Gest, & Tellegan, 1995; Sroufe & Rutter, 1984). This is particularly true at school, but also applies to compliance at home, peer interactions, extracurricular activities, and in a variety of other situations in which children interact with adults outside the family. Children's patterns of rule-abiding versus rule-breaking behavior that emerge during middle childhood appear to be remarkably stable into adolescence and early adulthood (Masten et al., 1995). The development of competency in this area, therefore, has lasting implications for mental health and adaptive functioning. Prosocial behavior is consistently linked to the prior development of moral emotions during early childhood, particularly empathy (Fabes, Eisenberg, & Eisenbud, 1993; Holmgren, Eisenberg, & Fabes, 1998). Indeed, the foundations of numerous aspects of emotionality and emotion regulation begin to develop during the preschool period, including emotional awareness, understanding of others' emotions, and patterns of emotional expressiveness and coping (Denham, 1998; Denham et al., 2003). The consolidation of these emotion regulation skills represents an additional developmental task during middle childhood, as patterns of emotionality and emotion regulation become more stable (Cole, Michel, & O'Donnell Teti, 1994; Eisenberg et al., 1997). As children engage with an increasing number of individuals outside the family, the ability to identify, understand, and adaptively modulate their emotional experiences in the service of goals becomes paramount. A final critical task of middle childhood involves the development of social competence, particularly within the context of peer relationships (Masten & Coatsworth, 1998; Masten et al., 1995; Sroufe & Rutter, 1984). Children begin to form friendships and must develop skills to ensure harmonious relationships with peers in the school setting. Social hierarchies begin to emerge, and peer acceptance plays an important role in shaping child adjustment during middle childhood.

## Childhood social environment and depressogenic deviations

Several environmental contexts influence children's ability to successfully accomplish the developmental tasks of middle childhood. The family environment continues to play a central role in shaping positive development during this period. Parenting styles that are warm and accepting and provide consistent structure, discipline, and expectations for behavior promote adaptive development in academic, social, and emotional realms (Macoby & Martin, 1983; Steinberg, Elmen, & Mounts, 1989; Steinberg, Mounts, Lamborn, & Dornbusch, 1991). Parenting quality is associated with depression, both in middle childhood and later in development (Berg-Nielson, Vikan, & Dahl, 2002; Garber, Robinson, & Valentiner, 1997; Oakley-Browne, Joyce, Wells,

Bushnell, & Hornblow, 1995), although recent evidence suggests that parenting explains only a small proportion of the variance in child depression (McLeod, Weisz, & Wood, 2007). Adverse family environments—including marital conflict, violence, parental psychopathology, and child maltreatment—are particularly powerful predictors of depression risk (Brown et al., 1999; Cicchetti & Toth, 2005; Cohen, Brown, & Smailes, 2001; Fantuzzo et al., 1991; Sternberg et al., 1993). We explore how deviations from adaptive parenting and disruptions in the family environment influence the primary developmental tasks of middle childhood in ways that increase risk of depression.

Children spend a substantial amount of time outside the home in middle childhood, and the school environment also contributes to children's development of autonomy and academic, and social success. In elementary school, the quality of teacher–student relationships are associated with academic performance as well as social and emotional competence (Birch & Ladd, 1997; Murray & Greenberg, 2000). School also provides the primary context for peer interactions. The landscape of the peer environment is a particularly important contributor to adjustment and maladjustment during middle childhood. The formation of stable friendships and positive interactions with peers is associated with positive developmental outcomes, whereas peer rejection and poor friendship quality contribute to maladjustment across numerous domains of functioning and are associated with risk of depression (Coie, Lochman, Terry, & Hyman, 1992; DeRosier, Kupersmidt, & Patterson, 1994; Hecht, Inderbitzen, & Bukowski, 1998; Hymel, Rubin, Rowden, & Lemare, 1990; Ladd, 1990; Oldenburg & Kerns, 1997; Parker & Asher, 1993). Peer victimization and bullying are particularly strong determinants of depression risk during this time period (Gladstone, Parker, & Malhi, 2006; Hawker & Boulton, 2000; Hodges & Perry, 1999; Olweus, 1993). We examine the consequences of peer rejection, victimization, and low friendship quality on developmental processes related to depression risk.

## Mechanisms linking the childhood environment to depression risk

Children's motivation, beliefs, and goals about academic achievement first develop in middle childhood. Children with learning goals focused on competency building exhibit greater motivation for achievement, seek out academic challenges, display greater behavioral persistence in academic tasks, and are characterized as having a mastery orientation toward academics (Dweck, 1986; Elliott & Dweck, 1988; Heyman & Dweck, 1992). In contrast, children whose goals focus on performance or evaluations of the adequacy of their competencies, particularly, those with low ability or confidence, exhibit a passive and helpless orientation, avoid challenging tasks, and have low behavioral persistence (Elliott & Dweck, 1988; Heyman & Dweck, 1992). This helpless and passive orientation to school predicts the onset of symptoms of depression following academic stressors, such as receiving a bad grade (Hilsman & Garber, 1995). Mastery of developmental tasks in early childhood also shapes academic achievement. In particular, children with better self-regulation skills—particularly effortful control— are more likely to transition successfully to kindergarten and have higher academic achievement throughout elementary school (Blair & Razza, 2007; Valiente, Lemery-Chalfant, Swanson, & Reiser, 2008). Children with poor academic competency in elementary school are more likely to develop symptoms of depression during this period (Cole, 1990, 1991).

Emotion regulation skills continue to develop throughout middle childhood, and the family environment plays an important role in the development of these skills. Children learn to regulate emotions by observation and modeling of parental emotional behavior and through socialization processes within the family (Eisenberg, Cumberland, & Spinard, 1998; Morris, Silk, Steinberg, Myers, & Robinson, 2007). Parent socialization of emotion is a critical factor in children's development of emotion regulation skills and prosocial behavior during this period (Denham, Mitchell-Copeland, Strandberg, Auerbach, & Blair, 1997; Eisenberg et al., 1998; Gottman, Katz, & Hooven, 1997). Parental emotion expression, responses to emotion in their children and others, and explicit teaching about emotion all drive the development of emotional competence in middle childhood. Children raised in families with high levels of negative affect expression, for example, exhibit poor emotional awareness, frequent anger displays, and poor regulation skills (Dunn & Brown, 1994; Eisenberg et al., 2001; Snyder, Stoolmiller, & Wilson, 2003). Moreover, difficulties in the formation of a secure attachment style may "carry over" to influence emotion regulation in middle childhood. Attachment behavior is organized by internal working models that guide emotion regulation throughout the life course, and failure to develop a secure attachment to a caregiver may preclude the development of adaptive emotion regulation skills in middle childhood (Cassidy, 1994; Contreras, Kerns, Weimer, Gentzler, & Tomich, 2000; Zimmerman, 1999). Children exposed to maltreatment and domestic violence exhibit deficits in numerous aspects of emotion regulation including recognition and awareness of emotions, emotion expression, and coping (Camras et al., 1988; Jungmeen & Cicchetti, 2010; Katz, Hessler, & Annest, 2007; Maughan & Cicchetti, 2002; Shipman & Zeman, 2001; Shipman, Zeman, Penza, & Champion, 2000). Peer experiences can also shape emotion regulation in middle childhood. Peer victimization experiences elicit negative emotions including anger, sadness, and contempt (Wilton, Craig, & Pepler, 2000), and youths who are the victims of peer aggression exhibit high levels of emotional arousal and reactivity (Schwartz, Dodge, & Coie, 1993). Emotion regulation deficits have consistently been identified as risk factors for depression (Garber, Braafladt, & Weiss, 1995; McLaughlin, Hatzenbuehler, Mennin, & Nolen-Hoeksema, 2011; Sheeber et al., 2009; Silk, Steinberg, & Morris, 2003), suggesting that they represent a key mechanism linking the childhood social environment to depression risk.

An additional mechanism linking the family, peer, and school environment to depression risk in middle childhood is social competence. Social competence encompasses a variety of behaviors and social information-processing patterns that contribute to successful interpersonal interactions and adaptive social functioning (Dodge, Pettit, McClaskey, Brown, & Gottman, 1986). Harsh, punitive, and inconsistent parenting can disrupt children's ability to develop socially appropriate and rule-governed behaviors, and exposure to conflict and stress within the family environment can negatively influence the development of social competence. Children exposed to harsh parenting and violence within the family are likely to develop a variety of social information-processing patterns that increase the risk for aggressive behavior, maladjustment in peer relationships, and social rejection (Dodge, Bates, & Pettit, 1990; Schwartz, Dodge, Pettit, & Bates, 1997; Weiss, Dodge, Bates, & Petit, 1992). Conflictual and violent family environments are also related to hostility, elevated peer conflict, and poor conflict resolution skills in children (Herrera & Dunn, 1997; Matthews, Woodall, Kenon, & Jacob, 1996; McCloskey & Stuewig, 2001). Prior development of emotion regulation skills plays a central role in shaping social competence during this period. Children with low negative emotionality and adaptive emotion regulation skills are consistently found to be more socially competent and have better social functioning than children with high emotional reactivity and poor regulation skills (Denham et al., 2003; Eisenberg et al., 1995; Eisenberg et al., 1997; Eisenberg et al., 2001; Spinard et al., 2006). Moreover, children who engage in greater levels of prosocial behavior and have developed a solid understanding of social norms regarding appropriate behavior, fairness, and equity are more likely to be considered socially competent by both adults and peers (Denham & Holt, 1993). Although adverse environments involving violence and conflict are most strongly associated with social competence difficulties, normal variations in parenting continue to be an important determinant of both emotion regulation and social competence in middle childhood. Parents with good awareness of emotion, particularly their child's emotions, who engage in appropriate emotion coaching have children who exhibit more positive and less negative behaviors in play with peers (Katz & Windecker-Nelson, 2004). Together, difficulties with social information processing and appropriate social behavior contribute to elevated risk for depression, both in childhood and in later developmental periods (Cole, 1990; Cole, Martin, & Powers, 1997; Cole, Martin, Powers, & Truglio, 1996; Dodge, 1993).

Finally, adverse family and peer environments in childhood can disrupt the development of physiological stress response systems. A substantial literature has examined the influence of adverse family environments on HPA axis functioning and reactivity. In middle childhood, converging evidence suggests that adversity is associated with blunted cortisol reactivity and a diurnal rhythm characterized by low morning values and a flattened decrease across the day, a pattern called hypocortisolism (Dozier et al., 2006; Gunnar & Vazquez, 2001; Hart, Gunnar, & Cicchetti, 1995; Heim, Ehlert, & Helhammer, 2000), although some studies have found an opposite pattern (Cicchetti & Rogosch, 2001; Gunnar, Morison, Chisolm, & Schuder, 2001). Dysregulated cortisol regulation has also been observed in depressed children, with the most commonly reported pattern involving elevated evening cortisol levels (Dahl et al., 1991; Goodyer, Park, & Herbert, 2001; Hart, Gunnar, & Cicchetti, 1996; Lopez-Duran, Kovacs, & George, 2009). The degree to which this dysregulation is a precursor to depression or a consequence of depression itself remains unclear, although one study found that afternoon cortisol values at the age of four are associated prospectively with elevated internalization of problems, social wariness, and withdrawal behaviors during kindergarten (Smider et al., 2002). Further research is needed to disentangle the relationship between environmental adversity, HPA axis regulation, and depression risk in middle childhood.

## Social ecological factors

Much of the research on broader social and ecological factors that influence development in middle childhood has focused on cognitive development, academic competence, and risk for externalizing problems (Leventhal & Brooks-Gunn, 2000). Indeed, concentrated neighborhood disadvantage has been shown to have lasting effects on children's cognitive ability (Sampson, Sharkey, & Raudenbush, 2007). Neighborhood disadvantage may thus contribute to depression risk indirectly by interfering with academic achievement and motivation. Neighborhood characteristics may also increase risk for more exposures that are associated strongly with child and adolescent depression, including violence and maltreatment (Coulton, Crampton, Irwin, Spilsbury, & Korbin, 2007; Gorman-Smith & Tolan, 1998). Moreover, family processes serve as a mechanism linking the broader social context to child adjustment during middle childhood. The development of informal social controls that promote positive bonds to societal institutions, including family, school, and work, is disrupted in families living in urban poverty (Sampson & Laub, 1994). The disruption of these social controls is associated with increased delinquency in children, an effect which is mediated through harsh and inconsistent parenting, poor supervision, and insecure child–parent attachment (Sampson & Laub, 1994). These same mechanisms are likely to increase risk of depression, both in middle childhood and adolescence. Concentrated poverty neighborhoods and neighborhoods with high residential instability have a notable absence of expectations for shared child control and collective efficacy for children, such as adult–child exchanges outside the home (Sampson, Morenoff, & Earls, 1999), as well as institutional resources to support parents, including access to educational, social, and recreational opportunities (Leventhal & Brooks-Gunn, 2000). The absence of social controls, social capital, and resources to support child rearing may directly influence children's ability to develop socially appropriate behavior and social competence, which may further contribute to risk for depression both concurrently and in later developmental periods.

# Adolescence

The prevalence of depression increases dramatically during adolescence, particularly for girls and for sexual-minority adolescents. Here, we define adolescence as the period spanning the onset of the pubertal transition through high school graduation (or the age equivalent for adolescents who do not complete high school). For comprehensive reviews on adolescent depression see Nolen-Hoeksema and Hilt (2009) and Strauman, Costanzo, and Garber (2011).

## Salient developmental tasks

Adolescence marks a period of remarkable change in cognitive, physiological, psychological, and social domains. Adolescents become increasingly autonomous and experience marked individuation from parents. The development of a stable identity and sense of self is thus a central task of adolescence. Adolescents develop an increasingly abstract self-concept centered around personal beliefs and values (Harter, 1998; Steinberg & Morris, 2001). Sexual orientation and ethnic identities also develop at this time (D'Augelli, 1994; Phinney, 1990). Adolescents develop relatively stable attitudes and attributional style, or patterns of interpreting events in the world (Garber, Weiss,

& Shanley, 1993; Gotlib, Lewinsohn, Seeley, Rohde, & Redner, 1993). Puberty is the hallmark of adolescent physiological development. Puberty consists of changes in secondary sexual characteristics in early adolescence, a salient developmental milestone that impacts both identity and relationship development. Maturational deviance, a misalignment between an individual's pubertal timing and that of their same-age peers, has been linked to depression and adjustment problems. Both prospective and cross-sectional studies have established a strong link between early pubertal onset and heightened risk for major depression in girls (Angold, Costello, & Worthman, 1998; Ge, Conger, & Elder, 2001; Graber, Lewinsohn, Seeley, & Brooks-Gunn, 1997; Graber, Nichols, & Brooks-Gunn, 2010; Mendle, Harden, Brooks-Gunn, & Graber, 2010; Negriff & Susman, 2011; Stice, Presnell, & Bearman, 2001). In contrast, late maturing boys may be at increased risk for depression (Conley & Rudolph, 2009; Graber et al., 1997). Social roles change dramatically during adolescence as relationships with parents become less close and more conflictual (Collins, 1990; Steinberg, 1987, 1988), relationships with peers become increasingly important and occupy more time (Buhrmester & Furman, 1987; Larson & Richards, 1991), and social acceptance is paramount. A central task of adolescence is to learn to regulate affect in adaptive ways, increasingly without the aid of the adults who provide guidance in childhood (Steinberg & Avenevoli, 2000; Steinberg et al., 2006). Changes in cognitive, physiological, and social systems present innumerable affectively laden situations in which emotions must be successfully managed to ensure adaptive functioning (Larson & Richards, 1991; Steinberg, 1987). For instance, increasing independent contact with peers introduces numerous challenges that require effective emotional response management (e.g., entry into romantic relationships, exposure to peer substance use).

## Adolescent social environment and depressogenic deviations

Although adolescents spend less time with parents and greater time with peers during this period, the family environment remains important in shaping adolescent development. The same parenting styles that promote positive adjustment in middle childhood continue to foster adaptive development in adolescence. In particular, authoritative parenting is associated with positive social, emotional, and academic functioning and psychosocial maturity in adolescence (Macoby & Martin, 1983; Steinberg et al., 1994; Steinberg et al., 1991). Authoritative parenting is defined as warm yet demanding; authoritative parents are responsive to their child's needs but have high expectations, clear rules for behavior, and firm discipline (Darling & Steinberg, 1993; Macoby & Martin, 1983). Adolescents who are securely attached to parents are at lower risk for depression during the transition to adolescence (Armsden, McCauley, Greenberg, Burke, & Mitchell, 1990). In contrast, adolescents from families characterized by greater conflict, nonacceptance, psychological control, parental criticism, and poor parent–child relationships are more likely to develop depression (Frye & Garber, 2005; Garber et al., 1997; Puig-Antich et al., 1993).

The family may play a particularly pivotal role in shaping depression risk for sexual-minority adolescents. Lesbian, gay, and bisexual (LGB) adolescents are at twice the risk of developing depression as their heterosexual peers (Fergusson, Horwood, &

Beautrais, 1999). The process of coming out to one's family is associated with psychological distress and suicidality, and LGB adolescents often experience parental nonacceptance of their sexual orientation (D'Augelli, Hershberger, & Pilkington, 1998, 2001). Many LGB adolescents experience homelessness (Cochran, Stewart, Ginzler, & Cauce, 2002; Fournier et al., 2009; Kruks, 1991; Van Leeuwen et al., 2006), at least in part due to expulsion from their homes following disclosure of their sexual orientation (Kruks, 1991). This transition thus exposes LGB adolescents to numerous risks for depression.

Peers are an especially salient socialization context in adolescence for multiple reasons, including increases in the amount of time spent with peers, the importance of peer relationships (Brown & Larson, 2009), and greater susceptibility to peer influence compared to earlier or later developmental periods (Steinberg & Monahan, 2007). As such, difficulties with peer and romantic relationships are robustly associated with depression in adolescents (Borelli & Prinstein, 2006; Daley & Hammen, 2002; LaGreca & Harrison, 2005; Rudolph & Clark, 2001). Interpersonal stressors are strong risk factors for adolescent depression. For example, romantic relationship loss predicts the subsequent first onset of major depression in adolescents (Monroe, Rohde, Seeley, & Lewinsohn, 1999). Peer stressors and peer rejection are also strongly linked to the onset of depressive symptoms, particularly for girls (Daley & Hammen, 2002; Hankin, Mermelstein, & Roesch, 2007; LaGreca & Harrison, 2005; Nolan, Flynn, & Garber, 2003). Peer victimization is a particularly salient stressor that has damaging effects on social and psychological adjustment in adolescents (Olweus, 1993; Prinstein, Boergers, & Vernberg, 2001). Peer victimization is associated with depression in both cross-sectional (Hawker & Boulton, 2000) and longitudinal studies (Storch, Masia-Warner, Crisp, & Klein, 2005; Vernberg, Abwender, Ewell, & Beery, 1992). Adolescent peer victimization also predicts depression in adulthood (Gladstone et al., 2006; Olweus, 1993), rendering these peer experiences particularly damaging. In addition to experiences of stigma and discrimination, peer victimization is elevated in LGB adolescents, who are more likely than heterosexual adolescents to be bullied, harassed, and to be victims of violence at school and in their communities (Faulkner & Cranston, 1998; Robin et al., 2002; Russell, Franz, & Driscoll, 2001; Williams, Connolly, Pepler, & Craig, 2005).

Finally, the school environment can contribute to depression risk in adolescents. Low student connectedness to school is associated prospectively with depressive symptoms in adolescents (Shochet, Dadds, Ham, & Montague, 2006). In contrast, positive student–teacher relationships increase perceptions of belonging, promote emotional functioning, and support the development of autonomy and other milestones (Kuperminc, Leadbeater, & Blatt, 2001; Roeser, Eccles, & Sameroff, 1998, 2000). Cross-sectional studies have consistently shown a negative relationship between measures of student belonging, including quality of relationships and involvement in extracurricular activities, and emotional distress (Anderman, 2002; Harrison & Narayan, 2003; Murray & Greenberg, 2000). Perceived teacher support declines over the middle school years and predicts subsequent increases in depressive symptoms (Reddy, Rhodes, & Mulhall, 2003). Chaotic school environments may be characterized by discipline problems and violence, which are in turn associated with risk for depression (O'Keefe, 1997).

## Mechanisms linking the adolescent environment to depression risk

For many adolescents, the biological and psychosocial changes of early adolescence come well before they have experienced cognitive maturation that would facilitate adaptive emotion regulation. Areas of the brain that facilitate cognitive control of emotion undergo substantial maturation during adolescence. Steinberg et al. (2006) suggest the disjunction among early adolescent change, the emotional arousal it creates, and the absence of fully developed emotion regulation skills is a major risk factor for the development of psychopathology in adolescence. Given the myriad of changes occurring during this period, it is not surprising that adolescents perceive increases in stressors and daily hassles (Larson & Ham, 1993; Seidman, Allen, Aber, Mitchell, & Feiman, 1994; Simmons & Blythe, 1987) and experience greater negative affect and emotional lability (Larson & Lampman-Petraitis, 1989; Larson, Moneta, Richards, & Wilson, 2002). Stressful events become more closely linked to the emergence of negative affect, rendering adolescents more emotionally vulnerable to the effects of stress (Larson & Ham, 1993; Larson et al., 2002). Because early adolescence is associated with a number of academic, social, and biological changes, increased stress, and greater experiences of negative affect and emotion variability, adolescents who have not developed adaptive ways to regulate and manage negative emotions may be particularly at risk for depression.

A specific aspect of emotion regulation that is consistently linked to adolescent depression is engagement in rumination (Abela, Brozina, & Haigh, 2002; Abela & Hankin, 2011; Broderick & Korteland, 2004; Nolen-Hoeksema, Stice, Wade, & Bohon, 2007; Schwartz & Koenig, 1996). Rumination involves passively focusing on feelings of distress and thinking about their causes and consequences without initiating problem-solving behaviors (Nolen-Hoeksema, Wisco, & Lyubomirsky, 2008). Although rumination may occur in childhood (Abela et al., 2002), the link between rumination and depression has been identified most consistently in adolescents and adults. Rumination predicts the development of depressive symptoms (Broderick & Korteland, 2004; Nolen-Hoeksema, Morrow, & Fredrickson, 1993; Nolen-Hoeksema, Parker, & Larson, 1994; Nolen-Hoeksema et al., 2004; Schwartz & Koenig, 1996) as well as the future onset, number, and duration of major depressive episodes (Abela & Hankin, 2011; Just & Alloy, 1997; Nolen-Hoeksema, 2000; Nolen-Hoeksema et al., 2004; Robinson & Alloy, 2008). Females are more likely to engage in rumination than males, which likely contributes to the emergence of the gender difference in depression during adolescence (Hankin & Abramson, 2001; Nolen-Hoeksema & Girgus, 1994; Nolen-Hoeksema, Larson, & Grayson, 1999). Engagement in rumination has also been shown to explain sexual orientation disparities in adolescent depressive symptoms (Hatzenbuehler, McLaughlin, & Nolen-Hoeksema, 2008). Recent evidence suggests that exposure to stressful life events and peer victimization is related to increases in rumination over time in adolescents, and that these increases in rumination mediate the association between stress exposure and depressive symptoms (McLaughlin & Hatzenbuehler, 2009; McLaughlin, Hatzenbuehler, & Hilt, 2009).

An extensive body of work has documented the role of cognitive factors in increasing risk for adolescent depression, including negative attributional style, dysfunctional attitudes, and hopelessness (Gladstone & Kaslow, 1995; Hankin, Abramson, & Siler, 2001; Joiner & Wanger, 1995; Nolen-Hoeksema, Girgus, & Seligman, 1992). Some evidence suggests that these cognitive vulnerability characteristics are associated most strongly with depression following exposure to stressful life events (Hankin & Abramson, 2001; Robinson, Garber, & Hilsman, 1995), presumably because adolescents with these cognitive characteristics are more likely to interpret stressful events in a negative manner. Some have argued that as negative schemas are accessed more frequently, their negative content becomes increasingly accessible following even minor stressors (Hammen, Henry, & Daley, 2000). Negative attributional style, dysfunctional attitudes, and hopelessness are more common among adolescents exposed to maltreatment or parenting characterized by low acceptance (Alloy et al., 2001; Garber & Flynn, 2001; Hankin, 2005). Moreover, although these cognitive characteristics do not appear to differ for male and female adolescents, some evidence suggests that negative attributional style is more strongly associated with depression among females (Gladstone, Kaslow, Seeley, & Lewinsohn, 1997).

Beliefs about academic ability, in particular, influence both school performance and emotional adjustment in adolescents. Poor school performance can disrupt perceived and actual academic achievement, as well as feelings of success in the transition to secondary schooling. Adolescents who experience repeated academic failure may incorporate academic- or career-related failure into permanent schemas surrounding their self-concept, increasing risk for depression. Students' perceived academic inefficacy has been shown to increase the risk of emotional distress and depression (Bandura, Pastorelli, Barbaranelli, & Caprar, 1999; Roeser et al., 2000). Conversely, perceived academic ability can serve as a moderator to mitigate the effects of stressful life events on the development of depression. Minority students face unique barriers to academic success. African-American students may distance themselves from their culture of origin, for example, changing their dialect or mannerisms, to succeed academically. The need to reject aspects of their culture in order to succeed academically is associated with depression (Arroyo & Zigler, 1995). Students who have had to repeat a grade or feel that they are older than most in their class experience heightened emotional distress (Resnick et al., 1997). Thus, adolescents are at increased risk for depression when they feel that they are not keeping up with their peers academically, or must compromise another aspect of their identity to do so.

Physiological factors also underlie the emergence of depression during adolescence. Adolescents with early pubertal onset experience accelerated physical development, with implications for their self-concept and relationships, yet without a parallel acceleration in social and emotional development to facilitate their adjustment (Mendle et al., 2010; Negriff & Susman, 2011). Although the association between early pubertal timing and depression risk in females has been consistently documented, the pathways linking pubertal onset and depression are not well delineated. One pathway related to poor quality family, peer, and romantic relationships has been considered as both a cause and consequence of early pubertal onset. Stressors in the family environment, such as low-quality family interactions or father absence, may lead to early pubertal onset (Graber et al., 2010). Early maturing girls have lower quality relationships with family and peers, and are at higher risk for physical and verbal abuse from romantic partners (Graber et al., 2010). The combination of early pubertal timing and subsequent stressful life events, particularly peer stressors, is associated with elevated risk for depression (Conley & Rudolph, 2009; Ge et al., 2001). The relationship between early puberty and depression may also be mediated by self-esteem and body dissatisfaction in girls (Negriff & Susman, 2011; Stice et al., 2001).

Adolescence is characterized by marked increases in physiological reactivity to stress, both in the HPA axis and autonomic nervous system (Gunnar, Wewerka, Frenn, Long, & Griggs, 2009; Stroud et al., 2009). This increase in stress reactivity occurs to a greater degree for females as compared to males (Stroud, Papandonatos, Williamson, & Dahl, 2004). As noted previously, adverse events and disruptions in the family and peer environments can lead to dysregulation in physiological stress response systems. As these systems become more attuned to the social environment in adolescence, disruptions related to adverse environmental experiences may culminate in the onset of major depression. Indeed, emotional reactivity to stress in adolescence is associated prospectively with risk for the onset of major depression and significantly mediates the relationship between markers of the childhood social environment and depression (McLaughlin et al., 2010). Evidence linking dysregulation in physiological stress response systems to the subsequent onset of depression is more limited; however, one prospective study found that elevated cortisol-to-DHEA ratio (a measure of anabolic balance) predicted major depression onset in a high risk adolescent sample (Goodyer, Herbert, & Tamplin, 2003).

## Social ecological factors

In earlier stages of development, socioeconomic status (SES) is associated more strongly with cognitive development and behavior problems than with depression. Beginning in adolescence, SES appears to play a more important role in the development of depression. Longitudinal evidence suggests that adolescents from low SES families are more likely to develop major depression than adolescents from families with greater economic resources (Johnson, Cohen, Dohrenwend, Link, & Brook, 1999). Data from national surveys also indicate that major depression is more common among adolescents from low SES families (Goodman, 1999; McLaughlin, Costello, Leblanc, Sampson, & Kessler, 2001). Neighborhood factors also impinge upon adolescent development. Adolescents living in low SES neighborhoods are exposed to numerous environmental risks including crime, violence, substance use, ambient noise, and physical disorders such as dilapidated and vacant housing, litter, and graffiti; these environmental hazards are associated with increased risk of depression (Aneshensel & Sucoff, 1996; Latkin & Curry, 2003). The broader social climate plays an increasingly important role in shaping risk for depression, particularly for sexual-minority adolescents. For example, LGB adolescents are at lower risk of depression in communities with a greater proportion of same-sex couples and schools with gay–straight alliances, anti-bullying policies, and anti-discrimination policies that include sexual orientation (Hatzenbuehler, 2011). The extent to which aspects of social climate influence risk for adolescent depression in other groups is unknown but represents an important area for future research.

## Conclusion

Major depression is a common condition in adults associated with substantial functional impairment. Unlike anxiety disorders and disruptive behavior disorders that have an average age of onset in childhood, depression typically begins in adolescence or early adulthood (Kessler et al., 2004). Despite the relatively late age of onset, a multitude of social, environmental, and contextual factors in childhood play a role in the etiology of depression. Beginning at birth, the social environment shapes neurobiological, psychological, and social developmental processes in ways that can increase risk for depression or protect against the disorder. Developmental psychopathology provides a framework for understanding the complex and reciprocal interplay between the developing child and the array of social contexts in which they are embedded that contribute to the accumulation of risk and protective factors for depression across the life course. Incorporating a developmental psychopathology approach into interventions targeting depression holds promise for generating innovative approaches to treat and prevent the disorder.

## References

Abela, J. R., Brozina, K., & Haigh, E. P. (2002). An examination of the response styles theory of depression in third- and sixth-grade children: A short-term longitudinal study. *Journal of Abnormal Child Psychology, 30*, 515–527.

Abela, J. R., & Hankin, B. L. (2011). Rumination as a vulnerability factor to depression during the transition from early to middle adolescence: A multiwave longitudinal study. *Journal of Abnormal Psychology, 120*, 259–271.

Ahnert, L., Gunnar, M. R., Lamb, M. E., & Barthel, M. (2004). Transition to child care: Associations with infant-mother attachment, infant negative emotion, and cortisol elevations. *Child Development, 75*, 639–650.

Ainsworth, M. D. S., Blehar, M. C., Waters, E., & Wall, S. (1978). *Patterns of attachment.* Hillsdale, NJ: Erlbaum.

Allen, J. P., Porter, M., McFarland, C., McElhaney, K. B., & Marsh, P. (2007). The relation of attachment security to adolescent's paternal and peer relationships, depression, and externalizing behavior. *Child Development, 78*, 1222–1239.

Alloy, L. B., Abramson, L. Y., Tashman, N. A., Berrebbi, D. S., Hogan, M. E., Whitehouse, W. G., & Morocco, A. (2001). Developmental origins of cognitive vulnerability to depression: Parenting, cognitive, and inferential feedback styles of the parents of individuals at high and low cognitive risk for depression. *Cognitive Therapy and Research, 25*, 397–423.

Anderman, E. M. (2002). School effects on psychological outcomes during adolescence. *Journal of Educational Psychology, 94*, 795–809.

Anderson, L. M., Shinn, C., Fullilove, M. T., Scrimshaw, S. C., Fielding, J., Normand, J., & Carande-Kulis, V. G.; Task Force on Community Preventive Services. (2003). The effectiveness of early childhood development programs: A systematic review. *American Journal of Preventive Medicine, 24*, 32–46.

Aneshensel, C. S., & Sucoff, C. A. (1996). The neighborhood context of adolescent mental health. *Journal of Health and Social Behavior, 37*, 293–310.

Angold, A., Costello, E. J., & Worthman, C. M. (1998). Puberty and depression: The roles of age, pubertal status and pubertal timing. *Psychological Medicine, 28,* 51–61.

Armsden, G. C., McCauley, E., Greenberg, M. T., Burke, P. M., & Mitchell, J. R. (1990). Parent and peer attachment in early adolescent depression. *Journal of Abnormal Child Psychology, 18,* 683–697.

Arroyo, C. G., & Zigler, E. (1995). Racial identity, academic achievement, and the psychological well-being of economically disadvantaged adolescents. *Journal of Personality and Social Psychology, 69,* 903–914.

Bandura, A., Pastorelli, C., Barbaranelli, C., & Caprar, G. V. (1999). Self-efficacy pathways to child depression. *Journal of Personality and Social Psychology, 76,* 258–269.

Beardslee, W. R., Versage, E. M., & Gladstone, T. R. (1998). Children of affectively ill parents: A review of the past 10 years. *Journal of the American Academy of Child and Adolescent Psychiatry, 37,* 1134–1141.

Berg-Nielson, T. S., Vikan, A., & Dahl, A. A. (2002). Parenting related to child and parental psychopathology: A descriptive review of the literature. *Clinical Child Psychology and Psychiatry, 7,* 529–552.

Birch, S. H., & Ladd, G. W. (1997). The teacher–child relationship and children's early school adjustment. *Journal of School Psychology, 35,* 61–79.

Blair, C., & Razza, R. P. (2007). Relating effortful control, executive function, and false belief understanding to emerging math and literacy ability in kindergarten. *Child Development, 78,* 647–663.

Borelli, J. L., & Prinstein, M. J. (2006). Reciprocal, longitudinal associations between adolescents' negative feedback-seeking, depressive symptoms, and friendship perceptions. *Journal of Abnormal Child Psychology, 34,* 159–169.

Bowlby, J. (1969). *Attachment and loss, Vol. 1: Attachment.* New York: Basic Books.

Bowlby, J. (1973). *Attachment and Loss, Vol. 2: Separation.* New York: Basic Books.

Bretherton, I., & Waters, E. (1985). *Growing points of attachment theory and research. Monographs for the Society for Research in Child Development, 50*(1–2), Serial No. 209.

Broderick, P. C., & Korteland, C. (2004). A prospective study of rumination and depression in early adolescence. *Journal of Clinical Child and Adolescent Psychology, 9,* 383–394.

Brown, B. B., & Larson, J. (2009). Peer relationships in adolescence. In R. M. Lerner, & L. Steinberg (Eds.), *Handbook of adolescent psychology: Contextual influences on adolescent development* (Vol. 2, pp. 74–103). Hoboken, NJ: John Wiley & Sons.

Brown, J., Cohen, P., Johnson, J. G., & Smailes, E. (1999). Childhood abuse and neglect: Specificity of effects on adolescent and young adult depression and suicidality. *Journal of the American Academy of Child & Adolescent Psychiatry, 38,* 1490–1496.

Brumariu, L. E., & Kerns, K. A. (2010). Parent–child attachment and internalizing symptoms in childhood and adolescence: A review of empirical findings and future directions. *Development and Psychopathology, 22,* 177–203.

Buhrmester, D., & Furman, W. (1987). The development of companionship and intimacy. *Child Development, 58,* 1101–1113.

Bureau, J. F., Easterbrooks, M. A., & Lyons-Ruth, K. (2009). Maternal depressive symptoms in infancy: Unique contribution to children's depressive symptoms in childhood and adolescence? *Development and Psychopathology, 21,* 519–537.

Camras, L. A., Ribordy, S., Hill, J., Martino, S., Spaccarelli, S., & Stefani, R. (1988). Recognition and posing of emotional expressions by abused children and their mothers. *Developmental Psychology, 24,* 776–781.

Carlson, V., Cicchetti, D., Barnett, D., & Braunwald, K. (1989). Disorganized/disoriented attachment relationships in maltreated infants. *Developmental Psychology, 25,* 525–531.

Cassidy, J. (1994). Emotion regulation: Influences of attachment relationships. *Monographs for the Society for Research in Child Development, 59*(2/3), 228–249.

Cicchetti, D. (1993). Developmental psychopathology: Reactions, reflections, projections. *Developmental Review, 13,* 471–502.

Cicchetti, D. (1996). Contextualism and developmental psychopathology. *Development and Psychopathology, 10,* 137–141.

Cicchetti, D., & Lynch, M. (1993). Toward an ecological/transactional model of community violence and child maltreatment: Consequences for children's development. *Psychiatry, 56,* 96–118.

Cicchetti, D., & Lynch, M. (1995). Failures in the expectable environment and their impact on individual development: The case of child maltreatment. In D. Cicchetti, & D. Cohen (Eds.), *Developmental psychopathology: Vol. 2. Risk, disorder, and adaptation* (pp. 32–71). New York: John Wiley & Sons.

Cicchetti, D., & Rogosch, F. A. (1996). Equifinality and multifinality in developmental psychopathology. *Development and Psychopathology, 8,* 597–600.

Cicchetti, D., & Rogosch, F. A. (1997). The role of self-organization in the promotion of resilience in maltreated children. *Development and Psychopathology, 9,* 797–815.

Cicchetti, D., & Rogosch, F. A. (2001). Diverse patterns of neuroendocrine activity in maltreated children. *Development and Psychopathology, 13,* 677–693.

Cicchetti, D., & Toth, S. L. (1998). The development of depression in children and adolescents. *American Psychologist, 53,* 221–241.

Cicchetti, D., & Toth, S. L. (2009a). A developmental psychopathology perspective on adolescent depression. In S. Nolen-Hoeksema, & L. M. Hilt (Eds.), *Handbook of depression in adolescents* (pp. 3–32). New York: Routledge.

Cicchetti, D., & Toth, S. L. (2009b). The past achievements and future promises of developmental psychopathology: The coming of age of a discipline. *Journal of Child Psychology and Psychiatry, 50,* 16–25.

Cicchetti, D., & Toth, T. L. (2005). Child maltreatment. *Annual Review of Clinical Psychology, 1,* 409–438.

Cochran, B. N., Stewart, A. J., Ginzler, J. A., & Cauce, A. M. (2002). Challenges faced by homeless sexual minorities: Comparison of gay, lesbian, bisexual, and transgender homeless adolescents with their heterosexual counterparts. *American Journal of Public Health, 92,* 773–777.

Cohen, P., Brown, J., & Smailes, E. (2001). Child abuse and neglect and the development of mental disorders in the general population. *Development and Psychopathology, 13,* 981–999.

Coie, J. D., Lochman, J. E., Terry, R., & Hyman, C. (1992). Predicting early adolescent disorder from childhood aggression and peer rejection. *Journal of Consulting and Clinical Psychology, 60,* 783–792.

Cole, D. A. (1990). Relation of social and academic competence to depressive symptoms in childhood. *Journal of Abnormal Psychology, 99,* 422–429.

Cole, D. A. (1991). Preliminary support for a competency-based model of depression in children. *Journal of Abnormal Psychology, 100,* 181–190.

Cole, D. A., Martin, J. M., & Powers, B. (1997). A competency-based model of child depression: A longitudinal study of peer, parent, and self-evaluations. *Journal of Child Psychology and Psychiatry, 38,* 504–514.

Cole, D. A., Martin, J. M., Powers, B., & Truglio, R. (1996). Modeling causal relations between academic and social competence and depression: A multitrait–multimethod longitudinal study of children. *Journal of Abnormal Psychology, 105,* 258–270.

Cole, P. M., Michel, M. K., & O'Donnell Teti, L. (1994). The development of emotion regulation and dysregulation: A clinical perspective. *Monographs for the Society for Research in Child Development, 59*(2/3), 73–100.

Collins, W. A. (1990). Parent-child relationships in the transition to adolescence: Continuity and change in interaction, affect, and cognition. In R. Monetmayor, G. Adams, & T. Gullotta (Eds.), *Advances in adolescent development: Vol. 2. From childhood to adolescence: A transitional period?* (pp. 85–106). Newbury Park, CA: Sage.

Conley, C. S., & Rudolph, K. D. (2009). The emerging sex difference in adolescent depression: Interacting contributions of puberty and peer stress. *Development and Psychopathology, 21,* 593–620.

Contreras, J. M., Kerns, K. A., Weimer, B. L., Gentzler, A. L., & Tomich, P. L. (2000). Emotion regulation as a mediator of associations between mother-child attachment and peer relationships in middle childhood. *Journal of Family Psychology, 14,* 111–124.

Costello, E. J., Erkanli, A., & Angold, A. (2006). Is there an epidemic of child or adolescent depression? *Journal of Child Psychology and Psychiatry, 47*(12), 1263–1271.

Coulton, C. J., Crampton, D. S., Irwin, M., Spilsbury, J. C., & Korbin, J. E. (2007). How neighborhoods influence child maltreatment: A review of the literature and alternative pathways. *Child Abuse and Neglect, 31,* 1117–1142.

Coyl, D. D., Roggman, L. A., & Newland, L. A. (2002). Stress, maternal depression, and negative mother-infant interactions in relation to infant attachment. *Infant Mental Health Journal, 23,* 145–163.

Dahl, R. E., Ryan, N. D., Puig-Antich, J., Nguyen, N. A., Al-Shabbout, M., Meyer, V. A., & Perel, J. (1991). 24-hour cortisol measures in adolescents with major depression: A controlled study. *Biological Psychiatry, 30,* 25–36.

Daley, S. E., & Hammen, C. (2002). Depressive symptoms and close relationships during the transition to adulthood: Perspectives from dysphoric women, their best friends, and their romantic partners. *Journal of Consulting and Clinical Psychology, 70,* 129–144.

Darling, N., & Steinberg, L. (1993). Parenting style as context: An integrative model. *Psychological Bulletin, 113,* 487–496.

D'Augelli, A. R. (1994). Identity development and sexual orientation: Toward a model of lesbian, gay, and bisexual development. In J. Edison, R. J. Watts, & D. Birman (Eds.), *Human diversity: Perspectives on people in context* (pp. 312–333). San Francisco, CA: Jossey-Bass Trickett.

D'Augelli, A. R., Hershberger, S. L., & Pilkington, N. W. (1998). Lesbian, gay, and bisexual youth and their families: Disclosure of sexual orientation. *American Journal of Orthopsychiatry, 68,* 361–371.

D'Augelli, A. R., Hershberger, S. L., & Pilkington, N. W. (2001). Suicidality patterns and sexual orientation-related factors among lesbian, gay, and bisexual youths. *Suicide and Life-Threatening Behavior, 31,* 250–264.

Davidson, R. J. (1992). Emotion and affective style: Hemispheric substrates. *Psychological Science, 3,* 39–43.

Davidson, R. J., Ekman, P., Saron, C. D., Senulis, J. A., & Friesen, W. V. (1990). Approach-withdrawal and cerebral asymmetry: Emotional expression and brain physiology. *Journal of Personality and Social Psychology, 58,* 330–341.

Davidson, R. J., & Fox, N. A. (1982). Asymmetrical brain activity discriminates between positive and negative affective stimuli in human infants. *Science, 218*(4578), 1235–1237.

Davidson, R. J., & Fox, N. A. (1989). Frontal brain asymmetry predicts infants' response to maternal separation. *Journal of Abnormal Psychology, 98,* 127–131.

Denham, S. A. (1998). *Emotional development in young children.* New York: Guilford Press.

Denham, S. A., Blair, K. A., DeMulder, E., Levitas, J., Sawyer, K., Auerbach-Major, S., & Queenan, P. (2003). Preschool emotional competence: Pathway to social competence. *Child Development, 74,* 238–256.

Denham, S. A., & Holt, R. W. (1993). Preschoolers' likeability as cause or consequence of their social behavior. *Developmental Psychology, 29,* 271–275.

Denham, S. A., Mitchell-Copeland, J., Strandberg, K., Auerbach, S., & Blair, K. (1997). Parental contributions to preschoolers' emotional competence: Direct and indirect effects. *Motivation and Emotion, 21,* 65–86.

DeRosier, M. E., Kupersmidt, J. B., & Patterson, C. J. (1994). Children's academic and behavioral adjustment as a function of the chronicity and proximity of peer rejection. *Child Development, 65,* 1799–1813.

Dodge, K. A. (1993). Social-cognitive mechanisms in the development of conduct disorder and depression. *Annual Review of Psychology, 44,* 559–584.

Dodge, K. A., Bates, J. E., & Pettit, G. S. (1990). Mechanisms in the cycle of violence. *Science, 250,* 1678–1683.

Dodge, K. A., Pettit, G. S., McClaskey, C. L., Brown, M. M., & Gottman, J. M. (1986). Social competence in children. *Monographs for the Society for Research in Child Development, 51,* 1–85.

Downey, G., & Coyne, J. C. (1990). Children of depressed parents: An integrative review. *Psychological Bulletin, 108,* 50–76.

Dozier, M., Manni, M., Gordon, M. K., Peloso, E., Gunnar, M. R., Stovall-McClough, K. C., & Levine, S. (2006). Foster children's diurnal production of cortisol: An exploratory study. *Child Abuse and Neglect, 11,* 189–197.

Duncan, G. J., Brooks-Gunn, J., & Kato Klebanov, P. (1994). Economic deprivation and early childhood development. *Child Development, 65,* 296–318.

Dunn, J., & Brown, J. (1994). Affect expression in the family, children's understanding of emotions, and their interactions with others. *Merrill-Palmer Quarterly, 40,* 120–137.

Dweck, C. S. (1986). Motivational processes affecting learning. *American Psychologist, 41,* 1040–1048.

Egeland, B., & Farber, E. A. (1984). Infant-mother attachment: Factors related to its development and changes over time. *Child Development, 55,* 753–771.

Eisenberg, N., Cumberland, A., & Spinard, T. L. (1998). Parental socialization of emotion. *Psychological Inquiry, 9,* 241–273.

Eisenberg, N., Cumberland, A., Spinard, T. L., Fabes, R. A., Shepard, S. A., Reiser, M., & Guthrie, I. K. (2001). The relations of regulation and emotionality to children's externalizing and internalizing problem behavior. *Child Development, 72,* 1112–1134.

Eisenberg, N., Fabes, R. A., Murphy, B. C., Maszk, P., Smith, M., & Karbon, M. (1995). The role of emotionality and regulation in children's social functioning: A longitudinal study. *Child Development, 66,* 1360–1384.

Eisenberg, N., Fabes, R. A., Shepard, S. A., Murphy, B. C., Guthrie, I. K., Jones, S., & Maszk, P. (1997). Contemporaneous and longitudinal prediction of children's social functioning from regulation and emotionality. *Child Development, 68,* 642–664.

Eisenberg, N., Gershoff, E. T., Fabes, R. A., Shepard, S. A., Cumberland, A. J., Losoya, S., & Murphy, B. C. (2001). Mother's emotional expressivity and children's behavior problems and social competence: Mediation through children's regulation. *Developmental Psychology, 37,* 475–490.

Eisenberg, N., Guthrie, I. K., Fabes, R. A., Shepard, S. A., Losoya, S., Murphy, B. C., & Reiser, M. (2000). Prediction of elementary school children's externalizing problem behaviors from attentional and behavioral regulation and negative emotionality. *Child Development, 71*, 1367–1382.

Eisenberg, N., Zhou, Q., Losoya, S. H., Fabes, R. A., Shepard, S. A., Murphy, B. C., & Cumberland, A. (2003). The relations of parenting, effortful control, and ego control to children's emotional expressivity. *Child Development, 74*, 875–895.

Elliott, E. S., & Dweck, C. S. (1988). Goals: An approach to motivation and achievement. *Journal of Personality and Social Psychology, 54*, 5–12.

Essex, M. J., Klein, M. J., Cho, E., & Kalin, N. H. (2002). Maternal stress beginning in infancy may sensitize children to later stress exposure: Effects on cortisol and behavior. *Biological Psychiatry, 52*, 776–784.

Fabes, R. A., Eisenberg, N., & Eisenbud, L. (1993). Behavioral and physiological correlates of children's reactions to others' distress. *Developmental Psychology, 29*, 655–663.

Fantuzzo, J. W., DePaola, L. M., Lambert, L., Martino, T., Anderson, G., & Sutton, S. (1991). Effects of interparental violence on the psychological adjustment and competencies of young children. *Journal of Consulting and Clinical Psychology, 59*, 258–265.

Faulkner, A. H., & Cranston, K. (1998). Correlates of same-sex behavior in a random sample of Massachusetts high school students. *American Journal of Public Health, 88*, 262–266.

Fergusson, D. M., Horwood, L. J., & Beautrais, A. (1999). Is sexual orientation related to mental health problems and suicidality in young people? *Archives of General Psychiatry, 56*, 876–880.

Field, T. (1998). Maternal depression effects on infants and early interventions. *Preventive Medicine, 27*, 200–203.

Field, T., Fox, N. A., Pickens, J., & Nawrocki, T. (1995). Relative right frontal EEG activation in 3- to 6-month old infants of "depressed mothers". *Developmental Psychology, 31*, 358–363.

Finkelhor, D., Ormrod, R., Turner, H., & Hamby, S. L. (2005). The victimization of children and youth: A comprehensive, national survey. *Child Maltreatment, 10*, 5–25.

Fournier, M. E., Austin, S. B., Samples, C. L., Goodenow, C. S., Wylie, S. A., & Corliss, H. L. (2009). A comparison of weight-related behaviors among high school students who are homeless and non-homeless. *Journal of School Health, 79*, 466–473.

Fox, N. A. (1991). If it's not left, it's right. *American Psychologist, 46*, 863–872.

Fox, N. A., Coplan, R. J., Rubin, K. H., Porges, S. W., Calkins, S. D., Long, J. M., & Stewart, S. (1995). Frontal activation asymmetry and social competence at four years of age. *Child Development, 66*, 1770–1784.

Fox, N. A., & Davidson, R. J. (1987). Electroencephalogram asymmetry in response to the approach of a stranger and maternal separation in 10-month-old infants. *Developmental Psychology, 23*, 233–240.

Frye, A. A., & Garber, J. (2005). The relations among maternal depression, maternal criticism, and adolescent's externalizing and internalizing symptoms. *Journal of Abnormal Child Psychology, 33*, 1–11.

Garber, J., Braafladt, N., & Weiss, B. (1995). Affect regulation in depressed and nondepressed children and young adolescents. *Development and Psychopathology, 7*, 93–115.

Garber, J., & Flynn, C. (2001). Predictors of depressive cognitions in young adults. *Cognitive Therapy and Research, 25*, 353–376.

Garber, J., Robinson, N. S., & Valentiner, D. (1997). The relation between parenting and adolescent depression: Self-worth as a mediator. *Journal of Adolescent Research, 12*, 12–33.

Garber, J., Weiss, B., & Shanley, N. (1993). Cognitions, depressive symptoms, and development in adolescents. *Journal of Abnormal Psychology, 102*, 47–57.

Ge, X., Conger, R. D., & Elder, G. H. (2001). Pubertal transition, stressful life events, and the emergence of gender differences in adolescent depressive symptoms. *Developmental Psychology, 37*, 404–417.

Gelfand, D. M., & Teti, D. M. (1990). The effects of maternal depression on children. *Clinical Psychology Review, 10*, 329–353.

Gladstone, G. L., Parker, G. B., & Malhi, G. S. (2006). Do bullied children become anxious and depressed adults? A cross-sectional investigation of the correlates of bullying and anxious depression. *Journal of Nervous and Mental Disease, 194*, 201–208.

Gladstone, T. R. G., & Kaslow, N. J. (1995). Depression and attributions in children and adolescents: A meta-analytic review. *Journal of Abnormal Child Psychology, 23*, 597–606.

Gladstone, T. R., Kaslow, N. J., Seeley, J. R., & Lewinsohn, P. M. (1997). Sex differences, attributional style, and depressive symptoms among adolescents. *Journal of Abnormal Child Psychology, 25*, 297–306.

Goodman, E. (1999). The role of socioeconomic status gradients in explaining differences in US adolescents' health. *American Journal of Public Health, 89*, 1522–1528.

Goodman, S. H., & Gotlib, I. H. (1999). Risk for psychopathology in the children of depressed mothers: A developmental model for understanding mechanisms of transmission. *Psychological Bulletin, 106*, 458–490.

Goodyer, I., Herbert, J., & Tamplin, A. (2003). Psychoendocrine antecedents of persistent first-episode major depression in adolescents: A community-based longitudinal enquiry. *Psychological Medicine, 33*, 601–610.

Goodyer, I., Park, R. J., & Herbert, J. (2001). Psychosocial and endocrine features of chronic first-episode major depression in 8–16 year olds. *Biological Psychiatry, 50*, 351–357.

Gorman-Smith, D., & Tolan, P. H. (1998). The role of exposure to community violence and developmental problems among inner-city youth. *Development and Psychopathology, 10*, 101–116.

Gotlib, I. H., & Goodman, S. H. (1999). Children of parents with depression. In W. K. Silverman, & T. Ollendick (Eds.), *Developmental issues in the clinical treatment of children and adolescents* (pp. 415–432). New York: Allyn & Bacon.

Gotlib, I. H., Lewinsohn, P. M., Seeley, J. R., Rohde, P., & Redner, J. E. (1993). Negative cognitions and attributional style in depressed adolescents: An examination of stability and specificity. *Journal of Abnormal Psychology, 102*, 607–615.

Gotlib, I. H., Ranganathand, C., & Rosenfeld, J. P. (1998). Frontal EEG alpha asymmetry, depression, and cognitive functioning. *Cognition and Emotion, 12*, 449–478.

Gottlieb, G. (1991a). Experiential canalization of behavioral development: Results. *Developmental Psychology, 27*, 35–39.

Gottlieb, G. (1991b). Experiential canalization of behavioral development: Theory. *Developmental Psychology, 27*, 4–13.

Gottman, J. M., Katz, L. F., & Hooven, C. (1997). *Meta-emotion: How families communicate emotionally.* Mahwah, NJ: Erlbaum.

Graber, J. A., Lewinsohn, P. M., Seeley, J. R., & Brooks-Gunn, J. (1997). Is psychopathology associated with the timing of pubertal development? *Journal of the American Academy of Child & Adolescent Psychiatry, 36*, 1768–1776.

Graber, J. A., Nichols, T. R., & Brooks-Gunn, J. (2010). Putting pubertal timing in developmental context: Implications for prevention. *Developmental Psychobiology, 52*, 254–262.

Green, J. G., McLaughlin, K. A., Berglund, P., Gruber, M. J., Sampson, N. A., Zaslavsky, A. M., & Kessler, R. C. (2010). Childhood adversities and adult psychopathology in the National Comorbidity Survey Replication (NCS-R) I: Associations with first onset of DSM-IV disorders. *Archives of General Psychiatry, 62*, 113–123.

Greene, B. A., & Miller, R. B. (1996). Influences on achievement: Goals, perceived ability and cognitive engagement. *Contemporary Educational Psychology, 21*, 181–192.

Gunnar, M. R., Morison, S. J., Chisolm, K., & Schuder, M. (2001). Salivary cortisol levels in children adopted from Romanian orphanages. *Development and Psychopathology, 13*, 611–628.

Gunnar, M. R., Tout, K., de Haan, M., Pierce, S., & Stanbury, K. (1997). Temperament, social competence, and adrenocortical activity in preschoolers. *Developmental Psychobiology, 31*, 65–85.

Gunnar, M. R., & Vazquez, D. M. (2001). Low cortisol and a flattening of expected daytime rhythm: Potential indices of risk in human development. *Development and Psychopathology, 13*, 515–538.

Gunnar, M. R., Wewerka, S., Frenn, K., Long, J. D., & Griggs, C. (2009). Developmental changes in hypothalamus-pituitary-adrenal activity over the transition to adolescence: Normative changes and associations with puberty. *Development and Psychopathology, 21*, 69–85.

Hammen, C., Henry, R., & Daley, S. E. (2000). Depression and sensitization to stressors among young women as a function of childhood adversity. *Journal of Consulting and Clinical Psychology, 68*, 782–787.

Hane, A. A., & Fox, N. A. (2006). Ordinary variations in maternal caregiving influence human infants' stress reactivity. *Psychological Science, 17*, 550–556.

Hane, A. A., Henderson, H. A., Reeb-Sutherland, B. C., & Fox, N. A. (2010). Ordinary variations in human maternal caregiving in infancy and biobehavioral development in early childhood: A follow-up study. *Developmental Psychobiology, 52*, 1–10.

Hankin, B. L. (2005). Childhood maltreatment and psychopathology: Prospective tests of attachment, cognitive vulnerability, and stress as mediating processes. *Cognitive Therapy and Research, 29*, 645–671.

Hankin, B. L., & Abramson, L. Y. (2001). Development of gender differences in depression: An elaborated cognitive vulnerability-transactional stress model. *Psychological Bulletin, 127*, 773–796.

Hankin, B. L., Abramson, L. Y., Moffitt, T. E., Silva, P. A., McGee, R., & Angell, K. E. (1998). Development of depression from preadolescence to young adulthood: Emerging gender differences in a 10-year longitudinal study. *Journal of Abnormal Psychology, 107*, 128–140.

Hankin, B. L., Abramson, L. Y., & Siler, M. (2001). A prospective test of the hopelessness theory of depression in adolescence. *Cognitive Therapy and Research, 25*, 607–632.

Hankin, B. L., Mermelstein, R., & Roesch, L. (2007). Sex differences in adolescent depression: Stress exposure and reactivity models. *Child Development, 78*, 279–295.

Harrison, P. A., & Narayan, G. (2003). Differences in behavior, psychological factors, and environmental factors associated with participation in school sports and other activities. *Journal of School Health, 73*, 113–120.

Hart, J., Gunnar, M. R., & Cicchetti, D. (1995). Salivary cortisol in maltreated children: Evidence of relations between neuroendocrine activity and social competence. *Development and Psychopathology, 7*, 11–26.

Hart, J., Gunnar, M. R., & Cicchetti, D. (1996). Altered neuroendocrine activity in maltreated children related to symptoms of depression. *Development and Psychopathology, 8*, 201–214.

Harter, S. (1982). The perceived competence scale for children. *Child Development, 53*, 87–97.

Harter, S. (1998). The development of self-representations. In W. Damon, & N. Eisenberg (Eds.), *Handbook of child psychology: Social, emotional, and personality development* (pp. 553–617). Hoboken, NJ: John Wiley & Sons.

Hartmann, H. (1958). *Ego psychology and the problem of adaptation*. New York: International Universities Press.

Hatzenbuehler, M. L. (2011). The social environment and suicide attempts in lesbian, gay, and bisexual youth. *Pediatrics, 127*, 896–903.

Hatzenbuehler, M. L., McLaughlin, K. A., & Nolen-Hoeksema, S. (2008). Emotion regulation and the development of internalizing symptoms in a longitudinal study of LGB adolescents and their heterosexual peers. *Journal of Child Psychology and Psychiatry, 49*, 1270–1278.

Hawker, D. S. J., & Boulton, M. J. (2000). Twenty years' research on peer victimization and psychosocial maladjustment: A meta-analytic review of cross-sectional studies. *Journal of Child Psychology and Psychiatry, 41*, 441–455.

Hecht, D. B., Inderbitzen, H. M., & Bukowski, A. L. (1998). The relationship between peer status and depressive symptoms in children and adolescents. *Journal of Abnormal Child Psychology, 26*, 153–160.

Heim, C., Ehlert, U., & Helhammer, D. H. (2000). The potential role of hypocortisolism in the pathophysiology of stress-related bodily disorders. *Psychoneuroendocrinology, 25*, 1–35.

Herrera, C., & Dunn, J. (1997). Early experiences with family conflict: Implications for arguments with a close friend. *Developmental Psychology, 33*, 869–881.

Heyman, G. D., & Dweck, C. S. (1992). Achievement goals and intrinsic motivation: Their relation and their role in adaptive motivation. *Motivation and Emotion, 16*, 231–247.

Hilsman, R., & Garber, J. (1995). A test of the cognitive diathesis-stress model of depression in children: Academic stressors, attributional style, perceived competence, and control. *Journal of Personality and Social Psychology, 69*, 370–380.

Hodges, E. V. E., & Perry, D. G. (1999). Personal and interpersonal antecedents and consequences of victimization by peers. *Journal of Personality and Social Psychology, 76*, 677–685.

Holmgren, R. A., Eisenberg, N., & Fabes, R. A. (1998). The relations of children's situational empathy-related emotions to dispositional prosocial behavior. *International Journal of Behavioral Development, 22*, 169–193.

Hymel, S., Rubin, K. H., Rowden, L., & Lemare, L. (1990). Children's peer relationships: Longitudinal prediction of internalizing and externalizing problems from middle to late childhood. *Child Development, 61*, 2004–2021.

Johnson, J. G., Cohen, P., Dohrenwend, B. P., Link, B. G., & Brook, J. S. (1999). A longitudinal investigation of social causation and social selection processes involved in the association between socioeconomic status and psychiatric disorders. *Journal of Abnormal Psychology, 108*, 490–499.

Joiner, T. E., Jr., & Wanger, K. D. (1995). Attributional style and depression in children and adolescents: A meta-analytic review. *Clinical Psychology Review, 15*, 777–798.

Jones, N. A., Field, T., Davalos, M., & Pickens, J. (1997). EEG stability in infants/children of depressed mothers. *Child Psychiatry and Human Development, 28*, 59–70.

Jones, N. A., Field, T., Fox, N. A., Lundy, B., & Davalos, M. (1997). EEG activation in 1-month-old infants of depressed mothers. *Development and Psychopathology, 9*, 491–505.

Jungmeen, K., & Cicchetti, D. (2010). Longitudinal pathways linking child maltreatment, emotion regulation, peer relations, and psychopathology. *Journal of Child Psychology and Psychiatry, 51*, 706–716.

Just, N., & Alloy, L. B. (1997). The response styles theory of depression: Tests and an extension of the theory. *Journal of Abnormal Psychology, 106*, 221–229.

Kaplan, S. J., Pelcovitz, D., & Labruna, V. (1999). A review of the past 10 year. Part I: Physical and emotional abuse and neglect. *Journal of the American Academy of Child and Adolescent Psychiatry, 38*, 1214–1222.

Katz, L. F., Hessler, D. M., & Annest, A. (2007). Domestic violence, emotional competence, and child adjustment. *Social Development, 16*, 513–538.

Katz, L. F., & Windecker-Nelson, B. (2004). Parental meta-emotion philosophy in families with conduct-problem children: Links with peer relations. *Journal of Abnormal Child Psychology, 32*, 385–398.

Keiley, M. K., Howe, T. R., Dodge, K. A., Bates, J. E., & Pettit, G. S. (2001). The timing of child physical maltreatment: A cross-domain growth analysis of impact on adolescent externalizing and internalizing problems. *Development and Psychopathology, 13*, 891–912.

Kessler, R. C., Berglund, P., Demler, O., Jin, R., Koretz, D., Merikangas, K. R., & National Comorbidity Survey Replication. (2003). The epidemiology of major depressive disorder: Results from the National Comorbidity Survey Replication (NCS-R). *Journal of the American Medical Association, 289*, 3095–3105.

Kessler, R. C., Berglund, P., Demler, O., Jin, R., Merikangas, K. R., & Walters, E. E. (2004). Lifetime prevalence and age-of-onset distributions of DSM-IV disorders in the National Comorbidity Survey Replication. *Archives of General Psychiatry, 62*, 593–602.

Kim-Cohen, J., Caspi, A., Moffitt, T. E., Harrington, H., Milne, B. J., & Poulton, R. (2003). Prior juvenile diagnoses in adults with mental disorder: Developmental follow-back of a prospective-longitudinal cohort. *Archives of General Psychiatry, 60*(7), 709–717.

Kochanska, G., Murray, K. T., & Harlan, E. T. (2000). Effortful control in early childhood: Continuity and change, antecedents, and implications for social development. *Developmental Psychology, 36*, 220–232.

Kopp, C. B. (1982). Antecedents of self-regulation: A developmental perspective. *Developmental Psychology, 18*, 199–214.

Kopp, C. B. (1989). Regulation of distress and negative emotions: A developmental view. *Developmental Psychology, 25*, 343–354.

Kruks, G. (1991). Gay and lesbian homeless/street youth: Special issues and concerns. *Journal of Adolescent Health, 12*, 515–518.

Kuperminc, G. P., Leadbeater, B. J., & Blatt, S. D. (2001). School social climate and individual differences in vulnerability to psychopathology among middle school students. *Journal of School Psychology, 39*, 141–159.

Ladd, G. W. (1990). Peer relationships and social competence during early and middle childhood. *Annual Review of Psychology, 50*, 333–359.

LaGreca, A. M., & Harrison, H. M. (2005). Adolescent peer relations, friendships, and romantic relationships: Do they predict social anxiety and depression? *Journal of Clinical Child and Adolescent Psychology, 34*, 49–61.

Larson, R., & Ham, M. (1993). Stress and "storm and stress" in early adolescence: The relationship of negative events with dysphoric affect. *Developmental Psychology, 29*, 130–140.

Larson, R., & Lampman-Petraitis, C. (1989). Daily emotional stress as reported by children and adolescents. *Child Development, 60*, 1250–1126.

Larson, R., Moneta, G., Richards, M. H., & Wilson, S. (2002). Continuity, stability, and change in daily emotional experience across adolescence. *Child Development, 73*, 1151–1165.

Larson, R., & Richards, M. H. (1991). Daily companionship in late childhood and early adolescence: Changing developmental contexts. *Child Development, 62*, 284–300.

Latkin, C. A., & Curry, A. D. (2003). Stressful neighborhoods and depression: A prospective study of the impact of neighborhood disorder. *Journal of Health and Social Behavior, 44*, 34–44.

Lemery, K. S., Essex, M. J., & Smider, N. A. (2002). Revealing the relation between tempera-ment and behavior problem symptoms by eliminating measurement confounding: Expert ratings and factor analyses. *Child Development, 73*, 867–882.

Lengua, L. J., Honorado, E., & Bush, N. R. (2007). Contextual risk and parenting as predic-tors of effortful control and social competence in preschool children. *Journal of Applied Developmental Psychology, 28*, 40–55.

Leventhal, T., & Brooks-Gunn, J. (2000). The neighborhoods they live in: The effects of neighborhood residence on child and adolescent outcomes. *Psychological Bulletin, 126*, 309–337.

Lopez-Duran, N., Kovacs, M., & George, C. J. (2009). Hypothalamic-pituitary-adrenal axis dysfunction in depressed children and adolescents: A meta-analysis. *Psychoneuroendocrinol-ogy, 34*, 1272–1283.

Lorant, V., Deliege, D., Eaton, W. W., Robert, A., Philippot, P., & Ansseau, M. (2003). Socioeconomic inequalities in depression: A meta-analysis. *American Journal of Epidemi-ology, 157*, 98–112.

Love, J. M., Kisker, E. E., Ross, C., Raikes, H., Constantine, J., Boller, K., & Vogel, C. (2005). The effectiveness of early head start for 3-year-old children and their parents: Lessons for policy and programs. *Developmental Psychology, 41*, 885–901.

Lynch, M., & Cicchetti, D. (1998). An ecological-transactional analysis of children and contexts: The longitudinal interplay among child maltreatment, community violence, and children's symptomatology. *Development and Psychopathology, 10*, 235–257.

Macoby, E., & Martin, J. (1983). Socialization in the context of the family: Parent–child interaction. In E. M. Hetherington, & P. H. Mussen (Eds.), *Handbook of child psychology: Socialization, personality, and social development* (Vol. 4, pp. 1–101). New York: John Wiley & Sons.

Mahady Wilton, M. M., Craig, W. M., & Pepler, D. J. (2000). Emotional regulation and display in classroom victims of bullying: Characteristic expressions of affect, coping styles and relevant contextual factors. *Social Development, 9*, 226–245.

Main, M., & Soloman, J. (1986). Discovery of an insecure-disorganized/disoriented attach-ment pattern. In T. B. Brazelton, & M. W. Yogman (Eds.), *Affective development in infancy* (pp. 121–160). Norwood, NJ: Ablex.

Martins, C., & Gaffan, E. A. (2000). Effects of early maternal depression on patterns of infant-mother attachment: A meta-analytic investigation. *Journal of Child Psychology and Psychi-atry, 41*, 737–746.

Masten, A., & Coatsworth, J. D. (1998). The development of competence in favorable and unfavorable environments: Lessons from research on successful children. *American Psy-chologist, 53*, 205–220.

Masten, A., Coatsworth, J. D., Neeman, J., Gest, S. D., & Tellegan, A. (1995). The structure and coherence of competence from childhood through adolescence. *Child Development, 66*, 1635–1659.

Matthews, K. A., Woodall, K. L., Kenon, K., & Jacob, T. (1996). Negative family environment as a predictor of boys' future status on measures of hostile attitudes, interview behavior, and anger expression. *Health Psychology, 15*, 30–37.

Maughan, A., & Cicchetti, D. (2002). Impact of child maltreatment and interadult violence on children's emotion regulation abilities and socioemotional adjustment. *Child Development, 73*, 1525–1542.

McCloskey, L. A., & Stuewig, J. (2001). The quality of peer relationships among children exposed to family violence. *Development and Psychopathology, 13*, 83–96.

McLaughlin, K. A., Costello, E. J., Leblanc, W., Sampson, N. A., & Kessler, R. C. (2012). Socioeconomic status and mental disorders in adolescents. *American Journal of Public Health, 102*, 1742–1750.

McLaughlin, K. A., Fox, N. A., Zeanah, C. H., & Nelson, C. A. (2011). Adverse rearing environments and neural development in children: The development of frontal EEG asymmetry. *Biological Psychiatry, 70*, 1008–1015.

McLaughlin, K. A., & Hatzenbuehler, M. L. (2009). Mechanisms linking stressful life events and mental health problems in a prospective, community-based sample of adolescents. *Journal of Adolescent Health, 44*, 153–160.

McLaughlin, K. A., Hatzenbuehler, M. L., & Hilt, L. M. (2009). Emotion dysregulation as a mechanism linking peer victimization to the development of internalizing symptoms among youth. *Journal of Consulting and Clinical Psychology, 77*, 894–904.

McLaughlin, K. A., Hatzenbuehler, M. L., Mennin, D. S., & Nolen-Hoeksema, S. (2011). Emotion regulation and adolescent psychopathology: A prospective study. *Behaviour Research and Therapy, 49*, 544–554.

McLaughlin, K. A., Kubzansky, L. D., Dunn, E. C., Waldinger, R. J., Vaillant, G. E., & Koenen, K. C. (2010). Childhood social environment, emotional reactivity to stress, and mood and anxiety disorders across the life course. *Depression and Anxiety, 27*, 1087–1094.

McLaughlin, K. A., Zeanah, C. H., Fox, N. A., & Nelson, C. A. (2012). Attachment security as a mechanism linking foster care placement to improved mental health outcomes in previously institutionalized children. *Journal of Child Psychology and Psychiatry, 53*, 46–55.

McLeod, B. D., Weisz, J. R., & Wood, J. J. (2007). Examining the association between parenting and childhood depression: A meta-analysis. *Clinical Psychology Review, 27*, 986–1003.

McLeod, J. D., & Shanahan, M. J. (1993). Poverty, parenting, and children's mental health. *American Sociological Review, 58*, 351–366.

McLoyd, V. C. (1998). Socioeconomic disadvantage and child development. *American Psychologist, 53*, 185–204.

Mendle, J., Harden, K. P., Brooks-Gunn, J., & Graber, J. A. (2010). Development's tortoise and hare: Pubertal timing, pubertal tempo, and depressive symptoms in boys and girls. *Development and Psychopathology, 46*, 1341–1353.

Monroe, S. M., Rohde, P., Seeley, J. R., & Lewinsohn, P. M. (1999). Life events and depression in adolescence: Relationship loss as a prospective risk factor for first onset of major depressive disorder. *Journal of Abnormal Psychology, 108*(4), 606–614.

Morris, A. S., Silk, J. S., Steinberg, L., Myers, E., & Robinson, L. R. (2007). The role of the family context in the development of emotion regulation. *Social Development, 16*, 361–368.

Moss, E., Smolla, N., Cyr, C., Dubois-Comtois, K., Mazzarello, T., & Berthiaume, C. (2006). Attachment and behavior problems in middle childhood as reported by adult and child informants. *Development and Psychopathology, 18*, 425–444.

Muris, P., Meesters, C., & Blijlevens, P. (2007). Self-reported reactive and regulative temperament in early adolescence: Relations to internalizing and externalizing problem behavior and "Big Three" personality factors. *Journal of Adolescence, 30*, 1035–1049.

Murray, C., & Greenberg, M. T. (2000). Children's relationship with teachers and bonds with school: An investigation of patterns and correlates in middle childhood. *Journal of School Psychology, 38*, 423–445.

Nachmias, M., Gunnar, M. R., Mangelsdorf, S., Parritz, R. H., & Buss, K. A. (1996). Behavioral inhibition and stress reactivity: The moderating role of attachment security. *Child Development, 67*, 508–522.

Negriff, S., & Susman, E. J. (2011). Pubertal timing, depression, and externalizing problems: A framework, review, and examination of gender differences. *Journal of Research on Adolescence, 21*, 717–746.

Newman, D. L., Moffitt, T. E., Caspi, A., Magdol, L., Silva, P. A., & Stanton, W. R. (1996). Psychiatric disorder in a birth cohort of young adults: Prevalence, comorbidity, clinical significance, and new case incidence from ages 11 to 21. *Journal of Consulting and Clinical Psychology, 64*(3), 552–562.

Nolan, S. A., Flynn, C., & Garber, J. (2003). Prospective relations between rejection and depression in young adolescents. *Journal of Personality and Social Psychology, 85*, 745–755.

Nolen-Hoeksema, S. (2000). The role of rumination in depressive disorders and mixed anxiety/depressive symptoms. *Journal of Abnormal Psychology, 109*, 504–511.

Nolen-Hoeksema, S., & Girgus, J. S. (1994). The emergence of gender differences in depression during adolescence. *Psychological Bulletin, 115*(3), 424–443.

Nolen-Hoeksema, S., Girgus, J. S., & Seligman, M. E. P. (1992). Predictors and consequences of childhood depressive symptoms: A 5-year longitudinal study. *Journal of Abnormal Psychology, 101*, 405–422.

Nolen-Hoeksema, S., & Hilt, L. M. (2009). *Handbook of depression in adolescents.* New York: Routledge.

Nolen-Hoeksema, S., Larson, J., & Grayson, C. (1999). Explaining the gender difference in depressive symptoms. *Journal of Personality and Social Psychology, 77*, 1061–1072.

Nolen-Hoeksema, S., Morrow, J., & Fredrickson, B. L. (1993). Response styles and the duration of episodes of depressed mood. *Journal of Abnormal Psychology, 102*, 20–28.

Nolen-Hoeksema, S., Parker, L. E., & Larson, J. (1994). Ruminative coping with depressed mood following loss. *Journal of Personality and Social Psychology, 67*, 92–104.

Nolen-Hoeksema, S., Stice, E., Wade, E., & Bohon, C. (2007). Reciprocal relations between rumination and bulimic, substance abuse, and depressive symptoms in female adolescents. *Journal of Abnormal Psychology, 116*(1), 198–207.

Nolen-Hoeksema, S., & Twenge, J. M. (2002). Age, gender, race, socioeconomic status, and birth cohort difference on the children's depression inventory: A meta-analysis. *Journal of Abnormal Psychology, 111*, 578–588.

Nolen-Hoeksema, S., Wisco, B. E., & Lyubomirsky, S. (2008). Rethinking rumination. *Perspectives on Psychological Science, 3*, 400–424.

Oakley-Browne, M., Joyce, P. R., Wells, J. E., Bushnell, J. A., & Hornblow, A. R. (1995). Adverse parenting and other childhood experience as risk factors for depression in women aged 18–44 years. *Journal of Affective Disorders, 34*, 13–23.

O'Keefe, M. (1997). Adolescents' exposure to community and school violence: Prevalence and behavioral correlates. *Journal of Adolescent Health, 20*, 368–376.

Oldenburg, C. M., & Kerns, K. A. (1997). Associations between peer relationships and depressive symptoms: Testing moderator effects of gender and age. *Journal of Early Adolescence, 17*, 319–337.

Olweus, D. (1993). *Bullying at school: What we know and what we can do.* Oxford: Blackwell.

Parker, J. G., & Asher, S. R. (1993). Friendship and friendship quality in middle childhood: Links with peer group acceptance and feelings of loneliness and social dissatisfaction. *Developmental Psychology, 29*, 611–621.

Phinney, J. S. (1990). Ethnic identity in adolescents and adults: Review of research. *Psychological Bulletin, 108*, 499–514.

Prinstein, M. J., Boergers, J., & Vernberg, E. M. (2001). Overt and relational aggression in adolescents: Social-psychological adjustment of aggressors and victims. *Journal of Clinical Child Psychology, 30*, 479–491.

Puig-Antich, J., Kaufman, J., Ryan, N. D., Williamson, D. E., Dahl, R. E., Lukens, E., & Nelson, B. (1993). The psychosocial functioning and family environment of depressed adolescents. *Journal of the American Academy of Child and Adolescent Psychiatry, 32*, 244–253.

Reddy, R., Rhodes, J. E., & Mulhall, P. F. (2003). The influence of teacher support on student adjustment in the middle school years: A latent growth curve study. *Development and Psychopathology, 15*, 119–138.

Resnick, M. D., Bearman, P. S., Blum, R. W., Bauman, K. E., Harris, K. M., Jones, J., & Udry, J. R. (1997). Protecting adolescents from harm: Findings from the National Longitudinal Study on Adolescent Health. *Journal of the American Medical Association, 278*, 823–832.

Robin, L., Brener, N. D., Donahue, S. F., Hack, T., Hale, K., & Goodenow, C. (2002). Associations between health risk behaviors and opposite-, same-, and both-sex sexual partners in representative samples of Vermont and Massachusetts high school students. *Archives of Pediatrics and Adolescent Medicine, 156*, 349–355.

Robinson, M. S., & Alloy, L. B. (2008). Negative cognitive styles and stress-reactive rumination interact to predict depression: A prospective study. *Cognitive Therapy and Research, 27*, 275–291.

Robinson, N. S., Garber, J., & Hilsman, R. (1995). Cognitions and stress: Direct and moderating effects on depressive versus externalizing symptoms during the junior high transition. *Journal of Abnormal Psychology, 104*, 453–463.

Roeser, R. W., Eccles, J. S., & Sameroff, A. J. (1998). Academic and emotional functioning in early adolescence: Longitudinal relations, patterns, and prediction by experience in middle school. *Development and Psychopathology, 10*, 321–352.

Roeser, R. W., Eccles, J. S., & Sameroff, A. J. (2000). School as a context of early adolescent's academic and social-emotional development: A summary of research findings. *The Elementary School Journal, 100*, 443–471.

Rothbart, M., Ahadi, S. A., & Evans, D. E. (2000). Temperament and personality: Origins and outcomes. *Journal of Personality and Social Psychology, 78*, 122–135.

Rothbart, M., & Derryberry, D. (1981). Development of individual differences in infant temperament. In M. E. Lamb, & A. Brown (Eds.), *Advances in developmental psychology* (Vol. 1, pp. 37–87). Hillsdale, NJ: Erlbaum.

Rudolph, K. D., & Clark, A. G. (2001). Conceptions of relationships in children with depressive and aggressive symptoms: Social-cognitive distortion or reality? *Journal of Abnormal Child Psychology, 29*, 41–56.

Russell, S. T., Franz, B. T., & Driscoll, A. K. (2001). Same-sex romantic attraction and experiences of violence in adolescence. *American Journal of Public Health, 91*, 903–906.

Sampson, R. J., & Laub, J. H. (1994). Urban poverty and the family context of delinquency: A new look at structure and process in a classic study. *Child Development, 65*, 523–540.

Sampson, R. J., Morenoff, J. D., & Earls, F. (1999). Beyond social capital: Spatial dynamics of collective efficacy for children. *American Sociological Review, 64*, 633–660.

Sampson, R. J., Sharkey, P., & Raudenbush, S. (2007). Durable effects of concentrated disadvantage on verbal ability among African-American children. *Proceedings of the National Academy of Sciences, 105*, 845–852.

Schmidt, L. A., Fox, N. A., Rubin, K. H., Sternberg, E. M., Gold, P. W., Smith, C. C., & Schulkin, J. (1997). Behavioral and neuroendocrine responses in shy children. *Developmental Psychobiology, 30*, 127–140.

Schwartz, D., Dodge, K. A., & Coie, J. D. (1993). The emergence of chronic peer victimization in boys' play groups. *Child Development, 64*, 1755–1772.

Schwartz, D., Dodge, K. A., Pettit, G. S., & Bates, J. E. (1997). The early socialization of aggressive victims of bullying. *Child Development, 68*, 665–675.

Schwartz, J. A. J., & Koenig, L. J. (1996). Response styles and negative affect among adolescents. *Cognitive Therapy and Research, 20,* 13–26.

Sedlak, A. J., & Broadhurst, D. D. (1996). *Executive summary of the Third National Incidence Study of Child Abuse and Neglect.* Washington, DC: U.S. Department of Health and Human Services.

Seidman, E., Allen, L., Aber, J. L., Mitchell, C., & Feiman, J. (1994). The impact of school transitions in early adolescence on the self-system and perceived social context of poor urban youth. *Child Development, 65,* 507–522.

Shankman, S. A., Tenke, C. E., Bruder, G. E., Durbin, C. E., Hayden, E. P., & Klein, D. N. (2005). Low positive emotionality in young children: Association with EEG asymmetry. *Development and Psychopathology, 17,* 85–98.

Sheeber, L. B., Allen, N. B., Leve, C., Davis, B., Shortt, J. W., & Katz, L. F. (2009). Dynamics of affective experience and behavior in depressed adolescents. *Journal of Child Psychology and Psychiatry, 50,* 1419–1427.

Shipman, K., & Zeman, J. (2001). Socialization of children's emotion regulation in mother-child dyads: A developmental psychopathology perspective. *Development and Psychopathology, 13,* 317–336.

Shipman, K., Zeman, J., Penza, S., & Champion, K. (2000). Emotion management skills in sexually maltreated and nonmaltreated girls: A developmental psychopathology perspective. *Development and Psychopathology, 12,* 47–62.

Shochet, I., Dadds, M. R., Ham, D., & Montague, R. (2006). School connectedness is an underemphasized parameter in adolescent mental health: Results of a community prediction study. *Journal of Clinical Child and Adolescent Psychology, 35,* 170–179.

Silk, J. S., Steinberg, L., & Morris, A. S. (2003). Adolescents' emotion regulation in daily life: Links to depressive symptoms and problem behaviors. *Child Development, 74,* 1869–1880.

Silverman, I. W., & Ragusa, D. M. (1992). A short-term longitudinal study of the early development of self-regulation. *Journal of Abnormal Child Psychology, 20,* 415–435.

Simmons, R. G., & Blythe, D. A. (1987). *Moving into adolescence: The impact of pubertal change and school context.* Hawthorne, NY: Aldine de Gruyter.

Smider, N. A., Essex, M. J., Kalin, N. H., Buss, K. A., Klein, M. H., Davidson, R. J., & Goldsmith, H. H. (2002). Salivary cortisol as a predictor of socioemotional adjustment during kindergarten: A prospective study. *Child Development, 73,* 75–92.

Snyder, J., Stoolmiller, M., & Wilson, M. (2003). Child anger regulation, parental responses to children's anger display, and early child antisocial behavior. *Social Development, 12,* 335–360.

Spinard, T. L., Eisenberg, N., Cumberland, A., Fabes, R. A., Valiente, C., Shepard, S. A., & Guthrie, D. (2006). Relation of emotion-related regulation to children's social competence: A longitudinal study. *Emotion, 6,* 498–510.

Sroufe, L. A. (1979). The coherence of individual development: Early care, attachment, and subsequent developmental issues. *American Psychologist, 34,* 834–841.

Sroufe, L. A. (1983). Infant-caregiver attachment and patterns of adaptation in preschool: The roots of maladaptation and competence. In M. Perlmutter (Ed.), *The Minnesota symposia on child psychology* (Vol. 16, pp. 41–83). Hillsdale, NJ: Erlbaum.

Sroufe, L. A. (1990). Considering normal and abnormal together: The essence of developmental psychopathology. *Development and Psychopathology, 2,* 335–347.

Sroufe, L. A. (1997). Psychopathology as an outcome of development. *Development and Psychopathology, 9,* 251–268.

Sroufe, L. A. (2009). The concept of development in developmental psychopathology. *Child Development Perspectives, 3,* 178–183.

Sroufe, L. A., Egeland, B., & Kreutzer, T. (1990). The fate of early experience following developmental change: Longitudinal approaches to individual adaptation in childhood. *Child Development, 61*, 1363–1373.

Sroufe, L. A., & Rutter, M. (1984). The domain of developmental psychopathology. *Child Development, 55*, 17–29.

Steinberg, L. (1987). Impact of puberty on family relations: Effects of pubertal status and pubertal timing. *Developmental Psychology, 23*, 451–460.

Steinberg, L. (1988). Reciprocal relation between parent-child distance and pubertal maturation. *Developmental Psychology, 24*, 122–128.

Steinberg, L., & Avenevoli, S. (2000). The role of context in the development of psychopathology: A conceptual framework and some speculative propositions. *Child Development, 71*, 66–74.

Steinberg, L., Dahl, R., Keating, D., Kupfer, D. J., Masten, A., & Pine, D. (2006). The study of developmental psychopathology in adolescence: Integrating affective neuroscience with the study of context. In D. Cicchetti, & D. Cohen (Eds.), *Developmental psychopathology* (Vol. 2, pp. 710–741). New York: John Wiley & Sons.

Steinberg, L., Elmen, J. D., & Mounts, N. S. (1989). Authoritative parenting, psychosocial maturity, and academic success among adolescents. *Child Development, 60*, 1424–1436.

Steinberg, L., & Monahan, K. C. (2007). Age differences in resistance to peer influence. *Developmental Psychology, 43*, 1531–1543.

Steinberg, L., & Morris, A. S. (2001). Adolescent development. *Annual Review of Psychology, 52*, 83–100.

Steinberg, L., Mounts, N. S., Lamborn, S. D., & Dornbusch, S. M. (1991). Authoritative parenting and adolescent adjustment across varied ecological niches. *Journal of Research on Adolescence, 1*, 19–36.

Sternberg, K. J., Lamb, M. E., Greenbaum, C., Cicchetti, D., Dawud, S., Cortes, R. M., Lorey, F. (1993). Effects of domestic violence on children's behavior problems and depression. *Developmental Psychology, 29*, 44–52.

Stice, E., Presnell, K., & Bearman, S. K. (2001). Relation of early menarche to depression, eating disorders, substance abuse, and comorbid psychopathology among adolescent girls. *Development and Psychopathology, 37*, 608–619.

Stifter, C. A., & Braungart, J. M. (1995). The regulation of negative reactivity in infancy: Function and development. *Developmental Psychology, 31*, 448–455.

Storch, E., Masia-Warner, C., Crisp, H., & Klein, R. G. (2005). Peer victimization and social anxiety in adolescence: A prospective study. *Aggressive Behavior, 31*, 437–452.

Strauman, T. J., Costanzo, P. R., & Garber, J. (2011). *Depression in adolescent girls: Science and prevention*. New York: Guilford Press.

Stroud, L. R., Foster, E., Papandonatos, G. D., Handwerger, K., Granger, D. A., Kivlighan, K. T., & Niaura, R. (2009). Stress response and the adolescent transition: Performance versus peer rejection stressors. *Development and Psychopathology, 21*, 47–68.

Stroud, L. R., Papandonatos, G. D., Williamson, D., & Dahl, R. (2004). Sex differences in the effects of pubertal development on responses to corticotropin-releasing hormone challenge. *Annals of the New York Academy of Sciences, 1021*, 348–351.

Teti, D. M., Gelfand, D. M., Messinger, D. S., & Isabella, R. (1995). Maternal depression and the quality of early attachment: An examination of infants, preschoolers, and their mothers. *Developmental Psychology, 31*, 364–376.

Valiente, C., Lemery-Chalfant, K., Swanson, J., & Reiser, M. (2008). Prediction of children's academic competence from their effortful control, relationships, and classroom participation. *Journal of Educational Psychology, 100*, 67–77.

Van Leeuwen, J. M., Boyle, S., Salomonsen-Sautel, S., Baker, D. N., Garcia, J. T., Hoffman, A., & Hopfer, C. J. (2006). Lesbian, gay, and bisexual homeless youth: An eight-city public health perspective. *Child Welfare, 85,* 151–170.

Vernberg, E. M., Abwender, D. A., Ewell, K. K., & Beery, S. H. (1992). Social anxiety and peer relationships in early adolescence: A prospective analysis. *Journal of Clinical Child Psychology, 21,* 189–196.

Watamura, S. E., Donzella, B., Alwin, J., & Gunnar, M. R. (2003). Morning-to-afternoon increases in cortisol concentrations for infants and toddlers at child care: Age differences and behavioral correlates. *Child Development, 74,* 1006–1020.

Watamura, S. E., Donzella, B., Kertes, D. A., & Gunnar, M. R. (2004). Developmental changes in baseline cortisol activity in early childhood: Relations with napping and effortful control. *Developmental Psychobiology, 45,* 125–133.

Weiss, B., Dodge, K. A., Bates, J. E., & Petit, G. S. (1992). Some consequences of early harsh discipline: Child aggression and a maladaptive social information processing style. *Child Development, 63,* 1321–1335.

Werner, H., & Kaplan, B. (1963). *Symbol formation: An organismic-developmental approach to language and the expression of thought.* New York: John Wiley & Sons.

Williams, T., Connolly, J., Pepler, D., & Craig, W. (2005). Peer victimization, social support, and psychosocial adjustment of sexual minority adolescents. *Journal of Youth and Adolescence, 34,* 471–482.

Zalewski, M., Lengua, L. J., Wilson, A. C., Trancik, A., & Bazinet, A. (2011). Emotion regulation profiles, temperament, and adjustment problems in preadolescents. *Child Development, 82,* 951–966.

Zeanah, C. H., Smyke, A. T., Koga, S. F., & Carlson, E. (The Bucharest Early Intervention Project Core Group). (2005). Attachment in institutionalized and community children in Romania. *Child Development, 76,* 1015–1028.

Zimmerman, P. (1999). Structure and functions of internal working models of attachment and their role for emotion regulation. *Attachment and Human Development, 1,* 291–306.

# 6

# Biological Treatment
# of Mood Disorders

Charlotte L. Allan,[1] Anya Topiwala,[1]
Klaus P. Ebmeier,[1] David Semple,[2] and
Douglas Steele[2]

[1]Oxford, UK
[2]Edinburgh, UK

## Pharmacotherapy of Unipolar Disorder

Certain pharmacological agents increase monoamine activity (noradrenaline, serotonin, and dopamine) and ameliorate depressive symptoms. This has led to the monoamine hypothesis of depression (Bunney & Davis, 1965; Schildkraut, 1965). Developments in neuroimaging have since demonstrated that antidepressants, particularly those of specific serotonergic action, can also modulate the volume, function, and biochemistry of brain structures, such as the dorsolateral prefrontal cortex, anterior cingulate, and amygdala (Bellani, Dusi, Yeh, Soares, & Brambilla, 2011; Delaveau et al., 2011). According to their chemical structure and mechanism of action, antidepressants can be divided into tricyclic antidepressants (TCAs), for example, amitriptyline and imipramine; monoamine oxidase inhibitors (MAOIs), for example, moclobemide, phenelzine; serotonin reuptake inhibitors (SSRIs), for example, fluoxetine, paroxetine; serotonin and noradrenaline reuptake inhibitors (SNRIs), for example, venlafaxine, duloxetine; noradrenaline reuptake inhibitors (NARIs), for example, reboxetine; as well as some miscellaneous drugs, for example, mirtazapine, trazodone.

Newer-generation antidepressant drugs, with improvements in safety and tolerability, have replaced TCAs as first-line treatment of depressive illness. However, no single antidepressant drug from any class has distinguished itself as the obvious first-line treatment of major depression. The choice of therapy is driven primarily by incidental effects, such as sedation, appetite stimulation, or other side effects, and depends centrally on patient's informed consent to accept the risks of adverse effects. In financially constrained times, cost has become an additional decision factor, as several of the newer antidepressant drugs are now becoming available in generic form.

Incomplete remission of depressive symptoms is associated with increased risk of relapse, decreased functioning in work and social settings, and increased risk of suicide. Strategies to manage patients who do not respond to an initial course of antidepressant

*The Wiley-Blackwell Handbook of Mood Disorders*, Second Edition. Edited by Mick Power.
© 2013 John Wiley & Sons, Ltd. Published 2013 by John Wiley & Sons, Ltd.

medication include optimizing the dose, switching antidepressants, or adding adjunctive treatment (psychotherapy or a second medication). Augmentation may be the preferred strategy for improving response if tolerability to the original agent is acceptable and the initial medication has had some beneficial effects. Possible augmentation strategies include lithium; an antipsychotic such as aripiprazole, olanzapine, quetiapine, or risperidone; or another antidepressant, such as mianserin or mirtazapine. However, there is a paucity of evidence to support one strategy over another.

Current National Institute for Health and Clinical Excellence (NICE) guidance only recommends pharmacological treatment as a first line for moderate or severe depression (National Institute for Health and Clinical Excellence [NICE], 2009). This is supported by a recent meta-analysis, which did not demonstrate the efficacy of antidepressants in minor depression (Barbui, Cipriani, Patel, Ayuso-Mateos, & van Ommeren, 2011). Recommendations also state that treatment should be continued for 6 months following remission of symptoms. Continuing treatment with antidepressants reduces the odds of relapse by 70% compared with treatment discontinuation (Geddes et al., 2003).

## Tricyclics

Despite solid evidence for the efficacy of TCAs in the treatment of depression, they are now rarely used as a first line. The reasons for this are twofold: first, their wide receptor affinity results in an extensive side-effect profile, and second, their cardiac toxicity in overdose. The commonest side effects are related to their anticholinergic activity, such as dry mouth, blurred vision, constipation, and urinary retention.

However, despite these concerns, there is still a place for TCAs in the arsenal against depression. In fact, a Cochrane review of trials conducted in primary care found that the numbers needed to treat (NNT) for TCAs ranged from 7 to 16 (median NNT 9) and for SSRIs from 7 to 8 (median NNT 7) (Arroll et al., 2009). Surprisingly, the numbers needed to harm (NNH; for withdrawal due to side effects) did not differ significantly between TCAs (4–30) and SSRIs (20–90).

## SSRIs

SSRIs have become the initial treatment of choice, in line with current NICE guidance, because of their efficacy, acceptability, and relative safety in overdose. However, their side effects include headache, nausea, increased bleeding risk, akathisia, and withdrawal syndrome. The latter is not associated with behavioral dependence (Haddad, 2001). Although much has been made of their extrapyramidal side effects, a recent review concluded that this is not a class-specific effect, they are not dose related, and can develop with short-term or long-term use (Madhusoodanan, Alexeenko, Sanders, & Brenner, 2010). The popular belief that antidepressant treatment takes up to 6 weeks, explained by alterations in monoamine receptor sensitivities (Charney, Krystal, Delgado, & Heninger, 1990), was refuted in 2006. A meta-analysis found that treatment with SSRIs compared with placebo was associated with clinical improvement by the end of the first week of use (Taylor, Freemantle, Geddes, & Bhagwagar, 2006).

In the early 2000s, it was claimed that SSRIs increased suicidal behavior that threatened their reputation as "safer" antidepressants. The US Food and Drug Administration issued a black box warning for antidepressants and suicidal thoughts and behavior in children and young adults following these concerns. Paroxetine has been particularly implicated, with its shorter half-life and increased discontinuation symptoms. The risk of suicidality associated with the use of antidepressants appears to be strongly age dependent, with adolescents at particular risk. In adults, the net effect seems to be neutral on suicidal behavior but possibly protective for suicidal ideation (Gibbons, Brown, Hur, Davis, & Mann, 2012; Stone et al., 2009). In a large Finnish cohort study, Tiihonen et al. (2006) found a substantially lower mortality during SSRI use. Among subjects who had ever used an antidepressant, there was an increased risk of attempted suicide (39%), but with a decreased risk of completed suicide (−32%). In those aged 10–19 years, there was an increased risk of death with paroxetine use (RR 5.44).

Choosing a specific agent within the class has not previously been evidence based, but a meta-analysis in 2009 has offered some guidance. Cipriani et al. (2009) investigated the acute treatment of unipolar major depression with 12 new-generation antidepressants. Mirtazapine, escitalopram, venlafaxine, and sertraline were significantly more efficacious than duloxetine, fluoxetine, fluvoxamine, paroxetine, and reboxetine. Escitalopram and sertraline were the best accepted and hence less discontinued (see Figure 6.1).

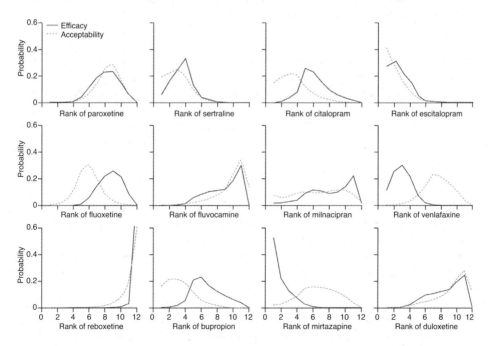

**Figure 6.1.** Ranking for Efficacy (solid line) and Acceptability (dotted line). Ranking Indicates the Probability to be the Best Treatment, the Second Best, the Third Best, and so on, among the 12 Antidepressants. Reproduced with permission from Cipriani et al. (2009)

## Other antidepressants

*SNRIs*   Although a potentially more efficacious alternative to SSRIs, venlafaxine and duloxetine are considered second-line choice because of their poorer tolerability (Schueler et al., 2011). Also of concern is their higher toxicity in overdose. In a meta-analysis of 15 head-to-head randomized controlled trials (RCTs) comparing SSRIs to SNRIs, although remission rates were higher with SNRIs (48.5% vs. 41.9%), dropouts due to adverse reactions were also higher. In a 2009 Cochrane review, meta-analysis of 16 RCTs showed no statistically significant difference in efficacy, acceptability, or tolerability of milnacipran compared with other antidepressants (Nakagawa et al., 2009). There were fewer dropouts than with TCAs.

*Mirtazapine*   A popular second-line choice or augmentation agent, mirtazapine has proven efficacy in treating depression. One meta-analysis has suggested a faster onset of action compared with SSRIs. Higher rates of remission were found at 2 weeks, although these were not sustained at increased time periods (Watanabe et al., 2008).

*NARIs*   Studies have shown reboxetine to be a poor choice of initial antidepressant. In the 2009 Lancet meta-analysis (Cipriani et al., 2009), it was the least efficacious of all the 12 antidepressants included. A later meta-analysis of published and unpublished data again showed reboxetine to be inferior to SSRIs for remission and response, and inferior to placebo for harm (Eyding et al., 2010).

*Lithium*   In a 2006 Cochrane review (Cipriani et al., 2006), lithium was shown to be efficacious at preventing hospital admission in unipolar depression. However, it was not significantly different from antidepressants according to other outcomes (quality of life, social functioning, occupational functioning, dropout rate, side effects, all-cause mortality, and suicides). Lithium has been demonstrated to decrease suicide and self-harm behavior in patients with mood disorders (Cipriani, Pretty, Hawton, & Geddes, 2005).

*Antiglucocorticoids—for example, mifepristone, ketoconazole, metyrapone, DHEA*   Gallagher et al. (2008) found a significant difference favoring treatment in psychotic depression. However, this sample included patients with bipolar as well as unipolar depression. There is as yet insufficient evidence to recommend these drugs as mainline treatment options.

*Folate*   Although mooted as novel treatment strategy, research so far has been unconvincing. In a review of three RTCs, Taylor, Carney, Goodwin, and Geddes (2004) found that folate decreased Hamilton depression rating scores by an average of 2.65 points, but not more so than trazodone. It remains to be seen whether supplementary folate has a role in those with normal folate levels, or just in those who are deficient.

## Augmentation strategies

Evidence for augmentation of antidepressants with other drugs remains widespread in clinical use, but lacks a solid evidence base to support it. A systematic review of the literature on augmentation strategies for major depression was conducted by Fleurence et al. (2009). There was no evidence of clinical efficacy, as measured by treatment response, in augmentation with buspirone, testosterone, methylphenidate, yohimbine, inositol, and atomoxetine. Although earlier work suggested a benefit of combined antidepressant therapy and lithium augmentation in treatment-resistant depression (Austin, Souza, & Goodwin, 1991), Fleurence et al. (2009) found that results were inconsistent across studies. The only eligible study of thyroid augmentation was positive, though this study evaluated patients treated with TCAs (Kelly & Lieberman, 2009). It is possible due to small sample sizes that some of the trials failed to detect significant differences versus placebo because of inadequate statistical power.

Adjunctive therapy with atypical antipsychotics has shown not only higher response rates compared with antidepressant monotherapy and placebo but also more withdrawals due to adverse events (Fleurence et al., 2009). TCA monotherapy has been reported to increase psychosis in psychotic depression compared with adjunctive antipsychotic (Kantrowitz & Tampi, 2008). However, in another meta-analysis of 10 RCTs, using an antipsychotic in addition to an antidepressant was no better at treating psychotic depression than an antidepressant alone (Wijkstra, Lijmer, Balk, Geddes, & Nolen, 2006). A post hoc analysis demonstrated that adjunctive aripiprazole treatment in patients with depression, with a history of an inadequate response to antidepressant medication, is associated with a decreased rate of suicidality in a group of subjects not at significant risk (Weisler et al., 2011). Prospective trials directly assessing suicidality are needed to further understand the benefits of an adjunctive antipsychotic in an at-risk population.

There is little evidence to guide the use of lamotrigine for depression that has not responded to a course of antidepressants. A meta-analysis found only one randomized double-blind study showing effectiveness for lamotrigine in treatment-resistant depression (Thomas, Nandhra, & Jayaraman, 2010). In this study, lamotrigine was found to be statistically superior to placebo on the CGI scale for severity and improvement; however, it was not on the HAM-D (primary end point) and MADRS scales.

## Novel agents

New targets have been identified in the battle against depression, for instance, the melatonin and glutamate (NMDA) receptors. Agomelatine, an $MT_1$ and $MT_2$ agonist and $5HT_{2c}$ antagonist, has now been licensed for the treatment of depression. Short-term studies have shown a good efficacy and tolerance (Green, 2011). It has fewer sexual side effects than SSRIs and no withdrawal symptoms (Kennedy & Rizvi, 2010). Ketamine, an established anesthetic agent, has been suggested as a novel antidepressant agent because of its antagonism of the NMDA receptor. As yet, there are no double-blinded controlled trials, but this may receive increasing focus in the years ahead (Mathew et al., 2012). Similarly, studies of psychostimulants, such as dexamphetamines, methylphenidate, have mostly been of low quality, but have shown a short-term decrease in depressive symptoms (Candy, Jones, Williams, Tookman, & King, 2008; Orr & Taylor, 2007). Longer term and higher quality trials are needed of these agents.

## St John's wort (*Hypericum perforatum*)

*Hypericum perforatum*, or St John's wort, has been used for its therapeutic effects for centuries and is now increasingly popular as a herbal antidepressant. It is widely available as a dietary supplement, or in some European countries, on prescription. This disparity in availability and licensing reflects a heterogeneous evidence base. We review the evidence for clinical use of hypericum extract focusing on recent meta-analyses and some of the larger, randomized trials.

In a Cochrane review of 29 randomized, double-blind trials, hypericum extract shows a good response rate when compared to placebo (1.28 (95% confidence interval (CI): 1.10–1.49)), though there was marked heterogeneity between trials (Linde, Berner, & Kriston, 2008). Trials comparing hypericum extract to standard antidepressants were homogeneous and demonstrated similar efficacy (response rate = 1.02 (95% CI: 0.90–1.15) for TCAs; and 1.00 (95% CI: 0.90–1.11) for SSRIs (Linde et al., 2008). Similar results are found in another recent meta-analysis (Rahimi, Nikfar, & Abdollahi, 2009). While these results appear favorable, compared to other pharmacological treatments for depression, the overall quality of evidence for hypericum extract is low; many studies have small subject numbers and are of short duration (less than 8 weeks). This is confounded by the use of differing doses and types of plant extract, which makes it difficult to draw clinically meaningful conclusions (Cipriani, Barbui, Butler, Hatcher, & Geddes, 2011). There is also a concern that (smaller) studies from countries which use hypericum extracts more widely are more likely to find favorable results, raising the question of systematic and publication bias (Linde et al., 2008). Although some larger studies have shown favorable results when comparing hypericum extract with placebo (Gastpar, Singer, & Zeller, 2006; Kasper, Anghelescu, Szegedi, Dienel, & Kieser, 2006; Lecrubier, Clerc, Didi, & Kieser, 2002) and similar efficacy compared to standard antidepressants (Gastpar et al., 2006; Woelk, 2000), others have not detected a difference between hypericum extracts and placebo (Hypericum Depression Trial Study Group, 2002; Shelton et al., 2001) or standard antidepressants (Hypericum Depression Trial Study Group, 2002). More recently, Mannel, Kuhn, Schmidt, Ploch, and Murck (2010) reported that hypericum extract may be useful in atypical depression. Rappaport et al. (2011) found no benefit of hypericum treatment for patients with mild depression. Relapse rates may be lower compared to placebo in mild depressive disorder (Singer, Schmidt, Hauke, & Stade, 2011) and moderate depressive disorder (Kasper, Volz, Möller, Dienel, & Kieser, 2008).

Despite conflicting evidence of its efficacy, the prospect of a "natural" remedy for depression is appealing to many patients, yet the use of hypericum extract presents a number of practical difficulties. Hypericum extracts available commercially contain a large number of constituents and it is unknown which is responsible for the antidepressant properties of the herb. Some of the most researched compounds are the napthodiathrones including hypericin and pseudohypericin, and phloroglucinols, such as hyperforin, tannins, and flavonoids. The concentrations of constituents vary among different extracts due to different plant types, growing conditions, preparations, and processing procedures, which make it difficult to establish active mechanisms of hypericum extracts. In addition to concerns regarding nature and purity of the extracts, there are additional concerns about drug interactions and side effects. St John's wort is a cytochrome inducer, and therefore, acts to reduce levels of many commonly prescribed drugs, for example, oral contraceptives, warfarin, theophylline, cyclosporine, and simvastatin. If used in addition to SSRI treatment, there is a risk of precipitating serotonin syndrome. These interactions are a particular concern if patients self-medicate without specialist prescribing knowledge. Studies to date show that despite these concerns, hypericum extracts are generally well tolerated compared to conventional antidepressants (Linde et al., 2008); common side effects include gastrointestinal and skin complaints (Brattström, 2009).

Current evidence suggests that hypericum extracts may be useful in mild–moderate depressive disorder; however, this evidence is relatively weak. Without further investigation of its components' antidepressant actions, and greater consistency surrounding dose and type of hypericum extract, it is unlikely to become more widely used. Larger, RCTs which use a standard preparation of hypericum extract are needed. Hypericum extract can interact dangerously with other medications, and though many studies report lower side effects compared to standard antidepressants (Linde et al., 2008), investigation of safety data in larger samples is also important. Given that existing evidence does not suggest superior efficacy of hypericum extracts compared to standard treatments, there seems to be limited impetus for such research.

## Pharmacotherapy of Bipolar Disorder

### Long-term prophylaxis

*Lithium and the anticonvulsants* The primary aim of long-term treatment is the prevention of recurrent episodes (either mania or depression) (see also Chapter 11). Despite problems with tolerability, lithium remains the "gold standard" against which other treatments are measured. The effectiveness of long-term treatment with lithium to prevent recurrences in bipolar disorder is supported by recent meta-analyses (Burgess et al., 2001; Geddes, Burgess, Hawton, Jamison, & Goodwin, 2004). The BALANCE study (Geddes et al., 2010) found that lithium plus valproate and lithium monotherapy were more likely to prevent relapse than valproate monotherapy in patients with "classical" bipolar I disorder. BALANCE could not say that lithium monotherapy was more effective than a combination but it was superior to valproate alone. In fact, despite common clinical practice, support for the use of valproate monotherapy (as sodium valproate, divalproex, or valproic acid) is surprisingly limited (Macritchie, Geddes, Scott, Haslam, & Goodwin, 2001). Initial enthusiasm for carbamazepine prophylaxis (Okuma & Kishimoto, 1998) has not stood the test of time although it may be effective in the treatment of "bipolar spectrum" (Greil et al., 1997; Hartong, Moleman, Hoogduin, Broekman, & Nolen, 2003). Despite promising reports on the efficacy of newer anticonvulsants such as oxcarbazepine, topiramate, gabapentin, and tiagabine, lamotrigine is the only new compound to be incorporated into recent bipolar guidelines (Goodwin, 2009). Maintenance trials, in patients who tolerate lamotrigine well, support a prophylactic effect against depressive relapse and, to a much lesser extent, mania, when compared to lithium and placebo (Goodwin et al., 2004).

*Antipsychotics*   Using similar continuation designs to the lamotrigine studies, the newer, second-generation antipsychotics, such as quetiapine (Vieta et al., 2008), aripiprazole (Keck et al., 2007), and olanzapine (Tohen et al., 2006) have been shown to be effective in placebo-controlled relapse prevention studies. Antipsychotic agents may be useful for the long-term management of bipolar patients especially where there are marked psychotic features. They may also have some utility in difficult-to-treat cases of rapid cycling or as an adjunct to lithium or anticonvulsants. For example, clozapine added to usual treatment was found to be superior to usual treatment alone over 1 year in treatment-resistant bipolar patients including those with rapid cycling and mixed states (Suppes et al., 1999). Similarly, in patients stabilized on quetiapine plus lithium or divalproex, continued treatment was associated with a significant risk reduction in the time to recurrence of any mood event compared with placebo and lithium or divalproex alone (Suppes, Vieta, Liu, Brecher, & Paulsson, 2009). The availability of depot formulations of the newer antipsychotics, such as Risperdal Consta®, may provide a useful alternative in poorly compliant bipolar patients at high risk of manic relapse (Malempati, Bond, & Yatham, 2008).

*Antidepressants*   There is continued debate over the role of antidepressants in the long-term management of bipolar disorder. Originally, concern over their use was sparked by a small maintenance study (Prien et al., 1984) that suggested that bipolar patients on imipramine alone experienced an unacceptably large number of manic relapses—an effect that was prevented by the addition of lithium. Subsequently, most guidelines have reflected a more or less cautious approach to recommending monotherapy with an antidepressant. Long-term treatment of bipolar patients with antidepressants is very common in clinical practice but evidence to confirm their role in the prevention of depressive episodes is lacking. There is some evidence for successful long-term prophylaxis with antidepressants in bipolar patients in combination with lithium, valproate, carbamazepine, and antipsychotics (Altshuler et al., 2001). There is even a suggestion that antidepressant monotherapy could be prophylactic, at least for some patients with bipolar II disorder (Parker, Tully, Olley, & Hadzi-Pavlovic, 2006). This is clearly an area that requires further study.

## Management of acute mania

*Antipsychotics*   The first-generation antipsychotics have been the mainstay of treatment globally but until recently there have been few controlled trials confirming their antimanic benefits (Johnstone, Crow, Frith, & Owens, 1988). Recent studies have fortunately included haloperidol as a comparator and meta-analysis of this data has shown risperidone, olanzapine, and haloperidol to be among the best of the available options for the treatment of manic episodes (Cipriani et al., 2011). It is usual to try and avoid significant extrapyramidal side effects, and for this reason most modern guidelines recommend the use of one of the second-generation antipsychotics as a first-line treatment in view of ease of use, rapidity of action, and tolerability. In the United Kingdom, olanzapine, quetiapine, risperidone, aripiprazole, and asenapine are all licensed for this purpose.

*Lithium and the anticonvulsants*   Lithium is highly effective as a treatment for acute mania (Poolsup, Li Wan Po, & de Oliveira, 2000). Up to 2 weeks of treatment with lithium may be necessary to reach maximal effectiveness for manic patients and due to this delayed effect, especially for severe episodes with marked behavioral disturbance, addition of an antipsychotic or a benzodiazepine is usually required. Evidence also supports valproate and carbamazepine (Smith, Cornelius, Warnock, Tacchi, & Taylor, 2007). Unlike carbamazepine, valproate is well tolerated and has very few drug interactions, making it more suitable for combined treatment regimes, but it should be used with caution in women of childbearing age. Oxcarbazepine is sometimes employed as an alternative to carbamazepine since it is less problematic in its interactions with other drugs (Baruzzi, Albani, & Riva, 1994), but it may not be as effective. There is no current evidence to recommend the use of any other anticonvulsant. The strongest evidence is for lamotrigine, but in depressive episodes, not mania or hypomania. Topiramate has shown some promise in both depressed and manic bipolar patients, with the added benefit of promoting weight loss. Overall, however, the evidence is not very convincing (Kushner, Khan, Lane, & Olson, 2006).

*Benzodiazepines*   Benzodiazepines such as diazepam, lorazepam, and clonazepam, are useful in the management of acutely agitated manic states (Allen et al., 2001) and are commonly included in local protocols for the management of acute behavioral disturbance along with antipsychotics. Their use can help avoid high doses of antipsychotics and safely induce sleep. The availability and rapid absorption of benzodiazepine intramuscular injections make them very useful for highly agitated acute mania (Chouinard, Annable, Turnier, Holobow, & Szkrumelak, 1993).

*Alternative strategies*   ECT should be strongly considered as first-line treatment and has been shown to be one of the best treatment options in acute mania (Mukherjee, Sackeim, & Schnur, 1994). Current practice reserves ECT for clinical situations where pharmacological treatments may not be possible, such as pregnancy or severe cardiac disease, when the patient's illness is refractory to drug treatments for very severe manic episodes that may be life-threatening, or if the patient has expressed a personal preference (Valenti et al., 2008).

## Management of depressive episodes

The pharmacological treatment of depressive episodes in bipolar disorder represents a particular challenge. Bipolar depression occurs more frequently, lasts longer, is more disruptive, and is associated with greater risk of suicide than mania. Until recently, research had focused more on the treatment of mania and prophylaxis (Hirschfeld, 2004). Most recent guidelines recommend the initiation or optimization of a prophylactic agent as a first step in the treatment of bipolar depression followed by augmentation strategies such as addition of an antidepressant or antipsychotic, if required (NICE, 2006). Lithium is usually recommended as first-line treatment rather than an antidepressant, even though the actual evidence for the acute efficacy of lithium in bipolar depression, either alone or in combination, is decidedly weak (Bhagwagar & Goodwin, 2002).

*Antidepressants*   Although almost all of the antidepressants used in the treatment of unipolar depression are effective in the treatment of bipolar depression, the response rates are lower and there is the risk of precipitating a manic episode or inducing/accelerating rapid cycling (Compton & Nemeroff, 2000). Evidence is scarce but recent studies have suggested that SSRIs may be better tolerated, work more quickly, and have lower potential of inducing mania or rapid cycling compared to TCAs (Nemeroff et al., 2001). In general, the choice will depend on issues such as previous beneficial response, side effects, and tolerability.

*Antipsychotics*   Quetiapine has been shown to be effective in the treatment of bipolar depression in two RCTs (BOLDER 1 and 2) and the EMBOLDEN I and II replication trials (Bogart & Chavez, 2009). In the United States (but not the United Kingdom), olanzapine as an olanzapine–fluoxetine combination (Symbyax®) is licensed for bipolar depression and may work well in mixed episodes (Benazzi, 2001). Olanzapine has a license for mania and prophylaxis in the United Kingdom and is recommended as a second-line treatment of bipolar depression after the SSRIs in the NICE guidelines (NICE, 2006). Preliminary data also suggest that aripiprazole may have utility (Thase et al., 2008).

*Anticonvulsants*   Recent meta-analysis supports monotherapy with lamotrigine (licensed in the United States but not yet in the United Kingdom), particularly for treatment-refractory bipolar depression (Geddes, Calabrese, & Goodwin, 2009). Gabapentin appears much less effective. Although controlled clinical trials comparing standard treatments for depression in patients with bipolar disorder are lacking, it is a widely accepted practice to add a second mood stabilizer to the treatment regimens of patients with bipolar disorder (e.g., carbamazepine or valproate).

*Alternative strategies*   Other suggested strategies include the use of adjunctive tri-iodothyronine ($T_3$), even if there is no evidence of clinical hypothyroidism (Bauer et al., 2002), and the novel use of inositol (Chengappa et al., 2000). Evidence for omega-3 fatty acids is equivocal at best (Montgomery & Richardson, 2008). For severe or life-threatening depressive episodes, ECT should not be overlooked, particularly if there is evidence of a previous good response or if the patient has made an advance statement of preference.

## Suicide prevention

Individuals with bipolar disorder are 20 times more likely to commit suicide than the general population with a lifetime prevalence of 3–6% (Bostwick & Pankratz, 2000).

For this reason, it is important to know whether any pharmacological treatments reduce the occurrence of suicidal acts. Effective long-term therapies for bipolar disorder do appear to have the added advantage of reducing the risk of suicide (Angst, Stassen, Clayton, & Angst, 2002). Lithium appears to be particularly beneficial in this regard and a meta-analysis of RCT data for lithium suggests an effect on suicide which is consistent across many studies (Cipriani et al., 2005). There are still very few studies on the antisuicidal effects of other treatments. Naturalistic studies do suggest similar beneficial effects on nonfatal suicidal behaviors with lithium, valproate, and carbamazepine, but not the antipsychotics or antidepressants (Yerevanian, Koek, & Mintz, 2007).

## Pharmacotherapy of Late-Life Depression

Late-life depression is commonly defined as depression occurring in those over the age of 60. Though it is not phenomenologically distinct from depression at other stages in life, there may be differences in etiology, with cardiovascular disease (Alexopoulos et al., 1997) and age-related social factors (e.g., retirement) playing a greater role. Use of pharmacotherapy is often more complex in this age group, and therefore, warrants more detailed consideration.

Biological changes with increasing age lead to altered pharmacokinetics and pharmacodynamics. There is increased body fat content and reduced water content, so hydrophobic compounds (e.g., antidepressants and antipsychotics) are more readily distributed, whereas distribution of hydrophilic compounds is reduced. Renal excretion is also reduced, leading to potentially increased concentrations of active compounds (Turnheim, 2003). Medical comorbidities are more common in this age group, and coupled with the physiological changes related to ageing, patients are more vulnerable to medication side effects. Polypharmacy is a risk and care is needed to minimize the effects of drug interactions (Mark et al., 2011). It is therefore particularly important that pharmacotherapy in late-life depression is based on a careful review of an individual's medical and psychiatric history.

SSRIs such as sertraline and citalopram are the most common first-line treatments, similar to younger populations (Alexopoulos et al., 2009; Cipriani et al., 2009). These have the advantage of a lower side-effect profile and can be used in those who have previously had stroke or cardiovascular disease (Apler, 2011), and in those with cognitive impairment. SSRIs should be avoided in patients with a history of gastrointestinal bleeding, and used with caution in those who are on other medications which may precipitate this (e.g., nonsteroidal anti-inflammatories). There are several options for second-line treatment of late-life depression: venlafaxine has evidence for efficacy (Lenox-Smith & Jiang, 2008; Rush et al., 2009), but may exacerbate hypertension, and mirtazapine has a growing evidence base with fewer cardiac side effects. Its common adverse effects of sedation and weight gain may be therapeutically beneficial in this patient population. TCAs are effective treatments but should be used with caution in late-life depression because of the risks of cardiac side effects (e.g., prolongation of QT interval with amitriptyline). In addition, the antimuscarinic effects of TCAs may be more likely to exacerbate cognitive impairment in this age group.

For patients with severe depression, especially those presenting with psychotic symptoms, antidepressant medication may need to be augmented. Antipsychotic medication can be an effective adjunctive treatment after careful consideration of the risks and benefits (Alexopoulos, 2011). If there is evidence of cognitive impairment antipsychotics should be avoided, if possible, because of the increased risk of stroke (Sacchetti et al., 2008). Use of lithium should be accompanied by careful monitoring of renal function, using lower doses than in younger populations.

Late-life depression shows good response to pharmacotherapy (Roose & Schatzberg, 2005), however, prescribing can be complex and requires lower doses and slow titrations of new medication, combined with more judicious monitoring. There is a high risk of depressive relapse in older patients, especially in those with comorbid medical illness (Beekman et al., 2002), so pharmacotherapy should be continued longer than for younger patients—at least 2 years.

## Interactions between Pharmacotherapy and Psychotherapy (Trial Evidence)

The focus of this chapter so far has been the pharmacological treatment of depression, with the implication that if one medication is not successful then a second can be added or an alternative started. However, the split between pharmacological and psychotherapeutic approaches may be unhelpful and several studies have reviewed the effectiveness of combined treatment.

This is a difficult field to evaluate effectively as there are multiple, frequently small studies, using a variety of pharmacological and psychological approaches which focus on different aspects of treatment, for example, recovery, maintenance of relapse, or relapse prevention. One systematic review tried to address this heterogeneity by summarizing results from 19 systematic reviews (Oestergaard & Møldrup, 2011); its focus was to review treatment for depression comparing pharmacotherapy and psychotherapy interventions to pharmacotherapy alone. Although combined therapy led to better overall care and reduced risk of relapse, the specific impact of combined therapy on depression remains uncertain (Oestergaard & Møldrup, 2011). A systematic review of 20 trials found that combined pharmacotherapy and psychotherapy led to a small improvement in efficacy, particularly for chronic or severely depressed patients, and helped to prevent depressive relapse (Friedman et al., 2004). A review of 16 trials found that patients receiving combined therapy improved significantly compared to pharmacological treatment alone (odds ratio: 1.86; 95% CI: 1.38–2.52) (Pampallona, Bollini, Tibaldi, Kupelnick, & Munizza, 2004). This finding was particularly marked for studies longer than 12 weeks (odds ratio: 2.21; 95% CI: 1.22–4.03), and was associated with fewer dropouts.

In terms of acute treatment response, there seems to be limited benefit of combined pharmacotherapy and psychotherapy. An RCT of adolescents with moderate-to-severe depressive disorder found no evidence of improved outcome when treatment included SSRIs and CBT (weekly sessions for 12 weeks, fortnightly sessions for 12 weeks, and a follow-up session at 28 weeks), compared to pharmacotherapy alone (Goodyer et al., 2007). A randomized controlled study of depressed inpatients who received interpersonal therapy (IPT) and pharmacotherapy, compared to pharmacotherapy alone found a significant difference in response rate at 5 weeks using Hamilton's rating scale, but not with Becks Depression Inventory, and there was no significant difference between groups at 3 or 12 months (Schramm et al., 2007). Likewise, an RCT in adults over 60 found no evidence of improved treatment response from escitalopram and IPT compared to escitalopram alone (Reynolds et al., 2010). Both these studies used pharmacotherapy in conjunction with a comprehensive package of supportive care, and it may be that this in itself provided a psychotherapeutic intervention.

There is some evidence that combined therapies may help to sustain remission or prevent relapse. In a randomized controlled study of IPT and pharmacotherapy in depressed inpatients, those receiving combined treatment who responded initially were more likely to show a sustained improvement in their symptoms (73% compared to 47%, $p = 0.012$ at 3 months; 69% compared to 36%, $p = 0.002$ at 12 months) (Schramm et al., 2007). Sustained remission rates were also found to be greater in those receiving combined IPT and pharmacotherapy, compared to pharmacotherapy alone, in another randomized trial assessing long-term follow-up (Zobel et al., 2011). Maintenance IPT combined with pharmacotherapy significantly reduces the recurrence rate of depression, compared with pharmacotherapy alone after successful treatment of acute depression (odds ratio: 0.37; 95% CI: 0.19–0.73) (Cuijpers et al., 2011). Although combined treatment may improve risk of relapse, these studies show that pharmacotherapy alone has greater efficacy than IPT alone.

Though there is no compelling evidence that IPT is more effective than cognitive behavioral therapy (CBT), the benefits of combined therapy with CBT have not been demonstrated. A randomized placebo-controlled trial of CBT and fluoxetine found that pharmacotherapy alone reduced recurrent rates by 18–21% compared to placebo, but that combined treatment did not reduce the risk of relapse of moderate depressive disorder (Petersen et al., 2004). In treatment-resistant depression, adjunctive treatment with quetiapine and CBT led to greater improvement compared to placebo and CBT; there was no comparison of quetiapine alone and CBT alone (Chaput, Magnan, & Gendron, 2008).

Pharmacotherapy and psychotherapy are both useful treatments for mood disorders (Cuijpers, van Straten, van Oppen, & Andersson, 2008). Combining pharmacotherapy (e.g., SSRIs) and psychotherapy (e.g., IPT or CBT) may lead to, at best, a modest improvement in acute treatment response; however, recent evidence suggests that pharmacotherapy and good supportive management is as effective as combined pharmacotherapy and formal psychological approaches. Combined therapy may increase rates of sustained remission and contribute to preventing depressive relapse.

## Physical Treatments

### Transcranial procedures

*Electroconvulsive treatment*  Although electroconvulsive treatment (ECT) is widely used in clinical practice, it is one of the more controversial treatments in psychiatry

(Read & Bentall, 2010): probably the most concerning criticism is its occasional effect on autobiographic memory (Fraser, O'Carroll, & Ebmeier, 2008). In spite of this, the clinical consensus is that in the right context and with state-of-the-art methodology it is a safe and effective treatment for severe depression (Carney et al., 2003; Keltner & Boschini, 2009; NICE, 2003; Scott, 2004). Up to 80% of patients recover and the remission rate can reach 60% even within 3 weeks (Bailine et al., 2010).

A variety of mechanisms of action have been proposed, ranging from specific effects on neurotransmitter action, for example, postsynaptic $5\text{-HTA}_{1A}$ receptor signaling (Savitz, Lucki, & Drevets, 2009) to $5\text{-HT}_2$ receptor downregulation (Yatham et al., 2010), or dopaminergic activation (Saijo et al., 2010) to increases in brain plasticity mediated by brain neurotrophic factor (BNDF) (Fernandes et al., 2009; Grønli, Stensland, Wynn, & Olstad, 2009), including activation of glial cells (Palmio et al., 2010). Increases in hippocampal volume, somewhat at odds with the notion of "brain damage," have been reported after ECT (Nordanskog et al., 2010).

The principles of good practice in applying ECT involve the induction of a seizure with the use of minimum current. This is achieved in part by restricting stimulation to one, preferably the nondominant right, brain hemisphere, as well as reducing electric energy by moving from the originally sine-wave-type stimulation to high frequency square-wave stimulation (0.5–2 ms), and most recently ultra-brief stimulation (0.3 ms). By minimizing current energy, the liability to induce cognitive side effects is minimized (Loo, Sainsbury, Sheehan, & Lyndon, 2008).

A recent systematic review with meta-analysis (Semkovska & McLoughlin, 2010) suggests that most cognitive side effects occur within the first 3 days after treatment, and after 15 days pretreatment functioning had recovered. In fact, in parallel with the improvement of depression, certain aspects of cognitive function significantly improve after treatment.

Clearly, patients with initially compromised brain function may suffer particularly from side effects and complications, but on the other hand, ECT is a relatively preferred treatment in the psychiatry of old age, where pharmacotherapy may be poorly tolerated.

*Magnetic seizure therapy*    Animal research (Dwork et al., 2004) and early human trials (Kirov et al., 2008) suggest that inducing seizures by magnetic induction is less likely to cause cognitive side effects than electrically induced seizures. New transcranial stimulation technology, which allows the application of high frequency (50–100 Hz) stimulation at full machine output, has made it possible to induce seizures with transcranial magnetic stimulation in a reliable fashion. Magnetic coils are positioned over central or frontal areas of the skull to stimulate motor or prefrontal cortex, respectively. Initial small trials (Kayser et al., 2011; Lisanby, Luber, Schlaepfer, & Sackeim, 2003) have shown promising results, but larger more convincing studies are awaited.

*Transcranial magnetic stimulation*    Transcranial magnetic stimulation (TMS) has been used (without seizure induction) with patients being fully conscious and cooperative during the intervention. A recent meta-analysis and systematic review identified 31 studies suitable for inclusion covering a total of 815 active and 716 sham TMS courses (Allan, Herrmann, & Ebmeier, 2011). TMS is approved for the treatment of depression in countries such as Canada, Australia, New Zealand, the European Union, and Israel (Marangell, Martinez, Jurdi, & Zboyan, 2007). The very few studies in mania have not been successful (Kaptsan, Yaroslavsky, Applebaum, Belmaker, & Grisaru, 2003). TMS is usually applied to frontal areas, in particular, dorsolateral prefrontal cortex, based on the hypothesis that increasing excitability in left prefrontal cortex (or less often reducing excitability in right prefrontal cortex) may counteract the underactivity observed in this area in depression. As TMS does not require an anesthetic, the operator merely needs to be trained in establishing motor threshold over the primary motor cortex with TMS, as treatment strength tends to be calibrated against motor threshold. Stimulation treatment tends to be given on a daily basis, ranging from 2 to 3 weeks or longer. Although there is limited long-term experience, in general, there are few untoward effects. The most common are headaches associated with repetitive stimulation over the frontal muscles and superficial nerves, and the risk of inducing an accidental seizure, which tends to be contained by adhering to safety guidelines (these include limiting stimulation strength, frequency, and duration of continuous stimulation periods (trains)) (Nyffeler & Müri, 2010; Rossi, Hallett, Rossini, & Pascual-Leone, 2009; Wassermann, 1998).

We computed a pooled odds ratio of 4.1 (95% CI: 2.9–5.9) for treatment response (reduction of depression scores to less than 50% of the initial value). While there was significant variability in study outcomes, there were no predictors detectable from regression between (mean) sample variables and effect sizes of different studies (Allan et al., 2011).

The main practical limitation of TMS as a clinical treatment is the fact that it is labor intensive. As ECT has been found to be more effective than TMS, at least for psychotic depression, this is no incentive to replace ECT with TMS (Eranti et al., 2007; Grunhaus, Schreiber, Dolberg, Polak, & Dannon, 2003; Hansen et al., 2011; Rosa et al., 2006). Operators need to be trained in neurophysiological techniques, emergency procedures need to be in place for the rare accidental seizure, but generally, TMS is viewed by patients as an attractive alternative to other treatment methods and may thus find a place in private or specialist health care settings.

*Transcranial direct current stimulation*  Transcranial direct current stimulation (tDCS) delivers low amplitude (1–2 mA) direct current to the underlying cerebral cortex via sponge electrodes placed on the scalp. It results in a modulation of cortical excitability and spontaneous neural activity (Nitsche, Boggio, Fregni, & Pascual-Leone, 2009). In trials of tDCS for the treatment of major depression, the anodal (−) electrode is usually placed over the left dorsolateral prefrontal cortex. This shifts the resting membrane potential of underlying neurons toward depolarization, enhancing cortical excitability and increasing the rate of neuronal firing. The cathodal (+) electrode is then placed over the right supraorbital area or dorsolateral prefrontal cortex and appears to shift the resting membrane potential toward hyperpolarization, reducing cortical excitability and decreasing the rate of neuronal firing. Such effects can outlast the duration of stimulation for up to an hour (Nitsche et al., 2009).

In a recent meta-analysis of RCTs of tDCS for depression we found that active tDCS reduced symptoms compared with sham tDCS significantly (Hedges' $g \approx 0.7$, 95% CI: $\approx 0.2$ to 1.2, $n = 165$) (Allan, Kalu, Sexton, & Ebmeier, 2012; Kalu, Sexton, Loo,

& Ebmeier, 2012). Optimal stimulus parameters (electrode placement, stimulation strength) and protocol (higher frequency and longer duration of treatment sessions) are as yet unclear. The largest study to date has recruited 64 depressed patients with a score of ≥20 on the MADRS, who received active or sham anodal tDCS to the left prefrontal cortex (2 mA, 15 × 20 min sessions over 3 weeks). Concurrent antidepressant medications were continued at stable doses 4 weeks prior to study entry. Hedges' *g* after treatment was 0.52 (95% CI: 0.01–1.03) (Loo et al., 2012).

Side effects associated with tDCS include headaches and skin irritation under the electrodes; skin lesions have been reported at 2 mA (Palm et al., 2008). Adverse cognitive effects have been reported rarely. Some studies have reported that working memory improves in the tDCS group (Fregni, Boggio, Nitsche, Rigonatti, & Pascual-Leone, 2006; Palm et al., 2008). As with transcranial stimulation techniques, in general, contraindications to tDCS are epilepsy, metallic implants, or severe eczema near electrodes.

> [tDCS] may provide a cheaper and more practical alternative [to TMS] that requires expertise similar to that necessary to administer ECT. Electrode positioning is standardised and stimulation strength follows protocol. tDCS equipment is easily transportable and can even be administered in the patient's own home. Assuming that it will pass scrutiny in large controlled naturalistic studies in the NHS, it may turn out to be the perfect future treatment in the community! (Allan et al., 2012)

## Implantation and invasive procedures

*Vagus nerve stimulation for mental disorder*   Vagus nerve stimulation (VNS) by an implanted pacemaker, a treatment used for the control of epileptic seizures, has been applied to the treatment of depression (George et al., 2000). Thirty treatment-resistant nonpsychotic depressed patients received an implant of a pacemaker stimulating the left cervical vagus nerve using bipolar electrodes. Initial follow-up appeared to support the efficacy of VNS (Marangell et al., 2002) and a larger follow-up study suggested a good response in about 50% patients with remission in about 30% (Andrade et al., 2010). However, it remains unclear whether such recovery rates are applicable to patients with the most treatment-resistant and severe mood disorders, for whom ablative neurosurgery may be indicated.

*Early deep brain stimulation*   A series of controversial studies by Heath beginning in the 1950s on animals, extending to humans in the 1970–1980s, reported correlations between neural activity (recorded using electrodes implanted deep within the brain) and subjective emotional experiences (Heath, 1985; Heath, Cox, & Lustick, 1974). Pleasurable/"rewarding" emotions correlated with "septal region" (subgenual cortex including Brodmann's area 25, BA25, from anterior commissure to the anterior tips of lateral ventricles), medial forebrain bundle, and lateral amygdala activity, whereas aversive emotions correlated with hippocampal, medial amygdala, cingulate, and periaqueductal/third-ventricle activity (Heath, 1985; Heath et al., 1974). These brain regions have subsequently been associated with normal and abnormal emotional experiences in many functional neuroimaging studies, although Heath's link with emotional valence is less clear, at least for some regions (Steele, Currie, Lawrie, & Reid, 2007; Steele & Lawrie, 2004).

Based on studies on animals indicating that deep brain stimulation (DBS) of a cerebellar region, the vermis, enhanced "rewarding" emotional experience and "septal" activity, plus inhibited aversive experience and medial temporal lobe activity, Heath, Llewellyn, and Rouchell (1980) developed a DBS cerebellar "pacemaker" and used it to treat a variety of psychiatric disorders. They reported the best results with patients whose symptoms were related to "profound negative emotion" such as intractable depression (Heath et al., 1980). In the late 1980s, DBS of the basal ganglia was introduced for the treatment of Parkinson's disease tremor and dystonia and is now very commonly used for the treatment of neurological disorders.

*Modern DBS for psychiatric disorder*   DBS has been used to treat a variety of psychiatric disorders (Andrade et al., 2010). For example, Mayberg et al. (2005) reported a clinical trial using bilateral DBS of the white matter tracts lateral to the subgenual cingulate (BA25), to treat otherwise refractory depression (Kennedy et al., 2011; Mayberg et al., 2005). Previous neuroimaging work had suggested overactivity of BA25 (Drevets et al., 1997; Mayberg et al., 2005), although this is controversial (Steele et al., 2007), and chronic *stimulation* of the white matter tracts lateral to BA25 was claimed to *reduce* abnormal brain activity (Mayberg et al., 2005). Whatever the mechanism, at least a 50% reduction in symptoms was reported in more than half of the patients (Mayberg et al., 2005). An international double-blind placebo-controlled DBS trial for treatment-resistant depression "BROADEN" (http://www.broadenstudy.com/) is underway. Interestingly, BA25 is part of the "septal" region that Heath aimed to stimulate indirectly (Heath et al., 1980).

*Ablative neurosurgery for mental disorder*   Ablative neurosurgery for mental disorder (NMD) is rarely undertaken. For example, between 1984 and 1994, a total of only 20 operations per year in the United Kingdom (CRAG Working Group, 1996) were done, with even fewer operations per year nowadays. However DBS interventions for psychiatric disorders have been increasing rapidly in recent years.

The only contemporary indications for ablative NMD in the United Kingdom are severe mood disorder or obsessive compulsive disorder (OCD), when the patient wants the operation, when all other reasonable treatments have repeatedly failed, and the patient remains ill but competent to provide sustained informed consent (CRAG Working Group, 1996). Under the Mental Health (Scotland) Act, independent certification by the Mental Welfare Commission of a patient's ability to consent and the appropriateness of treatment is required.

NMD operations comprise stereotactic subcaudate tractotomy (SST), anterior cingulotomy (ACING), anterior capsulotomy (ACAPS), and limbic leucotomy (CRAG Working Group, 1996). Operations such as amygdalotomy and hypothalamotomy are no longer practiced (CRAG Working Group, 1996).

*Early history of ablative NMD*   NMD developed because of a need to treat intractable severe psychiatric disorders when there were no effective treatments (Malhi & Bartlett, 2000). This remains the only indication.

Fulton and Jacobson (1935), investigating primate frontal lobe function, discovered that bilateral removal of the orbitofrontal cortex subdued the animals making them appear less anxious. Soon afterward, Lima operated on humans, and Freeman and Watts began "psychosurgery" in the United States, devising the prefrontal leucotomy (Fenton, 1999). Subsequently, 40,000 patients in the United States and 12,000 patients in the United Kingdom were operated on until the mid-1950s (Malhi & Bartlett, 2000). At this point, the number of such operations declined because of the development of the first effective drug treatments and reports of a "post-lobotomy syndrome" (Malhi & Bartlett, 2000). These operations had employed relatively crude "freehand" methods lesioning widespread and variable parts of the brain, reflecting neurosurgical practice at the time.

An early consensus arose that patients with mood disorders and OCD appeared to benefit most (Knight, 1964). In such patients it was thought that lesions confined to the white matter tracts deep to the orbitomedial prefrontal cortex had minimal effect on intellect and personality while illness recovery was maintained (Knight, 1964). A stereotactic operative procedure designed to make reproducible lesions was devised (Knight, 1964) with postmortem studies confirming reproducibility (Newcombe, 1975). The procedure, SST, became by far the most common modern ablative NMD used in the United Kingdom over the next 40 years (CRAG Working Group, 1996). Nowadays though, SST is no longer available in the United Kingdom.

In other countries two other stereotactic operations were developed: ACING and ACAPS (CRAG Working Group, 1996). The combination of what was essentially SST and cingulotomy was termed limbic leucotomy (Richardson, 1973). Patient follow-up studies indicated a significant improvement in 40–60% of otherwise treatment-refractory patients receiving SST (Bridges et al., 1994; Goktepe, Young, & Bridges, 1975).

*Modern ablative NMD practice*   ACING and perhaps ACAPS remain available for a small number of UK patients with treatment-refractory mood disorder and OCD (Christmas et al., 2011; Steele, Christmas, Eljamel, Matthews, 2008). Practice in other countries varies (Leiphart & Valone, 2010).

ACAPS is an established procedure for chronic treatment-refractory depression and OCD. While benefit has been claimed, previous ACAPS reports have provided limited information. However, a prospective study of therapeutic effect, mental status, quality of life, and social and neurocognitive functioning, has recently been published (Christmas et al., 2011). Data were collected preoperatively and at long-term follow-up. According to a priori criteria, 10% were "responders" and 40% "remitters" (Christmas et al., 2011). Neurocognitive and personality testing at long-term follow-up were not significantly different from preoperative baseline with a suggestion of a trend toward improved executive functioning (Christmas et al., 2011). ACING is similarly a treatment for chronic treatment-refractory depression and OCD, but has also been used to treat intractable pain (Steele et al., 2008). With regard to long-term clinical outcome, 25% were classified "responders" and 37.5% "remitters". Again, there were no significant differences between baseline and long-term follow-up on a range of neuropsychological tasks, with a suggestion of a trend toward improved executive functioning (Steele et al., 2008).

Overall, this suggests a 50% response rate with ACAPS and a 63% response rate with ACING (Christmas et al., 2011; Steele et al., 2008). The number of patients in these studies is small, reflecting its use as a procedure of last resort. Larger studies and studies by other groups are, therefore, required to confirm these findings.

Complicating this, psychiatric and surgical practice varies considerably from center to center, for example, ACAPS at one center (Rück et al., 2008) is very different from another (Christmas et al., 2011). Variation occurs with regard to patient inclusion and exclusion criteria (e.g., inclusion of patients with personality disorder and other comorbidities), extent of pre- and postoperative assessment (with the former often being incomplete), and surgical practice (e.g., whether radiosurgery is used in contrast to conventional thermal ablation, plus details of lesion placement and lesion volume). This makes comparison of reports between centers difficult. Conclusions from one center (Rück et al., 2008) are therefore not necessarily generalizable to another (Christmas et al., 2011).

*ACING lesion characteristics and clinical response*     Double-blind, placebo-controlled trials of *ablative* neurosurgical treatments for psychiatric disorders are unlikely to be done due to ethical considerations (Earp, 1979). Nevertheless, demonstration of a link between neurosurgical lesion characteristics and clinical outcome is evidence against the suggestion that NMD is a placebo. To date, there have been almost no such reports. However one study (Steele et al., 2008) reported a strong relationship between ACING lesion location and volume. Specifically, the best clinical response was obtained with more anterior lesions and smaller (down to a specific limit) lesion volumes. The former may be explained by more anterior lesions being located in brain regions specialized for emotional rather than cognitive or premotor functioning (Steele et al., 2008).

*National and international availability of NMD*     NMD has always been a controversial treatment and lack of space prevents detailed discussion of evidence for its efficacy and safety versus adverse outcome, plus the limitations of that knowledge. The CRAG Working Group for Mental Illness investigated this issue for the NMD procedures of interest here. Their report constitutes the largest inquiry into NMD in the United Kingdom (CRAG Working Group, 1996).

They concluded that "subject to existing and recommended additional safeguards and procedures, NMD should continue to be available in Scotland, but only as a treatment for intractable OCD and affective disorders (e.g., major depressive illness)." The Dundee Advanced Interventions Service (AIS) is currently the only center in the United Kingdom that regularly provides NMD and offers one ablative procedure (ACING) ans also participates in the BROADEN trial. In Scotland but not England, DBS procedures for mental disorder are controlled by the same laws as ablative NMD (Mental Health Care and Treatment Act, Scotland, 2003). Worldwide, most other countries allow ablative NMD and DBS, though with variable safeguards on its use (Fins et al., 2011).

# References

Alexopoulos, G. S. (2011). Pharmacotherapy for late-life depression. *Journal of Clinical Psychiatry, 72*(1), e04.

Alexopoulos, G. S., Meyers, B. S., Young, R. C., Campbell, S., Silbersweig, D., & Charlson, M. (1997). 'Vascular depression' hypothesis. *Archives of General Psychiatry, 54*, 915–922.

Alexopoulos, G. S., Reynolds, C. F., Bruce, M. L., Katz, I. R., Raue, P. J., Mulsant, B. H., ... PROSPECT Group. (2009). Reducing suicidal ideation and depression in older primary care patients: 24-month outcomes of the PROSPECT study. *American Journal of Psychiatry, 166*, 882–890.

Allan, C., Kalu, U. G., Sexton, C. E., & Ebmeier, K. P. (2012). Transcranial stimulation in depression. *British Journal of Psychiatry, 200*, 10–11.

Allan, C. L., Herrmann, L. L., & Ebmeier, K. P. (2011). Transcranial magnetic stimulation in the management of mood disorders. *Neuropsychobiology, 64*, 163–169.

Allen, M. H., Currier, G. W., Hughes, D. H., Reyes-Harde, M., Docherty, J. P., & Expert Consensus Panel for Behavioral Emergencies. (2001). The expert consensus guideline series. Treatment of behavioral emergencies. *Postgraduate Medicine*, 1–88; quiz 89–90.

Altshuler, L., Kiriakos, L., Calcagno, J., Goodman, R., Gitlin, M., Frye, M., & Mintz, J. (2001). The impact of antidepressant discontinuation versus antidepressant continuation on 1-year risk for relapse of bipolar depression: A retrospective chart review. *Journal of Clinical Psychiatry, 62*, 612–616.

Andrade, P., Noblesse, L. H. M., Temel, Y., Ackermans, L., Lim, L. W., Steinbusch, H. W., & Visser-Vandewalle, V. (2010). Neurostimulatory and ablative treatment options in major depressive disorder: A systematic review. *Acta Neurochirurgica, 152*, 565–577.

Angst, F., Stassen, H. H., Clayton, P. J., & Angst, J. (2002). Mortality of patients with mood disorders: Follow-up over 34–38 years. *Journal of Affective Disorders, 68*, 167–181.

Apler, A. (2011). Citalopram for major depressive disorder in adults: A systematic review and meta-analysis of published placebo-controlled trials. *BMJ Open, 1*, e000106.

Arroll, B., Elley, C. R., Fishman, T., Goodyear-Smith, F. A., Kenealy, T., Blashki, G., ... Macgillivray, S. (2009). Antidepressants versus placebo for depression in primary care. *Cochrane Database of Systematic Reviews*, (3), CD007954.

Austin, M. P., Souza, F. G., & Goodwin, G. M. (1991). Lithium augmentation in antidepressant-resistant patients. A quantitative analysis. *British Journal of Psychiatry, 159*, 510–514.

Bailine, S., Fink, M., Knapp, R., Petrides, G., Husain, M. M., Rasmussen, K., ... Kellner, C. H. (2010). Electroconvulsive therapy is equally effective in unipolar and bipolar depression. *Acta Psychiatrica Scandinavica, 121*, 431–436.

Barbui, C., Cipriani, A., Patel, V., Ayuso-Mateos, J. L., & van Ommeren, M. (2011). Efficacy of antidepressants and benzodiazepines in minor depression: Systematic review and meta-analysis. *British Journal of Psychiatry, 198*(1), 11–16.

Baruzzi, A., Albani, F., & Riva, R. (1994). Oxcarbazepine: Pharmacokinetic interactions and their clinical relevance. *Epilepsia, 35*(Suppl. 3), S14–S19.

Bauer, M., Berghofer, A., Bschor, T., Baumgartner, A., Kiesslinger, U., Hellweg, R., ... Müller-Oerlinghausen, B. (2002). Supraphysiological doses of L-thyroxine in the maintenance treatment of prophylaxis-resistant affective disorders. *Neuropsychopharmacology, 27*, 620–628.

Beekman, A. T. F., Geerlings, S. W., Deeg, D. J. H., Smit, J. H., Schoevers, R. S., de Beurs, E., ... van Tilburg, W. (2002). The natural history of late-life depression: A 6-year prospective study in the community. *Archives of General Psychiatry, 59*, 605–611.

Bellani, M., Dusi, N., Yeh, P. H., Soares, J. C., & Brambilla, P. (2011). The effects of antidepressants on human brain as detected by imaging studies. Focus on major depression. *Progress in Neuro-Psychopharmacology & Biological Psychiatry, 35*, 1544–1552.

Benazzi, F. (2001). Prevalence and clinical correlates of residual depressive symptoms in bipolar II disorder. *Psychotherapy and Psychosomatics, 70*, 232–238.

Bhagwagar, Z., & Goodwin, G. M. (2002). Role of mood stabilizers in bipolar disorder. *Expert Review of Neurotherapeutics, 2*, 239–248.

Bogart, G. T., & Chavez, B. (2009). Safety and efficacy of quetiapine in bipolar depression. *Annals of Pharmacotherapy, 43*, 1848–1856.

Bostwick, J. M., & Pankratz, V. S. (2000). Affective disorders and suicide risk: A reexamination. *American Journal of Psychiatry, 157*, 1925–1932.

Brattström, A. (2009). Long-term effects of St. John's wort (*Hypericum perforatum*) treatment: A 1-year safety study in mild to moderate depression. *Phytomedicine, 16*, 277–283.

Bridges, P. K., Bartlett, J. R., Hale, A. S., Poynton, A. M., Malizia, A. L., & Hodgkiss, A. D. (1994). Psychosurgery: Stereotactic subcaudate tractomy. An indispensable treatment. *British Journal of Psychiatry, 165*, 599–611; discussion 612–613.

Bunney, W. E., Jr., & Davis, J. M. (1965). Norepinephrine in depressive reactions. A review. *Archives of General Psychiatry, 13*, 483–494.

Burgess, S., Geddes, J., Hawton, K., Townsend, E., Jamison, K., & Goodwin, G. (2001). Lithium for maintenance treatment of mood disorders. *Cochrane Database of Systemic Reviews*, (3), CD003013.

Candy, M., Jones, L., Williams, R., Tookman, A., & King, M. (2008). Psychostimulants for depression. *Cochrane Database of Systematic Reviews*, (2), CD006722.

Carney, S., Cowen, P., Geddes, J., Goodwin, G., Rogers, R., Dearness, K., . . . Scott, A. (2003). Efficacy and safety of electroconvulsive therapy in depressive disorders: A systematic review and meta-analysis. *Lancet, 361*, 799–808.

Chaput, Y., Magnan, A., & Gendron, A. (2008). The co-administration of quetiapine or placebo to cognitive-behavior therapy in treatment refractory depression: A preliminary trial. *BMC Psychiatry, 8*, 73.

Charney, D. S., Krystal, J. H., Delgado, P. L., & Heninger, G. R. (1990). Serotonin-specific drugs for anxiety and depressive disorders. *Annual Review of Medicine, 41*, 437–446.

Chengappa, K. N., Levine, J., Gershon, S., Mallinger, A. G., Hardan, A., Vagnucci, A., . . . Kupfer, D. J. (2000). Inositol as an add-on treatment for bipolar depression. *Bipolar Disorders, 2*, 47–55.

Chouinard, G., Annable, L., Turnier, L., Holobow, N., & Szkrumelak, N. (1993). A double-blind randomized clinical trial of rapid tranquilization with I.M. clonazepam and I.M. haloperidol in agitated psychotic patients with manic symptoms. *Canadian Journal of Psychiatry, 38*(Suppl. 4), S114–S121.

Christmas, D., Eljamel, M. S., Butler, S., Hazari, H., MacVicar, R., Steele, J. D., . . . Matthews, K. (2011). Long term outcome of thermal anterior capsulotomy for chronic, treatment refractory depression. *Journal of Neurology, Neurosurgery, and Psychiatry, 82*, 594–600.

Cipriani, A., Barbui, C., Butler, R., Hatcher, S., & Geddes, J. (2011). Depression in adults: Drug and physical treatments. *Clinical Evidence, 5*, 1003.

Cipriani, A., Barbui, C., Salanti, G., Rendell, J., Brown, R., Stockton, S., . . . Geddes, J. R. (2011) Comparative efficacy and acceptability of antimanic drugs in acute mania: A multiple-treatments meta-analysis. *Lancet, 378*, 1306–1315.

Cipriani, A., Furukawa, T. A., Salanti, G., Geddes, J. R., Higgins, J. P., Churchill, R., . . . Barbui, C. (2009). Comparative efficacy and acceptability of 12 new-generation antidepressants: A multiple-treatments meta-analysis. *Lancet, 373*, 746–758.

Cipriani, A., Pretty, H., Hawton, K., & Geddes, J. R. (2005). Lithium in the prevention of suicidal behavior and all-cause mortality in patients with mood disorders: A systematic review of randomized trials. *American Journal of Psychiatry, 162*, 1805–1819.

Cipriani, A., Smith, K., Burgess, S., Carney, S., Goodwin, G., & Geddes, J. (2006). Lithium versus antidepressants in the long-term treatment of unipolar affective disorder. *Cochrane Database of Systematic Reviews*, (4), CD003492.

Compton, M. T., & Nemeroff, C. B. (2000). The treatment of bipolar depression. *Journal of Clinical Psychiatry, 61*(Suppl. 9), 57–67.

Crag Working Group. (1996). *Neurosurgery for mental disorder*. Edinburgh, UK: Scottish Office.

Cuijpers, P., Geraedts, A. S., van Oppen, P., Andersson, G., Markowitz, J. C., & van Straten, A. (2011). Interpersonal psychotherapy for depression: A meta-analysis. *American Journal of Psychiatry, 168*, 581–592.

Cuijpers, P., van Straten, A., van Oppen, P., & Andersson, G. (2008). Are psychological and pharmacologic interventions equally effective in the treatment of adult depressive disorders? A meta-analysis of comparative studies. *Journal of Clinical Psychiatry, 69*, 1675–1685; quiz 1839–1841.

Delaveau, P., Jabourian, M., Lemogne, C., Guionnet, S., Bergouignan, L., & Fossati, P. (2011). Brain effects of antidepressants in major depression: A meta-analysis of emotional processing studies. *Journal of Affective Disorders, 130*, 66–74.

Drevets, W. C., Price, J. L., Simpson, J. R., Jr., Todd, R. D., Reich, T., Vannier, M., & Raichle, M. E. (1997). Subgenual prefrontal cortex abnormalities in mood disorders. *Nature, 386*, 824–827.

Dwork, A. J., Arango, V., Underwood, M., Ilievski, B., Rosoklija, G., Sackeim, H. A., & Lisanby, S. H. (2004). Absence of histological lesions in primate models of ECT and magnetic seizure therapy. *American Journal of Psychiatry, 161*, 576–578.

Earp, J. D. (1979). Psychosurgery: The position of the Canadian Psychiatric Association. *Canadian Journal of Psychiatry, 24*, 353–364.

Eranti, S., Mogg, A., Pluck, G., Landau, S., Purvis, R., Brown, R. G., ... McLoughlin, D. M. (2007). A randomized, controlled trial with 6-month follow-up of repetitive transcranial magnetic stimulation and electroconvulsive therapy for severe depression. *American Journal of Psychiatry, 164*, 73–81.

Eyding, D., Lelgemann, M., Grouven, U., Härter, M., Kromp, M., Kaiser, T., ... Wieseler, B. (2010). Reboxetine for acute treatment of major depression: Systematic review and meta-analysis of published and unpublished placebo and selective serotonin reuptake inhibitor controlled trials. *BMJ (Clinical Research Ed.), 341*, c4737.

Fenton, G. W. (1999). Neurosurgery for mental disorder: Past and present. *Advances in Psychiatric Treatment, 5*, 261–270.

Fernandes, B., Gama, C. S., Massuda, R., Torres, M., Camargo, D., Kunz, M., ... Inês Lobato, M. (2009). Serum brain-derived neurotrophic factor (BDNF) is not associated with response to electroconvulsive therapy (ECT): A pilot study in drug resistant depressed patients. *Neuroscience Letters, 453*, 195–198.

Fins, J. J., Mayberg, H. S., Nuttin, B., Kubu, C. S., Galert, T., Sturm, V., ... Schlaepfer, T. E. (2011). Misuse of the FDA's humanitarian device exemption in deep brain stimulation for obsessive-compulsive disorder. *Health Affairs (Project Hope), 30*, 302–311.

Fleurence, R., Williamson, R., Jing, Y., Kim, E., Tran, Q. V., Pikalov, A. S., & Thase, M. E. (2009). A systematic review of augmentation strategies for patients with major depressive disorder. *Psychopharmacology Bulletin, 42*, 57–90.

Fraser, L. M., O'Carroll, R. E., & Ebmeier, K. P. (2008). The effect of electroconvulsive therapy on autobiographical memory: A systematic review. *Journal of ECT*, *24*, 10–17.

Fregni, F., Boggio, P. S., Nitsche, M. A., Rigonatti, S. P., & Pascual-Leone, A. (2006). Cognitive effects of repeated sessions of transcranial direct current stimulation in patients with depression. *Depression and Anxiety*, *23*, 482–484.

Friedman, M. A., Detweiler-Bedell, J. B., Leventhal, H. E., Horne, R., Keitner, G. I., & Miller, I. W. (2004). Combined psychotherapy and pharmacotherapy for the treatment of major depressive disorder. *Clinical Psychology: Science and Practice*, *11*, 47–68.

Fulton, J. E., & Jacobsen, C. F. (1935). The functions of the frontal lobes. A comparative study in monkey, chimpanzee and man. *Abstracts of the Second International Neurological Congress*, 70–71.

Gallagher, P., Malik, N., Newham, J., Young, A. H., Ferrier, I. N., & Mackin, P. (2008). Antiglucocorticoid treatments for mood disorders. *Cochrane Database of Systematic Reviews*, (1), CD005168.

Gastpar, M., Singer, A., & Zeller, K. (2006). Comparative efficacy and safety of a once-daily dosage of hypericum extract STW3-VI and citalopram in patients with moderate depression: A double-blind, randomised, multicentre, placebo-controlled study. *Pharmacopsychiatry*, *39*, 66–75.

Geddes, J. R., Burgess, S., Hawton, K., Jamison, K., & Goodwin, G. M. (2004). Long-term lithium therapy for bipolar disorder: Systematic review and meta-analysis of randomized controlled trials. *American Journal of Psychiatry*, *161*, 217–222.

Geddes, J. R., Calabrese, J. R., & Goodwin, G. M. (2009). Lamotrigine for treatment of bipolar depression: Independent meta-analysis and meta-regression of individual patient data from five randomised trials. *British Journal of Psychiatry*, *194*, 4–9.

Geddes, J. R., Carney, S. M., Davies, C., Furukawa, T. A., Kupfer, D. J., Frank, E., & Goodwin, G. M. (2003). Relapse prevention with antidepressant drug treatment in depressive disorders: A systematic review. *Lancet*, *361*, 653–661.

Geddes, J. R., Goodwin, G. M., Rendell, J., Azorin, J. M., Cipriani, A., ... Juszczak, E.; BALANCE investigators and collaborators. (2010). Lithium plus valproate combination therapy versus monotherapy for relapse prevention in bipolar I disorder (BALANCE): A randomised open-label trial. *Lancet*, *375*, 385–395.

George, M. S., Nahas, Z., Bohning, D. E., Lomarev, M., Denslow, S., Osenbach, R., & Ballenger, J. C. (2000). Vagus nerve stimulation: A new form of therapeutic brain stimulation. *CNS Spectrums*, *5*, 43–52.

Gibbons, R. D., Brown, C. H., Hur, K., Davis, J. M., & Mann, J. J. (2012). Suicidal thoughts and behavior with antidepressant treatment: Reanalysis of the randomized placebo-controlled studies of fluoxetine and venlafaxine. *Archives of General Psychiatry*, *69*, 580–587.

Goktepe, E. O., Young, L. B., & Bridges, P. K. (1975). A further review of the results of stereotactic subcaudate tractotomy. *British Journal of Psychiatry*, *126*, 270–280.

Goodwin, G. M. (2009). Evidence-based guidelines for treating bipolar disorder: Revised second edition—Recommendations from the British Association for Psychopharmacology. *Journal of Psychopharmacology*, *23*, 346–388.

Goodwin, G. M., Bowden, C. L., Calabrese, J. R., Grunze, H., Kasper, S., White, R., ... Leadbetter, R. (2004). A pooled analysis of 2 placebo-controlled 18-month trials of lamotrigine and lithium maintenance in bipolar I disorder. *Journal of Clinical Psychiatry*, *65*, 432–441.

Goodyer, I., Dubicka, B., Wilkinson, P., Kelvin, R., Roberts, C., Byford, S., ... Harrington, R. (2007). Selective serotonin reuptake inhibitors (SSRIs) and routine specialist care with and without cognitive behaviour therapy in adolescents with major depression: Randomised controlled trial. *BMJ (Clinical Research Ed.)*, *335*, 142.

Green, B. (2011). Focus on agomelatine. *Current Medical Research and Opinion*, *27*, 745–749.

Greil, W., Ludwig-Mayerhofer, W., Erazo, N., Schöchlin, C., Schmidt, S., Engel, R. R., . . . Wetterling, T. (1997). Lithium versus carbamazepine in the maintenance treatment of bipolar disorders—A randomised study. *Journal of Affective Disorders*, *43*, 151–161.

Grønli, O., Stensland, G. Ø., Wynn, R., & Olstad, R. (2009). Neurotrophic factors in serum following ECT: A pilot study. *World Journal of Biological Psychiatry*, *10*, 295–301.

Grunhaus, L., Schreiber, S., Dolberg, O. T., Polak, D., & Dannon, P. N. (2003). A randomized controlled comparison of electroconvulsive therapy and repetitive transcranial magnetic stimulation in severe and resistant nonpsychotic major depression. *Biological Psychiatry*, *53*, 324–331.

Haddad, P. M. (2001). Antidepressant discontinuation syndromes. *Drug Safety: An International Journal of Medical Toxicology and Drug Experience*, *24*, 183–197.

Hansen, P. E., Ravnkilde, B., Videbech, P., Clemmensen, K., Sturlason, R., Reiner, M., . . . Vestergaard, P. (2011). Low-frequency repetitive transcranial magnetic stimulation inferior to electroconvulsive therapy in treating depression. *Journal of ECT*, *27*, 26–32.

Hartong, E. G., Moleman, P., Hoogduin, C. A., Broekman, T. G., & Nolen, W. A. (2003). Prophylactic efficacy of lithium versus carbamazepine in treatment-naive bipolar patients. *Journal of Clinical Psychiatry*, *64*, 144–151.

Heath, R. G. (1985). Neural substrate for emotion: Relationship of feelings, sensory perception, and memory. *International Journal of Neurology*, *19–20*, 144–155.

Heath, R. G., Cox, A. W., & Lustick, L. S. (1974). Brain activity during emotional states. *American Journal of Psychiatry*, *131*, 858–862.

Heath, R. G., Llewellyn, R. C., & Rouchell, A. M. (1980). The cerebellar pacemaker for intractable behavioral disorders and epilepsy: Follow-up report. *Biological Psychiatry*, *15*, 243–256.

Hirschfeld, R. M. (2004). Bipolar depression: The real challenge. *European Neuropsychopharmacology*, *14*(Suppl. 2), S83–S88.

Hypericum Depression Trial Study Group. (2002). Effect of *Hypericum perforatum* (St John's wort) in major depressive disorder: A randomized controlled trial. *Journal of the American Medical Association*, *287*, 1807–1814.

Johnstone, E. C., Crow, T. J., Frith, C. D., & Owens, D. G. (1988). The Northwick Park "functional" psychosis study: Diagnosis and treatment response. *Lancet*, *2*, 119–125.

Kalu, U. G., Sexton, C. E., Loo, C. K., & Ebmeier, K. P. (2012). Transcranial direct current stimulation in the treatment of major depression: A meta-analysis. *Psychological Medicine*, *42*, 1791–1800.

Kantrowitz, J. T., & Tampi, R. R. (2008). Risk of psychosis exacerbation by tricyclic antidepressants in unipolar major depressive disorder with psychotic features. *Journal of Affective Disorders*, *106*, 279–284.

Kaptsan, A., Yaroslavsky, Y., Applebaum, J., Belmaker, R. H., & Grisaru, N. (2003). Right prefrontal TMS versus sham treatment of mania: A controlled study. *Bipolar Disorders*, *5*, 36–39.

Kasper, S., Anghelescu, I.-G., Szegedi, A., Dienel, A., & Kieser, M. (2006). Superior efficacy of St John's wort extract WS 5570 compared to placebo in patients with major depression: A randomized, double-blind, placebo-controlled, multi-center trial [ISRCTN77277298]. *BMC Medicine*, *4*, 14.

Kasper, S., Volz, H. P., Möller, H. J., Dienel, A., & Kieser, M. (2008). Continuation and long-term maintenance treatment with *Hypericum* extract WS 5570 after recovery from an acute episode of moderate depression–a double-blind, randomized, placebo controlled long-term trial. *European Neuropsychopharmacology, 18*, 803–813.

Kayser, S., Bewernick, B. H., Grubert, C., Hadrysiewicz, B. L., Axmacher, N., & Schlaepfer, T. E. (2011). Antidepressant effects, of magnetic seizure therapy and electroconvulsive therapy, in treatment-resistant depression. *Journal of Psychiatric Research, 45*, 569–576.

Keck, P. E., Jr., Calabrese, J. R., McIntyre, R. S., McQuade, R. D., Carson, W. H., Eudicone, J. M., ... Aripiprazole Study Group. (2007). Aripiprazole monotherapy for maintenance therapy in bipolar I disorder: A 100-week, double-blind study versus placebo. *Journal of Clinical Psychiatry, 68*, 1480–1491.

Kelly, T. F., & Lieberman, D. Z. (2009). Long term augmentation with T3 in refractory major depression. *Journal of Affective Disorders, 115*, 230–233.

Keltner, N. L., & Boschini, D. J. (2009). Electroconvulsive therapy. *Perspectives in Psychiatric Care, 45*, 66–70.

Kennedy, S. H., Giacobbe, P., Rizvi, S. J., Placenza, F. M., Nishikawa, Y., Mayberg, H. S., & Lozano, A. M. (2011). Deep brain stimulation for treatment-resistant depression: Follow-up after 3 to 6 years. *American Journal of Psychiatry, 168*, 502–510.

Kennedy, S. H., & Rizvi, S. J. (2010). Agomelatine in the treatment of major depressive disorder: Potential for clinical effectiveness. *CNS Drugs, 24*, 479–499.

Kirov, G., Ebmeier, K. P., Scott, A. I., Atkins, M., Khalid, N., Carrick, L., ... Lisanby, S. H. (2008). Quick recovery of orientation after magnetic seizure therapy for major depressive disorder. *British Journal of Psychiatry, 193*, 152–155.

Knight, G. (1964). The orbital cortex as an objective in the surgical treatment of mental illness. The results of 450 cases of open operation and the development of the stereotactic approach. *British Journal of Surgery, 51*, 114–124.

Kushner, S. F., Khan, A., Lane, R., & Olson, W. H. (2006). Topiramate monotherapy in the management of acute mania: Results of four double-blind placebo-controlled trials. *Bipolar Disorders, 8*, 15–27.

Lecrubier, Y., Clerc, G., Didi, R., & Kieser, M. (2002). Efficacy of St. John's wort extract WS 5570 in major depression: A double-blind, placebo-controlled trial. *American Journal of Psychiatry, 159*, 1361–1366.

Leiphart, J. W., & Valone, F. H. (2010). Stereotactic lesions for the treatment of psychiatric disorders. *Journal of Neurosurgery, 113*, 1204–1211.

Lenox-Smith, A. J., & Jiang, Q. (2008). Venlafaxine extended release versus citalopram in patients with depression unresponsive to a selective serotonin reuptake inhibitor. *International Clinical Psychopharmacology, 23*, 113–119.

Linde, K., Berner, M. M., & Kriston, L. (2008). St John's wort for major depression. *Cochrane Database of Systematic Reviews (Online)*, (4), CD000448.

Lisanby, S. H., Luber, B., Schlaepfer, T. E., & Sackeim, H. A. (2003). Safety and feasibility of magnetic seizure therapy (MST) in major depression: Randomized within-subject comparison with electroconvulsive therapy. *Neuropsychopharmacology, 28*, 1852–1865.

Loo, C. K., Alonzo, A., Martin, D., Mitchell, P. B., Galvez, V., & Sachdev, P. (2012). Transcranial direct current stimulation for depression: 3-week, randomised, sham-controlled trial. *British Journal of Psychiatry, 200*, 52–59.

Loo, C. K., Sainsbury, K., Sheehan, P., & Lyndon, B. (2008). A comparison of RUL ultrabrief pulse (0.3 ms) ECT and standard RUL ECT. *International Journal of Neuropsychopharmacology, 11*, 883–890.

Macritchie, K. A., Geddes, J. R., Scott, J., Haslam, D. R., & Goodwin, G. M. (2001). Valproic acid, valproate and divalproex in the maintenance treatment of bipolar disorder. *Cochrane Database of Systematic Reviews*, (3), CD003196.

Madhusoodanan, S., Alexeenko, L., Sanders, R., & Brenner, R. (2010). Extrapyramidal symptoms associated with antidepressants—A review of the literature and an analysis of spontaneous reports. *Annals of Clinical Psychiatry, 22,* 148–156.

Malempati, R. N., Bond, D. J., & Yatham, L. N. (2008). Depot risperidone in the outpatient management of bipolar disorder: A 2-year study of 10 patients. *International Clinical Psychopharmacology, 23,* 88–94.

Malhi, G. S., & Bartlett, J. R. (2000). Depression: A role for neurosurgery? *British Journal of Neurosurgery, 14,* 415–422; discussion 423.

Mannel, M., Kuhn, U., Schmidt, U., Ploch, M., & Murck, H. (2010). St. John's wort extract LI160 for the treatment of depression with atypical features—A double-blind, randomized, and placebo-controlled trial. *Journal of Psychiatric Research, 44,* 760–767.

Marangell, L. B., Martinez, M., Jurdi, R. A., & Zboyan, H. (2007). Neurostimulation therapies in depression: A review of new modalities. *Acta Psychiatrica Scandinavica, 116,* 174–181.

Marangell, L. B., Rush, A. J., George, M. S., Sackeim, H. A., Johnson, C. R., Husain, M. M., . . . Lisanby, S. H. (2002). Vagus nerve stimulation (VNS) for major depressive episodes: One year outcomes. *Biological Psychiatry, 51,* 280–287.

Mark, T. L., Joish, V. N., Hay, J. W., Sheehan, D. V., Johnston, S. S., & Cao, Z. (2011). Antidepressant use in geriatric populations: The burden of side effects and interactions and their impact on adherence and costs. *American Journal of Geriatric Psychiatry, 19,* 211–221.

Mathew, S. J., Shah, A., Lapidus, K., Clark, C., Jarun, N., Ostermeyer, B., & Murrough, J. W. (2012). Ketamine for treatment-resistant unipolar depression: Current evidence. *CNS Drugs, 26,* 189–204.

Mayberg, H. S., Lozano, A. M., Voon, V., McNeely, H. E., Seminowicz, D., Hamani, C., . . . Kennedy, S. H. (2005). Deep brain stimulation for treatment-resistant depression. *Neuron, 45,* 651–660.

Montgomery, P., & Richardson, A. J. (2008). Omega-3 fatty acids for bipolar disorder. *Cochrane Database of Systematic Reviews,* (2), CD005169.

Mukherjee, S., Sackeim, H. A., & Schnur, D. B. (1994). Electroconvulsive therapy of acute manic episodes: A review of 50 years' experience. *American Journal of Psychiatry, 151,* 169–176.

Nakagawa, A., Watanabe, N., Omori, I. M., Barbui, C., Cipriani, A., McGuire, H., . . . Furukawa, T. A. (2009). Milnacipran versus other antidepressive agents for depression. *Cochrane Database of Systematic Reviews,* (3), CD006529.

National Institute for Health and Clinical Excellence. (2003). *Technology appraisal (TA59): The clinical effectiveness and cost effectiveness of electroconvulsive therapy (ECT) for depressive illness, schizophrenia, catatonia and mania.* London: National Collaborating Centre for Mental Health.

National Institute for Health and Clinical Excellence. (2006). *The management of bipolar disorder in adults, children and adolescents, in primary and secondary care.* London: National Collaborating Centre for Mental Health.

National Institute for Health and Clinical Excellence. (2009). *The treatment and management of depression in adults* (NICE clinical guideline 90). London: National Institute for Health and Clinical Excellence.

Nemeroff, C. B., Evans, D. L., Gyulai, L., Sachs, G. S., Bowden, C. L., Gergel, I. P., . . . Pitts, C. D. (2001). Double-blind, placebo-controlled comparison of imipramine and paroxetine in the treatment of bipolar depression. *American Journal of Psychiatry, 158,* 906–912.

Newcombe, R. (1975). The lesion in stereotactic subcaudate tractotomy. *British Journal of Psychiatry, 126,* 478–481.

Nitsche, M. A., Boggio, P. S., Fregni, F., & Pascual-Leone, A. (2009). Treatment of depression with transcranial direct current stimulation (tDCS): A review. *Experimental Neurology, 219*, 14–19.

Nordanskog, P., Dahlstrand, U., Larsson, M. R., Larsson, E.-M., Knutsson, L., & Johanson, A. (2010). Increase in hippocampal volume after electroconvulsive therapy in patients with depression: A volumetric magnetic resonance imaging study. *Journal of ECT, 26*, 62–67.

Nyffeler, T., & Müri, R. (2010). Comment on: Safety, ethical considerations, and application guidelines for the use of transcranial magnetic stimulation in clinical practice and research, by Rossi et al. (2009). *Clinical Neurophysiology, 121*, 980.

Oestergaard, S., & Møldrup, C. (2011). Improving outcomes for patients with depression by enhancing antidepressant therapy with non-pharmacological interventions: A systematic review of reviews. *Public Health, 125*, 357–367.

Okuma, T., & Kishimoto, A. (1998). A history of investigation on the mood stabilizing effect of carbamazepine in Japan. *Psychiatry and Clinical Neurosciences, 52*, 3–12.

Orr, K., & Taylor, D. (2007). Psychostimulants in the treatment of depression: A review of the evidence. *CNS Drugs, 21*, 239–257.

Palm, U., Keeser, D., Schiller, C., Fintescu, Z., Nitsche, M., Reisinger, E., & Padberg, F. (2008). Skin lesions after treatment with transcranial direct current stimulation (tDCS). *Brain Stimulation, 1*, 386–387.

Palmio, J., Huuhka, M., Laine, S., Huhtala, H., Peltola, J., Leinonen, E., ... Keränen, T. (2010). Electroconvulsive therapy and biomarkers of neuronal injury and plasticity: Serum levels of neuron-specific enolase and S-100b protein. *Psychiatry Research, 177*, 97–100.

Pampallona, S., Bollini, P., Tibaldi, G., Kupelnick, B., & Munizza, C. (2004). Combined pharmacotherapy and psychological treatment for depression: A systematic review. *Archives of General Psychiatry, 61*, 714–719.

Parker, G., Tully, L., Olley, A., & Hadzi-Pavlovic, D. (2006). SSRIs as mood stabilizers for Bipolar II Disorder? A proof of concept study. *Journal of Affective Disorders, 92*, 205–214.

Petersen, T., Harley, R., Papakostas, G. I., Montoya, H. D., Fava, M., & Alpert, J. E. (2004). Continuation cognitive-behavioural therapy maintains attributional style improvement in depressed patients responding acutely to fluoxetine. *Psychological Medicine, 34*, 555–561.

Poolsup, N., Li Wan Po, A., & de Oliveira, I. R. (2000). Systematic overview of lithium treatment in acute mania. *Journal of Clinical Pharmacy and Therapeutics, 25*, 139–156.

Prien, R. F., Kupfer, D. J., Mansky, P. A., Small, J. G., Tuason, V. B., Voss, C. B., & Johnson, W. E. (1984). Drug therapy in the prevention of recurrences in unipolar and bipolar affective disorders. Report of the NIMH Collaborative Study Group comparing lithium carbonate, imipramine, and a lithium carbonate-imipramine combination. *Archives of General Psychiatry, 41*, 1096–1104.

Rahimi, R., Nikfar, S., & Abdollahi, M. (2009). Efficacy and tolerability of *Hypericum perforatum* in major depressive disorder in comparison with selective serotonin reuptake inhibitors: A meta-analysis. *Progress in Neuro-Psychopharmacology & Biological Psychiatry, 33*, 118–127.

Rapaport, M. H., Nierenberg, A. A., Howland, R., Dording, C., Schettler, P. J., & Mischoulon, D. (2011). The treatment of minor depression with St. John's Wort or citalopram: Failure to show benefit over placebo. *Journal of Psychiatric Research, 45*, 931–941.

Read, J., & Bentall, R. (2010). The effectiveness of electroconvulsive therapy: A literature review. *Epidemiologia e Psichiatria Sociale, 19*, 333–347.

Reynolds, C. F., III, Dew, M. A., Martire, L. M., Miller, M. D., Cyranowski, J. M., Lenze, E., ... Frank, E. (2010). Treating depression to remission in older adults: A controlled evaluation of combined escitalopram with interpersonal psychotherapy versus escitalopram with depression care management. *International Journal of Geriatric Psychiatry, 25,* 1134–1141.

Richardson, A. (1973). Stereotactic limbic leucotomy: Surgical technique. *Postgraduate Medical Journal, 49,* 860–864.

Roose, S. P., & Schatzberg, A. F. (2005). The efficacy of antidepressants in the treatment of late-life depression. *Journal of Clinical Psychopharmacology, 25,* S1–S7.

Rosa, M. A., Gattaz, W. F., Pascual-Leone, A., Fregni, F., Rosa, M. O., Rumi, D. O., ... Marcolin, M. A. (2006). Comparison of repetitive transcranial magnetic stimulation and electroconvulsive therapy in unipolar non-psychotic refractory depression: A randomized, single-blind study. *International Journal of Neuropsychopharmacology, 9,* 667–676.

Rossi, S., Hallett, M., Rossini, P. M., & Pascual-Leone, A. (2009). Safety, ethical considerations, and application guidelines for the use of transcranial magnetic stimulation in clinical practice and research. *Clinical Neurophysiology, 120,* 2008–2039.

Rück, C., Karlsson, A., Steele, J. D., Edman, G., Meyerson, B. A., Ericson, K., ... Svanborg, P. (2008). Capsulotomy for obsessive-compulsive disorder: Long-term follow-up of 25 patients. *Archives of General Psychiatry, 65,* 914–921.

Rush, A. J., Warden, D., Wisniewski, S. R., Fava, M., Trivedi, M. H., Gaynes, B. N., & Nierenberg, A. A. (2009). STAR*D: Revising conventional wisdom. *CNS Drugs, 23,* 627–647.

Sacchetti, E., Trifirò, G., Caputi, A., Turrina, C., Spina, E., Cricelli, C., ... Mazzaglia, G. (2008). Risk of stroke with typical and atypical anti-psychotics: A retrospective cohort study including unexposed subjects. *Journal of Psychopharmacology, 22,* 39–46.

Saijo, T., Takano, A., Suhara, T., Arakawa, R., Okumura, M., Ichimiya, T., ... Okubo, Y. (2010). Electroconvulsive therapy decreases dopamine $D_2$ receptor binding in the anterior cingulate in patients with depression: A controlled study using positron emission tomography with radioligand [C]FLB 457. *Journal of Clinical Psychiatry, 71,* 793–799.

Savitz, J., Lucki, I., & Drevets, W. C. (2009). 5-HT(1A) receptor function in major depressive disorder. *Progress in Neurobiology, 88,* 17–31.

Schildkraut, J. J. (1965). The catecholamine hypothesis of affective disorders: A review of supporting evidence. *American Journal of Psychiatry, 122,* 509–522.

Schramm, E., van Calker, D., Dykierek, P., Lieb, K., Kech, S., Zobel, I., ... Berger, M. (2007). An intensive treatment program of interpersonal psychotherapy plus pharmacotherapy for depressed inpatients: Acute and long-term results. *American Journal of Psychiatry, 164,* 768–777.

Schueler, Y. B., Koesters, M., Wieseler, B., Grouven, U., Kromp, M., Kerekes, M. F., ... Weinmann, S. (2011). A systematic review of duloxetine and venlafaxine in major depression, including unpublished data. *Acta Psychiatrica Scandinavica, 123,* 247–265.

Scott, A. (2004). *The ECT Handbook: The third report of the Royal College of Psychiatrists' Special Committee on ECT.* London: The Royal College of Psychiatrists.

Semkovska, M., & Mcloughlin, D. M. (2010). Objective cognitive performance associated with electroconvulsive therapy for depression: A systematic review and meta-analysis. *Biological Psychiatry, 68,* 568–577.

Shelton, R. C., Keller, M. B., Gelenberg, A., Dunner, D. L., Hirschfeld, R., Thase, M. E., ... Halbreich, U. (2001). Effectiveness of St John's wort in major depression: A randomized controlled trial. *Journal of the American Medical Association, 285,* 1978–1986.

Singer, A., Schmidt, M., Hauke, W., & Stade, K. (2011). Duration of response after treatment of mild to moderate depression with *Hypericum* extract STW 3-VI, citalopram and placebo: A reanalysis of data from a controlled clinical trial. *Phytomedicine, 18,* 739–742.

Smith, L. A., Cornelius, V., Warnock, A., Tacchi, M. J., & Taylor, D. (2007). Pharmacological interventions for acute bipolar mania: A systematic review of randomized placebo-controlled trials. *Bipolar Disorders, 9*, 551–560.

Steele, J. D., Christmas, D., Eljamel, M. S., & Matthews, K. (2008). Anterior cingulotomy for major depression: Clinical outcome and relationship to lesion characteristics. *Biological Psychiatry, 63*, 670–677.

Steele, J. D., Currie, J., Lawrie, S. M., & Reid, I. (2007). Prefrontal cortical functional abnormality in major depressive disorder: A stereotactic meta-analysis. *Journal of Affective Disorders, 101*, 1–11.

Steele, J. D., & Lawrie, S. M. (2004). Segregation of cognitive and emotional function in the prefrontal cortex: A stereotactic meta-analysis. *NeuroImage, 21*, 868–875.

Stone, M., Laughren, T., Jones, M. L., Levenson, M., Holland, P. C., Hughes, A., . . . Rochester, G. (2009). Risk of suicidality in clinical trials of antidepressants in adults: Analysis of proprietary data submitted to US Food and Drug Administration. *BMJ (Clinical Research Ed.), 339*, b2880.

Suppes, T., Vieta, E., Liu, S., Brecher, M., & Paulsson, B. (2009). Maintenance treatment for patients with bipolar I disorder: Results from a North American study of quetiapine in combination with lithium or divalproex (trial 127). *American Journal of Psychiatry, 166*, 476–488.

Suppes, T., Webb, A., Paul, B., Carmody, T., Kraemer, H., & Rush, A. J. (1999). Clinical outcome in a randomized 1-year trial of clozapine versus treatment as usual for patients with treatment-resistant illness and a history of mania. *American Journal of Psychiatry, 156*, 1164–1169.

Taylor, M. J., Carney, S. M., Goodwin, G. M., & Geddes, J. R. (2004). Folate for depressive disorders: Systematic review and meta-analysis of randomized controlled trials. *Journal of Psychopharmacology, 18*, 251–256.

Taylor, M. J., Freemantle, N., Geddes, J. R., & Bhagwagar, Z. (2006). Early onset of selective serotonin reuptake inhibitor antidepressant action: Systematic review and meta-analysis. *Archives of General Psychiatry, 63*, 1217–1223.

Thase, M. E., Jonas, A., Khan, A., Bowden, C. L., Wu, X., McQuade, R. D., . . . Owen, R. (2008). Aripiprazole monotherapy in nonpsychotic bipolar I depression: Results of 2 randomized, placebo-controlled studies. *Journal of Clinical Psychopharmacology, 28*, 13–20.

Thomas, S. P., Nandhra, H. S., & Jayaraman, A. (2010). Systematic review of lamotrigine augmentation of treatment resistant unipolar depression (TRD). *Journal of Mental Health, 19*, 168–175.

Tiihonen, J., Lonnqvist, J., Wahlbeck, K., Klaukka, T., Tanskanen, A., & Haukka, J. (2006). Antidepressants and the risk of suicide, attempted suicide, and overall mortality in a nationwide cohort. *Archives of General Psychiatry, 63*, 1358–1367.

Tohen, M., Calabrese, J. R., Sachs, G. S., Banov, M. D., Detke, H. C., Risser, R., . . . Bowden, C. L. (2006). Randomized, placebo-controlled trial of olanzapine as maintenance therapy in patients with bipolar I disorder responding to acute treatment with olanzapine. *American Journal of Psychiatry, 163*, 247–256.

Turnheim, K. (2003). When drug therapy gets old: Pharmacokinetics and pharmacodynamics in the elderly. *Experimental Gerontology, 38*, 843–853.

Valenti, M., Benabarre, A., Garcia-Amador, M., Molina, O., Bernardo, M., & Vieta, E. (2008). Electroconvulsive therapy in the treatment of mixed states in bipolar disorder. *European Psychiatry, 23*, 53–56.

Vieta, E., Suppes, T., Eggens, I., Persson, I., Paulsson, B., & Brecher, M. (2008). Efficacy and safety of quetiapine in combination with lithium or divalproex for maintenance of patients with bipolar I disorder (international trial 126). *Journal of Affective Disorders*, *109*, 251–263.

Wassermann, E. M. (1998). Risk and safety of repetitive transcranial magnetic stimulation: Report and suggested guidelines from the International Workshop on the Safety of Repetitive Transcranial Magnetic Stimulation, June 5–7, 1996. *Electroencephalography and Clinical Neurophysiology*, *108*, 1–16.

Watanabe, N., Omori, I. M., Nakagawa, A., Cipriani, A., Barbui, C., McGuire, H., . . . Multiple Meta-Analyses of New Generation Antidepressants (MANGA) Study Group. (2008). Mirtazapine versus other antidepressants in the acute-phase treatment of adults with major depression: Systematic review and meta-analysis. *Journal of Clinical Psychiatry*, *69*, 1404–1415.

Weisler, R. H., Khan, A., Trivedi, M. H., Yang, H., Eudicone, J. M, Pikalov, A., . . . Carlson, B. X. (2011). Analysis of suicidality in pooled data from 2 double-blind, placebo-controlled aripiprazole adjunctive therapy trials in major depressive disorder. *Journal of Clinical Psychiatry*, *72*, 548–555.

Wijkstra, J., Lijmer, J., Balk, F. J., Geddes, J. R., & Nolen, W. A. (2006). Pharmacological treatment for unipolar psychotic depression: Systematic review and meta-analysis. *British Journal of Psychiatry*, *188*, 410–415.

Woelk, H. (2000). Comparison of St John's wort and imipramine for treating depression: Randomised controlled trial. *BMJ (Clinical Research Ed.)*, *321*, 536–539.

Yatham, L. N., Liddle, P. F., Lam, R. W., Zis, A. P., Stoessl, A. J., Sossi, V., . . . Ruth, T. J. (2010). Effect of electroconvulsive therapy on brain 5-HT(2) receptors in major depression. *British Journal of Psychiatry*, *196*, 474–479.

Yerevanian, B. I., Koek, R. J., & Mintz, J. (2007). Bipolar pharmacotherapy and suicidal behavior. Part I: Lithium, divalproex and carbamazepine. *Journal of Affective Disorders*, *103*, 5–11.

Zobel, I., Kech, S., van Calker, D., Dykierek, P., Berger, M., Schneibel, R., & Schramm, E. (2011). Long-term effect of combined interpersonal psychotherapy and pharmacotherapy in a randomized trial of depressed patients. *Acta Psychiatrica Scandinavica*, *123*, 276–282.

# 7

# CBT for Depression

## Mick Power
### Edinburgh University, UK

## Introduction

Depression has been known as a disorder for thousands of years. Its earliest known description comes from the Egyptian wisdom text, *The Dialogue of a Man with His Ba*, the papyrus manuscript of which is held in the Berlin Sate Museum (translation downloaded from Nederhof, 2009; see also Power, 2012). In this manuscript, a depressed man argues with his soul (in Ancient Egyptian, the *ba*):

> Look, my soul is disobeying me, while I do not listen to him, is dragging me toward death, before I have come to it, and is throwing me on the fire to burn me up (lines 11–13).

The man then goes on to complain:

> Whom can I talk to today? Faces are blank, every man has his face downcast concerning his brothers. Whom can I talk to today? Hearts have become greedy and there is no man's heart on which one may rely (lines 118–121).

Another early vivid description of depression is presented in the Bible when Job loses his possessions and his family, and then laments:

> My days are past, my purposes are broken off, even the thoughts of my heart. They change the night into day: the light is short because of darkness. If I wait, the grave is mine house: I have made my bed in the darkness. I have said to corruption, Thou art my father: to the worm, Thou art my mother, and my sister. And where is now my hope?

Hippocrates, in the fifth century BC, coined the term "melancholia" (the Latinized form of the original Greek term) to cover this disorder, though he considered it to result from an excess of one of the four humors, black bile. The term "depression" (from the Latin word "deprimere" meaning "to press down") was not introduced into English until the seventeenth century. It was popularized by Dr. Johnson in the eighteenth century, but it was only in the late nineteenth century and early twentieth century in the writings of Griesinger and Kraepelin that the term began to replace "melancholia" as a diagnostic label (see Jackson, 1986, for a detailed history).

*The Wiley-Blackwell Handbook of Mood Disorders*, Second Edition. Edited by Mick Power.
© 2013 John Wiley & Sons, Ltd. Published 2013 by John Wiley & Sons, Ltd.

The term "depression" now refers to a wide range of disorders and a number of different classification systems. Nevertheless, the majority of these systems consider depression to be a combination of depressed mood together with at least some of the following symptoms:

1. Loss of interest in normal activities (anhedonia)
2. Slowness in thinking and, in severe cases, slowness in movement (retardation)
3. Feelings of self-condemnation
4. Appetite disturbance
5. Excessive tiredness
6. Sleep disturbance
7. Loss of libido
8. Suicidal thoughts and attempts

There have been various attempts at classification that have included distinctions such as *reactive–endogenous* and *neurotic–psychotic*. However, it has now been shown that the majority of depressions of all types are preceded by negative life events, so the attempts to distinguish reactive from nonreactive types has largely been abandoned (see Champion, 2000). One distinction that does appear to be useful though is that between unipolar and bipolar depressions. Bipolar disorders typically show periods of mania or hypomania in addition to periods of severe depression; in contrast to unipolar depression, bipolar disorders have a high genetic loading; and the primary form of treatment is with lithium (Goodwin & Jamison, 2007). There are interesting signs, nevertheless, that even such an apparently biologically determined form of depression may also demonstrate considerable sensitivity to psychosocial factors both in relation to the first onset and to the course of the disorder, and that approaches such as CBT and interpersonal psychotherapy (IPT) are useful adjunctive therapies (see Chapters 13, 14, and 15).

## Cognitive-Behavioral Models

There are a number of theoretical and clinical models of depression in both the behavioral and the cognitive literature. Early behavioral models (Lewinsohn, 1974) tended to focus on the symptoms of anhedonia, with the general assumption that reduced rates of positive reinforcement, or lower rates of self-reinforcement that would follow from a withdrawal from everyday activities, would lead to a state of depression. Seligman's (1975) Learned Helplessness model initially argued that it was the lack of control over reinforcement that was more important than whether or not you received reinforcement. However, as we have pointed out elsewhere (Wykes & Power, 1996), the Learned Helplessness model would predict that people should become depressed if an anonymous well-wisher dropped £100 through their letter box every week, an idea that we definitely find counter-intuitive. Although it has become clear, as we will discuss in detail below, that the straightforward behavioral models are too simplistic in their accounts of depression because they focus primarily on anhedonia, in the treatment of depression the early assessment and, if needed, intervention in activity levels has become a standard part of cognitive-behavioral approaches.

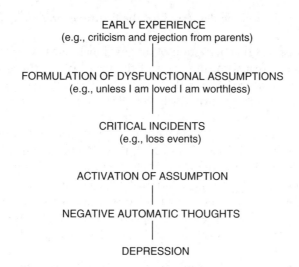

EARLY EXPERIENCE
(e.g., criticism and rejection from parents)

FORMULATION OF DYSFUNCTIONAL ASSUMPTIONS
(e.g., unless I am loved I am worthless)

CRITICAL INCIDENTS
(e.g., loss events)

ACTIVATION OF ASSUMPTION

NEGATIVE AUTOMATIC THOUGHTS

DEPRESSION

**Figure 7.1.** A Summary of Beck's Model of Depression

We will concentrate, in this chapter, on the main CBT approach to depression, that of Beck (1976), and then review some of the latest developments in CBT. However, it should first be pointed out that Beck's theory was in fact presaged by the work of the ego analyst Bibring (1953), who revised Freud's original psychoanalytic formulation (presented in his classic work, *Mourning and Melancholia,* 1917/1984). Bibring proposed that it was the failure of certain aspirations, such as to be loved or to be admired, that was the primary cause of depression in vulnerable individuals. Although it is unclear as to what extent Beck was influenced by Bibring's work (see Weishaar, 1993), this idea lies at the core of Beck's cognitive therapy.

The general cognitive therapy model of depression is outlined in Figure 7.1. The figure shows that dysfunctional schemas are typically formed in childhood as a consequence of socialization processes developed in interactions with parents and other significant individuals within the child's social network. These early socialization processes lead the child to believe that his or her worth is especially dependent on the views of others or that self-worth can only be achieved through the successful pursuit of certain goals and through gaining the admiration of others. Beck (1983) has characterized dependent individuals as "sociotropic" and the achievement-oriented individuals who often avoid dependency on others as "autonomous," with men in our culture being more likely to be the "autonomous" type and women, the "sociotropic" type. Within the model, both types of individuals are considered to have dysfunctional schemas which are normally latent, but which become activated when a negative event occurs that matches that particular schema. For example, the adolescent who has an excessive need to be loved by others may find that the first rejection in a love relationship leads to a state of depression in which the self is believed to be unlovable and worthless. Of course, not everyone who has the dysfunctional schemas need become depressed; the successful pursuit of a role or goal may prevent some individuals from becoming depressed despite their vulnerability. It may also explain why some individuals might only become depressed for the first time later in life (Champion & Power, 1995).

Figure 7.1 also shows that activation of dysfunctional schemas leads to a range of cognitive phenomena that form the focus of the main part of therapy. One of the innovations of Beck's approach was the focus on the so-called negative automatic thoughts (NATs), the experience of which typically leads the individual to believe that he or she is a failure. For example, a thought such as "I'm worthless" or "No-one will ever love me" can lead to a sudden downturn in mood; one of the aims of therapy, therefore, is to help the individual identify what these NATs are and, subsequently, to learn how to challenge them rather than simply treat them as absolute truths.

A second feature of cognitive processes that are consequent on the activation of the dysfunctional schemas are that they lead to so-called logical errors of thinking. These logical errors have been variously grouped into the following sorts of categories (Beck, Rush, Shaw, & Emery, 1979):

1. All-or-nothing thinking: "If I can't do it perfectly, there's no point in doing it at all"
2. Overgeneralization: "I always get things wrong"
3. Discounting the positive (selective abstraction): "I've finished my work today, but I should have done more"
4. Jumping to conclusions (mind reading): "Everyone is fed up with me because I'm depressed again"
5. Catastrophizing (magnification and minimization): "It's all going to go wrong and I can't change it"
6. Emotional reasoning: "I feel bad; therefore, I must have done something wrong"
7. Shoulds: "I should pull my socks up and get on with it"
8. Personalization: "It always rains when I arrange to go out"

In the early writings on cognitive therapy, these logical errors were presented in a way that implied that depressed individuals were irrational and illogical in their thinking, with the implication that normal individuals were rational and logical. However, more recent analyses have accepted the demonstrations from studies of reasoning in normal individuals that such individuals may also demonstrate characteristic biases (Kahneman, 2011) and even that under certain conditions depressed individuals may be *more* accurate rather than less accurate than normal controls (Alloy & Abramson, 1979). Therefore, cognitive therapists now assume that depression causes self-related information processing to be biased in a negative way (Haaga, Dyck, & Ernst, 1991; Weishaar, 1993). A negative bias does not, however, invariably imply a distortion of information processing (see Power & Dalgleish, 2008). In fact, normal nondepressed individuals are typically mildly positively biased for self-related information processing and are also prone to the same types of logical errors as are depressed individuals, but in the opposite direction, as the following examples illustrate (Wykes & Power, 1996):

1. All-or-nothing thinking: "This place would fall apart without me"
2. Overgeneralization: "You know I'm always right"
3. Discounting the negative (selective abstraction): "I was just doing my duty and following orders"

4. Jumping to conclusions (Mind reading): "I feel happy and everyone thinks I'm wonderful"
5. Magnification and minimization: "If I were running the country, I'd soon sort this mess out"
6. Emotional reasoning: "I feel so good I know I'm going to win the National Lottery today"
7. Shoulds: "Other people should pay me more respect and recognize my talents"
8. Personalization: "The sun always shines when I arrange to go out"

The moral of this story is that both normal and depressed individuals can be biased in how they process information, though the biases are typically positive for normal individuals and negative for depressed individuals (Power & Dalgleish, 2008). The task for the therapist is made even more difficult, therefore, than the original cognitive therapy approach implied in that some of the depressed client's negative statements may be incisively accurate. The therapist should not be misled into thinking, however, that the accuracy of some negative statements means that all negative statements are true, for therein lies the therapist's skill in distinguishing one from the other (Power, 2002).

## The Practice of Therapy

### General comments

As in work with any client group, there are a number of issues that are general to work in therapy and a number of issues that are specific to the client group in particular. The most general issue for any therapy is, of course, the development of a collaborative therapeutic relationship; without such a relationship, effective therapeutic work is well nigh impossible (Frank, 1982; Gilbert & Leahy, 2007). In fact, the establishment of a good relationship is typically easier in depression than with some other client groups, especially in those clients with strong dependency needs. Even in the case of the "autonomous" depressed individuals mentioned above who normally aim to be self-sufficient, when they enter therapy it is often because their attempts at self-sufficiency have broken down under the pressure of a significant life crisis; they may experience their need for help from the therapist as shameful or humiliating, but, nevertheless, one of the functions of depression may be to force individuals to question interpersonal and other goal-related issues which they have attempted to deny. It is more likely to be on recovery from depression that the autonomous individual becomes difficult to work with in therapy. The issue of the therapeutic relationship remains, of course, an important factor throughout therapy and is particularly relevant in short-term work for depression where termination issues are always just around the corner, a problem that we will return to subsequently.

### Assessment

The functions of the initial assessment sessions with any client are twofold and involve the collection of basic information about the individual's background and history in addition to testing likely problems in the establishment of the collaborative therapeutic relationship (see Power, 2002). The cognitive model of depression (Beck et al., 1979) highlights issues about the individual's early background and relationships with significant others (see Figure 7.1); therefore, careful attention needs to be paid both to early losses which have been followed by experiences of neglect (see Rutter, 1972), and to subtler issues about the acceptability of the individual or characteristics of the individual to those significant others. Of course, it is not uncommon for clients to initially report that they had happy childhoods with loving parents. However, as Bowlby (1980) and a number of subsequent commentators have observed, the client may often report what they have been instructed to say by a parent, "I'm doing this because I love you dear … "; thus, the client may have conflicting schematic models (Power, 2010) and it may only be in the reporting of specific incidents from childhood that the nature of the different and inconsistent parental models come to light.

Turning to more specific aspects of the assessment, it is necessary for the therapist to assess the severity and chronicity of depression. Severity is commonly measured with the Beck depression inventory (BDI) (Beck, Ward, Mendelsohn, Mock, & Erbaugh, 1961), though as Kendall, Hollon, Beck, Hammen, and Ingram (1987) noted, the BDI is not a diagnostic instrument and it is only in conjunction with a clinical diagnosis of depression that the scale can be assumed to measure depression. In conjunction with the assessment of the severity of depression, particular care needs to be taken with the assessment of suicide risk in depressed individuals; thus, an estimated 15% of depressed individuals succeed in killing themselves, and above 40% of depressed clients may attempt suicide (Champion, 2000). We would also note that although the BDI is the most widely used self-report measure of depression, like other depression measures it fails to consider the interpersonal dimension, so more recent measures may be preferable if they become widely used (Cheung & Power, 2012). It is incumbent on the therapist, therefore, to help a client feel safe about the discussion of current suicide ideation and any past attempts, in order to both gauge the severity of the attempts and identify the high-risk situations in which such attempts may be likely to occur in the future. Where such a risk is identified, clear action plans must be in place and be agreed upon with the client and other key individuals, where appropriate.

Other features of depression that should be addressed during the assessment include the experience of recent negative life events which are known to be significantly increased prior to the onset of depression (Brown & Harris, 1978). One of the risks of depression, however, is that not only may there have been an increase in the so-called independent events prior to the episode of depression, but subsequent to the episode there may have been an increase in the number of dependent events (i.e., events dependent on the individual's own actions). These dependent events may be especially destructive for the person's relationships and career, but may be preventable with an appropriate intervention in therapy (Champion, 2000).

Information should also be collected about the individual's current sources of social support, in particular, whether or not the person is able to mobilize support during a crisis, or, indeed, whether, for example, the lack of support from the person's partner may be one of the reasons for the depressive episode.

In our own attempts to put emotion back into cognition (Power, 2010; Power & Dalgleish, 2008), an additional feature that we emphasized for the assessment for therapy is the person's beliefs about their own emotional states. In the case of depression, we have suggested that the maintenance of the depressed state may, in part, be due to the coupling of emotion states, especially sadness and shame (i.e., self-disgust in our analysis). The experience of self-disgust may arise in a number of ways, not only in the ways emphasized traditionally in cognitive therapy because of a belief of being worthless, unlovable, or a failure. In addition, the person may be depressed because they have, in their own view, allowed themselves to experience an unacceptable emotional state. For example, in many cultures men are not supposed to experience or express sadness because it is a weak effeminate emotion and women are not supposed to express anger because it is not "ladylike" (Power, 1999). Although we know better, clients often enter therapy ashamed of the emotions that they are experiencing, perhaps because of familial and societal reasons they have been brought up to reject these emotions. The task for the therapist is to enable the person to accept the experience and expression of these rejected emotional states and to integrate the states into the normal experience of the self (see Greenberg, Rice, & Elliott, 1993).

## The educational component

One of the strengths of the cognitive behavioral approach (Beck et al., 1979) is that the therapist presents the client with a rationale for therapy and also presents relevant educational information or bibliotherapy about the problems being experienced. The booklet, *Coping with Depression*, was designed by Beck and his colleagues in order to provide information to depressed clients about the likely experiences they may be having in addition to introducing the main characteristics of the cognitive approach. The booklet is handed out during the first or second session to be read for homework. The client's response to the booklet has been shown to be a good predictor of whether or not the cognitive approach is likely to be effective with that particular client (Fennell & Teasdale, 1987), such that a client who clearly disagrees or does not relate to the description of the model in any way is unlikely to do well in cognitive therapy. In such a case, the therapist might be advised to discuss alternative forms of treatment with the client to see if one of these might be more suitable.

One of the frequent experiences that therapists report is that clients may have little or no information about the problems that they are experiencing and, indeed, may even have mistaken beliefs. For example, the person may believe that he or she is the only person to have had this experience, that depression will never go away, or that depression is cured by pulling your socks up. Therefore, a crucial aspect of the early stages of cognitive therapy is to explore the person's own model of depression and to provide facts and information with, when appropriate, additional reading material relevant to the person's problems. This additional information can range from specific handouts to workbooks such as Greenberger and Padesky (1995) which presents useful information and includes relevant exercises. A meta-analysis of the use of CBT bibliotherapy showed a clear benefit for this approach even in the absence of other interventions (Cuijpers, 1997).

## Daily activities

In addition to handing out the *Coping with Depression* manual early on in therapy, the therapist should also ask the client to complete an Activities Schedule for at least the first few weeks of therapy. In those cases where there has been a reduction in the usual activities, this can be quickly identified from the completed schedule. Exploration should then be made of what normal activities have been dropped and why this has occurred. For example, some people who are depressed believe that they would be a burden on other people and that they would spoil other people's fun; others think that there is no point in trying because they would not enjoy any of their former activities. Using this information, the therapist can identify a range of graded tasks that starts with the easiest one that the person is both most likely to succeed at and perhaps even enjoy. In cases where the person has become extremely inactive, one of the early aims of therapy should be to help the individual increase his or her activity levels. In very extreme cases, the depressed individual may perceive almost any activity or even physical movement as "too much effort." In such cases, it may first be necessary to focus on beliefs about effort, while encouraging the individual to practice small tasks that no longer seem to be carried out under automatic control, but have to be consciously controlled throughout; this situation may parallel a similar problem that is experienced in Chronic Fatigue Syndrome in which everyday physical and mental activities are perceived to be excessively effortful and therefore are no longer carried out (Lawrie, MacHale, Power, & Goodwin, 1997).

In the case of some depressed clients, it is not the reduction in activity that is the problem, but rather the excessive focus on one type of activity. A classic case is that of a workaholic whose waking hours are all spent in the pursuit of ambition and success, often of an unrealistic nature. In such cases, the Activities Schedule is full of so-called mastery items, combined with an absence of pleasurable activities. The focus on one dominant role or goal and the undervaluing of other roles and goals is, of course, a classic presentation in depression (Champion & Power, 1995), so the therapist may have to identify and explore long-held quasi-religious beliefs about the importance of such an approach. Indeed, the focus of therapy may become those schematic models that lead the person to exclude happiness or pleasure from day-to-day life.

## Monitoring thoughts and feelings

After the client has been recording daily activities for a week or two, it is then useful to introduce the idea of structured diaries (Greenberger & Padesky, 1995). The technique provides individuals with a new way of approaching and thinking about distressing situations because of the way in which they are taught to structure these experiences. With the collection of a number of such situations, the therapist and client may become aware of certain themes that may emerge from the material. The first column in a structured diary typically asks for a brief description of the situation that led up to the experience of distress. The second column asks the individual to list the emotions experienced in the situation; it can usefully include a percentage rating of the strength of the emotions so that the therapist can readily gauge exactly how distressing the situation was. The third column is designed for the recording of NATs that occurred in the situation. The identification of NATs is straightforward for some people with depression (and other emotional disorders) and within a week or two such individuals readily make the distinction between feelings and automatic thoughts.

However, some individuals need more practice before they can make the distinction, but it is important to continue the monitoring exercise until the distinction becomes clearer. Some individuals, even with practice, report that they have no thoughts to record and that the emotional reactions simply occur "out of the blue." We will return to this problem shortly.

Once clients have mastered the simpler three-column technique, the next step is to introduce a more complex monitoring form which expands the structured monitoring to five columns. The additional two columns require clients to find one or more alternative interpretations to the interpretation that is reflected in their automatic thoughts. Having found an alternative interpretation, the clients are then asked to re-rate their degree of belief in the original interpretation. We have also presented a more detailed diary record form that should also be used within the first few sessions of therapy (Power, 2010).

The crucial part of the five-column technique obviously depends on the clients' willingness to search for alternative interpretations for situations that they may have interpreted in a particular way for many years. It is well known from studies of reasoning that individuals (in whatever mood state) find it difficult to draw alternative conclusions when they have already reached a conclusion that is congenial with a current mental model and, indeed, many biases reflect the early termination of a search for conclusions when such an interpretation has been found (Kahneman, 2011; Wykes & Power, 1996). For example, if someone's currently dominant schematic model represents the self as a failure, then the interpretation of a situation as another instance of failing is congenial with this model and no alternatives will normally be sought. The converse occurs for someone whose dominant schematic model of the self is as a success, when situations will be readily interpreted to reflect instances of further success, even though such interpretations may not necessarily be accurate. Depressed clients may need considerable encouragement to search for alternative explanations to their favored conclusions in many situations. The therapist should carefully avoid being drawn in to dispute and argue against these cherished interpretations, but, instead, as Padesky (1994) has cogently argued, should try to use the process of guided discovery which enables clients themselves to identify alternatives, rather than the alternatives being thrust upon them.

One of the key problems that we noted above with the three- and the five-column technique is that clients sometimes report that emotions "come out of the blue" without any prior automatic thoughts. The early cognitive therapy view of this problem was that it was merely a matter of time and of practice before such clients would be able to identify their NATs. Such a strategy does, of course, run the risk that has sometimes been leveled against psychoanalytic therapies, namely, of bringing about the phenomenon rather than the phenomenon having genuine causal validity; that is, cognitive therapy clients might come to experience NATs, just as Freudian patients come to have Freudian dreams and Jungian patients come to have Jungian dreams. An alternative approach that we have spelled out in our SPAARS model is the possibility that some emotions really do come "out of the blue" (Power & Dalgleish, 2008). Although some emotional reactions follow the occurrence of conscious appraisals, there appear to be a number of phenomena that do not require such conscious processes (see Figure 7.2). In addition, we propose that emotions can also result from

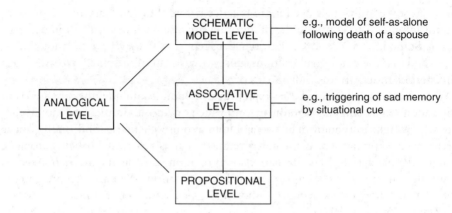

**Figure 7.2.**    The SPAARS Model of Emotion Showing Sadness-related Outcomes

automatic processes that occur outside of awareness; these automatic processes may be the consequence of the frequent repetition of particular appraisal–emotion sequences, such as the child who is shouted at repeatedly comes to be afraid of anyone shouting and this reaction continues into adulthood as an automatic reaction. In such cases, the best way forward is to explore where the reactions have originated rather than insist that the NATs are there, while, nevertheless, continuing to encourage the client to record as much information as possible about these automatic responses.

## Schematic models of self and others

One of the key aims of cognitive therapy is to explore the underlying assumptions that people have of themselves and of significant others in their lives. The continued monitoring of critical situations week to week in therapy will soon provide the therapist with clear indications of the themes underlying a particular client's difficulties, information that can be supplemented with assessments of attitudes such as using the Dysfunctional Attitudes Scale (Weissman & Beck, 1978) and the Schema Question-naire (Young, 1999). Let us imagine that we have a client, part of whose formulation is that he has a fear of success in competitive situations because of other people's envy that would ensue from winning. Exploration of the origins of this schematic model might indicate that the client's father reacted in a very overbearing manner whenever there was a competitive situation in which the client was involved. The client may also back down or appear to withdraw statements in therapy in order to avoid imagined conflict with the therapist. The therapist therefore accrues information from a variety of past and present situations, including the therapeutic relationship, which supports the existence of this key self-defeating schematic model which had a particular value in a previous significant relationship, but which unfortunately has been generalized now to cover all relationships that are perceived to be competitive. Having reached such clarity, the therapist has a variety of options all of which probably should be explored in parallel.

First, there may be a number of experiments that can be set as homework in which the client puts to the test his belief that any competitive situation will lead to destructive attacks from other individuals; thus, there are many situations in which, in theory, there is no limit on the number of winners or losers because the outcome is primarily dependent on the individual's own performance (e.g., taking a driving test).

Second, the therapist may also explore the client's thoughts and feelings where schematic models become obvious in therapy, for example, in an apparent conflict over who is right in therapy. The therapist can also use these situations in therapy as indications of past and present other relationships and how significant others might react in relation to the client's actions; in addition, the client's perceptions of how the other person really feels about him winning can also be explored (see Safran & Segal, 1990).

Third, the therapist can help the client restrict the range of applicability of the self–other schematic model, or, alternatively, may help the client to develop a more sophisticated and appropriate mental model of why his father related to him in the way he did (see Padesky, 1994). In fact, his father reacted badly toward *anyone's* success, not just the client's; his father covered up his own feelings of being a failure with attacks on other people's success, not only his son's. While the client had believed that he was the only one that his father had related to in this manner, when for the first time he began to talk to other relatives about his father's reactions, he realized that they all felt similar to the client, but were not prepared to fail in order to avoid his father's envy and destructive attacks.

This example illustrates that schematic models are complex, have their origins in the past, and typically relate the self and one or more significant others in a rigid repeating pattern (Power & Dalgleish, 2008). The themes involved in depression normally relate to issues of loss, failure, and shame. The self is viewed positively when an overinvested role or goal is being pursued successfully, for example, being the perfect wife or mother, the high-flying student, the executive who can deal with everything, or the would-be pop star who will finally get the recognition that she deserves. Unfortunately, the experience of events and difficulties that are a threat to such goals or roles leaves the person feeling worthless, unlovable, and shameful because the self-concept is so bound up with them and little or nothing else is seen to be of value.

## Termination issues, including relapse prevention

Issues related to termination may be more critical for individuals suffering from depression than for most other disorders because of the role that loss and abandonment plays in the onset of depression (Power, 2002). In addition, in short-term treatments such as CBT, the therapist may have had little or no opportunity to observe a client's reactions to natural breaks in therapy, such as those caused by vacations, which normally occur in longer-term treatments and provide invaluable clues about how the client deals with issues related to loss. In working with short-term therapies for depression, it is therefore essential that termination issues are considered early in therapy and that the therapist remains vigilant throughout. Of course, many short-term therapies have a prespecified number of sessions so that the client knows from the start the number of sessions involved. In other cases, however, the therapist may need to make some judgment about when the client is likely to be ready for the end of therapy. Such judgments must obviously take into account the client's own views; they may include some formal assessment of symptomatology and relevant cognitive variables; and they should also include a judgment of the extent to which the client has understood and been able to put the CBT model into practice. Casement's (1985) notion of the internalization of a positive model of the therapist also seems like a useful proposal that can be applied to any form of therapy. Clues that the client has internalized a model of the therapist can be gleaned, for example, when the client reports something along the following lines:

> I was just about to jump over the till in the supermarket on Friday and escape in a panic, when I suddenly thought to myself 'Oh, I wonder what my therapist would say to me now'. I then managed to calm down and continue with my shopping.

Such statements are, of course, powerful indicators that the client has an internal model of both the therapist and the skills of therapy, in that the model is being applied in critical situations (see also Power, 2012).

However, the real risk in short-term CBT for depression is that the therapy will merely have been palliative and would not have dealt with the high risk of relapse, which runs at approximately 50% over 2 years following recovery from depression (Hammen & Watkins, 2008). One of the tasks toward the end of CBT is therefore to develop potential relapse prevention measures with clients, which include the identification of and working through potential high-risk situations (Segal, Williams, & Teasdale, 2002). An additional focus of relapse prevention is the client's reactions to the situations. For example, if a client begins to feel miserable because of an upset at work, but then begins to worry that feeling moderately miserable means that serious long-term depression will inevitably follow, a vicious downward cycle will have begun that can pull the client further down into depression (see Teasdale, 1988). The focus of relapse prevention should therefore be on the possible events or situations that could lead to the client feeling miserable, and also on how the client reacts to such feelings when they occur (Segal et al., 2002). As we noted above, many individuals with emotional disorders have unrealistic beliefs about their emotional states in that they often want to rid themselves of feelings of anxiety, depression, or sadness, and live a future filled only with the experience of happiness. Relapse prevention must therefore emphasize to clients that living happily ever after only happens in fairytales, not in real life, and that our emotional reactions are as inherent and essential a part of us as the experience of physical pain.

Finally, on a more practical level, it is useful to include one or two "booster" sessions approximately 3 to 6 months after the end of therapy. These sessions allow a review of the successes and the problems that the client has faced since the end of therapy. They allow the therapist to assess how well the client has worked with the model without the support of therapy. Booster sessions also provide a tangible lifeline for the client at times when things feel difficult and may help the client to pull through without the need for additional professional intervention.

# New Developments and the Evaluation of CBT for Depression

Theory and practice in CBT continues to evolve and the last decade has seen the emergence of a number of "third generation" approaches, some of which have been applied in the treatment of depression. We will briefly review three new approaches: cognitive-behavioral analysis system of psychotherapy (CBASP), acceptance and commitment therapy (ACT), and emotion-focused cognitive therapy (EFCT).

## Cognitive-behavioral analysis system of psychotherapy

This approach to therapy was developed by McCullough (2000). The therapy takes interpersonal avoidance and problems in interpersonal functioning as its focus; thus, CBASP represents an interesting blend of both CBT and IPT approaches (see Chapter 9). The therapist's task is to help understand what previous trauma and interpersonal problems have led to the current interpersonal avoidance using analysis of significant interpersonal episodes. The building of interpersonal skills helps the client to function more optimally in interpersonal situations in a variety of family and work domains. A large RCT reported by Keller et al. (2000) in which CBASP was tested against an antidepressant showed significant benefit for chronic depression with both CBASP and medication combined.

## Acceptance and commitment therapy

This approach to psychotherapy was developed by Hayes, Strosahl, and Wilson (1999). The therapy emphasizes the use of mindfulness and acceptance in which the client is helped to experience previously avoided experiences in a flexible and safe manner. Cognitive defusion is used as a process whereby the proposed fusion between thought and behavior is loosened, so that behavior is not seen as inevitable from thought. The therapeutic approach is based on a theory called relational frame theory (RFT) that Hayes and colleagues have derived as a neo-Skinnerian associationist approach to language. If ACT were to be judged on its theory alone, then the approach would be an out-and-out failure; fortunately for its proponents, it does much better on the practical front with support, with a recent meta-analysis showing medium-to-large effective sizes for ACT in comparison to placebo control and other active treatments (Hayes, Luoma, Bond, Masuda, & Lillis, 2006).

## Emotion-focused cognitive therapy

Aspects of this therapy have been mentioned throughout this chapter, but a full presentation of the approach can be found in Power (2010). As shown in Figure 7.2, EFCT is based on the SPAARS approach to cognition and emotion in which two routes, the schematic model and the automatic routes, can run in parallel in the generation of emotion (Power & Dalgleish, 2008). The emotion system is built on the five basic emotions of anger, anxiety, sadness, disgust, and happiness, with complex emotions and mood states typically involving a combination of two or more basic emotions. For example, depression can result from a combination of sadness and self-disgust, though other combinations are also possible. The aim of the short-term therapy is to identify a problem-focus, which typically consists of an emotion, an interpersonal context, and the perceived problem.

## Evaluation of CBT

There have now been a number of meta-analytic reviews of the comparative effectiveness of CBT for depression that have clearly demonstrated the effectiveness of CBT (Dobson, 1989; Robinson, Berman, & Neimeyer, 1990; Reinecke, Ryan, & DuBois, 1998). These studies show a reduction in symptom severity across treatment by about two-thirds in comparison to pre-treatment depression levels. The meta-analysis by Reinecke et al. (1998) is of interest in that they demonstrated the effectiveness of CBT for the treatment of adolescent depression with effect sizes compared to controls of 1.02 at immediate post-treatment, and continuing at 0.61 at short-to-medium length follow-up (see Chapter 5). Laidlaw (2001) (see Chapter 21) has summarized the work to date with CBT for depression in older adults and reached the conclusion that CBT is probably efficacious, but that more large-scale studies are needed. A meta-analysis of psychotherapies for depression carried out by Cuijpers, van Straten, Andersson, and van Oppen (2008) examined 53 studies in which 7 major types of psychotherapy had been compared with other psychological treatments. The meta-analyses showed that all forms of psychotherapy were generally efficacious for treatment of depression in adults, though there was an indication that IPT was somewhat more efficacious ($d = 0.20$) and that nondirective supportive treatment was somewhat less efficacious ($d = -0.13$) than other treatments. There was also an indication that the dropout rate was higher in CBT than in other therapies. However, in the interpretation of these meta-analysis results we need to be mindful of two more recent meta-analyses also published by Cuijpers and colleagues. In the first, they reported that when the quality of an RCT is taken into account in the meta-analyses, they found only 11 studies that met the quality criteria and that these studies showed much smaller standardized effect sizes ($d = 0.22$) than the studies that were of poorer quality and did not meet the criteria ($d = 0.74$) (Cuijpers, van Straten, Bohlmeijer, Hollon, & Andersson, 2010b). The quality criteria included that participants met diagnostic criteria, there was manualized treatment, trained therapists, checked treatment integrity, randomization done by an independent party, blind assessors, intention-to-treat analyses, and $N$ greater than 50. A second meta-analysis reported by Cuijpers, Li, Hofmann, and Andersson (2010) compared self-reported versus clinician-rated depression outcome measures and found that significantly higher effect sizes were found with clinician-rated measures than with self-report, including those studies that used the two commonest measures, the Hamilton Rating Scale for Depression (HRSD) and the Beck Depression Inventory (BDI).

The American Psychological Association Task Force (see Crits-Christoph, 1998 for a revised summary) concluded that both CBT and IPT were well-established treatments for adult depression. The NICE (2009) depression guideline has suggested a so-called stepped-care approach be taken to support people with depression. This approach suggests the offer of CBT self-help for mild to moderately severe symptoms, and the offer of medication for moderate-to-severe depression. Antidepressants, however, are sometimes either not wanted or are not tolerated by patients because of side effects and drug interactions.

The results from these studies have, however, been overshadowed by the large-scale NIMH multisite study of cognitive therapy, IPT, imipramine, and placebo (Elkin et al., 1989). In this study, 250 patients with major depressive disorders were randomly assigned to one of the four treatment types at one of the three treatment centers. The immediate post-treatment results showed that there were no overall significant differences between any of the treatment types, the surprising comparison being that imipramine was no more effective than placebo. Only on a post hoc division of cases into moderate versus severe levels of depression did some effects emerge for the more severe group, with imipramine being clearly more effective than placebo and there being some possible benefits for IPT in comparison to placebo. More recent analyses of follow-up over 18 months have again shown surprisingly few significant comparisons, though there was some evidence that CBT was slightly more effective than imipramine or placebo in relation to a range of measures of relapse, need for further treatment, and length of time free of symptom (Shea et al., 1992). Perhaps one of the more interesting revelations from this large-scale study has been comments about *site* differences for the various therapies (Elkin, 1994); a more revealing analysis might, however, be of *therapist* differences rather than leaving the differences attributed to sites, though, understandably, individual therapists may wish to avoid such direct scrutiny. Perhaps one of the most intriguing of the subsequent analyses of this large dataset has been the recent study by Ablon and Jones (2002). In their analyses of therapy process in transcripts of CBT and IPT sessions, they developed a rating system of the "ideal CBT prototype" and the "ideal IPT prototype." They found, however, that *both* CBT and IPT corresponded more closely to the CBT prototype rather than the IPT prototype. Moreover, the better the correspondence to the CBT prototype the better the outcome for both types of therapy. Of course, this finding highlights many issues that have been long discussed about theory versus actual practice in therapy, with findings such as those going back to Sloane, Staples, Cristol, Yorkston, and Whipple (1975) that expert therapists of different therapy types are more similar to each other than predicted when the content of their therapy sessions is analyzed (see Holmes & Bateman, 2002, for a recent summary).

## Conclusions

The evidence to date for the effectiveness of CBT shows that CBT is clearly an effective treatment for depression and that it may be particularly beneficial for the prevention of relapse, especially with training in relapse-prevention strategies. The approach is now well established and may be the treatment of choice for many groups. Notwithstanding these strengths, however, there are a number of aspects of both the theory and the practice of CBT that can yet be improved. One important such area is that of the role of emotion in the therapy and the theoretical models of understanding cognition and emotion. Modern multilevel theories of emotion (Power & Dalgleish, 2008; Teasdale & Barnard, 1993) provide more sophisticated models on which to base CBT and, in the process, offer different implications for practice (Power, 2010). In addition, there is the continuing accumulation of evidence that good therapists of all persuasions may be more similar in their practice than bad therapists who simply follow textbook accounts of therapy. Future large-scale studies, such as those funded in the United States by NIMH, will provide unique opportunities to disentangle mechanisms of change common across therapies; these analyses will take us to the next level of evidence and beyond the mere percentage game that the current level of evidence provides.

# References

Ablon, J. S., & Jones, E. E. (2002). Validity of controlled clinical trials of psychotherapy: Findings from the NIMH Treatment of Depression Collaborative Research Program. *American Journal of Psychiatry, 159*, 775–783.

Alloy, L. B., & Abramson, L. Y. (1979). Judgment of contingency in depressed and non-depressed students: Sadder but wiser? *Journal of Experimental Psychology: General, 108*, 441–485.

Beck, A. T. (1976). *Cognitive therapy and the emotional disorders*. New York: Meridian.

Beck, A. T. (1983). Cognitive therapy of depression: New perspectives. In P. J. Clayton, & J. E. Barrett (Eds.), *Treatment of depression: Old controversies and new approaches*. New York: Raven Press.

Beck, A. T., Rush, A. J., Shaw, B. F., & Emery, G. (1979). *Cognitive therapy of depression: A treatment manual*. New York: Guilford Press.

Beck, A. T., Ward, C. H., Mendelsohn, M., Mock, J., & Erbaugh, J. (1961). An inventory for measuring depression. *Archives of General Psychiatry, 4*, 561–571.

Bibring, E. (1953). The mechanism of depression. In P. Greenacre (Ed.), *Affective disorders*. New York: International Universities Press.

Bowlby, J. (1980). *Attachment and loss, Vol. III. Loss: Sadness and depression*. Harmondsworth, UK: Penguin.

Brown, G. W., & Harris, T. O. (1978). *Social origins of depression: A study of psychiatric disorder in women*. London: Tavistock.

Casement, P. (1985). *On learning from the patient*. London: Tavistock.

Champion, L. A. (2000). Depression. In L. A. Champion, & M. J. Power (Eds.), *Adult psychological problems: An introduction* (2nd ed., pp. 29–54). Hove, UK: Psychology Press.

Champion, L. A., & Power, M. J. (1995). Social and cognitive approaches to depression: Towards a new synthesis. *British Journal of Clinical Psychology, 34*, 485–503.

Cheung, H. N., & Power, M. J. (2012). The development of a new multidimensional depression assessment scale: Preliminary results. *Clinical Psychology and Psychotherapy, 19*, 170–178.

Crits-Christoph, P. (1998). Training in empirically validated treatments: The Division 12 APA Task Force recommendations. In K. S. Dobson, & K. D. Craig (Eds.), *Empirically supported therapies: Best practice in professional psychology* (pp. 3–25). Thousand Oaks, CA: Sage.

Cuijpers, P. (1997). Bibliotherapy in unipolar depression: A meta-analysis. *Journal of Behavior Therapy and Experimental Psychiatry, 28*, 139–147.

Cuijpers, P., Li, J., Hofmann, S. G., & Andersson, G. (2010). Self-reported versus clinician-rated symptoms of depression as outcome measures in psychotherapy research on depression: A meta-analysis. *Clinical Psychology Review, 30*, 768–778.

Cuijpers, P., van Straten, A., Andersson, G., & van Oppen, P. (2008). Psychotherapy for depression in adults: A meta-analysis of comparative outcome studies. *Journal of Consulting and Clinical Psychology, 76*, 909–922.

Cuijpers, P., van Straten, A., Bohlmeijer, E., Hollon, S. D., & Andersson, G. (2010). The effects of psychotherapy for adult depression are overestimated: A meta-analysis of study quality and effect size. *Psychological Medicine, 40*, 211–223.

Dobson, K. S. (1989). A meta-analysis of the efficacy of cognitive therapy for depression. *Journal of Consulting and Clinical Psychology, 57*, 414–419.

Elkin, I. (1994). The NIMH treatment of depression collaborative research program: Where we began and where we are now. In A. E., Bergin, & S. L., Garfield (Eds.), *Handbook of psychotherapy and behavior change* (4th ed., pp. 114–135). New York: Wiley.

Elkin, I., Shea, T., Watkins, J. T., Imber, S. D., Sotsky, S. M., Collins, J. F., ... Parloff, M. B. (1989) National Institute of Mental Health treatment of Depression Collaborative Research Program. General effectiveness of treatments. *Archives of General Psychiatry, 46*, 971–982.

Fennell, M. J. V., & Teasdale, J. D. (1987). Cognitive therapy for depression: Individual differences and the process of change. *Cognitive Therapy and Research, 11*, 253–271.

Frank, J. D. (1982). Therapeutic components shared by all psychotherapies. In J. H. Harvey, & M. M. Parks (Eds.), *Psychotherapy research and behavior change* (pp. 9–37). Washington, DC: American Psychological Association.

Freud, S. (1917/1984). Mourning and melancholia. *Pelican Freud Library* (Vol.11). Harmondsworth, UK: Penguin.

Gilbert, P., & Leahy, R. L. (Eds.). (2007). *The therapeutic relationship in the cognitive behavioral psychotherapies*. London: Routledge.

Goodwin, F. K., & Jamison, K. R. (2007). *Manic-depressive illness: Bipolar disorders and recurrent depression* (2nd ed.). Oxford: Oxford University Press.

Greenberg, L. S., Rice, L. N., & Elliott, R. (1993). *Facilitating emotional change: The moment by moment process*. New York: Guilford Press.

Greenberger, D., & Padesky, C. (1995). *Mind over mood: A cognitive therapy treatment manual for clients*. New York: Guilford Press.

Haaga, D. A. F., Dyck, M. J., & Ernst, D. (1991). Empirical status of cognitive therapy of depression. *Psychological Bulletin, 110*, 215–236.

Hammen, C., & Watkins, E. (2008). *Depression* (2nd ed.). Hove, UK: Psychology Press.

Hayes, S. C., Luoma, J., Bond, F., Masuda, A., & Lillis, J. (2006). Acceptance and commitment therapy: Model, processes, and outcomes. *Behaviour Research and Therapy, 44*, 1–25.

Hayes, S. C., Strosahl, K. D., & Wilson, K. G. (1999). *Acceptance and commitment therapy: An experiential approach to behavior change*. New York: Guilford Press.

Holmes, J., & Bateman, A. (2002). *Integration in psychotherapy: Models and methods*. Oxford, UK: Oxford University Press.

Jackson, S. W. (1986). *Melancholia and depression: From hippocratic times to modern times*. New Haven, CT: Yale University Press.

Kahneman, D. (2011). *Thinking, fast and slow*. London: Penguin Books.

Keller, M. B., McCullough, J. P., Klein, D. N., Arnow, B., Dunner, D. L., Gelenberg, A. J., & Zajecka, J. (2000). A comparison of nefazodone, the cognitive behavioral-analysis system of psychotherapy, and their combination for the treatment of chronic depression. *New England Journal of Medicine, 342*, 1462–1470.

Kendall, P. C., Hollon, S. D., Beck, A. T., Hammen, C. L., & Ingram, R. E. (1987). Issues and recommendations regarding use of the Beck Depression Inventory. *Cognitive Therapy and Research, 11*, 289–300.

Laidlaw, K. (2001). An empirical review of cognitive therapy for late life depression: Does research evidence suggest adaptations are necessary for cognitive therapy with older adults? *Clinical Psychology and Psychotherapy, 8*, 1–14.

Lawrie, S. M., MacHale, S. M., Power, M. J., & Goodwin, G. M. (1997). Is the chronic fatigue syndrome best understood as a primary disturbance of the sense of effort? *Psychological Medicine, 27*, 995–999.

Lewinsohn, P. (1974). A behavioural approach to depression. In R. Friedman, & M. Katz (Eds.), *The psychology of depression: Contemporary theory and research* (pp. 157–185). New York: Winston-Wiley.

McCullough, J. P. (2000). *Treatment for chronic depression: Cognitive behavioral analysis system of psychotherapy.* New York: Guilford Press.

Nederhof, M.-J. (2009). *Dispute of a man with his ba.* http://www.cs.st-andrews.ac.uk/~mjn/egyptian/texts/corpus/pdf/Dispute.pdf. Accessed 21/1/13.

NICE. (2009). *Depression: The treatment and management of depression in adults.* London: NICE.

Padesky, C. A. (1994). Schema change processes in cognitive therapy. *Clinical Psychology and Psychotherapy, 1*, 267–278.

Power, M. J. (1999). Sadness and its disorders. In T. Dalgleish, & M. J. Power (Eds.), *Handbook of cognition and emotion* (pp. 497–520). Chichester, UK: Wiley.

Power, M. J. (2002). Integrative therapy from a cognitive-behavioural perspective. In J. Holmes, & A. Bateman (Eds.), *Integration in psychotherapy: Models and methods* (pp. 27–48). Oxford, UK: Oxford University Press.

Power, M. J. (2010). *Emotion-focused cognitive therapy.* Chichester, UK: Wiley-Blackwell.

Power, M. J. (2012). *Adieu to God: Why psychology leads to atheism.* Chichester, UK: Wiley-Blackwell.

Power, M. J., & Dalgleish, T. (2008). *Cognition and emotion: From order to disorder* (2nd ed.). Hove, UK: Psychology Press.

Reinecke, M. A., Ryan, N. E., & DuBois, D. L. (1998). Cognitive-behavioral therapy of depression and depressive symptoms during adolescence: A review and meta-analysis. *Journal of the American Academy of Child and Adolescent Psychiatry, 37*, 26–34.

Robinson, L. A., Berman, J. S., & Neimeyer, R. A. (1990). Psychotherapy for the treatment of depression: A comprehensive review of controlled outcome research. *Psychological Bulletin, 108*, 30–49.

Rutter, M. (1972). *Maternal deprivation reassessed.* Harmondsworth, UK: Penguin.

Safran, J. D., & Segal, Z. V. (1990). *Interpersonal process in cognitive therapy.* New York: Basic Books.

Segal, Z. V., Williams, J. M. G., & Teasdale, J. D. (2002). *Mindfulness-based cognitive therapy for depression.* New York: Guilford Press.

Seligman, M. E. P. (1975). *Helplessness: On depression, development and death.* San Francisco, CA: Freeman.

Shea, T. M., Elkin, I., Imber, S. D., Sotsky, S. M, Watkins, J. T., Collins, J. F., & Parloff, M. B. (1992). Course of depressive symptoms over follow-up: Findings from the National Institute of Mental Health Treatment of Depression Collaborative Research Program. *Archives of General Psychiatry, 49*, 782–787.

Sloane, R. B., Staples, F. R., Cristol, A. H., Yorkston, N. J., & Whipple, K. (1975). *Psychotherapy versus behavior therapy.* Cambridge, MA: Harvard University Press.

Teasdale, J. D. (1988). Cognitive vulnerability to persistent depression. *Cognition and Emotion, 2*, 247–274.

Teasdale, J., & Barnard, P. (1993). *Affect, cognition and change*. Hove, UK: Lawrence Erlbaum Associates.

Weishaar, M. (1993). *Aaron T. Beck*. London: Sage.

Weissman, A. N., & Beck, A. T. (1978, March). *Development and validation of the Dysfunctional Attitude Scale: A preliminary investigation*. Paper presented at the meeting of the American Educational Research Association, Toronto.

Wykes, T., & Power, M. J. (1996). The mental health of mental models and the mental models of mental health. In J. Oakhill, & A. Garnham (Eds.), *Mental models in cognitive science: Essays in honour of Phil Johnson-Laird* (pp. 197–222). Hove, UK: Psychology Press.

Young, J. E. (1999). *Cognitive therapy for personality disorders: A schema-focused approach* (3rd ed.). Sarasota, FL: Professional Resource Press.

# 8

# Interpersonal Psychotherapy of Depression

John C. Markowitz

Columbia University College of Physicians and Surgeons, USA
New York State Psychiatric Institute, USA

Interpersonal psychotherapy (IPT) is a time-limited, diagnosis-targeted, empirically tested treatment. Relative to most psychotherapies, it has been carefully studied, but until the last 15 years or so, relatively little practiced; most of its practitioners were researchers. The success of IPT in the treatment of outpatients with major depression has led to its testing for an expanded range of diagnostic indications and to its increasing clinical dissemination.

In our current era, both the empirical grounding of treatments and economic pressures on treatment have gained increasing importance, according greater stature to treatments like IPT. This has been reflected in a growing interest in clinical training in IPT and in treatment guidelines from several countries and professional organizations.

This chapter is intended for clinicians in the United Kingdom who are interested in exploring IPT as one of the available interventions for mood and other disorders. Readers should know that there is a British Interpersonal Psychotherapy Society (IPTUK; http://www.interpersonalpsychotherapy.org.uk) as well as an international one (http://www.interpersonalpsychotherapy.org). IPT training requirements for clinicians and supervisors have advanced farther in the United Kingdom than elsewhere in the world.

This chapter provides a brief overview of IPT for clinicians. For greater depth of discussion, the reader is referred to the IPT manual (Weissman, Markowitz, & Klerman, 2000, 2007) and the new Casebook for Interpersonal Psychotherapy (Markowitz & Weissman, 2012a).

## Background

Klerman, Weissman, and colleagues developed IPT as a treatment arm for a pharmacotherapy study of depression. They recognized that many outpatients in clinical practice received talking therapy as well as medication and felt that their study would gain face validity by including both modalities. They realized that they had no idea what psychotherapy was actually practiced in the surrounding offices of New England—as indeed we know little of what is presumably eclectic community practice today. Being

*The Wiley-Blackwell Handbook of Mood Disorders*, Second Edition. Edited by Mick Power.
© 2013 John Wiley & Sons, Ltd. Published 2013 by John Wiley & Sons, Ltd.

researchers, they developed a psychotherapy based on research data, as well as on existing interpersonal theory.

IPT is based on principles derived from psychosocial and life events research of depression, which has demonstrated connections between depression and complicated bereavement, role disputes (e.g., bad marriages), role transitions (meaningful life changes), and interpersonal deficits (social isolation). Life stressors can trigger depressive episodes in vulnerable individuals, and conversely depressive episodes impair psychosocial functioning, leading to further negative life events. In contrast, social supports protect against depression. IPT theory borrows from the post–World War II work of Adolph Meyer, Sullivan (1953), as well as the attachment theory of Bowlby (1973) and others. Sullivan, who popularized the term "interpersonal," emphasized that life events occurring after the early childhood years influenced psychopathology. This idea, which seems commonplace today, was radical in an era dominated by psychoanalysis, when the focus was almost exclusively on early childhood experiences. IPT uses this principle for practical, not etiological purposes. Without presuming to know the *cause* of a depressive episode, whose etiology is presumably multifactorial, IPT therapists pragmatically use the connection between current life events and onset of depressive symptoms to help patients understand and combat their episode of illness. They help patients to build social supports and develop social skills.

## Conducting IPT

IPT therapists use a few basic principles to explain the patient's situation and illness. These are simple enough that dysphoric patients with poor concentration can grasp them. First, they define depression as a *medical illness*, a treatable condition that is not the patient's fault. This definition displaces the burdensome guilt of depression from the patient to her illness, making the symptoms ego-dystonic and discrete. It also provides hope for a response to treatment. The therapist uses ICD-10 or DSM-IV (American Psychiatric Association, 1994) criteria to make the mood diagnosis, and rating scales such as the Hamilton Depression Rating Scale (HAM-D; Hamilton, 1960) or Beck Depression Inventory (BDI; Beck, 1978) to assess symptoms.

Indeed, the therapist temporarily gives the patient the "sick role" (Parsons, 1951), which helps the patient to recognize that he/she suffers from a common mood disorder with a predictable set of symptoms—not the personal failure, weakness, or character flaw that the depressed patient often believes is the problem. The sick role excuses the patient from what the illness prevents him or her from doing, but also obliges the patient to work as a patient in order to ultimately recover the lost healthy role. I have heard that in the United Kingdom (unlike the United States), clinicians hear the term "sick role" as a tainted term associated with long-term psychiatric disability. This is not at all its intended IPT connotation. On the contrary, the sick role is intended as a temporary role, coincident with the term of a time-limited treatment, to relieve self-blame while focusing the patient on a medical diagnosis. The time limit and brief duration of IPT, and the IPT therapist's frequent encouragement of the patient to take social risks and improve his or her situation, guard against regression and passivity.

A second IPT principle is to focus the treatment on an interpersonal crisis in the patient's life, a problem area connected to the patient's episode of illness. By solving an interpersonal problem—complicated bereavement, a role dispute or transition—the IPT patient can both improve his or her life situation and simultaneously relieve the symptoms of the depressive episode. Since randomized controlled outcome studies have repeatedly validated this coupled formula (Cuijpers et al., 2011), IPT can be offered with confidence and optimism equivalent to that accompanying an antidepressant prescription. This therapeutic optimism, while hardly specific to IPT, very likely provides part of its power in remoralizing the patient.

IPT is an eclectic therapy, using techniques seen in other treatment approaches. It uses the so-called common factors of psychotherapy (Frank, 1971). These include building a therapeutic alliance, helping the patient feel understood (through use of the medical disease model and relating mood to event), facilitation of affect, a rationale for improvement (if you fix your situation, your mood should improve), support and encouragement, a treatment ritual, and success experiences (viz, actual life changes). Its medical model of depressive illness is consistent with pharmacotherapy (and makes IPT highly compatible with medication in combination treatment). IPT shares role playing and a "here and now" focus with cognitive behavior therapy (CBT) and addresses interpersonal issues in a manner marital therapists would find familiar. It is not its particular techniques but its overall strategies that make IPT a unique and coherent approach. Although IPT overlaps to some degree with psychodynamic psychotherapies, and many of its early research therapists came from psychodynamic backgrounds, IPT meaningfully differs from them: it focuses on the present, not the past; on real life change rather than self-understanding; it employs a medical model; and it avoids exploration of the transference and genetic and dream interpretations (Markowitz, Svartberg, & Swartz, 1998). Like CBT, a time-limited treatment targeting a syndromal constellation (e.g., major depression), IPT is considerably less structured, assigns no explicit homework, and focuses on affect and interpersonal problem areas rather than automatic thoughts. Each of the four IPT interpersonal problem areas has discrete, if somewhat overlapping, goals for therapist and patient to pursue.

IPT techniques help the patient to pursue these interpersonal goals. The therapist repeatedly helps the patient relate life events to mood and other symptoms. These techniques include an *opening question*, which elicits an interval history of mood and events; *communication analysis*, the reconstruction and evaluation of recent, affectively charged life circumstances; *exploration of patient wishes and options*, in order to pursue these goals in particular interpersonal situations; *decision analysis*, to help the patient choose which options to employ; and *role playing*, to help patients prepare interpersonal tactics for real life.

IPT deals with current interpersonal relationships, focusing on the patient's immediate social context rather than on the past. The IPT therapist attempts to intervene in depressive symptom formation and social dysfunction rather than enduring aspects of personality. Indeed, it is difficult to accurately assess personality traits in the context of the state changes of an Axis I disorder such as a depressive episode (Hirschfeld et al., 1983). IPT builds new social skills (Weissman, Klerman, Prusoff, Sholomskas, & Padian, 1981), which may be as valuable as changing personality traits.

## Phases of treatment

Acute IPT treatment has three phases. The *first phase*, usually one to three sessions, involves diagnostic evaluation, psychiatric anamnesis, and setting the treatment framework. The therapist reviews symptoms, gives the patient a diagnosis as depressed, by standard criteria (e.g., ICD-10, DSM-IV), and gives the patient the "sick role." The psychiatric history includes the *interpersonal inventory*, which is not a structured instrument but a careful review of the patient's past and current social functioning and close relationships, their patterns, and mutual expectations. The therapist should gain a sense of who the patient is with other people, how he or she interacts with them, and how relationships may have contributed to or have been altered by the depressive episode. Depressed patients often have difficulty in asserting their needs, confronting others or getting angry effectively, and taking social risks. The therapist elicits changes in relationships proximal to the onset of symptoms: for example, the death of a loved one (potential complicated bereavement), children leaving home (a role transition), or worsening marital strife (a role dispute). Therapist and patient determine which relationships might be contributing to the depressed mood and which might provide important social support. The interpersonal inventory thus supplies a framework for understanding the social and interpersonal context in which the depressive symptoms occur and should lead to a treatment focus.

The therapist assesses the need for medication based on symptom severity, past illness history, treatment response, and patient preference, then provides psychoeducation by discussing the constellation of symptoms that define major depression, their psychosocial concomitants, and what the patient may expect from treatment. The therapist links the depressive syndrome to the patient's interpersonal situation in a formulation (Markowitz & Swartz, 2007) targeting one of four interpersonal problem areas: (1) *grief*, (2) interpersonal *role disputes*, (3) *role transitions*, or (4) *interpersonal deficits* (social isolation). With the patient's explicit acceptance of the formulation as the treatment focus, therapy enters the middle phase.

Any formulation necessarily simplifies a patient's complex situation. It is important nonetheless to keep antidepressant treatment focused on a simple theme that even a highly distractible depressed patient can grasp. When patients present with multiple interpersonal problems, the goal of formulation is to isolate one or at most two salient problems that are related (either as precipitant or consequence) to the patient's depressive episode. More than two foci mean an unfocused treatment. Choosing the focal problem area requires clinical acumen, although research has shown IPT therapists agree in choosing such areas (Markowitz et al., 2000), and patients find the foci credible.

In the *middle phase*, the IPT therapist follows strategies specific to the chosen interpersonal problem area. For **grief**—complicated bereavement following the death of a loved one—the therapist encourages the catharsis of mourning, exploring positive and negative feelings about the deceased and the lost relationship; as that affect is released, the therapist helps the patient to find new activities and relationships to compensate for the loss. For **role disputes**, which are overt or covert conflicts with a spouse, other family member, coworker, or close friend, the therapist helps the patient explore the relationship, the nature of the dispute, whether it has reached an impasse, and available options to resolve it. Improving the relationship tends to improve social supports, the patient's life, and his or her mood. Should these options fail, therapist and patient may conclude that the relationship has reached an impasse and consider ways to change or live with the impasse or to end the relationship.

A **role transition** is a change in life status defined by a life event: Beginning or ending a relationship or career, a geographic move, job promotion or demotion, retirement, graduation, or diagnosis of a medical illness. The patient learns to manage the change by mourning the loss of the old role while recognizing positive and negative aspects of the new role he or she is assuming, and taking steps to gain mastery over the new role. Frequently the new role, while undesired, is discovered to have previously unseen benefits. **Interpersonal deficits**, the residual fourth IPT problem area, is reserved for patients who lack one of the first three problem areas: that is, patients who report no recent life events. Poorly named, the category really means that the patient is presenting without the kind of defining recent life event on which IPT usually focuses. Interpersonal deficits indicate that the patient is usually quite socially isolated. It defines the patient as lacking social skills, including having problems in initiating or sustaining relationships, and focuses on helping the patient to develop new relationships and skills. Some, if not most, patients who might fall into this category suffer from dysthymic disorder, for which separate strategies have been developed (Markowitz, 1998).

IPT sessions address current, "here and now" problems rather than childhood or developmental issues. Each session after the first begins with the question: "How have things been since we last met?" This focuses the patient on recent mood and events, which the therapist helps the patient to connect. The therapist provides empathic support for the patient's suffering, but takes an active, non-neutral, supportive, and hopeful stance to counter depressive pessimism. The therapist asks what feelings an interpersonal encounter has evoked, normalizing them, and asking what the patient wanted to happen in that situation. Blaming the depressive disorder and the patient's social situation for the patient's distress, the therapist elicits options that the patient has to change his or her life in positive ways in order to resolve the focal interpersonal problem, and options that the depressive episode may have kept the patient from seeing or exploring fully.

Simply understanding the situation does not suffice: Therapists stress the need for patients to test these options in order to improve their lives and simultaneously treat their depressive episodes. They role-play the options to rehearse the patient's social skills. If the patient tries out a new approach and it goes well, the therapist provides congratulations and reinforces the patient's new social capacity. If things go badly, the therapist offers empathy, gives the patient credit for trying, blames the situation or other person when appropriate, and helps the patient to explore further options for change. It can be seen why this focus on interpersonal functioning might build social skills and lead the patient to make meaningful life changes in a relatively brief treatment interval.

The *final phase* of IPT occupies the last few sessions of acute treatment (or the last months of a maintenance phase). Here the therapist's goal is to build the patient's newly regained sense of independence and competence by having him or her recognize and consolidate therapeutic gains. The therapist anchors self-esteem by elucidating how the patient's depressive episode has improved because of the changes the patient has made in his or her life situation and in resolving the interpersonal problem area ("Why do you think you're feeling so much better? . . . It's impressive what you've accomplished!")—at a time when the patient had felt weak and impotent. The therapist helps the patient to anticipate depressive symptoms that might arise in the future and their potential triggers and remedies. Relative to psychodynamic psychotherapy, IPT de-emphasizes termination, seeing it as simply a graduation from successful treatment. The therapist helps the patient see the sadness of parting as a normal interpersonal response to separation, distinct from depressive feelings. If the patient has not improved, the therapist emphasizes that it is the treatment that has failed, not the patient, and that alternative effective treatment options exist. This is analogous to a failed pharmacotherapy trial; if one treatment fails, it is the illness rather than the patient who is resistant, and thankfully other treatment options remain. Patients who respond to IPT, but whose multiple prior depressive episodes leave them at high risk for recurrence, may contract for maintenance therapy as acute treatment draws to a close. Another strength of IPT is that its maintenance form has also demonstrated efficacy in rigorous trials.

## IPT for Unipolar Mood Disorders: Efficacy and Adaptations

The history of IPT has been a sequence of manual-based clinical trials, often adapting IPT to the particular psychosocial problems and needs of the target treatment population. These studies have repeatedly demonstrated its efficacy for major depressive disorder in various patient populations across the life span and are supported by two meta-analyses (Cuijpers et al., 2011; de Mello, de Jesus Mari, Bacaltchuk, Verdeli, & Neugebauer, 2005).

### Acute treatment of major depression

The first acute study of IPT was a four-cell, 16-week randomized trial comparing IPT, amitriptyline (AMI), combined IPT and AMI, and a nonscheduled control treatment for 81 outpatients with major depression (DiMascio et al., 1979; Weissman et al., 1979). AMI more rapidly alleviated symptoms, but at treatment completion, IPT and AMI did not differ in symptom reduction. Each reduced symptoms more efficaciously than the control condition, and combined AMI–IPT was more efficacious than either active monotherapy. Patients with psychotic depression did poorly on IPT alone. One-year follow up found that many patients remained improved after the brief IPT intervention. Moreover, IPT patients had developed significantly better psychosocial functioning at 1 year, whether or not they received medication. This effect on social function was not found for AMI alone, nor was it evident for IPT immediately after the 16-week trial (Weissman et al., 1981).

The ambitious, multisite National Institute of Mental Health Treatment of Depression Collaborative Research Program (NIMH TDCRP; Elkin et al., 1989) randomly assigned 250 outpatients with major depression to 16 weeks of IPT, CBT, or either imipramine (IMI) or placebo plus clinical management. Most subjects completed at least 15 weeks or 12 sessions. Mildly depressed patients (17-item HAM-D score <20) showed equal improvement in all treatments. For more severely depressed patients (HAM-D ≥ 20), IMI worked fastest and most consistently outperformed placebo. IPT fared comparably to IMI on several outcome measures, including HAM-D, and was superior to placebo for more severely depressed patients. This study's great surprise was that CBT was not superior to placebo (albeit not significantly worse than IPT or IMI) among more depressed patients. Reanalyzing the NIMH TDCRP data using the Johnson–Neyman technique, Klein and Ross (1993) found "medication superior to psychotherapy, [and] the psychotherapies somewhat superior to placebo... particularly among the symptomatic and impaired patients" (p. 241), and "CBT relatively inferior to IPT for patients with BDI scores greater than approximately 30, generally considered the boundary between moderate and severe depression" (p. 247).

Shea et al. (1992) conducted an 18-month naturalistic follow-up study of TDCRP patients and found no significant differences in recovery among remitters (who had responded with minimal or no symptoms by end of treatment, sustained during follow up) across the four treatments. Overall, 26% of IPT, 30% of CBT, 19% of IMI, and 20% of placebo subjects who had acutely remitted remained in remission 18 months later. Among acute remitters, relapse over the 18 months was 33% for IPT, 36% for CBT, 50% for IMI (medication having been stopped at 16 weeks), and 33% for placebo. The authors concluded that 16 weeks of specific treatments were insufficient to achieve full and lasting recovery for many patients.

Blom et al. (2007) randomized 193 patients with major depression to 12–16 weeks of treatment with IPT, nefazodone plus clinical management, combined IPT/nefazodone, or IPT plus pill placebo. All treatments appeared effective and no differences emerged on the HAM-D. On the Montgomery–Asberg Depression Rating Scale (MADRS), however, combined IPT/nefazodone reduced symptoms more effectively than nefazodone alone, but not more than the other IPT conditions.

## Maintenance treatment

IPT was first developed and tested in an eight-month, six-cell study (Klerman, DiMascio, Weissman, Prusoff, & Paykel, 1974; Markowitz & Weissman, 2012b; Paykel, DiMascio, Haskell, & Prusoff, 1975). Today this study would be considered "continuation" treatment, as the concept of maintenance antidepressant treatment has lengthened. In total, 150 acutely depressed women outpatients who responded (with ≥50% symptom reduction rated by a clinical interviewer) to 4–6 weeks of AMI were randomly assigned to receive 8 months of weekly IPT alone, AMI alone, placebo alone, combined IPT–AMI, IPT–placebo, or no pill. Randomization to IPT or a low contact psychotherapy condition occurred at entry into the continuation phase, followed by randomization to medication, placebo, or no pill occurred at the end of the second month of continuation. Maintenance pharmacotherapy prevented relapse and symptom exacerbation, whereas IPT improved social functioning (Weissman, Klerman, Paykel, Prusoff, & Hanson, 1974). Effects of IPT on social functioning were not apparent for 6–8 months and combined psychotherapy–pharmacotherapy had the best outcome.

Several studies in Pittsburgh, Pennsylvania, have assessed longer antidepressant maintenance trials of IPT. Frank et al. (1990) and Frank, Kupfer, Wagner, McEachran, and Cornes (1991) studied 128 outpatients with multiply, rapidly recurrent depression. Patients who had on average seven episodes of major depression were initially treated with combined high dose IMI (>200 mg/day) and weekly IPT. Responders remained on high dosage medication while IPT was tapered to a monthly frequency during a 4-month continuation phase. Patients remaining remitted were then randomly assigned to 3 years of either: (1) ongoing high dose IMI plus clinical management; (2) high dose IMI plus monthly IPT; (3) monthly IPT alone; (4) monthly IPT plus placebo; or (5) placebo plus clinical management. High dose IMI, with or without maintenance IPT, was the most efficacious treatment, protecting more than 80% of patients over 3 years. In contrast, most patients on placebo relapsed within the first few months. Once-monthly IPT, while less efficacious than medication, was statistically and clinically superior to placebo in this high-risk patient population. Reynolds et al. (1999) essentially replicated these maintenance findings in a study of geriatric patients with major depression comparing IPT and nortriptyline. It is notable that both of these studies used unusually high doses (i.e., maintenance of acute levels, rather than a dosage taper) of antidepressant medications while employing the lowest ever (albeit only ever) monthly maintenance dosage of a psychotherapy.

The modal depressed patient is a woman of childbearing age, and many depressed pregnant or nursing women prefer to avoid pharmacotherapy. Frank and colleagues (1990) found that an 82-week survival time without recurrence with monthly maintenance IPT alone would suffice to protect many women with recurrent depression through pregnancy and nursing without medication.

It is easy to misinterpret the comparison of high-dose tricyclic antidepressants to low-dose monthly IPT (IPT-M) in both the early maintenance studies. First, it should be noted that no patients in this study received only medication or IPT: Even patients in the "medication only" maintenance phase had received a longer course of acute and continuation IPT than most patients ever get. Second, had the tricyclics been lowered comparably to the reduced psychotherapy dosage, as had been the case in earlier antidepressant medication maintenance trials, recurrence in the medication groups might well have been greater. Meanwhile, there were no precedents for dosing maintenance psychotherapy, for which the choice of a monthly interval for IPT-M was reasonable, and indeed somewhat clinically beneficial. For less severely recurrent major depression, or at somewhat higher IPT doses, how might maintenance IPT fare? In a follow-up study, Frank et al. (2007) found no difference among frequency of weekly, fortnightly, and monthly maintenance IPT doses; all tended to preserve acute gains in depressed women.

## Geriatric depressed patients

IPT was initially used to augment a pharmacotherapy trial of geriatric patients with major depression to enhance compliance and to provide some treatment for the placebo control group (Rothblum, Sholomskas, Berry, & Prusoff, 1982; Sholomskas, Chevron, Prusoff, & Berry, 1983). Investigators noted that grief and role transition specific to aging were the prime interpersonal treatment foci. These researchers suggested modifying IPT to include more flexible duration of sessions, more use of practical advice and support (e.g., arranging transportation, calling physicians), and recognizing that major role changes (e.g., divorce at age 75) may be impractical and detrimental. The 6-week trial compared standard IPT to nortriptyline in 30 geriatric depressed patients. Results showed some advantages for IPT, largely due to higher attrition from side effects in the medication group (Sloane, Stapes, & Schneider, 1985).

Reynolds et al. (1999) conducted a 3-year maintenance study for geriatric patients with recurrent depression in Pittsburgh using IPT and nortriptyline in a design similar to the Frank et al. (1990) study. The IPT manual was modified to allow greater flexibility in session length under the assumption that some elderly patients might not tolerate 50-min sessions. The authors found older patients needed to address early life relationships in psychotherapy in addition to the usual "here and now" IPT focus. The study treated 187 patients, aged 60 years or older, with recurrent major depression using combination of IPT and nortriptyline. The 107 who acutely remitted and then achieved recovery after continuation therapy were randomly assigned to one of four 3-year maintenance conditions: (1) medication clinic with nortriptyline alone, with steady-state nortriptyline plasma levels maintained in a therapeutic window of 80–120 ng/ml; (2) medication clinic with placebo; (3) monthly maintenance IPT with placebo; or (4) IPT-M plus nortriptyline. Recurrence rates were 20% for combined treatment, 43% for nortriptyline alone, 64% for IPT with placebo, and 90% for placebo alone. Each monotherapy was statistically superior to placebo, whereas combined therapy was superior to IPT alone and had a trend for superiority over medication alone. Patients aged 70 years or older were more likely to have a depressive recurrence and to do so more quickly than patients in their sixties. This study corroborated the maintenance results of Frank and colleagues, except that in this geriatric trial, combined treatment had advantages over pharmacotherapy alone as well as psychotherapy alone.

In subsequent studies, Reynolds et al. (2010, 2006) found that maintenance IPT was not helpful for depressed patients aged 70 years and older, whereas maintenance serotonin reuptake inhibitors were. Cognitive dysfunction in old-old patients may account for this.

## Depressed adolescents (IPT-A)

Mufson, Moreau, and Weissman (1993) modified IPT to address developmental issues of adolescence, including family and school contacts. The researchers conducted an open feasibility trial before completing a controlled 12-week clinical trial comparing IPT-A to clinical monitoring in 48 clinic-referred, 12- to 18-year-old patients who met DSM-III-R criteria for major depressive disorder. Thirty-two patients completed the protocol (21 IPT-A, 11 controls). Patients who received IPT-A reported significantly greater improvement in depressive symptoms and social functioning, including interpersonal functioning and problem-solving skills. In the intent-to-treat sample, 75% of IPT-A patients met the criterion for recovery (HAM-D score $\leq 6$) compared to 46% of controls (Mufson, Weissman, Moreau, & Garfinkel, 1999). Mufson et al. (2004) then conducted a trial of IPT-A in a large-scale effectiveness study in school-based clinics, showing its superiority to usual school-based treatment, and is piloting it in a group format for depressed adolescents.

Rossello and Bernal compared 12 weeks of randomly assigned IPT ($n = 22$), CBT ($n = 25$), and a waiting list control condition ($n = 24$) for adolescents aged 13–18 years in Puerto Rico who met DSM-III-R criteria for major depression, dysthymia, or both. The investigators did not use Mufson's IPT-A modification. Both IPT and CBT were more efficacious than the waiting list in improving adolescents' self-rated depressive symptoms. IPT was more efficacious than CBT in increasing self-esteem and social adaptation (effect size for IPT $= 0.73$, for CBT $= 0.43$) (Rossello & Bernal, 1999).

## Depressed medically ill patients

Recognizing that medical illness is the kind of serious life event that might lend itself to IPT treatment, Markowitz, Klerman, Perry, Clougherty, and Mayers (1992) modified IPT for depressed HIV patients (IPT-HIV), emphasizing common issues among this population including concerns about illness and death, grief and role transitions. Formulations emphasized that patients had two medical illnesses, of which depression was the more easily treatable. A pilot open trial found that 21 of the 24 depressed patients responded. In a 16-week controlled study, 101 subjects were randomized to IPT-HIV, CBT, supportive psychotherapy (SP), or IMI plus SP (Markowitz et al., 1998). All treatments were associated with symptom reduction, but IPT and IMI–SP produced symptomatic and functional improvement significantly greater than CBT or SP. These results recall those of more severely depressed subjects in the NIMH TDCRP study (Elkin et al., 1989). Many HIV-positive patients responding to treatment reported improvement of neurovegetative physical symptoms that they had mistakenly attributed to HIV infection. A recent study of telephone IPT for rural depressed HIV-positive individuals also found benefits for IPT (Ransom et al., 2008).

## Primary care

Many depressed individuals will accept medical but not mental health treatment. Schulberg and colleagues compared IPT with nortriptyline pharmacotherapy for depressed ambulatory medical patients in a primary care setting (Schulberg & Scott, 1991; Schulberg, Scott, Madonia, & Imber, 1993). IPT was integrated into the routine of the primary care center: Nurses took vital signs before each session, and if patients were medically hospitalized, IPT was continued in the hospital when possible.

Patients with current major depression ($n = 276$) were randomly assigned to IPT, nortriptyline, or primary care physicians' usual care (UC). They received 16 weekly sessions followed by 4 monthly sessions of IPT (Schulberg et al., 1996). Depressive symptoms improved more rapidly with IPT or nortriptyline than in UC. About 70%

of treatment completers receiving nortriptyline or IPT recovered after 8 months, compared to 20% in UC. This study, which brought mental health treatment into medical clinics, was oddly designed for treatment in the United States but might inform treatment in the United Kingdom, where a greater proportion of antidepressant treatments are delivered in primary care settings.

In the study by Brown, Schulberg, Madonia, Shear, and Houck (1996), subjects with a lifetime history of comorbid panic disorder had a poor response across treatments compared to those with major depression alone. Frank et al. (2000) later corroborated these predictive findings on comorbid panic disorder. Meanwhile, several samples (Mossey, Knott, Higgins, & Talerico, 1996; Neugebauer et al., 2006; van Schaik et al., 2006) but not all depressed medically ill patients have responded to IPT: A study with cardiac patients was negative (Lesperance et al., 2007).

## Conjoint IPT for depressed patients with marital disputes (IPT-CM)

It is well established that marital conflict, separation, and divorce can precipitate or complicate depressive episodes (Rounsaville, Weissman, Prusoff, & Herceg-Baron, 1979). Some clinicians have feared that individual psychotherapy for depressed patients in marital disputes can lead to premature rupture of marriages (Gurman & Kniskern, 1978). To test and address these concerns, Klerman and Weissman (1993) developed an IPT manual for conjoint therapy of depressed patients with marital disputes. Both spouses participate in all sessions, and treatment focuses on the current marital dispute. Eighteen patients with major depression linked to the onset or exacerbation of marital disputes were randomly assigned to 16 weeks of either individual IPT or IPT-CM. Patients in both treatments showed similar improvement in depressive symptoms, but patients receiving IPT-CM reported significantly better marital adjustment, marital affection, and sexual relations than did individual IPT patients (Foley, Rounsaville, Weissman, Sholomskas, & Chevron, 1989). These pilot findings require replication in a larger sample and with other control groups.

## Antepartum/postpartum depression

Pregnancy and the postpartum period are times of heightened depressive risk when patients may wish to avoid pharmacotherapy. Moreover, treating depressed mothers may protect the mental health of their children (Markowitz, 2008; Swartz et al., 2006, 2008).

Spinelli at Columbia University used IPT to treat women with antepartum depression. Pregnancy is a role transition that involves the depressed pregnant woman's self-evaluation as a parent, physiologic changes of pregnancy, and altered relationships with the spouse or significant other and with other children. Spinelli added "complicated pregnancy" as a fifth potential interpersonal problem area. Session timing and duration are adjusted for bed rest, delivery, obstetrical complications, and childcare, and postpartum mothers may bring children to sessions. As with depressed HIV-positive patients, therapists use telephone sessions and hospital visits as necessary (Spinelli, 1997). In a controlled clinical trial, 16 weeks of acute IPT and 6 monthly follow-up sessions were superior to a didactic parent education group for depressed pregnant women (Spinelli & Endicott, 2003).

O'Hara, Stuart, Gorman, and Wenzel (2000) compared 12 weeks of IPT with a waiting list for 120 women with postpartum depression. The investigators assessed both the mothers' symptom states and their interactions with their infants (Stuart & O'Hara, 1995). In the IPT group, 38% met HAM-D and 44% met BDI remission criteria, whereas remission on each measure in the waiting list control group was 14%. Overall, 60% of IPT patients and 16% of controls reported more than a 50% BDI improvement. Postpartum women receiving IPT also improved significantly on social adjustment measures relative to the control group.

Klier, Muzik, Rosenblum, and Lenz (2001) adapted IPT to a 9-week, 90-min group format and treated 17 women with postpartum depression. Scores on the 21-item HAM-D fell from 19.7 to 8.0, suggesting efficacy. Still more intriguingly, Zlotnick, Johnson, Miller, Pearlstein, and Howard (2001) treated 37 women at risk for postpartum depression with either four 60-min sessions of an IPT-based group approach or usual treatment. This preventive application resembles a group form of interpersonal counseling (IPC, Klerman et al., 1987), a simplified version of IPT. Six of 18 women in the control condition, but none of 17 in the interpersonal group, developed depression 3 months postpartum.

In other small studies, IPT has shown benefits for women with depressive symptoms post miscarriage (Neugebauer et al., 2006) and with women confronting infertility.

## Dysthymic disorder (IPT-D)

IPT was modified for dysthymic disorder, a disorder less responsive than major depression to all antidepressants, and whose chronicity does not fit the standard IPT model. This adaptation also may provide a better fit for dysthymic patients without acute life events who previously would have been put in the interpersonal deficits category of acute IPT. IPT-D encourages patients to reconceptualize what they have considered lifelong character flaws as egodystonic, chronic mood-dependent symptoms; as chronic but treatable "state" rather than immutable "trait." Therapy itself was defined as an "iatrogenic role transition," from believing oneself flawed in personality to recognizing and treating the mood disorder. Markowitz (1994, 1998) openly treated 17 pilot subjects with 16 sessions of IPT-D, of whom none worsened and 11 remitted. Medication benefits many dysthymic patients (Kocsis et al., 1988; Thase et al., 1996), but nonresponders may need psychotherapy, and even medication responders may benefit from combined treatment (Markowitz, 1994).

Based on these pilot results, Markowitz, Kocsis, Bleiberg, Christos, and Sacks (2005) treated 94 subjects with "pure" dysthymic disorder (i.e., no major depressive episode within the past 6 months) with 16 weeks of randomly assigned IPT-D alone, supportive therapy (SP), sertraline plus clinical management, or combined IPT/sertraline cell. All groups showed improvement, but sertraline cells yielded better outcomes than psychotherapies alone. Response rates were 58% for sertraline alone, 57% for combined treatment, 35% for IPT, and 31% for SP. In a pilot trial ($N = 26$) comparing IPT to SP for chronically depressed patients with comorbid alcohol abuse/dependence, IPT showed advantages in treating chronic depression but no advantage for comorbid alcoholism compared to supportive therapy (Markowitz, Kocsis, Christos, Bleiberg, & Carlin, 2008).

Browne et al. (2002) at McMaster University in Hamilton, Canada, treated more than 700 dysthymic patients in the community with 12 sessions of standard IPT over 4 months, sertraline for 2 years, or their combination. Patients were followed for 2 years. Based on an improvement criterion of at least a 40% reduction in MADRS score at 1 year follow-up, 51% of IPT-alone subjects improved, fewer than the 63% taking sertraline and 62% in combined treatment. On follow-up, however, IPT was associated with significant economic savings in use of health care and social services. Combined treatment was thus most cost-effective, equally efficacious to but less expensive than sertraline alone.

In a comparison of medication to combined treatment, de Mello, Myczowisk, and Menezes (2001) randomly assigned 35 dysthymic outpatients to moclobemide with or without 16 weekly sessions of IPT. Both groups improved, but with a nonsignificant trend for greater improvement on the HAM-D and MADRS in the combined treatment group.

The chronicity of dysthymic disorder and other forms of chronic depression make them more difficult to treat with both medication and psychotherapy. Chronic depression may be an indication for combining pharmacotherapy with IPT: the former relieves symptoms while the latter helps patients rehabilitate their social functioning (Markowitz, 1993; Rush & Thase, 1999).

### Subsyndromally depressed hospitalized elderly patients

Recognizing that subthreshold symptoms for major depression impeded recovery of hospitalized elderly patients, Mossey et al. (1996) conducted a trial using IPC (Klerman et al., 1987), a simplification of IPT. Nonpsychiatric nurses treated geriatric, medically hospitalized patients with minor depressive symptoms for ten 1-hour sessions flexibly scheduled to accommodate the patient's medical status. Seventy-six hospitalized patients aged 60 years and older who had subsyndromal depressive symptoms on two consecutive assessments were randomly assigned to either IPC or UC. A euthymic, untreated control group was also followed. Patients found IPC feasible and tolerable. Three-month assessment showed nonsignificantly greater improvement in depressive symptoms and on all outcome variables for IPC relative to UC, whereas controls showed mild symptomatic worsening. In the IPC and euthymic control groups, rates of rehospitalization were similar (11–15%), and significantly less than the subsyndromally depressed group receiving UC (50%). Differences between IPC and UC became statistically significant after 6 months on depressive symptoms and self-rated health, but not physical or social functioning. The investigators felt 10 sessions did not suffice for some patients, and that maintenance IPC might have been useful.

## Other Applications

The success of IPT in treatment of unipolar mood disorders has led to its expansion to treat other psychiatric disorders. Frank and colleagues in Pittsburgh have demonstrated the benefits of a behaviorally modified version of IPT as a treatment adjunctive to pharmacotherapy for bipolar disorder (Frank et al., 2005; Miklowitz et al., 2007).

Furthermore, IPT is increasingly being applied to a range of non-mood disorders. There are intriguing applications of IPT as treatment for bulimia (Agras, Walsh, Fairburn, Wilson, & Kraemer, 2000; Fairburn, Jones, Peveler, Hope, & O'Connor, 1993; Wilfley et al., 1993; Wilfley, MacKenzie, Welch, Ayres, & Weissman, 2000) and anorexia nervosa, social phobia (Lipsitz, Markowitz, Cherry, & Fyer, 1999), post-traumatic stress disorder (Bleiberg & Markowitz, 2005; Krupnick et al., 2008), and other conditions. Life events, the substrate of IPT, are ubiquitous, but how useful it is to focus on them may vary from disorder to disorder. There have been negative trials of IPT for substance disorders (Carroll, Rounsaville, & Gawin, 1991; Markowitz et al., 2008; Rounsaville, Glazer, Wilber, Weissman, & Kleber, 1983), and it seems unlikely that an outwardly focused treatment such as IPT would be useful for such an internally focused diagnosis as obsessive compulsive disorder. In continuing the IPT tradition, clinical outcome research should determine utility. IPT is also being modified for use in other formats, for example, as group therapy (Klier, Muzik, Rosenblum, & Lenz, 2001; Wilfley et al., 1993, 2000; Zlotnick et al., 2001) and as a telephone intervention (e.g., Neugebauer et al., 2006). Weissman (1995) developed an IPT patient guide with worksheets for depressed readers that may be used in conjunction with IPT.

In summary, IPT is one of the best tested psychotherapies, particularly for mood disorders: It has repeatedly demonstrated efficacy as both an acute and maintenance monotherapy and as a component of combined treatment for major depressive disorder. It appears beneficial for other mood and non-mood syndromes, although evidence for these is sparser. As monotherapy with either IPT or pharmacotherapy is likely to successfully treat most patients with major depression, combined treatment should be reserved for more severely or chronically ill patients (Rush & Thase, 1999). How best to combine time-limited psychotherapy with pharmacotherapy is an exciting area for future research: when is it indicated, in what sequence, and for which patients.

Comparative trials have begun to reveal moderating factors that predict treatment outcome. The NIMH Treatment of Depression Collaborative Research Program, which compared IPT and CBT, suggested factors that might predict better outcome with either IPT or CBT. Sotsky et al. (1991) found that depressed patients with low baseline social dysfunction responded well to IPT, whereas those with severe social deficits (probably reflecting the "interpersonal deficits" problem area) responded less well. Greater symptom severity and difficulty in concentrating responded poorly to CBT. Initial severity of major depression and of impaired functioning responded best in that study to IPT and to IMI. IMI worked most efficaciously for patients with difficulty functioning at work, reflecting its faster onset of action. Patients with atypical depression responded better to IPT or CBT than to IMI or placebo (Shea, Elkin, & Sotsky, 1999).

Barber and Muenz (1996), studying TDCRP completers, found IPT more efficacious than CBT for patients with obsessive personality disorder, whereas CBT fared better for avoidant personality disorder. This finding did not hold for the intent to treat sample. The degree to which patients resolved their interpersonal problem area (e.g., role dispute) appears to correlate with symptom remission (Markowitz, Bleiberg, Christos, & Levitan, 2006). Biological factors, such as abnormal sleep profiles on EEG, predicted significantly poorer response to IPT than for patients with normal sleep parameters (Thase et al., 1997). Frank et al. (1991) found that psychotherapist adherence to a focused IPT approach may enhance outcome. Moreover, sleep EEG and adherence, the first a biological and the latter a psychotherapy factor, had additive effects in that study. Replication and further elaboration of these predictive factors deserve ongoing study.

Another exciting development is the use of neuroimaging to compare IPT and pharmacotherapy outcomes. Martin, Martin, Rai, Richardson, and Royall (2001), in Sunderland, using SPECT, found that IPT and venlafaxine had overlapping but also differing effects on right posterior cingulate (IPT), right posterior temporal (venlafaxine), and right basal ganglia activation (both treatments). Brody et al. (2001) in Los Angeles reported roughly analogous findings using PET scanning of patients treated with IPT and paroxetine.

# Training

Until fairly recently, IPT was well studied but delivered almost entirely by research study therapists. As the research base of IPT grew and it became included in treatment guidelines, clinical demand for this empirically supported treatment swelled. IPT training is now increasingly included in professional workshops and conferences, with training courses conducted at university centers in the United Kingdom, Canada, continental Europe, Asia, New Zealand, and Australia in addition to the United States. An International Society for Interpersonal Psychotherapy (ISIPT; http://www.interpersonalpsychotherapy.org) now holds regular meetings. IPT is taught in a still small but growing number of psychiatric residency training programs in the United States (Lichtmacher, Eisendrath, & Haller, 2006; Markowitz, 1995) and has been included in family practice and primary care training. It was not, however, included in a mandate for psychotherapy proficiency of US psychiatric residency programs, as CBT was.

The principles and practice of IPT are straightforward. Yet, any psychotherapy requires innate therapeutic ability, and IPT training requires more than reading the manual (Rounsaville, O'Malley, Foley, & Weissman, 1988; Weissman, Rounsaville, & Chevron, 1982). Therapists learn psychotherapies by practicing them. IPT training programs are generally designed to help already experienced therapists refocus their treatment by learning new techniques, not to teach novices psychotherapy. This makes sense, given its development as a focal research therapy: IPT has never been intended as a universal treatment for all patients, a conceptualization of psychotherapy that in any case seems naive in the modern era.

IPT candidates should have a graduate clinical degree (MD, PhD, MSW, RN), several years of experience conducting psychotherapy, and clinical familiarity with the diagnosis of patients they plan to treat. The training developed for the TDCRP (Elkin et al., 1989) became the model for subsequent research studies. It included a brief didactic program, review of the manual, and a longer practicum in which the therapist treated two to three patients under close supervision monitored by videotapes of the sessions (Chevron & Rounsaville, 1983). Rounsaville, Chevron, Weissman, Prusoff, and Frank (1986) found that psychotherapists who successfully conducted an initial supervised IPT case often did not require further intensive supervision and that experienced therapists committed to the approach required less supervision than others (Rounsaville et al., 1988). Some clinicians have taught themselves IPT using the IPT manual (Klerman, Weissman, Rounsaville, & Chevron, 1984) and peer supervision to guide them. For research certification, we recommend at least two or three successfully treated cases with hour-for-hour supervision of taped sessions (Markowitz, 2001).

There has been no formal certificate for IPT proficiency and no accrediting board. When the practice of IPT was restricted to a few research settings, this was not a problem, one research group taught another as described above. As IPT spreads into clinical practice, issues arise about standards for clinical training, and questions of competence and accreditation gain greater urgency. Training programs in IPT are still not widely available, as a recent US Surgeon General's report noted (Satcher, 1999). Many psychiatry residency and psychology training programs still focus exclusively on long-term psychodynamic psychotherapy or on CBT. In these programs too, the lack of exposure to time-limited treatment has been noted.

The educational process for IPT in clinical practice requires further study. We do not know, for example, what levels of education and experience are required to learn IPT, nor how much supervision an already experienced psychotherapist is likely to require. The ISIPT is currently debating how best to set standards for clinical practice of IPT, which doubtless varies from country to country. The United Kingdom is in better shape than most: IPT therapists in Britain have agreed on standards for clinical training and practice that are essentially equivalent to those for researchers (http://www.iptuk.org/Main/HomePage?action=download&upname=Accredita tion%20Standards%20July%202010.pdf). These rigorous standards should ensure high quality of IPT in the United Kingdom.

# References

Agras, W. S., Walsh, B. T., Fairburn, C. G., Wilson, G. T., & Kraemer, H. C. (2000). A multicenter comparison of cognitive-behavioral therapy and interpersonal psychotherapy for bulimia nervosa. *Archives of General Psychiatry, 57*, 459–466.

American Psychiatric Association. (1994). *Diagnostic and statistical manual of mental disorders (DSM-IV)* (4th ed.). Washington, DC: Author.

Barber, J. P., & Muenz, L. R. (1996). The role of avoidance and obsessiveness in matching patients to cognitive and interpersonal psychotherapy: Empirical findings from the Treatment for Depression Collaborative Research Program. *Journal of Consulting and Clinical Psychology, 64*, 951–958.

Beck, A. T. (1978). *Depression inventory*. Philadelphia, PA: Center for Cognitive Therapy.

Bleiberg, K. L., & Markowitz, J. C. (2005). A pilot study of interpersonal psychotherapy for posttraumatic stress disorder. *American Journal of Psychiatry, 162*, 181–183.

Blom, M. B., Jonker, K., Dusseldorp, E., Spinhoven, P., Hoencamp, E., Haffmans, J., & van Dyck, R. (2007). Combination treatment for acute depression is superior only when psychotherapy is added to medication. *Psychotherapy and Psychosomatics, 76,* 289–297.

Bowlby, J. (1973). *Attachment and loss.* New York: Basic Books.

Brody, A. L., Saxena, S., Stoessel, P., Gillies, L. A., Fairbanks, L. A., Alborzian, S., . . . Baxter, L. R., Jr., (2001). Regional brain metabolic changes in patients with major depression treated with either paroxetine or interpersonal therapy: Preliminary findings. *Archives of General Psychiatry, 58,* 631–640.

Brown, C., Schulberg, H. C., Madonia, M. J., Shear, M. K., & Houck, P. R. (1996). Treatment outcomes for primary care patients with major depression and lifetime anxiety disorders. *American Journal of Psychiatry, 153,* 1293–1300.

Browne, G., Steiner, M., Roberts, J., Gafni, A., Byrne, C., Dunn, E., . . . Kraemer, J. (2002). Sertraline and/or interpersonal psychotherapy for patients with dysthymic disorder in primary care: 6-month comparison with longitudinal 2 year follow-up of effectiveness and costs. *Journal of Affective Disorders, 68,* 317–330.

Carroll, K. M., Rounsaville, B. J., & Gawin, F. H. (1991). A comparative trial of psychotherapies for ambulatory cocaine abusers: Relapse prevention and interpersonal psychotherapy. *American Journal of Drug and Alcohol Abuse, 17,* 229–247.

Chevron, E. S., & Rounsaville, B. J. (1983). Evaluating the clinical skills of psychotherapists: A comparison of techniques. *Archives of General Psychiatry, 40,* 1129–1132.

Cuijpers, P., Geraedts, A. S., van Oppen, P., Andersson, G., Markowitz, J. C., & van Straten, A. (2011). Interpersonal psychotherapy of depression: A meta-analysis. *American Journal of Psychiatry, 168,* 581–592.

de Mello, M. F., de Jesus Mari, J., Bacaltchuk, J., Verdeli, H., & Neugebauer, R. (2005). A systematic review of research findings on the efficacy of interpersonal psychotherapy for depressive disorders. *European Archives of Psychiatry and Clinical Neuroscience, 255,* 75–82.

de Mello, M. F., Myczowisk, L. M., & Menezes, P. R. (2001). A randomized controlled trial comparing moclobemide and moclobemide plus interpersonal psychotherapy in the treatment of dysthymic disorder. *Journal of Psychotherapy Practice and Research, 10,* 117–123.

DiMascio, A., Weissman, M. M., Prusoff, B. A., Neu, C., Zwilling, M., & Klerman, G. L. (1979). Differential symptom reduction by drugs and psychotherapy in acute depression. *Archives of General Psychiatry, 36,* 1450–1456.

Elkin, I., Shea, M. T., Watkins, J. T., Imber, S. D., Sotsky, S. M., Collins, J. F., . . . Parloff, M. B. (1989). National Institute of Mental Health treatment of depression collaborative research program: General effectiveness of treatments. *Archives of General Psychiatry, 46,* 971–982.

Fairburn, C. G., Jones, R., Peveler, R. C., Hope, R. A., & O'Connor, M. (1993). Psychotherapy and bulimia nervosa: Longer-term effects of interpersonal psychotherapy, behavior therapy, and cognitive behavior therapy. *Archives of General Psychiatry, 50,* 419–428.

Foley, S. H., Rounsaville, B. J., Weissman, M. M., Sholomskas, D., & Chevron, E. (1989). Individual versus conjoint interpersonal psychotherapy for depressed patients with marital disputes. *International Journal of Family Psychiatry, 10,* 29–42.

Frank, E., Kupfer, D. J., Buysse, D. J., Swartz, H. A., Pilkonis, P. A., Houck, P. R., . . . Stapf, D. M. (2007). Randomized trial of weekly, twice-monthly, and monthly interpersonal psychotherapy as maintenance treatment for women with recurrent depression. *American Journal of Psychiatry, 164,* 761–767.

Frank, E., Kupfer, D. J., Perel, J. M., Cornes, C., Jarrett, D. B., Mallinger, A. G. . . . Grochocinski, V. J. (1990). Three-year outcomes for maintenance therapies in recurrent depression. *Archives of General Psychiatry, 47,* 1093–1099.

Frank, E., Kupfer, D. J., Thase, M. E., Mallinger, A. G., Swartz, H. A., Fagiolini, A. M., . . . Monk, T. (2005). Two-year outcomes for interpersonal and social rhythm therapy in individuals with bipolar I disorder. *Archives of General Psychiatry, 62,* 996–1004.

Frank, E., Kupfer, D. J., Wagner, E. F., McEachran, A. B., & Cornes, C. (1991). Efficacy of interpersonal psychotherapy as a maintenance treatment of recurrent depression. Contributing factors. *Archives of General Psychiatry, 48,* 1053–1059.

Frank, E., Shear, M. K., Rucci, P., Cyanowski, J. M., Endicott, J., Fagiolini, A., . . . Cassano, G. B. (2000). Influence of panic-agoraphobic spectrum symptoms on treatment response in patients with recurrent major depression. *American Journal of Psychiatry, 157,* 1101–1107.

Frank, J. (1971). Therapeutic factors in psychotherapy. *American Journal of Psychotherapy, 25,* 350–361.

Gurman, A. S., & Kniskern, D. P. (1978). Research on marital and family therapy: Progress, perspective, and prospect. In S. B. Garfield, & A. B. Bergen (Eds.), *Handbook of psychotherapy and behavior change* (pp. 817–902). New York: John Wiley & Sons.

Hamilton, M. (1960). A rating scale for depression. *Journal of Neurology, Neurosurgery, and Psychiatry, 23,* 56–62.

Hirschfeld, R. M., Klerman, G. L., Clayton, P. J., Keller, M. B., McDonald-Scott, P., & Larkin, B. H. (1983). Assessing personality: Effects of the depressive state on trait measurement. *American Journal of Psychiatry, 140,* 695–699.

Klein, D. F., & Ross, D. C. (1993). Reanalysis of the National Institute of Mental Health treatment of depression collaborative research program general effectiveness report. *Neuropsychopharmacology, 8,* 241–251.

Klerman, G. L., Budman, S., Berwick, D., Weissman, M. M., Damico-White, J., Demby, A., & Feldstein, M. (1987). Efficacy of a brief psychosocial intervention for symptoms of stress and distress among patients in primary care. *Medical Care, 25,* 1078–1088.

Klerman, G. L., DiMascio, A., Weissman, M. M., Prusoff, B. A., & Paykel, E. S. (1974). Treatment of depression by drugs and psychotherapy. *American Journal of Psychiatry, 131,* 186–191.

Klerman, G. L., & Weissman, M. M. (1993). *New applications of interpersonal psychotherapy.* Washington, DC: American Psychiatric Press.

Klerman, G. L., Weissman, M. M., Rounsaville, B. J., & Chevron, E. S. (1984). *Interpersonal psychotherapy of depression.* New York: Basic Books.

Klier, C. M., Muzik, M., Rosenblum, K. L., & Lenz, G. (2001). Interpersonal psychotherapy adapted for the group setting in the treatment of postpartum depression. *Journal of Psychotherapy Practice and Research, 10,* 124–131.

Kocsis, J. H., Frances, A. J., Voss, C., Mann, J. J., Mason, B. J., & Sweeney, J. (1988). Imipramine treatment for chronic depression. *Archives of General Psychiatry, 45,* 253–257.

Krupnick, J. L., Green, B. L., Stockton, P., Miranda, J., Krause, E., & Mete, M. (2008). Group interpersonal psychotherapy for low-income women with posttraumatic stress disorder. *Psychotherapy Research, 18,* 497–507.

Lesperance, F., Frasure-Smith, N., Koszycki, D., Laliberte, M. A., van Zyl, L. T., Baker, B., . . . Guertin, M. C.; CREATE Investigators. (2007). Effects of citalopram and interpersonal psychotherapy on depression in patients with coronary artery disease: The Canadian Cardiac Randomized Evaluation of Antidepressant and Psychotherapy Efficacy (CREATE) trial. *Journal of the American Medical Association, 297,* 367–379.

Lichtmacher, J. E., Eisendrath, S. J., & Haller, E. (2006). Implementing interpersonal psychotherapy in a psychiatry residency training program. *Academic Psychiatry, 30,* 385–391.

Lipsitz, J. D., Markowitz, J. C., Cherry, S., & Fyer, A. J. (1999). An open trial of interpersonal psychotherapy for social phobia. *American Journal of Psychiatry, 156,* 1814–1816.

Markowitz, J. C. (1993). Psychotherapy of the post-dysthymic patient. *Journal of Psychotherapy Practice and Research, 2,* 157–163.

Markowitz, J. C. (1994). Psychotherapy of dysthymia. *American Journal of Psychiatry, 151,* 1114–1121.

Markowitz, J. C. (1995). Teaching interpersonal psychotherapy to psychiatric residents. *Academic Psychiatry, 19,* 167–173.

Markowitz, J. C. (1998). *Interpersonal psychotherapy for dysthymic disorder.* Washington, DC: American Psychiatric Press.

Markowitz, J. C. (2001). Learning the new psychotherapies. In M. M. Weissman (Ed.), *Treatment of depression: Bridging the 21st century* (pp. 281–300). Washington, DC: American Psychiatric Press.

Markowitz, J. C. (2008). Depressed mothers, depressed children. *American Journal of Psychiatry, 165,* 1086–1088.

Markowitz, J. C., Bleiberg, K. L., Christos, P., & Levitan, E. (2006). Solving interpersonal problems correlates with symptom improvement in interpersonal psychotherapy: Preliminary findings. *Journal of Nervous and Mental Disease, 194,* 15–20.

Markowitz, J. C., Klerman, G. L., Perry, S. W., Clougherty, K. F., & Mayers, A. (1992). Interpersonal therapy of depressed HIV-seropositive patients. *Hospital and Community Psychiatry, 43,* 885–890.

Markowitz, J. C., Kocsis, J. H., Bleiberg, K. L., Christos, P. J., & Sacks, M. (2005). A comparative trial of psychotherapy and pharmacotherapy for "pure" dysthymic patients. *Journal of Affective Disorders, 89,* 167–175.

Markowitz, J. C., Kocsis, J. H., Christos, P., Bleiberg, K., & Carlin, A. (2008). Pilot study of interpersonal psychotherapy versus supportive psychotherapy for dysthymic patients with secondary alcohol abuse or dependence. *Journal of Nervous and Mental Disease, 196,* 468–474.

Markowitz, J. C., Kocsis, J. H., Fishman, B., Spielman, L. A., Jacobsberg, L. B., Frances, A. J., . . . Perry, S. W. (1998). Treatment of HIV-positive patients with depressive symptoms. *Archives of General Psychiatry, 55,* 452–457.

Markowitz, J. C., Leon, A. C., Miller, N. L., Cherry, S., Clougherty, K. F., & Villalobos, L. (2000). Rater agreement on interpersonal psychotherapy problem areas. *Journal of Psychotherapy Practice and Research, 9,* 131–135.

Markowitz, J. C., Svartberg, M., & Swartz, H. A. (1998). Is IPT time-limited psychodynamic psychotherapy? *Journal of Psychotherapy Practice and Research, 7,* 185–195.

Markowitz, J. C., & Swartz, H. A. (2007). Case formulation in interpersonal psychotherapy of depression. In T. D. Eells(Ed.), *Handbook of psychotherapy case formulation* (2nd ed., pp. 221–250). New York: Guilford Press.

Markowitz, J. C., & Weissman, M. M. (Eds.). (2012a). *Casebook of interpersonal psychotherapy.* New York: Oxford University Press.

Markowitz, J. C., & Weissman, M. M. (2012b). Interpersonal pschyotherapy: Past, present, and future. *Clinical Psychology and Psychotherapy, 19,* 99–105.

Martin, S. D., Martin, E., Rai, S. S., Richardson, M. A., & Royall, R. (2001). Brain blood flow changes in depressed patients treated with interpersonal psychotherapy or venlafaxine hydrochloride: Preliminary findings. *Archives of General Psychiatry, 58,* 641–648.

Miklowitz, D. J., Otto, M. W., Frank, E., Reilly-Harrington, N. A., Wisniewski, S. R., Kogan, J. N., . . . Sachs, G. S. (2007). Psychosocial treatments for bipolar depression: A 1-year randomized trial from the systematic treatment enhancement program. *Archives of General Psychiatry, 64,* 419–427.

Mossey, J. M., Knott, K. A., Higgins, M., & Talerico, K. (1996). Effectiveness of a psychosocial intervention, interpersonal counseling, for subdysthymic depression in medically ill elderly. *Journals of Gerontology. Series A, Biological Sciences and Medical Sciences, 51*(4), M172–M178.

Mufson, L., Dorta, K. P., Wickramaratne, P., Nomura, Y., Olfson, M., & Weissman, M. M. (2004). A randomized effectiveness trial of interpersonal psychotherapy for depressed adolescents. *Archives of General Psychiatry, 61*, 577–584.

Mufson, L., Moreau, D., & Weissman, M. M. (1993). *Interpersonal therapy for depressed adolescents.* New York: Guilford Press.

Mufson, L., Weissman, M. M., Moreau, D., & Garfinkel, R. (1999). Efficacy of interpersonal psychotherapy for depressed adolescents. *Archives of General Psychiatry, 56*, 573–579.

Neugebauer, R., Kline, J., Markowitz, J. C., Bleiberg, K., Baxi, L., Rosing, M.,... Keith, J. (2006). Pilot randomized controlled trial of interpersonal counseling for subsyndromal depression following miscarriage. *Journal of Clinical Psychiatry, 67*, 1299–1304.

O'Hara, M. W., Stuart, S., Gorman, L. L., & Wenzel, A. (2000). Efficacy of interpersonal psychotherapy for postpartum depression. *Archives of General Psychiatry, 57*, 1039–1045.

Parsons, T. (1951). Illness and the role of the physician: A sociological perspective. *American Journal of Orthopsychiatry, 21*, 452–460.

Paykel, E. S., & DiMascio, A., Haskell, D., & Prusoff, B. A. (1975). Effects of maintenance amitriptyline and psychotherapy on symptoms of depression. *Psychological Medicine, 5*, 67–77.

Ransom, D., Heckman, T. G., Anderson, T., Garske, J., Holroyd, K., & Basta, T. (2008). Telephone-delivered, interpersonal psychotherapy for HIV-infected rural persons with depression: A pilot trial. *Psychiatric Services, 59*, 871–877.

Reynolds, C. F., III, Dew, M. A., Martire, L. M., Miller, M. D., Cyranowski, J. M., Lenze, E.,... Frank, E. (2010). Treating depression to remission in older adults: A controlled evaluation of combined escitalopram with interpersonal psychotherapy versus escitalopram with depression care management. *International Journal of Geriatric Psychiatry, 25*, 1134–1141.

Reynolds, C. F., III, Dew, M. A., Pollock, B. G., Mulsant, B. H., Frank, E., Miller, M. D.,... Kupfer, D. J. (2006). Maintenance treatment of major depression in old age. *New England Journal of Medicine, 354*, 1130–1138.

Reynolds, C. F., III, Frank, E., Perel, J. M., Imber, S. D., Cornes, C., Miller, M. D.,... Kupfer, D. J. (1999). Nortriptyline and interpersonal psychotherapy as maintenance therapies for recurrent major depression: A randomized controlled trial in patients older than fifty-nine years. *JAMA, 281*, 39–45.

Rossello, J., & Bernal, G. (1999). The efficacy of cognitive-behavioral and interpersonal treatments for depression in Puerto Rican adolescents. *Journal of Consulting and Clinical Psychology, 67*, 734–745.

Rothblum, E. D., Sholomskas, A. J., Berry, C., & Prusoff, B. A. (1982). Issues in clinical trials with the depressed elderly. *Journal of American Geriatric Society, 30*, 694–699.

Rounsaville, B. J., Chevron, E. S., Weissman, M. M., Prusoff, B. A., & Frank, E. (1986). Training therapists to perform interpersonal psychotherapy in clinical trials. *Comprehensive Psychiatry, 27*, 364–371.

Rounsaville, B. J., Glazer, W., Wilber, C. H., Weissman, M. M., & Kleber, H. D. (1983). Short-term interpersonal psychotherapy in methadone-maintained opiate addicts. *Archives of General Psychiatry, 40*, 629–636.

Rounsaville, B. J., O'Malley, S. S., Foley, S. H., & Weissman, M. M. (1988). The role of manual-guided training in the conduct and efficacy of interpersonal psychotherapy for depression. *Journal of Consulting and Clinical Psychology, 56*, 681–688.

Rounsaville, B. J., Weissman, M. M., Prusoff, B. A., & Herceg-Baron, R. L. (1979). Marital disputes and treatment outcome in depressed women. *Comprehensive Psychiatry, 20*, 483–490.

Rush, A. J., & Thase, M. E. (1999). Psychotherapies for depressive disorders: A review. In M. Maj, & N. Sartorius (Eds.), *Depressive disorders: WPA series evidence and experience in psychiatry* (pp. 161–206). Chichester, UK: John Wiley & Sons.

Satcher, D. (1999). *Surgeon General's reference: Mental Health: A report of the Surgeon General.* Rockville, MD: U.S. Department of Health and Human Services.

Schulberg, H. C., Block, M. R., Madonia, M. J., Scott, C. P., Rodriguez, E., Imber, S. D.,... Coulehan, J. L. (1996). Treating major depression in primary care practice. *Archives of General Psychiatry, 53*, 913–919.

Schulberg, H. C., & Scott, C. P. (1991). Depression in primary care: Treating depression with interpersonal psychotherapy. In C. S. Austad, & W. H. Berman (Eds.), *Psychotherapy in managed health care: The optimal use of time & resources* (pp. 153–170). Washington, DC: American Psychological Association.

Schulberg, H. C., Scott, C. P., Madonia, M. J., & Imber, S. D. (1993). Applications of interpersonal psychotherapy to depression in primary care practice. In G. L. Klerman, & M. M. Weissman (Eds.), *New applications of interpersonal psychotherapy* (pp. 265–291). Washington, DC: American Psychiatric Press.

Shea, M. T., Elkin, I., Imber, S. D., Sotsky, S. M., Watkins, J. T., Collins, J. F.,... Parloff, M. B. (1992). Course of depressive symptoms over follow-up: Findings from the National Institute of Mental Health Treatment for Depression Collaborative Research Program. *Archives of General Psychiatry, 49*, 782–794.

Shea, M. T., Elkin, I., & Sotsky, S. M. (1999). Patient characteristics associated with successful treatment: Outcome findings from the NIMH Treatment of Depression Collaborative Research Program. In D. S. Janowsky (Ed.), *Psychotherapy indications and outcomes* (pp. 71–90). Washington, DC: American Psychiatric Press.

Sholomskas, A. J., Chevron, E. S., Prusoff, B. A., & Berry, C. (1983). Short-term interpersonal therapy (IPT) with the depressed elderly: Case reports and discussion. *American Journal of Psychotherapy, 36*, 552–566.

Sloane, R. B., Stapes, F. R., & Schneider, L. S. (1985). Interpersonal therapy versus nortriptyline for depression in the elderly. In G. D. Burrows, T. R. Norman, & L. Dennerstein (Eds.), *Clinical and pharmacological studies in psychiatric disorders* (pp. 344–346). London: John Libbey.

Sotsky, S. M., Glass, D. R., Shea, M. T., Pilkonis, P. A., Collins, J. F., Elkin, I.,... Oliveri, M. E. (1991). Patient predictors of response to psychotherapy and pharmacotherapy: Findings in the NIMH Treatment of Depression Collaborative Research Program. *American Journal of Psychiatry, 148*, 997–1008.

Spinelli, M. G. (1997). Interpersonal psychotherapy for depressed antepartum women: A pilot study. *American Journal of Psychiatry, 154*, 1028–1030.

Spinelli, M. G., & Endicott, J. (2003). Controlled clinical trial of interpersonal psychotherapy versus parenting education program for depressed pregnant women. *American Journal of Psychiatry, 160*, 555–562.

Stuart, S., & O'Hara, M. W. (1995). IPT for postpartum depression. *Journal of Psychotherapic Practice and Research, 4*, 18–29.

Sullivan, H. S. (Ed.). (1953). *The interpersonal theory of psychiatry.* New York: W. W. Norton.

Swartz, H. A., Frank, E., Zuckoff, A., Cyranowski, J., Houck, P., Cheng, Y.,... Shear, M. K. (2008). Brief interpersonal psychotherapy for depressed mothers whose children are seeking psychiatric treatment. *American Journal of Psychiatry, 165*, 1155–1162.

Swartz, H. A., Zuckoff, A. M., Frank, E., Spielvogle, H. N., Shear, M. K., Fleming, M. A., & Scott, J. (2006). An open-label trial of enhanced brief interpersonal psychotherapy in depressed mothers whose children are receiving psychiatric treatment. *Depression and Anxiety, 23,* 398–404.

Thase, M. E., Buysse, D. J., Frank, E., Cherry, C. R., Cornes, C. L., Mallinger, A. G., & Kupfer, D. J. (1997). Which depressed patients will respond to interpersonal psychotherapy? The role of abnormal EEG sleep profiles. *American Journal of Psychiatry, 154,* 502–509.

Thase, M. E., Fava, M., Halbreich, U., Kocsis, J. H., Koran, L., Davidson, J., . . . Harrison, W. (1996). A placebo-controlled, randomized clinical trial comparing sertraline and imipramine for the treatment of dysthymia. *Archives of General Psychiatry, 53,* 777–784.

van Schaik, D. J., van Marwijk, H. W., Ader, H., van Dyck, R., de Haan, M., Penninx, B., . . . Beekman, A. (2006). Interpersonal psychotherapy for elderly patients in primary care. *American Journal of Geriatric Psychiatry, 14,* 777–786.

Weissman, M. M. (1995). *Mastering depression: A patient guide to interpersonal psychotherapy.* Albany, NY: Graywind Publications, Inc.

Weissman, M. M., Klerman, G. L., Paykel, E. S., Prusoff, B. A., & Hanson, B. (1974). Treatment effects on the social adjustment of depressed patients. *Archives of General Psychiatry, 30,* 771–778.

Weissman, M. M., Klerman, G. L., Prusoff, B. A., Sholomskas, D., & Padian, N. (1981). Depressed outpatients: Results one year after treatment with drugs and/or interpersonal psychotherapy. *Archives of General Psychiatry, 38,* 51–55.

Weissman, M. M., Markowitz, J. C., & Klerman, G. L. (2000). *Comprehensive guide to interpersonal psychotherapy.* New York: Basic Books.

Weissman, M. M., Markowitz, J. C., & Klerman, G. L. (2007). *Clinician's quick guide to interpersonal psychotherapy.* New York: Oxford University Press.

Weissman, M. M., Prusoff, B. A., DiMascio, A., Neu, C., Goklaney, M., & Klerman, G. L. (1979). The efficacy of drugs and psychotherapy in the treatment of acute depressive episodes. *American Journal of Psychiatry, 136,* 555–558.

Weissman, M. M., Rounsaville, B. J., & Chevron, E. S. (1982). Training psychotherapists to participate in psychotherapy outcome studies: Identifying and dealing with the research requirement. *American Journal of Psychiatry, 139,* 1442–1446.

Wilfley, D. E., Agras, W. S., Telch, C. F., Rossiter, E., Schneider, J., Cole, A. C., . . . Raeburn, S. (1993). Group cognitive-behavioral therapy and group interpersonal psychotherapy for the nonpurging bulimic individual: A controlled comparison. *Journal of Consulting and Clinical Psychology, 61,* 296–305.

Wilfley, D. E., MacKenzie, R. K., Welch, R. R., Ayres, V. E., & Weissman, M. M. (2000). *Interpersonal psychotherapy for group.* New York: Basic Books.

Zlotnick, C., Johnson, S. L., Miller, I. W., Pearlstein, T., & Howard, M. (2001). Postpartum depression in women receiving public assistance: Pilot study of an interpersonal-therapy-oriented group intervention. *American Journal of Psychiatry, 158,* 638–640.

# 9

# Marital Therapy for Dealing with Depression

Guy Bodenmann[1] and Ashley Randall[2]

[1]University of Zurich, Switzerland
[2]University of Arizona, USA

## Introduction

Depression is typically categorized as a mental illness that affects one individual (*intrapsychic phenomenon;* Whiffen & Aube, 1999); nevertheless, it is important that one understands the interpersonal effects depression may have on both partners and their relationship. A large body of research illustrates the association between depression and relationship distress, suggesting that there is a significant negative connection between relationship functioning and the onset, course, and relapse of depression (Banawan, O'Mahen, Beach, & Jackson, 2001; Coyne, Thompson, & Palmer, 2002; Hooley, 2007; Joiner, Brown, & Kistner, 2006). The correlations between depressed mood and marital quality are moderate (women: $r = -0.30$; men: $r = -0.27$; Bodenmann & Ledermann, 2008), and are stronger for diagnosed depression ($r = -0.66$ for both genders; Whisman, 2001).

Several theories have been proposed to explain how depression at an individual level may affect the marital relationship. The most widespread and influential models are the *marital distress model of depression* by Beach, Sandeen, and O'Leary (1990), Coyne's (1975) *interactional model,* and Hammen's (1991) *stress generation model.* While Beach et al. (1990) give causal primacy to marital distress leading to depression, Coyne (1976) and Hammen (1991) posit that depression is one factor that contributes to and maintains negative affect within the dyad, which contributes to increased conflicts between partners—furthering symptoms of depression.

### Depression and marital distress

Individuals suffering from depression show a variety of symptoms such as depressed mood, lack of motivation and energy, loss of libido, sleeping problems, and even suicidal thoughts (DSM-IV, 1994). Indefinitely, these symptoms could be a heavy burden for their partner. For example, the nondepressed partner could have to take over as caregiver for their partner or take on other family roles that the depressed partner is

*The Wiley-Blackwell Handbook of Mood Disorders*, Second Edition. Edited by Mick Power.
© 2013 John Wiley & Sons, Ltd. Published 2013 by John Wiley & Sons, Ltd.

no longer able to complete. This is in addition to the natural tendency for one's partner to worry about the patient, and his/her well-being. Often sexual intimacy is also negatively affected by one partner's depression (Bodenmann & Ledermann, 2008; Trudel, Landry, & Larose, 1997). Taken together, the effects depression has on the relationship may help explain the link between depression and decreased relationship satisfaction. One question, however, remains: What comes first, depression or marital distress? Empirical evidence is inconsistent about the direction of causality between depression and marital distress, as most studies are cross-sectional and do not allow us to draw causal links between variables (Rehman, Gollan, & Mortimer, 2007). Yet, as Kurdek (1998) and others indicate, it seems that depression and marital distress have a bidirectional link, such that depression can lead to marital distress or marital distress can further exacerbate symptoms of depression (Davila, Karney, Hall, & Bradbury, 2003). Nevertheless, in many cases marital problems and distress predict subsequent depressive episodes (Whisman & Bruce, 1999). Specifically, Whisman (2007) showed, based on data of 2,237 subjects, that marital distress increased the risk for affective disorders by 2.3 (odds ratio). Additionally, in a longitudinal study over 16 months, marital discord was found to predict future depressive symptoms, while depression did not predict future marital distress (Cano, Christian-Herman, O'Leary, & Avery-Leaf, 2002), a finding that was also supported by a longitudinal study by Choi and Marks (2008). Recently, however, Brock and Lawrence (2011) reported that only for men, marital discord during the transition into marriage predicted internalizing problems over the first 7 years of marriage.

For treatment of depression, the direction of association is irrelevant; either way of causality may justify an intervention focusing on interpersonal aspects, including both partners into treatment. Previous findings showed that the association between depression and relationship quality is consistent and that only couple therapy but not individual-oriented treatment of depression lead to an improvement of relationship quality (Beach et al., 1990). This indicates that an improvement of depression does not necessarily covary with higher relationship quality, but inversely an increase of relationship quality after therapy also improves depression (Beach & O'Leary, 1992; Jacobson, Fruzzetti, Dobson, Whisman, & Hops, 1993).

### Depression as an interpersonal construct: How it affects both partners' negativity and negative attitudes

*Expressed emotion* is an interpersonal concept that has immerged in the discussion of how the marital relationship may impact relapse of depression (or other mental disorders such as schizophrenia). A large body of research supports the assumption that a negative attitude toward the partner is relevant for the course of depression and the likelihood for relapse (Butzlaff & Hooley, 1998; Hooley, 2007). In couples with a depressed partner, the nondepressed partner's attitude toward the depressed patient is often characterized by high negativity such as criticism, hostility, and overprotection. These three aspects describe the concept of expressed emotion. While expressed emotion has been discussed mainly with regard to relapse prediction, more recent studies show that it also covaries with the course of depression (Brummett et al., 2000). Additionally, expressed emotion has been shown to activate and foster dysfunctional thinking in the depressed partner and maintains depression. Partners showing high expressed emotion activated more negative thinking in their depressed patients going along with higher scores in depression (Brummett et al., Meuwly, Coyne, & Bodenmann, in press). Benazon (2000) further showed that negative attitudes toward the depressed partner do not simply reflect low marital satisfaction but are predicted by depressed partner's reassurance seeking and own mood. Thus, the attitude toward the depressed partner seems important for understanding the development, maintenance, and remission of depression.

In addition to negative expressed emotion (reflecting an attitude toward the partner), couples with a depressed partner are often also characterized by more behavioral negativity in their relationships that arises in the form of open criticism, contempt, belligerence, defensiveness, and withdrawal. In addition to this, both partners may also experience less caring, fondness, intimacy, and overall support from the other (Biglan et al., 1985; Gotlib & Whiffen, 1989; Jacob & Leonard, 1992; Johnson & Jacob, 1997; McCabe & Gotlib, 1993). Interestingly, nondepressed partners are less likely to suppress their negative emotions if the discord has existed for a long period of time, which could have a particularly negative impact on the symptomatology of the depressed patient (Nelson & Beach, 1990). However, very often marital distress is responsible for negative dyadic interaction behavior and not so much depression per se (Schmaling & Jacobson, 1990).

## Reinforcing and supporting behavior in couples with a depressed partner

Historically, behavioral psychologists have argued that the partner plays a role in reinforcing depressive symptoms by showing empathy, understanding, caring, and helping following complaints, lethargy, and lack of motivation in the depressed patient (Coyne, 1976; Lewinsohn, 1974). Thus, apart from negative interaction behavior and negative attitudes (expressed emotion), positive, reinforcing behaviors of the partner may also be problematic. When the partner provides support (such as empathic behavior, caring, taking over tasks that usually the depressed patient accomplishes) with regard to depressive symptoms (complaining, passivity, etc.) this behavior may even increase depression. Thus, unaware reinforcement of depressive symptomatology may be a serious problem in couples where the partner tries to be empathic and supportive. Empathic reactions on complaining and passivity usually exacerbate symptoms of depression, leading to experiences of exhaustion and motivational deficits, ambivalence, and withdrawal in the supporting partner. Instead, promoting activity and problem-solving behavior would be needed to help the depressed patient overcome depressive symptoms. Thus, often dyadic coping is not functional in couples with a depressed partner. While, in general, spousal support and joint dyadic coping are beneficial for relationship functioning (Bodenmann, 2005), in the context of depression, other rules govern. Bodenmann, Widmer, Charvoz, and Bradbury (2004) reported deficits in partner's coping together with stressors (dyadic coping), mainly in highly depressed patients. Often partners of depressed patients support him or her, forced by social expectancies from society, medical staff, and relatives, but do so in an uninspired, exhausted, cynic, or critical way, especially in situations of recurrent depression. Obviously, this ambivalent support is adverse for depressed patient's well-being. Hence, Tower and Krasner's (2006) finding that marital closeness was protective against depression, revealing a buffering effect of support and intimacy for becoming depressed seems less evident in long-term depression.

### Reciprocity of depressed mood in couples with a depressed partner

Another argument for viewing depression as an interpersonal phenomenon in couples is that depression affects both partners and both show emotional contagion (Larson & Almeida, 1999). Well-being and behaviors of both partners are mutually influencing each other and are interdependent. Acitelli and Badr (2005) suggest that this interdependence is best reflected in the term "we-disease", meaning that both partners are affected by the disorder in multiple ways and that both partners need to be considered, validated, and supported in treatment. Benazon and Coyne (2000) showed that spouses living with a depressed patient reported significantly higher scores in depressed mood and subjective burden than nonclinical couples due to worries, insecurity, and anxiety related to depression, financial and social constraints, and significant changes in life conditions.

In sum, depression is not an isolated individual problem but has an impact on the partner and vice versa, suggesting a treatment including the partner.

## Seeking Therapeutic Treatment for Depression

Psychological treatment for depression such as cognitive-behavioral therapy (CBT) (Beck, Rush, Shaw, & Emery, 1979) or interpersonal therapy (IPT) (Weissman, Markowitz, & Klerman, 2000) has proven to be effective in alleviating symptoms of depression (Elkin et al., 1989). However, both interventions are primarily individual centered and do not specifically focus on depression as an interpersonal construct, and how it affects both partners. Although findings reported above recommend such an approach, many therapists are not aware of the benefit of including the partner in the therapy process. For this integration two modalities are recommended: (a) including the partner from time to time into the treatment process in the framework of individual-oriented therapy or (b) couple therapy for the treatment of depression. The selection of either strategy depends on: (a) the relationship status of the patient (whether he/she is in a close relationship), (b) the severity of depression, (c) the relationship quality, (d) the willingness of the partner to participate, and (e) the appropriate training and skills of the therapist to conduct couple therapy.

The inclusion of the partner into individual therapy aims to teach the depressed patient and their nondepressed partner about the role of the partner in maintaining depressive symptoms by means of positive and negative reinforcement (i.e., caring for patient, listening to complaints of the patient, sharing negative feelings with the patient, taking over responsibilities of the patient, protective buffering, etc.). In addition, this interpersonal approach helps educate the nondepressed partner in effective coping techniques and problem-solving skills and in reinforcing active problem-solving of the patient and his/her activity in everyday life. The focus of couple therapy, on the other hand, is the enhancement of relationship quality (positive dyadic coping, adequate communication) and the decrease of expressed emotion by the partner, both associated with depression and its development.

## Couple therapy for the treatment of depression

In the 1990s, Beach et al. (1990) started to question individual-oriented treatment of depression based on research findings on the significance of the partner for mood disorders. Consequently, different authors developed manuals for couple therapy of couples with a depressed partner (Banawan et al., 2001; Beach et al., 1990; Cordova & Gee, 2001; Craighead, Craighead, & Ilardi, 1998; Gollan, Friedman, & Miller, 2002; Jacobson, Dobson, Fruzzetti, Schmaling, & Salusky, 1991). Key elements of these treatments include: (1) psychoeducation, (2) the enhancement of positive dyadic interaction and the feeling of security and closeness by means of behavioral exchange techniques, and (3) the improvement of communication and problem-solving skills.

In psychoeducation, the primary goal is to teach the couple about the roles of both partners and the importance of positive reciprocity. Both partners should maintain a balance in sacrifices within the relationship, specifically in daily responsibilities. Additionally, the nondepressed partner is educated on how to give proper support, without reinforcing symptoms of depression (Coyne, 1976; Lewinsohn, 1974). Other key elements are the enhancement of positivity in daily interaction by means of behavioral exchange techniques and the improvement of dyadic communication by teaching partners appropriate communication techniques such as speaker and listener rules. The therapist prompts the couple in applying these rules in guided role plays and exercises and allows learning new communication behaviors under his/her supervision. Often cognitive elements (understanding information processing in the patient; see Beck et al., 1979) also complete couple therapy (Beach et al., 1990).

More recent developments within couple therapy represent the *integrative approach* by Cordova and Gee (2001), based upon the acceptance work approach by Jacobson and Christensen (1996) and the *coping-oriented couple therapy* (COCT), developed by Bodenmann (2007, 2010). Cordova and Gee (2001) work with the couple toward a view of depression as a joint problem that needs both partners' efforts to fight this common enemy in order to overcome, together, difficulties related to the disorder. Feelings of guilt and culpability as well as reproach and regret are recognized as not useful and instead both partners are taught to understand depression as a dyadic issue that can best be resolved by mutual efforts. Thus reciprocal understanding, flexibility, and joint support processes are trained and the activity level of the depressed partner increased.

The coping-oriented approach is based upon cognitive-behavioral couple therapy (Baucom & Epstein, 1990; Beach, Fincham, & Katz, 1998; Beach et al., 1990), integrative couple therapy (Jacobson & Christensen, 1996) as well as techniques derived from research on stress and coping in couples (Bodenmann, 2007, 2010; Boden-mann & Shantinath, 2004). Based upon vulnerability–stress models of depression, this approach focuses on the role of stress for: (a) the development and maintenance of depression and (b) the impact of stress on close relationship functioning in gen-eral (Randall & Bodenmann, 2009). It is assumed that either a critical life event (loss of a significant person, job loss, movement, severe illness, etc.) or the pileup of chronic external everyday stress (stressful job, multiple stressors in different areas of life) plays a crucial role in depression going along with relationship deterioration. It is assumed that stress negatively affects relationship quality consequently leading to increased marital tensions, relationship strains, and depression. For these reasons, the significance of stress and coping is a primary target of COCT (Bodenmann, 2010).

Based on the stress–divorce model by Bodenmann et al. (2004, 2008), the adverse effects of stress on close relationship are manifold by: (1) reducing the time spent together (going along with less shared experiences, a lower feeling of intimacy and closeness, and less opportunities for dyadic coping), (2) deteriorating couple's com-munication (decrease of positivity and increase of negativity in times of stress), (3) increasing the likelihood for physical and psychological health problems in both part-ners (e.g., depression), and (4) by unmasking partners under stress. By these different mechanisms, chronic everyday stress leads to alienation, relationship dissatisfaction, and an increased likelihood for divorce. These deleterious effects of stress can be moderated by individual and dyadic coping. As dyadic communication skills often break down under stress (Ledermann, Bodenmann, Ruaz, & Bradbury, 2010), the enhancement of individual and dyadic coping is essential for the maintenance of constructive communication and relationship quality over time. In the systemic trans-actional model (STM) (Bodenmann, 2005), dyadic coping is conceptualized as an interactive and systemic process of dealing with stress in couples by means of stress communication, supportive, delegated, and common dyadic coping[1]. Furthermore, dyadic coping may also buffer between stress experience and expressed emotion. It is assumed that partners engage more frequently and easily in expressed emotion in times of stress, as patient's behavior (lack of motivation and energy, withdrawal, complaining, etc.) may be experienced as even more difficult and annoying in these situations when personal resources are limited and challenged. Thus, a supporting and caring partner may be challenged by the depression of his/her partner when he/she is dealing with high levels of stress of their own.

*Strengthening dyadic coping in the treatment of depression*   We know from a large body of studies that dyadic coping is positively associated with positive relationship

---

[1]The main assumption of this approach is that stress in couples can be described as a direct or indirect dyadic phenomenon. External stress (usually experienced by one partner outside of the relationship) is either communicated by the stressed partner or is perceived by the other partner. Subsequently, the stress triggers dyadic coping in addition to each partner's individual coping attempts. According to the profile of the situation (external or internal stress, involvement and personal concern of each partner, attribution of causes of the stress, possible contributions to problem resolution, etc.) and the individual and dyadic appraisal and goals, various forms of coping (*common dyadic coping*, *supportive dyadic coping*, or *delegated dyadic coping*) can be differentiated (Bodenmann, 2007).

functioning (for an overview see Bodenmann, 2005). Thus, strengthening dyadic coping in the treatment of depression reduces two important predictors of depression—expressed emotion and behavioral negativity in dyadic interaction—by simultaneously increasing positive resources of the couple (positive exchange, dyadic communication, dyadic coping), which ultimately reduces symptoms of depression and prevents relapse (Bodenmann et al., 2008). In addition to communication training and problem-solving training, couples obviously benefit significantly from being taught how to deal with daily stress more effectively (Bodenmann & Shantinath, 2004). A key element of the COCT is strengthening dyadic coping by adhering to the 3-phase method. In the first phase of the 3-phase method, the therapist facilitates deepened stress-related self-disclosure in one partner (speaker) and deepened understanding and empathy in the other partner (listener). In the second phase, the listening partner is now invited to support the stressed partner mostly on an emotional level by expressing understanding and empathy and encouraging and helping the partner to reframe the situation. In the third phase, the supported partner provides feedback about how helpful, effective, and satisfying the support provision of the partner was. The whole process lasts 45 min and afterward roles are changed, allowing both partners to experience being speaker as well as listener. The aims of the 3-phase method are: (a) to enhance each partner's ability to communicate explicitly his/her stress experienced outside the close relationship to the other (phase 1, 30 min: stress-related self-disclosure); (b) to adapt their support to the specific needs of the other (phase 2, 10 min: emotion-focused and problem-focused support provision by the listening partner); and (c) to refine the support they offer based on the partner's feedback (phase 3, 5 min: feedback toward the supporting partner how helpful his/her dyadic coping was for the partner who had self-disclosed) (Bodenmann, 2007). Based on the concept of central hassles or schemata (Beck et al., 1979), partners learn that external daily hassles are most often not the real cause for enduring stress experience but only activate central schemata, which, consequently, flood the individual with stress emotions. Thus, the 3-phase method tries to make both partners aware of these personally important schemata (e.g., "I am only appreciated when I am perfect," "I am only valuable when I am beloved," "I am only okay when I deliver great performance," "I feel only well when I have complete control over my environment," etc.) by exploring emotions, thoughts, and physiological reactions that emerge when one faces the stressful situation. Importantly, the 3-phase method is only applied when a sufficient level of mutual positivity and respect between partners has been installed, which is usually done by the enhancement of positive reciprocity and communication training. Additionally, the method is only applied when both partners indicate their commitment to one another and the longevity of the relationship.

The therapist's role during the first phase is to guide both partners in the direction of schemata exploration in the speaker, to supervise the appropriate application of the speaker and listener rules, to help the speaker to dive into deeper emotions and to explore his/her personal schemata by asking open-ended questions such as "How did you feel?," "What happened to you?," "What did this mean to you?," "Why was this so stressful?," and to facilitate stress exploration. The therapist is always coaching both partners simultaneously (the speaker as well as the listener). On the listener's side, the therapist is joining him/her with feedback and by asking him/her from time to time to summarize when new elements of self-exploration were presented by the speaker. Overall, the therapist engages in (1) supervising the partners' roles and their application of speaker and listener rules; (2) prompting the partners in their attempts to explore and summarize emotions and meanings associated with the stress event; (3) promoting mutual understanding in a discrete and nonintrusive way; and (4) offering structure with regard to time frame, roles, setting, and phases.

The method is similarly applied in the context of couples with a depressed partner as with nonclinical couples. Both partners (nondepressed and depressed) engage in both roles (speaker and listener) and make the experience such that the depressed patient is also able to listen empathically and to support the other and that reciprocity is still possible to some degree in the context of psychological disorder (e.g., depression). Not only receiving but also providing support means being equal, important, and valued and give the depressed patient the sense of utility and significance.

## Efficacy of couple therapy as a treatment for depression

Several studies document the efficacy of couple therapy in the treatment for depression (Beach & O'Leary, 1992; Bodenmann et al., 2008; Emanuels-Zuurveen & Emmelkamp, 1996; Foley, Rounsaville, Weissman, Sholomaskas, & Chevron, 1989; Jacobson et al., 1991; Jacobson & Christensen, 1996; Teichman, Bar-El, Shor, Sirota, & Elizur, 1995). Couple therapy seems as efficacious as CBT and IPT and enhances effects of pharmacological treatment of depression, because medication often adversely affects libido (Denton, Golden, & Walsh, 2003). Positive outcomes of couple therapy are found on self-report (e.g., Beck Depression Inventory) as well as on clinical rating scales (e.g., Hamilton Depressive Symptoms Rating Scale), yielding effect sizes of $d = 1.67$ (Jacobson et al., 1991). Bodenmann et al. (2008) found effect sizes of $d = 1.19$ directly after the treatment (post-measurement), $d = 1.46$ (after 6 months), $d = 1.74$ (after 1 year), and $d = 1.37$ (after 1.5 years). Couple therapy was found to be as effective as CBT or IPT—two approaches that are known for their efficacy in treating depression (Elkin et al., 1989). Although, usually effects are stronger when depressed patients are in distressed relationships (Beach & O'Leary, 1992; Foley et al., 1989) and seem less efficacious when depressed patients are not in currently unhappy relationships (Jacobson et al., 1991), the fact that most depressed patients live in dissatisfied relationships (see correlations reported above) suggests that couple therapy is beneficial for many depressed patients living in a close relationship.

Recovery rates for couple therapy range from 37% to 55% (Jacobson & Christensen, 1996). In the recent study done by Bodenmann et al. (2008), 32% of couples recovered until the post-measurement (compared to 37% in CBT or IPT) and another 16% until the follow-up of 6 months (compared to 10% in both other treatment conditions). Thus, overall, 53% of patients treated with couple therapy recovered within 6 months. Similarly, Teichman et al. (1995) reported recovery rates of 42% in marital therapy compared to 55% in the cognitive therapy group at 6-month follow-up.

As expressed emotion figures among the best predictor of relapse, one main purpose of couple therapy is to improve depression by reducing this risk factor. It is noteworthy that relapse rates for individuals seeking individual therapy for depression range between 30% and 50% (Belsher & Costello, 1988). In couple therapy, relapse rates are usually lower. Jacobson et al. (1993) report a relapse rate between 10% and 15% for behavioral marital therapy, and Bodenmann et al. (2008) found a relapse rate of 28.6% for COCT.

## Summary

There is a strong and consistent association between relationship distress and depression that led to the assumption that couple therapy might be an adequate treatment for this disorder (Banawan et al., 2001; Beach et al., 1990). Although both directions of causality (depression causing relationship problems as well as relationship distress producing depression) are plausible, independently from this question of causality, how the partner interacts with the depressed patient is highly predictive for maintenance of depression (Lewinsohn, 1974; Meuwly et al., in press) and relapse (Butzlaff & Hooley, 1998; Hooley, 2007). Therefore, psychoeducation is of particular importance in helping couples deal with their depressed partner. Additionally, negative attitudes (expressed emotion), dysfunctional interaction behaviors as well as inadequate dyadic coping should be targeted. The fact that expressed emotion, which increases the likelihood for relapse in a reliable way (Hooley, 2007) and activates dysfunctional attitudes in the patient along with higher depression (Meuwly et al., in press) are strong arguments for strengthening couple relationship. Happy couples are less prone to develop depression (Tesser & Beach, 1998) and thus the enhancement of couple's functioning is a valuable possibility to improve well-being (Pihet, Bodenmann, Cina, Widmer, & Shantinath, 2007).

The strong link between depression and relationship distress allows defining depression as a "we-disease" (Acitelli & Badr, 2005; Cordova & Gee, 2001). Such a conceptualization is an important step in framing the problem in a systemic perspective demanding the inclusion of both partners into the therapeutic process. As has been shown, both partners benefit from an interpersonal view of the disorder and a therapeutic approach where resources of the couple (e.g., dyadic communication, dyadic coping) are stimulated and strengthened. In return, the couple climate may ameliorate, life conditions become more satisfactory and favorable circumstances for well-being increase, and conditions to recover from depression increase.

Although there are many advantages of a couple-oriented approach in treating depression, there are also some limitations. First, as several authors pointed out, couple therapy is primarily indicated when relationship quality is low and thus an improvement of relationship quality is only found in couple therapy and not CBT (Beach et al., 1990; Schmaling & Jacobson, 1990). Second, not all therapists are capable of conducting couple therapy as many do not have the specific training that is required for best treatment. Third, couple therapy requires the commitment of both partners to engage in the therapeutic process; in cases where one partner is not willing to contribute, this approach is not possible. Fourth, often insurances do not cover costs for couple therapy, rather only individual therapy, and expenses can be higher in a couple intervention, which can place a financial burden and increase stress within the relationship.

Nevertheless, we believe that arguments for an inclusion of the partner are more powerful. Increasing evidence has shown the efficacy of using couple therapy as a means to alleviate depressive symptomatology (Beach & O'Leary, 1992; Beach et al., 1990; Bodenmann et al., 2008). We are convinced that couple therapy is an important option for treating depression, a mental disorder that has significant interpersonal effects, or that including the partner from time to time in individual-oriented treatment is beneficial.

# References

Acitelli, L. K., & Badr, H. J. (2005). My illness or our illness? Attending to the relationship when one partner is ill. In T. A. Revenson, K. Kayser, & G. Bodenmann (Eds.), *Couples coping with stress* (pp. 121–136). Washington, DC: American Psychological Association.

Banawan, S. F., O'Mahen, H. A., Beach, S. R. H., & Jackson, M. H. (2001). The empirical underpinnings of marital therapy for depression. In J. H. Harvey, & A. Wenzel (Eds.), *A clinician's guide to maintaining and enhancing close relationships.* Mahwah, NJ: Lawrence Erlbaum Associates.

Baucom, D. H., & Epstein, N. (1990). *Cognitive behavioral marital therapy.* New York: Brunner & Mazel.

Beach, S. R. H., Fincham, F. D., & Katz, J. (1998). Marital therapy in the treatment of depression: Toward a third generation of therapy and research. *Clinical Psychology Review*, *18*, 635–661.

Beach, S. R., & O'Leary, K. D. (1992). Treating depression in the context of marital discord: Outcome and predictors of response for marital therapy vs. cognitive therapy. *Behaviour Therapy*, *23*, 507–528.

Beach, S. R. H., Sandeen, E. E., & O'Leary, K. D. (1990). *Depression in marriage. A model for etiology and treatment.* New York: Guilford Press.

Beck, A. T., Rush, A. J., Shaw, B. L., & Emery, G. (1979). *Cognitive therapy of depression.* New York: Guilford Press.

Belsher, G., & Costello, C. G. (1988). Relapse after recovery from unipolar depression: A critical review. *Psychological Bulletin*, *104*, 84–96.

Benazon, N. R. (2000). Predicting negative spouse attitudes toward depressed persons: A test of Coyne's interpersonal model. *Journal of Abnormal Psychology*, *109*, 550–554.

Benazon, N. R. & Coyne, J. C. (2000). Living with a depressed spouse. *Journal of Family Psychology*, *14*, 71–79.

Biglan, A., Hops, H., Sherman, L., Friedman, L. S., Arthur, J., & Osteen, V. (1985). Problem solving interactions of depressed women and their spouses. *Behavior Therapy*, *16*, 431–451.

Bodenmann, G. (2005). Dyadic coping and its significance for marital functioning. In T. Revenson, K. Kayser, & G. Bodenmann (Eds.), *Couples coping with stress: Emerging perspectives on dyadic coping* (pp. 33–50). Washington, DC: American Psychological Association.

Bodenmann, G. (2007). Dyadic coping and the 3-phase-method in working with couples. In L. VandeCreek (Ed.), *Innovations in clinical practice: Focus on group and family therapy* (pp. 235–252). Sarasota, FL: Professional Resources Press.

Bodenmann, G. (2010). New themes in couple therapy: The role of stress, coping and social support. In K. Hahlweg, M. Grawe, & D. H. Baucom (Eds.), *Enhancing couples. The shape of couple therapy to come* (pp. 142–156). Cambridge, MA: Hogrefe Publishing.

Bodenmann, G., & Ledermann, T. (2008). Depressed mood and sexual functioning. *International Journal of Sexual Health*, *19*, 63–73.

Bodenmann, G., Plancherel, B., Beach, S. R. H., Widmer, K., Gabriel, B. Meuwly, N., ... Schramm, E. (2008). Effects of coping-oriented couples therapy on depression: A randomized clinical trial. *Journal of Consulting and Clinical Psychology, 76*, 944–954.

Bodenmann, G., & Shantinath, S. D. (2004). The Couples Coping Enhancement Training (CCET): A new approach to prevention of marital distress based upon stress and coping. *Family Relations, 53*(5), 477–484.

Bodenmann, G., Widmer, K., Charvoz, L., & Bradbury, T. N. (2004). Differences in individual and dyadic coping in depressed, non-depressed and remitted persons. *Journal of Psychopathology and Behavioral Assessment, 26*, 75–85.

Brock, R. L., & Lawrence, E. (2011). Marriage as a risk factor for internalizing disorders: Clarifying scope and specificity. *Journal of Consulting and Clinical Psychology, 79*, 577–589.

Brummett, B. H., Barefoot, J. C., Feaganes, J. R., Yen, S., Bosworth, H. B., Williams, R. B., & Siegler, I. C. (2000). Hostility in marital dyads: Associations with depressive symptoms. *Journal of Behavioral Medicine, 23*, 95–105.

Butzlaff, R. L., & Hooley, J. M. (1998). Expressed emotion and psychiatric relapse. A meta-analysis. *Archives of Genetic Psychiatry, 55*, 547–552.

Cano, A., Christian-Herman, J., O'Leary, K. D., & Avery-Leaf, S. (2002). Antecedents and consequences of negative marital stressors. *Journal of Marital and Family Therapy, 28*, 145–151.

Choi, H., & Marks, N. F. (2008). Marital conflicts, depressive symptoms, and functional impairment. *Journal of Marriage and Family, 70*, 377–390.

Cordova, J. V., & Gee, C. B. (2001). Couples therapy for depression: Using healthy relationships to treat depression. In S. R. H. Beach (Ed.), *Marital and family processes in depression: A scientific foundation for clinical practice* (pp. 185–203). Washington, DC: American Psychological Association.

Coyne, J. C. (1976). Toward an interactional description of depression. *Psychiatry, 39*, 28–40.

Coyne, J. C., Thompson, R., & Palmer, S. C. (2002). Marital quality, coping with conflicts, marital complaints, and affection in couples with a depressed wife. *Journal of Family Psychology, 16*, 26–37.

Craighead, W. E., Craighead, L. W., & Ilardi, S. S. (1998). Psychosocial treatments of major depressive disorder. In P. E. Nathan, & J. M. Gorman (Eds.), *A guide to treatments that work* (pp. 226–239). Oxford, UK: Oxford University Press.

Davila, J., Karney, B. R., Hall, T. W., & Bradbury, T. N. (2003). Depressive symptoms and marital satisfaction: Within subject associations and the moderating effect of gender and neuroticism. *Journal of Family Psychology, 17*, 557–570.

Denton, W. H., Golden, R. N., & Walsh, S. R. (2003). Depression, marital discord, and couple therapy. *Current Opinions in Psychiatry, 16*, 29–34.

DSM-IV, American Psychiatric Association. (1994). *Diagnostic and statistical manual of mental disorders (DSM-IV)* (4th ed.). Washington, DC: Author.

Elkin, I., Shea, T., Watkins, J. T., Imber, S. D., Stuart, M. S., Collins, J. F., ... Parloff, M. B. (1989). National institute of mental health treatment of depression collaborative research program. *Archives of General Psychiatry, 46*, 971–982.

Emanuels-Zuurveen, L., & Emmelkamp, P. M. (1996). Individual behavioral-cognitive therapy versus marital therapy for depression in maritally distressed couples. *British Journal of Psychiatry, 169*, 181–188.

Foley, S. H., Rounsaville, B. J., Weissman, M. M., Sholomaskas, D., & Chevron, E. (1989). Individual versus conjoint interpersonal therapy for depressed patients with marital disputes. *International Journal of Family Psychology, 10*, 29–42.

Gollan, J. K., Friedman, M. A., & Miller, I. W. (2002). Couple therapy in the treatment of major depression. In A. S. Gurman, & N. S. Jacobson (Eds.), *Clinical handbook of couple therapy* (pp. 653–676). New York: Guilford Press.

Gotlib, I. H., & Whiffen, V. E. (1989). Depression and marital functioning: An examination of specificity and gender differences. *Journal of Abnormal Psychology, 98*, 23–30.

Hammen, C. (1991). The generation of stress in the course of unipolar depression. *Journal of Abnormal Psychology, 100*, 555–561.

Hooley, J. M. (2007). Expressed emotion and relapse of psychopathology. *Annual Review of Clinical Psychology, 3*, 329–352.

Jacob, T., & Leonard, K. (1992). Sequential analysis of marital interactions involving alcoholic, depressed, and nondistressed men. *Journal of Abnormal Psychology, 101*, 647–656.

Jacobson, N. S., & Christensen, A. (1996). *Integrative behavioral couple therapy.* New York: Norton.

Jacobson, N. S., Dobson, K. S., Fruzzetti, A. E., Schmaling, K. B., & Salusky, S. (1991). Marital therapy as a treatment for depression. *Journal of Consulting and Clinical Psychology, 59*, 547–557.

Jacobson, N. S., Fruzzetti, A. E., Dobson, K., Whisman, M., & Hops, H. (1993). Couple therapy as a treatment for depression: II. The effects of relationship quality and therapy on depressive relapse. *Journal of Consulting and Clinical Psychology, 61*, 516–519.

Johnson, S. L., & Jacob, T. (1997). Marital interactions of depressed men and women. *Journal of Consulting and Clinical Psychology, 65*, 15–23.

Joiner, T. E., Brown, J. S., & Kistner, J. (2006). *The interpersonal, cognitive, and social nature of depression.* Mahwah, NJ: Lawrence Erlbaum Associates.

Kurdek, L. A. (1998). The nature and predictors of the trajectory of change in marital quality over the first four years of marriage and for first-married husbands and wives. *Journal of Family Psychology, 12*, 494–510.

Larson, R. W., & Almeida, D. M. (1999). Emotional transmission in the daily lives of families: A new paradigm for studying family process. *Journal of Marriage and the Family, 61*, 5–20.

Ledermann, T., Bodenmann, G., Rudaz, M., & Bradbury, T. N. (2010). Stress, communication, and marital quality in couples. *Family Relations, 59*, 195–206.

Lewinsohn, P. M. (1974). A behavioral approach to depression. In R. J. Friedman, & M. M. Katz (Eds.), *The psychology of depression: Contemporary theory and research* (pp. 157–185). New York: John Wiley & Sons.

McCabe, S. B., & Gotlib, I. H. (1993). Interactions of couples with and without a depressed spouse: Self-report and observations of problem-solving situations. *Journal of Personality and Social Psychology, 10*, 589–599.

Meuwly, N., Coyne, J., & Bodenmann, G. (in press). The association between partner's expressed emotion and depression: Mediated by patient's dysfunctional attitudes? *Journal of Clinical and Social Psychology.*

Nelson, G. M., & Beach, S. R. H. (1990). Sequential interaction in depression: Effects of depressive behavior on spousal aggression. *Behavior Therapy, 21*, 167–182.

Pihet, S., Bodenmann, G., Cina, A., Widmer, K., & Shantinath, S. D. (2007). Can prevention of marital distress improve well-being? Results of a 1-year longitudinal study. *Clinical Psychology and Psychotherapy, 14*, 79–88.

Randall, A. K., & Bodenmann, G. (2009). The role of stress on close relationships and marital satisfaction. *Clinical Psychology Review, 29*, 105–115.

Rehman, U. S., Gollan, J., & Mortimer, A. R. (2007). The marital context of depression: Research, limitations, and new directions. *Clinical Psychology Review, 28*, 179–198.

Schmaling, K. B., & Jacobson, N. S. (1990). Marital interaction and depression. *Journal of Abnormal Psychology, 99*, 229–236.

Teichman, Y., Bar-El, Z., Shor, H., Sirota, P., & Elizur, A. (1995). A comparison of two modalities of cognitive therapy (individual and marital) in treating depression. *Psychiatry, 58*, 136–148.

Tesser, A., & Beach, S. R. H. (1998). Life events, relationship quality, and depression: An investigation of judgment discontinuity in vivo. *Journal of Personality and Social Psychology, 74*, 36–52.

Tower, R. B., & Krasner, M. (2006). Marital closeness, autonomy, mastery, and depressive symptoms in a U.S. Internet sample. *Personal Relationships, 13*, 429–449.

Trudel, G., Landry, L., Larose, Y. (1997). Low desire: The role of anxiety, depression and marital adjustment. *Journal of Sex and Marital Therapy, 12*, 95–99.

Weissman, M. M., Markowitz, J. C., & Klerman, G. L. (2000). *Comprehensive guide to interpersonal psychotherapy.* New York: Basic Books.

Whiffen, V. E., & Aube, J. A. (1999). Personality, interpersonal context, and depression in couples. *Journal of Social and Personal Relationships, 16*, 369–383.

Whisman, M. A. (2001). The association between depression and marital satisfaction. In S. R. H. Beach (Ed.), *Marital and family processes in depression: A scientific foundation for clinical practice* (pp. 3–24). Washington, DC: American Psychological Association.

Whisman, M. A. (2007). Marital distress and DSM-IV psychiatric disorders in a population-based national survey. *Journal of Abnormal Psychology, 116*, 638–643.

Whisman, M. A., & Bruce, M. L. (1999). Marital distress and incidence of major depressive episode in a community sample. *Journal of Abnormal Psychology, 108*, 674–678.

# 10

# Depression

## The Challenges of an Integrative, Biopsychosocial Evolutionary Approach

### Paul Gilbert
#### Kingsway Hospital, UK

## Introduction

For many centuries, different cultures have had a myriad of descriptions and explanations for suffering and its alleviation, including and especially depression (Radden, 2000). Beliefs about causes include bad luck, life events and losses, poor childhoods, consequences of past misdeeds (bad karma), anger of God (sinner), a test of spirit, attachment and cravings, soul loss, possession, social oppression, guilt, and black bile (Radden, 2000; Shweder, Much, Mahapatra, & Park, 1997). More recently (see below) we have seen genes, hormones, immune functioning, and an array of psychological processes, both conscious and unconscious, furnished as explanations for suffering. Depending on the meanings given to depression, different people have tried different things to alleviate and prevent depression such as changing one's luck, working off bad karma, passing the spiritual tests, earning the love or forgiveness of God, communing with dead ancestors, seeking release from oppression, exercise, various diets, bodily cleansings, bloodletting, whipping, spinning and cold water immersions, atonements, hard work, self-harm, herbs, pills, potions, and alcohol, and more recently the increasing use of antidepressants, electric shocks, light therapy, and a variety of psychotherapies focusing on conscious or unconscious attention, thinking, feeling, motivations, or behaviors, and working with individuals, groups, couples, and families—and that is far from exhaustive! Yet depression is still increasing and an American community-based study found that of those with "self-diagnosed" depression and anxiety, 53.6% with severe depression and 56.7% with anxiety reported using complimentary medicine and alternative therapies to try to treat their conditions (Kessler et al., 2001).

We have problems! Although depression has been recognized as a common disorder for more than 2,000 years, with many sharp and insightful descriptions (Radden, 2000), unlike certain physical illnesses, there is still no consensus about its cause and the treatment is tenuous. There remains doubt about its physiology and whether (or which type of) depression can be construed as a defect/error, a normal reaction to abnormal circumstances, or the extreme of a normally distributed variation in defensive strategies (Gilbert, 2001, 2006). For some peoples and social groups, life is so harsh that depression may be a common experience. For others, genes and/or early life traumas may drive depression, even for people whose current environments appear to be not so bad. The biopsychosocial approach focuses on the *interactions* between different types of biological, psychological, and social processes. About 35 years ago, Akiskal and McKinney (1975) suggested that depression is best seen as a final common pathway of many different processes. Today its heterogeneity makes this seem less certain.

## The Heterogeneity of Depression

Our understanding of the nature, varieties and complexities of the state of mind we call "depression," has been growing exponentially as witnessed by the comprehensive edition of Ingram's (2009) *The International Encyclopaedia of Depression*. This heterogeneity in symptom variation, triggers, and genetic vulnerabilities poses major problems for animal models too, and is a reason why consensus has been slow to emerge (Anisman & Matheson, 2005). Depression can be classified in various ways and can take many forms, including bipolar or manic depression (Akiskal & Pinto, 1999; Goodwin & Jamison, 1990), major depression (Beckham, Leber, & Youll, 1995), and dysthymia (Griffiths, Ravindran, Merrali, & Anisman, 2000), and according to ICD-10 can be "mild, moderate, or severe." The symptoms of major depression include loss of pleasure (anhedonia) (Clark, 2000; Willner, 1993), loss of motivation/interest (Klinger, 1975, 1993; Watson & Clark, 1988), negative thinking about the self, world, and future (Beck, Rush, Shaw, & Emery, 1979), increased negative emotions (e.g., anxiety and anger; van Praag, 1998), problems in cognitive functions such as memory, attention, and concentration (Gotlib, Gilboa, & Sommerfeld, 2000; Watts, 1993), dysfunctional changes in sleep and restorative processes (Moldofsky & Dickstein, 1999) with dreams becoming more fearful and "nightmarish" (Cukrowicz et al., 2006). There is also a host of biological changes in various neurotransmitter and hormonal systems (Cowen, 2010; McGuade & Young, 2000; Thase & Howland, 1995), immune systems (Raison & Miller, 2012), and various brain areas, such as the frontal cortex (Davidson, 2000).

Although highly heterogeneous, major depression is a common disorder with a point prevalence of around 5% (Kaelber, Moul, & Farmer, 1995) and a 12-month prevalence twice this, with a rate of 7.7% for men and 12.9% for women (Kessler et al., 1994); but both points and yearly prevalence can be much higher in some disadvantaged and traumatized communities (Bebbington, Katz, McGuffin, Sturt, & Wing, 1989). Recent research has also indicated much higher rates in communities when one uses prospective versus retrospective measures of assessment (Moffitt et al., 2010). One in 4–5 women and one in 7–10 men will have an episode at some time in their lives (Bebbington, 1998). Though it is a point of controversy it does seem that depression is increasing (Fombonne, 1994, 1999; Murray & Lopex, 1996) especially in younger cohorts (Twenge et al., 2010). The World Health Organization has pointed out that depression constitutes one of the most common mental health problems (shortly to be rated as the second most burdensome disorder), is a major personal, social, and economic burden, and is associated with the risk of a variety of physical disorders.

At least 50% of people with major depression will have more than one episode with early-onset depression (on or before 20 years) being particularly vulnerable to relapse (Giles, Jarrett, Biggs, Guzick, & Rush, 1989). Early onset is linked to child adversities. Indeed, major depression is regarded as a relapsing condition and about 20% of cases can become chronic (McCullough, 2000; Scott, 1988). However, recently Monroe and Harkness (2011) pointed out that around 50% of people will only have one episode and that research into the single life event episodes is scant. Research has yet to clarify distinctions between relapse, recurrences, and new (unrelated) episodes. They say,

> depression very often does not take a severe lifelong course.... single lifetime cases have fallen between the cracks of theory, research, and practice,.... This class of formerly depressed persons requires detailed attention and analysis. For example, do such persons recover completely and lead "normal" lives? Do they experience chronic or recurring subsyndromal symptoms that impair functioning and impede full participation in and enjoyment of life? Do they develop other comorbid psychiatric conditions? How can it be that someone of proven vulnerability to depression escapes any further episodes? (p. 671)

In 2008 the journal, *Dialogues in Clinical Neuroscience* (downloadable from the Internet at www.dialogues-cns.org), provided a number of scholarly state-of-the-art reviews on treatments for depression—of which there are vast varieties (see above). Although rather focused on psychopharmacology there is growing recognition that our treatments are far from adequate with perhaps only 50% making full recoveries, but the risk of relapse remains high and many patients continue to have residual symptoms. Problems in social functioning can persist well after symptoms have reduced. Also, as Otte (2008) notes,

> In depressed patients, psychiatric and medical comorbidity is the rule rather than exception. About 60% to 70% of depressed patients have at least one comorbid psychiatric condition, about 30% to 40% have two or more comorbid psychiatric disorders. Furthermore, two thirds of depressed patients have at least one concurrent general medical condition.... Currently, several studies have demonstrated that 65% to 90% of treatment-seeking depressed patients would be excluded from a randomized controlled efficacy trials. (p. 458)

Otte (2008) suggests that one of the main reasons for exclusion is comorbidity, meaning we have to be very careful as to the conclusions we draw from highly selective randomized controlled trials. It is not just comorbidity, but also a failure to contextualize "depression" in a much broader context. For example, there is evidence that some treatments like antidepressants may be less effective in people with major social adversities (Brown et al., 2010); people from abusive environments may do poorly with all kinds of interventions (Nanni, Uhser, & Danese, 2012); feeling trapped in environments (such as loveless marriages or stressful jobs one feels unable to get away from) may contribute to chronicity, treatment resistance, and relapse vulnerability (Gilbert, 2007; Gilbert, Gilbert, & Irons, 2004), as may personality and interpersonal style (see below) (Cain et al., 2012).

## Types, categories, dimensions, and discontinuities

Despite the undoubted usefulness of syndromic approaches to mental disorders, from which the above is derived, there is a serious concern with them, partly because depression needs to be understood in its personal and social contexts. This is also because classification systems tend to see symptom clusters as disorders and distinct categories that can overlap with other disorders, and vary in levels of severity, but are distinct nonetheless (Gilbert, 1984, 1992, 2007). But even syndromic approaches recognize that depression is a highly heterogeneous disorder with a variety of proposed subtypes such as neurotic–psychotic, bipolar–unipolar, endogenous–reactive, primary–secondary, early onset–late onset, angry versus anxious, agitated–retarded, serotonin versus noradrenalin based, and various mixed states (Gilbert, 1984, 1992, 2007) with a new category of atypical depression also being suggested (Posternak & Zimmerman, 2002)—to name just a few. Various personality distinctions that texture the triggers, symptom profiles, and treatment needs of depressed people have also been suggested (Zuroff, Mongrain, & Santor, 2004). It is also clear that relapse vulnerability is another important dimension of variation in depression (Monroe & Harkness, 2011).

Depressions vary with different patterns of symptom clusters (e.g., of sadness, anhedonia, fatigue, and sleep disturbance). In a study of 4,856 individuals (53% female) over 12 years, Keller, Neale, and Kendler (2007) reported,

> Deaths of loved ones and romantic breakups were marked by high levels of sadness, anhedonia, appetite loss, and (for romantic breakups) guilt. Chronic stress and, to a lesser degree, failures were associated with fatigue and hypersomnia, but less so with sadness, anhedonia, and appetite loss. Those who reported that no adverse life events caused their dysphoric episodes reported fatigue, appetite gain, and thoughts of self-harm, but less sadness or trouble concentrating. (p. 1512)

Andrews (1998) has shown that chronic depression in women is linked to childhood sexual abuse and the history of abuse in depression is associated with increased risk of PTSD symptoms, impulsivity, self-destructive behaviors, and self-harm (Boudewyn & Liem, 1995). People with depressions associated with abuse have less favorable treatment outcomes than nonabused people (Nanni et al., 2012).

To further complicate the picture, Akiskal and Pinto (1999) suggest that a substantial minority of depressions are related to a spectrum of bipolar disorders, some of which may be destabilized on traditional antidepressants. In a recent study, Smith et al. (2011) found that between 3.3% and 21.6% of patients in primary care settings diagnosed with unipolar disorders may actually have different variants of bipolar disorders (depending on how it is measured) with major implications for treatment and relapse prevention. And as noted, depression is also, more often than not, comorbid with other (especially anxiety) disorders (Brown, Campbell, Lehman, Grisham, &

Mancill, 2001). For these sorts of reasons Coyne (1994) raised major concerns about dimensional approaches (e.g., mild, moderate, and severe), assuming that studying mildly depressed or dysphoric people (e.g., some students) can be extrapolated to more severe depression; there may be a quite different process involved.

Coyne's view has been challenged (Vredenburg, Flett, & Krames, 1993; Zuroff et al., 2004); but this debate, on types of depressions, spectra of the disorder, and variations in physiological, psychological, and social processes, raises key issues about the models we use to investigate complex interacting processes. We can, for example, consider the question of discontinuities in severity of depression (i.e., some people have more severe depressions than others) and whether discontinuities necessarily suggest different processes (e.g., causes and vulnerability factors) and/or different relationships (interactions) between processes. For example, catastrophe theory (Zeeman, 1977; and chaos theory) points out that processes that are themselves dimensional and linear can produce discontinuous effects according to the state of the system. Many systems are like this in fact; the straw that breaks the camel's back, the wave breaking on the beach, or the animal that is fighting and then suddenly, as fear gets the better of it, turns tail and runs away; and in anxiety disorders we talk of "panic attacks" as a sudden onset of a major change in the system. These, then, are points of sudden shifts and discontinuities. Hence, in 1984 I argued that taking a dimensional approach to depression is *not to assume linearity* (i.e., a bit more of this causes a bit more of that). I used what is called the *Cusp Catastrophe* (Zeeman, 1977) to explore this (Gilbert, 1984, pp. 199–215). Hence, although there are different types of depressions, with different severities there may still be *similarities in the processes and types of stressors that trigger them*. However, due to system organization factors (e.g., genes or types of early trauma) small variations in one dimension (e.g., a rejection that makes one feel unloved) can produce catastrophic effects in another part of the system (e.g., stress hormones). This concept, of nonlinear discontinuities of states linked to stress, is now well formulated (Ganzel, Morris, & Wethington, 2010). The concept of discontinuities is also stressed by Raison et al. to explain how small variations in immune system functioning, for some individuals, can actually have big effects "downstream" on systems such as the stress system (Raison, Lowry, & Rook, 2010; Raison & Miller, 2012). So small variations in the process in systems set up in a certain way can cause a system to spiral down or dramatically shift to a new equilibrium (catastrophic shift) way different (below) from what (say) someone else might experience. We often call these predepression factors *vulnerability* factors but another way to think of them is as *system setters*, that is, they set a system up in a certain way to be capable of producing "catastrophic" shifts of state and effects in some contexts.

Cognitive therapists also have sometimes suggested mechanisms by which sudden switches of state can arise in depression. For example, they suggest that people develop core beliefs and schema as a result of childhood experiences, which can be reactivated and which produced "catastrophic" changes. For example, a child who is often rejected or abandoned can develop a core belief that they will be abandoned, with the associated feelings of abandonment. Certain events may trigger interpersonal conflicts which then activate the abandonment schema and "reorganizes" the person's state of mind. Beck (1967, p. 277) described this type of vulnerability as "negative latent schema" that can persist and be "like an explosive charge ready to be detonated by an appropriate set of conditions." *Explosions* are not smooth transitions, and it points again to the issue of potential discontinuity in switching from nondepressed to depressed states. Meehl (1995) offered an important discussion of these difficulties in classification (e.g., categorical vs. dimensional) and called for new mathematical models for their study. However, the fact that discontinuities can arise from dimensional processes does not imply that all depressions should be understood as variations along shared dimensions or even as a common pathway. Indeed, our understanding of individual variation now argues against this.

## Gender

Another source of variation between depressions is of course gender. Explanations of the 2:1 or 3:1 gender differences in rates of depression are given in terms of biological differences such as sex hormones (especially important is the mood linked to menstrual cycles and menopause, which may represent specific types of mood disorders; Hartlage, Freels, Gotman, & Yonkers, 2012); differences in emotional processing; differences in ruminative styles, vulnerabilities to shame, inhibition of anger; social differences (such that women occupy more subordinate positions in society), vulnerability to domestic violence, childhood sexual abuse; differences in the importance of affiliative relationships for well-being (Harris, Surtees, & Bancroft, 1991). McQuire and Troisi (1998) offered an important ecological–evolutionary idea that since males dominate the creation of cultural forms and economic relationships, they have created these to benefit themselves at the expense of the more socially integrative and supportive relationships that benefit women. In a biopsychosocial approach, *interactions* between any or *all* of these variables may be important but differ for individual cases.

In regard to the manifestation of depression there has been consideration that women show more somatic symptoms than men. However, in a recent major study of matched men–women scores on BDI-11, Delisle, Beck, Dobson, Dozois, and Thombs (2012) found that such differences were small and inconsequential. There are also suggestions that actually the differences in rates are simple differences in manifestation and expression of depression, with men having more externalizing symptoms such as irritability and aggression, are more likely to use alcohol, more likely to close down on emotions, in contrast to women who tend to be more internalizing, tearful, submissive, and emotionally open. However, in a large student population Möller-Leimkühler and Yücel (2010) found that women were just as likely to have externalizing symptoms as men—although we do not know if there is a historical change or cultural version on this. A more complex insight comes from a study of 54 depressed men and 50 depressed women by Gilbert, Irons, Olsen, Gilbert, and McEwan (2006) who looked at three components of depression: mood (including anxiety and depression); internalization (related to self-blame and feelings of low rank/inferiority); and externalization (related to anger and blaming others). For both men and women, internalization was significantly correlated with depression. However, externalization was negatively related to depression in women, but positively related in men. So the link between depression and internalization may be similar for men and women but externalization may operate differently for men and women.

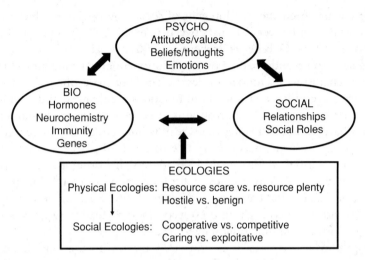

**Figure 10.1.** A Biopsychosocial and Ecological Model. Reproduced from Gilbert (2004), with permission from Wiley

## Biopsychosocial Approaches

One of the reasons that our models and treatments of *the depressions* are still lacking arises from difficulties in studying interactive processes, and a lack of an integrating evolutionary framework which gives insight into function (Gilbert, 1992, 1995, 2007; Panksepp, 2010). This has recently been discussed as a problem for studies in psychopathology in general (Brune et al., 2012). Yet we know that systems (including physiological systems) change as a function of both the forces acting upon them and their own internal dynamics (Gilbert, 1984). There is now increasing recognition that depression is typically related to a host of processes in the domains of physiology (genes and stress hormones), psychology (negative beliefs, rumination, and social withdrawal), and social factors (life events and social support or hostility) that interact over time (Akiskal & McKinney, 1975; Hammen, Garber, & Ingram, 2010). We also know that these in turn are contextualized within certain ecologists—such as ones of high social adversity (Brown et al., 2010). A model for interaction is depicted in Figure 10.1.

Early forerunners of the biopsychosocial approach can be found in Meyers' psychobiology approach (Rutter, 1986), behavioral medicine, and psychosomatic medicine (Kiesler, 1999), and there is growing interest in depression as a vulnerability factor to various physical conditions such as diabetes and cardiovascular disease (Kupfer, Frank, & Phillips, 2011). The influence goes the other way too as it is now known that various mood-linked (neurochemical) systems are influenced by cardiovascular (Porges, 2007) and immune system functioning (Kupfer et al., 2011; Miller, Maletic, & Raison, 2009; Raison et al., 2010). Depression is associated with lower heart rate variability, which in turn is associated with heart disease (Kemp, Quintana, Felmingham, Matthews, & Jelinek, 2012).

More recent has been the development of social neuroscience, which is focused on the interaction and coregulation between neurophysiology and social relationships (Cozolino, 2007; Ochsner & Lieberman, 2001; Ward, 2011). Biopsychosocial approaches need to be underpinned by an evolutionary understanding of the origins (when the mechanisms that underpin depression begin to evolve), *functions* (what problems they solved then and how those functions are retained and operate now), *structures* (what brain systems are involved in the mechanisms underpinning depression and how have they been adapted, and are now (may be) under different regulatory mechanisms)—that is their current *regulation* (Brune et al., 2012; Gilbert, 1995). As we will see later, various models could help address this issue: learned helplessness, coping with poor resource environments, disruption and loss of attachment and affiliative bonds, and defeat and entrapment (Gilbert, 2006). Such models are applicable across species and provide insight into evolved mood regulating systems (see Raison & Miller, 2012 for an immune system hypothesis).

The biopsychosocial approach is critical of narrow focused or single process approaches and is critical of "the dualisms" (mind vs. body; nature vs. nuture)—which Eisenberg (2000) aptly termed *brainless versus mindless* science—that still plague our theorizing. One thing is clear, however—although many clinicians of all types pay lip service to a biopsychosocial approach, few clinicians are actually trained in it or adopt it in their clinical practice or research (Gilbert, 1995; Kiesler, 1999) government policies also fail to reflect biopsychosocial models and focus instead on providing people with individual solutions, be they drugs and/or therapies. This has huge and very negative effects on prevention (as we have seen rates of depression are extraordinarily high and increasing) and treatments because single treatments (such as antidepressants vs. cognitive behavior therapy), which tend to be highly focused on individuals completely outside of the social context, are often played off against each other and then one type of therapy can suddenly become the flavor of the month and is adopted nationwide! To engage in this debate though would be to engage in controversies over the research agenda itself, including randomized controlled trials. The point here is simpler and calls for *radical* shifts in research, training, and practice (Gilbert, 1995, 2009a; Kiesler, 1999; World Health Organization (WHO), 2010).

## Genotypes and phenotypes

Many clinicians, especially psychologists, do not grasp some of the most basic principles and evolutionary psychology and key to biopsychosocial approach is the concept of phenotype (Brune et al., 2012). At its simplest (and there are more complex definitions) a phenotype is created by the interaction between the potential carried by the genes of an organism and its environmental shaping (Boyce & Ellis, 2005; Boyce, Essex, & Ellis, 2005; Gilbert & Miles, 2000). It is complicated because genes interact and the environment can affect their interaction, turning some genes on and some off at different times; even the environment of the womb may affect genetic expression (Harper, 2005). Phenotypes are manifestations of potential, so the potential to learn to speak a language (with all the appropriate neurophysical structures such as the larynx and cortical coding systems) is a genotype; the language that is spoken and *how that language influences thinking* is the phenotype. The potential to develop attachment relationships is a genotype while the types of relationships and relating styles people develop, according to whether they experienced love, abuse, and neglect, is the phenotype. Obesity and diabetes are increasing rapidly but this is not due to some change in genes in the population but the (food availability) environments in which our genes are now operating (Smith, 2002). It is recognized that any serious effort at prevention (of obesity) will have to target not only individual behaviors, but also the social contexts, which in this case is the food industry. This kind of analysis enables us to recognize that people can become quite "ill" as a result of "normal genes" encountering abnormal environments. Given the very high rates of depression, which seems to be increasing, especially in younger cohorts, we need to look much more closely to environmental factors such as shift from community values to individualistic, materialistic, competitive values (Twenge et al., 2010). Biopsychosocial models are essential to understand cause, prevention, and treatment. In an effort to raise the importance of biopsychosocial approaches, and in particular, the social contexts which give rise to the causes of illness, the WHO (2010) has been focusing on efforts to understand the "social determinants of disease" and recognizes the important training implications, particularly for medicine that has (partly due to pressure of numbers) become more and more focused on diagnosis and biological interventions.

However, the influence of the social environment can also be very indirect. Raison et al. (2010) and Raison and Miller (2012) have made the important observation that our environments have also changed significantly in regard to the microorganisms to which we are exposed. There is increasing evidence that microorganisms played a fundamental role in our evolution. Indeed, we are evolved to anticipate and to be regulated by microorganisms in various ways, in particular the immune system, which can influence a whole range of neurophysiological processes. They make the argument that although we usually think about the way different alleles (such as the short versions of monoamine transporter genes) interact with *social* environments to increase vulnerability to depression, we can also think about their interaction in regard to microorganic environments. Looked at in this way, although certain alleles might appeared to increase the risk of psychological disorders they could also confer benefit in environments where appropriate microorganisms are present. This opens up completely new dimensions of thinking about biopsychosocial interactions and how "in cleaning up" microorganisms may actually be part of the problem. They also raise the important issue of the linkage between immune system functioning and mood states, which also promise novel and potentially important treatment pathways. Again, the concept of phenotype is essential here.

So for the biopsychosocial approach, and for the development of the science of understanding disorders like depression, the concept of phenotype is more useful as an integrating concept than say that the concept of schema (beloved by cognitive therapists) because it helps us think about how a whole range of physiological and psychological processes emerge and become organized to fit certain ecological niches, and how, as niches change, they can provide unexpected or unusual challenges to the adapting organism (Ganzel et al., 2010). Yet clinicians very rarely use the concept of phenotype or think of its implications. For example, given the science of neuroplasticity and gene sensitivity to environmental contingencies (Belsky & Pluess, 2009), including microorganisms (Raison et al., 2010) is it possible to change phenotypes once formed? Should phenotypic change be the real focus for treatments? How would one measure that?

## Emergence

A second major biopsychosocial construct is the (un)predictability of the *emergence* of states of mind. Perhaps one of the greatest mysteries is why certain combinations of elements produce the patterns they do; for instance, why two atoms of hydrogen and one of oxygen produce a totally different molecule "water" with very specific and different properties to either hydrogen or oxygen. This emergence arises through the higher-level organization of lower-level interactions (Johnson, 2002). For example, genes build bodies and physiological systems that together create brains and "conscious feeling" minds and these are themselves responding to external influences that stimulate or inhibit physiological pathways (literally shaping themselves in feedback loops)—but crucial to the emergence of patterns in a brain, there is no overall "coordinating gene or process," no master director. An anthill emerges because of the interactions of millions of ants; there is no master controller—it simply emerges from the interactions of the multitude, and no two anthills are the same. Multilevel organization then allows patterns to emerge but while patterns are sometimes predictable, sometimes they are not.

Psychologists point to the emergence of "the self" as a coordinating system to provide consistency and coherence (McGregor & Marigold, 2003) but while important this does not ensure voluntary control over complex motives or emotions; we often find ourselves feeling, thinking, and behaving in ways we would rather not. The biopsychosocial approach is therefore also the study of the emergence of states of mind from multilevel, dynamic reciprocal interacting processes that are coregulating and coshaping each other—and the medium (physical and social environments) in which they are acting.

## Biological–Social Interactive Processes

Among some of the most fascinating advances in the study of the link between social context and biology has also been studies of the polymorphisms of different genes, particularly serotonin and dopamine transporter genes. Early evidence suggested that the short alleles of these genes conveyed depression risk in the context of early stress (Caspi & Moffit, 2006; Kupfer et al., 2011). However, a biopsychosocial model has proved essential because there is now good evidence that while social relationships affect gene expression, certain gene alleles may actually reflect increased potential for *phenotypic variation*. It is not the case that people with short alleles are doomed to depression because in fact they tend to do poorly or *well* according to the benignness or adversity of certain, especially early environments (Belsky & Pluess, 2009; Brody et al., 2009). So short alleles seem to be more responsive *to both positive and negative environments*. It is possible that such alleles become advantaged if neuroplasticity increases (see Liu et al., 2012).

In addition to gene expression, early social environments influence a whole range of maturating neurophysiological processes, including important pathways between frontal cortex and affect regulating systems such as the amygdala (Cozolinio, 2007; Schore, 2010). Two types of processes need to be considered here. One is linked to structural processes (how the brain actually wires itself), which may or may not be open to change later in life thanks to a new understanding of the importance of neuroplasticity. A second process is linked to the potential for type of change within the system; what I called the system setters (see above). For example, the capacity for, and potential patterns of, affect variation within an individual are linked to early life experiences. People who have been subjected to severe adverse (early) life events will have experienced high stress and possibly low positive affect states as a consequence. Key brain systems may then have greater potential for "remembering" and thus reactivating these patterns in times of stress or for other reasons. This is important because while a whole range of neurophysiological processes are involved in depression, and depressed brains are different from nondepressed brains, these differences tend to disappear on recovery (Kupfer et al., 2011). This suggests (the obvious point) that brains switch states, under certain conditions (Gilbert, 1984), and generate certain patterns (e.g., patterns of activity in the dorsal lateral, orbital, and medial prefrontal cortexes, in relationship to amygdala and hypothalamic processing associated with various neurotransmitter systems). The question then, is understanding the availability and potential for these types of switches in brain states and how to switch them to more desired states.

Throughout life social relationships play major roles in people's physiological regulation with many and major impacts on various brain circuits and other systems such as immune, cardiovascular, and lymphatic (Cacioppo, Bernston, Sheridan, & McClintock, 2000; Cacioppo & Patrick, 2008; Cozolino, 2008; Raison et al., 2010). Individuals, as physiological systems, are constantly socially contextualized and choreographed, and while cognitive systems allow some autonomy it may be more limited than we think.

## Biosocial–Psychological Interface: The Implications of Humans Getting "Smart"

The human brain is similar to other animals in terms of both its emotional and motivational systems but also fundamentally different. We share with other animals a whole range of social motives for belonging, attachment, sex, and status-seeking, dominant, and subordinate behavioral systems. Also humans have a whole variety of subgoals that are linked more or less to these evolved biosocial goals such as studying at university to get a good job to earn the money to buy the car to impress potential sexual partner and bring up children (Gilbert, 1989, 2009b). We also share a range of potential emotions with animals such as anger, anxiety, joy, lust—indeed, if this were not the case then animal brains would not be used for research into these basic processes (sadly for them). We can call these old brain functions (Gilbert, 2009b).

However about 2 million years ago, a line of primates who led eventually to homo sapiens, began to evolve cognitive competencies that would allow us to get smart (Geary & Huffman, 2002). Researchers are revealing that this was not just development of new structures such as the frontal cortex but also in changes and genetic regulation of synaptic development, especially in the early years (see Liu et al., 2012). This obviously raises issues in regard to developmental experiences that will also affect synaptic development and the evolution of different alleles (see above).

Another question, regarding our evolved cognitive abilities (with implications for depression), is the degree to which our reasoning and thinking can be modular; and that the way "we reason" really depends upon the task at hand (Gilbert, 1998a). This is important because different types of problems require us to integrate different types of information (Buss, 2003). So the way we reason when it comes to looking after our children is quite different to how we reason, and the memories and emotions we recruit, when competing for status or fighting with our enemies. Reasoning about who represents a desirable sexual partner uses different processing systems than those used when engaged in theory of mind (ToM), mentalizing, and empathy processing (Liotti & Gilbert, 2011). The way young children pay attention and reason when suddenly abandoned is different to how they pay attention and reason when safe and content. Many of the ways we process evolutionary important situations are believed to be partly innate and algorithmic, and they come with *specific heuristic algorithms and biases* that are not the result of learned cognitive schemas. Moreover, they operate across species (Tobena, Marks, & Dar, 1999). That humans often reason on the basis of heuristics rather than logic has been suggested for some time. For example, Kahneman and Tversky (1972) note,

> In making predictions and judgements under uncertainty, people do not appear to follow the calculus of chance or statistical theory of prediction. Instead, they rely on a limited number of heuristics which sometimes yield reasonable judgements and sometimes lead to severe and systematic errors. (p. 237)

So for example, the young of all mammals show distress, seek attention, search, and lose interest in positives like food when abandoned. These are not learned behaviors or ways of thinking and attending to the world, but are part of innate algorithms they are thinking of attending: "if A happens focus on that, and think like this" (Buss, 2003). The stress system also shows elevated cortisol to these kinds of events in most species studied. Again, animals are not learning to respond with a cortisol elevation to separation from the parent—it's a biological given defensive response. This is important because cortisol itself has an impact on cognitive processing and biases. The fact that people make "errors" in reasoning as they get depressed should not surprise us; therefore, it may indicate some defensive algorithms at work, especially since depressed people can have very similar ways of thinking. One model that makes this explicit is the social risk model of depression (see Allen & Badcock, 2003).

So the evolutionary view is that human psychology is (partly) made up of "modules" or special-purpose algorithms designed to certain things. Selecting a sexual partner is not based on logic, nor is empathic reasoning. The key here is that if certain kinds of difficulties (like separation, social defeat, loss of control) activate specific types of heuristics and algorithms rather than reasoned and verbally accessible sequencing in thinking, this will have implications for treatment. Some of our defensive heuristics and algorithms may not be easily accessible to consciousness or insight and can create all kinds of problems (Gilbert, 1998a). The degree to which people's cognitive systems become "encapsulated" in specific "narrow" and focused ways, stuck in a train of thinking and feeling choreographed (partly) by the innate defenses for coping with the defeat abandonment or social threat, is yet to be properly investigated (Gilbert, 1989, ch. 14). Space does not allow us to enter this debate in detail but these issues have been recently explored by Bolhuis, Brown, Richardson, and Laland (2011), with a growing consensus that we do have specialized processing systems, especially when it comes to evolutionarily important motives and goals, but we also have general processing systems that can be used across a multitude of tasks. These insights have implications for understanding the regulators of depressed mood, because "thinking" may have evolved to function differently in different social contexts (e.g., hostility vs. friendliness). General-purpose cognitive abilities that can be applied to multiple tasks and motivations may also be a source of depression because of the creation of thought–feeling recursive loops, as suggested in cognitive therapy ideas. Here again, however, these problematic feedback loops between thinking and feeling exist because of how our brain has evolved, not just because we learn certain schemas.

## Cognition as general-purpose abilities

Cognitive therapy for depression (Beck et al., 1979) became very popular because of its simple and straightforward axioms and promise of therapeutic benefit (Gilbert, 1992). The idea was relatively simple; that consciously available, negative thoughts are symptoms of acquired negative beliefs about the self, world, and future learned in childhood. Once triggered, these negative beliefs bias thinking to form maladaptive feedback loops that drive down mood. The cognitive approach favors a focus on consciously available, general-purpose cognitive abilities rather than modularized, specific algorithms. General-purpose cognitive abilities involve competencies for conscious thinking that enable reasoning, anticipation, imagination, rumination, reflection, and planning. In effect, we can run simulations of potential opportunistic or threatening situations in our minds where outcomes can be anticipated without actually having to risk engagement and experience failure, threat, or harm. Simulations are also powerful aids for problem-solving; for instance, with how to get the shelter built, find food, date one's desired mate, or look after the children. From these abilities to simulate and imagine we can be creative and create tools, clothes, weapons, buildings, art, and so on—to modern science.

Importantly, though these "new brain" competencies also interact with (much older) motives and emotional systems in complex ways. Motives obviously play key roles in the forms of simulations we create: the "what" we think about rather than the "how" we think. Obvious too is that many of our simulations, where we predict the links between events and outcomes, or predict the future, are not necessarily accurate and can be unhelpful (Beck et al., 1979; Gilbert, 1998a). Although Beck has been very keen to link cognitive models with our understanding of evolutionary processes (see Beck, 1987 for his discussion of cognition-linked abandonment and defeat state biases) the way CBT is taught today rather strips the mind of evolved motivational systems and the importance of specific algorithmic ways of processing information (Gilbert, 1992).

Consciously and purposely created simulations are very important, however, and can work in another way by replaying and reanalyzing. For example, a zebra will be frightened when chased by a lion and run away, but once out of sight the zebra will gradually get back to grazing again. Humans, however, could well ruminate about "what would have happened if" they had not escaped and fantasize most terrible outcomes (being eaten alive!). They may find their minds full of unwanted memories or unpleasant intrusions and can ruminate on what could happen if they do not spot the lion in the future. As Wells (2000) and Fisher and Wells (2009) suggest, humans engage in a lot of "what if... thoughts." Depressed people in particular also engage in a lot of counterfactual thinking—"if only I had... ; If only I hadn't... "—going over and over past harms and getting locked into cycles of regret and frustration.

It is as if we have a kind of "go back and repair function" linked to regret. Clearly the (evolved) ability to recognize damage and to repair has advantages. Sometimes it is possible to repair and make amends, and this is essentially important for the guilt or repairing relationships—the ability to apologize or put it right (Gilbert, 1989). However, the same motives and focus may get stuck—leaving us constantly wanting to change something in the past that is not changeable—an example where regret and trying to work out what one can do to repair/change something becomes maladaptive (see Dalgleish, Hill, Morant, & Golden, 2011). People crave time machines—although as the film the "Butterfly Effect" noted, sometimes changing the past makes things worse. Instead, therapists help us to "let go" or "come to terms" with the past as the past and unchangeable, in effect removing it from the constant stimulation and "find and repair" algorithmic ways of thinking.

So human rumination does seem to be able to operate outside any "modularized" cognitive competency. In fact, evolutionary approaches also argue that the evolution of human capacities for thinking, reasoning, planning, and mental simulations influence not only mental health problems but also physical ones, as outlined in Sapolsky's (2004) famous book *Why Zebras Don't Get Ulcers*. The point is, though, that these cognitive abilities have evolved because the advantage motives link to reproduction and survival.

Although there are specific brain areas that regulate it, the focus of rumination can range over simply trying to solve a problem to all kinds of fears, possibilities to come, threats, and harms passed. We should also note that rumination may have an algorithm behind it which is something like "run simulation again and again until threat/harm is removed/reduced." However, although depressed people cannot easily turn off or away from negative simulations of self, future, and world (Beck et al., 1979; Fischer & Wells, 2009), this may not have (just) a "cognitive" source (Panksepp, 2010). In fact, simulations can be partly driven by motivational and emotional processes in the limbic system, which give rise to intrusions; indeed, a ruminative simulation may itself maintain threat processing rather than resolve it. Grief is a classic example where one may not want to keep thinking about the lost person and feel the pain of loss, but it keeps returning unbidden. It is also possible that some of the power of a simulation is driven by emotional memory and past trauma. Here we need different models of emotion–cognition linkage that takes account of conditioning and associative learning (Power & Dalgleish, 2008). In any event, understanding how the stimulations have got stuck in recursive feedback loops, and the degree to which modular and nonmodular cognitive processing is involved, provide key research avenues to depression.

A key problem for depression then becomes immediately obvious; old brain motives, emotions, and emotional memories and new brain "reasoning" competencies get locked together in *maladaptive loops*. Note that this is a modern take on what is essentially a well-recognized problem, which the Greeks regarded as the problem of "rationality versus passion" and their mutual influence, and was the seedbed for cognitive therapies (Beck et al., 1979; Dryden, 2012; Power & Dalgleish, 2008). The issue for depression then is that as one becomes depressed there is a shift in brain states and patterns that direct attention, thinking, and behavior in certain ways—mostly linked to threats and losses (Gilbert, 1992, 2007). Memories of previous threats and losses are activated and attention and focusing on positive events become more difficult, while attention and focusing on negative events, including those in autobiographical memory become more easily accessible (Dalgleish et al., 2011). Once attention gets locked into "negative memories and classes of information, and ruminating then one is stuck in a depression loop" (Fischer & Wells, 2009).

It is this loop (between new brain capacities for awareness, having a sense of self, rumination and old brain, deeply rooted emotional motivational systems of the body and "felt" experience) which recent mindfulness approaches attempt to interrupt (Kuyken et al., 2010; Williams, Teasdale, Segal, & Kabat-Zinn, 2007). Mindfulness teaches us to put our attention *into observation* of these inner loops as opposed to being part of them. Whether these loops are linked to evolved brain algorithm functions that create certain simulations under certain conditions or are a link to general-purpose "cognitive processes" of attention is not considered within the mindfulness tradition. For example, questions have been raised about whether targeting *the way* people reason, by helping them take on more evidence-based approach, is necessary for change (Longmore & Worrell, 2007), while the mindfulness tradition advocates that one should change people's *relationships* to their thoughts and not worry too much about the content of the thoughts themselves (Davis & Hayes, 2011). In principle, all thoughts are treated the same, as parts of a wandering mind, whether one is thinking about what to have for dinner or how one is going to cope with having just lost one's job. One implication, however, is that to reduce activity in one algorithm or module you may need to set another one running. Returning attention to focus on the breath may be quite helpful for a cluttered mind, thinking about what to buy the kids for dinner, but developing (say) compassion, focusing may be important when dealing with the fear of having lost one's job—where compassion is seen as an innate algorithm linked to specific physiological systems that could counteract self-criticism or the sense of being alone (Gilbert, 2010).

The new brain capacity for rumination is also linked to another new brain human function: *imagination*. The importance of imagination as a creative competency is, of course, key to human success. However, humans can be plagued by distressing, intrusive ruminations and imaginations, and there is increasing evidence that depressed people can be haunted by intrusive images and memories (Brewin, 2006; Hackmann,

Bennet-Levy, & Holmes, 2011), which again can be understood in terms of algorithms that repeat simulations until they are resolved. It is important that imagination can drive physiological processes, for example, if one lies in bed and *deliberately* imagines a hot sexual fantasy this will stimulate the *specific* cell bodies and physiological systems, causing release of hormones from the pituitary, giving rise to feelings, body change, urges, and more fantasies—and of course people use imagery and fantasies precisely because they know *it can* stimulate physiological processes. This is using imagery on purpose for physiological effect. Note that this is a biologically wired-in connection, and although I suppose you could develop sexual fantasies about bananas or motorbikes and conditioning is always possible (hence fetishes), in general the strength of the linkage between image and physiology has to do with the evolved design.

So images and thoughts that are linked to depression are probably also linked in some way to evolved design, such that certain kinds of stimuli would trigger "depressed" patterns and the brain—subject of course to many individual variations. In depression, images tend to be intrusive, ruminative, dark, and unpleasant (Hackmann et al., 2011). As intrusive images enter into consciousness, they may be capable of stimulating important physiological systems (e.g., depressogenic). This is no different from saying that a spontaneous sexual image may stimulate the pituitary. Not surprisingly then our new brain function for imagination has also become a target for intervention with specifically developed imagery-based therapies and imagery work, and these are thought to be more powerful than verbal interventions (Hackmann et al., 2011). This research is looking at the medium of processing (e.g., verbal, behavioral, imaginal) that most specifically links to physiology.

Another new brain competency that links to attention, imagination, reasoning, and rumination is *meta-cognition*. This is the ability to be aware of thinking, to think about the nature (source and functions) of one's thinking, the sources and nature of one's emotions and motives, and even the nature of one's mind; it is "taking a view from the balcony." Wells (2000) and Fisher and Wells (2009) point out that while traditional cognitive therapy tends to focus on distortions and biases in reasoning and helping people "correct" them, meta-cognitive processes and therapies are similar to mindfulness in that they help people change *their relationships* to their thinking. They focus on the way people's attentional mechanisms get caught in loops and how one can help people identify this, and switch their attentional strategies. This is more like an algorithmic-type intervention of trying to change the process itself not the content. However, rather than focusing on innate algorithms, most meta-cognitive therapists stick with the idea that maladaptive attentional strategies can be kept in place by meta-cognitive beliefs such as "only by worrying can I solve the problem." or "I have to work out why I am depressed."

## Some difficulties

While cognitive approaches have made and continue to make important contributions to our understanding and treatment of depression that is not without difficulties. One is that some cognitive models lack specificity. So a concept like "core beliefs or schema" risks becoming rarefied "entities in the mind" rather than part of the way the brain processes information. More problematically, cognitive therapists tend to use the concept of "cognition" and "information processing" interchangeably. However, your computer, DNA, and amygdala are all information processing systems but they do not have cognitions. If one is not careful cognition comes to stand for any psychological or "information" process and so it is unclear what one gains by calling some process a "cognitive" process. You also risk losing linkage to more multilayered reciprocal concepts like phenotype. This problem has been resolved to some extent recently by psychologists being much more precise in defining attention, rumination, imagination, and intrusions. These can then be understood as psychologies in their own right and how they operate in the brain and link to a whole range of other processing systems, such as emotional and behavioral outputs.

Beck (1996) was aware of the problem of rarefied cognitive concepts and suggested ideas of *integrated modes*, which are different from schemas. Beck (2008) has also tried to locate how and where distortions in processing arise. He places them close to our emotional core (such as the amygdala) but some might see this as emotion biasing rather than cognitive biasing. At their core though all these approaches recognize the importance of loops between "old brain emotions and motives" and "new brain cognitive functions" and helping clients develop more "frontal cortical control" for their patients—breaking these loops—either by switching of attention or creating alternatively different emotional systems (as compassion-focused therapy would attempt to do—see below)—or both.

Another problem that psychologies face in developing a better understanding of and therapies for depression is the old chestnut of the conscious and "un" or nonconscious interface. There is now good research showing that what appears in "conscious attention" may be very late in the processing sequence and that what appears in conscious attention may be very different from unconscious and preconscious attention (Hassin, Uleman, & Bargh, 2005). Psychodynamic theories argue that it is not only that "attention" can pick up on information unconsciously, but also we can have fantasies and images operating unconsciously; they are warded off from consciousness and the therapeutic task is to enable the patient to develop a capacity for acknowledging, engaging, thinking, and reflecting on them—especially aggressive and sexual fantasies (Davenloo, 2005). Getting evidence for this is tricky but not impossible. There is, for example, evidence that people's own judgments of their abilities can be influenced by subliminal priming of faces showing approval or disapproval of (in one research case) the university professor (Baldwin & Dandeneau, 2005). People who are primed with an approving face judge their ideas more positively than those who are primed with a disapproving face. People fully believe that they are making their own judgments when actually they have been primed by social approval/disapproval.

## The Social Brain

Most of the cognitive models do not distinguish between social and nonsocial processing (negative views of the world can be treated the same as negative views of self or others) but in fact this is a fundamental distinction. The evolved expansion of the human brain was, as noted above, linked to changes in synaptic development and expansions in frontal cortical systems. However, brains are extremely "expensive" to maintain, so there must have been important payoffs for this evolution. A growing consensus suggests that what drove this was the cognitive demands of increasingly complex *social* relating (Dunbar, 2007, 2010; Whiten, 1999). For example, birds who pair bond for life have bigger brains than those who do not, and this is because pair-bonded birds have to coordinate their behavior in much more complex ways over long periods of time (Dunbar, 2010). So another reason (and may be the principal reason) we got smart was developing particular abilities for *social intelligence* and processing that included capacities for empathy, ToM, and higher-order thinking, and inferences (e.g., I believe in X; I want you to believe that I believe in X; I want to believe that you believe that I believe in X, and so on). Again, the issue of how modular they are and how algorithmic they are is important if we are to think about therapy.

These are complex competencies enabling us to understand each other, make simulations of, judge and predict social behavior, and coordinate our interactions. These are highly specialized competencies and *different* from general reasoning abilities (Dunbar, 2007, 2010). Some individuals can have high general intelligence and well developed problem-solving abilities but have very little capacity for empathy or understanding of their own or other people's feelings, motives, and thoughts (Baron-Cohen, 2011). There is evidence that, specialized for social relating, these competencies operate through different neural systems (such as the medial frontal cortex) compared to general reasoning (see Decety & Ickes, 2011 for discussions).

With ToM abilities one can think about someone else—what they may know and don't know (as in the classic studies of ToM in children): what motivates *their* behaviour, what they might value, what they know, and what they don't know, and we can *think* how to manipulate them to like us or be wary of us, or help them. Whiten (1999) argues that "Reading others' minds makes minds deeply social in that those minds *interpenetrate* each other." (p. 177)

Dunbar (2007) puts it this way:

> The social brain hypothesis, then, argues that maintaining and servicing the kinds of intense relationships found in pairbonds (in most birds and mammals) and friendships (among anthropoid primates) involves serious cognitive work, which in turn, is reflected in the size of a species brain. But it is, at the same time, apparent, both from the human social psychology literature on friendships and from the ethological literature on how primates service their relationships, that cognition is only part of the story. There is a deeply emotional component to relationships that derives in both cases from doing things together. This leads us, perhaps inevitably, into the issue of how primates bond their social groups. (p. 409)

Importantly, there are all kinds of biases linked into how we read other people's minds and problems of projection—assuming they think and feel as we do (Nickerson, 1999); again these algorithms do not always follow strict logic. These types of biases have a different source, are different from the simple biases in general cognitive reasoning, and may not be seen easily corrected by logic because they operate through a better-safe-than-sorry principle (Gilbert, 1998a, 2007). Believing that I can trust you requires a different set of cognitive abilities than believing that the sun will come up tomorrow.

The way people think about their own and other people's behavior is known to be problematic in people with mental health problems (Allen & Fonagy, 1995). Recently, there have been therapies developed that specifically target ToM and capacities to mentalize; that is, to be able to reflect and think about one's own thoughts, motivations, and emotions and those of others. Over a number of years Peter Fonagy and his colleagues have been developing the concept of mentalizing and generating therapies that target this algorithm (Allen & Fonagy, 1995). In depression, the capacity for this type of reflection may be compromised although the data are mixed. Part of the reason for this is that researchers recognize that mentalizing and ToM are not just competencies that people have or do not have, but rather there are levels of these competencies which can vary, come, and go, within the same person as they shift between different states of mind. Liotti and Gilbert (2011) suggested that people may be able to reflect and mentalize as long as they are not under too much threat, because threat can interfere with frontal cortical abilities and mentalizing. Different states of mind, but also different relationships, can compromise people's ability to be empathic and mentalize. Mentalizing may even change moment-to-moment as threats rise or fall during the therapeutic interaction, for example, a person may be able to mentalize quite well when with friends, (or patients) but struggle when they run into conflicts with loved and wanted (sexual/attachment) partners. If researchers do not capture this essential difference in the nature of the general-purpose thinking versus thinking about relationships, then we are missing important data on mentalizing in different social relationships (Liotti & Gilbert, 2011). Note that mentalizing is more like an algorithm-processing competency than a general-purpose cognitive competency.

These insights offer different ways of thinking about cognitive processes in depression. Some people's capacities are not (just) compromised simply because they cannot reason accurately, because their minds are dominated by reactivated schema or because their attention has got caught in loops, but also because certain heuristic and algorithmic systems that underpin the ability for social cognition and mentalizing may have become compromised, and they can get stuck in evolved "attention focusing and reasoning" algorithms for coping with, for example, loss and defeat. Some of the simplistic ways in which "depressive cognitive processes" are presented as "errors in reasoning" are now outdated and future researchers can be more mindful of the complexities of social cognitions, their algorithmic basis, and their links to evolved social motives and needs.

## Becoming a Self in Social Contexts

As noted above a sense of self is important if one is to become a reasoning, thinking, and mentalizing social agent. Hence, a third reason we got smart was linked to our abilities to think about *ourselves as objects* and be able to evaluate ourselves within the contexts of our social world. I can think about myself as I am (too fat and unfit in my case), as what I would like to be, what I need to do to become what I want to be, and things I have done that might stop me being who I want to be. I can also think of myself as a social agent, of how I think others see think/feel of me, and how I want them to see me. It is a high-level organizing system. Leary (2005) calls our evolved ability to have a sense of self *The Curse of the Self* because it is another process where we can develop emotion–cognition loops—particularly in areas of shame and humiliation (see below). There is no doubt that depression involves a disturbed and at times distressing experience of the self.

Fears of rejection and social marginalization can have us running countless, unhelpful simulations in our mind, imagining this, that, and the other. However, a sense of self and a self-identity are necessary in order for us to coordinate a huge range of potential phenotypes: ways of being, thinking, feeling, and behaving in any context. Otherwise, without a sense of self-identity that allows us to think and root ourselves in memory and consistency, we would be beset with complex questions: what should we value, what can we aspire to, what should we focus on, how should we act in this context, and so on. We would simply be overwhelmed with complex, chaotic, incoherent, and unpredictable possibilities (McGregor & Marigold, 2003). However, as we will see, this construction of the self, in a social context, comes with a cost, especially if it becomes linked to self-evaluations of inferiority and shame.

To capture the social dynamic of the sense of self we can note that it is unlikely that chimpanzees "worry" much about where they are in the social hierarchy; more likely they operate automatically, being wary of those that could hurt or block them from above, and ready to dominate those who are subordinate to them. Although there is more to primate politics than this, and grooming is a central to the bonding of relationships (Dunbar, 2010), it is unlikely that chimpanzees deliberately think about how to make themselves into a good and desired grooming partner! Things change enormously, however, when the mechanisms of rank and resource sharing change from aggressive to strategies for affiliation and attraction (Barkow, 1989; Gilbert, 1989). It is likely that a combination of adaptations advanced our human capacity for sharing and caring but also concerns to be accepted by others. This in turn may have had an impact on mood (see below).

Interestingly about 1 million years ago, the fossil record suggests that elderly, frail, injured, and diseased people were being cared for by (presumably) relatives. Other mammals will care for their young but not their old or diseased; in fact ill individuals are usually avoided (Spikins, Rutherford, & Needham, 2010). In child rearing too, humans are apparently the only primates that allow multiple caring of their infant (to be held and cared for by sisters, aunts, grandmothers); other primates are very protective and exclusive (Hrdy, 2009). In fact, human infants (for a variety of reasons) may be less likely to survive without multiple caregivers (e.g., from relatives, grandparents). Thus multiple caregiving may also have had an impact on human's ability to process the emotions and intentions of others because they would be interacting with many others from the earliest days of life (Hrdy, 2009). The point of these two observations is that being part of a caring affiliative network would be enormously beneficial to survival and therefore prominent in our motivations. We also know that affiliation has very powerful impacts on a whole range of physiological processes conducive to well-being (see below; Dunbar, 2010; Macdonald & Macdonald, 2010). Keeping in mind that depressed people often feel cut off from sources of support, these observations, of the extraordinary importance of affiliative relationships to human survival, can be crucial.

Researchers have shown that affiliative relationships are fundamental to so many aspects of human functioning. As noted above they play a major role in genetic expression so that even people with certain alleles can have very different outcomes according to their affection histories (Belsky & Pluess, 2009). Affiliative relationships help shape the brain (Cozolini, 2007), influence the development of affect regulation systems, and develop a sense of self and personal values (Baldwin & Dandeneau, 2005; Cozolino, 2008). The loss of, reduction in, and disengagement or exclusion from cooperative and affiliative relationships are known to be extremely painful, and may well go through brain systems *linked to pain* (Abram, Hogg, & Marques, 2005).

Cooperative and affiliative relationships are so important in so many ways that humans spend a lot of time focusing on their sense of self, and on how they exist in the minds of others and in their social arenas in general. The fact that these social and evaluative systems are also linked to social rank can be seen by the fact that when people make negative evaluations about themselves, perceive themselves to be inferior, unattractive, undesirable, and rejectable they showed decrements in mood (Gilbert, 1992, 2007). Today, outside of violent gangs perhaps, few humans worry about their aggressive status and much more about their desirability, acceptance, and being esteemed by others. This ability to think of oneself *in relation to others* and give oneself social value is an important evolutionary adaptation, and helps to explain the way in which shame (a self feeling inferior inadequate or rejectable) is linked to a whole range of emotional regulating processes (see below).

Evolutionary approaches therefore outline how we can come to understand basic motivational and emotional systems and their regulations through more recently evolved cognitive and socially cognitive competencies. So while there are general-purpose processing systems, there are also specialist social processing systems that give rise to capacities for empathy, ToM, and mentalizing.

## Behavioral and Emotion Adaptations

Many behavioral approaches to depression (and psychopathology in general) are less focused on new brain "thinking" competencies and more on the direct links between external and internal events and emotional outputs. This is particularly true for those who are concerned with the importance of classical and associative conditioning in emotional experiences (Gilbert, 1992, 2007; Power & Dalgleish, 2008). Many years ago, Ferster (1973) argued that one emotion can become conditioned to another so that it can be difficult to experience and process a primary emotion. For example, Sam was punished as a child if he showed anger or distress and "learned" to inhibit feelings. Over time, because distress and anger had been associated with fear and punishment they become difficult to access, because when anger arose so did fear. Now cognitive therapists may focus on Sam's "beliefs" about feelings with the assumption that people will be able to articulate the fears they have about emotions (Leahy, Tirch, & Napolitano, 2011). Psychodynamic theorists, however, posit the existence feelings (e.g., distress or anger at lack of care) becoming "unconscious" but possibly able to experience reactions to unconscious emotions such as guilt (Davenloo, 2005). Freud (1917) argued that depressed people struggle with, and can be unconscious of anger toward those they also depend on for fear of driving them away. The point is that conditioned fear responses can block conscious access to emotions but not remove them—and in behavioral terms this can become a source of depression (Ferster, 1973; Gilbert, 1992).

There are now increasingly sophisticated models that address these issues, such as the Schematic Propositional Analogical Associative Representation System (SPAARS) model developed by Power and Dalgleish (2008) for understanding how one emotion can be fused with and block out another and render emotions difficult to experience, articulate, or work through (for a helpful overview of how this model links to emotions in the case of eating disorders with implications for depression, see Fox & Power, 2009). Emotion-focused therapies have also noted how emotions can become welded together making them difficult to process, but it is the gradual distinguishing and the processing of them that can be most beneficial in depression (Pascual-Leone & Greenberg, 2007). In the therapy, they argue, one needs to use one emotion to change another emotion (of course that assumes people are able to engage consciously with what might be feared emotions). Emotions are closer to basic algorithms and therefore finding a way to directly influence emotion processing holds promise for improving our therapies for depression. But as I will argue below, we must keep an eye on the fact that it has been a need to experience, track, and process *affiliative* relationships that has driven social intelligence, and a lot of our algorithms for emotion regulation are socially focused.

Another approach that recognizes the importance of physiological systems and body processes, and in particular "amygdala-based body memories" or emotional memories, was put forward by Rothschild (2000) in her well-named book, *The Body Remembers*. The last decade has also seen major progress in understanding the way in which cognitive systems can be influenced and even completely thrown off track by arousal in affect and trauma memory (Van der Hart, Nijenhuis, & Steele, 2006). Hence, therapists need to focus on the physiological state of the person (and may have to work directly with physiological state) as they undergo therapeutic change and intervention. In an effort to integrate the importance of understanding the nature of competing memories and conditioned emotional responses, Brewin (2006) offered a "memory competing hypotheses" as explanations for some of the cognitive phenomena reported in depression. In this model, depression can reemerge as an emotional memory that changes brain states. Also, unprocessed and unconscious feelings might be a source for unpleasant intrusions and aversive dreams (Cukrowicz et al., 2006).

Today our understanding of emotional processing, and in particular classical conditioning, the physiological effects of early trauma and the complexity of that regulation are increasingly understood. It is hoped that improved therapies for depression will integrate this psychological knowledge better into therapies rather than getting trapped in specific models.

## Ecologies

Ecologies provide the context that will deliver a range of situations, opportunities, and stressors to organisms (Gilbert, 1995). As noted above (e.g., in the case of obesity) humans are creating ecologies which are not necessarily helpful. They may also create maladaptive phenotypes and this is why it is important to take a biopsychosocial approach (Smith, 2002). We also noted that ecologies need to take into consideration microorganisms that may influence maturation of physiological processes (Raison et al., 2010). In addition, the World Health Organization is increasingly keen on developing our understanding of what they call Social *Determinants of Health* because the evidence is that the social context of ecological factors plays a major role in health and disease (WHO, 2010). There is in fact considerable evidence that the social ecology, which can be linked to poverty and/or exposure to crime and violence, constitutes major risk factors for a whole range of mental health problems including depression (Andrade et al., 2012). In contrast the experience of genuine social safeness contributes to well-being and is different from social support (Andrade et al., Kelly, Zuroff, Leybman, & Gilbert, in press).

Phenotypes leading to depression are shaped in social environments (Belsky & Pluess, 2009), but these themselves are contextualized in historical and ecological contexts. So, for example, children growing up in poverty, or in families who have historical cultural styles of abuse, will be subjected to environments that will shape their phenotypes. In hostile environments, becoming quick to anger, anxiety, or depression might be adaptive and protective; whereas being open, laid-back, and trusting might be the adaptive phenotype in safe, loving, and supportive environments. There is a lot of literature, of course, on the importance of background experience for subsequent vulnerability to all kinds of mental health difficulties (Ingram & Price, 2010). Sometimes, especially when working with patients who are self-critical and have a great amount of shame, it helps to (loosely) explain the concept of phenotype and reflect just how much they (indeed all of us) have been shaped outside of their (and our) control. One can explain that we are biologically built by our genes and shaped by our environments. I often use the following example: if I had been swapped as a 3-day-old baby and brought up in a violent drug gang, I would not be a clinician but more likely an aggressive person, low in empathy, possibly having killed others, possibly dead myself, or in prison, because this is destiny of many who grow up in these hostile environments. Work is just beginning on understanding how ecologies shape phenotypes and personal values, identities, and a range of psychological competencies, such as affect regulation (Cohen, 2001), the very basis of the biopsychosocial approach.

## Life events

Ecologies deliver life events and there is a major genre of literature on the way in which life events interact with an individual's sensitivities to produce outcomes such as depression brain states (Ingram & Price, 2010). We know that people are far more likely to suffer depression if they live in poverty than in relative wealth. Subversive life events and experiences of frustration and defeat are much higher in environments of poverty than they are in relative wealth (Gilbert, 1995). Over many years, George Brown and Tirrel Harris have shown how depression, especially in women, is related to life events, and chronic stress that arises within certain social contexts. Their original seminal model (Brown & Harris, 1978; Brown et al., 2010) distinguished between

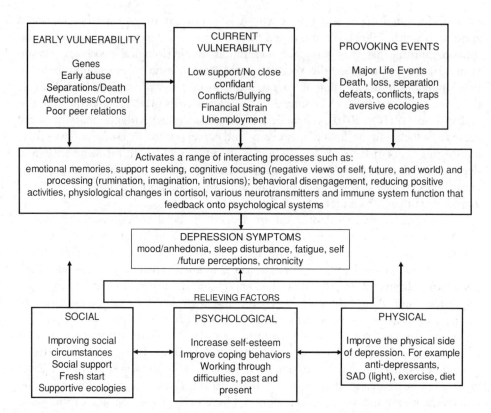

**Figure 10.2.** A Biopsychosocial Integration. Adapted from Gilbert (2004), with permission from John Wiley & Sons

vulnerability factors (often in a person's history), triggering and onset factors (such as loss of the job or break up of a relationship), and symptom formation factors (such as early parental loss). This model remains a most useful model, linking ecological and life events to personal experiences of depression. They found that it is chronic life difficulties that link to depression rather than acute events, and that fresh start events, particularly of new opportunities such as relationships, are associated with remission of depression (Brown, Adler, & Bifulco, 1988). They make the point that we should study the *natural* causes of remission and recovery more than we do. An example of this model can be seen in Figure 10.2.

Ecologies that give rise to all manner of difficulties, including depression, are created through complex interactions of individuals over time. So, for example, the link between mental health and disparities in wealth is the result of complex social, economic, and political forces operating since World War II and before (Wilkinson & Picket, 2010). More fine-grained analysis is starting to suggest that indicators of mental health including depression, homicide, and suicide actually change according to the political policies—that as politicians pursue less egalitarian policies so these indicators increase, but reduce in times of greater fairness (Gilligan, 2011). Certainly, the links between economics such as employment, job security, and job stress are now known to be linked to mental health, especially depression; at one level then, the greed of the few creates the ecologies for the misery of the many. This is not a moral statement because many of us might rather bask in the delights of excessive wealth than poverty; it is a reflection about how ecologies influence psychology and patterns of disorders like depression.

## Summary

Taken together then the biopsychosocial approach to disorders like depression seeks to understand genetic vulnerability in the context of phenotypic variability, and how phenotypic variability can be impacted by the social and physical ecologies in which people grow and mature, form their relationships, and give rise to psychologies that can be threat-focused and easily trigger depressed states. Phenotypes can reflect algorithmic patterns that influence a range of psychological processes (e.g., thinking, imagination, attending feelings). The next section explores more closely the motivational and emotional systems that become dysregulated in depression and something of which evolutionary mechanisms might be at play.

# What Motives and Emotions Are Dysregulated in Depression?

As argued, depression is best regarded as a complex shift in brain states and patterns of organization that are possibly linked to different phenotypic, defensive strategies. The rest of this chapter will take a closer look at exactly what and how different motives and affect systems may be dysregulated.

## Blocked and thwarted motives

First though, it is important to distinguish between motives and emotions. Motives "aim" behavior and are object or goal seeking. We might be motivated to secure a date with a desired partner, advance our career, or have a nice holiday. Motives give rise to goals, plans, and values. Unlike emotions, which respond to specific events that come and go, motives can be present over a lifetime, and some of them may not be fully articulated or conscious. Many are focused on evolutionarily important domains, such as the motives for attachments and close affiliative relationships, gaining status and avoiding rejection, seeking sexual partners, and acquiring material resources to make a comfortable life. Many years ago, George Mandler (1975) outlined a psychology of how motivations, and the formation of personal goals, and their success or failure/interruption, was linked to moods and emotions. Key to depression is the importance of the motivation/goal that is interrupted. So, for example, the death of a loved person would have a far more destructive and depressive effect than the death of an acquaintance. This is partly because certain motives/goals and values are highly integrated into *networks of motivations.* Losing a loved partner means that you lose somebody you talked to everyday, someone you shared plans with, shared the news with, planned meals with, went to restaurants and parties and on holidays with, shared problems with, and made decisions with of what color to paint the bedroom. You lose someone who you regularly turned to for comfort, and who was perhaps the biggest source of shared pleasure. When the motives and goals (in this case, to continue these activities with a loved one) are blocked a lot depends on the interconnectedness with other motivational systems. These concepts are not easily captured with a concept-like schema unless one understands the complex link between "motivations" and personal meaning. This was essentially the idea put forward by Champion and Power (1995) who focused on depression as linked to the loss of (control over) core roles which are important for a person's sense of self and offered a sense of status, value, or prestige. Their analysis links motivations and core goals to experience of the self, helping to explain why the sense of self can feel fragmented and fractured in depression. Helping people understand their basic motivation systems and personal goals and to realign them with obtainable goals has become a key focus in Acceptance Commitment Therapy (ACT) (Hayes, Strosahl, & Wilson, 2004).

There is a range of theories of depression that focus on blocked or thwarted motives. A classic model is learned helplessness, which looks at what happens when you block an animal's ability to escape from the threat—you thwart escape (Seligman, 1975) and eventually the animal gives up trying. Over many years, learned helplessness explanations of the way animals and people become passive, give up, and have a kind of mental collapse in the face of difficulties, have inspired considerable research into the similarities and differences between helplessness states and depression—both physiological and psychological processes.

A slightly different approach was taken by Klinger (1975) who developed the incentive disengagement theory of depression. He argued that it is maladaptive for animals to continue to pursue goals that are unlikely to pay off (be rewarded) and therefore there must be mechanisms that enable animals to disengage from the unobtainable. In his view, this is the mechanism of reduced reward sensitivity, a lowered tone of positive emotion and motives to continue to pursue the goal, and depression. Nesse (2000) developed Klinger's idea and argued that depression is due to an innate defensive strategy for hunkering down and withdrawing effort from engaging in environments that have very low or potentially aversive payoffs. It follows that individuals who show mild depression in some contexts might actually be at an advantage when it comes to changing goals and giving up on unproductive pursuits. A twist to this was offered by Gilbert (1984), who noted that some depressed people remain highly motivated to achieve goals that they are unlikely to achieve, and therefore constantly experience frustration and defeat. Yet another take on this line of thinking on depression is Allen and Badcocks' (2003) social risk hypothesis where they have posited basic evolved algorithms for calculating social risk, linked to contingencies like social rejection, connection, and defeat, which then automatically mood and behavior accordingly.

Other researchers, interested in the concept of blocked goals and motives, focus more on the *social dynamic*, suggesting that it is when *social and interpersonal* motivational systems get thwarted, lost, or blocked that are specifically depressogenic. There are many reasons for this, one being that so much of human evolution has focused on achieving positive social relationships. Another is because depression has a social signaling function (out of action) and comes with a way of thinking about oneself in relationship to other people. Thus depressed people typically see themselves as inferior, vulnerable to shame, rejection, and marginalization. These are such common social cognitions that they are probably linked to basic defensive, strategic phenotypes.

## Attachment and affiliative approaches to depression

There are two major *social theories* of depression (for a review of their interaction, see Gilbert, 2006). The first is disruption of important affiliative relationships, especially attachment ones. Bowlby (1969, 1973, 1980) argued that mammalian infants/young are totally reliant on parents for protection, food warmth, comfort, emotional regulation, and social learning. There is good evidence that the quality of the customer relationship linked to the degree of physical closeness and availability of food influences the maturation of specific physiological systems (Hofer, 1994). Recent research has shown that in humans the attachment relationships also play a fundamental role in the maturation of many brain areas, especially those involved social cognition, emotional regulation, and self-regulating processes (Cozolino, 2007). Without access to a caring parent, mammalian survival is severely compromised; uncared for infants simply do not survive. Disruptions in attachment are therefore a very serious threat indeed, and one can expect that evolution has built in some major defensive strategies—which it has.

Disruption to the attachment relationship activates what Bowlby (1969) called the *protest–despair* reaction. In protest, the infant first seeks for the lost parent, moving around in the territory, with anxiety, pining, crying, and distress calling. They show heightened threat processing associated with major changes in cardiovascular and immune functions (Porges, 2007). If reunion occurs, then usually this defensive strategy is turned off and the infant returns to a more relaxed state and will eventually explore/play again. However, if reunion is not possible, then a very different defensive phenotype is activated, called the *despair state*. In this state, it is important that the infant stops distress calling, stops moving, and searching, signaling its unprotected status, and hunkers down out of sight. The reason for this is that to continue will attract predators, risk getting lost, getting injured, and dehydrated. It is far better therefore for the infant to stop acting and wait for the parent's return. Keep in mind that most mammals have a strong sense of smell and can recognize their offspring via scent from some way off, so that being out of sight is not necessarily a disadvantage. Despair states therefore turn drive and "seeking" motivational systems off—a kind of pushing one to the back of the cave and waiting for better times or rescue. Activations of these phenotypic strategies are likely to come with a particular kind of social experience which is one of separation, abandonment, or aloneness, because this is the context that would normally (over millions of years) trigger them. There is some evidence for genetic differences in susceptibility to the intensity of protest–despair responses (Suomi, 1997). It is possible that more intense responses represent phenotypic variations that are sensitive to hostile environments (Boyce & Ellis, 2005; Belsky & Pluess, 2009).

As we will see shortly, depression is commonly associated with the feelings of being emotionally distant and separate from others. Depressed people can have desires to be "rescued"—even if they know it is illogical, and even if they try to avoid those feelings out of shame. Helping people understand the historical (if there have been attachment failures in the past) and phylogenetic (of the defensive strategy) source of these experiences can help people validate, accept, and engage with them rather than see them as say "distortions"—or simply as childish wishes. Rather, they can be fundamental to the human experience. So again we are picking up here how governance of thinking evolved rather than (just) changes in general cognitive processing systems.

## Social rank theory: Defeat, subordination, and arrested defenses in depression

There is increasing evidence that our judgment of our social rank automatically biases attention and processing and neurophysiological responses to certain tasks (Boksem, Kostermans, Milivojevic, & De Cremer, 2011). It regulates our optimism and confidence (Gilbert, Allan, Ball, & Bradshaw, 1996), the way we deal with conflicts (Fournier, Moskowitz, & Zuroff, 2002), and is linked to a whole range of motivations for advancement and the avoidance of inferiority (Gilbert, 2007). Because many animals live within social hierarchies, it would not be unreasonable to assume that there are evolved heuristic algorithms for guiding attention, processing, and behavior in accord with hierarchies. Focusing on behavior within hierarchies led Price (1972; Price & Sloman, 1987) to formulate a different social model of depression focusing on *social* relationships that was based upon the observation that depressed people showed similarities to animals who have been in conflict and were defeated or harassed. He noted that these animals seemed slower, wary, and lacking confidence, expressed postural changes of trying to make the body smaller by crouching, curling up, and hunching, typical of a very submissive posture and hiding (see Gilbert, 2000 for a review of these changes). The idea of there being an evolved processing systems for regulating one's behavior and social rank that is involved in depression was also suggested by depressed people being very cognitively focused on feelings of defeat and inferiority, very avoidant, and passive to those more powerful than themselves (Gilbert, 1992; Gilbert & Allan, 1998). However, depressed people (like defeated animals) could be irritable and aggressive down rank; for example, to their subordinates or children. Price argued that depressed states reflected defensive strategies for dealing with defeats and hostility one could not otherwise defend against. In order for animals not to injure each other in fights, one (the weaker) needed to submit, lose the desire to try again and again (with risk or repeated injury), and then indicate that it was not thinking of a comeback. The idea was that there is an automatic regulator of emotion and motivation, according to the level of conflicts and hostility and the animal/person's encounters can deal with. This is important because it helps us recognize why depression has been commonly associated with bullying and hostile/abusive environments both currently and in the past. The mechanisms involved may share processing systems of those learned helplessness but it is the added social signaling and social evaluation that is important for this model (Gilbert, 1992).

Gilbert (1992, 2007) added three features to this model. The first was that human social competition is far less focused on aggressiveness (though hostility/abuse plays a role in some depressions, of course) because human competition is via attractiveness; *we compete to be chosen*. The idea that human competition became focused on influencing the minds of others positively in one's favor, has been around for a long time reaching back to George Herbert Mead's concepts of the looking glass self. It was further developed by Barkow (1989) in his discussion of *competition for prestige and reputation*. Competition then becomes focused on the impact you have in the minds of other people. This is why we can see social intelligence becoming greatly important as an evolved competency. So today, be it for employment, selected for a sports team, going to university, forming certain types of friends, engaging certain types of sexual partners, or earning the money to buy a house, there is an underlying competition that depends on being desired, wanted, and valued by others. Indeed, being successful at securing supportive, affiliative, and cooperative relationships became so important to human survival that it was probably a powerful driver for our evolved social intelligence (Dunbar, 2007, 2010; Gilbert, 1989, 2009b).

The competition for social attractiveness is a bridge between some of the innate mechanisms that regulate competitive processing systems and evaluations of one's personal rank, and the affect-regulating processes that go with it in social arenas. These social evaluative systems include processes such as social comparison, the regulation of submissive or assertive behavior, and the whole dynamic of shame (Gilbert, 1998b). There is now considerable evidence that depression is associated with unfavorable social comparison, seeing oneself as inferior, and also a tendency to behave submissively (see Allan & Gilbert, 1995; Gilbert & Allan, 1998; Gilbert, Allan, Brough, Melley, & Miles, 2002). Recently, unaware of social rank theory, Cain et al. (2012) used the interpersonal circumplex model to explore different interpersonal patterns in depression and identified six (extroverted, dominant, arrogant, cold, submissive, and unassuming). All these textured depression in slightly different ways. However, they found that it was the submissive interpersonal styles that particularly predicted the risk of depression and poorer outcomes, as suggested by social rank theory (Gilbert, 1992, 2007).

Gardner (1982) proposed that bipolar depression might also be specifically linked to social rank mechanisms, with a (dopamine) mechanism that evolved to invigorate activity in the context winning rank and depress activity in the context of losing. Indeed, it is known that seasonal variation in breeding produces marked changes in some species activity levels. There is also evidence that winning (e.g., important competitions) has profound effects on a range of physiological processes including various monoamines. The advantage is that winning provides the energy to make use of one's win and engage in resource-acquiring behaviors. If bipolar depression is linked to some mechanism for social rank then we should see social comparison change with mood in people with this condition. Indeed, this seems to be the case. As people with bipolar disorder begin to experience elevations of mood they can also start to rate themselves as superior (Gilbert, McEwan, Hay, Irons, & Cheung, 2007), suggesting that the self-evaluative system for social ranking has got caught up in this affect system in a way that is yet to be understood.

In this approach, that focuses social competition via social attractiveness, low rank experiences are linked to shame. It is, however, important, to separate *external* shame (linked to the feelings we experience when we believe we are devalued in the eyes of others) and internal shame (linked to our own self-evaluation). In a major meta-analysis of external and internal shame, Kim, Thibodeau, and Jorgensen (2011) found that one of the strongest predictors of depression was external shame. They say:

> External shame, which involves negative views of self as seen through the eyes of others, was associated with larger effect sizes (r =.56) than internal shame (r = .42), which involves negative views of self as seen through one's own eyes. (p. 68)

So feeling devalued, inadequate, or unworthy in the eyes of others seems to be significantly associated with the experience of depression for many people. In evolutionary terms, external shame is like "being seen as subordinate." Suggesting a link between shame, concerns with one social rank or social standing (ability to compete for social place in the hearts and minds of others) and depression leads to a testable hypothesis that those vulnerable to depressed states will have elevated drives to compete for social position and avoid rejection. It is important to recognize that competing for superiority is different to competing to avoid inferiority and rejection. In a series of studies (Gilbert et al., 2007; Gilbert, McEwan, Irons, et al., 2009), we develop scales to measure *striving to avoid inferiority*, which we called insecure striving, fears of missing out, being overlooked, and active rejection. We found that you could indeed identify an insecure striving motivation where people believe that they must strive to compete for their social place and avoid mistakes and inferiority. This can be contrasted with a second factor, which we labeled as *secure nonstriving*, where people believed that whether they succeed or fail others still accept and value them. In students, insecure striving was significantly associated with various fears of rejection, feeling inferior, submissive behavior, need for validation and depression. Secure nonstriving was negatively associated with these variables (Gilbert et al., 2007). In depressed people striving to avoid inferiority was significantly linked to feeling inferior, external shame, submissive behavior, anxious attachment and depression, stress, and anxiety (Gilbert, McEwan, Mitra, et al., 2009). Mediator analyses revealed that the relationship between striving to avoid inferiority and depression was mediated by external shame, and anxious attachment. It would appear then that people vulnerable to depression are indeed aware of the competitive dynamics of life, and of being rejected if they do not prove themselves or "measure up." When they feel they are failing, a sense of defeat with self-experiences of, "I can't make it"; "I can't achieve this standard"; "I can't be the person I'm trying to be" begins to become activated (Gilbert & Allan, 1998). This may link with early life memories of being in a fearful subordinate position (Gilbert, Cheung, Wright, Campey, & Irons, 2003) or inferior compared to siblings (Gilbert & Gelsma, 1999) and with a sense of being cut off from sources of support and affiliation.

The second adaptation to Price's model was to focus more on: (1) the experience of personal defeat and (2) the importance of entrapment in defeating and thwarting environments. The concept of entrapment as a depressogenic process was actually first articulated by Dixon (1998), a neuroethologist working on developing antidepressants. He noted that when animals are trying to escape but escape is blocked, they can show depressed-like behaviors. Although similar to learned helplessness (Seligman, 1975) he termed the process *arrested flight*—because the flight motivation is very active but inhibited—with important physiological consequences. Distinguishing arrested flight from learned helplessness (though they are not competitive models; see Gilbert 1992, pp. 175–184) is important because flight motivation can stay power-fully activated in people's consciousness and fantasies and at times even drive suicide (Taylor, Gooding, Wood, & Tarrier, 2011). To the best of my knowledge, no one has explored unconscious defeat and escape fantasies' potential role in vulnerability to depression. So even if a person appears to be passive they might be ruminating on how to get away from the pain or life difficulties they are in (see also Baumeister, 1990).

This model was expanded to suggest that different types of defensive behaviors could be arrested including arrested anger—a psychodynamic concept. The entrap-ment model therefore covers both arrested flight and arrested fight (and in some conditions arrested submissiveness) (Gilbert, 2001, 2007). Arrested anger can be related to a whole range of processes to do with fear of retaliation but also of course guilt and fear of one's own anger (Davenloo, 2005). In a study to explore the themes and timelines for entrapment, arrested fight, and arrested flight, Gilbert et al. (2004) used Brown et al.'s (1988) life events and difficulties schedule (LEDS) in relation to a specially designed semistructured interview for assessing these arrested defenses in 50 depressed people. A summary of the results were:

> In regard to arrested flight, 88% of the group acknowledged strong desires to escape difficulties in their life but many felt unable to. Transcript analysis from the LEDS also indicated strong themes of entrapment. 38.7% felt trapped before becoming depressed. Fantasies of escaping were common, but making actual plans to get away less common. A variety of reasons were given for not escaping: In regard to arrested anger, 82% felt they suppressed their anger and 56% felt this problem predated their depression. A number of different reasons were given for not expressing anger. Despite self-blame often being seen as important to depression, we found that for many severe life events and difficulties patients did not blame themselves. Rather they blamed external circumstances or other people and saw these as the source of their entrapment. (p. 149)

In a focus group analysis of depressed people and nurses, the themes of entrapment and arrested anger were seen as an important part of the depressive experience (Gilbert & Gilbert, 2003). Nurses in the study, however, thought that entrapment was due to patients fearing changing what they needed to change (e.g., get a job or leave an unsupportive relationship). Taken together these data suggest that arrested defenses are common in depression and this is important because it suggests that within the threat system these behavioral output systems may stay in an activated state (see Taylor et al., 2011 for review). It was also notable that depressed people did not seem unconscious of (or at least some of their) anger but did acknowledge substantial fear of expressing it, making it difficult to process or translate into assertiveness.

Central to the original Price model was the notion of defeat—a mental state that arose when individuals were unable to resolve or regulate a stressor (especially con-flict). Similarities have been identified between defeat states and learned helplessness and experimental neurosis (where animals show disorganized and disturbed behavior in the context of being able to discriminate stimuli that signaled different rewards for approach avoidance conflicts; Gilbert 1992). However, in Price's model the central aspect of defeat was that it usually occurs in a social context and goes with having to signal to potential victors that one is not about to make a comeback. This is why defeat/depression typically goes with feeling inferior and behaving submissively with the closing down of positive (acquisitive) affect. In 1998, Gilbert and Allan developed a self-report scale for defeat and two scales entrapment: (1) feeling trapped and wanting to escape from situations in one's life and (2) feeling trapped and wanting to escape from repetitive thoughts, feelings, and intrusions. In a major review of a number of studies on the defeat and entrapment model, Taylor et al. (2011) highlighted considerable evidence that both defeat and entrapment play powerful roles in depression, suicidality, and other psychopathologies such as posttraumatic stress disorder.

We did not make the distinction between feeling defeated and mental defeat, which we saw as equivalent. However, it is important to distinguish the objective fact of suffering a defeat from personal experiences that go with it. Important research in the field of posttraumatic disorders following torture has found that severity of symptoms and duration are related to experiences of mental defeat. Ehlers, Maercker, and Boos (2000) point out that many victims of torture may feel defeated and sign false confessions, but may not feel *inwardly or personally defeated* in the sense that one has lost autonomy. Mental defeat, however, is defined as "the perceived loss of all autonomy, a state of giving up in one's mind all efforts to retain one's identity as a human being with a will of one's own" (p. 45). Mental defeat, in this context, was also associated with total subordination such as feeling merely an object to the other, loss of self-identity, preparedness to do whatever the other asked, and not caring if one lives or dies. Those who experienced mental defeat had more chronic PTSD symptoms and higher depression. In the social rank model, mental defeat would be related to feeling personally inferior in some way. Indeed Ehlers et al. (2000) indicated that refusing to feel personally inferior to one's torturers (or perhaps others in the same situation) might help to avoid mental defeat.

Gilbert (1992, pp. 209–217) noted that similar themes (of feeling controlled by others and not caring if one lives or dies) as common in some depressions. Clearly, for humans, who make symbolic representations of the self and develop identities, the mechanisms of defeat will operate in and through these competencies (see below). Scott's (1990) anthropological studies indicate that even though groups can be beaten down (for example, slaves in North America) their ability to hold on to their own identities and values affected their adjustment and resistance. Clearly, more research is needed on the differences between feeling defeated, loss of status and control, and mental defeat related to an internal sense of inferiority and a loss of self-identity. Interestingly, severely depressed people can feel that the illness itself robs them of their identity and makes them into a "no-thing" and feel mental defeat as part of the experience of being depressed. Such experiences raise questions of what evolved mechanisms may underpin defeat states and can be trigger by various routes.

Gilbert and Allan (1998) also looked at whether people felt they needed to get away from *their own thoughts or painful states of mind*. This has some similarity to Baumeister's (1990) concept of escape from the self, and also less specific concepts such as experiential avoidance (Hayes et al., 2004). The point was to articulate the activation of the flight motivation system but being in the state of arrest because one could not get away—and also the degree to which not being able to regulate one's feelings and intrusive unpleasant thoughts left one with the feelings of defeat—"I can't even control my own mind" as some clients reflected. So some people can feel defeated by the "depression" itself. Feeling trapped with negative thoughts or in a state of mind one could not get out of seem to be linked to defeat entrapment and depression.

## The Importance of Understanding Different Phases and Stages of Defensive Strategies in Aversive Environments

What both the attachment and defeat models suggest is that the defensive phenotypes to certain types of stresses are biphasic or triphasic (Gilbert, 1984, 1988). For example, in the learned helplessness model when animals are first confronted by stressors, there is an invigorated activity as the animal struggles to overcome the stress, but then subsequently, if it cannot escape systems become helpless and more passive (Seligman, 1975). These "helpless" states are also conditionable so that when confronted by the certain cues an individual is more rapidly likely switch to "helplessness or motor deactivation" brain state (Gilbert 1992, 2007).

As noted already, in the attachment loss model, the first defensive response to the loss of the parent or threat is "protest," which involves invigorated activity of distress calling, wondering, seeking, anxiety, and at times, protest anger. If this does not work then the despair state switches on, which turns off all those behaviors that could be very threatening to the individual (get lost, injured, and attract predators). In the defeat and arrested defenses model there is again the proposition that when individuals are first confronted by stressors, they will try to overcome them and it is when they find they cannot escape, and/or switch to new positive goals, that they feel trapped and defeated. Once again, the defeat state is a change as a result of failed struggle.

These types of models are important because they help us to link the processes in the way the brain is designed to protect itself and how, because of new brain–old brain mechanisms, it can get stuck in loops, constantly stimulating the sense of affiliative disengagement, defeat (and low rank/inferiority), and entrapment. Once we can begin to identify the strategic phenotypic defenses, their triggers and forms, we may get close to the core processes in depression (Panksepp, 2010).

### Summary

This section has focused on innate motivational systems and their regulation, especially the defensive strategies that can be activated when motives and social (self-identity) roles are blocked. Important here is to try to identify heuristic and algorithmic processes that can be triggered in depression. The cognitive content of depressions can be understood as reflecting these innate mechanisms rather than (just) being based on learning and general-purpose cognitive processing systems. If this has merit then of course the question becomes how do you change or switch off innate algorithmic ways of thinking and behaving—when sometimes it is defensive and may not be fully conscious—as can arise in the case of self-deception. One answer has been to activate a different motivational system such as one based on affiliation and compassion because these were evolved for different social niches and have very important neurophysiological regulating properties, especially on the threat system (see below).

## Emotional Patterns in Depression: Exploring Three Types of Emotions

Motives and goals of course do not themselves have emotions or feelings, rather feelings are linked to how motives are doing, and the current state of an organism (Panksepp, 2003, 2010). We can work away on a goal, such as studying for an examination and may neither be excited nor anxious but simply absorbed in the task. Our emotions change, however, when we experience that we are learning the material very well and think we will give an excellent answer or we cannot make head nor tail of what we are trying to study. So in general emotions track motives, and when motives are being successfully pursued we experience positive emotions, but when they are blocked we experience emotions that warn of harm or threat.

The link between emotions and motives, however, is not straightforward. This is because evolution has designed different types of emotions to do different things, and it is these functions that are linked to moods. There is no agreed upon functional analysis of emotional systems but Panksepp (2003), for example, uses neurophysiological studies to distinguish between a number of different functions for emotions. These include (1) a seeking system, which is basically linked to drives to go out and achieve things necessary for survival; (2) an anger/rage system that is triggered when motives and drives are blocked; (3) a fear system that is triggered when the animal is under threat of harm or loss; (4) a sexuality/lust system that is orientated to specific targets with specific behavioral outputs; (5) a care and maternal nurturance system; (6) a grief system for attachment loss that is linked to protest–despair; and (7) a play system that is linked to joyfulness. Panskepp (2010) sees depression as compromised problems with the seeking and grief system but also recognizes that there are problems in all these systems (see below).

Another way of looking at our emotions is to focus on evolutionary functions in a different but uncompetitive way. Here it is possible to identify just three types of emotional experiences and regulation derived from the work of attachment theorists Mikluciner and Shaver (2007) and the neuroscience work of Depue and Morrone-Strupinsky (2005). These are:

- *Threat and self-protection focused systems*—enables detecting, attending, processing, and responding to threats. There is a menu of threat-based emotions such as anger, anxiety, and disgust, and a menu of defensive behaviors such as fight, flight, submission, freeze, and so on. Various subdivisions as suggested by Panksepp are possible.
- *Drive, seeking, and acquisition focused system*—enables the paying of attention to advantageous resources, and with some degree of "activation"—an experience of

Driven, excited, vitality      Content, safe, connected

Incentive/resource-focused

Wanting, pursuing, achieving, consuming

Activating

Non wanting/
Affiliative-focused

Safeness-kindness

Soothing

Threat-focused

Protection and
safety-seeking

Activating/inhibiting

Anger, anxiety, disgust

**Figure 10.3.** Three Types of Affect Regulation System. Reprinted from Gilbert (2009a), with permission from Constable & Robinson Ltd

pleasure in pursuing and securing them. Most theories of positive affect have this positive emotion system identified.

- *Contentment, soothing, and affiliative focused system*—enabling a state of peacefulness and openness when individuals are no longer threat focused or seeking resources—but are satisfied. Also linked to feelings of well-being. Over evolutionary time, this system of calming has been adapted for many functions of attachment and affiliative behavior. The system is linked to the endorphin–oxytocin dimensions which function to promote trust, affiliative behavior, and recipients of affiliation experience of calming in the threat system (Macdonald & Macdonald, 2010).

These three systems are depicted in Figure 10.3.

## The Threat System and Depression

The threat detection and protection system links to emotions such as anger, anxiety, disgust, and their variants (e.g., envy, apprehension/dread, and contempt); attentional focusing and behaviors such as fight, flight, and vomit/expel. The threat-protection system has been studied for many years, so we understand something of its neurophysiology and physiological processing—what it does to the body, attention, cognition, feeling, and behavior (LeDoux, 1998; Panksepp, 2003).

    Much research suggests that major depression is a state of *chronic* stress and threat system activation as measured by subjective reports, life events (Morriss & Morriss, 2000), physiological indicators of ANS hyperarousal (Toates, 1995), and overactivity in the hypothalmic–pituitary–adrenal system (HPA), which results in high cortisol, called hypercortisolemia (Cowen, 2010; Levitan, Hasey, & Sloman, 2000; McGuade & Young, 2000; Nemeroff, 1998; Raadsheer, Hoogendijk, Stam, Tilders, Swaab, 1994). Importantly, hypercortisolemia has many detrimental effects on the immune system (Maes, 1995; Raison et al., 2010), various internal organs, and brain areas (Sapolsky, 1996, 2000) and by feedback interactions downgrades serotonin (5-HT), an important neurotransmitter in mood regulation (McGuade & Young, 2000). There is good evidence that even in the less severe depression of dysthymia there are significant physiological disturbances of functioning of the threat system (e.g., in HPA, immune systems, and neurotransmitters; Griffiths et al., 2000). Although there are a variety of regulators of the HPA system (Nemeroff, 1996; Raison et al., 2010) that may operate differently in different types of depressions (Posener et al., 2000), so important is the HPA system in depression that new therapeutic efforts are being targeted at hypercortisolemia (Cowen, 2010; McGuade & Young, 2000).

There is also evidence that people vulnerable to depression have a history of threat activation, especially during their maturational years (see Hammen, Bistricky, & Ingram, 2010). Kessler and Magee (1993), in a large epidemiological study, found that childhood adversities are related to both onset and recurrent episodes of depression. In a follow-up study of 121 women students, Hammen, Henry, and Daley (2000) found that women with a history of childhood adversity needed less stress to trigger depression than those without childhood adversity. Andrews (1998) has shown that chronic depression in women is linked to childhood sexual abuse. Hence, aversive early relationships can skew development of the threat system toward anxiety, suspiciousness, shame sensitivity, nonaffiliation (poor help-seeking), aggressiveness, and social wariness or avoidance. Nanni et al. (2012) suggest that people from abusive backgrounds do less well in standard therapies. Children who have adversities such as health problems, even pain, but experience these in the context of high degrees of love and affection, appear to be much less vulnerable to depression although good data is hard to find. In fact, some childhood adversity in the context of high love and caring may well build resilience. So it seems that it is social stresses, and specifically those that impact on the experience of the self as a social being, that are key for the regulation of mood. This makes sense when you consider the "social brain" hypothesis, which indicates just how many processes are linked into social relationships.

However, we should keep in mind that it is not just abusive environments that can have disruptive effects on the maturational brain and vulnerability to depression. For example, there has been a long tradition of exploring the concepts of overprotection and affectionless control, neglect, growing up with depressed parents or anxious parents. In these cases it may not be that the threat–stress system is over-stimulated but rather that certain types of positive and especially affiliative affect are under-stimulated (Gilbert, 2007, 2010).

## Depression and the Drive System

Depression is typically seen as a disorder of positive emotion where individuals lose the ability to experience pleasure. Before we consider the role of positive emotion on the loss of positive affect and depression, it is important to note that many researchers now suggest that there are *different types of positive* emotions. For example, Davidson (2000) suggested a difference between the anticipation of rewards with the drive to achieve them, and the pleasure of having achieved and consuming. Panksepp (2010) distinguishes the positive emotions of drive/seeking, sexuality/lust, and play/affiliation. Depue and Morrone-Strupinsky (2005) pointed out that energy and drive are necessary for moving toward and securing (achieving) resources important for survival but once obtained those systems need to be toned down. Such a state would be one's contentment or satisfaction (not seeking and not being threatened), quiescence, and rest. Without toning down the "hyped feelings of drive" we would simply be on the go the whole time, never satisfied and quick to burnout. The drive system is linked to dopamine function (although dopamine function is not only linked to drive emotions but is important for other affect systems too) (Panksepp, 2003, 2010).

This system is very responsive to the success or thwarting of personal motives/goals and access to resources. When exceptional things happen to people they can have a dopamine flush and become briefly and mildly hypomanic. For example, imagine winning the Euro lottery so that you are now worth €100 million—the chances are you would become quite "activated," have racing thoughts and would struggle sleeping for a few nights. You would find this excitement almost impossible to regulate through "thinking" cognitive systems; because it is operating on the algorithm that "when good things happen make the most of them; do a lot." This is a typical behavior that arises in changes of season in animals that they become much more activated in the summer the times for breeding—that is, be active when conditions are good; less active when they are not so good (Nesse, 2000). However, in the normal course of events our hypomania would be a self-regulating system and would settle. This self-regulating, self-correcting dopaminergic drive system, however, can be problematic for people with disorders like bipolar affective disorder because once the drive system becomes destabilized it risks swinging too high or too low (King, Rases, & Barchas, 1981).

In contrast, suffering major defeats, losses, setbacks, or being very subordinate is linked to depressed mood. There is clearly a loss of drive-based emotions such that individuals find it difficult to derive pleasure from, or anticipate deriving pleasure from, normally enjoyable things. This is the experience of anhedonia, the core symptom of depression. There are, however, slightly different conceptualizations of anhedonia. One focuses on anhedonia as a broad category encompassing general apathy with a marked lack of motivation to engage in almost all activities (Klinger, 1993) and diminished interest or pleasure in activities reflecting a generalized lack of positive affect (Watson & Clark, 1988; Watson et al., 1995a, 1995b). This definition views depression as the result of reductions in a range of positive affects such as joy, energy, enthusiasm, alertness, self-confidence, and interest. Others (Willner, 1993) have suggested that anhedonic patients can remain "interested" in hedonic experiences (they would like to engage in certain activities—in other words motivations remain intact and may even be elevated), but people anticipate that they will be unable to enjoy them if they do engage in them; or they are just too tired or too anxious to try. Loss of interest or lack of motivation may *develop* from repeated experiences of wanting but failing to feel pleasure or reward from various activities, and getting frustrated or anxious (Snaith et al., 1995).

New research has shown evidence of problems in the processing of rewards in depressed people as measured by various means, including fMRI studies. In line with suggestions in this chapter, there seem to be differences in responding to social rewards as opposed to nonsocial rewards as outlined in the major review by Forbes (2009), Forbes and Dahl (2012), and Gilbert, McEwan, Mitra, et al. (2009). They developed a scale to measure pleasure experienced in social relationships and pleasure from nonsocial relationships (e.g., enjoying a pleasant sunset). Our data showed that in both a recovered bipolar group and student group, nonsocial positive affect has few correlations with other types of positive affect and temperament. In contrast, the pleasures derived for social relationships significantly related to other types of positive affect and mood-linked temperaments. Such studies suggest then that we should not assume that all rewarding stimuli are operating in the same way. This would fit with the evolutionary model that suggests that the processing and emotional responding to *social* stimuli will overlap with systems designed for nonsocial but also be different because in the latter social communication, and possible adjustments to one's own self-evaluation and social presentation are key whereas these are not involved in the former. Indeed as argued above, depression is very linked into people's social cognitive processing styles, such as with shame and social cognitive competencies such as mentalizing and ToM.

The drive system is especially linked to social rank stress. Rygula et al. (2005) found that chronic social stress is a source of anhedonia in rats. Primates who are in subordinate positions are more stressed or harassed and more vulnerable to having the drive systems downgraded. For example, Grant et al. (1998) found lower D2 receptors among subordinate monkeys, hypothesizing that the stress of subordination produced a downregulation of D2 receptors in monkeys. Shively (1999) also found that the stress of social subordination is associated with downregulation of D2 receptors and poorer regulation of HPA system. Shively et al. (2005) explored the link between depression and social/subordinate status in female monkeys over a period of 27 months and found very clear links between social status and depression, leading them to recommend social status as good model for the psychological and physiological study of depression. In humans too, there is also a considerable evidence that social stress and particularly, the stresses that are associated with inequity are linked to depression (Ostler et al., 2001; Wilkinson & Pickett, 2010).

Positive emotion systems need stimulating, by thought or action, and many early behavioral theorists noted that in depression there is a drop in positively reinforcing behavior (for a review, see Gilbert, 1992). In other words, due partly to increased threat sensitivity (anxiety), shamed or fatigued individuals stop stimulating positive emotions and engage instead in threat-based ruminations (rather than positive planning or anticipating) and behavioral withdrawal and avoidance. This compounds the problem. Hence, behavior-focused therapies such as behavioral activation therapy, seek to address these difficulties directly and encourage people to "act as if one is not depressed and engage with activities that could be reinforcing" (Martell, Addis, & Jacobson, 2001).

## Contentment, Soothing, Affiliation, and Safeness

In discussions of anhedonia, what is often neglected is the fact that there is also another very different type of positive affect system that has its own evolved functions and neurophysiology; with the endorphins and oxytocin playing especially important roles (Carter, 1998; Depue & Morrone-Strupinsky, 2005; Macdonald & Macdonald, 2010). This system also seems to be compromised in depression although the neurophysiological data are less clear.

When animals are not engaged in pursuing or enjoying rewards, and not under any threat, they can enter states of quiescence and contentment. Subjectively, this is associated with peaceful well-being and calmness. Endorphins are especially important for this system and are well known to induce feelings of well-being, contentment, and social connectedness (Depue & Morrone-Strupinsky, 2005; Panskepp, 1998, 2010). Indeed, this is one of the reasons why heroin can be a drug of choice for people who seek experiences of well-being; it provides experiences very different from the more activating drive–dopamine-based drugs of amphetamine and cocaine.

There is also increasing evidence that endorphins have been very important in the development of affiliation, typically through the two processes: (1) infant–parent attachment and (2) primate grooming (Dunbar, 2010). Grooming and cleaning of newborns and infants is common in mammals, as is self-grooming, but it is mostly only primates in whom social grooming plays a major role in the development of affiliative bonds. Moreover, primates spend considerable time in affiliative grooming interactions (Dunbar, 2010) with increasing evidence that affiliative behavior and grooming trigger endorphins (among other neurotransmitters). Abbott et al. (2003) found that cortisol levels in subordinates were predicted by two key variables: first, the rates of conflicts and stressors experienced, and second, subordinate opportunities for affiliative kin and supportive interactions—where a lot of these were grooming interactions. Panksepp (2010) also points out that the endorphin system is increasingly looking like an important system in regard to antidepressant action. However as we will note, the neurophysiology of affiliative and attachment system is complex because some people can have a fear of these emotions, and when activated you get fear not affiliation.

Another important hormone for affiliation, which works in conjunction with endorphins, is oxytocin (Macdonald & Macdonald, 2010). During evolution, oxytocin came to play an important role in bonding. It also came to have a significant regulatory function on the threat system. For example, when infants are distressed, kind comfort will soothe them and tone down the threat system. In fact, there are oxytocin receptors in the amygdala to do exactly this (Kirsch et al., 2005).

Although the neurophysiology is complex there is now good evidence that affiliative emotion and affiliative interactions (or lack of them) play important roles in both the vulnerability to depression, its maintenance, and recovery (Cacioppo & Patrick, 2008; Cozolino, 2008). The experience of affiliation and secure attachment in early life is known to influence genetic expression (Belsky & Pluess, 2009), and the maturation of physiological systems that are going to be important in emotion and mood regulation (Boyce & Ellis, 2005; Boyce et al., 2005). Put simply, individuals who experience their caregivers as loving, affiliative, available, and caring have their brains stimulated by these interactions, can internalize a sense of self as lovable and other people as loving, build neurophysiological systems, and support positive affects. These form the basis of resilience (Atwool, 2006).

Above we noted that vulnerability to depression may arise not just because of overstimulation of stress in threat systems in early life but also because of the under-development of affiliative systems—especially since they may well act as a buffer when confronted by stress. Indeed we now know that the endorphin system is particularly linked to touch and grooming behavior (Dunbar, 2010), rats handled early in life tend to be calmer than those who are not. There are of course also many anecdotal stories of how parents were not abusive but they certainly were not very physically affectionate. The neuroscientist Robert Sapolsky observed:

> Touch is one of the central experiences of an infant, whether rodent, primate, or human. We readily think of stressors as consisting of various unpleasant things that can be done to an organism. Sometimes a stressor can be the *failure* to provide something to an organism, and the absence of touch is seemingly one of the most marked of developmental stressors that we can suffer. (p. 92)

These observations have been very poorly integrated into research on depression if at all, and certainly not in terms of thinking about treatment implications (Gilbert, 2010). These data are even more worrying in the context of our society as we are moving away from "comforting touch" in school because of fears of pedophilia. It is unclear if we are depriving ourselves of a very important bonding and endorphin-regulating interaction. Questions have also been raised in regard to modern forms of communication through such means as texting—which are essentially relating with our visual or physical signals—signals which actually would normally be biologically activating.

Study of the affiliative motions, the underlying neurophysiological regulators, and their evolved functions obviously link into a major area called attachment theory. We now know that attachment styles can vary in terms of secure anxious ambivalence, avoidant fearfulness, avoidant dismissing, and disorganization (Mikulincer & Shaver, 2007). While insecurely attached individuals are neither doomed to depression, nor are securely attached individuals guaranteed freedom from it, there is no doubt that attachment is a risk factor. More complex so is the fact that different types of insecure attachment may be linked to different types of depressions. For example, people with abuse or neglect histories can be vulnerable to disorganized attachment where the parent has been both a source of threat and calming at the same time, producing intense conflict (Liotti, 2010). These attachment styles have profound effects on the internal organization of emotion, the ability to form, maintain, and mature adaptive supporters' interpersonal relationships, which in turn are affect regulating. All these factors can significantly influence the expression and presentation of depression and compromise various therapies. To date there is little research or clinical guidance on how attachment styles might influence presentation and treatment for depression.

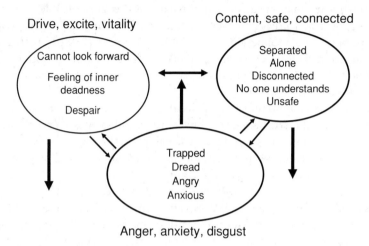

**Figure 10.4.** Disruption and Experiences Associated with Three Major Affect Regulation Systems in Depression

## The Patterns of Emotional Disturbance in Depression

The biopsychosocial view focuses on patterns and interactions rather than honing in on one specific process. Using the three-circle model of different emotional systems we can conceptualize depression as a change of brain state that involves all three systems in different combinations to different degrees. This is depicted in Figure 10.4.

As noted above, depression involves elevated threat processing. This makes sense because depression is usually in the context of some life events, past or present, which are threatening or harmful. The subjective experience of an elevated threat system offered by patients who talk about their feelings is having a sense of dread, anxiety, irritability, being on the short fuse, disgust, shame, and even horror with a sense of self.

As noted above, drive systems and especially dopamine systems, are typically compromised in the context of defeats (including social losses) in both humans and animals (Gilbert, 2007). Typically, early in the depression, there may be a slight increase in drive (as part of the biphasic response to stress; see above) so individuals become agitated, trying to sort out difficulties and confront problems; however, as these efforts begin to fail then more defeat like "dips in dopamine" may occur. Indeed, there are a number of studies in learned helplessness and other stress areas that show that dopamine and other monoamines begin to become depleted in chronic stress situations and produced discontinuities and sudden shifts and mental states (Ganzel et al., 2010). Indeed, the link between an inner experience of intense social threat, defeat, and anhedonia may be especially important for understanding depression in people with psychosis. The subjective experience of a disrupted drive system deems to be feeling of lacking drive/energy, empty, washed-up, feeling emotionally flat, frozen, and fatigued. These are typical experiences of depressed people (Keller & Nesse, 2006).

Moreover, rather than trying to enjoy what rewards are available in the current environment, or how to make the best of things as they are, depressed people tend to be escape motivated (Gilbert & Allan 1998; Taylor et al., 2011). Interestingly, gratitude and appreciation exercises, where people directly pay attention to the things they can enjoy, does have some antidepressant effect on at least at mild levels (White, Laithwaite, & Gilbert, in press).

However, it is also important to recognize that the contentment and social affiliative system, with the ability to experience connectedness and safeness in relationships, also seems compromised in depression. Here, the subjective experience presents as one of yearning for closeness, feeling unloved, loneliness, tearfulness, and may be a want to be protected and looked after. Again these are typical experiences of depressed people and may constitute a variant of depression more closely linked to protest attachment difficulties (Keller & Nesse, 2006). We also know that social and emotional feelings of loneliness are very common and mental health problems are indeed highly associated with them (Cacioppo & Patrick, 2008). A complexity is that some people are fearful of affiliative feelings, and find these difficult to process and acknowledge.

As noted above, there is a strong link between early history of the abuse and vulnerability to depression, but such depressions are often textured with personality-disorder-like symptoms. There is growing evidence that the affiliative system and in particular the endorphin and oxytocin regulators have been compromised in certain personality disorders especially those with the problems such as impulsivity, self-harming, emotional instability, aggressive outbursts, sensitivity to rejection, and poor self-identity (Stanley & Siever, 2010). It is quite possible that these systems need urgent attention to provide the basis for working on drive and threat reduction. One of the reasons that these individuals may do poorly in therapy is that very few therapies recognize or pay attention to the repair of this specific positive affect system (Gilbert 2010). People who generally struggle with affiliative feelings and do not feel safe may not benefit so much from dopamine and serotonin drugs—or just focusing on cognitive distortions, or processing anger. Rather, they actually require therapies that will help them to begin to feel and experience affiliative emotion, because affiliative emotion and attachment evolved the fundamental regulators and threat and positive affect.

## Complications

### The relationship of self with self

It is very unlikely that any other animal can feel self-pride or be self-critical. Although chimpanzees may well get frustrated with their efforts it is unlikely that they feel anger or disgust *with themselves*. However, these newly evolved capabilities for objectifying the self and forming self-judgments and evaluations play a key role in generating and maintaining low mood. There is now considerable evidence that self-criticism is linked to a range of psychopathologies especially depression (Bulmash, Harkness, Stewart, & Bagby, 2009; Gilbert & Irons, 2005; Zuroff, Santor, & Mongrain, 2005) and interferes with recovery (Bulmash et al., 2009).

Importantly, humans not only objectify the self and judge "the self" but we also have *feelings* about "oneself" that are no different from feelings for other social relationships. Hence, we feel liking, anger, disappointment, or even disgust with "ourselves"; or aspects of it. Whelton and Greenberg (2005) showed that when people are being self-critical, the emotion *in the criticism* tended to be anger and/or contempt. Individuals vulnerable to depression felt beaten down by their own self-criticism; and it appears to be the strength of *the emotion* in the criticism and not the content of a criticism that is key. Gilbert (2004) identified different types of self-criticism with different emotions. One type of self-criticism seems linked to desires to avoid mistakes and to self-improve; however, another type of self-criticism is linked self-contempt and even self-hatred. The latter was more pathogenic.

Longe et al. (2010), using fMRI, showed that there were clear differences in the brain systems activated when people were being self-reassuring or self-critical about potentially shaming events. There is increasing evidence that the self-criticisms are physiologically powerful and stimulate the threat system. This being the case, then depressed people may need to develop a different emotional relationship with themselves; based on more positive emotions such as self-compassion and kindness to replace the anger and contempt of self-criticisms (Gilbert, 2000, 2010).

Another depressogenic aspect of self-criticism is that it can be regularly activated, sometimes many times in a day. Hence, a self-criticism may regularly stimulate the threat system and activate aversive memories. In a sense, this is like (internal) bullying and harassing oneself into depression.

In contrast, self-criticism depression is associated with low rates of self-reassurance (Gilbert, 2004) and self-compassion (Neff, Kirkpatrick, & Rude, 2007). The implication is that individuals struggle to stimulate positive affect systems, especially those associated with affiliation, internal self-evaluation, or some kind of positive feelings of self.

People also have beliefs that they need to hang onto self-criticism even when it is doing a lot of harm (Gilbert & Irons, 2005). Gilbert and Irons (2005; Gilbert, 2009b) drew attention to Bowlby's (1980) concept, the *defense of exclusion,* whereby the child blames himself for the parent's bad behavior (defensively avoids processing the idea that the parent could be bad and dangerous) in order not to threaten the attachment. The parent tells the child that it is the child's own bad behavior that caused them to be beaten, not because the parent has loss control of his/her anger. This submissive strategy in the face of a potentially powerful dominant is also seen in religion. For example, people appeal to their gods for help or support to deal with famines, diseases, or hardships and if things get worse rather than believing their gods unreasonable or spiteful (which would be very threatening) they prefer to believe that they have done something wrong and try to find ways to be more submissive and win back their gods' favor. The medical historian Roy Porter (2003) pointed out that in the Middle Ages, a lot of the focus of depression was on the idea that the sufferer had, like Job, offended God and was now cast out; the depressed person focused on their badness, wickedness, and desperate wish for forgiveness—a highly subordinate terror of punitive authority. The point is that self-criticism cannot be approached only from a logical point of view but needs to be understood in terms of its emotional origins and function—especially in the context of power dynamics.

Therefore, self-criticism can be depressogenic because: (1) it sends "put down signals" (you are stupid, your behavior was dreadful) that can active "defeat" states; (2) it comes with intense attacking emotions (e.g., anger and contempt); (3) it stimulates threat processing systems; (4) it can be regularly activated (sometimes many times a day) especially when things go wrong; (5) it blocks out positive affect for the self; (6) people hold metacognitive beliefs of the need to remain self-critical; and (7) self-criticisms can be a cover for being fearful of process anger to (powerful) others that maintain low rank and a vulnerable sense of self cutoff from affiliative and supportive relationships.

## The Fear of Positive Emotion—An Important but Commonly Unforeseen Complication in the Treatment of Depression

If depression represents a pattern of increased threat processing, reduced drive, and affiliative processing, then a commonsense view would be that we simply need to activate these positive systems again. This is key to the behavioral activation approaches (Martell et al., 2001). The complication here, however, is that the positive affect itself is not necessarily experienced "positively." When I started trying to help people develop more affiliative emotion to themselves nearly 20 years ago (I was surprised to find) many depressed patients were quite resistant to this idea. In the early days we simply asked people to generate alternative thoughts to depressing ones but to imagine the emotional tone of kindness, warmth, and encouragement—building inner warmth (Gilbert, 2000). Trying to generate "kind, supportive, and warm" emotional textures into alternative thoughts proved very tricky, with some depressed people becoming anxious and resistant (see Gilbert, 2010, 2012 for a historical review).

Clinical experience with these patients and indeed many other therapists (Liotti, 2000, 2010; Van der Hart et al., 2006) have drawn attention to the *fear of affiliation* and attachment. In CFT, it is not just fear of affiliative feelings from other people but also fear of *self*-compassion. Some years ago I heard a lecture by John Bowlby who noted that for some people, the kindness and support of the therapist can activate the attachment system. When this happens the "system" will open to what memories have been encoded there. This leads to a simple memory defense-activation model.

So if a person has experienced neglect, fear, abandonment, and/or sadness in early life, then when the therapist stimulates affiliative and attachment feelings, those aversive of emotional textured memories can also be activated (see Figure 10.5). This is no different from saying that normally one's sexual feelings are pleasant and stimulate approach behavior, but if one has been raped then one's *own sexual arousal* can be deeply traumatic. Emotional systems that should be felt positively can (via aversive emotional experiences) become very distressing. This simple classical conditioning phenomenon has huge implications for both psychological and pharmacological therapies. Psychotherapy is now understanding the importance of stimulus activation of aversive emotions in trauma and the importance of desensitization and rescripting (Ehlers, Clark, Hackmann, McManus, & Fennell, 2005). This type of approach may be important for the aversive conditioning of positive emotion too.

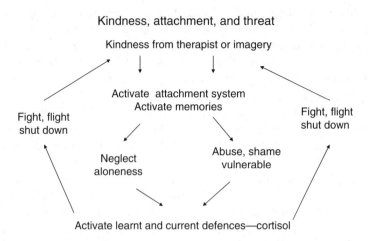

Kindness, attachment, and threat

Kindness from therapist or imagery

Activate attachment system
Activate memories

Fight, flight
shut down

Fight, flight
shut down

Neglect
aloneness

Abuse, shame
vulnerable

Activate learnt and current defences—cortisol

**Figure 10.5.** Ways of Kindness and Compassion can Relate to Threat and Avoidance. Reprinted from Gilbert (2009c), with permission from Routledge

Indeed we have begun to explore fear of affiliation toward self, others, and from others. We have shown that in self-critics in particular asking them to generate an image of an individual being kind and caring to them actually activates the threat system as measured by heart rate variability (Rockliff, Gilbert, McEwan, Lightman, & Glover, 2008). In another study using fMRI (Longe et al., 2010) we found that when self-critics where asked to be kind to themselves in a potentially shaming situation, again they showed threat (amygdala) responses rather less (insula) soothing response (in contrast to low self-critics). And when we did a study where we provided students with a nasal infusion of oxytocin (the hormone associated with affiliation and trust) we found that self-critics were more likely to find this unpleasant or might remind them of feeling lonely (Rockliff et al., 2011). Any simple idea then that oxytocin or opiate-derived drugs could be a treatment for depression should be handled extremely careful, because much may depend upon the emotional memories that are in the affiliative and attachment system that these hormones may activate.

Work on exactly what the fears of affiliative emotion are is in its infancy. Some suggest that beginning to feel affiliative emotions also activates the fear of being harmed or hurt again in some way (Liotti, 2000, 2010); some suggest that it activates unprocessed needs and a complex grief process (Gilbert & Irons, 2005)—and indeed is noticeable when people start to learn to be kind to themselves or to imagine kindness they can become very tearful but also highly avoidant of sadness. Other therapists suggest closeness activates awareness of how angry they have felt at childhood neglect or abuse but can be very frightened of the degree of this rage and its potential destructiveness, feel guilt, keep distant, or might try to be excessively "nice" (Davenloo, 2005). And of course the obvious connection is with avoidant attachment and disorganized attachment (Mikulincer & Shaver, 2007). It is likely that different patients will have different combinations of these threats and while clinical anecdotes abound careful study is yet to be undertaken.

Gilbert, McEwan, Matos, and Rivis (2011) also explored metacognitive beliefs tapping fears of (1) being compassionate to others, (2) being open and receptive to the compassion from others, and (3) being self-compassionate. Fear of compassion to oneself and being open to and from others is highly correlated with depression in both clinical and nonclinical populations. Fear of being compassionate to others is less so and may be indicated as a different mechanism.

We also wondered if the fear of positive emotion was only for affiliative emotions or was it more general? Could people fear the experience of being happy? I certainly thought so because patients had often talked about emotional memories where they were happy and then something bad happened. For example, Carol remembered being very happy playing in the garden and then her alcoholic mother rushed into the garden screamed at her hit about the head for making a noise. "You must never let your guard down, and when you're feeling happy that is the most dangerous time," she said. Now you could see that as core belief—but in CFT it is a very powerful emotional memory (classical conditioning) that may require careful desensitization.

In a recent study, Gilbert, McEwan, Matos, and Rivis (2011); Gilbert et al. (2012) found that in students, fear of happiness correlated with depression surprisingly highly at $r = 0.70$. In an ongoing study, we find a very similar association in a depressed population. We therefore need further studies on the fears of positive feelings in general and those associated with social relationships in particular. This has clear implications for all kinds of therapies, be it pharmacological, psychological, or social. Compassion-focused therapy (Gilbert, 2010) seeks to address self-criticism and the fears of positive emotion, and build compassion capacity and tolerance. Without positive emotion systems accessible, and certainly without the affiliative system (which from an evolutionary point of view has been evolving as a threat regulator for millions of years), people are going to struggle. So we take the view that for over 120 million years, the mammalian brain has been evolving capacities (brain systems and algorithms) for developing and responding to affiliative relationships. These have come to play key roles in a whole range of phenotypic development and that for our patients and in our treatments for people with mental health problems these require our most urgent attention.

# Conclusion

I noted at the beginning of this chapter that the field of "depression" is something of a mess. This is not the lack of effort, but psychiatry and clinical psychology remain fragmented, too mindlessness versus brainless, with poor understanding of individual differences and evolved mechanisms. We have not been very successful at instigating biopsychosocial approaches that can illuminate the importance and source of individual variation of phenotypes in either training or treatment. Understanding the natural regulators of positive emotion is a start to thinking about depression but from there the complexity in the variation of causes, types, expression, and treatments for depression can operate in any dimension of the biopsychosocial model. So, for example, depressive phenotypes can vary in terms of their genes and how different genes become expressed differently in different environments. People with short alleles for the serotonin gene might be different from those with short alleles for dopamine or oxytocin. Depressions can vary in terms of whether dopamine, serotonin, endorphin, oxytocin, and/or immune system functioning (to name just a few) play the crucial role. They can vary in terms of their life history—with physical and sexual abuse, neglect, lack of physical affection, anxious or depressed parents, and sibling and peer bullying all having unique shaping effects on phenotypes. Early-onset depression may shape personality development, and personality may shape the forms and expressions of depression. Personality types with submissive interpersonal styles and prone to social anxiety seeming particularly vulnerable for later depression. People from traumatic and abusive backgrounds tend to have more PTSD symptoms and commit more self-harm. Depression can vary in terms of the environment in which it takes root, such as in poverty or violent environments. Depressions can vary in terms of the degree to which people feel trapped in states of mind or aversive situations they cannot get out of. Researchers are looking at the link between fatigue (which can have multiple causes including poor diet) and how that can trigger depressive thinking and behavior. Fatigue states are important because they can be indicators of some underlying pathology, such as thyroid dysfunction or diabetes, which can be misdiagnosed as depression.

Research into depression often fails to consider what the normal adaptive mechanisms of mood variation are or why many depressed people will only have one episode. Candidates for causes and relapse signatures have been associated with lack of control over stresses, involuntary subordination, management and social risk, hostile and critical relationships, defeat, entrapment, separation, loneliness, and social disconnection. These turn out to be major affect regulators. Researchers interested in the psychology of depression focus on general-purpose cognitive processes (reasoning, attention, ruminating, imagination), others are more interested in algorithms (like social comparison) linked to evolved outcomes such as involuntary low rank, defeat, or separation. Others focus more on motivational systems and the blocking of desired values, goals, and ambitions.

The treatments for depression are more variable than they have ever been, with many people turning to alternative therapies. There is evidence for the benefits of exercise through to music therapy. While drug therapies push their own brands of antidepressants, evidence is accumulating that some people might do better with the dopaminergic as opposed to serotonergic drug, that a range of compounds can be helpful for some depressions some of the time. Candidates here include folic acid, omega-3, vitamin D, vitamin Bs, chromium picolinate, St. Johns wort, and ginkgo (to name a few). Evidence is increasing too that modern diets might contribute to depression vulnerability and a change of diet can be helpful. Light therapy might be useful for some people with seasonal affective disorder.

While drug treatments have had an impact, they are not the panacea that people might hope for. Psychotherapy too is a bit of a mess, with many different schools therapy emerging all claiming some degree of efficacy. Far more research is needed to identify those individuals who only can have one episode from those who can have more. If study happens to have many "single episode cases" then their relapse rates will look good but it will not be due to the therapy but to the nature of the case.

Most therapists recognize that "tribalism" is a problem in psychotherapy. This leads the problem where we have different schools/approaches therapy (rather than understanding specific symptom difficulties in developing specific therapies for those problems) addressing broad, and as we are seeing here, unhelpful symptom clusters for depression—all trying to get some RCT data to prove their worth. It may be better for us to simply start the psychology with depression and test different interventions with different problems in a much more specific way.

Psychotherapy too often fails to connect itself to an appropriate biopsychosocial model rooted in the science of mind and especially in the evolutionary and neurological sciences. It is important because these help us understand how the mind *actually* processes information (Gilbert, 1995). If we simply rely on different psychotherapy models, we will have myriad ways of thinking about how the mind works. Physiotherapy without some understanding of how the muscular system works would seem nonsensical but some psychotherapists think you can train in and understand therapy without any recourse to the concept of a phenotype or physiological process—or understand how physiological processes can significantly influence cognitive and emotional systems—as in the case of the physiological adaptations that individuals who have grown up in abusive environments have had to make. Psychotherapy is going to have to understand the issue of the hardware and not just the software of the brain, even thinking about developing training that can interact with hardware processes (e.g., meditation training is showing ways by which frontal cortical mechanisms could be changed).

Equally, whatever school of psychotherapy is our personal evidence-based flavor we should all be vocal in terms of the social determinants of depression and push for social solutions. Hundreds of years ago, we made significant advances in the prevention of disease not by having more and more individual doctors pushing pills and potions, but with the concept of hygiene and better sanitation. We are long overdue in thinking about creating environments that are socially and psychologically hygienic! What would they look like? How would we instigate them?

About 35 years ago, Akiskal and McKinney (1975) wrote their landmark and influential paper on *depression as a final common pathway*. Today though, this concept is looking less secure and is actually problematic because there are many different types of depressions that are interacting with different types of "systems" and may require different types of therapies. "Depression" may not be best viewed as a final common pathway, but as representing a whole range of different pathways, different processes, and different treatment requirements. Only by studying complex interactions in the context of a brain that has evolved to function in certain ways can we begin to address these complexities and individual variations.

When confronted by the epidemic of depression we keep turning to disease models that recommend individual solutions, be these drugs or training graduate workers to do simple individualized interventions. This is probably our biggest failure, arising from a lack of a biopsychosocial model, and highlights the importance of the World Health Organization's concerns about identifying the social determinants of disease—except that by disease, we need to understand pathological states produced by pathogenic environments. Social psychiatry and community clinical psychology focus on prevention and social solutions have rather been lost in the decades of the brain and yet it is the study of the brain that has shown us just how important our social relationships are to our well-being.

# References

Abbott, D. H., Keverne, E. B., Bercovitch, F. B., Shively, C. A., Mendoza, S. P., & Saltzman, W. (2003). Are subordinates always stressed? A comparative analysis of rank differences in cortisol levels among primates. *Hormones and Behavior, 43*, 67–82.

Abram, D., Hogg, M. A., & Marques, J. M. (2005). *The social psychology of inclusion and exclusion*. Hove, UK: Psychology Press.

Akiskal, H. S., & McKinney, W. T. (1975). Overview of recent research in depression: Integration of ten conceptual models into a comprehensive frame. *Archives of General Psychiatry, 32*, 285–305.

Akiskal, H. S., & Pinto, O. (1999). The evolving bipolar spectrum: Prototypes I, II, III, and IV. *Psychiatric Clinics of North America, 22*, 517–534.

Allan, S., & Gilbert, P. (1995). A social comparison scale: Psychometric properties and relationship to psychopathology. *Personality and Individual Differences, 19*, 293–299

Allen, J. G., & Fonagy, P. (Eds.). (2007). *Handbook of mentalization-based treatment*. Chichester, UK: Wiley.

Allen, N. B., & Badcock, P. B. T. (2003). The social risk hypothesis of depressed mood: Evolutionary, psychosocial, and neurobiological perspective. *Psychological Bulletin, 129*, 887–913.

Andrade, L. A., Wang, Y. P., Andreon, S., Silva, C., Siu, E. R., Anthony, J. C., . . . Viana, M. C. (2012). Mental disorders in megacities: Findings from the São Paulo megacity mental health survey, Brazil. *PLoS One, 7*(2), e31879.

Andrews, B. (1998). Shame and childhood abuse. In P. Gilbert, & B. Andrews (Eds.), *Shame: Interpersonal behavior, psychopathology and culture* (pp. 176–190). New York: Oxford University Press.

Anisman, H., & Matheson, K. (2005). Stress, depression, and anhedonia: Caveats concerning animal models. *Neuroscience and Biobehavioral Reviews, 29*, 525–546. doi:10.1016/j.neubiorev

Atwool, N. (2006). Attachment and resilience: Implications for children in care. *Child Care in Practice, 12*, 315–330. doi:10.1080/13575270600863226

Baldwin, M. W., & Dandeneau, S. D. (2005). Understanding and modifying the relational schemas underlying insecurity. In M. W. Baldwin (Ed.), *Interpersonal cognition* (pp. 33–61). New York: Guilford Press.

Barkow, J. H. (1989). *Darwin, sex and status: Biological approaches to mind and culture*. Toronto: University of Toronto Press.

Baron-Cohen, S. (2011). *Zero degrees of empathy: A new theory of cruelty*. London: Allen Lane.

Baumeister, R. F. (1990). Suicide as escape from self. *Psychological Review, 97*, 90–133.

Bebbington, P. (1998). Editorial: Sex and depression. *Psychological Medicine, 28*, 1–8.

Bebbington, P., Katz, R., McGuffin, P., Sturt, E., & Wing, J. K. (1989). The risk of minor depression before age 65: Results from a community survey. *Psychological Medicine, 19*, 393–400.

Beck, A. T. (1967). *Depression: Clinical, experimental and theoretical aspects*. New York: Harper & Row.

Beck, A. T. (1987). Cognitive models of depression. *Journal of Cognitive Psychotherapy: An International Quarterly, 1*, 5–38.

Beck, A. T. (1996). Beyond belief: A theory of modes, personality and psychopathology. In P. Salkovskis (Ed.), *Frontiers of cognitive therapy* (pp. 1–25). New York: Oxford University Press.

Beck. A. T. (2008). The evolution of the cognitive model of depression and its neurobiological correlates. *American Journal of Psychiatry, 165,* 969–977. doi:10.1176/appi.ajp.2008.08050721

Beck, A. T., Rush, A. J., Shaw, B. F., & Emery, G. (1979). *Cognitive therapy of depression.* New York: John Wiley & Sons.

Beckham, E. E., Leber, W. R., & Youll, L. K. (1995). The diagnostic classification of depression. In E. E. Beckham, & W. R. Leber (Eds.), *Handbook of depression* (2nd ed., pp. 36–60). New York: Guilford Press.

Belsky, J., & Pluess, M. (2009). Beyond diathesis stress: Differential susceptibility to environmental influences. *Psychological Bulletin, 135,* 885–908. doi:10.1037/a0017376

Boksem, M., Kostermans, E., Milivojevic, B., & De Cremer, D. (2011). Social status determines how we monitor and evaluate our performance. *Social, Cognitive and Affective Neuroscience, 7,* 304–313. doi:10.1093/scan/nsr010

Bolhuis, J. J., Brown, G. R., Richardson, R. C., & Laland, R. N. (2011). Darwin in mind: New opportunities for evolutionary psychology. *PLoS Biology, 9,* 1–8. doi:10.1371/journal.pbio.1001109

Boudewyn, A. C., & Liem, J. H. (1995). Childhood sexual abuse as a precursor to depression and self-destructive behavior in adulthood. *Journal of Traumatic Stress, 8,* 445–459. doi:10.1007/BF02102969

Bowlby, J. (1969). *Attachment: Attachment and loss* (Vol. 1). London: Hogarth Press.

Bowlby, J. (1973). *Separation, anxiety and anger: Attachment and loss* (Vol. 2). London: Hogarth Press.

Bowlby, J. (1980). *Loss: Sadness and depression. Attachment and loss* (Vol. 3). London: Hogarth Press.

Boyce, W. T., & Ellis, B. J. (2005). Biological sensitively to context 1: An evolutionary-developmental theory of the origins and functions of stress reactivity. *Development and Psychopathology, 17,* 271–302.

Boyce, W. T., Essex, M. J., & Ellis, B. J. (2005). Biological sensitively to context 11: Empirical explorations of an evolutionary-developmental theory. *Development and Psychopathology, 17,* 271–302.

Brewin, C. R. (2006). Understanding cognitive behaviour therapy: A retrieval competition account. *Behaviour Research and Therapy, 44,* 765–784. doi:10.1016/j.brat.2006.02.005

Brody, G. H., Beach, S. R. H., Philibert, R. A., Chen, Y., Lei, M. L., Murry, V. M., & Brown, A. C. (2009). Parenting moderates a genetic vulnerability factor in longitudinal increases in youths' substance use. *Journal of Consulting and Clinical Psychology, 77,* 1–11. doi:10.1037/a0012996

Brown, G. B., Harris, T. O., Kendrick, T., Chatwin, J., Craig, T. K., Kelly, V., . . . Uher, R.; Thread Study Group. (2010). Antidepressants, social adversity and outcome of depression in general practice. *Journal of Affective Disorders, 121,* 239–246. doi:10:1016/j.jad.2000.06.004

Brown, G. W., Adler, W. Z., & Bifulco, A. (1988). Life events, difficulties and recovery from chronic depression. *British Journal of Psychiatry, 152,* 487–498.

Brown, G. W., & Harris, T. O. (1978). *The social origins of depression.* London: Tavistock.

Brown, T., Campbell, L. A., Lehman, C. L., Grisham, J. R., & Mancill, R. B. (2001). Current and life time comorbidity of the DSM-IV anxiety and mood disorders in a large clinical sample. *Journal of Abnormal Psychology, 110,* 585–599.

Brune, M., Belsky, J., Fabrega, H., Feierman, J. R., Gilbert, P., Glantz, K., . . . Wilson, D. R. (2012). The crisis of psychiatry—insights and prospects from evolutionary theory. *World Psychiatry, 11*, 55–57.

Bulmash, E., Harkness, K. L., Stewart, J. G., & Bagby, R. M. (2009). Personality, stressful life events, and treatment response in major depression. *Journal of Consulting and Clinical Psychology, 77*, 1067–1077.

Buss, D. M. (2003). *Evolutionary psychology: The new science of mind* (2nd ed.). Boston: Allyn & Bacon.

Cacioppo, J. T., Berston, G. G., Sheridan, J. F., & McClintock, M. K. (2000). Multilevel integrative analysis of human behavior: Social neuroscience and the complementing nature of social and biological approaches. *Psychological Bulletin, 126*, 829–843.

Cacioppo, J. T., & Patrick, B. (2008). *Loneliness: Human nature and the need for social connection.* New York: Norton.

Cain, N. M., Ansell, E. B., Wright, A. G., Hopwood, C. J., Thomas, K. M., Pinto, A., . . . Grilo, C. M. (2012). Interpersonal pathoplasticity in the course of major depression. *Journal of Consulting and Clinical Psychology, 80*, 78–86. doi:10.1037/a0026433

Carter, C. S. (1998). Neuroendocrine perspectives on social attachment and love. *Psychoneuroendocrinology, 23*, 779–818.

Caspi, A., & Moffit, T. E. (2006). Gene-environment interactions in psychiatry: Joining forces with neuroscience. *Nature Reviews: Neuroscience, 7*, 583–590.

Champion, L. A., & Power, M. J. (1995). Social and cognitive approaches to depression. *British Journal of Clinical Psychology, 34*, 485–503.

Clark, L. A. (2000). Mood, personality and personality disorder. In R. J. Davidson (Ed.), *Anxiety, depression and emotion* (pp. 171–200). New York: Oxford University Press.

Cohen, D. (2001). Cultural variation: Considerations and implications. *Psychological Bulletin, 127*, 451–471.

Coyne, J. C. (1994). Self-reported distress: Analog or ersatz depression? *Psychological Bulletin, 116*, 29–45.

Cowen. P. J. (2010). Not fade away: The HPA axis and depression. *Psychological Medicine, 40*, 1–4. doi:10.1017/S0033291709005558

Cozolino, L. (2007). *The neuroscience of human relationships: Attachment and the developing brain.* New York: Norton.

Cozolino, L. (2008). *The healthy aging brain: Sustaining attachment, attaining wisdom.* New York: Norton.

Cukrowicz, K. C., Otamendi, A., Pinto, J. V., Bernert, R. A., Krakow, B., & Joiner, T. E. (2006). The impact of insomnia and sleep disturbances on depression and suicidality. *Dreaming, 16*, 1–10.

Dalgleish, T., Hill, E., Morant, N., & Golden, A. M. J. (2011). The structure of past and future lives in depression. *Journal of Abnormal Psychology, 120*, 1–15. doi:10.1037/a0020797

Davenloo, H. (2005). Intensive short-term dynamic psychotherapy. In B. J. Sadock, & V. A. Sadock (Eds.), *Kaplan & Sadock's comprehensive textbook of psychiatry* (8th ed.). New York: Lippincott Williams & Wilkins.

Davidson, R. J. (2000). Affective style, mood, and anxiety disorders: An affective neuroscience approach. In R. J. Davidson (Ed.), *Anxiety, depression and emotion* (pp. 88–108). New York: Oxford University Press.

Davis, D. M., & Hayes, J. A. (2011). What are the benefits of mindfulness? A practice review of psychotherapy-related research. *Psychological Bulletin, 48*, 198–208. doi:10.1037/a0022062

Delisle, V. C., Beck, A. T., Dobson, K. S., Dozois, D. J. A., & Thombs, B. D. (2012). Revisiting gender differences in somatic symptoms of depression: Much ado about nothing? *PLoS One*, *7*(2), e32490. doi:10.1371/journal.pone.0032490

Depue, R. A., & Morrone-Strupinsky, J. V. (2005). A neurobehavioral model of affiliative bonding. *Behavioral and Brain Sciences*, *28*, 313–395.

Dixon, A. K. (1998). Ethological strategies for defence in animals and humans: Their role in some psychiatric disorders. *British Journal of Medical Psychology*, *71*, 417–445.

Dryden, W. (2012). *CBT approaches to counselling and psychotherapy*. London: Sage.

Dunbar, R. I. M. (2007). Mind the bonding gap: Or why humans aren't just great apes. *Proceedings of the British Academy*, *154*, 403–433.

Dunbar, R. I. M. (2010). The social role of touch in humans and primates: Behavioural function and neurobiological mechanisms. *Neuroscience and Biobehavioral Reviews*, *34*, 260–268. doi:10.1016/j.neubiorev.2008.07.001

Ehlers, A., Clark, D. M., Hackmann, A., McManus, F., & Fennell, M. (2005). Cognitive therapy for PTSD: Development and evaluation. *Behaviour Research and Therapy*, *43*, 413–431.

Ehlers, A., Maercker, A., & Boos, S. (2000). Posttraumatic stress disorder following imprisonment: Role of mental defeat, alienation, and perceived permanent change. *Journal of Abnormal Psychology*, *109*, 45–55.

Eisenberg, L. (2000). Is psychiatry more mindful or brainier than it was a decade ago? *British Journal of Psychiatry*, *176*, 1–5.

Ferster, C. B. (1973). A functional analysis of depression. *American Psychologist*, *28*, 857–870.

Fisher, P., & Wells, A. (2009). *Metacognitive therapy*. London: Routledge.

Fombonne, E. (1994). Increased rates of depression: Update of epidemiological findings and analytical problems. *Acta Psychiatrica Scandinavica*, *90*, 145–156.

Fombonne, E. (1999). Time trends in affective disorders. In P. Cohen, C. Slomkowski, & L. Robins (Eds.), *Historical and geographical influences on psychopathology* (pp. 115–140). Mahwah, NJ: Erlabum.

Forbes, E. E. (2009). Where's the fun in that? Broadening the focus on reward function in depression. *Biological Psychiatry*, *66*, 199–200. doi:10.1016/j.biopsych.2009.05.001

Forbes, E. E., & Dahl, R. E. (2012). Research review: Altered reward function in adolescent depression: What, when and how? *Journal of Child Psychology and Psychiatry*, *53*(1), 3–15.

Fournier, M. A., Moskowitz, D. S., & Zuroff, D. C. (2002). Social rank strategies in hierarchical relationships. *Journal of Personality and Social Psychology*, *83*, 425–433

Fox, J. R. E., & Power, M. J. (2009). Eating disorders and multi-level models of emotion: An integrated model. *Clinical Psychology and Psychotherapy*, *16*, 240–267. doi:10.1002/cpp.626

Freud, S. (1917). Mourning and melancholia. In J. Strachey (Ed. & Trans.), *Standard edition of the complete psychological works of Sigmund Freud* (Vol. 14, pp. 237–260). London: Hogarth Press.

Ganzel, B. L., Morris, P. A., & Wethington, E. (2010). Allostasis and the human brain: Integrating models of stress from the social and life sciences. *Psychological Review*, *117*, 134–174. doi:10.1037/a0017773

Gardner, R. (1982). Mechanisms of manic-depressive disorder: An evolutionary model. *Archives of General Psychiatry*, *39*, 1436–1441.

Geary, D. C., & Huffman, K. J. (2002). Brain and cognitive evolution: Forms of modularity and functions of the mind. *Psychological Bulletin*, *128*, 667–698.

Gilbert, P. (1984). *Depression: From psychology to brain state*. London: Lawrence Erlbaum Associates Ltd.

Gilbert, P. (1988). Emotional disorders, brain state and psychosocial evolution. In W. Dryden, & P. Trower (Eds.), *Recent developments in cognitive psychotherapy* (pp. 41–70). London: Sage.

Gilbert, P. (1989). *Human nature and suffering.* Hove, UK: Lawrence Erlbaum Associates.

Gilbert, P. (1992). *Depression: The evolution of powerlessness.* New York: Guilford Press.

Gilbert, P. (1995). Biopsychosocial approaches and evolutionary theory as aids to integration in clinical psychology and psychotherapy. *Clinical Psychology and Psychotherapy, 2,* 135–156.

Gilbert, P. (1998a). The evolved basis and adaptive functions of cognitive distortions. *British Journal of Medical Psychology, 71,* 447–463.

Gilbert, P. (1998b). What is shame? Some core issues and controversies. In P. Gilbert, & B. Andrews (Eds.), *Shame: Interpersonal behavior, psychopathology and culture* (pp. 3–38). New York: Oxford University Press.

Gilbert, P. (2000). Varieties of submissive behaviour: Their evolution and role in depression. In L. Sloman, & P. Gilbert (Eds.), *Subordination and defeat. An evolutionary approach to mood disorders* (pp. 3–46). Hillsdale, NJ: Lawrence Erlbaum Associates.

Gilbert, P. (2001). Depression and stress: A biopsychosocial exploration of evolved functions and mechanisms. *Stress, 4,* 121–135.

Gilbert, P. (2004). Depression: A biopsychosocial, integrative and evolutionary approach. In M. Power (Ed.), *Mood disorders: A handbook of science and practice* (pp. 99–142). Chichester, UK: John Wiley & Sons.

Gilbert, P. (2006). Evolution and depression: Issues and implications. *Psychological Medicine, 36,* 287–297.

Gilbert, P. (2007). *Psychotherapy and counselling for depression* (3rd ed.). London: Sage.

Gilbert, P. (2009a). *The compassionate mind.* London: Constable-Robinson.

Gilbert, P. (2009b). *Overcoming depression* (3rd ed.). London: Constable-Robinson.

Gilbert, P. (2009c). Evolved minds and compassion focused imagery in depression. In L. Stropa (Ed.), *Imagery and the threatened self: Perspectives on mental imagery in cognitive therapy* (pp. 206–231). London: Routledge.

Gilbert, P. (2010). *Compassion focused therapy: The CBT distinctive features series.* London: Routledge.

Gilbert, P. (2012). Compassion focused therapy. In W. Dryden (Ed.), *Cognitive behaviour therapies* (pp. 140–165). London: Sage.

Gilbert, P., & Allan, S. (1998). The role of defeat and entrapment (arrested flight) in depression: An exploration of an evolutionary view. *Psychological Medicine, 28,* 584–597.

Gilbert, P., Allan, S., Ball, L., & Bradshaw, Z. (1996). Overconfidence and personal evaluations of social rank. *British Journal of Medical Psychology, 69,* 59–68.

Gilbert, P., Allan, S., Brough, S., Melley, S., & Miles, J. (2002). Anhedonia and positive affect: Relationship to social rank, defeat and entrapment. *Journal of Affective Disorders, 71,* 141–151.

Gilbert, P., Broomhead, C., Irons, C., McEwan, K., Bellew, R., Mills, A., & Gale, C. (2007). Striving to avoid inferiority: Scale development and its relationship to depression, anxiety and stress. *British Journal of Social Psychology, 46,* 633–648.

Gilbert, P., Cheung, M., Wright, T., Campey, F., & Irons, C. (2003). Recall of threat and submissiveness in childhood: Development of a new scale and its relationship with depression, social comparison and shame. *Clinical Psychology and Psychotherapy, 10,* 108–115.

Gilbert, P., & Gelsma, C. (1999). Recall of favouritism in relation to psychopathology. *British Journal of Clinical Psychology, 38,* 357–373.

Gilbert, P., & Gilbert, J. (2003). Entrapment and arrested fight and flight in depression: An exploration using focus groups. *Psychology and Psychotherapy: Theory Research and Practice, 76*, 173–188.

Gilbert, P., Gilbert, J., & Irons, C. (2004). Life events, entrapments and arrested anger in depression. *Journal of Affective Disorders, 79*, 149–160. doi:10.1016/S0165-0327(02)00405-6

Gilbert, P., & Irons, C. (2005). Focused therapies and compassionate mind training for shame and self-attacking. In P. Gilbert (Ed.), *Compassion: Conceptualisations, research and use in psychotherapy* (pp. 263–325). London: Routledge.

Gilbert, P., Irons, C., Olsen, K., Gilbert, J., & McEwan, K. (2006). Interpersonal sensitivities: Their link to mood, anger and gender. *Psychology and Psychotherapy: Theory Research and Practice, 79*, 37–51.

Gilbert, P., McEwan, K., Gibbons, L., Chotai, S., Duarte, J., & Matos, M. (2012). Fears of compassion and happiness in relation to alexithymia, mindfulness and self-criticism. *Psychology and Psychotherapy, 85*(4), 374–390.

Gilbert, P., McEwan, K., Hay, J., Irons, C., & Cheung, M. (2007). Social rank and attachment in people with a bipolar disorder. *Clinical Psychology and Psychotherapy, 14*, 48–53.

Gilbert, P., McEwan, K., Irons, C., Broomhead, C., Bellew, R., Mills, A., & Gale, C. (2009). The dark side of competition: How competitive behaviour and striving to avoid inferiority, are linked to depression, anxiety, stress and self-harm. *Psychology and Psychotherapy, 82*, 123–136.

Gilbert, P., McEwan, K., Matos, M., & Rivis, A. (2011). Fears of compassion: Development of three self-report measures. *Psychology and Psychotherapy, 84*, 239–255. doi:10.1348/147608310×526511

Gilbert, P., McEwan, K., Mitra, R., Richter, A., Franks, L., Mills, A., . . . Gale, C. (2009). An exploration of different types of positive affect in students and in patients with bipolar disorder. *Clinical Neuropsychiatry, 6*, 135–143.

Gilbert, P., & Miles, J. N. V. (2000). Evolution, genes, development and psychopathology. *Clinical Psychology and Psychotherapy, 7*, 246–255.

Giles, D., Jarrett, R., Biggs, M., Guzick, D., & Rush, J. (1989). Clinical predictors of reoccurrence in depression. *American Journal of Psychiatry, 146*, 764–767.

Gilligan, J. (2011). *Why some politicians are more dangerous than others*. Cambridge: Polity Press.

Grant, K. A., Shively, C. A., Nader, M. S., Ehrenkaufer, R. L., Line, S. W., Morton, T. E., . . . Mach, R. H. (1998). Effects of social status on striatal dopamine D2 receptor binding characteristics in cynomologus monkeys assesses with positron emission tomography. *Synapse, 29*, 80–83.

Goodwin, D., & Jamison, K. R. (1990). *Manic depressive illness*. Oxford: Oxford University Press.

Gotlib, I. H., Gilboa, E., & Sommerfeld, B. K. (2000). Cognitive functioning in depression. In R. J. Davidson (Ed.), *Anxiety, depression and emotion* (pp. 133–165). New York: Oxford University Press.

Griffiths, J., Ravindran, A. V., Merali, Z., & Anisman, H. (2000). Dysthymia: A review of pharmacological and behavioral factors. *Molecular Psychiatry, 5*, 242–261.

Hackmann, A., Bennett-Levy, J., & Holmes, E. A. (2011). *The Oxford guide to imagery in cognitive therapy*. Oxford: Oxford University Press.

Hammen, C. L., Bistricky, S. L., & Ingram, R. E. (2010). Vulnerability to depression in adulthood. In R. E. Ingram, & J. M. Price (Eds.), *Vulnerability to psychopathology: Risks across the lifespan* (pp. 248–281). New York: Guilford Press.

Hammen, C. L., Garber, J., & Ingram, R. E. (2010). Vulnerability to depression across the lifespan. In R. E. Ingram, & J. M. Price (Eds.), *Vulnerability to psychopathology: Risks across the lifespan* (pp. 282–287). New York: Guilford Press.

Hammen, C. L., Henry, R., & Daley, S. E. (2000). Depression and sensitization to stressors among young women as a function of childhood adversity. *Journal of Consulting and Clinical Psychology, 68,* 782–787

Harper, L. V. (2005). Epigenetic inheritance and the intergenerational transfer of experience. *Psychological Bulletin, 131,* 340–360.

Harris, T. O., Surtees, P., & Bancroft, J. (1991). Is sex necessarily a risk factor to depression? *British Journal of Psychiatry, 158,* 708–712.

Hartlage, S. A., Freels, S., Gotman, N., & Yonkers, K. (2012). Criteria for premenstrual dysphoric disorder: Secondary analyses of relevant data sets. *Archives of General Psychiatry. 69,* 300–305.

Hassin, R. R., Uleman, J. S., & Bargh, J. A. (2005). *The new unconscious.* New York: Oxford University Press.

Hayes, S. C., Strosahl, K. D., & Wilson, K. G. (2004). *Acceptance and commitment therapy: An experiential approach to behavior change.* New York: Guilford Press.

Hofer, M. A. (1994). Early relationships as regulators of infant physiology and behavior. *Acta Paediatrica Supplement, 397,* 9–18.

Hrdy, S. B. (2009). *Mothers and others: The evolutionary origins of mutual understanding.* Harvard: Harvard University Press.

Ingram, R. E. (2009). *The International encyclopedia of depression.* New York: Springer.

Ingram, R. E., & Price, J. M. (2010). *Vulnerability to psychopathology.* New York: Guilford Press.

Johnson, S. (2002). *Emergence: The connected lives of ants, brains, cities and software.* Harmondsworth: Penguin.

Kaelber, C. T., Moul, D. E., & Farmer, M. E. (1995). Epidemiology of depression. In E. E. Beckham, & W. R. Leber (Eds.), *Handbook of depression* (2nd ed., pp. 3–35). New York: Guilford Press.

Kahneman, D., & Tversky, A. (1972). Subjective probability: A judgement of representativeness. *Cognitive Psychology, 3,* 430–454.

Keller, M. C., Neale, M. C., & Kendler, K. S. (2007). Association of different adverse life events with distinct patterns of depressive symptoms. *American Journal of Psychiatry, 164,* 1521–1529.

Keller, M. C., & Nesse, R. M. (2006). The evolutionary significance depressive symptoms: Different adverse situations lead to different depressive symptom patterns. *Journal of Personality and Social Psychology, 91,* 316–330. doi:10.1037/0022-3514.91.2.316

Kelly, A. C., Zuroff, D. C., Leybman, M. J., & Gilbert, P. (in press). Social safeness, received social support, and maladjustment: Testing a tripartite model of affect regulation. *Cognitive Therapy and Research.* doi:10.1007/s10608-011-9432-5

Kemp, A. H., Quintana, D. S., Felmingham, K. L., Matthews, S., & Jelinek, H. F. (2012). Depression, comorbid anxiety disorders, and heart rate variability in physically healthy, unmediated patients: Implications for cardiovascular risk. *PLoS One, 7*(2), e31879. Retrieved from http://www.plosone.org

Kessler, R. C., & Magee, W. (1993). Childhood adversities and adult depression: Basic patterns of association in a U.S. national survey. *Psychological Medicine, 23,* 679–690.

Kessler, R. C., McGonagle, K. A., Zhao, S., Nelson, C. B., Hughes, M., Eshelman, S.,... Kendler, K. S. (1994). Lifetime and 12-month prevalence of DSM-111R psychiatric disorders in the United States: Results from the National Comorbidity Survey. *Archives of General Psychiatry, 51,* 8–19.

Kessler, R. C., Soukup, J., Davis, R. B., Foster, D. F., Wilkey, S. A., Van Rompay, M. I., & Eisenberg, D. M. (2001). The use of complementary and alternative therapies to treat anxiety and depression in the United States. *American Journal of Psychiatry, 158,* 289–294.

Kiesler, D. J. (1999). *Beyond the disease model of mental disorders.* New York: Praeger.

Kim, S., Thibodeau, R., & Jorgensen, R. S. (2011). Shame, guilt, and depressive symptoms: A meta-analytic review. *Psychological Bulletin, 137,* 68–96. doi:10.1037/a0021466

King, R., Rases, J. D., & Barchas, J. D. (1981). Catastrophe theory of dopamine transmission. A revised dopamine hypothesis if schizophrenia. *Journal of Theoretical Biology, 92,* 373–400.

Kirsch, P., Esslinger, C., Chen, Q., Mier, D., Lis, S., Siddanti, S., . . . Meyer-Lindenberg, A. (2005). Oxytocin modulates neural circuitry for social cognition and fear in humans. *Journal of Neuroscience, 25,* 11489–11493.

Klinger, E. (1975). Consequences and commitment to aid disengagement from incentives. *Psychological Review, 82,* 1–24.

Klinger, E. (1993). Loss of interest. In C. G. Costello (Ed.), *Symptoms of depression* (pp. 43–62). New York: John Wiley & Sons.

Kupfer, D. J., Frank, E., & Phillips, M. L. (2011). Major depressive disorder: New clinical neurobiological, and treatment perspectives. *Lancet, 20,* 1–11. doi:10.1016/50140-6736(11)60602-8

Kuyken, W., Watkins, E., Holden, E., White, K., Taylor, R. S., Byford, S., . . . Dalgleish, T. (2010). How does mindfulness-based cognitive therapy work? *Behaviour Research and Therapy, 48,* 1105–1112.

Leahy, R. L., Tirch, D., & Napolitano, L. A. (2011). *Emotion regulation in psychotherapy: A practitioner's guide.* New York: Guilford Press.

Leary, M. R. (2005). *The Curse of the self: Self-awareness, egotism and the quality of human life.* New York: Oxford University.

LeDoux, J. (1998). *The emotional brain.* London: Weidenfeld & Nicolson.

Levitan, R., Hasey, G., & Sloman, L. (2000). Major depression and the involuntary defeat strategy; biological correlates. In L. Sloman, & P. Gilbert (Eds.), *Subordination and defeat: An evolutionary approach to mood disorders and their therapy* (pp. 95–114). Mahwah, NJ: Lawrence Erlbaum Associates.

Liotti, G. (2000). Disorganised attachment, models of borderline states and evolutionary psychotherapy. In P. Gilbert, & B. Bailey (Eds.), *Genes on the couch: Explorations in evolutionary psychotherapy* (pp. 232–256). Hove, UK: Brunner-Routledge.

Liotti, G. (2010). Attachment and dissociation. In P. F. Dell, & J. A. O'Neil (Eds.), *Dissociation and the dissociative disorders: DSM-V and beyond* (pp. 53–66). London: Routledge.

Liotti. G., & Gilbert, P. (2011). Mentalizing, motivations and social mentalities: Theoretical considerations and implications for psychotherapy. *Psychology and Psychotherapy, 84,* 9–25.

Liu, X., Somel, M., Tang, L., Yan, Z., Jiang, X., Guo, S., . . . Khaitovich, P. (2012). Extension of cortical synaptic development distinguishes humans from chimpanzees and macaques. *Genome Research.* Retrieved from http://genome.cshlp.org/content/early/2012/01/30/gr.127324.111.abstract

Longe, O., Maratos, F. A., Gilbert, P., Evans, G., Volker, F., Rockliffe, H., & Rippon, G. (2010). Having a word with yourself: Neural correlates of self-criticism and self-reassurance. *NeuroImage, 49,* 1849–1856.

Longmore, R. J., & Worrell, M. (2007). Do we need to challenge thoughts in cognitive behavior therapy? *Clinical Psychology Review, 27,* 173–187. doi:10.1016/j.cpr.2006.08.001

Macdonald, K., & Macdonald, T. M. (2010). The peptide that binds: A systematic review of oxytocin and its prosocial effects in humans. *Harvard Review of Psychiatry, 18*, 1–21.

Maes, M. (1995). Evidence for an immune response in major depression: A review and hypothesis. *Progress in Neuro-Psychopharmacology and Biological Psychiatry, 19*, 11–38.

Mandler, G. (1975). *Mind and emotion*. Chichester, UK: John Wiley & Sons.

Martell, C. R., Addis, M. E., & Jacobson, N. S. (2001). *Depression in context: Strategies for guided action*. New York: Norton.

McCullough, J. P., Jr. (2000). *Treatment for chronic depression: Cognitive behavioral analysis system of psychotherapy*. New York: Guilford Press.

McGregor, I., & Marigold, D. C. (2003). Defensive zeal and the uncertain self: What makes you so sure? *Journal of Personality and Social Psychology, 85*, 838–852.

McGuade, R., & Young, A. H. (2000). Future therapeutic targets in mood disorders: The glucocorticoid receptor. *British Journal of Psychiatry, 177*, 390–395.

McQuire, M. T., & Troisi, A. (1998). Prevalence differences in depression among males and females: Are there evolutionary explanations? *British Journal of Medical Psychology, 71*, 479–491.

Meehl, P. E. (1995). Bootstrap taxometrics: Solving the classification problem in psychopathology. *American Psychologist, 50*, 266–275.

Mikulincer, M., & Shaver, P. R. (2007). *Attachment in adulthood: Structure, dynamics, and change*. New York: Guilford Press.

Miller, A. H., Maletic, V., & Raison, C. L. (2009). Inflammation and its discontents: The role of cytokines in the pathophysiology of major depression. *Biological Psychiatry, 65*, 732–74. doi:10.1016/j.biopsych.2008.11.029

Moffitt, T. E., Caspi, A., Taylor, A., Kokaua, J., Milne, B. J., Polanczyk, G., & Poulton, R. (2010). How common are common mental disorders? Evidence that lifetime prevalence rates are doubled by prospective versus retrospective ascertainment. *Psychological Medicine, 40*, 899–909.

Moldofsky, H., & Dickstein, J. B. (1999). Sleep and cytokine-immune functions in medical, psychiatric and primary sleep disorders. *Sleep Medicine Reviews, 3* (4), 325–337.

Möller-Leimkühler, A. M., & Yücel, M. (2010). Male depression in females? *Journal of Affective Disorders, 121*, 22–29. doi:10.1016/j.jad.2009.05.007

Monroe, S. M., & Harkness, K. L. (2011). This is recurrence in major depression: A conceptual analysis. *Psychological Review, 118*, 655–674. doi:10.1037/a0025190

Morriss, R. K., & Morriss, E. E. (2000). Contextual evaluation of social adversity in the management of depressive disorder. *Advances in Psychiatric Treatment, 6*, 423–431.

Murray, C. J. L., & Lopex, A. D. (1996). *The global burden of disease: A comprehensive assessment of mortality and disability from diseases. Injuries and risk factors in 1990 and projected to 2020*. Cambridge, MA: Harvard University Press.

Nanni, V., Uhser, R., & Danese, A. (2012). Childhood maltreatment predicts unfavorable course of illness and treatment outcome in depression: A meta-analysis. *American Journal of Psychiatry, 169*, 141–151.

Neff, K. D., Kirkpatrick, K., & Rude, S. S. (2007). Self-compassion and its link to adaptive psychological functioning. *Journal of Research in Personality, 41*, 139–154.

Nemeroff, C. B. (1996). The corticotropin-releasing factor (CRF) hypothesis of depression: New findings and new directions. *Molecular Psychiatry, 1*, 336–342.

Nemeroff, C. B. (1998). The neurobiology of depression. *Scientific American, 278*, 28–35.

Nesse, R. (2000). Is depression an adaptation? *Archives of General Psychiatry, 57*, 14–20.

Nickerson, R. S. (1999). How we know—and sometimes misjudge—what others know: Inputting one's own knowledge to others. *Psychological Bulletin, 125*, 737–759.

Ochsner, K. N., & Lieberman, M. D. (2001). The emergence of cognitive social neuroscience. *American Psychologist, 56*, 717–734.

Ostler, K., Thompson, C., Kinmonth, A. L. K., Peveler, R. C., Stevens, L., & Stevens, A. (2001). Influence of socio-economic deprivation on the prevalence and outcome of depression in primary care: The Hampshire Depression Project. *British Journal of Psychiatry, 178*, 12–17.

Otte, C. (2008). Incomplete remission in depression: Role of psychiatric and somatic comorbidity. *Dialogues in Clinical Neuroscience, 10*, 450–458.

Panksepp, J. (1998). *Affective neuroscience*. New York: Oxford University Press.

Panksepp, J. (2010). Affective neuroscience of the emotional brainmind: Evolutionary perspectives and implications for understanding depression. *Dialogues in Clinical Neuroscience, 12*, 383–399.

Pascual-Leone, A., & Greenberg, L. S. (2007). Emotional processing in experiential therapy: Why "the only way out is through". *Consulting and Clinical Psychology, 75*, 875–887. doi:10.1037/0022-006X.75.6.875

Porges, S. W. (2007). The polyvagal perspective. *Biological Psychology, 74*, 116–143.

Porter, R. (2003). *Madness: A brief history*. Oxford: Oxford University press.

Posener, J. A., deBattista, C., Willimans, G. H., Chmura, H., Kalehzan, M., & Scatzberg, A. F. (2000). 24-hour monitoring of cortisol and corticotropin secretion in psychotic and nonpsychotic major depression. *Archives of General Psychiatry, 57*, 755–760.

Posternak, M. A., & Zimmerman, M. (2002). Partial validation of the atypical features subtype of major depressive disorders. *Archives of General Psychiatry, 59*, 70–76.

Power, M., & Dalgleish, T. (2008). *Cognition and emotion: From order to disorder*. Hove, UK: Psychology Press.

Price, J. S. (1972). Genetic and phylogenetic aspects of mood variations. *International Journal of Mental Health, 1*, 124–144.

Price, J. S., & Sloman, L. (1987). Depression as yielding behaviour: An animal model based on Schjelderup-Ebb's pecking order. *Ethology and Sociobiology, 8*(Suppl. 1), 85–98.

Raadsheer, F. C., Hoogendijk, W. J. G., Stam, F. C., Tilders, F. J. H., & Swaab, D. F. (1994). Increased numbers of corticotropin-releasing hormone expressing neurons in the hypothalamic paraventricular nucleus of depressed patients. *Clinical Neuroendocrinology, 60*, 436–444.

Radden, J. (2000). *The nature of melancholy: From Aristotle to Kristeva*. New York: Oxford University Press.

Raison, C. L., Lowry, C. A., & Rook, G. A. W. (2010). Inflammation, sanitation and consternation: Loss of contact with co-evolved, tolerogenic microorganisms and the pathophysiology and treatment of major depression. *Archives of General Psychiatry, 67*, 1211–1223.

Raison, C. L., & Miller, A. H. (2012). The evolutionary significance of depression in Pathogen host defense (PATHOS-D). *Molecular Psychiatry*. doi:10.1038/mp.2012.2

Rockliff, H., Gilbert, P., McEwan, K., Lightman, S., & Glover, D. (2008). A pilot exploration of heart rate variability and salivary cortisol responses to compassion-focused imagery. *Journal of Clinical Neuropsychiatry, 5*, 132–139.

Rockliff, H., Karl, A., McEwan, K., Gilbert, J., Matos, M., & Gilbert, P. (2011). Effects of intranasal oxytocin on compassion focused imagery. *Emotion, 11*, 1388–1396. doi:10.1037/a0023861

Rothschild, B. (2000). *The body remembers: The psychophysiology of trauma and trauma treatment*. New York: Norton.

Rutter, M. (1986). Meyerian psychobiology, personality development and the role of life experiences. *American Journal of Psychiatry, 143*, 1077–1087.

Rygula, R., Abumaria, N., Flügge, G., Fuchs, E., Rüther, E., & Havemann-Reinecke, U. (2005). Anhedonia and motivational deficits in rats: Impact of chronic social stress. *Behavioural Brain Research, 162*, 127–134.

Sapolsky, R. M. (1996). Why stress is bad for your brain. *Science, 273*, 749–750.

Sapolsky, R. M. (2000). Gluocorticoids and hippocampus atrophy in neuropsychiatric disorders. *Archives of General Psychiatry, 57*, 925–935.

Sapolsky, R. M. (2004). *Why zebras don't get ulcers* (3rd ed.). London: St Martin's Press.

Schore, A. N. (2010). Attachment trauma and the developing right brain: Origins of pathological dissociation. In P. F. Dell, & J. A. O'Neil (Eds.), *Dissociation and the dissociative disorders: DSM-V and beyond* (pp. 107–141). London: Routledge.

Scott, J. (1988). Chronic depression. *British Journal of Psychiatry, 153*, 287–297.

Scott, J. C. (1990). *Domination and the arts of resistance*. New Haven, CT: Yale University Press.

Seligman, M. E. P. (1975). *Helplessness: On depression development and death*. San Francisco, CA: Freeman & Co.

Shively, C. A. (1999). Social subordination stress, behavior, and central monoaminergic function in cynomolgus monkeys. *Biological Psychiatry, 44*, 882–891.

Shively, C. A., Register, T. C., Friedman, D. P., Morgan, T. M., Thompson, J., & Lanier, T. (2005). Social stress-associated depression in adult female cynomolgus monkeys (*Macaca fascicularis*). *Biological Psychology, 69*(1), 67–84. doi:10.1016/j.biopsycho.2004.11.006

Shweder, R. A., Much, N. C., Mahapatra, M., & Park, L. (1997). The "big three" of morality (autonomy, community and divinity) and the "big three" explanations of suffering. In A. M. Brandt, & P. Rozin (Eds.), *Morality and health* (pp. 119–169). New York: Routledge.

Smith, D. J., Griffiths, E., Kelly, M., Hood, K., Craddock,N., & Simpson, S. A. (2011). Unrecognised bipolar disorder in primary care patients with depression. *British Journal of Psychiatry, 199*, 49–56. doi:10.1192/bjp.bp.110.083840

Smith, E. O. (2002). *When culture and biology collide: Why we are stressed, depressed and self-obsessed*. New Brunswick, NJ: Rutgers University Press.

Snaith, R. P., Hamilton, M., Morley, S., Humayan, A., Hargreaves, D., & Trigwell, P. (1995). A scale for the assessment of hedonic tone. The Snaith Hamilton Pleasure Scale. *British Journal of Psychiatry, 167*, 99–103.

Spikins, P. A., Rutherford, H. E., & Needham, A. P. (2010). From homininity to humanity: Compassion from the earliest archaics to modern humans. *Journal of Archaeology, Conscious and Culture, 3*, 303–326.

Stanley, B., & Siever, L. J. (2010). The interpersonal dimension of borderline personality disorder towards a neuropeptide model. *American Journal of Psychiatry, 167*, 24–39.

Suomi, S. J. (1997). Early determinants of behavior: Evidence from primate studies. *British Medical Bulletin, 53*, 170–184.

Taylor, P., Gooding, P., Wood, A. N., & Tarrier, N. (2011). The role of defeat and entrapment in depression, anxiety and suicide. *Psychological Bulletin, 137*, 391–420. doi:10.1037/a0022935

Thase, M. E., & Howland, R. H. (1995). Biological processes in depression: An update and integration. In E. E. Beckham, & W. R. Leber (Eds.), *Handbook of depression* (2nd ed., pp. 213–279). New York: Guilford Press.

Toates, F. (1995). *Stress: Conceptual and biological aspects*. Chichester, UK: John Wiley & Sons.

Tobena, A., Marks, I., & Dar, R. (1999). Advantages of bias and prejudice: An exploration of their neurocognitive templates. *Neuroscience and Behavioral Reviews, 23*, 1047–1058.

Twenge, J. M., Gentile, B., DeWall, C. N., Ma, D., Lacefield, K., & Schurtz, D. R. (2010). Birth cohort increases in psychopathology among young Americans,

1938–2007: A cross-temporal meta-analysis of the MMPI. *Clinical Psychology Review*, *30*, 145–154.

Van der Hart, O., Nijenhuis, E. R. S., & Steele, K. (2006). *The haunted self: Structural dissociation and treatment of chronic traumatisation*. New York: Norton.

van Praag, H. M. (1998). Anxiety and increased aggression as pacemakers of depression. *Acta Psychiatrica Scandinavica*, *98*(Suppl. 393), 81–88.

Vredenburg, K., Flett, G. L., & Krames, L. (1993). Analogue versus clinical depression: A critical reappraisal. *Psychological Bulletin*, *113*, 327–344.

Ward, J. (2011). *The student's guide to social neuroscience*. London: Psychology Press.

Watson, D., & Clark, L. A. (1988). Positive and negative affectivity and their relation to anxiety and depressive disorders. *Journal of Abnormal Psychology*, *97*, 346–353.

Watson, D., Clark, L. A., Weber, K., Assenheimer, J., Strauss, M. E., & McCormick, R. A. (1995a). Testing a tripartite model I: Evaluating the convergent and discriminate validity of anxiety and depression symptom scales. *Journal of Abnormal Psychology*, *104*, 3–14.

Watson, D., Clark, L. A., Weber, K., Assenheimer, J., Strauss, M. E., & McCormick, R. A. (1995b). Testing a tripartite model II: Exploring the symptom structure of anxiety and depression in student, adult and patient samples. *Journal of Abnormal Psychology*, *104*, 15–25

Watts, F. (1993). Problems with memory and concentration. In C. G. Costello (Ed.), *Symptoms of depression* (pp. 113–1140). New York: John Wiley & Sons.

Wells, A. (2000). *Emotional disorders and metacognition: Innovative cognitive therapy*. Chichester, UK: John Wiley & Sons.

Whelton, W. J., & Greenberg, L. S. (2005). Emotion in self-criticism. *Personality and Individual Differences*, *38*, 1583–1595.

White, R., Laithwait, H., & Gilbert, P. (in press). Negative symptoms in schizophrenia: The role of social defeat. In A. Gumley, A. Gillham, K. Taylor, & M. Schwannauer (Eds.), *Psychosis and emotion: The role of emotions in understanding psychosis, therapy and recovery*. London: Routledge.

Whiten, A. (1999). The evolution of deep social mind in humans. In M. C. Corballis, & S. E. G. Lea (Eds.), *The descent of mind: Psychological perspectives on humanoid evolution* (pp. 173–193). New York: Oxford University Press.

Wilkinson, R., & Picket, K. (2010). *The spirit level: Why equality is better for everyone*. London: Penguin.

Williams, M., Teasdale, J., Segal, Z., & Kabat-Zinn, J. (2007). *The mindful way through depression: Freeing yourself from chronic unhappiness*. New York: Guilford Press.

Willner, P. (1993). Anhedonia. In C. G. Costello (Ed.), *Symptoms of depression* (pp. 63–84). New York: John Wiley & Sons.

World Health Organization (WHO). (2010). A conceptual framework for action on the social determinants of health. Retrieved from http://whqlibdoc.who.int/publications/2010/9789241500852_eng.pdf

Zeeman, E. C. (1977). *Catastrophe theory: Selected papers 1972–1977*. Reading, MA: Addison-Wesley Publishing.

Zuroff, D. C., Mongrain, M., & Santor, D. A. (2004). Conceptualizing and measuring personality vulnerability to depression: Comment on Coyne and Whiffen (1995). *Psychological Bulletin*, *130*, 489–511.

Zuroff, D. C., Santor, D., & Mongrain, M. (2005). Dependency, self-criticism, and maladjustment. In J. S. Auerbach, K. N. Levy, & C. E. Schaffer (Eds.), *Relatedness, self-definition and mental representation. Essays in honour of Sidney J. Blatt* (pp. 75–90). London: Routledge.

# Part II
# Bipolar Depression

# 11

# Classification and Epidemiology of Bipolar Disorder

Sameer Jauhar[1] and Jonathan Cavanagh[2]

[1]London, UK
[2]Glasgow, UK

## Introduction

The concept of bipolar disorder has undergone significant changes over the years, and continues to be marked by controversy and uncertainty. Significant attempts have been made to reclassify bipolar disorder, and in this chapter we will discuss these developments, their empirical basis, and future directions in the classification of bipolar disorder. Throughout, we will use the epidemiological data available to illustrate the inherent difficulties within the classification of bipolar disorders.

## Historical Roots

Recognition of the signs and symptoms of what we would now consider bipolar disorder dates back to Hippocrates and his school of writers, in the fourth and fifth centuries BC, who recognized mania, melancholia, and paranoia. The first description of it as one disease entity is credited to Aretaeus of Cappadocia, who stated in his books *The treatment of chronic diseases* and *Symptomatology of chronic diseases,* "The development of mania is really a worsening of the disease [melancholia], rather than a change into another disease ... In most of them [melancholics], the sadness became better after various lengths of time and changed into happiness; the patients then develop a mania" (Goodwin & Marneros, 2005; examples being William Cullen and Esquirol). It was not until the advent of the infamous German school of psychiatry in the late 1800s that the classification of bipolar disorder (and psychiatric classification) took a significant leap forward.

Kahlbaum's (1874) assertion that the classification of psychosis consisted of a nosological entity signified a clearer conceptualization of mental illness. He put forward the concept of a close correspondence between clinical symptoms, course and outcome, cerebral pathology, and etiology as the criteria for correlated clinical states constituting a "natural disease entity." In using the term, "cyclical insanity," he is also credited as the first person to use the term cyclothymia (Howland & Thase, 1993).

*The Wiley-Blackwell Handbook of Mood Disorders*, Second Edition. Edited by Mick Power.
© 2013 John Wiley & Sons, Ltd. Published 2013 by John Wiley & Sons, Ltd.

This set the stage for the father of modern psychiatric classification, Emil Kraepelin, whose contribution to the classification of bipolar disorder rests on his splitting of psychoses into manic–depressive insanity and dementia praecox, and his unitary concept of manic–depressive illness (Kraepelin, 2010).

Kraepelin's concept of manic–depressive insanity has been described in terms of excitement or inhibition (increase or decrease) of three basic areas: mood, thinking, and activity (Benazzi, 2007). All three can move in the same direction, leading to episodes of manic, hypomanic, or depressive states; or move in opposite directions, resulting in mixed states, defined as combinations of manic or hypomanic and depressive symptoms in the same episode. Crucially, mood did not have to be increased for a diagnosis of mania to be made (the two other symptoms of activity and thinking could be increased). An emphasis was placed on *recurrence*, family history, episodic course (episodes including mixed states, recurrent depression, hypomania or mania), and young age of onset (Jablensky, Hugler, Von Cranach, & Kalinov, 1993).

This view, in which manic–depressive insanity is conceptualized as a broader group than that espoused in ICD-10 and DSM-IV is reflected in the relative frequencies of the two diagnoses (of psychoses) in Kraepelin's Munich University Clinic—manic–depressive illness accounted for 18.6% but dementia praecox for only 7.3% of all admissions in 1908 (Jablensky et al., 1993).

Although better known for his contribution to the classification of schizophrenia, the Swiss psychiatrist, Eugen Bleuler, also played a part in the modern classification of bipolar illness, broadening manic–depressive insanity into categories of affective illness (Goodwin & Jamison, 2007). Leonhard then took this further, making the distinction between unipolar and bipolar depression, a distinction that continues to the contemporary classification systems of DSM-IV and ICD-10. In 1980, the term bipolar disorder replaced that of manic–depressive disorder in DSM-III, reflecting the observation that not all those with the illness developed psychosis, and clearly differentiating it from schizophrenia.

## The Current Classification of Bipolar Disorder

The prevailing current classification of bipolar disorder (DSM-IV) is summarized in Table 11.1, and encompasses the following:

In DSM-IV (2000), it is split into bipolar I, bipolar II, bipolar disorder not otherwise specified, and cyclothymic disorder. A diagnosis can be made on the basis of one episode of mania, or a single episode of hypomania and a major depressive episode.

ICD-10 requires two discrete mood episodes, one of which must include mania. The classical symptoms of mania are well documented in DSM-IV (see Table 11.2) though it is worth noting comments made by one of the subgroups of the International Society for Bipolar Disorders Diagnostic Guidelines Task Force (Ghaemi et al., 2008) who, while acknowledging the classic nature of mania, emphasized the importance of recognizing "mixed" manic features, such as irritability and aggression.

It is worth noting that, despite the above classification systems, Kraepelin's unitary view of manic–depressive insanity is the one favored by Goodwin and Jamison (2007),

**Table 11.1.**
DSM-IV-TR Classification of Bipolar Disorders

|  | *Bipolar I disorder* | *Bipolar II disorder* | *Cyclothymic disorder* |
|---|---|---|---|
| Mania and MDE | + | − | +/− |
| Hypomania and MDE | − | + | +/− |
| Hypomanic and MDE symptom frequently switching | − | − | + |
| Duration | At least 4 days for hypomania, 2 weeks for MDE | At least 4 days for hypomania, 2 weeks for MDE | At least 2 years |

*Source:* Benazzi (2007).
MDE, major depressive episode; +, present; −, absent.

who in the second edition of their book, "Manic Depressive Illness," specifically acknowledge his contribution to classification.

## Classifying psychiatric disorders

Current classification systems in psychiatry, as described above, have evolved largely from clinical data on psychopathology and treatment outcome, and have hinged on various statistical models applied to these, from demographic data to the use of multivariate statistical methods, including factor analysis and the fitting of statistical models to identify classes within a disorder. The criteria for classification has largely been built on the influential Robins–Guze criteria, proposed over 40 years ago, in their seminal papers published in the *American Journal of Psychiatry*, first on the classification of schizophrenia and later on psychiatric illness in general (Feighner et al., 1972; Robins & Guze, 1970). Though more modern criteria, building on advances in neuroscience, are underway (Insel et al., 2010), see below, the following remain the mainstay of current classification:

1. clinical description—this not only includes not only symptoms, but also natural history of the illness;
2. laboratory studies (including radiological and psychological tests, and what could now be termed neuroimaging, electrophysiological, and neuropsychological tests);
3. delimitation from other disorders—distinguishing homogeneous cases;
4. follow-up study; and
5. family study.

## Evaluating the current classification system

A critical look at recent debates on the classification of bipolar disorder center around a number of "fuzzier" areas, assembled around the borders of the current classification

**Table 11.2.**

Tabular Summary Deliberations of the Diagnostic Guidelines Task Force of the International Society for Bipolar Disorders

| Diagnostic validators | Mania | Bipolar | Rapid cycling | Type II | Bipolar spectrum illness | Pediatric bipolar disorder | Schizoaffective disorder |
|---|---|---|---|---|---|---|---|
| Phenomenology | ++++ | ++ | + | ++++ | ++ | +++ | ++++ |
| Course | +/− | +++ | ++++ | ++ | ++ | ++ | +++ |
| Genetics | + | +++ | +/− | ++ | + | ++ | +++ |
| Treatment response | ++ | +++ | ++ | + | ++ | + | +/− |
| Neurobiology | ++ | +/− | +/− | + | +/− | +/− | ++ |
| Special topics | Pure mania often includes dysphonic/irritable presentations | Probabilistic differentiation from unipolar depression proposed | Dimensional approach to ultradian cycling merits investigation | Value judgment in identifying it versus mania or normality | Clinical utility important | Key diagnostic overlap with ADHD and ODD | Dimensional model of psychosis is suggested |
| Areas of consensus | Broaden definition to include irritable/dysphoric states | Some key features are more common than in unipolar depression | Importance for prognosis | Severe depressive morbidity is prominent | Importance for future investigation | Narrow grandiose euphoric phenotype is similar to adult bipolar disorder | Does not represent a separate categorical disease entity |
| Areas of dissensus | None | Relevance for treatment response | Association with antidepressant use | Relevance for treatment response | Underlying validity of broadened model, and relevance for treatment response | Diagnostic validity of broad irritable/aggressive phenotype; relevance for treatment response | Whether a dimensional one-psychosis model is implied versus comorbidity of schizophrenia and severe affective disorder |

*Source:* Ghaemi et al. (2008).

++++, data strongly informative for diagnostic validity; +++, data moderately informative for diagnostic validity; ++, data mildly informative for diagnostic validity; +, data slightly informative for diagnostic validity; +/−, equivocal or no data informative for diagnostic validity; COD, oppositional defiant disorder; ADHD, attention deficit-hyperactivity disorder.

systems. These have been proposed by Cassano, Giovanni, Mantua, and Fagiolini (2011) as:

1. the schizophrenia/bipolar I border;
2. the continuum of schizophrenia–schizoaffective-mixed psychotic bipolar–unipolar psychotic illness; and
3. the continuum between unipolar and bipolar depression.

The schizophrenia/bipolar I border has been fairly well demarcated, on the basis of outcome and treatment. Specifically, in a cohort of those with functional psychosis, response to lithium treatment distinguished those with mania from those with non-affective psychosis (Johnstone, Crow, Frith, & Owens, 1988). Furthermore, when looking at outcome in a cohort of patients from the International Pilot Study of Schizophrenia (IPSS), Brockington et al. were able to distinguish a similar cohort of patients on the basis of 2-year outcome data, using discriminant function analysis (Brockington, Kendell, Wainwright, Hillier, & Walker, 1979). This finding was replicated by Johnstone et al. a few years later, who applied DSM-III criteria to a cohort of patients enrolled in the original functional psychosis trial (Johnstone et al., 1992). This distinction has now essentially been dropped in favor of the second continuum stated below.

The second continuum, an expanded version of the schizophrenia/bipolar I distinction, encompassing schizoaffective disorder and affective psychoses has been the subject of recent debate, with recent findings in molecular genetics prompting some (e.g., Craddock & Owen, 2007) to propose an expanded continuum between schizophrenia and affective psychoses. However, the main nosological debate of recent times has been the distinction made between bipolar and unipolar depression, and this will be focused on here. In essence, this centers on the concept of the "bipolar spectrum."

## The Bipolar Spectrum

For a number of years, Akiskal and others have been calling for a radical extension of the boundaries of bipolar disorder to include various subcategories such as bipolar II and bipolar III. Akiskal and Mallya (1987) estimated that 4–5% of the general population belongs to a broad bipolar spectrum with chiefly depressive phenomenology coupled with less-than-manic excitements. The clinical reality of these "less-than-manic" patients has led to various reclassifications. For example, Dunner, Gershon, and Goodwin (1976) described less-than-manic patients as bipolar II on the basis of hospitalization for depression and excited periods that did not require hospitalization. It should be remembered that "less-than-manic" excitements are very controversial concepts and the debate remains active (see the section on Epidemiology, below).

The "soft bipolar spectrum" (Akiskal & Mallya, 1987) is a more inclusive term for bipolar conditions beyond classical mania, which revises previous definitions of BP II by incorporating depression with hypomanic episodes, cyclothymic and hyperthymic traits, as well as depression with familial bipolarity. The spectrum also includes hypomanic episodes which occur during pharmacotherapy or other somatic treatments.

Other terms used for "less-than-manic" bipolar conditions with depressive presentations include "Dm" (Angst, Frey, Lohmeyer, & Zerbin-Rüdin, 1980), "Unipolar-L" (Kupfer, Pickar, Himmelhoch, & Detre, 1975), and "pseudo-unipolar" depression (Mendels, 1976).

In a series of more formal bipolar spectrum proposals (Akiskal, 2003; Akiskal & Akiskal, 1992), bipolarity is categorized into the following:

Type I: Mania with or without depression
Type II: Depression with hypomania and/or cyclothymia
Type III: Hypomania associated with antidepressants as well as depressions with hyper-
    thymic temperament and/or bipolar family history

Angst et al. (1980) demonstrated a high prevalence of brief hypomanic episodes below the 4-day requirement of DSM-IV. This work argues in favor of broadening the bipolar concept to include both the severe psychotic mania end of the spectrum and the subthreshold—brief hypomania end.

Subthreshold does not equate with the subclinical nor the clinically insignificant. Indeed, subthreshold episodes have been shown to have significant psychosocial consequences. However, the question of whether this constitutes inclusion criteria in a categorical classification remains unanswered.

Arguments given against adoption of the bipolar spectrum have included the lack of an adequate treatment response to antidepressants in patients classified with bipolar spectrum disorder and depression in the recent STEP-BD trial (Sachs et al., 2007), and the lack of evidence to show an improvement in the treatment of this cohort of patients when treated according to bipolar, as opposed to unipolar guidelines (Strakowski, Fleck, & Maj, 2011). Further arguments against the spectrum made by Strakowski et al. include the observation of lack of specificity of genetic studies and the clear differences seen in tests of neurocognition, with bipolar I patients having deficits in verbal learning, memory, executive function, and attention, in addition to clinically significant cognitive impairment compared to bipolar II patients, who exhibit working memory and executive impairment. They make the point that if bipolar spectrum, in the wider sense, were to be included this would lead to more heterogeneity in terms of the clinical picture, with no clear research currently available to fully validate the concept. The real question might be whether categories are appropriate for these criteria or whether they are better placed in the context of continua.

## Cyclothymia, hypomania, hyperthymia, and personality disorder

Although most are aware of the clinical picture of mania, the above "outer edges" of the classification system are worthy of further scrutiny.

Kraepelin (2010) and Kretschmer (1936), both described affective states which ranged from the severest to the mildest and which existed on a continuum that included personal predisposition or temperament.

Both described cyclothymic people in whom low-grade subdepressive and hypomanic presentations occurred.

*Descriptions of cyclothymia*  Some people with cyclothymia exhibit depressive or irritable moodiness, while in others hypomanic traits (hyperthymic temperament) predominate. These characteristics can present throughout life but never progress to major episodes of affective illness. Upon recovery, patients customarily return to baseline temperament.

Some large-scale studies have investigated cyclothymia. These studies differ from more typical epidemiology in that they concentrate on student or clinical populations. Examples of these studies include the following:

1. Akiskal, Djenderedjian, Rosenthal, and Khani (1977) reported that just less than 10% of the mental health clinic conformed to subsyndromal mood changes over extended periods of time.
2. Placidi et al. (1998) in Italy found subthreshold variation between hypomanic and subdepressive periods occurring in 6.3% of the population.

It should be remembered, however, that these two studies employed operationalized criteria developed at the University of Tennessee by Akiskal et al., a group which favors the broadening of bipolar criteria. Nevertheless, all of the studies tend to show very similar levels of "bipolar diathesis."

*Personality disorder*  One of the practical difficulties of classification is the separation on the continuum between personality disorder features and the point at which symptoms become a disorder in terms of bipolar disorder rather than abnormalities of personality or temperament. An awareness of boundaries is important as personality tests in common use have been known to misattribute subthreshold mood changes to borderline personality disorder (O'Connell, Mayo, & Sciutto, 1991), a feature of which clinicians will be all too aware. Furthermore, as detailed clearly in large population surveys, such as the ECAS (see section on Epidemiology), the level of comorbidity of personality disorder with axis I disorders is high, especially with bipolar disorder. Recent calls for borderline personality disorder to be reclassified in the "bipolar spectrum," based on some evidence of shared etiology would appear premature based on current evidence, although a recent 4-year follow-up study showed a modest increase in reclassification of borderline patients as having bipolar disorder (7.9% reclassified as bipolar I or II), significantly more than other personality disorders (Gunderson et al., 2006).

*Descriptions of hypomania*  There is also a very real clinical problem in separating hypomania from mania using the criteria laid down in DSM-IV. One point of contention focuses on the length of time during which the symptoms must be present. Those studies validating a shorter than 4 days duration for hypomania were all conducted before the availability of DSM-IV. For example, a study by Wicki and Angst (1991) found a modal duration of 1–3 days.

Cassano, Akiskal, Savino, Musetti, and Perugi (1992) used a definition of 2 days in a study of bipolar II disorder and found that these patients had rates of bipolar family history statistically indistinguishable from that of bipolar I disorder—both of which were significantly higher than that of major depressive disorders.

The most common manifestations of hypomania in a community study (from Angst, 1998) are:

- less sleep;
- more energy, strength;
- more self-confidence;
- increased activities (including working more);
- enjoying work more than usual;
- more social activities;
- spending too much money;
- more plans and ideas;
- less shy, less inhibited;
- more talkative than usual;
- increased sex drive;
- increased consumption of coffee, cigarettes, and alcohol;
- overly optimistic;
- increased laughter; and
- thinking fast/sudden ideas.

*The distinction between mania and hypomania*   In an editorial commentary, Goodwin (2002) clearly described the difficulties surrounding contemporary use of these two descriptors. The outstanding issue remains of where the boundary falls between hypomania and mania, and between hypomania and normalcy. DSM-IV defines both hypomania and cyclothymia to be milder conditions than ICD-10.

The boundary between hypomania and mania pivots on a definition of functional disturbance that is different between DSM-IV and ICD-10 but is dependent upon qualifications such as "severe" and "marked" whose meaning is open to interpretation.

Goodwin argues that DSM-IV splits mania from hypomania in a clinically significant way. The community cohort study carried out by Angst (1998) exerts a major influence in terms of lifetime prevalence estimates. This study found DSM-IV diagnoses of mania and hypomania in 5.5% of the population. But extending the boundaries resulted in the inclusion of a further 14.1% of the population. The Angst study also revealed a population rate of bipolar I of 0.5% and of bipolar II of 3%.

Although the inclusion or exclusion of bipolar spectrum disorders is the subject of contemporary controversy, findings from US studies (Carlson & Kashani, 1988; Lewinsohn, Klein, & Seeley, 1995) support the views of Angst. Despite the epidemiological and nosological caveats, Goodwin emphasizes that something is being detected that requires explanation and clarification. Moreover, the diagnosis of hypomania is not merely one of abundant good health and while it may at times be benign it often is less so. As Goodwin concludes, accurate diagnosis has become clinically important for elated states. Also, the challenge remains of defining where hypomania ends and individual differences begin. Goodwin states that to make the distinction between hypomania and mania as it is drawn in DSM-IV appears to have important advantages.

*Descriptions of hyperthymia*   Clinically, hyperthymia is regarded as subthreshold life-long hypomanic symptoms. Psychometrically established traits in hyperthymia are:

- warm, people-seeking, or extroverted;
- cheerful, overoptimistic, or exuberant;
- uninhibited, stimulus-seeking, or promiscuous;
- overinvolved and meddlesome;
- vigorous, full of plans, improvident, or carried away by restless impulses;
- overconfident, self-assured, boastful, bombastic, or grandiose; and
- articulate and eloquent.

Current data cast an uncertain light on the boundary between hyperthymic temperament and normalcy and this temperament may be considered abnormal only in the presence of clinical depression, with one study suggesting a significant increase in family history of bipolar disorder in patients with depression and five of the seven criteria (Cassano et al., 1992).

*Descriptions of bipolar II*   A common clinical situation involves a patient presenting with a major depressive episode and on further examination reveals a history of hypomania. The accuracy of the diagnosis is dependent on the sharpness of the patient's memory and recall bias can be a significant problem. It can be seen as with a problem-state-dependent memory in particular. When high, all previous highs are remembered and when low, only previous depressions are remembered (Kelsoe, personal communication to Akiskal, March 31, 2000).

Bipolar II is a complex diagnosis owing to the reportedly high levels of comorbidity; for example, anxiety, bulimia, substance misuse, and personality disorder (Benazzi, 2007; Perugi et al., 1997). There is also some evidence that so-called atypical depressions frequently progress to bipolar spectrum disorders.

An analysis of the NIMH Collaborative Depression Study on unipolar patients who switched to bipolar II examined 559 patients with unipolar depression at entry during a prospective observation period of 11 years. Of these, 48 converted to bipolar II—that is, just over 8.5%. It has been suggested that mood lability is a key variable in the cyclothymic temperament and the hallmark of those unipolar patients who switch to bipolar II. According to Coryell et al., in those with at least a 5-year history of affective illness, those with a diagnosis of bipolar II represent a stable condition, which rarely progresses to bipolar I. To date, the best evidence of the longitudinal symptom course of bipolar II disorder comes from a longitudinal study, conducted over a median of 13.4 years, with interviews conducted at 6- and 12-month intervals. Symptomatic inquiry revealed that subjects were symptomatic for 53.9% of the follow-up time. Specifically, depressive symptoms dominated the clinical picture (50.3% of weeks), compared to symptoms of hypomania, which lasted for 1.3% of weeks. Factors that predicted increased chronicity of symptoms included longer episodes, poor prior psychosocial functioning, and family history of affective illness (Judd et al., 2003).

A similar study, in those with bipolar I disorder, following up 148 subjects from the NIMH Collaborative Depression Study illustrated that bipolar I patients were symptomatically ill for 47.3% of weeks, over a median of 12.8 years follow-up, with change of polarity noted on more than three occasions a year (Judd et al., 2002).

*Pharmacological hypomania*    This is a form of hypomania that manifests itself on treatment with antidepressants. Neither of the major classification systems (ICD-10 and DSM-IV) has accorded bipolar status to these patients. Some authors disagree and regard this as a separate bipolar state and name it "bipolar III." At the current time there is no clear consensus on this, with recent data from the STEP-BD trial (Sachs et al., 2007) suggesting that, in bipolar I and II patients at least, the use of newer antidepressants did not worsen the outcome of bipolar depression. (This is also tempered by the fact that no clinically significant treatment response was seen in bipolar patients treated with antidepressants in the trial.)

*Rapid-cycling bipolar disorder*    According to standard classification systems (ICD-10 and DSM-IV), those with rapid cycling suffer a minimum of four episodes of illness per year. The term "alternating" has been advocated as preferable as many patients have no remission from episodes during a rapid-cycling phase.

There are degrees of cycling severity: rapid ($\geq 4$/year), ultrarapid ($\geq 4$/month), and ultradian ($\geq$ within a day). Coryell et al. (1995) regard rapid cycling as a phase in the illness rather than a distinct subtype. There is no clear indication from current literature on what risk factors exist for rapid cycling. Those highlighted include female gender, cyclothymic temperament, borderline hypothyroidism, and excessive use of antidepressants. By no means are all these agreed upon. Indeed, in one meta-analysis, Tondo and Baldessarini found an inconsistent association with female gender. One important factor in this literature is the difficulty associated with what is essentially a post hoc diagnosis.

One retrospective analysis of a large sample showed that bipolar illness with depression as the primary onset illness was significantly more likely than manic/mixed onsets to develop rapid cycling, suicidal behavior, and psychotic symptoms. However, as noted above, there is no clear consensus as to the specific role of antidepressants in precipitating rapid-cycling illness.

*Mixed states*    Mixed states of bipolar affective disorder have been recognized since the earliest days of modern classification (Kraepelin, 2010; Weyngandt, n.d.). Kraepelin described depressive admixtures occurring during mania as well as hypomanic intrusions into depression. His categorization included six subtypes. Mixed states are not fully reflected in ICD-10 and the DSM-IV definition requires manic and depressive symptoms in their full manifestations.

In their review of the phenomenology of mania, Goodwin and Jamison (2007) found that symptoms of depression and irritability, rather than elation, occur in 70–80% of patients with mania. Since then research has attempted to define mixed states with greater precision (Cassidy, Forest, Murry, & Carroll, 1998; McElroy et al., 1992). Various conceptualizations have included transitional states between mania and depression, an intermediate state; a distinct affective state. However, little consensus has emerged on how best to diagnose mixed states. DSM-IV remains the most widely accepted convention, but there is criticism of its rigidity (Perugi et al., 1997). This has prompted alternative definitions, for example: using the criteria derived from existing depression rating scales (Prien, Himmelhoch, & Kupfer, 1988; Secunda et al., 1985; Swann et al., 1993); the use of depression items or subscales from general rating instruments (Himmelhoch & Garfinkel, 1986) and a reduction in the number of DSM-IV major depression criteria required to make the diagnosis (McElroy et al., 1992; Tohen, Waternaux, & Tsuang, 1990). Another approach has involved revisiting the essential constituents of mania. Cassidy et al. (1998), in their comprehensive factor analysis of manic symptoms in a sample of 237 patients with DSM-III, defined bipolar disorder and identified five independent factors. Importantly, the most significant factor, dysphoric mood, was found to have a bimodal distribution. This finding raises the possibility that mixed bipolar disorder is a distinct entity. Although little studied, estimates have been made of the clinical epidemiology of mixed states (Cassidy & Carroll, 2001). They concluded that an earlier age of first hospitalization and increased duration of illness were compatible with the view that mixed manic episodes occur more frequently later in the course of bipolar. Also, differences in ethnicity, gender, and clinical history add to the evidence supporting the separation of mixed mania as a diagnostic subtype. The degree of difficulty in classifying "mixed states" was eloquently summarized by Ghaemi, who, in an editorial, commented on the "mixed state" as the orphan of bipolar disorder. The ISBD subgroup on mixed states, that he had been a part of, had wished to broaden the concept, noting that DSM-IV required "full" depression and "full" mania, and that this excluded a significant number of people with, for example, depression with some symptoms of mania, leading to a "bloating" of the diagnosis of bipolar depression (Ghaemi, 2008).

*Distinguishing bipolar depression from unipolar depression*   The evidence for this is best summarized by the ISBD Task Force (Ghaemi et al., 2008) who makes this dimensional distinction based primarily on phenomenology. Predominant features include hypersomnia, hyperphagia, psychomotor disturbance, and psychotic features. Family history appears to be more relevant in bipolar depression, and clinical diagnosis has been emphasized in recent times by the licensing of a number of treatments for bipolar depression, including a number of second-generation antipsychotics and other psychotropic agents, such as Lamotrigine.

*Pediatric bipolar disorder*   The identification of pediatric bipolar disorder is both appealing (in terms of picking up those who will develop significant impairment) and controversial (with regard to misdiagnosis/overdiagnosis). This was brought into focus by data from the American National Hospital Discharge Survey, that showed an increase in hospital discharge diagnoses for bipolar disorder in children, from 1.3 per 10,000 in 1996 to 7.3 per 100,000 in 2004 (Ghaemi, 2008). At the current time, while there is appreciation of the comorbidity between this and attention deficit-hyperactivity disorder (ADHD), there is acknowledgment of the difficulties in evaluating symptoms such as irritability, which may represent normal childhood development (Ghaemi, 2008). Furthermore, at the current time there is no clear data showing a link in terms of treatment response, or longer term follow up in this cohort of patients who share symptoms of both disorders.

*Is bipolar disorder overdiagnosed or underdiagnosed?*    An interesting recent debate has centered on whether bipolar disorder is over- or underdiagnosed. This was recently addressed in the *British Medical Journal*, in which Smith and Ghaemi (2010) put the case forward for its underdiagnosis, and Zimmerman for overdiagnosis. Despite different assertions, all authors found, in their own cohort studies, that the use of a structured diagnostic interview had significantly more reliability than symptom check-lists or everyday clinical practice, Smith and Ghaemi make the point that overdiagnosis did not occur when the initial diagnosis was made using a structured interview. Taking all the evidence together and bearing in mind routine clinical practice, it is reasonable to surmise that both over- and underdiagnosis of bipolar disorder occur, depending on a wide range of factors such as setting, stage of illness, and concurrent substance misuse.

*Can biological markers help in our classification of bipolar disorder?*    As has been pointed out (Insel et al., 2010), classification systems for psychiatric illnesses in the future will take into account recent trends in neuroscience and molecular genetics, with the express aim of helping to predict treatment response and target treatments at components of what we currently consider psychiatric illnesses (e.g., use of clinically relevant circuitry behavior relationships within functional neuroimaging).

# Epidemiology

Classification and epidemiology are intimately linked. The accuracy of the latter is essentially dependent on the former. In psychiatry, a branch of medicine currently devoid of objective physical signs and testing, classification, and clinical assessment is all we have. The epidemiology of bipolar disorder is therefore governed by what classification system is in place and in what way the diagnosis is reached.

Modern epidemiology must also take into account the elasticity of diagnostic boundaries, both in terms of broadening and narrowing the definition of bipolar disorder.

A broad summary of factors which influence rates of psychiatric disorders are as follows:

- breadth of criteria;
- instruments used;
- lay versus clinical interviewers;
- population studied;
- sample size;
- single versus repeated observations;
- interview of patients versus relatives; and
- timing of interviews.

In the best of circumstances, epidemiological data can be a measure of the distribution of an illness in the population, its extent, and associated risk factors. Epidemiological data can also link genetic, psychological, environmental, biological, and sociological factors.

While accepting these limitations, establishing the epidemiology of a disorder is an essential part of researching the condition itself. A crucial factor in this is the completeness of case ascertainment. To achieve complete ascertainment, the options include total population surveys, which are expensive and difficult, especially if the condition under study is rare. An alternative is random sampling, which can have problems surrounding the yield obtained.

There are problems with the epidemiology of bipolar affective disorder. There are inconsistencies in diagnosis, treatment, and research design. For example, bipolar disorder is not always included as a separate diagnostic class in epidemiological studies; consequently, the true epidemiological picture remains unclear. Further problems include the ascertainment of "polarity" itself. There is an intrinsic problem in establishing the prevalence of a disorder that can only be recognized at an unpredictable point in its course, namely when polarity changes.

That said, Goodwin and Jamison (2007) argue that most of the biases in the literature are in the direction of underestimating, rather than overestimating the incidence and prevalence of bipolar disorder, a view that has found favor recently among epidemiologists in the field (Merikangas & Pato, 2009; Smith & Ghaemi, 2010; see above).

Despite methodological variation and consequent interpretative difficulties, a level of agreement is evident. Bipolar disorder is a relatively common condition affecting men and women equally, with a lifetime prevalence, across studies, of around 1%. Cultural, marital, social, and ethnic variations are less clearly defined. An updated summary of the incidence and prevalence rates of bipolar disorder is given in Table 11.3, taken from a recent review by Merikangas, who contributed to a number of the largest epidemiological studies of bipolar disorder.

Taking data from this table, the median 12-month prevalence rate (in the United States) is only slightly lower than lifetime prevalence (0.8%), using DSM-IV criteria. There is less available data pertaining to bipolar II disorder, the best estimate of lifetime prevalence being 1.1%, taking data from the National Comorbidity Survey replication (Merikangas et al., 2007). This lack of data on bipolar II is most probably due to concern over whether the sampling method (lay interview) is able to detect cases in a robust fashion (e.g., dealing with false positives), though the validity of this method can probably be estimated by evaluating factors such as help-seeking in identified cases.

Clinical significance is increasingly important, especially from the perspective of service provision. Interestingly, clinical significance has been part of the DSM definition of mental disorder. DSM-IV defines a mental disorder as: "a clinically significant behavioural or psychological syndrome or pattern that occurs in an individual and that is associated with present distress (e.g., a painful symptom) or disability (i.e., impairment in one or more important areas of functioning) or with a significantly increased risk of suffering death, pain, disability, or an important loss of freedom."

**Table 11.3.**

Rates of DSM-IV Bipolar Disorders in Community Samples of Adults

| Location | Study | Age (years) | Sample size | Method | Diagnosis | Lifetime prevalence (%) | | | 12-month prevalence (%) | | |
|---|---|---|---|---|---|---|---|---|---|---|---|
| | | | | | | Male | Female | Total | Male | Female | Total |
| China | Lee et al. (2007) | 18–70 | 5,201 | WMH-CIDI/DSM-IV | Bipolar I/bipolar II | – | – | 0.1 | – | – | – |
| Germany | Jacobi et al. (2004) | 18–65 | 4,181 | M-CIDI/DSM-IV | Any bipolar | 0.8 | 1.2 | 1.0 | 0.6 | 1.1 | 0.8 |
| | Wittchen et al. (1998) | 14–24 | 3,021 | M-CIDI/DSM-IV | Bipolar I | 1.1 | 1.7 | 1.4 | 0.9 | 1.6 | 1.3 |
| | | | | | Bipolar II | 0.2 | 0.7 | 0.4 | 0.2 | 0.7 | 0.4 |
| Japan | Kawakami et al. (2005) | ≥20 | 1,664 | WMH-CIDI/DSM-IV | Bipolar I/bipolar II | – | – | – | – | – | 0.1 |
| Lebanon | Karam et al. (2008) | ≥18 | 2,857 | CIDI 3.0/DSM-IV | Bipolar disorder | 2.6 | 2.3 | 2.4 | – | – | – |
| Mexico | Medina-Mora et al. (2007) | 18–65 | 5,826 | WMH-CIDI/DSM-IV | Bipolar I/bipolar II | – | – | 1.9 | – | – | – |
| New Zealand | Baxler et al. (2006) | 16–64 | 12,992 | CIDI 3.0/DSM-IV | Bipolar disorder | – | – | – | – | – | 1.8 |
| Nigeria | Gureje et al. (2006) | ≥18 | 4,984 | WMH-CIDI/DSM-IV | Bipolar I/bipolar II | – | – | 0.0 | – | – | 0.0 |
| Switzerland | Angst et al. (2005) | – | 591 | SPINKE/DSM-IV | Bipolar I, bipolar II | – | – | 1.7 | – | – | – |
| United States | Grant et al. (2005) | ≥12 | 43,093 | NESARC/DSM-IV | Bipolar I | 3.2 | 3.4 | 3.3 | 1.8 | 2.2 | 2.0 |
| | Ford et al. (2007) | ≥55 | 6,082 | WMH-CIDI/DSM-IV | Bipolar I/bipolar II | – | – | 0.8 | – | – | 0.4 |
| | Merikangas et al. (2007) | ≥18 | 9,282 | CIDI/DSM-IV | Bipolar I | 0.8 | 1.1 | 1.0 | – | – | 0.6 |
| | | | | | Bipolar II | 0.9 | 1.3 | 1.1 | – | – | 0.8 |
| | | | | | Subthreshold bipolar disorder | 2.6 | 2.1 | 2.4 | – | – | – |

*Source:* Merikangas and Pato (2009).

Clinical significance has also been incorporated in the diagnostic criteria for many disorders in DSM-IV in the context of distress or impairment in social, occupational, or other important areas of functioning. However, despite this prominence of clinical significance as a concept, there is no consensus as to its definition nor are there any operationalized criteria.

In the study by Narrow, Rae, Robins, and Regier (2002), the use of data on clinical significance *lowered* the past year prevalence rates of "any (psychiatric) disorder" among 18–54 by 17% in the Epidemiological Catchment Area Survey (ECA) and 32% in the National Comorbidity Survey (NCS). For adults older than 18 years, the revised estimate for any disorder was 18.5%. The use of the clinical significance criterion reduced disparities between estimates in the two surveys. The validity of the criterion was supported by the positive associations between clinical significance with disabilities and suicidal behavior. The discrepancies between the ECA and NCS, a source of considerable controversy, were largely attributed to methodological differences. In bipolar I disorder, when clinically significant criteria were applied to the use of the Composite International Diagnostic Interview (CIDI), the rate decreased from 1.3% to 0.3%. Clinical significance has also been used to explore the validity of data pertaining to the wider definition of bipolar spectrum disorder.

Epidemiological estimates of bipolar spectrum, using data from studies such as the Zurich Cohort and ECAS studies have shown an increase in rates to around 5% (Angst, Gamma, & Lewinsohn, 2002; Judd & Akiskal, 2003). This was replicated with data from the NCS (Merikangas et al., 2007), which estimated these rates at 4.5%. Of note is the observation that rates of disability associated with subthreshold symptoms were similar to that of mania and depression, suggesting a degree of validity to the concept.

Another way of validating population data is to ascertain what proportion of "cases" has received treatment. From the studies presented above, it has been pointed out that, in US populations, around half are receiving treatment, this figure dropping by around half in other countries (Merikangas & Pato, 2009), which questions the generalizability of some of these findings.

## Comorbidity

The issue of comorbid conditions has been more readily recognized in contemporary studies. For example, McElroy et al. (2001, p. 1), evaluated 288 outpatients with bipolar I or bipolar II using structured diagnostic interviews to determine the diagnosis of bipolar, comorbid axis I diagnoses, and demographics. They found that 187 (65%) with bipolar also met DSM-IV criteria for at least one comorbid lifetime axis I disorder. More had anxiety (42%) and substance misuse (42%) than eating disorders (5%). There were no differences in terms of comorbidity between bipolar I and bipolar II. Both lifetime and current axis I comorbidity were associated with an earlier age of onset. Current axis I comorbidity was associated with history of both cycle acceleration and more severe episodes over time. This was underlined in the NCS-R (Merikangas et al., 2007), which identified that 80% of those with bipolar disorder also fulfilled criteria for DSM-IV anxiety disorder, particularly panic attacks and social phobia (70% and 50%, respectively). Using data from the Zurich follow-up study, in which structured interviews were given to a cohort of young adults over the course of 20 years, Merikangas et al. (2008) found that manic symptoms were an independent risk factor for later alcohol, cannabis, and benzodiazepine abuse/dependency.

## Synthesis

In an edition of the *British Medical Journal*, its editor Richard Smith (2002) attempted to define the concept of "non-disease." Its conclusions are summarized as follows: "The concept of 'disease' is a slippery one"—so is "medicine." "Health is also impossible to define. To have a condition labeled as a disease may bring considerable benefit—both material and emotional. But the diagnosis of a disease may also create problems in the denial of insurance, mortgage, and employment. Also a diagnosis may lead to the individual regarding themselves as forever flawed and unable to 'rise above' their problem."

There is increasing evidence of a neurobiological, genetic, psychological, and social nature, which indicates that bipolar disorder is at the very least a disorder. If disease is defined as the presence of clear and reproducible pathology, this is not yet available in the case of bipolar disorder. However, modern biotechnology is providing methods that can provide information in vivo concerning the nature of the functional abnormalities in conditions such as schizophrenia and the affective disorders.

The main issue for the future is the question of whether a broad or narrow definition of bipolar is the most useful from both a clinical and a research viewpoint.

The central diagnostic importance placed on alterations in mood distracts from the more subtle but nevertheless meaningful symptoms such as changes in psychomotor function and cognition. Advances in neuroimaging paradigms, which incorporate neuropsychological tests, have revealed some of the neurofunctional similarities and differences between diagnostic subgroups. Importantly, more information than ever is available concerning the correlation between structural and functional brain changes and symptoms expressed by patients suffering from bipolar disorder and schizophrenia. One of the great challenges ahead is the separation of state from trait phenomena and the increase in understanding of common fundamentals in mental disorder. In other words, what are the first principles which underlie mental functions and abnormalities therein? Cognition, emotion, and behavior offer templates with which to examine the symptoms in disorders such as bipolar. Clinical observation, while useful, is no longer sufficient for exploring the baseline abnormalities in these disabling disorders. Debates surrounding definitions, broad versus narrow, inclusive versus exclusive, may be answered by greater understanding of the common pathways that underlie the symptoms expressed. We are, unfortunately, still far from grasping what these pathways might be. The notion of "mechanism" in the mental health sciences remains controversial and agreement on what defines it, elusive. To the extent that this remains the case, we may find the gap between treatment necessity and scientific precision ever widening.

## References

Akiskal, H. S. (2003). Validating "hard" and "soft" phenotypes within the bipolar spectrum: Continuity or discontinuity? *Journal of Affective Disorders, 73*(1–2), 1–5.

Akiskal, H. S., & Akiskal, K. (1992). Cyclothymic, hyperthymic and depressive temperaments as subaffective variants of mood disorders. *Annual Review of Psychiatry, 11*, 43–62.

Akiskal, H. S., Djenderedjian, A. M., Rosenthal, R. H., & Khani, M. K. (1977). Cyclothymic disorder: Validating criteria for inclusion in the bipolar affective group. *American Journal of Psychiatry, 134*(11), 1227–1233.

Akiskal, H. S., & Mallya, G. (1987). Criteria for the 'soft' bipolar spectrum: Treatment implications. *Psychopharmacology Bulletin, 23*(1), 68–73.

Angst, J. (1998). The emerging epidemiology of hypomania and bipolar II disorder. *Journal of Affective Disorders, 50*(2), 143–151.

Angst, J., Frey, R., Lohmeyer, B., & Zerbin-Rüdin, E. (1980). Bipolar manic-depressive psychoses: Results of a genetic investigation. *Human Genetics, 55*(2), 237–254.

Angst, J., Gamma, A., & Lewinsohn, P. (2002). The evolving epidemiology of bipolar disorder. *World Psychiatry, 1*(3), 146–148.

Benazzi, F. (2007). Bipolar disorder—Focus on bipolar II disorder and mixed depression. *Lancet, 369*(9565), 935–945.

Brockington, I., Kendell, R.E., Wainwright, S., Hillier, V. F., & Walker, J. (1979). The distinction between the affective psychoses and schizophrenia. *British Journal of Psychiatry, 135*(3), 243–248.

Carlson, G. A., & Kashani, J. H. (1988). Manic symptoms in a non-referred adolescent population. *Journal of Affective Disorders, 15*(3), 219–226.

Cassano, G. B., Akiskal, H. S., Savino, M., Musetti, L., & Perugi, G. (1992). Proposed subtypes of bipolar II and related disorders: With hypomanic episodes (or cyclothymia) and with hyperthymic temperament. *Journal of Affective Disorders, 26*(2), 127–140.

Cassano, G.B., Mantua, V., & Fagiolini, A. (2011). Bipolar spectrum: Just broadening or an integration between categories and dimensions? *World Psychiatry, 10*(3), 192–193.

Cassidy, F., & Carroll, B. J. (2001). The clinical epidemiology of pure and mixed manic episodes. *Bipolar Disorders, 3*(1), 35–40.

Cassidy, F., Forest, K., Murry, E., & Carroll, B. J. (1998). A factor analysis of the signs and symptoms of mania. *Archives of General Psychiatry, 55*(1), 27–32.

Coryell, W., Endicott, J., Maser, J. D., Leon, A. C. & Akiskal, H. S. (1995). Long-term stability of polarity distinctions in the affective disorders. *American Journal of Psychiatry, 152*, 385–390.

Craddock, N., & Owen, M. J. (2007). Rethinking psychosis: The disadvantages of a dichotomous classification now outweigh the advantages. *World Psychiatry, 6*(2), 84–91.

DSM-IV, American Psychiatric Association. (2000). *Diagnostic and statistical manual of mental disorders: DSM-IV-TR*. Washington, DC: Author.

Dunner, D. L., Gershon, E. S., & Goodwin, F. K. (1976). Heritable factors in the severity of affective illness. *Biological Psychiatry, 11*(1), 31–42.

Feighner, J. P., Robins, E., Guze, S. B., Woodruff, R. A., Jr., Winokur, G., & Munoz, R. (1972). Diagnostic criteria for use in psychiatric research. *Archives of General Psychiatry, 26*(1), 57–63.

Ghaemi, S. N. (2008). All mixed up: On the absence of diagnostic guidelines for mixed states in the ISBD Diagnostic Guidelines Task Force Report. *Bipolar Disorders, 10*(1 Pt 2), 129–130.

Ghaemi, S. N., Bauer, M., Cassidy, F., Malhi, G. S., Mitchell, P., Phelps, J., . . . Youngstrom, E.; ISBD Diagnostic Guidelines Task Force. (2008). Diagnostic guidelines for bipolar disorder: A summary of the International Society for Bipolar Disorders Diagnostic Guidelines Task Force Report. *Bipolar Disorders, 10*(1 Pt 2), 117–128.

Goodwin, G. (2002). Hypomania: What's in a name? *British Journal of Psychiatry, 181*(2), 94–95.

Goodwin, F. K., & Jamison, K. R. (2007). *Manic-depressive illness: Bipolar disorders and recurrent depression.* New York: Oxford University Press.

Goodwin, F., & Marneros, A. (2005). *Bipolar disorders: Mixed states, rapid cycling and atypical forms.* New York: Cambridge University Press.

Gunderson, J. G., Weinberg, I., Daversa, M. T., Kueppenbender, K. D., Zanarini, M. C., Shea, M.T., . . . Dyck, I. (2006). Descriptive and longitudinal observations on the relationship of borderline personality disorder and bipolar disorder. *American Journal of Psychiatry, 163*(7), 1173–1178.

Himmelhoch, J. M., & Garfinkel, M. E. (1986). Sources of lithium resistance in mixed mania. *Psychopharmacology Bulletin, 22*(3), 613–620.

Howland, R. H., & Thase, M. E. (1993). A comprehensive review of cyclothymic disorder. *Journal of Nervous and Mental Disease, 181*(8), 485–493.

Insel, T., Cuthbert, B., Garvey, M., Heinssen, R., Pine, D. S., Quinn, K., . . . Wang, P. (2010). Research domain criteria (RDoC): Toward a new classification framework for research on mental disorders. *American Journal of Psychiatry, 167*(7), 748–751.

Jablensky, A., Hugler, H., Von Cranach, M., & Kalinov, K. (1993). Kraepelin revisited: A reassessment and statistical analysis of dementia praecox and manic-depressive insanity in 1908. *Psychological Medicine, 23*(4), 843–858.

Johnstone, E. C., Crow, T. J., Frith, C. D., & Owens, D. G. (1988). The Northwick Park 'functional' psychosis study: Diagnosis and treatment response. *Lancet, 2*(8603), 119–125.

Johnstone, E. C., Frith, C. D., Crow, T. J., Owens, D. G., Done, D. J., Baldwin, E. J., & Charlette, A. (1992). The Northwick Park 'functional' psychosis study: Diagnosis and outcome. *Psychological Medicine, 22*(2), 331–346.

Judd, L. L., & Akiskal, H.S. (2003). The prevalence and disability of bipolar spectrum disorders in the US population: Re-analysis of the ECA database taking into account subthreshold cases. *Journal of Affective Disorders, 73*(1–2), 123–131.

Judd, L. L., Akiskal, H. S., Schettler, P. J., Coryell, W., Endicott, J., Maser, J. D., . . . Keller, M. B. (2003). A prospective investigation of the natural history of the long-term weekly symptomatic status of bipolar II disorder. *Archives of General Psychiatry, 60*(3), 261–269.

Judd, L. L. Akiskal, H. S., Schettler, P. J., Endicott, J., Maser, J., Solomon, D. A., . . . Keller, M. B. (2002). The long-term natural history of the weekly symptomatic status of bipolar I disorder. *Archives of General Psychiatry, 59*(6), 530–537.

Kahlbaum, K. (1874). *Die Katatonie oder das Spannungsirresein.* Berlin: Verlag August Hirshwald.

Kraepelin, E. (2010). *Manic-depressive insanity and paranoia.* London: Forgotten Books.

Kretschmer, E. (1936). *Physique and character.* London: Routledge.

Kupfer, D. J., Pickar, D., Himmelhoch, J. M., & Detre, T. P. (1975). Are there two types of unipolar depression? *Archives of General Psychiatry, 32*(7), 866–871.

Lewinsohn, P. M., Klein, D. N., & Seeley, J. R. (1995). Bipolar disorders in a community sample of older adolescents: Prevalence, phenomenology, comorbidity, and course. *Journal of the American Academy of Child and Adolescent Psychiatry, 34*(4), 454–463.

McElroy, S. L., Altshuler, L. L., Suppes, T., Keck, P. E., Jr., Frye, M. A., Denicoff, K.D., . . . Post, R. M. (2001). Axis I psychiatric comorbidity and its relationship to historical illness variables in 288 patients with bipolar disorder. *American Journal of Psychiatry, 158*(3), 420–426.

McElroy, S. L., Keck, P. E., Jr., Pope, H. G., Jr., Hudson, J. I., Faedda, G. L., & Swann, A. C. (1992). Clinical and research implications of the diagnosis of dysphoric or mixed mania or hypomania. *American Journal of Psychiatry, 149*(12), 1633–1644.

Mendels, J. (1976). Lithium in the treatment of depression. *American Journal of Psychiatry, 133*(4), 373–378.

Merikangas, K. R., Akiskal, H. S., Angst, J., Greenberg, P. E., Hirschfeld, R. M., Petukhova, M., & Kessler, R. C. (2007). Lifetime and 12-month prevalence of bipolar spectrum disorder in the National Comorbidity Survey replication. *Archives of General Psychiatry*, 64(5), 543–552.

Merikangas, K. R., Herrell, R., Swendsen, J., Rössler, W., Ajdacic-Gross, V., & Angst, J. (2008). Specificity of bipolar spectrum conditions in the comorbidity of mood and substance use disorders: Results from the Zurich cohort study. *Archives of General Psychiatry*, 65(1), 47–52.

Merikangas, K. R., & Pato, M. (2009). Recent developments in the epidemiology of bipolar disorder in adults and children: Magnitude, correlates, and future directions. *Clinical Psychology: Science and Practice*, 16(2), 121–133.

Narrow, W. E., Rae, D. S., Robins, L. N., & Regier, D. A. (2002). Revised prevalence estimates of mental disorders in the United States: Using a clinical significance criterion to reconcile 2 surveys' estimates. *Archives of General Psychiatry*, 59(2), 115–123.

O'Connell, R. A., Mayo, J. A., & Sciutto, M. S. (1991). PDQ-R personality disorders in bipolar patients. *Journal of Affective Disorders*, 23(4), 217–221.

Perugi, G., Akiskal, H. S., Micheli, C., Musetti, L., Paiano, A., Quilici, C., ... Cassano, G. B. (1997). Clinical subtypes of bipolar mixed states: Validating a broader European definition in 143 cases. *Journal of Affective Disorders*, 43(3), 169–180.

Placidi, G., Signoretta, S., Liguori, A., Gervasi, R., Maremmani, I., & Akiskal, H. S. (1998). The semi-structured affective temperament interview (TEMPS-I). Reliability and psychometric properties in 1010 14–26 year old students. *Journal of Affective Disorders*, 47(1–3), 1–10.

Prien, R. F., Himmelhoch, J. M., & Kupfer, D. J. (1988). Treatment of mixed mania. *Journal of Affective disorders*, 15(1), 9–15.

Robins, E., & Guze, S. B. (1970). Establishment of diagnostic validity in psychiatric illness: Its application to schizophrenia. *American Journal of Psychiatry*, 126(7), 983–987.

Sachs, G. S., Nierenberg, A. A., Calabrese, J. R., Marangell, L. B., Wisniewski, S. R., Gyulai, L., ... Thase, M. E. (2007). Effectiveness of adjunctive antidepressant treatment for bipolar depression. *New England Journal of Medicine*, 356(17), 1711–1722.

Secunda, S. K., Katz, M. M., Swann, A., Koslow, S. H., Maas, J. W., Chuang, S., & Croughan, J. (1985). Mania. Diagnosis, state measurement and prediction of treatment response. *Journal of Affective Disorders*, 8(2), 113–121.

Smith, D. J., & Ghaemi, N. (2010). Is underdiagnosis the main pitfall when diagnosing bipolar disorder? Yes. *British Medical Journal*, 340, c854.

Smith, R. (Ed.). (2002). In search of "non-disease." *British Medical Journal*, 324(7642), 883–885.

Strakowski, S. M., Fleck, D. E., & Maj, M., 2011. Broadening the diagnosis of bipolar disorder: Benefits vs. risks. *World Psychiatry*, 10(3), 181–186.

Swann, A. C., Secunda, S. K., Katz, M. M., Croughan, J., Bowden, C. L., Koslow, S. H., ... Stokes, P. E. (1993). Specificity of mixed affective states: Clinical comparison of dysphoric mania and agitated depression. *Journal of Affective Disorders*, 28(2), 81–89.

Tohen, M., Waternaux, C. M., & Tsuang, M. T. (1990). Outcome in mania: A 4-year prospective follow-up of 75 patients utilizing survival analysis. *Archives of General Psychiatry*, 47(12), 1106–1111.

Weyngandt, W. (n.d.). Ueber das manisch-depressive Irresein. *Berliner Klinischer Wochenschrift*, 4, 105–106.

Wicki, W., & Angst, J. (1991). The Zurich Study. X. Hypomania in a 28- to 30-year-old cohort. *European Archives of Psychiatry and Clinical Neuroscience*, 240(6), 339–348.

# 12

# Neurobiological Theories of Bipolar Disorder

## Karine Macritchie and Douglas Blackwood
### Edinburgh, UK

## Introduction

The neurobiological basis of bipolar disorder remains poorly understood. However, the past decade has witnessed a remarkable expansion in the range of investigative techniques available to researchers in this field. Through the recognition of risk genes, the identification of abnormalities in neural circuits serving mood regulation and neurocognition, and the exploration of neurotransmitter systems and intracellular neurochemistry, considerable progress has been made in our understanding of the processes likely to be involved in the pathogenesis of this heterogeneous illness.

## Genetic Studies

Neurobiological systems fundamental to the etiology of bipolar disorder may be identified by studying its associated genes. Bipolar disorder is clearly familial. A first-degree relative carries a tenfold increase in the risk of developing the illness compared with the general population; adoption and twin studies have repeatedly confirmed that this risk is largely due to genetic factors and not upbringing. However, the observation that concordance between identical twins is less than complete suggests that environmental and possibly epigenetic factors are also influential in determining the way that genetic risk is expressed in each individual. The disorder is not usually caused by the dysfunction of a single gene although instances have been found where illness in an individual or family is associated with a single genetic locus. More commonly the illness is likely to be caused by multiple additive or interacting genes, although how many genes are involved is not known.

Various approaches have been used to identify genes implicated in bipolar disorder. Cytogenetic analyses have examined individuals with the illness who also have rare chromosomal rearrangements. Linkage studies focus on families with several affected members. Association studies now involve cohorts comprising several thousand cases and control subjects. Most recently, the direct analysis of the complete sequence of the genome of individuals from selected groups and families is becoming possible.

Genetic linkage studies with families where two or more family members are affected by illness aim to detect the co-segregation of a particular genetic marker with the disease phenotype. In a typical linkage study, DNA obtained from family members is typed using a series of single nucleotide polymorphisms (SNPs) evenly spaced across the region of interest or across the whole genome. Several chromosome regions likely to harbor genes implicated in bipolar disorder have been identified in this way. A meta-analysis of data from 11 whole-genome linkage studies of bipolar disorder included over 5,000 individuals from more than 1,000 families. Significant linkage to bipolar disorder was found on the long arm of chromosome 6 and the long arm of chromosome 8 (McQueen et al., 2005). However, a limitation of the linkage approach is that the chromosome regions identified are usually large and contain many genes, any one (or several) of which may be related to the disease.

Association studies have the advantage that they can detect much smaller regions down to the level of single genes by comparing the frequency of DNA variants (alleles) between affected and unaffected populations (Cardon & Bell, 2001). The limitations of association studies include much reduced power to detect disease-related loci in the presence of genetic heterogeneity as is the case for bipolar disorder. Secondly, very large numbers of cases and controls are required to detect genetic variants that are relatively common in the population and make very small contributions to genetic risk. It is now thought that a substantial part of the genetic risk in bipolar disorder is due to the additive or interactive effects of multiple common risk variants, each with a very small effect (odds ratios less than about 1.5): very large sample sizes are needed to detect these. To achieve this, large international collaborations have pooled data from genome-wide association studies in bipolar disorder, strengthening the power of these analyses. A recent study of data from nearly 12,000 bipolar cases and over 51,000 controls not only confirmed evidence of association for the gene *CACNA1C* which codes an L-type voltage-dependent calcium channel protein, but also revealed association of other related calcium channel subunits with bipolar disorder (Psychiatric GWAS Consortium Bipolar Disorder Working Group, 2011). These genetic findings provide valuable clues about the neurobiology of bipolar disorder which may guide future research into the mechanisms that translate variation in a gene into the clinical expression of mood disorder. In addition, it is likely that in this process, traditional psychiatric diagnostic boundaries will be challenged: for instance, there is strong evidence that the gene *CACNA1C* also shows association with schizophrenia.

## The Structure and Function of Neural Circuitry in Bipolar Disorder

Histopathological and neuroimaging abnormalities have been found in prefrontal, temporal, and subcortical regions of the brain in bipolar disorder, particularly in those regions associated with mood regulation, emotional processing, and cognition.

## Histopathological studies

Postmortem studies on brain tissue from patients with bipolar disorder have revealed no gross pathological features. However, subtle changes in neuron density and morphology in regions including the prefrontal cortex, the hippocampus, and the amygdala have been observed. Decreased neuronal size and density occur in the dorsolateral prefrontal cortex (Cotter et al., 2002; Rajkowska, Halaris, & Selemon, 2001). Changes in neuronal density in regions of the anterior cingulate cortex are described (Benes, Vincent, & Todtenkopf, 2001; Bouras, Kövari, Hof, Riederer, & Giannakopoulos, 2001). Pyramidal cells are reported to be smaller in the CA1 region of the hippocampus (Liu, Schulz, Lee, Reutiman, & Fatemi, 2007) and neuronal somal size is reduced in the lateral amygdalar nucleus (Bezchlibnyk et al., 2007). Synaptic abnormalities are observed in the anterior cingulate and in the hippocampus (Eastwood & Harrison, 2001, 2010; Gray, Dean, Kronsbein, Robinson, & Scarr, 2010). Glial cell changes have also been reported. Glial density, particularly oligodendrocyte density, is decreased in prefrontal cortical areas, perhaps contributing to the neuronal abnormalities described above (Öngür, Drevets, & Price, 1998; Rajkowska et al., 2001; Uranova, Vostrikov, Orlovskaya, & Rachmanova, 2004; Vostrikov, Uranova, & Orlovskaya, 2007). Abnormal myelination in prefrontal deep white matter is observed (Regenold et al., 2007). Bowley, Drevets, Öngür, and Price (2002) found that amygdalar glial density and the glia/neuron ratio were substantially reduced in major depressive disorder cases and in the few bipolar subjects who had not received lithium or valproate. Together, these findings demonstrate that both neuronal and glial cell abnormalities occur in bipolar disorder.

## Neuroimaging studies on brain structure

Neuroimaging studies have identified brain structural changes in patients with bipolar disorder. Meta-analyses of such studies highlight whole brain, prefrontal lobe, and insular volume reductions, lateral ventriculomegaly, and increased pallidal volumes (Arnone et al., 2009; Bora, Fornito, Yücel, & Pantelis, 2010; Ellison-Wright & Bullmore, 2010). Medication may have a confounding effect on these analyses: for instance, patients with bipolar disorder taking the mood stabilizer lithium are reported to have larger amygdalae and hippocampi than other patients (Hallahan et al., 2011).

White matter structural anomalies are another interesting finding. In addition to the histopathological findings outlined above, magnetic resonance brain scans from patients with bipolar disorder show regions of hyperintensity in both periventricular and deep (particularly the deep frontal) white matter (see Mahon, Burdick, & Szeszko, 2010, for review). These hyperintensities are seen even in young patients and in those suffering their first acute affective episode (Botteron, Vannier, Geller, Todd, & Lee, 1995; Strakowski et al., 1993). The underlying pathology of these lesions remains unclear, but they may represent areas of demyelination, edema, and gliosis. In the broader medical literature, similar abnormalities are reported in association with cardiovascular risk factors and increasing age, a fact that makes their discovery in young people with bipolar disorder particularly significant. Diffusion tensor imaging provides evidence of impaired white matter network connectivity in bipolar disorder, particularly in the prefrontal regions and in projection, association, and commissural fibers (see Heng, Song, & Sim, 2010, for review).

In summary, histopathological and neuroimaging studies suggest that bipolar disorder is associated with neuronal, glial cell, and synaptic pathology. Subtle abnormalities have been found in both gray and white matter, predominantly in areas of the brain which regulate mood and serve cognition.

## Neuropsychological studies

Structural abnormalities have the potential to compromise cognitive function and emotional processing. Numerous studies record impairments across most cognitive domains in depressed patients with bipolar disorder (Martínez-Arán et al., 2000). During mania, patients show deficits in verbal learning, executive function, and sustained attention (Clark, Iversen, & Goodwin, 2002; Morice, 1990; Sweeney, Kmiec, & Kupfer, 2000). Impairments in cognitive function persist after remission. A meta-analysis of neuropsychological studies in euthymic bipolar disorder found impairments in executive function, attention, psychomotor speed, and immediate memory (Robinson et al., 2006). Emotional processing involves the activation of limbic, prefrontal, and subcortical areas. A meta-analysis of functional magnetic resonance imaging studies using facial affect processing reported increased engagement in limbic regions, the thalamus, and the basal ganglia and decreased engagement in the ventrolateral prefrontal region in patients with bipolar disorders (Delvecchio et al., 2012).

## Candidate Risk Genes Regulating Brain Regional Structure

The structural and functional abnormalities observed in bipolar disorder raise the possibility that abnormal neurodevelopment and/or impaired neuronal plasticity and survival occur over the course of the illness. Several susceptibility genes for bipolar disorder are implicated in neurodevelopment and neural plasticity. For example, the *ODZ4* gene located on chromosome 11 encodes a member of the teneurin family of cell surface proteins which are thought to modulate cell surface signaling and neuronal pathfinding (Psychiatric GWAS Consortium Bipolar Disorder Working Group, 2011; Tucker & Chiquet-Ehrismann, 2006). The previously mentioned *CACNA1C* gene encodes an L-type voltage-dependent calcium channel protein. Calcium modulates the expression of the gene for the neurotrophin brain-derived neurotrophic factor (BDNF), thus the *CACNA1C* gene may indirectly influence neuronal plasticity (see Wang, McIntosh, He, Gelernter, & Blumberg, 2011, for brief description). Several candidate genes for bipolar disorder affect white matter structure. Neuregulin-1 influences oligodendrocyte function, axonal migration, and myelination. Variants of this gene are associated with reductions in white matter density and integrity (McIntosh, Hall, Lymer, Sussmann, & Lawrie, 2009). Abnormalities of oligodendrocyte and myelination gene expression have been found in subjects with bipolar disorder and schizophrenia (Tkachev et al., 2003).

## Neurotrophic and Gliotrophic Factors

Neuronal growth, development, plasticity, and survival are modulated by neurotrophins, proteins which are synthesized by neurons in response to neuronal stimulation: reduction in neurotrophin activity may lead to neuronal atrophy. Perhaps the most extensively investigated neurotrophin in affective disorders is BDNF. BDNF levels are reduced during manic and depressive episodes in bipolar disorder (Fernandes et al., 2011). Lithium is reported to increase BDNF levels in the treatment of acute mania (de Sousa et al., 2011). Variants of the BDNF gene, especially the Val66Met polymorphism, appear to have a modest association with vulnerability to bipolar disorder (Fan & Sklar, 2008). Glial cell line-derived neurotrophic factor (GDNF) is another neurotrophic factor of interest. Serum GDNF levels are lower during mania and depression (Zhang et al., 2010). Animal studies demonstrate an increase in GDNF levels with lithium (Angelucci, Aloe, Jimenez-Vasquez, & Mathe, 2003).

## The Hypothalamic–Pituitary–Adrenal Axis

Excess cortisol activity may contribute to the neuropathological features of bipolar disorder. Glucocorticoid receptors are abundant in the prefrontal cortex, the amygdala, and the hippocampus. Prefrontal cortical and hippocampal neuronal atrophy occur in animal models of stress, while in contrast, the amygdala exhibits an enhanced neuronal growth response (see McEwen, 2005 for review). Animal studies show that elevated glucocorticoids inhibit astrocyte and oligodendrocyte proliferation (see Rajkowska & Miguel-Hidalgo, 2007 for review).

Hypothalamic–pituitary–adrenal (HPA) axis dysfunction is an established feature of affective disorders, reflected in hypersecretion of cortisol and corticotrophin-releasing hormone (CRH) and glucocorticoid receptor hypofunction (see Ceulemans et al., 2011 for review). Hypercortisolemia, disrupted diurnal cortisol secretion, and abnormal dexamethasone/CRH tests are seen in acute episodes of bipolar disorder (Bond & Young, 2007). Abnormally enhanced cortisol responses in dexamethasone/CRH tests have also been demonstrated in euthymic patients with bipolar disorder (Watson, Gallagher, Ritchie, Ferrier, & Young, 2004).

Genes that influence the regulation of the HPA axis have been studied most extensively in major depression. However, an association between bipolar disorder and the glucocorticoid receptor gene, *NR3C1*, has recently been reported (Ceulemans et al., 2011). Furthermore, variants of this gene may influence the burden of depressive symptoms in the course of bipolar disorder (Szczepankiewicz et al., 2011).

## Neurochemical Theories of Bipolar Disorder

Until recently, neurobiological theories of affective disorders largely focused on three interacting neurotransmitter systems, the norepinephrine, serotonin, and dopamine systems, which radiate throughout the prefrontal, limbic, and striatal circuitry. Interest in these systems originally arose from the observations that dopamine agonists may trigger mania, agents which deplete monoamines may precipitate depression, and antidepressants appear to act through the modulation of synaptic concentrations of norepinephrine and serotonin. The earliest theory, that depression was the consequence of a deficiency of monoamine neurotransmitters, was only partly supported by subsequent work. The realization that antidepressant response is delayed by several weeks led to the idea that therapeutic efficacy first required a series of changes to neurotransmitter receptors and their intracellular systems. The focus of research moved from neurotransmitters and their metabolites to their receptors, and then to the control of gene expression and the regulation of postsynaptic intracellular signaling cascades. These complex cascades, modulated by neurotransmitter systems, are strong pathophysiological candidates in bipolar disorder.

Recently, new neurotransmitter candidates have emerged, in particular glutamate and gamma-aminobutyric acid (GABA). Several studies on mood disorders report increases in glutamate metabolites (glutamate, glutamine, and GABA) variously in prefrontal, hippocampal, insular, and occipital regions, irrespective of affective state (see Yüksel & Öngür, 2010, for review). One study reported an increase in the expression of the glutamate transporter 1 in the anterior cingulate cortex of the postmortem brains of patients with bipolar disorder, reflecting increased glutamatergic synaptic activity (Eastwood & Harrison, 2010). Excessive glutamatergic activation of $N$-methyl-D-aspartate receptors may lead to a neurotoxic influx of calcium, a potential mechanism for some of the neuropathological features of bipolar disorder as described above. Existing antiglutamatergic agents such as lamotrigine have mood-stabilizing effects. This mechanism clearly offers a promising therapeutic target for future drug development.

The inhibitory neurotransmitter GABA is another candidate for several psychiatric illnesses including affective disorders and schizophrenia (Brambilla, Perez, Barale, Schettini, & Soares, 2003; Coyle, 2004). Valproate, an agent with antimanic and mood-stabilizing effects, has GABAergic actions. One genome-wide association study reported that variation in a GABA$_A$ receptor subunit gene was one of the most strongly associated polymorphisms for bipolar disorder (Wellcome Trust Case Control Consortium, 2007).

A new working model of the neurochemical systems involved in mood regulation has been advanced recently (see Garakani, Charney, & Anand, 2007, for a detailed description). It is proposed that in health, mood is regulated by a core circuit comprising the medial prefrontal and limbic cortices, the striatum, the globus pallidus, midbrain dopaminergic neurons, and the thalamus. Among the many neurotransmitters involved in the circuit, the principal "fast conductance" neurotransmitters are glutamatergic (the frontostriatal projections) and GABAergic (the striatopallidal and pallidothalamic projections). Within the circuit, feedback connections under GABAergic drive play a fundamental role in the maintenance of mood stability.

## Cell Membrane and Signal Transduction Pathways

Signal transduction pathways are the means by which the effects of many neurotransmitters and other molecules such as hormones and neurotrophic factors elicit intracellular functional effects in their target neurons. Some of these signal transduction pathways are involved in the regulation of neuroplasticity and cell survival: several have been implicated in the pathophysiology of bipolar disorder (Chen & Manji, 2007; Schloesser, Huang, Klein, & Manji, 2008).

These complex pathways are triggered through a second messenger system; the cascades, which are subsequently activated, generate a vast range of biological responses. Signal transduction usually includes a series of phosphorylation reactions precipitated by the activation of protein kinases. Four types of pathways have been categorized by their first and second messengers and are described in detail by Stahl (2009):

1. *G protein-linked cascades.* Neurotransmitters may stimulate cascades through the activation of guanine nucleotide-binding proteins (G proteins). G protein-linked systems use cyclic AMP and inositol triphosphate as second messengers.
2. *Ion channel-linked cascades.* Alternatively, neurotransmitters may stimulate cascades through the activation of ion channels. These systems use calcium ions as a second messenger.
3. *Nuclear hormone receptor cascades.* Hormones bind to nuclear hormone receptors and the resulting hormone–nuclear receptor complex acts as a second messenger.
4. *Receptor tyrosine kinase cascades.* Neurotrophic factors activate a series of kinase enzymes which in turn lead to the activation of the extracellular receptor-coupled kinase (ERK) and glycogen synthase kinase-3 systems.

Abnormalities in these pathways have been identified in mood disorders and the effects of psychotropic medications have been investigated.

## G proteins and inositol

Among several abnormalities of the G protein system demonstrated in mood disorders, increases in a G protein subtype G$\alpha$s, have been reported in the frontal and occipital cortices of patients with bipolar disorder. Elevated G$\alpha$s mRNA and protein levels have been reported in the blood cells of patients with bipolar disorder both during acute affective episodes and in euthymia. Lithium is thought to stabilize the inactive conformation of G proteins (see Chen & Manji, 2007 for review). In addition, lithium and two other mood stabilizers, carbamazepine and valproate, are reported to produce inositol depletion through a cytoplasmic inositol-regulating protein, prolyl oligopeptidase and so to modulate signal transduction (Williams, Cheng, Mudge, & Harwood, 2002).

## Extracellular receptor-coupled kinase signaling cascade

The extracellular signal-related kinase (ERK) pathway also mediates synaptic plasticity and neurotrophic action. The cascade is precipitated by the binding of neurotrophins such as BDNF and nerve growth factor (NGF). Inactivation of the ERK pathway results in manic-like behavior in animals. In brain regions associated with mood regulation, mood stabilizers such as lithium and valproate modify the ERK pathway.

Typical and atypical antipsychotics stimulate the pathway, effects apparently mediated through $D_2$ and $5HT_{1A}$ receptors: this has been proposed as a possible mechanism for the antimanic action of these agents (see Chen & Manji, 2007, for review).

## Glycogen synthase kinase 3

Glycogen synthase kinase 3 (GSK-3) is an enzyme situated at the meeting point of several signal pathways. It has important effects on progenitor cell fate determination, neuronal survival, apoptosis, and synaptic plasticity. GSK-3 has been the subject of considerable research in bipolar disorder. Lithium and valproate inhibit GSK-3 activity. Animal models of depression and mania suggest that GSK-3 inhibition mediates effects similar to both antidepressant and antimanic agents. The mechanisms through which these mood-stabilizing effects are mediated remain to be clarified (see Chen & Manji, 2007, for review). Interestingly, it is reported that copy-number variants involving the gene GSK-3$\beta$ are significantly increased in patients with bipolar disorder compared with controls (Lachman et al., 2007).

# Broader Questions on the Nature and Course of Bipolar Disorder

As our understanding of the pathological processes involved in bipolar disorder develops, important questions arise regarding the nature and course of the disorder, and its relationship to other psychiatric illnesses.

## Neurodevelopmental traits or scars?

One important question is whether some structural abnormalities and neuropsychological deficits are neurodevelopmental traits associated with bipolar disorder or whether they develop as the illness progresses. The potential role of candidate risk genes associated with abnormal neurodevelopment has already been discussed. Volumetric abnormalities which could be considered traits of the illness are seen in the unaffected relatives of patients with bipolar disorder: these abnormalities have been reported in the anterior cingulate, the thalamus, and the striatum. In addition, children and adolescents in the early stages of bipolar disorder are reported to show volumetric abnormalities in the subgenual prefrontal cortex, the striatum, the amygdala, the hippocampus, and the lateral ventricles (see Hajek, Carrey, & Alda, 2005, for review). White matter hyperintensities are seen in young patients with bipolar disorder, including children (Lyoo et al., 2002). Abnormalities of white matter integrity are reported in medication-naive adolescents with a first manic episode (Adler et al., 2006) and in unaffected relatives of patients with bipolar disorder (Sprooten et al., 2011). These findings suggest that structural vulnerability factors do exist in bipolar disorder and may be present as early as childhood and adolescence in affected individuals. They support the hypothesis that, at least in a subgroup, bipolar disorder is associated with abnormalities in brain development occurring from an early age.

Whether these abnormalities progress with the illness is not clear but this question is of considerable clinical significance, raising the possibility that early treatment may prevent further deterioration. Putative mechanisms for disease progression include impaired neurotrophic activity, apoptosis, and glutamate and glucocorticoid neuro-toxicity. Certain volumetric features may change over the course of the illness. The amygdala is reported to be smaller in children and adolescents with bipolar disor-der compared to healthy controls (Caetano et al., 2005). Strakowski, Delbello, and Adler (2005) speculated that enlargement of the amygdala might occur as the ill-ness progresses, in early adulthood. In their meta-analysis of volumetric studies in bipolar disorder, Hallahan et al. (2011) reported an association between reduction in cerebral volume and the duration of illness. There is evidence that patients with chronic, multiple-episode illness exhibit more severe cognitive impairment than young patients or those suffering less frequent recurrence: In a review of cross-sectional stud-ies, Robinson and Ferrier (2006) found that a worse previous course of bipolar illness (in terms of the length of illness, the number of manic episodes, and the number of hospitalizations) was associated with greater neuropsychological impairment. These structural and functional observations support the hypothesis that bipolar disorder is progressive, at least in some cases. However, longitudinal studies following high-risk subjects and patients with the disorder are required before the nature and develop-ment of these neuroanatomical and neurocognitive abnormalities can be established with any certainty.

## Schizophrenia and bipolar disorder: genetic, neuropathological, and neurocognitive similarities

In the course of the past decade, genetic, neuroanatomical, and neurocognitive simi-larities between bipolar disorder and schizophrenia have been uncovered. The results of genome-wide association studies are consistent with a significant overlap between the genetic risk factors for schizophrenia and affective disorders (Williams et al., 2011). Certain histopathological similarities are reported between schizophrenia and bipolar disorder involving neurones and oligodendrocytes in the prefrontal cortex (Benes et al., 2001; Uranova et al., 2004; Vostrikov et al., 2007). Some volumetric abnormal-ities may be features of both affective disorder and schizophrenia. For instance, a large meta-analysis of volumetric studies found that decreased whole brain and pre-frontal lobe volumes, lateral ventriculomegaly, and enlargement of the globus pallidus occurred in bipolar disorder compared to healthy controls. However, on compari-son with data on schizophrenia patients, the only significant differences between the groups were that the bipolar group had smaller lateral ventricles and larger amygdalae (Arnone et al., 2009). Cognitive deficits occur across several of the same domains in both schizophrenia and bipolar disorder, including verbal fluency, working memory, verbal and visual memory, mental speed, and executive control. Although these deficits appear to be of greater magnitude in schizophrenia, these differences in magnitude do not fully differentiate between the two disorders (Bora, Yücel, & Pantelis, 2010). These findings suggest that bipolar disorder and schizophrenia may not be discrete nosological entities but may in fact share certain pathophysiological features.

# Conclusion

The past decade has seen major advances in the neuroscience of bipolar disorder with encouraging progress in our understanding of the illness. Subtle neuronal, glial cell, and synaptic pathology has been identified. Neurotransmitter systems, neurotrophic factors, the HPA axis, and intracellular cascades have all been implicated in its etiology: abnormalities in each of these elements potentially impact on key neuronal circuits serving mood regulation and neurocognition. There is growing evidence for the view that, at least in some cases, the disorder has a neurodevelopmental component. Although preliminary findings suggest that in some, the illness may be progressive, large longitudinal studies are necessary to examine this hypothesis further. Neurobiological research has already borne fruit but much remains to be discovered about the pathophysiological processes of this complex illness.

# References

Adler, C. M., Adams, J., DelBello, M. P., Holland, S. K., Schmithorst, V., Levine, A., & Strakowski, S. M. (2006). Evidence of white matter pathology in bipolar disorder adolescents experiencing their first episode of mania: A diffusion tensor imaging study. *American Journal of Psychiatry*, *163*(2), 322–324.

Angelucci, F., Aloe, L., Jimenez-Vasquez, P., & Mathe, A. A. (2003). Lithium treatment alters brain concentrations of nerve growth factor, brain-derived neurotrophic factor and glial cell line-derived neurotrophic factor in a rat model of depression. *International Journal of Neuropsychopharmacology*, *6*(3), 225–231.

Arnone, D., Cavanagh, J., Gerber, D., Lawrie, S. M., Ebmeier, K. P., & McIntosh, A.M. (2009). Magnetic resonance imaging studies in bipolar disorder and schizophrenia: Meta-analysis. *British Journal of Psychiatry*, *195*(3), 194–201.

Benes, F. M., Vincent, S. L., & Todtenkopf, M. (2001). The density of pyramidal and nonpyramidal neurons in anterior cingulate cortex of schizophrenic and bipolar subjects. *Biological Psychiatry*, *50*(6), 395–406.

Bezchlibnyk, Y. B., Sun, X., Wang, J. F., MacQueen, G. M., McEwen, B. S., & Young, L. T. (2007). Neuron somal size is decreased in the lateral amygdalar nucleus of subjects with bipolar disorder. *Journal of Psychiatry & Neuroscience*, *32*(3), 203–210.

Bond, D. J., & Young, A. H. (2007). The hypothalamic–pituitary–adrenal axis in bipolar disorder. In J. C. Soares, & A. H. Young (Eds.), *Bipolar disorders. Basic mechanisms and therapeutic implications* (2nd ed., pp. 145–160). London: Informa Healthcare.

Bora, E., Fornito, A., Yücel, M., & Pantelis, C. (2010). Voxelwise meta-analysis of gray matter abnormalities in bipolar disorder. *Biological Psychiatry*, *67*(11), 1097–1105.

Bora, E., Yücel, M., & Pantelis, C. (2010). Cognitive impairment in schizophrenia and affective psychoses: Implications for DSM-V criteria and beyond. *Schizophrenia Bulletin*, *36*(1), 36–42.

Botteron, K. N., Vannier, M. W., Geller, B., Todd, R. D., & Lee, B. C. (1995) Preliminary study of magnetic resonance imaging characteristics in 8- to 16-year-olds with mania. *Journal of the American Academy of Child and Adolescent Psychiatry*, *34*(6), 742–749.

Bouras, C., Kövari, E., Hof, P. R., Riederer, B. M., & Giannakopoulos, P. (2001). Anterior cingulate cortex pathology in schizophrenia and bipolar disorder. *Acta Neuropathologica*, *102*(4), 373–379.

Bowley, M. P., Drevets, W. C., Ongür, D., & Price, J. L. (2002). Low glial numbers in the amygdala in major depressive disorder. *Biological Psychiatry*, *52*(5), 404–412.

Brambilla, P., Perez, J., Barale, F., Schettini, G., & Soares, J. C. (2003). GABAergic dysfunction in mood disorders. *Molecular Psychiatry*, *8*(8), 721–737.

Caetano, S. C., Olvera, R. L., Glahn, D., Fonseca, M., Pliszka, S., Soares, J. C. (2005). Fronto-limbic brain abnormalities in juvenile onset bipolar disorder. *Biological Psychiatry*, *58*(7), 525–531.

Cardon, L. R., & Bell, J. I. (2001). Association study designs for complex diseases. *Nature Reviews Genetics*, *2*(2), 91–99.

Ceulemans, S., De Zutter, S., Heyrman, L., Norrback, K. F., Nordin, A., Nilsson, L. G., & Claes, S. (2011). Evidence for the involvement of the glucocorticoid receptor gene in bipolar disorder in an isolated northern Swedish population. *Bipolar Disorders*, *13*(7–8), 614–623.

Chen, G., & Manji, H.K. (2007). Cell membrane and signal transduction pathways-implications for the pathophysiology of bipolar disorder. In J. C. Soares, & A. H. Young (Eds.), *Bipolar disorders. Basic mechanisms and therapeutic implications* (2nd ed., pp. 109–129). London: Informa Healthcare.

Clark, L., Iversen, S. D., & Goodwin, G. M. (2002). Sustained attention deficit in bipolar disorder. *British Journal of Psychiatry*, *180*(4), 313–319.

Cotter, D., Mackay, D., Chana, G., Beasley, C., Landau, S., & Everall, I. P. (2002). Reduced neuronal size and glial cell density in area 9 of the dorsolateral prefrontal cortex in subjects with major depressive disorder. *Cerebral Cortex*, *12*(4), 386–394.

Coyle, J.T. (2004). The GABA-glutamate connection in schizophrenia: Which is the proximate cause? *Biochemical Pharmacology*, *68*(8), 1507–1514.

de Sousa, R. T., van de Bilt, M. T., Diniz, B. S., Ladeira, R. B., Portella, L. V., Souza, D. O., & Machado-Viera, R. (2011). Lithium increases plasma brain-derived neurotrophic factor in acute bipolar mania: A preliminary 4-week study. *Neuroscience Letters*, *494*(1), 54–56.

Delvecchio, G., Fossati, P., Boyer, P., Brambilla, P., Falkai, P., Gruber, O., & Frangou, S. (2012). Common and distinct neural correlates of emotional processing in bipolar disorder and major depressive disorder: A voxel-based meta-analysis of functional magnetic resonance imaging studies. *European Neuropsychopharmacology*, *22*(2), 100–113.

Eastwood, S. L., & Harrison, P. J. (2001). Synaptic pathology in the anterior cingulate cortex in schizophrenia and mood disorders. A review and a Western blot study of synaptophysin, GAP-43 and the complexins. *Brain Research Bulletin*, *55*(5), 569–578.

Eastwood, S. L., & Harrison, P. J. (2010). Markers of glutamate synaptic transmission and plasticity are increased in the anterior cingulate cortex in bipolar disorder. *Biological Psychiatry*, *67*(11), 1010–1016.

Ellison-Wright, I., & Bullmore, E. (2010) Anatomy of bipolar disorder and schizophrenia: A meta-analysis. *Schizophrenia Research*, *117*(1), 1–12.

Fan, J., & Sklar, P. (2008). Genetics of bipolar disorder: Focus on BDNF Val66Met polymorphism. In N. Foundation (Ed.), Novartis Foundation Symposium 289. *Growth factors and psychiatric disorders* (pp. 60–73, 87–93). Chichester, UK: Wiley.

Fernandes, B. S., Gama, C. S., Maria Ceresér, K., Yatham, L. N., Fries, G. R., Colpo, G., & Kapczinski, F. (2011). Brain-derived neurotrophic factor as a state-marker of mood episodes in bipolar disorders: A systematic review and meta-regression analysis. *Journal of Psychiatric Research*, *45*(8), 995–1004.

Garakani, A., Charney, D. S., & Anand, A. (2007). Abnormalities in catecholamines and pathophysiology of bipolar disorder. In J. C. Soares, & A. H. Young (Eds.), *Bipolar disorders. Basic mechanisms and therapeutic implications* (2nd ed., pp. 33–65). New York, London: Informa Healthcare.

Gray, L. J., Dean, B., Kronsbein, H. C., Robinson, P. J., & Scarr, E. (2010). Region and diagnosis-specific changes in synaptic proteins in schizophrenia and bipolar I disorder. *Psychiatry Research, 178*(2), 374–380.

Hajek, T., Carrey, N., & Alda, M. (2005). Neuroanatomical abnormalities as risk factors for bipolar disorder. *Bipolar Disorders, 7*(5), 393–403.

Hallahan, B., Newell, J., Soares, J. C., Brambilla, P., Strakowski, S. M., Fleck, D. E., & McDonald, C. (2011). Structural magnetic resonance imaging in bipolar disorder: An international collaborative mega-analysis of individual adult patient data. *Biological Psychiatry, 69*(4), 326–335.

Heng, S., Song, A. W., & Sim, K. (2010). White matter abnormalities in bipolar disorder: Insights from diffusion tensor imaging studies. *Journal of Neural Transmission, 117*(5), 639–654.

Lachman, H. M., Pedrosa, E., Petruolo, O. A., Cockerham, M., Papolos, A., Novak, T., & Stopkova, P. (2007). Increase in GSK-3beta gene copy number variation in bipolar disorder. *American Journal of Medical Genetics. Part B, Neuropsychiatric Genetics, 144B*(3), 259–265.

Liu, L., Schulz, S. C., Lee, S., Reutiman, T. J., & Fatemi, S. H. (2007). Hippocampal CA1 pyramidal cell size is reduced in bipolar disorder. *Cell and Molecular Neurobiology, 27*(3), 351–358.

Lyoo, I. K., Lee, H. K., Jung, J. H., Noam, G. G., & Renshaw, P. F. (2002). White matter hyperintensities on magnetic resonance imaging of the brain in children with psychiatric disorders. *Comprehensive Psychiatry, 43*(5), 361–368.

Mahon, K., Burdick, K. E., & Szeszko, P. R. (2010). A role for white matter abnormalities in the pathophysiology of bipolar disorder. *Neuroscience and Biobehavioral Reviews, 34*(4), 533–554.

Martínez-Arán, A., Vieta, E., Colom, F., Reinares, M., Benabarre, A., Gastó, C., & Salamero, M. (2000). Cognitive dysfunctions in bipolar disorder: Evidence of neuropsychological disturbances. *Psychotherapy and Psychosomatics, 69*(1), 2–18.

McEwen, B. S. (2005). Glucocorticoids, depression, and mood disorders: Structural remodeling in the brain. *Metabolism, 54*(5), 20–23.

McIntosh, A. M., Hall, J., Lymer, G. K., Sussmann, J. E., & Lawrie, S. M. (2009). Genetic risk for white matter abnormalities in bipolar disorder. *International Review of Psychiatry, 21*(4), 387–393.

McQueen, M. B., Devlin, B., Faraone, S. V., Nimgaonkar, V. L., Sklar, P., Smoller, J. W., & Laird, N. M. (2005). Combined analysis from eleven linkage studies of bipolar disorder provides strong evidence of susceptibility loci on chromosomes 6q and 8q. *American Journal of Human Genetics, 77*(4), 582–595.

Morice, R. (1990). Cognitive inflexibility and pre-frontal dysfunction in schizophrenia and mania. *British Journal of Psychiatry, 157*(3), 50–54.

Öngür, D., Drevets, W. C., & Price, J. L. (1998). Glial reduction in the subgenual prefrontal cortex in mood disorders. *Proceedings of the National Academy of Sciences of USA, 95*(22), 13290–13295.

Psychiatric GWAS Consortium Bipolar Disorder Working Group. (2011). Large-scale genome-wide association analysis of bipolar disorder identifies a new susceptibility locus near *ODZ4. Nature Genetics, 43*(10), 977–983.

Rajkowska, G., Halaris, A., & Selemon, L. D. (2001). Reductions in neuronal and glial density characterize the dorsolateral pre-frontal cortex in bipolar disorder. *Biological Psychiatry*, *49*(9), 741–752.

Rajkowska, G., & Miguel-Hidalgo, J. (2007). Gliogenesis and glial pathology in depression. *CNS & Neurological Disorders Drug Targets*, *6*(3), 219–233.

Regenold, W. T., Phatak, P., Marano, C. M., Gearhart, L., Viens, C. H., & Hisley, K. C. (2007). Myelin staining of deep white matter in the dorsolateral pre-frontal cortex in schizophrenia, bipolar disorder and unipolar major depression. *Psychiatry Research*, *151*(3), 179–188.

Robinson, L.J., & Ferrier, I.N. (2006) Evolution of cognitive impairment in bipolar disorder: A systematic review of cross-sectional evidence. *Bipolar Disorders*, *8*(2), 103–116.

Robinson, L. J., Thompson, J. M., Gallagher, P., Goswami, U., Young, A. H., Ferrier, I. N., & Moore, P. B. (2006). A meta-analysis of cognitive deficits in euthymic patients with bipolar disorder. *Journal of Affective Disorders*, *93*(1-3), 105–115.

Schloesser, R. H., Huang, J., Klein, P. S., & Manji, H. K. (2008). Cellular plasticity cascades in the pathophysiology and treatment of bipolar disorder. *Neuropsychopharmacology*, *33*(1), 110–133.

Sprooten, E., Sussmann, J. E., Clugston, A., Peel, A., McKirdy, J., Moorhead, T. W., & McIntosh, A. M. (2011). White matter integrity in individuals at high genetic risk of bipolar disorder. *Biological Psychiatry*, *70*(4), 350–356.

Stahl, S. (2009). Signal transduction and the chemically addressed nervous system. In S. M. Stahl (Ed.), *Stahl's essential psychopharmacology. Neuroscientific basis and practical applications* (pp. 51–89). Cambridge: Cambridge University Press.

Strakowski, S. M., Wilson, D. R., Tohen, M., Woods, B. T., Douglass, A. W., & Stoll, A. L. (1993). Structural brain abnormalities in first-episode mania. *Biological Psychiatry*, *33*(8), 602–609.

Strakowski, S. M., Delbello, M. P., & Adler, C. M. (2005). The functional neuroanatomy of bipolar disorder: A review of neuroimaging findings. *Molecular Psychiatry*, *10*(1), 105–116.

Sweeney, J. A., Kmiec, J. A., & Kupfer, D. J. (2000). Neuropsychological impairments in bipolar and unipolar mood disorders on the CANTAB neurocognitive battery. *Biological Psychiatry*, *48*(7), 674–685.

Szczepankiewicz, A., Leszczyzyńska-Rodziewica, A., Pawlak, J., Rajewska-Rager, A., Dmitrzak-Weglarz, M., Wilkosc, M., & Hauser, J. (2011). Glucocorticoid receptor polymorphism is associated with major depression and predominance of depression in the course of bipolar disorder. *Journal of Affective Disorders*, *134*(1–3), 138–144.

Tkachev, D., Mimmack, M. L., Ryan, M. M., Wayland, M., Freeman, T., Jones, P. B., & Bahn, S. (2003). Oligodendrocyte dysfunction in schizophrenia and bipolar disorder. *Lancet*, *362*(9386), 798–805.

Tucker, R. P., & Chiquet-Ehrismann, R. (2006). Teneurins: A conserved family of trans-membrane proteins involved in intercellular signaling during development. *Developmental Biology*, *290*(2), 237–245.

Uranova, N. A., Vostrikov, V. M., Orlovskaya, D. D., & Rachmanova, V. I. (2004). Oligoden-droglial density in the prefrontal cortex in schizophrenia and mood disorders: A study from the Stanley Neuropathology Consortium. *Schizophrenia Research*, *67*(2–3), 269–275.

Vostrikov, V. M., Uranova, N. A., & Orlovskaya, D. D. (2007). Deficit of perineuronal oligo-dendrocytes in the prefrontal cortex in schizophrenia and mood disorders. *Schizophrenia Research*, *94*(1–3), 273–280.

Wang, F., McIntosh, A. M., He, Y., Gelernter, J., & Blumberg, H. P. (2011). The association of genetic variation in *CACNA1C* with structure and function of a frontotemporal system. *Bipolar Disorders*, *13*(7–8), 696–700.

Watson, S., Gallagher, P., Ritchie, J. C., Ferrier, I. N., & Young, A. H. (2004). Hypothalamic-pituitary-adrenal axis function in patients with bipolar disorder. *British Journal of Psychiatry, 184*(6), 496–502.

Wellcome Trust Case Control Consortium (2007). Genome-wide association study of 14,000 cases of seven common diseases and 3,000 shared controls. *Nature, 447*(7145), 661–678.

Williams, H. J., Craddock, N., Russo, G., Hamshere, M. L., Moskvina, V., Dwyer, S., & O'Donovan, M. C. (2011). Most genome-wide significant susceptibility loci for schizophrenia and bipolar disorder reported to date cross-traditional diagnostic boundaries. *Human Molecular Genetics, 20*(2), 387–391.

Williams, R. S., Cheng, L., Mudge, A. W., & Harwood, A. J. (2002). A common mechanism of action for three mood-stabilising drugs. *Nature, 417*(6886), 292–295.

Yüksel, C., & Öngür, D. (2010). Magnetic resonance spectroscopy studies of glutamate-related abnormalities in mood disorders. *Biological Psychiatry, 68*(9), 785–794.

Zhang, X., Zhang, Z., Sha, W., Xie, C., Xi, G., Zhou, H., & Zhang, Y. (2010). Effect of treatment on serum glial cell line-derived neurotrophic factor in bipolar patients. *Journal of Affective Disorders, 126*(1–2), 326–329.

# 13

# Psychological Theories of and Therapies for Bipolar Disorder

## Kim Wright
### Exeter, UK

Compared to psychological approaches to unipolar depression and anxiety disorders, the development of psychological models of, and corresponding treatments for, bipolar disorders (BDs) has a relatively brief history. This chapter describes four broad perspectives on psychological disorder that have generated influential theories of the psychological processes underlying both vulnerability to BD and the maintenance of episodes. The status of each perspective with respect to empirical support for the theory and for linked psychological intervention programmes is discussed. Finally, it is argued that there are important points of convergence between the accounts.

## Cognitive Theories

According to the hugely influential theory of the etiology and maintenance of depression advanced by Beck (1967, 1976), depression results when latent negative schemata, formed on the basis of early experiences, are activated by congruent trigger events, resulting in information-processing biases that influence the individual's thoughts, feelings, and behavior to produce the cognitive, emotional, somatic, and behavioral symptoms of depression. Beck (1996) later advanced the notion of modes, which are integrated networks of information about cognition, affect, and behavior that are activated by congruent life events and dictate patterns of thinking and behavioral response. Building upon this framework, Beck and colleagues (Newman, Leahy, Beck, Reilly-Harrington, & Gyulai, 2002) have proposed that schemata are bidirectional, such that a schema focusing upon worthiness, for example, would manifest as a sense of extreme unworthiness during depression and a sense of extreme worthiness during mania. As with Beck's model of depression, these schemata, or modes, are proposed to be activated by congruent life events, resulting in biases in information processing and consequent changes in thinking and behavior. Commensurate with this account, individuals with BD have been found to show evidence of information-processing biases during mania: Currently manic individuals have been found to show a bias toward rewarding stimuli (Murphy et al., 1999), while currently hypomanic individuals have been found to show impaired memory for depression-relevant

*The Wiley-Blackwell Handbook of Mood Disorders*, Second Edition. Edited by Mick Power.
© 2013 John Wiley & Sons, Ltd. Published 2013 by John Wiley & Sons, Ltd.

material (Lex, Hautzinger, & Meyer, 2011). In support of the notion that schemata are bidirectional in BD, currently manic individuals have been found to show elevated endorsement of over-positive beliefs about the self, as well as elevated levels of self-esteem on a repertory grid task, while currently bipolar depressed individuals showed reduced self-esteem (Ashworth, Blackburn, & McPherson, 1982; Goldberg, Wenze, Welker, Steer, & Beck, 2005). Furthermore, two studies (Alloy, Reilly-Harrington, Fresco, Whitehouse, & Zechmeister, 1999; Ashworth, Blackburn, & McPherson, 1985) have found self-perceptions to vary across mood states in BD and to be more positive in hypomanic than in depressed phases. However, less compatible with the view of schema as bidirectional and unidimensional in terms of valence, self-esteem has been found to be no higher in individuals currently experiencing mania than in individuals without BD (van der Gucht, Morris, Lancaster, Kinderman, & Bentall, 2009), while findings from several studies report elevations in negative self-concept in mania when assessed using an implicit recall-based task (Lyon, Startup, & Bentall, 1999) and a self-report measure of self-esteem (Scott & Pope, 2003). Furthermore, while negative attributional style has been found to be associated with both depressive and manic symptom level, positive attributional style was not found to be elevated in mania (Reilly-Harrington et al., 2010).

Thus, while some aspects of self-perception may become more positive in mania, particularly when compared to self-perception during depression, the evidence does not seem to support the presence of unequivocally positive self-concept during mania. Indeed, it may be the case that some "depressogenic" cognitive styles are retained or even enhanced during mania.

Alternative cognitive accounts have proposed that vulnerability to mania is contributed to by overly positive appraisals of internal states, rather than by a generalized tendency toward positive self-concept. Healy and Williams (1989) and Jones (2001) have the tendency to misattribute pleasant, activated physical states to positive, global, stable, internal causes that characterizes individuals vulnerable to mania, and have highlighted the potential of circadian rhythm disruption (see below) to produce such states. In support of this perspective, a tendency to make positive self-dispositional appraisals for hypomania-relevant internal states has been found to be elevated in individuals with BD, as compared to individuals without (Jones, Mansell, & Waller, 2006).

The concept of misinterpretation of certain internal states is a key to the cognitive model of mood swings proposed by Mansell, Morrison, Reid, Lowens, and Tai (2007), which suggests that extreme appraisals of internal state, for example, believing that increases in energy are a signal that anything can be achieved, contribute to the development and maintenance of bipolar episodes. Similarly to Beck, they suggest that these appraisal tendencies are the result of beliefs about the self, the world, and others, which are formed on the basis of life experiences. However, the Mansell model emphasizes the potential of ongoing experiences during adulthood to shape beliefs and appraisals. Episodes are developed and maintained as a result of extreme appraisals leading to behaviors intended to increase or decrease activation levels, and thus prevent disaster or attain success. These behaviors lead to changes in internal state, which then become the subject of further extreme appraisals. In support of the model, endorsement of extreme appraisals of internal states has been found to be associated with presence of, or vulnerability to BD (Alatiq, Crane, Williams, & Goodwin, 2010;

Mansell, 2006; Mansell & Jones, 2006; Mansell et al., 2011), and to predict bipolar symptoms 4 weeks later (Dodd, Mansell, Morrison, & Tai, 2011). With respect to the prediction that individuals with BD target behaviors toward modifying positive and negative mood states, there is evidence that in response to positive mood, individuals with BD are more likely to engage both in thought processes that might be expected to enhance positive mood and in those that might dampen it than individuals without BD (Gruber, Eidelman, Johnson, Smith, & Harvey, 2011; Johnson et al., 2008).

In summary, cognitive theories of BD propose that the symptoms of BD are the result of faulty appraisal of immediate experience, arising from underlying beliefs that are formed on the basis of life experience. The models differ in what they view as the key focus of faulty appraisal, furthermore, the Mansell model particularly emphasizes the role of behavior in driving the maintenance cycle of both depression and mania.

## Cognitive therapy

Cognitive behavioral therapy (CBT), which has been used extensively in the treatment of depression, has more recently been adapted for use with individuals with BD as a means of relapse prevention (Ball et al., 2006; Basco & Rush, 1996; Lam, Hayward, Watkins, Wright, & Sham, 2005; Lam, Jones, Hayward, & Bright, 1999; Lam et al., 2003; Newman et al., 2002; Scott, Garland, & Moorhead, 2001; Scott et al., 2006). Components of CBT for BD often include psychoeducation, relapse prevention including identification and management of prodromes, social rhythm stabilization, work on dysfunctional beliefs and thoughts, medication adherence work, and management of stressful life events (cf. Gutierrez & Scott, 2004). The study by Ball et al. (2006) differed from the others in that it adopted a schema-focused approach. To date, the findings from randomized controlled trials of CBT for BD have been mixed, with the largest study (Scott et al., 2006) failing to find a benefit. With respect to the other trials, the benefit appears to be the strongest with respect to reductions in depressive symptoms and reductions in risk of depressive relapse. Similarly, in a comparison of psychoeducation plus CBT with psychoeducation alone, additional benefit conferred by CBT was with respect to reduced time spent in depression (Zaretsky, Lancee, Miller, Harris, & Parikh, 2008). There have been a small number of trials of CBT for acute bipolar depression. Zaretsky, Segal, and Gemar (1999) compared the efficacy of CBT for bipolar versus unipolar depression, and found both groups to show a similar reduction in levels of depressive symptoms following CBT. The Systematic Treatment Enhancement Program for Bipolar Disorder (STEP-BD) involved a comparison of three intensive psychological therapies (CBT, IPSRT, and FFT) against collaborative care, among individuals with acute bipolar depression. All three intensive psychological therapy conditions were associated with faster time to recovery and greater probability of staying well over 1 year than was collaborative care (Miklowitz et al., 2007).

In common with most psychological therapies for BD, CBT tends to include a substantial "psychoeducation" component. This component has been tested as an intervention in its own right, in both individual and group formats. Individual psychoeducation has been found to reduce rates of manic relapse (Perry, Tarrier, Morris,

McCarthy, & Limb, 1999), while group psychoeducation has been found to increase time to episode recurrence, reduce rates of recurrence, and decrease time spent in bipolar episodes over 5 years (Colom et al., 2003, 2009), while group psychoeducation involving both individuals with BD and a companion has been found to increase time to relapse and decrease rates of relapse over 60 weeks (D'Souza, Piskulic, & Sundram, 2010). The success of psychoeducation-based interventions, combined with the prominence of psychoeducation within the treatment protocol for both CBT and focused family therapy (FFT) for BD, has led some proponents of psychoeducation to argue that psychoeducation is the primary active ingredient in both approaches (Colom, Pacchiarotti, & Vieta, 2006).

Recent developments in cognitive therapy for BD include early-phase testing of a cognitive behavioral intervention derived from the model proposed by Mansell and colleagues (Searson, Mansell, Lowens, & Tai, 2012). In addition, mindfulness-based cognitive therapy (MBCT), originally developed for individuals with recurrent unipolar depression, has been tested in individuals with BD in several pilot studies (Mirabel-Sarron et al., 2009; Weber et al., 2010; Williams et al., 2008). While initial findings are encouraging with respect to both new approaches, definitive randomized controlled trials are yet to be conducted.

## Behavioral Perspectives

While there is no comprehensive behavioral model of BD, a theory of vulnerability to depression that emphasizes the role of behavior has been advanced as a reformulation of the psychodynamic construct of the manic defense. Neale (1988) proposed that when life events occur that pose a threat to fragile self-esteem, an individual with BD may react by experiencing grandiose thoughts that serve the function of preventing depressive cognitions from entering cognitive awareness. In this way, mania represents a last effort at exerting control in the face of possible hopelessness and despair. If the individual is unable to employ such a cognitive defense mechanism, depression results. In a "behavioral" reworking of this idea, Bentall and colleagues have suggested that individuals with BD may engage in activating behaviors as a means of avoiding depression (Thomas, Knowles, Tai, & Bentall, 2007). In support of this, they note the evidence for negative cognitive style in mania, as well as evidence that individuals with, or vulnerable to, mania self-report responding to negative emotions with behaviors that likely to increase high-activation positive affect, for example, risk-taking (Thomas & Bentall, 2002; Thomas et al., 2007). They suggest that engaging in such behaviors may increase risk of a manic episode developing, for example, because of the interaction between these behaviors with biobehavioral vulnerabilities (see below) such as circadian rhythm instability and dysregulation of the behavioral activation system (BAS).

## Family-Based Perspectives

The results of studies investigating the impact of the family environment upon individuals diagnosed with schizophrenia (e.g., Brown, Birley, & Wing, 1972; Brown,

Monck, Carstairs, & Wing, 1962) suggest that the emotional quality of this environment is an important predictor of the course of the illness. These studies have tended to measure aspects of a construct termed "expressed emotion" (EE). The EE construct is derived from empirical findings rather than from a theoretical background. It relates to incidences, measured by the above studies, of expressed criticism, hostility, and emotional over-involvement by family members. The EE construct also includes an inverse component that of expressed emotional warmth. Studies of the relapse rates of individuals returning to high and low EE families following an episode of schizophrenia have found that those in high contact with a high EE family show a higher rate of relapse (cf. review by Bebbington & Kuipers, 1994). These findings appear to support a role for expressed emotion in the maintenance rather than the onset of schizophrenia.

Several studies have investigated the impact of high EE upon the course of BD. These have found that high levels of critical, hostile, or emotionally over-involved attitudes in families are associated with elevated rates of relapse and poor symptomatic outcomes in individuals with the disorder, particularly with respect to depression (Honig, Hofman, Rozendaal, & Dingemans, 1997; Miklowitz, Goldstein, Nuechterlein, Snyder, & Mintz, 2003; O'Connell, Mayo, Flatow, Cuthbertson, & O'Brien, 1991; Priebe, Wildgrube, & Muller-Oerlinghausen, 1989; Kim & Miklowitz, 2004; Yan, Hammen, Cohen, Daley, & Henry, 2004).

## Family-based interventions

Correspondingly, family-based interventions for BD have been developed. Such treatments have tended to include elements of psychoeducation, training in communication skills, coping skills and problem-solving, and emphasis upon the need for support by both individuals with BD and family members (e.g., Goldstein & Miklowitz, 1997). Several randomized controlled trials of FFT have been conducted, and these have found FFT to decrease risk of relapse over 2 years (Miklowitz, George, Richards, Simoneau, & Suddath, 2003) and, when compared to individual psychoeducation-based therapy, to reduce hospitalization rates at 1- to 2-year follow-up (Rea et al., 2003). While one study of FFT and medication, versus multifamily therapy and medication, compared to medication alone found no additional benefit of either form of family therapy for individuals currently experiencing a bipolar episode, individuals in families with greater difficulty at baseline (higher conflict or lower problem-solving skills) showed a greater benefit of either form of FFT on depression (Miller, Solomon, Ryan, & Keitner, 2004; Miller et al., 2008).

## Biobehavioral Theories

As is evident from the above review, several psychological accounts of BD make reference to interaction between psychological processes and vulnerabilities in biobehavioral systems. Two biobehavioral accounts have been particularly influential in this respect, and in guiding the content of psychological interventions. The first account proposes that vulnerability to depressive and manic episodes is, at least in part, a result of severe disruptions to the functioning of the system governing circadian rhythms. The second hypothesizes that dysregulation of the system governing approach motivation is a fundamental vulnerability factor.

## Circadian rhythm hypotheses

It has been proposed that bipolar episodes represent periods of external desynchronization of circadian rhythms (Wehr & Goodwin, 1983), and that individuals with BD have heightened sensitivity to events which disrupt circadian rhythms, including shift work or trans-meridian travel. While clear evidence that BD is characterized by pervasive desynchronization between biological rhythms and environmental cycles has not been forthcoming, a number of studies report disturbances in activity patterns, body temperature rhythms, and the secretion rhythms of some hormones in the acute and remitted phases of BD (e.g., Jones, Hare, & Evershed, 2005; Kennedy, Kutcher, Ralevski, & Brown, 1996; Linkowski et al., 1994; Meyer & Maier, 2006; Sachar, 1975; Salvatore et al., 2008; Tsujimoto, Yamada, Shimoda, Hanada, & Takahashi, 1990). Also, events that would be expected to cause acute disturbances to circadian rhythms have been found to be associated with the development of mania (Malkoff-Schwartz et al., 1998), and eastwards air travel, an event likely to delay the endogenous circadian rhythm relative to environmental sleep–wake cues, appear to be particularly potent in promoting mania (Jauhar & Weller, 1982; Young, 1995). Stabilization of circadian rhythm phase has been proposed as a mechanism by which lithium and other medications used in BD exert a mood-stabilizing effect (e.g., Abe, Herzog, & Block, 2000; Hallonquist, Goldberg, & Brandes, 1986; Yin, Wang, Klein, & Lazar, 2006), while there is evidence that bright light, a powerful zeitgeber, may be more effective in hastening recovery from bipolar as compared to unipolar depression (Benedetti, Colombo, Barbini, Campori, & Smeraldi, 2001; Deltito, Moline, Pollack, Martin, & Maremmani, 1991). To date, the precise pathway by which circadian disrupting events may provoke affective episodes is not clear, however, the mechanism may include psychological processes. As outlined previously, it has been suggested that the physical sensations and behavioral effects of severe circadian disruption may constitute an internal event which is then misinterpreted as evidence for positive personal qualities or potential (e.g., "this buzzy feeling is a sign that I am a creative, dynamic person who can accomplish a lot"), which may then lead to activating behaviors (such as staying up late working on projects) likely to hasten affective relapse through their disruptive effect upon circadian rhythms (Healy & Williams, 1989; Jones, 2001).

Interpersonal therapy (IPT) is an approach that has been used in the treatment of depression, and interpersonal and social rhythm therapy (IPSRT) represents an adaptation of IPT for individuals with BD. In addition to psychoeducation and a focus upon strategies for managing interpersonal events, such as social role changes or disputes, IPSRT includes work upon regulation of social rhythms.

Frank et al. (1997, 1999, 2005) have carried out a two-stage randomized, controlled trial of IPSRT and clinical management (CM), which comprised support, education, and review of symptoms and treatment. Participants were allocated to one of four conditions (IPSRT–IPSRT, CM–CM, IPSRT–CM, or CM–IPSRT) in addition to receiving standard pharmacotherapy. Stage I occurred during the acute phase of the illness. Individuals receiving IPSRT were found to achieve more stable social rhythms than those receiving CM. No differences between the treatment strategies were found with regard to time to stabilization. However, after controlling for covariates of survival time, time to relapse was found to be significantly longer in those who received IPSRT during the acute phase (Stage I), regardless of treatment modality during Stage II, and increased ability to regulate social rhythms was found to be associated with reduced likelihood of recurrence during the stabilization phase (Frank et al., 2005). In addition, in individuals with acute bipolar depression, the STEP-BD study found IPSRT not to differ from CBT or FFT in terms of time to recovery and probability of staying well over 1 year, and to be superior to collaborative care. Furthermore, the stabilization of social rhythms forms part of a number of intervention packages for BD, including CBT and psychoeducation (Miklowitz, Goodwin, Bauer, & Geddes, 2008).

## Approach system dysregulation hypotheses

The past few decades have seen a proliferation of research into the possibility that dysregulation of the system that governs approach behavior, the BAS, contributes significantly to the development and maintenance of bipolar episodes. Specifically, it has been hypothesized that in individuals vulnerable to BD, the BAS is more sensitive to challenges, namely potential reward and frustrative nonreward, and that following such a challenge BAS activation—or deactivation—persists for an extended period of time (Depue & Iacono, 1989; Depue, Krauss, & Spoont, 1987). An attractive aspect of this account is that the BAS can be described in terms of neurobiology as well as in terms of cognition, behavior, and emotional experience. Correspondingly, studies that have tested the BAS dysregulation hypothesis span a range of levels of explanation. A number of studies report an association between BD and differences in the structure of key brain areas implicated in reward processing including the ventral striatum and prefrontal cortex (see Urosevic, Abramson, Harmon-Jones, & Alloy, 2008, for a review). Fewer studies of the functioning of such brain areas have been conducted in individuals with BD, however, currently euthymic individuals with BD have been found to show exaggerated elevations in relative left frontal cortical activity when faced with a challenging task, relative to individuals without BD (Harmon-Jones et al., 2008). Individuals vulnerable to hypomania, but without clinically diagnosed BD, have been found to show elevated relative left frontal activation in response to an anger-inducing event (Harmon-Jones et al., 2002) and to differ from nonvulnerable individuals in terms of the pattern of striatal activity during a reinforcement learning task (O'Sullivan, Szczepanowski, El-Deredy, Mason, & Bentall, 2011). At the level of self-reported affect and behavior, individuals with BD have been found to self-report greater trait sensitivity of the BAS system to potential reward (Alloy et al., 2006, 2008; Salavert et al., 2007), and this trait sensitivity has been found to prospectively predict symptom levelsamong individuals with BD-I (Meyer, Johnson, & Winters, 2001) and time until hypomania onset in individuals with bipolar spectrum disorders (Alloy et al.,

2008). Experimental and observational studies have found vulnerability to mania to be associated with increased positive emotional reactivity (Gruber, Harvey, & Purcell, 2011), increased sensitivity to positive stimuli (Pavlova, Uher, Dennington, Wright, & Donaldson, 2011), greater surges in self-reported approach motivation or approach tendencies when faced with a challenge (Harmon-Jones et al., 2008; Meyer, Beevers, Johnson, & Simmons, 2007), and sustained self-reported positive affect or approach motivation following reward (Farmer et al., 2006; Wright, Lam, & Brown, 2008), while levels of high, rather than low, activation positive mood states predict manic symptoms 6 months prospectively (Gruber et al., 2009). Furthermore, onset of mania has been found to be associated with achievement-related, rather than more general, positive life events (Johnson et al., 2000, 2008).

While the BAS dysregulation hypothesis can be viewed as a "biological" account of vulnerability, it includes an important role for cognition and behavior in conferring vulnerability to BD and in the maintenance of episodes. Cognition and behavior are viewed as intrinsic aspects of this biobehavioral system: In order to organize behavior toward goals, the individual would usually need to focus attention upon the potential reward, and to direct his or her behavior in service of the goal. Cognitive and behavioral processes also have the potential to influence BAS activation because these processes can create opportunities for potential reward, for example, the behavior of going out to a party creates opportunities for exciting social interaction. In addition, directing attention toward potential opportunities and dwelling upon or constructing ambitious goals also create further "input" to the BAS.

Correspondingly, a number of studies have investigated reward or goal-related cognition and behavior in individuals with BD, at both a trait level, and in terms of changes in cognition or behavior following a goal-striving event or an increase in positive mood. In relation to long-term goals, a history of mania has been found to be associated with elevated expectancies of achievement in domains relating to public recognition (Johnson, Eisner, & Carver, 2009). Following an initial success, individuals at risk of BD have been found to show increases in confidence and optimism (Johnson, Ruggero, & Carver, 2005; Stern & Berrenberg, 1979) that appear to extend beyond the confines of the prompting event (Eisner, Johnson, & Carver, 2008). In an experience-sampling study looking at striving behavior in relation to personal goals, Johnson and Fulford (2009) found that following unexpectedly high goal progress, individuals with BD persisted in striving toward that goal, whereas individuals without BD reduced their efforts. In summary then, individuals vulnerable to mania not only appear to hold trait-like high achievement expectancies, but also, following BAS activation, show exaggerated increases in, and expansiveness of, cognitive processes linked to reward striving, as well as sustained goal striving behavior. Importantly, these differences are apparent during euthymia, and as such may be processes that contribute toward the development of a manic episode. Nevertheless, research has yet to test the hypothesis that these processes do indeed play a causal role in the development of mania.

Several recent models of BD highlight the potential for BAS dysregulation to both drives and are fuelled by goal-relevant cognition. Urosevic et al. (2008) have argued that vulnerability to manic episodes is contributed to by a combination of an overly sensitive, chronometrically dysregulated BAS, and extreme relevance and efficacy appraisals. They propose that, compared to individuals without BD, individuals with BD create more BAS activating and deactivating events (e.g., through engaging in intense reward-striving behavior) and show an exaggerated and sustained BAS response. This process is contributed to by a tendency to appraise a wider range of events as potentially BAS relevant (resulting in more frequent activation or deactivation of the BAS) and to hold more extreme views on personal efficacy (contributing to a stronger BAS response).

In another model that makes reference to the potential impact of differences in reward sensitivity, Johnson (2005) has proposed that vulnerability to mania is contributed to by unrealistically high confidence, resulting from a reward-sensitive individual experiencing a goal attainment life event, which interacts with the individual's ambitions to lead to intense goal striving. At this point, the resulting behaviors and their sequelae further activate the reward system, triggering an upward spiral to hypomania.

To date, only one published study reports the evaluation of a psychological therapy arising directly from this body of research. The GOALS program was designed to help participants to improve goal regulation skills. An open, uncontrolled trial revealed significant decreases in manic symptoms from pre- to posttreatment, and high levels of participant satisfaction with the intervention (Johnson & Fulford, 2009). Further investigation of the intervention within randomized, controlled trials is needed before strong conclusions can be drawn; however, the GOALS program appears to represent a promising, theoretically grounded intervention specifically aimed at reducing mania vulnerability.

## Points of Integration

As is clear above, the psychological and biopsychological processes that may contribute to BD have been conceptualized from a number of different perspectives; correspondingly, a range of psychological interventions has been developed or adapted. Despite this apparent plurality, research highlights the high degree of overlap between different psychological intervention packages (Milkowitz et al., 2008) in terms of the techniques deployed. This is reflected in the guidance issued by the UK National Institute for Health and Clinical Excellence (NICE), which recommends "structured psychological interventions (including) psychoeducation about the illness, the importance of regular daily routine and sleep and concordance with medication monitoring of mood, detection of early warning signs, and strategies to prevent progression into full-blown episodes (and enhancement of) general coping strategies" for people with BD recovering from an acute episode (NICE, 2006, pp. 38). Less often noted are the points of convergence between the theories that guide current treatments. The section below elaborates upon some of the themes common to several theoretical perspectives, and speculates upon the implications of these for psychological interventions for BD.

A number of accounts are suggestive of a close interrelationship between the functioning of biobehavioral systems, cognition, and behavior across the life span. This interaction may go beyond a relatively simple diathesis–stress model in which dysregulation of biological systems, or of belief systems formed early in life, represent underlying vulnerability factors that are triggered by corresponding life events, such as schedule-disrupting events or achievement striving opportunities. Instead, several accounts speak to a process whereby the individual's belief systems and behavioral repertoires are shaped over time by the experience of her own mood fluctuations. For example, the cognitive model of Mansell et al. (2007) proposes that underlying beliefs about the catastrophic potential of mood swings can be shaped by the negative consequences of affective episodes. A corollary to this might be that positive beliefs about what one is capable of when feeling energetic are driven by genuine experiences of greatly increased productivity during hypomania. Furthermore, the depression avoidance hypothesis (Thomas et al., 2007), which represents a more behavioral formulation of this interactive process, views mania vulnerability to be at least in part determined by the tendency to meet emerging depressive symptoms with behaviors that have the effect of driving mood upward. These behaviors are negatively reinforced due to the reduction in the aversive depression state. Presumably, for those individuals with a sensitive reward system, this learning process will be particularly powerful; not only are downward mood swings avoided through stimulating behavior, but also such individuals may experience a strong, positively reinforcing, surge in approach motivation as a result of such behavior, potentially strengthening the tendency to engage in stimulating behaviors over time. Thus, inherent in the depression avoidance hypothesis is the potential for one's behavioral repertoires to be shaped by one's biology.

Is it also possible that the reverse is true, in other words that patterns of thinking and behavior characteristic of mania and depression shape the functioning of biological systems? Certainly, this seems likely with regard to immediate impact on the activity of the approach or circadian systems. For example, as suggested by Urosevic et al. (2008), individuals who strive more, appraise more events as goal relevant, and have more extreme personal efficacy appraisals are likely to create more events which activate or deactivate the approach system. Whether over time such patterns of behavior have the potential to bring about enduring changes in the functioning of biobehavioral systems remains to be investigated.

A second point of convergence is the view that the behaviors that "drive" the development of mood episodes are carried out in reaction to particular internal states. Urosevic et al. (2008) and Johnson (2005) both propose that dysregulation of the reward or approach system promotes goal-striving behavior, which further activates this system. More specifically, however, several accounts propose that this behavior is a strategic response to internal state. The model proposed by Jones (2001) hypotheses that some of the energetic sensations associated with circadian rhythm disturbance trigger over-positive schemas about the self, which promote striving and risk-taking behaviors that have the effect of disrupting daily rhythms further, with a corresponding process with respect to depression. More broadly, Mansell et al. (2007) use the term "ascent" and "descent" behaviors to refer to actions carried out by the individual in response to extreme appraisals of particular internal states; these actions have the effect of pushing mood up or down. Similarly, the depression avoidance hypothesis (Thomas et al., 2007) views risk-taking or stimulating behaviors as attempts to avoid the aversive state of depression.

At a more abstract level, these accounts converge upon the idea that BD may be associated with a tendency for mood, or at least certain types of mood, to "organize" behavior. As described above, this may be through both the shaping of behavior *over time* by the enduring experience of mood swings, and *in the moment* whereby individuals are frequently motivated to take action to modify current mood state. A similar, more specific, suggestion is made by Gruber who proposes that individuals with BD may be motivated to feel consistently good, and thus pursue hedonic over instrumental goals.

## Implications for Therapy and Research

In terms of implications of the above analysis for therapy, first, it is possible that nonpsychological interventions that have the effect of stabilizing mood and energy levels may indirectly bring about changes in the patterns of behaviors that could contribute to mood swings. This is because behaviors and activities that were previously highly reinforced (or aversive) because of their effects upon internal state are no longer so. Thus, it is possible that mood stability may contribute to the formation of new behavioral responses to mood, as well as vice versa.

Second, the above discussion highlights convergence around the prediction that behavioral response to mood and internal state plays a key role in the maintenance of mood episodes. However, interrupting the connection between mood and action is likely to be challenging. First, the transition from internal state to behavioral response, for example, from feeling tired and sluggish to retreating from social contact, or taking substances to increase energy, may be the product of "low level" associative learning processes (Jones, 2001; Thomas et al., 2007), and thus, interventions that rely upon verbal debate and discussion may be less effective in changing these associations than those using repeated practice of alternatives. In addition, some behavioral responses may be part and parcel of very high or low levels of activity of the approach system, in other words, they may be a normal part of a "hardwired" behavioral repertoire that is prompted at extreme states of engagement or disengagement. Indeed, this is inherent in the multilevel conceptualization of the approach system advanced by Depue and Collins (1999). This has several implications for intervention. Techniques that help clients to learn the meta-skill of observing mood without immediately responding to it may be helpful. A number of therapies, some of which have been adapted for people with BD, explicitly emphasize the importance of responding to a goal, plan, or value rather than engaging in mood-dependent behavior. These include behavioral activation (Martell, Addis, & Jacobson, 2001), MBCT (Segal, Williams & Teasdale, 2002), acceptance and commitment therapy (Hayes, Strosahl, & Wilson, 1999), and dialectical behavior therapy (Linehan, 1993), but this general principle is not exclusive to these approaches. In addition, however, expecting individuals experiencing powerful fluctuations in approach motivation to be able to consistently and effectively "ignore" their mood state in order to act effectively may be asking too much: There may be some occasions when it is helpful for individuals to be able to access simple strategies to down- or upregulate a state in order to be able to access a state of mind that allows a "cooler" decision-making process to take place.

Given the prominence placed by a number of the accounts reviewed here upon the interaction between mood or internal state and behavior, further testing of some of the key theoretical predictions seems warranted. In particular, that striving, stimulating, and risk-taking behaviors play a causal role in the development and maintenance of hypomania, that low mood is a potential trigger for these behaviors, and that patterns of thinking and behavior directly contribute to vulnerability to biobehavioral dysregulation. In parallel, it would be of interest to measure whether changes in the mood–behavior relationship mediate reduction in problematic mood fluctuation following psychological therapy, or whether the presence and uptake of techniques that explicitly target this relationship have a bearing upon the individual's response to therapy. Finally, though it is important to note that this chapter has focused upon a relatively narrow area of theory and research within the broad domain of psychological understandings of BD, and as such further research in this area is likely to compliment research into a multitude of other factors that contribute toward, and could enhance, the effectiveness of psychological interventions for individuals with BD.

# References

Abe, M., Herzog, E. D., & Block, G. D. (2000). Lithium lengthens the circadian period of individual suprachiasmatic nucleus neurons. *Neuroreport, 11*, 3261–3264.

Alatiq, Y., Crane, C., Williams, J. M. G., & Goodwin, G. M. (2010). Dysfunctional beliefs in bipolar disorder: Hypomanic vs. depressive attitudes. *Journal of Affective Disorders, 122*, 294–300.

Alloy, L. B., Abramson, L. Y., Walshaw, P. D., Cogswell, A., Grandin, L. D., Hughes, M. E., & Hogan, M. E. (2008). Behavioral approach system and behavioral inhibition system sensitivities and bipolar spectrum disorders: Prospective prediction of bipolar mood episodes. *Bipolar Disorders, 10*, 310–322.

Alloy, L. B., Abramson, L. Y., Walshaw, P. D., Cogswell, A., Smith, J. M., Neeren, A. M., & Nusslock, R. (2006). Behavioral approach system (BAS) sensitivity and bipolar spectrum disorders: A retrospective and concurrent behavioral high-risk design. *Motivation and Emotion, 30*, 143–155.

Alloy, L. B., Reilly-Harrington, N., Fresco, D. M., Whitehouse, W. G., & Zechmeister, J. S. (1999). Cognitive styles and life events in subsyndromal unipolar and bipolar disorders: Stability and prospective prediction of depressive and hypomanic mood swings. *Journal of Cognitive Psychotherapy, 13*, 21–40.

Ashworth, C. M., Blackburn, I. M., & McPherson, F. M. (1982). The performance of depressed and manic patients on some repertory grid measures: A cross-sectional study. *British Journal of Medical Psychology, 55*, 247–255.

Ashworth, C. M., Blackburn, I. M., & McPherson, F. M. (1985). The performance of depressed and manic patients on some repertory grid measures: A longitudinal study. *British Journal of Medical Psychology, 58*, 337–342.

Ball, J. R., Mitchell, P. B., Corry, T. C., Skillecorn, A., Smith, M., & Malhi, G. S. (2006). A randomized controlled trial of cognitive therapy for bipolar disorder: Focus on long-term change. *Journal of Clinical Psychiatry, 67*, 277–286.

Basco, M. R., & Rush, A. J. (1996). *Cognitive-behavioural therapy for bipolar disorders.* New York: Guilford Press.

Bebbington, P., & Kuipers, E. (1994). The predictive utility of expressed emotion in schizophrenia: An aggregate analysis. *Psychological Medicine, 24*, 707–718.

Beck, A. T. (1967). *Depression: Clinical, experimental and theoretical aspects*. New York: Harper & Row.

Beck, A. T. (1976). *Cognitive therapy and the emotional disorders*. New York: International Universities Press.

Beck, A. T. (1996). Beyond belief: A theory of modes, personality, and psychopathology. In P. M. Salkovskis (Ed.), *Frontiers of cognitive therapy* (pp. 1–25). New York: Guilford Press.

Benedetti, F., Colombo, C., Barbini, B., Campori, E., & Smeraldi, E. (2001). Morning sunlight reduces length of hospitalisation in bipolar depression. *Journal of Affective Disorders, 62,* 221–223.

Brown, G. W., Birley, J., & Wing, J. (1972). Influence of family life on the course of schizophrenia disorder. *British Journal of Psychiatry, 121,* 241–258.

Brown, G. W., Monck, E. M., Carstairs, G. M., & Wing, J. K. (1962). Influence of family life on the course of schizophrenic illness. *British Journal of Preventive and Social Medicine, 16,* 55–68.

Colom, F., Pacchiarotti, I., & Vieta, E. (2006). Treatment arsenal for **bipolar** disorders: The role of psychoeducation in good clinical practice. *Psichiatria e Psicoterapia, 25,* 3–6.

Colom, F., Vieta, E., Martinez-Aran, A., Reinares, M., Goikolea, J. M., Benebarre, A., & Corominas, J. (2003). A randomized trial on the efficacy of group psychoeducation in the prophylaxis of recurrences in bipolar patients whose disease is in remission. *Archives of General Psychiatry, 60,* 402–407.

Colom, F., Vieta, E., Sanchez-Moreno, J., Palomino-Otiniano, R., Reinares, M., Goikolea, J. M., & Martinez-Aran, A. (2009). Group psychoeducation for stabilised bipolar disorders: 5-year outcome of a randomised clinical trial. *British Journal of Psychiatry, 194,* 260–265.

Deltito, J. A., Moline, M., Pollack, J. A., Martin, L. Y., & Maremmani, I. (1991). Effects of phototherapy on non-seasonal unipolar and bipolar depressive spectrum disorders. *Journal of Affective Disorders, 23,* 231–237.

Depue, R. A., & Collins, P. F. (1999). Neurobiology of the structure of personality: Dopamine, facilitation of incentive motivation, and extraversion. *Behavioral and Brain Sciences, 22,* 451–569.

Depue, R. A., & Iacono, W. G. (1989). Neurobehavioral aspects of affective disorders. In M. R. Rosenweig, & L. W. Porter (Eds.), *Annual review of psychology* (Vol. 40, pp. 457–492). Palo Alto, CA: Annual Reviews.

Depue, R. A., Krauss, S. P., & Spoont, M. R. (1987). A two-dimensional threshold model of seasonal bipolar affective disorder. In D. Magnusson, & A. Ohman (Eds.), *Psychopathology: An interactionist perspective* (pp. 95–123). New York: Academic Press.

Dodd, A. L., Mansell, W., Morrison, A. P., & Tai, S. (2011). Extreme appraisals of internal states and bipolar symptoms: The hypomanic attitudes and positive predictions inventory. *Psychological Assessment, 23,* 635–645.

D'Souza, R., Piskulic, D., & Sundram, S. (2010). A brief dyadic group based psychoeducation program improves relapse rates in recently remitted bipolar disorder: A pilot randomised controlled trial. *Journal of Affective Disorders, 120,* 272–276.

Eisner, L. R., Johnson, S. L., & Carver, C. S. (2008). Cognitive responses to failure and success relate uniquely to bipolar depression versus mania. *Journal of Abnormal Psychology, 117,* 154–163.

Farmer, A., Lam, D., Sahakian, B., Rosier, J., Burke, A., O'Neill, N., & McGuffin, P. (2006). A pilot study of positive mood induction in euthymic bipolar subjects compared with healthy controls. *Psychological Medicine, 26,* 1213–1218.

Frank, E., Hlastala, S., Ritenour, A., Houck, P., Tu, X. M., Monk, T. H., & Kupfer, D. J. (1997). Inducing lifestyle regularity in recovering bipolar patients: Results from the maintenance therapies in bipolar disorder protocol. *Biological Psychiatry, 41,* 1165–1173.

Frank, E., Kupfer, D. J., Thase, M. E., Mallinger, A. G., Swartz, H. A., Eagiolini, A. M., & Monk, T. (2005). Two-year outcomes for interpersonal and social rhythm therapy in individuals with bipolar I disorder. *Archives of General Psychiatry, 62,* 996–1004.

Frank, E., Schwartz, H. A., Mallinger, A. G., Thase, M. E., Weaver, E. V., & Kupfer, D. J. (1999). Adjunctive psychotherapy for bipolar disorder: Effects of changing treatment modality. *Journal of Abnormal Psychology, 108,* 579–587.

Goldberg, J. F., Wenze, S. J., Welker, T. M., Steer, R. A., & Beck, A. T. (2005). Content-specificity of dysfunctional cognitions for patients with bipolar mania versus unipolar depression: A preliminary study. *Bipolar Disorders, 7,* 49–56.

Goldstein, M. J., & Miklowitz, D. J. (1997). *Bipolar disorder: A family-focused treatment approach.* New York: Guilford Press.

Gruber, J., Culver, J. L., Johnson, S. L., Nam, J. Y., Keller, K. L., & Ketter, T. A. (2009). Do positive emotions predict symptomatic change in bipolar disorder? *Bipolar Disorders, 11,* 330–336.

Gruber, J., Eidelman, P., Johnson, S. L., Smith, B., & Harvey, A. G. (2011). Hooked on a feeling: Rumination about positive and negative emotion in inter-episode bipolar disorder. *Journal of Abnormal Psychology, 120,* 956–961.

Gruber, J., Harvey, A. G., & Purcell, A. (2011). What comes up can come down? A preliminary investigation of emotion reactivity and emotion recovery in bipolar disorder. *Journal of Affective Disorders, 134,* 102–111.

Gutierrez, M. J., & Scott, J. (2004). Psychological treatment for bipolar disorders. *European Archives of Psychiatry and Clinical Neuroscience, 254,* 92–98.

Hallonquist, J. D., Goldberg, M. A., & Brandes, J. S. (1986). Affective disorders and circadian rhythms. *Canadian Journal of Psychiatry, 31,* 259–272.

Harmon-Jones, E., Abramson, L. Y., Nusslock, R., Sigelman, J. D., Urosevic, S., Turonie, L. D., & Fearn, M. (2008). Effect of bipolar disorder on left frontal cortical responses to goals differing in valence and task difficulty. *Biological Psychiatry, 63,* 693–698.

Harmon-Jones, E., Abramson, L. Y., Sigelman, J. D., Bohlig, A., Hogan, M. E., & Harmon-Jones, C. (2002). Proneness to hypomania/mania symptoms or depression symptoms and asymmetrical frontal cortical responses to an anger-evoking event. *Journal of Personality and Social Psychology, 82,* 610–618.

Hayes, S. C., Strosahl, K. D., & Wilson, K. G. (1999). *Acceptance and commitment therapy.* New York: Guilford Press.

Healy, D., & Williams, J. M. G. (1989). Moods, misattributions and mania: An interaction of biological and social factors in the pathogenesis of mania. *Psychiatric Developments, 1,* 49–70.

Honig, A., Hofman, A., Rozendaal, N., & Dingemans, P. (1997). Psycho-education in bipolar disorder: Effect of expressed emotion. *Psychiatry Research, 72,* 17–22.

Jauhar, P., & Weller, M. P. I. (1982). Psychiatric morbidity and time zone changes: A study of patients from Heathrow airport. *British Journal of Psychiatry, 140,* 231–235.

Johnson, S. L. (2005). Mania and dysregulation in goal pursuit: A review. *Clinical Psychology Review, 25,* 241–262.

Johnson, S. L., Cueller, A. K., Ruggero, C., Winett-Perlman, C., Goodnick, P., White, R., & Miller, I. (2008). Life events as predictors of mania and depression in bipolar I disorder. *Journal of Abnormal Psychology, 117,* 268–277.

Johnson, S. L., Eisner, L. R., & Carver, C. S. (2009). Elevated expectancies among persons diagnosed with bipolar disorder. *British Journal of Clinical Psychology, 48,* 217–222.

Johnson, S. L., & Fulford, D. (2009). Preventing mania: A preliminary examination of the GOALS Program. *Behavior Therapy, 40,* 103–113.

Johnson, S. L., Ruggero, C. J., & Carver, C. S. (2005). Cognitive, behavioral, and affective responses to reward: Links with hypomanic symptoms. *Journal of Social and Clinical Psychology*, 24, 894–906.

Johnson, S. L., Sandrow, D., Meyer, B., Winters, R., Miller, I., Solomon, D., & Keitner, G. (2000). Increases in manic symptoms after life events involving goal attainment. *Journal of Abnormal Psychology*, 109, 721–727.

Jones, S. (2001). Circadian rhythms, multilevel models of emotion and bipolar disorder—an initial step towards integration? *Clinical Psychology Review*, 21, 1193–1209.

Jones, S. H., Hare, D. J., & Evershed, K. (2005). Actigraphic assessment of circadian activity and sleep patterns in bipolar disorder. *Bipolar Disorders*, 7, 176–186.

Jones, S., Mansell, W., & Waller, L. (2006). Appraisal of hypomania-relevant experiences: Development of a questionnaire to assess positive self-dispositional appraisals in bipolar and behavioural high risk samples. *Journal of Affective Disorders*, 93, 19–28.

Kennedy, S. H., Kutcher, S. P., Ralevski, E., & Brown, G. M. (1996). Nocturnal melatonin and 24-hour 6-sulphatoxymelatonin levels in various phases of bipolar affective disorder. *Psychiatry Research*, 63, 219–222.

Kim, E. Y., & Miklowitz, D. J. (2004). Expressed emotion as a predictor of outcome among bipolar patients undergoing family therapy. *Journal of Affective Disorders*, 82, 343–352.

Lam, D. H., Hayward, P., Watkins, E. R., Wright, K., & Sham, P. (2005). Relapse prevention in patients with bipolar disorder: Cognitive therapy outcome after 2 years. *American Journal of Psychiatry*, 162, 324–329.

Lam, D. H., Jones, S. H., Haywood, P., & Bright, J. A. (1999). *Cognitive therapy for manic depression*. Chichester, UK: John Wiley & Sons, Ltd.

Lam, D. H., Watkins, E. R., Hayward, P., Bright, J., Wright, K., Kerr, N., & Sham, P. (2003). A randomized controlled study of cognitive therapy for relapse prevention for bipolar affective disorder: Outcome of the first year. *Archives of General Psychiatry*, 60, 145–152.

Lex, C., Hautzinger, M., & Meyer, T. D. (2011). Cognitive styles in hypomanic episodes of bipolar I disorder. *Bipolar Disorders*, 13, 355–364.

Linehan, M. M. (1993). *Cognitive-behavioral treatment of borderline personality disorder*. New York: Guilford Press.

Linkowski, P., Kerkhofs, M., Van Onderbergen, A., Hubain, P., Copinschi, G., L'Hermite-Baleriaux, M., & Van Caute, E. (1994). The 24-hour profiles of cortisol, prolactin, and growth hormone secretion in mania. *Archives of General Psychiatry*, 51, 616–624.

Lyon, H. M., Startup, M., & Bentall, R. P. (1999). Social cognition and the manic defense: Attributions, selective attention, and self-schema in bipolar affective disorder. *Journal of Abnormal Psychology*, 108, 273–282.

Malkoff-Schwartz, S., Frank, E., Anderson, B., Sherrill, J., Siegel, L., Patterson, D., & Kupfer, D. J. (1998). Stressful life events and social rhythm disruption in the onset of manic and depressive bipolar episodes. *Archives of General Psychiatry*, 55, 702–707.

Mansell, W. (2006). The hypomanic attitudes and positive predictions inventory (HAPPI): A pilot study to select cognitions that are elevated in individuals with bipolar disorder compared to non-clinical controls. *Behavioural and Cognitive Psychotherapy*, 34, 467–476.

Mansell, W., & Jones, S. H. (2006). The brief-HAPPI: A questionnaire to assess cognitions that distinguish between individuals with a diagnosis of bipolar disorder and non-clinical controls. *Journal of Affective Disorders*, 93, 29–34.

Mansell, W., Morrison, A. P., Reid, G., Lowens, I., & Tai, S. (2007). The interpretation of, and response to, changes in internal states: An integrative cognitive model of mood swings and Bipolar Disorders. *Behavioural and Cognitive Psychotherapy*, 35, 515–539.

Mansell, W., Paszek, G., Seal, K., Pedley, R., Jones, S., Thomas, N., & Dodd, A. (2011). Extreme appraisals of internal states in bipolar I disorder: A multiple control group study. *Cognitive Therapy and Research*, *35*, 87–97.

Martell, C. R., Addis, M. E., & Jacobson, N. S. (2001). *Depression in context: Strategies for guided action*. New York: W. W. Norton & Company Ltd.

Meyer, B., Beevers, C. G., Johnson, S. L., & Simmons, E. (2007). Unique association of approach motivation and mania vulnerability. *Cognition and Emotion*, *21*, 1647–1668.

Meyer, B., Johnson, S. L., & Winters, R. (2001). Responsiveness to threat and incentive in bipolar disorder: Relations of the BIS/BAS scales with symptoms. *Journal of Psychopathology and Behavioral Assessment*, *23*, 133–143.

Meyer, T., & Maier, S. (2006). Is there evidence for social rhythm instability in people at risk of affective disorders? *Psychiatry Research*, *141*, 103–114.

Miklowitz, D. J., George, E. L., Richards, J. A., Simoneau, T. L., & Suddath, R. L. (2003). A randomized study of family-focused psychoeducation and pharmacotherapy in the outpatient management of bipolar disorder. *Archives of General Psychiatry*, *60*, 904–912.

Milkowitz, D. J., Goldstein, M. J., Nuechterlein, K. H., Snyder, K. S., & Mintz, J. (1988). Family factors and the course of bipolar affective disorder. *Archives of General Psychiatry*, *45*, 225–231.

Miklowitz, D. J., Goodwin, G. M., Bauer, M. S., & Geddes, J. R. (2008). Common and specific elements of psychosocial treatments for bipolar disorder: A survey of clinicians participating in randomized trials. *Journal of Psychiatric Practice*, *14*, 77–85.

Miklowitz, D. J., Otto, M. W., Frank, E., Reilly-Harrington, N. A., Wisneiwski, S. R., Kogan, J. N., & Sachs G. S. (2007). Psychosocial treatments for bipolar depression: A 1-year randomized trial from the systematic treatment enhancement program. *Archives of General Psychiatry*, *64*, 419–426.

Miller, I. W., Keitner, G. I., Ryan, C. E., Uebelacker, L. A., Johnson, S. L., & Solomon, D. A. (2008). Family treatment for bipolar disorder: Family impairment by treatment interactions. *Journal of Clinical Psychiatry*, *69*, 732–740.

Miller, I. W., Solomon, D. A., Ryan, C. E., & Keitner, G. I. (2004). Does adjunctive family therapy enhance recovery from bipolar I mood episodes? *Journal of Affective Disorders*, *82*, 431–436.

Mirabel-Sarron, C., Siobuda Dorocant, E., Sala, L., Bachelart, M., Guelfi, J.-D., & Rouillon, F. (2009). Mindfulness based cognitive therapy (MBCT): A pilot study in bipolar patients. *Annales Médico-Psychologiques, Revue Psychiatrique*, *167*, 686–692.

Murphy, F. C., Sahakian, B. J., Rubinsztein, J. S., Michael, A., Rogers, R. D., Robbins, T. W., & Paykel, E. S. (1999). Emotional bias and inhibitory control processes in mania and depression. *Psychological Medicine*, *29*, 1307–1321.

National Institute for Health and Clinical Excellence (NICE). (2006). *Bipolar disorder clinical guideline*. London: Author.

Neale, J. M. (1988). Defensive function of manic episodes. In T. F. Oltmanns, & B. A. Maher (Eds.), *Delusional beliefs* (pp. 131–148). New York: Wiley.

Newman, C. F., Leahy, R. L., Beck, A. T., Reilly-Harrington, N. A., & Gyulai, L. (2002). *Bipolar disorder: A cognitive therapy approach*. Washington, DC: APA Books.

O'Connell, R. A., Mayo, J. A., Flatow, L., Cuthbertson, B., & O'Brien, B. E. (1991). Outcome of bipolar disorder on long-term treatment with lithium. *British Journal of Psychiatry*, *159*, 123–129.

O'Sullivan, N., Szczepanowski, R., El-Deredy, W., Mason, L., & Bentall, R. P. (2011). fMRI evidence of a relationship between hypomania and both increased goal-sensitivity and positive outcome-expectancy bias. *Neuropsychologia*, *49*, 2825–2835.

Pavlova, B., Uher, R., Dennington, L., Wright, K., & Donaldson, C. (2011). Reactivity of affect and self-esteem during remission in bipolar affective disorder: An experimental investigation. *Journal of Affective Disorders, 134*, 102–111.

Perry, A., Tarrier, N., Morris, R., McCarthy, E., & Limb, K. (1999). Randomised controlled trial of efficacy of teaching patients with bipolar disorder to identify early symptoms of relapse and obtain treatment. *British Medical Journal, 318*, 149–153.

Priebe, S., Wildgrube, C., & Muller-Oerlinghausen, B. (1989). Lithium prophylaxis and expressed emotion. *British Journal of Psychiatry, 154*, 396–399.

Rea, M. M., Tompson, M., Miklowitz, D. J., Goldstein, M. J., Hwang, S., & Mintz, J. (2003). Family focused treatment vs. individual treatment for bipolar disorder: Results of a randomized clinical trial. *Journal of Consulting and Clinical Psychology, 71*, 482–492.

Reilly-Harrington, N., Miklowitz, D. J., Otto, E. F., Wisniewski, S. R., Thase, M. E., & Sachs, G. S. (2010). Dysfunctional attitudes, attributional styles and phase of illness in bipolar disorder. *Cognitive Therapy and Research, 34*, 24–34.

Sachar, E. J. (1975). Twenty-four-hour cortisol secretory patterns in depressed and manic patients. *Progress in Brain Research, 42*, 81–91.

Salavert, J., Caseras, X., Torrubia, R., Furrest, S., Arranz, B., Duenas, R., & San, L. (2007). The functioning of the behavioral activation and inhibition systems in bipolar I euthymic patients and its influence in subsequent episodes over an eighteen-month period. *Personality and Individual Differences, 42*, 1323–1331.

Salvatore, P., Ghidni, S., Zita, G., De Panfilis, C., Lambertino, S., Maggini, C., & Baldessarini, R. J. (2008). Circadian activity rhythm abnormalities in ill and recovered bipolar I disorder patients. *Bipolar Disorders, 10*, 256–265.

Scott, J., Garland, A., & Moorhead, S. (2001). A pilot study of cognitive therapy in bipolar disorders. *Psychological Medicine, 31*, 459–467.

Scott, J., Paykel, E., Morriss, R., Bentall, R., Kinderman, P., Johnson, T., & Hayhurst, H. (2006). Cognitive therapy for severe and recurrent bipolar disorders: Randomised controlled trial. *British Journal of Psychiatry, 188*, 313–320.

Scott, J., & Pope, M. (2003). Cognitive styles in individuals with bipolar disorders. *Psychological Medicine, 31*, 459–467.

Searson, R., Mansell, W., Lowens, I., & Tai, S. J. (2012). Think effectively about mood swings (TEAMS): A case series of cognitive behavioural therapy for bipolar disorders. *Journal of Behavior Therapy and Experimental Psychiatry, 43*, 770–779.

Segal, Z. V., Williams, J. M. G., & Teasdale, J. D. (2002). *Mindfulness-based cognitive therapy for depression*. New York: Guilford Press.

Stern, G. S., & Berrenberg, J. L. (1979). Skill-set, success outcome, and mania as determinants of the illusion of control. *Journal of Research in Personality, 13*, 206–220.

Thomas, J., & Bentall, R. P. (2002). Hypomanic traits and response styles to depression. *British Journal of Clinical Psychology, 41*, 309–313.

Thomas, J., Knowles, R., Tai, S., & Bentall, R. P. (2007). Response styles to depressed mood in bipolar affective disorder. *Journal of Affective Disorders, 100*, 249–252.

Tsujimoto, T., Yamada, N., Shimoda, K., Hanada, K., & Takahashi, S. (1990). Circadian rhythms in depression. Part II: Cicadian rhythms in inpatients with various mental disorders. *Journal of Affective Disorders, 18*, 199–210.

Urosevic, S., Abramson, L. Y., Harmon-Jones, E., & Alloy, L. B. (2008). Dysregulation of the behavioral approach system (BAS) in bipolar spectrum disorders: Review of theory and evidence. *Clinical Psychology Review, 28*, 1188–1205.

van der Gucht, E., Morris, R., Lancaster, G., Kinderman, P., & Bentall, R. P. (2009). Psychological processes in bipolar affective disorder: Negative cognitive style and reward processing. *British Journal of Psychiatry, 194*, 146–151.

Weber, B., Jermann, F., Gex-Fabry, M., Nallet, A., Bondolfi, G., & Aubry, J. M. (2010). Mindfulness-based cognitive therapy for bipolar disorder: A feasibility trial. *European Psychiatry*, 25, 334–337.

Wehr, T. A., & Goodwin, F. K. (1983). Biological rhythms in manic-depressive illness. In T. A. Wehr & F. K. Goodwin(Eds.), *Circadian rhythms in psychiatry* (pp. 129–184). Pacific Grove, CA: Boxwood Press.

Williams, J. M. G., Alatiq, Y., Crane, C., Barnhofer, T., Fennell, M. J. V., Duggan, D. S., & Goodwin, G. M. (2008). Mindfulness-based Cognitive Therapy (MBCT) in bipolar disorder: Preliminary evaluation of immediate effects on between-episode functioning. *Journal of Affective Disorders*, 107, 275–279.

Wright, K. A., Lam, D., & Brown, R. G. (2008). Dysregulation of the behavioral activation system in remitted bipolar I disorder. *Journal of Abnormal Psychology*, 117, 838–848.

Yan, L. J., Hammen, C., Cohen, A. N., Daley, S. E., & Henry, R. M. (2004). Expressed emotion versus relationship quality variables in the prediction of recurrence in bipolar patients. *Journal of Affective Disorders*, 83, 199–206.

Yin, L., Wang, J., Klein, P. S., & Lazar, M. A. (2006). Nuclear receptor Rev-erbα is a critical lithium-sensitive component of the circadian clock. *Science*, 311, 1002–1005.

Young, D. M. (1995). Psychiatric morbidity in travelers to Honolulu, Hawaii. *Comprehensive Psychiatry*, 36, 224–228.

Zaretsky, A., Lancee, W., Miller, C., Harris, A., & Parikh, S. (2008). Is cognitive-behavioural therapy more effective than psychoeducation in bipolar disorder? *Canadian Journal of Psychiatry*, 53, 441–448.

Zaretsky, A. E., Segal, Z. V., & Gemar, M. (1999). Cognitive therapy for bipolar depression: A pilot study. *Canadian Journal of Psychiatry*, 44, 491–494.

# 14

# Further Integration of Patient, Provider, and Systems Treatment Approaches in Bipolar Disorder
## *Where New Evidence Meets Practice Reality*

Sagar V. Parikh[1] and Sidney H. Kennedy[2]

[1]Continuing Mental Health Education, Canada
[1,2]University of Toronto, Canada
[1,2]University Health Network, Canada

Bipolar disorder (BD) is often characterized by grandiosity as a cardinal symptom of mania, but grandiosity may also characterize the illness from another perspective: Virtually no other psychiatric disorder is as grand in its plethora of clinical presentations (Goldberg & Harrow, 1999; Goodwin & Jamison, 2007). Depression, mania, and mixed states each require substantially different biological, psychological, and social interventions, and management of the same episode can be approached very differently by two biological psychiatrists or two psychotherapists (Prien & Potter 1990; Prien & Rush, 1996). How is a practitioner to choose among the many pathways to treatment? The science of medicine identifies the efficacy of each particular path, but only the art of medicine—the weighing of individual circumstances with clinical judgment and the capacity to integrate approaches—allows for truly effective treatment. Adding to the complexity, Leboyer and Kupfer (2010) have expanded the very definition of BD to incorporate the central role of multiple medical comorbidities and the persistence of various abnormalities even in the euthymic state, calling BD a "chronic and progressive multisystem disorder." Developing a treatment approach for an illness that is promiscuous in presentation, perniciously progressive even during apparent euthymia, and inducing health impact in multiple physiologic domains—cardiac, inflammatory, and endocrine, to name a few—requires a complex approach. Given the enormous public health burden of BD, a complex approach that offers interventions at the level of the patient, the provider, and the service delivery system is required. This chapter explores several dominant approaches to treatment, each of which has been discussed in detail in this book—but then, attempts to provide a model for weaving a therapeutic tapestry.

*The Wiley-Blackwell Handbook of Mood Disorders*, Second Edition. Edited by Mick Power.
© 2013 John Wiley & Sons, Ltd. Published 2013 by John Wiley & Sons, Ltd.

The challenges of treatment are perhaps best provoked by examining a common clinical scenario, illustrating how different experts might approach the problem and then offering a sequence of recommendations based on the integration of approaches at the end of the chapter.

*Vignette: Bipolar depression.* Mr. Y is a 22-year-old college student with a previous history of a psychotic manic episode requiring 3 weeks of inpatient treatment at age 19. He had discontinued lithium and antipsychotics after 6 months of treatment originally because he "didn't need pills to be well." He was successful in his studies, was in a serious relationship, and had become an impassioned animal rights activist. He was particularly skeptical of medical research for its reliance on animals, and was fond of movies that depicted psychiatric problems as a result of individuals struggling to assert individuality in the face of oppressive societal norms. Two months prior to the current assessment, he developed low energy and difficulty in concentrating; this had evolved to a more explicit major depressive episode with excessive sleepiness, overeating, severe depressive ruminations, social withdrawal, hopelessness, and suicidal ideation. Nevertheless, he felt that it was not right to kill—either animals or himself—and so he sought help to "get over the suicidal urges and get my energy back."

How should he be treated?

Most psychiatrists would agree that a medication with first-line efficacy for bipolar depression—such as lithium or quetiapine—would be a critical first step (Yatham et al., 2009). Major treatment guidelines on BD stress the importance of this step, often emphasizing the utility of lithium or quetiapine as monotherapies, also signal caution in the use of antidepressants in this situation (Yatham et al., 2009). Common clinical practice, however, is to start with two medications, such as an established mood stabilizer with an antidepressant to fully treat the depression. While use of two medications is also recognized as a first-line treatment, it raises prospects of additional side effects and potential additional perturbations of other physiologic systems—a concern for a "multisystem" disorder. Further complicating the biological approach is the lack of agreement on which antidepressant should be used. Finally, most if not all biological psychiatrists would likely agree on adding a psychosocial intervention to medications for the depression.

Psychotherapists might take a more complex approach (Roth & Fonagy, 2005). Most would accept the need for a mood stabilizer, but the target and technique for psychotherapy would differ markedly (Swartz & Frank, 2001). Cognitive behavior therapy (CBT) practitioners would target the depressive ruminations, social withdrawal, hopelessness, and suicidality. Interpersonal therapy (IPT) practitioners might attend to the sleep changes while searching for evidence of interpersonal deficits or conflicts underlying this particular episode. Still other therapists would also look to family/couple or even psychodynamic issues for intervention. Members of the public and self-help advocates might counsel on the wisdom of avoiding the formal health care system and looking to time, social support, and environmental change as key steps to be pursued. Stigma as a barrier to recovery in particular would be targeted by some (Perlick, 2001). The Recovery Movement in Mental Health has inspired a specific bipolar guide that would suggest other psychosocial interventions (OBAD, 2010). For each intervention—biological, psychological, and social—guidance would be available in the literature, and indeed in this volume—yet how to decide what is right for this person? Furthermore, how would one design a bipolar treatment service that would best suit situations such as this?

## A Theoretical Framework: Medical Models and Chronic Disease Management

Evidence-based medicine remains a dominant mantra and correctly stresses the importance of using a systematic search for efficacious treatments (Sackett, Straus, Richardson, Rosenberg, & Haynes, 2000). As an afterthought of this approach, larger factors that may also influence outcomes may be considered, such as patient treatment preference (Bedi et al., 2000; Lin & Parikh, 1999), local health system resources, as well as practitioner characteristics and training (Donohoe, 1998; Parikh, Lin, & Lesage, 1997). Several theoretical models provide guidance on how to understand these other relevant factors—models looking at "population health" (Ibrahim, Savitz, Carey, & Wagner, 2001) or the "determinants of health" and models explicitly designed for chronic disease management. In fact, in the leading model of chronic disease management (Coleman, Austin, Brach, & Wagner, 2009; Wagner, Austin, & Von Korff, 1996), four categories of intervention have been identified: (1) practice design (reorganization); (2) patient education; (3) expert systems (provider education, guidelines, and decision support); and (4) computer-based support (reminder programs, feedback of automated clinical measures, or alerts to the clinician on matters such as nonrenewal of prescribed medications). By blending these models into a hybrid, which reflects the perspective of the clinician, it is possible to look at treatment success as a product of successful negotiation of barriers at three key levels: patient, provider, and system. Furthermore, one can then use the three windows of intervention to address BD as a "chronic and multisystem disease."

## Patient Interventions

Medication remains the cornerstone of treatment for BD, so prescription of at least a mood stabilizer would be routine. Furthermore, while there may be cost factors in seeing a physician and filling a prescription, such interventions are feasible in virtually all health care environments in the developed world. Specific medication recommendations are outlined elsewhere in this volume, and would be combined with basic clinical management (supportive therapy including specifying treatment and monitoring outcome, offering practical advice for immediate problems such as work or school stressors, and instilling hope for relief of symptoms).

Unfortunately, abundant data demonstrate poor medication adherence in BD (Berk et al., 2010; Cohen, Parikh, & Kennedy, 2000); thus, the next level of intervention would be compliance-enhancing strategies. Such strategies would generally fall into the category of psychoeducation (PE), where multiple studies have demonstrated that PE improves medication compliance and overall treatment adherence (Sperry, 1995). Key studies have also shown that PE improves clinical outcomes; a median of nine sessions designed to educate the patient on the signs and symptoms of early relapse and the development of an early warning strategy dramatically reduced time to relapse into mania and improved quality of life in a randomized controlled trial (RCT; Perry, Tarrier, Morriss, McCarthy, & Limb, 1999). Multiple RCTs now have incorporated a specific PE intervention for BD, namely the "Life Goals" program (Bauer & McBride, 1996, 2003). These trials use a variety of approaches and some blend other interventions with the PE, but all demonstrate reductions in relapse into mania and reduction of overall symptom burden (Aubry et al., 2012; Bauer et al., 2006; Parikh et al., 2012; Simon, Ludman, Bauer, Unutzer, & Operskalski, 2006). A more intensive form of PE from Barcelona has also demonstrated striking persistence in the efficacy of the intervention over 5 years (Colom et al., 2003, 2009).

Beyond PE, specific psychotherapeutic interventions are now well described and moderately researched. At the time of our earlier reviews (Huxley, Parikh, & Baldessarini, 2000; Parikh et al., 1997), we found 32 peer-reviewed reports involving just 1,052 bipolar patients (average N per study just 33), with only 13 studies having some form of control group. Since 1999, multiple reports of psychosocial interventions have been published, including many RCTs, some of which involved close to 100 subjects each.

Within psychological disorders, major models exist to explain the etiology and symptoms of some anxiety disorders and depression. The negative cognitive triad model of Beck for depression, for instance, not only has been tested for validity, but also provides a rationale for treatment maneuvers such as Automatic Thought Records (Beck, 2008; Beck, Rush, Shaw, & Emery, 1979). Such theoretical models for BD are relatively scarce, based in part on the lack of basic research that identifies plausible psychosocial causes or moderators. Furthermore, existing models show considerable overlap, which in turn leads to considerable overlap in the design of psychosocial interventions designed on the basis of these models.

A further challenge to develop a theoretical model is the inherent complexity of the disorder in terms of phases of the illness, and the specific targets for intervention based on phase, symptoms, and sequelae. While BD is currently understood as a single illness, no unitary theory explains all the different types of symptoms. As a consequence, a different model may be necessary to explain the illness in acute depression, in acute mania, and in maintenance. Even within the maintenance phase, any bipolar intervention would have to be designed with possibly two different agenda: either to prevent relapse or to treat the sequelae of acute episodes, be they a damaged self-concept, a broken relationship, or a lost job. It may be that many of these concerns lead to a unitary model—for instance, treating the sequelae may be directly linked to relapse prevention—but it is also possible that several separate models need to be retained.

Since 2000, one important pilot study and three major published RCTs of CBT (Ball et al., 2006; Lam, Hayward, Watkins, Wright, & Sham, 2005; Lam, McCrone, Wright, & Kerr, 2005; Scott, 2001; Scott et al., 2006) have been published, one of which generated separate outcome papers at 12 and 30 months (Lam, Hayward, et al.,

2005; Lam, McCrone, et al., 2005). Here, the term "CBT" is used, although some prefer to use "CT" to signify cognitive therapy; in fact, all the bipolar CBT or CT manuals include behavioral techniques, and so "CBT" more accurately describes the interventions. While the results of initial studies in CBT for BD were generally positive, the results have often been modest; some did not show maintenance of gains over longer follow-up intervals (e.g., Lam, McCrone, et al., 2005), while others did not show any gains over control groups (e.g., Scott et al., 2006). In addition, there have not always been associated changes in the central mechanism of action underlying this therapeutic strategy—namely changes in underlying dysfunction beliefs (Zaretsky, Lancee, Miller, Harris, & Parikh, 2008). Given that the central and distinguishing focus of CBT is its emphasis on ameliorating dysfunctional thoughts, the very modestly positive clinical outcomes and modest effects on dysfunctional attitudes suggest that CBT is of limited value to the average bipolar patient. Studies involving CBT as one arm of multiple psychosocial interventions are considered separately, later in this chapter.

Prior to 2000, there were only two reports of interpersonal and social rhythm therapy (IPSRT) in the treatment of BD, both from Frank et al. (1997, 1999). The most systematic of the two reported no differences in symptoms, or time to relapse between patients receiving IPSRT versus clinical management. Since 2000, there have been three publications all stemming from the same study, a complex one also from Frank et al. (2005). Initial results from the study (Frank, Swartz, & Kupfer, 2000; Frank et al., 1999) pointed to the importance of continuity of treatment; individuals who were relapsing were more likely to have switched treatment modalities between the acute and the maintenance phase. Somewhat surprisingly, the first primary outcome of time to stabilization was no different for acute intense clinical management (ICM) versus acute IPSRT. Similarly, individuals receiving maintenance ICM did not differ in terms of time to recurrence compared to those receiving maintenance IPSRT. However, individuals treated with IPSRT in the acute treatment phase experienced longer survival time without a new affective episode and were more likely to remain well for the full 2 years of the preventative maintenance phase (regardless of the treatment received in the preventative maintenance phase). Similarly, recipients of acute phase IPSRT had greater regularity of social rhythms at the end of the acute phase, and the ability to increase regularity of social rhythms during acute treatment was associated with reduced likelihood of recurrence, suggesting a mechanism of action that was consistent with the theory of IPSRT.

Since 2000, six RCTs employing family-focused therapy (FFT) have demonstrated that FFT improves relapse rates and time to relapse as well as reduces overall mood symptoms (Miklowitz & Goldstein, 1997; Miklowitz, et al., 2000; Miklowitz, Wendel, & Simoneau, 1998; Miklowitz, George, Richards, Simoneau, & Suddath, 2003; Miklowitz, Richards, et al., 2003). However, there was no demonstrable advantage for FFT compared to treatment as usual in treating the symptoms of mania or hypomania. Unlike other psychosocial interventions that are largely geared to being delivered to patients during times of relative mood stability with the intent of reducing relapse or recurrence, FFT is designed for delivery to the family and the patient during a mood episode to promote a more effective recovery. The value of FFT as well as other interventions in acute bipolar depression is reviewed later in this chapter. One drawback of the FFT studies is the relatively small number of subjects who have actually received the treatment, given the small size of the studies and the use of larger control groups. While it is encouraging to witness the benefits of FFT in coping with depressive symptoms and recurrences, FFT treatment may be more limited when it comes to preventing hypomanic or manic symptoms and relapse in general. As with other individual intervention research, there is limited information on the persistence of gains at follow-up, as well as the applicability of the treatment to patients who have little or no contact with their families.

## Comparison of psychosocial interventions

Studies reviewed so far have compared a single major treatment modality to a control condition. Three key studies have now examined the comparative benefits of different psychosocial interventions.

In the largest study of psychosocial interventions in the acute phase of illness, Miklowitz et al. (2007) involved multiple sites from the Systematic Treatment Enhancement Program for Bipolar Disorder (STEP-BD) (Sachs et al., 2003). This program enrolled 4,361 bipolar subjects in a variety of studies, some open and some RCTs. From this large sample, 15 sites contributed 293 subjects to a study of acute psychosocial interventions. Adding to the complexity was that 236 of these subjects were also enrolled simultaneously in an RCT of a mood stabilizer plus either an antidepressant or placebo for bipolar depression. The remaining 57 subjects (293 − 236) were not eligible for the antidepressant study, but were treated openly with pharmacotherapy according to common treatment guidelines.

Psychosocial treatment options included IPSRT, FFT, and CBT. However, assignment of the psychosocial treatment was further complicated by the fact that some members did not have family members available ($n = 134$, or almost half of the 293 subjects). Furthermore, for practical reasons, few sites could offer treatment in all three modalities. Therefore, the study was designed so that at any one site, only two intensive psychosocial treatments would be offered. Thus, 10 sites offered CBT, 9 provided FFT, while 11 offered IPSRT. All 15 sites offered the control condition, which was three individual sessions of "Collaborative Care (CC)." CC was described as "a brief version of the most common psychosocial strategies shown to offer benefit for bipolar disorder" (Miklowitz et al., 2007). Thus, it is worth noting that CC is not a specific brief intervention for bipolar depression, but a more general brief psychosocial maneuver. As such, it would be reasonable to regard the CC control condition as a type of enhanced treatment as usual rather than a depression-specific intervention. These three sessions of CC were compared to intensive psychosocial interventions with up to 30 sessions given over a 9-month period, with a total study period of 12 months (including the 9-month treatment time). Primary outcomes were time to recovery and the proportion of patients classified as well during each of the 12 study months. Major findings of the study were that all three intensive interventions, versus the CC control, were able to achieve higher recovery rates by year end, and also shorten the time to recovery. No differences were seen among the three intensive treatments. The authors concluded that intensive psychosocial intervention was more beneficial than brief intervention for bipolar depression, but acknowledged that cost effectiveness merited further study.

Finally, our group has conducted two RCTs which involve PE in comparison to CBT in the maintenance phase. In our first study (Zaretsky et al., 2008), 79 subjects were randomized to receive individual interventions, either PE ($n = 39$) or PE plus additional CBT ($n = 40$). The same manual (Basco & Rush, 1996) was used to deliver both the PE (the first seven PE sessions) and the PE plus CBT treatment (the same first seven PE sessions plus 13 additional CBT sessions). There were no differences in the primary outcome of relapses over a 1-year period, but on the measure of the number of days of depressed mood (of any severity, not necessarily in a full depressive episode), there was an advantage to CBT.

Our second comparative study (Parikh et al., 2012) was also a study in the maintenance phase. However, it was designed more explicitly as an effectiveness study, with broad entry criteria, multiple sites, and sensitivity to cost and efficiency of treatment delivery. A total of 204 participants (aged 18–64 years) with either BD type I or II participated from four Canadian academic centers. Participants were assigned to receive either 20 individual sessions of CBT ($n = 95$) or six sessions of group PE ($n = 109$). Primary outcomes of symptom course and morbidity were assessed prospectively over 78 weeks using the Longitudinal Interval Follow-up Evaluation, which yields depression and mania symptom burden scores for each week. Time to relapse was an additional outcome. Both treatments had similar outcomes with respect to the reduction of symptom burden and the likelihood of relapse. Approximately 8% of subjects dropped out prior to receiving PE, while 64% were treatment completers; rates were similar for CBT (6% and 66%, respectively). PE costs $180 per subject, compared to a cost of $1,200 per subject for CBT. Despite longer treatment duration and individualized treatment, CBT did not show a significantly greater clinical benefit compared to group PE. Similar efficacy but lower cost and potential ease of dissemination suggest that the group PE intervention may be preferable from a public health perspective as an adjunct to medication for BD. Keeping in mind earlier findings about persistent negative cognitions in many patients with bipolar depression (Lam, Wright, & Smith, 2004; Zaretsky, Segal, & Gemar, 1999) and further, abnormal cognitive styles (Reilly-Harrington, Alloy, Fresco, & Whitehouse, 1999; Reilly-Harrington et al., 2010), a picture may be emerging that suggests brief group PE for all nonpsychotic bipolar patients as an initial step, with CBT being relegated to a secondary role for individuals with persistent problems and, in particular, persistent dysfunctional attitudes.

Finally, as alluded to above, the issue of cost and ease of dissemination of intensive psychosocial treatments will play a major role in the adoption of these interventions. Further research should clarify which mechanisms of action may be most potent, and should also explicitly examine the question of cost and efficiency of delivery of treatment. For instance, we noted that the excellent Barcelona Bipolar Disorders Psychoeducation program (Colom, Vieta, & Scott, 2006) was designed and delivered originally by psychologists, while the Life Goals program was designed to be taught by psychiatric nurses. In addition to the higher cost of psychologists versus nurses, the vastly larger number of nurses and their distribution across different treatment settings—in both rural and urban areas and both academic and community settings—argues for the use of such well-placed providers. Furthermore, given the training traditions of each profession, it is worth noting our experience in training primarily nurses, as well as some other professionals, in the Life Goals program for our multisite study of group PE versus individual CBT. After carefully inviting only experienced psychiatric nurses and master's level trained psychotherapists, we used a one-day training event, then accompanied the trainee through a single cycle of six PE group sessions. Additional supervision was provided as needed, but typically totalled no more than 1 hour over the six sessions. In contrast, providing training in FFT or CBT takes much longer and involves much more supervision, as both of the pivotal trials in FFT and CBT acknowledge in the key papers. In our PE versus CBT study, we noted that the cost of delivery was $180 per participant for PE, as opposed to $1,200 for the individual CBT. While the true cost of each therapy in real practice would necessitate a trial properly powered to establish financial outcomes (which would require thousands of subjects), it is still reasonable to conclude that group PE is going to be much less expensive than individual CBT.

Similar considerations would apply to family therapy, which typically involves 20–30 sessions with both patient and family members expected to attend. Both the feasibility of such an intervention for a strained health care system and the likelihood of many patients and families being able to attend must surely be low. By respecting such financial parameters, it would then be possible to follow a model of "stepped care" (Parikh & Kennedy, 2004), where all patients would be offered group PE, and the more expensive individual treatments would be reserved for those with persistent needs after finishing PE. Ideally, individuals might be evaluated after completion of PE for the presence of persistent dysfunctional attitudes, disrupted sleep cycles, or highly negative family situations, and then respectively referred to CBT, IPSRT, or FFT. For those with enduring deficits about sense of self, or comorbid problems like anxiety, personality, or substance use, additional psychodynamic therapy or targeted therapy for the comorbidity could be invoked. Emerging psychotherapies such as schema therapy offer new promise in treating BD (Hawke, Provencher, & Arntz, 2011; Hawke & Provencher, 2012).

## Provider Interventions

Specific provider interventions in BD are limited. However, the larger context of medical care, and depression in particular, has been studied exhaustively with respect to provider interventions, such as providing education in the form of treatment guidelines and continuing medical education events. Another common research intervention, involving the routine administration of screening tools by a third party and providing feedback on the results to the provider, has not been successful in altering clinical outcomes. From medicine as a whole, traditional education in the form of conventional continuing medical education events, distribution and teaching of guidelines, grand rounds, and conferences have shown little impact on clinical practice (Bloom, 2005; Davis, Thomson, Oxman, & Haynes, 1995; Davis et al., 1999). As summarized by Von Korff and Goldberg (2001), RCTs of interventions to improve depression treatment in primary care have been negative when the intervention focused only on provider or provider plus patient interventions. In the same spirit, single session training events in depression did not change practice patterns, but there is evidence that longitudinal programs alter practice (Hodges, Inch, & Silver, 2001; Parikh & Parker, 1999). However, simple mass screening with rating scales and provision of results to the relevant primary care physician have not been found particularly effective in altering disease outcomes (Gilbody, House, & Sheldon, 2001).

With respect to BD, we conducted a pilot study (Parikh, 2003) of a "Bipolar Treatment Optimization Program" that incorporated a patient intervention and a simultaneous provider education and support intervention for the patient's primary care physician. Patients benefited, as did the physicians, who demonstrated improved knowledge about BD and also greater confidence in managing it. Three bipolar studies involving complex interventions with careful attention to provider education did demonstrate improved concordance to treatment guidelines but limited clinical impact (Bauer, Biswas, & Kilbourne, 2009; Dennehy, Bauer, Perlis, Kogan, & Sachs, 2007; Suppes et al., 2003; Toprac et al., 2006). Taken together and extrapolated, these findings suggest that provider interventions may be a necessary, but clearly not a sufficient, intervention to make an improvement in the treatment of BD.

## System Interventions

System interventions incorporate multiple elements and inevitably overlap with the domains of patient and provider maneuvers. Furthermore, studies of system reorganization strategies do not easily allow "unbundling" of the different components to identify the most potent elements. Nonetheless, such system interventions are clear to specify and clear to study. Historically, the establishment of "lithium clinics" for BD was an early example of a relatively pure system intervention, as reviewed by Gitlin and Jamison (1984). Staff of these clinics fostered a clear understanding of the medical model for BD, built care along multidisciplinary lines, and established routines for the evaluation and monitoring of patients as well as the provision of basic PE. Virtually no advances in system interventions in BD had been reported until the publication of two randomized controlled studies (comparison condition is treatment as usual), one of which had modest results, with the other only moderate results. In the first program, Bauer and colleagues (Bauer, 2001; Bauer et al., 2006) compared a "comprehensive patient education package" with specific treatment guidelines for providers, and a special nurse providing care facilitation versus treatment as usual. Modest results in terms of the reduction of time spent in depression were found, without major changes in relapse. In the second similar study, Simon and colleagues (Simon, Lundman, Unutzer, & Bauer, 2002; Simon et al., 2006) used a collaborative treatment model involving the same structured PE for patients; feedback of "automatic" monitoring results and algorithm-based medication recommendations to providers; and a nurse care manager involved in providing monthly telephone monitoring, outreach, PE, and care coordination. Significant reductions in the frequency and severity of mania, but not depression, were found. Yet another development where a systems intervention may be helpful involves the simultaneous management of medical illnesses and BD, starting with attention to metabolic issues (Kilbourne, Lai, Bowersox, Pirraglia, &

Bauer, 2011; Leboyer & Kupfer, 2010). Finally, the enormous STEP-BD blended systems interventions with many other treatments, with complex findings (Parikh, LeBlanc, & Ovanessian, 2010; Sachs et al., 2003).

While results for BD are modest, the findings from the depression literature are very clear: Nine randomized controlled treatment involving depressed patients in primary care show strong positive results from the adoption of a model where therapeutic maneuvers include some degree of case management, reorganization of typical care pathways, and incorporation of patient and provider education and support (Von Korff & Goldberg, 2001). Similarly, in a U.S. multicentre clinical trial involving practice nurses in care management over 24 months was effective in improving remission rates by 33 percentage points compared to the "treatment-as-usual group" (a remarkable 74% remission rate vs. 41% at 24 months; Rost, Nutting, Smith, Elliott, & Dickinson, 2002). Such results, paralleling the success in employing chronic disease management strategies for diabetes (Renders et al., 2001), suggest that BD will be best served by a chronic disease model involving an emphasis on system reorganization to include nurse care facilitation, telephone interventions, and full use of a multidisciplinary "patient care team" (Coleman et al., 2009; Wagner, 2000)—but in conjunction with the patient and provider programs described earlier.

## Integration of Patient, Provider, and System Approaches

This chapter began by citing the example of a young man with BD and posed a question about the best treatment approach. Surely the start of the answer is rooted in evidence and some of the evidence has been reviewed briefly earlier. But clinical reality is influenced by a number of variables that extend beyond research evidence or "best practices." Patient attitudes, stigma both on the part of the patient and the provider, costs, availability of suitable providers, convenience, transportation access, the enthusiasm of providers, the nature of the treatment alliance, and the specific treatment preferences of a local environment are among the determinants of treatment initiation and continuation. Large epidemiological surveys, such as the U.S. National Comorbidity Survey (Kessler et al., 1994; Kessler, Merikangas, & Wang, 2007) and the Mental Health Supplement to the Ontario Health Survey (Lin & Parikh, 1999; Parikh et al., 1997; Parikh, Wasylenki, Goering, & Wong, 1996) document that many individuals who fulfill diagnostic criteria for various mood disorders are not receiving treatment; among those in treatment, the median annual treatment frequency is less than 10 visits to any type of provider. Faced with this evidence and cognizant of the cost of high-intensity services, recommendations for treatment should reflect what is readily achievable as well as what might constitute "best practice."

Integration of all these perspectives would suggest that treatment be conceptualized in a pyramid form, much like Maslow's hierarchy of needs (Maslow, 1987), as noted in Figure 14.1. At the base of the pyramid is the need for pharmacotherapy and clinical management (supportive therapy including specifying treatment and monitoring outcome, offering practical advice for immediate problems such as work or school stressors and instilling hope for relief of symptoms), essential for all patients. The second layer, involving appropriate health system design (tailored health services),

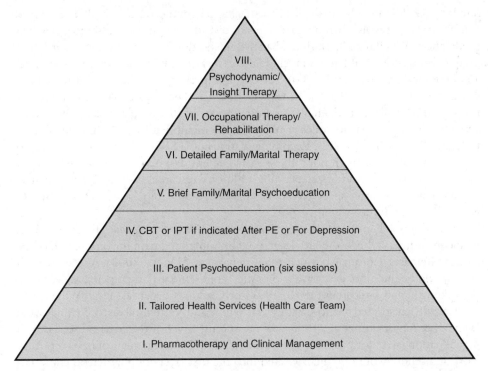

VIII.
Psychodynamic/
Insight Therapy

VII. Occupational Therapy/
Rehabilitation

VI. Detailed Family/Marital Therapy

V. Brief Family/Marital Psychoeducation

IV. CBT or IPT if indicated After PE or For Depression

III. Patient Psychoeducation (six sessions)

II. Tailored Health Services (Health Care Team)

I. Pharmacotherapy and Clinical Management

**Figure 14.1.**    Hierarchy of Treatment Interventions for Bipolar Disorder (Parikh, 2002)

would benefit most patients and would involve specific suggestions on the use of the chronic disease model for bipolar disorder, with the creation of a health care team for bipolar disorder. The treatment team likely would include nurse care coordinators/practitioners as key members, together with the ready availability of educational and other support for both patients and health care providers. The third layer, necessary for almost all patients, would be patient PE; based on the evidence and cost, brief group PE would be the ideal model. Multiple studies are employing the Bauer and McBride manual (Bauer & McBride, 1996, 2003) for group psychotherapy, from which a six-session psychoeducational component (phase I of the Life Goals Program) may be extracted. The highly readable and scripted format of the manual, its use in multiple studies, and even its translation into French and adoption in multiple clinical sites in Quebec and Europe suggest that this manual may be a prime model for cost-effective group PE; its revised 2nd edition in 2003 (Bauer & McBride) provides an improved format in English. This edition is also available in French, unpublished, and can be obtained by contacting the team that updated it (Provencher, St-Amand, Thienot, & Hawke, 2007).

The fourth layer of the pyramid, now necessary for fewer patients, would be specific individual psychotherapy, most likely CBT or IPSRT. However, in reality, the benefits of both these treatments include the fact that a key component of CBT includes illness education, relapse prevention drills, and attention to sleep and other behavioral routines; in other words, topics already covered through the basic PE.

Similarly, IPSRT includes many psychoeducational components as well. The unique features of CBT revolve around challenges to distorted cognitions and more detailed modulation of behavioral routines than would be done in basic PE. Similarly, the unique features of IPSRT would include the extremely meticulous attention to social and biological rhythms, and to some extent, interpersonal conflict/deficit resolution (Malkoff-Scwartz et al., 1998). In view of this, CBT perhaps could be reserved for those with poor illness management despite receipt of PE and particularly those with very high dysfunctional attitudes at outset (easily quantified by a Dysfunctional Attitudes Scale, Weissman, 1979). Recommendations of IPSRT would also be limited to those individuals both with poor illness management despite PE and with prominent interpersonal issues. In addition, pending additional research, both CBT and IPT may be appropriate to target-specific types of episodes, that is, bipolar depression (Swartz & Frank, 2001; Zaretsky et al., 1999).

Above the CBT and IPT layers of the pyramid, family and marital interventions would include basic PE as the fifth layer, possibly integrated with the original PE of the patient (Reinares, Colom, Martinez-Aran, Benabarre, & Vieta, 2002). A separate sixth layer would be the more extensive and costly "gold standard" treatments as described by Miklowitz and Goldstein (1990, 1997) or Clarkin, Carpenter, Hull, Wilner, and Glick (1998), restricted to those with severe family and/or marital discord (Miklowitz, Wendel, & Simoneau, et al., 1998). At the seventh level of the pyramid would be a rehabilitation layer; for purposes of this model, simple management of basic return to work and school would be incorporated into the first layers of pharmacotherapy and clinical management as well as in individual PE. In layer seven, rehabilitation refers to much more complex and detailed efforts to restore functioning, suitable for a small group of patients. Finally, the last layer of the pyramid would utilize psychotherapy models such as psychodynamic therapy to deal with more complex issues, personality problems, and so on.

To return to the example cited at the beginning of the chapter, describing the young man with bipolar depression on a background of medication noncompliance and skepticism about the medical model, we can now develop some recommendations.

1. Start a mood stabilizer; consider adding an antidepressant, offer practical advice (i.e., consider time off work or school, spend time with friends, etc.) and instill hope.
2. In addition to the treating physician, consider enlisting a nurse who will more closely monitor the patient and may be able to form a more detailed treatment alliance that permits other interventions as below.
3. Add basic PE (six sessions from the Bauer and McBride Manual).
4. Consider phase-specific psychotherapy: CBT for bipolar depression, particularly if a simple administration of the Dysfunctional Attitudes Scales shows an extremely high score.
5. Consider adding IPSRT if the above measures are insufficient, particularly after medication and CBT interventions.
6. Evaluate for family discord; provide one to two sessions of family PE.
7. Consider an occupational therapy consult if difficulty returning to work or school is anticipated.

8. Initiate family interventions as acute episode stabilizes, if indicated.
9. Consider detailed psychotherapy if indicated after episode stabilizes; issues such as shame, stigma, and diminished self-esteem and future potential are common.

This sequence of steps assumes that treatment expertise is available in each modality; in reality, many jurisdictions will not be able to provide all treatments. But based on the treatment pyramid model, and keeping in mind the fact that the most basic layers of the pyramid are those with both evidence and feasibility with respect to cost and practicality, it is then advisable for any clinic undertaking to treat BD to attempt to organize resources to provide as many of the basic layers of treatment as possible. To invest clinic resources heavily in IPSRT or family interventions, for example, without adequate efforts to offer more basic interventions would result in a mismatch between treatment needs and treatment availability. The challenges of BD are many; so too are the methods of treatment. Construction of a treatment model incorporating chronic disease management principles allows for rational clinic planning and for wise delivery of care to patients.

# References

Aubry, J. M., Charmillot, A., Aillon, N., Bourgeois, P., Mertel, S., Nerfin, F., . . . de Andrés, R. D. (2012). Long-term impact of the life goals group therapy program for bipolar patients. *Journal of Affective Disorders*, *136*(3), 889–894.

Ball, J. R., Mitchell, P. B., Corry, J. C., Skillecorn, A., Smith, M., & Malhi, G. S. (2006). A randomized controlled trial of cognitive therapy for bipolar disorder: Focus on long-term change. *Journal of Clinical Psychiatry*, *67*(2), 277–286.

Basco, M. R., & Rush, A. J. (1996). *Cognitive-behavioral therapy for bipolar disorder*. New York: Guildford Press.

Bauer, M. S. (2001). The collaborative practice model for bipolar disorder: Design and implementation in a multi-site randomized controlled trial. *Bipolar Disorders*, *3*, 233–244.

Bauer, M. S., Biswas, K., Kilbourne, A. M. (2009). Enhancing multiyear guideline concordance for bipolar disorder through collaborative care. *American Journal of Psychiatry*, *166*(11):1244–1250.

Bauer, M. S., & McBride, L. (1996). *Structured group psychotherapy for bipolar disorder*. New York: Springer.

Bauer, M. S., & McBride, L. (2003). *Structured group psychotherapy for bipolar disorder: The life goals program* (2nd ed.). New York: Springer.

Bauer, M. S., McBride, L., Williford, W. O., Glick, H., Kinosian, B., Altshuler, L., . . . Sajatovic, M. (2006). Collaborative care for bipolar disorder: Part II. Impact on clinical outcome, function, and costs. *Psychiatric Services*, *57*, 937–945.

Beck, A. T. (2008). The evolution of the cognitive model of depression and its neurobiological correlates. *American Journal of Psychiatry*, *165*, 969–977.

Beck, A. T., Rush, A. J., Shaw, B. F., & Emery, G. (1979). *Cognitive therapy of depression*. New York: Guilford Press.

Bedi, N., Chilvers, C., Churchill, R., Dewey, M., Duggan, C., Fielding, K., . . . Williams, I. (2000). Assessing effectiveness of treatment of depression in primary care. Partially randomised preference trial. *British Journal of Psychiatry*, *177*, 312–318.

Berk, L., Hallam, K. T., Colom, F., Vieta, E., Hasty, M., Macneil, C., . . . Berk, M. (2010). Enhancing medication adherence in patients with bipolar disorder. *Human Psychopharmacology, 25*(1), 1–16.

Bloom, B. S. (2005). Effects of continuing medical education on improving physician clinical care and patient health: A review of systematic reviews. *International Journal of Technology Assessment in Health Care, 21*(3), 380–385.

Clarkin, J. F., Carpenter, D., Hull, J., Wilner, P., & Glick, I. (1998). Effects of psychoeducational intervention for married patients with bipolar disorder and their spouses. *Psychiatric Services, 49*, 531–533.

Cohen, N. L., Parikh, S. V., & Kennedy, S. H. (2000). Medication compliance in unipolar depression and bipolar disorder: Determinants and methods of assessment. *Primary Care Psychiatry, 6*(3), 101–110.

Coleman, K., Austin, B. T., Brach, C., & Wagner, E. H. (2009). Evidence on the chronic care model in the new millennium. *Health Affairs (Millwood), 28*(1), 75–85.

Colom, F., Vieta, E., Martinez-Aran, A., Reinares, M., Goikolea, J. M., Benabarre, A., . . . Corominas, J. (2003). A randomized trial on the efficacy of group psychoeducation in the prophylaxis of recurrences in bipolar patients whose disease is in remission. *Archives of General Psychiatry, 60*, 402–407.

Colom, F., Vieta, E., Sánchez-Moreno, J., Palomino-Otiniano, R., Reinares, M., Goikolea, J. M., . . . Martínez-Arán, A. (2009). Group psychoeducation for stabilised bipolar disorders: 5-year outcome of a randomised clinical trial. *British Journal of Psychiatry, 194*(3), 260–265.

Colom, F., Vieta, E., & Scott, J. (2006). *Psychoeducation manual for bipolar disorder*. Cambridge: Cambridge University Press.

Davis, D., O'Brien, M. A., Freemantle, N., Wolf, F. M., Mazmanian, P., & Taylor-Vaisey, A. (1999). Impact of formal continuing medical education: Do conferences, workshops, rounds, and other traditional continuing education activities change physician behavior or health care outcomes? *Journal of American Medical Association, 282*, 867–874.

Davis, D. A., Thomson, M. A., Oxman, A. D., & Haynes, R. B. (1995). Changing physician performance: A systematic review of the effect of continuing medical education strategies. *Journal of American Medical Association, 274*, 700–705.

Dennehy, E. B., Bauer, M. S., Perlis, R. H., Kogan, J. N., & Sachs, G. S. (2007). Concordance with treatment guidelines for bipolar disorder: Data from the systematic treatment enhancement program for bipolar disorder. *Psychopharmacology Bulletin, 40*(3), 72–84.

Donohoe, M. T. (1998). Comparing generalist and specialty care: Discrepancies, deficiencies, and excesses. *Archives of Internal Medicine, 158*, 1596–1608.

Frank, E., Hlastala, S., Ritenour, A., Houck, P., Tu, X. M., Monk, T. H., . . . Kupfer, D. J. (1997). Inducing lifestyle regularity in recovering bipolar disorder patients: Results from the maintenance therapies in bipolar disorder protocol. *Biological Psychiatry, 41*, 1165–1173.

Frank, E., Kupfer, D. J., Thase, M. E., Mallinger, A. G., Swartz, H. A., Fagiolini, A. M., . . . Monk, T. (2005). Two-year outcomes for interpersonal and social rhythm therapy in individuals in bipolar IV. *Archives of General Psychiatry, 62*, 996–1004.

Frank, E., Swartz. H. A., & Kupfer, D. J. (2000). Interpersonal and social rhythm therapy: Managing the chaos of bipolar disorder. *Biological Psychiatry, 48*(6), 593–604.

Frank, E., Swartz, H. A., Mallinger, A. G., Thase, M. E., Weaver, E. V., & Kupfer, D. J. (1999). Adjunctive psychotherapy for bipolar disorder: Effects of changing treatment modality. *Journal of Abnormal Psychology, 108*, 579–587.

Gilbody, S. M., House, A. O., & Sheldon, T. A. (2001). Routinely administered questionnaires for depression and anxiety: Systematic review. *British Medical Journal, 322,* 406–409.

Gitlin, M. J., & Jamison, K. R. (1984). Lithium clinics: Theory and practice. *Hospital and Community Psychiatry, 35,* 363–368.

Goldberg, J. F., & Harrow, M. (1999). *Bipolar disorders: Clinical course and outcome.* Washington, DC: American Psychiatric Association Press.

Goodwin, F. K., & Jamison, K. R. (2007). *Manic-depressive illness: Bipolar disorders and recurrent depression* (2nd ed.). New York: Oxford.

Hawke, L. D., & Provencher, M. D. (2012). Early maladaptive schemas among patients diagnosed with bipolar disorder. *Journal of Affective Disorders, 136*(3), 803–811.

Hawke, L. D., Provencher, M. D., & Arntz, A. (2011). Early maladaptive schemas in the risk for bipolar spectrum disorders. *Journal of Affective Disorders, 133*(3), 428–436.

Hodges, B., Inch, C., & Silver, I. (2001). Improving the psychiatric knowledge, skills, and attitudes of primary care physicians, 1950–2000: A review. *American Journal of Psychiatry, 158,* 1579–1586.

Huxley, N. A., Parikh, S. V., & Baldessarini, R. J. (2000). Effectiveness of psychosocial treatments in bipolar disorder: State of the evidence. *Harvard Review of Psychiatry, 8,* 126–140.

Ibrahim, M. A., Savitz, L. A., Carey. T. S., & Wagner. E. H. (2001). Population-based health principles in medical and public health practice. *Journal of Public Health Management and Practice, 7*(3), 75–81.

Kessler, R. C., McGonagle, K. A., Zhao, S., Nelson, C. B., Hughes, M., Eshleman, S., . . . Kendler, K. S. (1994). Lifetime and 12-month prevalence of DSM-III-R psychiatric disorders in the United States. *Archives of General Psychiatry, 51,* 8–19.

Kessler, R. C., Merikangas, K. R., & Wang, P. S. (2007). Prevalence, comorbidity, and service utilization for mood disorders in the United States at the beginning of the twenty-first century. *Annual Review of Clinical Psychology, 3,* 137–158.

Kilbourne, A. M., Lai, Z., Bowersox, N., Pirraglia, P., & Bauer, M. S. (2011). Does colocated care improve access to cardiometabolic screening for patients with serious mental illness? *General Hospital Psychiatry, 33*(6), 634–636.

Lam, D. H., Hayward, P., Watkins, E. R., Wright, K., & Sham, P. (2005). Relapse prevention in patients with bipolar disorder: Cognitive therapy outcome after 2 years. *American Journal of Psychiatry, 162,* 324–329.

Lam, D. H., McCrone, P., Wright, K., & Kerr, N. (2005). Cost-effectiveness of relapse-prevention cognitive therapy for bipolar disorder: 30-month study. *British Journal of Psychiatry, 186,* 500–506.

Lam, D., Wright, K., & Smith, N. (2004). Dysfunctional assumptions in bipolar disorder. *Journal of Affective Disorders, 79,* 193–199.

Leboyer, M., & Kupfer, D. J. (2010). Bipolar disorder: New perspectives in health care and prevention. *Journal of Clinical Psychiatry, 71*(12):1689–1695.

Lin, E., & Parikh, S. V. (1999). Sociodemographic, clinical, and attitudinal characteristics of the untreated depressed in Ontario. *Journal of Affective Disorders, 53,* 153–162.

Malkoff-Schwartz, S., Frank, E., Anderson, B., Sherrill, J. T., Siegel, L., Patterson, D., . . . Kupfer, D. J. (1998). Stressful life events and social rhythm disruption in the onset of manic and depressive bipolar episodes. A preliminary investigation. *Archives of General Psychiatry, 55,* 702–707.

Maslow, A. H. (1987). *Motivation and personality* (3rd ed.). New York: Harper & Row.

Miklowitz, D. J., George, E. L., Richards, J. A., Simoneau, T. L., & Suddath, R. L. (2003). A randomized study of family-focused psychoeducation and pharmacotherapy in the outpatient management of bipolar disorder. *Archives of General Psychiatry, 60,* 904–912.

Miklowitz, D. J., & Goldstein, M. J. (1990). Behavioral family treatment for patients with bipolar affective disorder. *Behavior Modification, 14,* 457–489.

Miklowitz, D. J., & Goldstein, M. J. (1997). *Bipolar disorder: A family focused treatment approach.* New York: Guildford Press.

Miklowitz, D. J., Otto, M. W., Frank, E., Reilly-Harrington, N. A., Wisniewski, S. R., Kogan, J. N., . . . Sachs, G. S. (2007). Psychosocial treatments for bipolar depression: A 1-year randomized trial from the systematic treatment enhancement program. *Archives of General Psychiatry, 64*(4), 419–426.

Miklowitz, D. J., Richards, J. A., George, E. L., Frank, E., Suddath, R. L., Powell, K. B., . . . Sacher, J. A. (2003). Integrated family and individual therapy for bipolar disorder: Results of a treatment development study. *Journal of Clinical Psychiatry, 64,* 182–191.

Miklowitz, D. J., Simoneau, T. L., George, E. L., Richards, J. A., Kalbag, A., Sachs-Ericsson, N., . . . Suddath, R. (2000). Family-focused treatment of bipolar disorder: 1-year effects of a psychoeducational program in conjunction with pharmacotherapy. *Biological Psychiatry, 48*(6), 582–592.

Miklowitz, D. J, Wendel, J. S., & Simoneau, T. L. (1998). Targeting dysfunctional family interactions and high expressed emotion in the psychosocial treatment of bipolar disorder. *In-Session: Psychotherapy in Practice, 4*(3), 25–38.

Organization for Bipolar Affective Disorder (OBAD). (2010). *Bipolar affective disorder: A guide to recovery.* Calgary, Canada: Author.

Parikh, S. V. (2003, November). *Treating mood disorders more effectively: A health systems approach.* Canadian Psychiatric Association Annual Meeting, Halifax.

Parikh, S. V., & Kennedy, S. H. (2004). Integration of patient, provider, and systems treatment approaches in bipolar disorder. In M. Power (Eds.), *Mood disorders: A handbook of science and practice* (pp. 247–258). London: Wiley.

Parikh, S. V., Kusumakar, V., Haslam, D. R., Matte, R., Sharma, V., & Yatham, L. N. (1997). Psychosocial interventions as an adjunct to pharmacotherapy in bipolar disorder. *Canadian Journal of Psychiatry, 42*(Suppl. 2): 74S–78S.

Parikh, S. V., LeBlanc, S. R., & Ovanessian, M. M. (2010). Advancing bipolar disorder: Key lessons from the systematic treatment enhancement program for bipolar disorder (STEP-BD). *Canadian Journal of Psychiatry, 55*(3), 136–143.

Parikh, S. V., Lin, E., & Lesage, A. D. (1997). Mental health treatment in Ontario: Selected comparisons between the primary care and specialty sectors. *Canadian Journal of Psychiatry, 42,* 929–934.

Parikh, S. V., & Parker, K. (1999, January). *Improving detection and management of psychiatric illnesses: Linking family medicine and psychiatry with an innovative longitudinal course.* Alliance for Continuing Medical Education Annual Meeting, Atlanta.

Parikh, S. V., Wasylenki, D., Goering, P., & Wong, J. (1996). Mood disorders: Rural/urban differences in prevalence, health care utilization, and disability in Ontario. *Journal of Affective Disorders, 38,* 57–65.

Parikh, S. V., Zaretsky, A., Beaulieu, S., Yatham, L. N., Young, L. T., Patelis-Siotis, I., . . . Streiner, D. L. (2012). A randomized controlled trial of psychoeducation or cognitive-behavioral therapy in bipolar disorder: A canadian network for mood and anxiety treatments (CANMAT) study. *Journal of Clinical Psychiatry, 73*(6), 803–810.

Perlick, D. A. (2001). Special section on stigma as a barrier to recovery: Introduction. *Psychiatric Services, 52,* 1613–1614.

Perry, A., Tarrier, N., Morriss, R., McCarthy, E., & Limb, K. (1999). Randomized controlled trial of efficacy of teaching patients with bipolar disorder to identify early symptoms of relapse and obtain treatment. *British Medical Journal, 318,* 149–153.

Prien, R. F., & Potter, W. Z. (1990). NIMH workshop report on treatment of bipolar disorders. *Psychopharmacology Bulletins, 26*, 409–427.

Prien, R. F., & Rush, A. J. (1996). National Institute of Mental Health workshop report on the treatment of bipolar disorder. *Biological Psychiatry, 40*, 215–220.

Provencher, M. D., St-Amand, J., Thienot, E., & Hawke, L. D. (2007). Groupe psychoéducatif pour le traitement du trouble bipolaire: Révision et adaptation québécoise de la phase psychoéducative de la deuxième édition anglophone du manuel de Bauer, M. S., & McBride, L. (2003). *Structured group psychotherapy for bipolar disorder: The life goals program* (2nd ed.). Unpublished document, Université Laval.

Reilly-Harrington, N. A., Alloy, L. B., Fresco, D. M., & Whitehouse, W. G. (1999). Cognitive styles and life events interact to predict bipolar and unipolar symptomatology. *Journal of Abnormal Psychology, 108*, 567–578.

Reilly-Harrington, N. A., Miklowitz, D. J., Otto, M. W., Frank, E., Wisniewski, S. R., Thase, M. E., ... Sachs, G. S. (2010). Dysfunctional attitudes, attributional styles, and phase of illness in bipolar disorder. *Cognitive Therapy and Research, 34*(1), 24–34.

Reinares, M., Colom, F., Martinez-Aran, A., Benabarre, A., & Vieta, E. (2002). Therapeutic interventions focused on the family of bipolar patients. *Psychotherapy and Psychosomatics, 71*(1), 2–10.

Renders, C. M., Valk, G. D., Griffin, S. J., Wagner, E. H., Eijk Van, J. T. M., & Assendelft, W. J. (2001). Interventions to improve the management of diabetes in primary care, outpatient, and community settings: A systematic review. *Diabetes Care, 24*, 1821–1833.

Rost, K., Nutting, P., Smith, J. L., Elliott, C. E., & Dickinson, M. (2002). Managing depression as a chronic disease: A randomized trial of ongoing treatment in primary care. *British Medical Journal, 325*, 934.

Roth, A., & Fonagy, P. (2005). *What works for whom? A critical review of psychotherapy research* (2nd ed.). New York: Guilford Press.

Sachs, G. S., Thase, M. E., Otto, M. W., Bauer, M., Miklowitz, D., Wisniewski, S. R., ... Rosenbaum, J. F. (2003). Rationale, design, and methods of the systematic treatment enhancement program for bipolar disorder (STEP-BD). *Biological Psychiatry, 53*, 1028–1042.

Sackett, D. L., Straus, S. E., Richardson, W. S., Rosenberg, W., & Haynes, R. B. (2000). *Evidence-based medicine. How to practice and teach EBM*. Edinburgh, UK: Churchill Livingstone.

Scott, J. (2001). Cognitive therapy as an adjunct to medication in bipolar disorder. *British Journal of Psychiatry, 178*(Suppl. 41), S164–S168.

Scott, J., Paykel, E., Morriss, R., Bentall, R., Kinderman, P., Johnson, T., ... Hayhurst, H. (2006). Cognitive behavioural therapy for severe and recurrent bipolar disorders: Randomised controlled trial. *British Journal of Psychiatry, 188*, 313–320.

Simon, G. E., Ludman, E. J., Bauer, M. S., Unutzer, J., & Operskalski, B. (2006). Long-term effectiveness and cost of a systematic care program for bipolar disorder. *Archives of General Psychiatry, 63*, 500–508.

Simon, G. E., Ludman, E. J., Unutzer, J., & Bauer, M. S. (2002). Design and implementation of a randomized trial evaluating systematic care for bipolar disorder. *Bipolar Disorders, 4*, 226–236.

Sperry, L. (1995). *Psychopharmacology and psychotherapy: Strategies for maximizing outcomes*. New York: Brunner/Mazel.

Suppes, T., Rush, A. J., Dennehy, E. B., Cirsmon, M. L., Kashner, T. M., Toprac, M. G., ... Shon, S. P. (2003). Texas medication algorithm project, phase 3 (TMAP-3): Clinical results for patients with a history of mania. *Journal of Clinical Psychiatry, 64*, 370–382.

Swartz, H. A., & Frank, E. (2001). Psychotherapy for bipolar depression: A phase-specific treatment strategy? *Bipolar Disorders, 3*(1), 11–22.

Toprac, M. G., Dennehy, E. B., Carmody, T. J., Crismon, M. L., Miller, A. L., Trivedi, M. H., … Rush, A. J. (2006). Implementation of the Texas medication algorithm project patient and family education program. *Journal of Clinical Psychiatry, 67*, 1362–1372.

Von Korff, M., & Goldberg, D. (2001). Improving outcomes in depression. *British Medical Journal, 323*, 948–949.

Wagner, E. H. (2000). The role of patient care teams in chronic disease management. *British Medical Journal, 320*, 569–572.

Wagner, E. H., Austin, B. T., & Von Korff, M. (1996). Organizing care for patients with chronic illness. *The Millbank Quarterly, 74*, 511–544.

Weissman, A. N. (1979). The dysfunctional attitudes scale: A validation study. *Disserations Abstracts International, 40*, 1389–1390.

Yatham, L. N., Kennedy, S. H., Schaffer, A., Parikh, S. V., Beaulieu, S., O'Donovan, C., … Kapczinski, F. (2009). Canadian network for mood and anxiety treatments (CANMAT) and international society for bipolar disorders (ISBD) collaborative update of CANMAT guidelines for the management of patients with bipolar disorder: Update 2009. *Bipolar Disorders, 11*(3), 225–255.

Zaretsky, A., Lancee, W., Miller, C., Harris, A., & Parikh, S. V. (2008). Is cognitive-behavioural therapy more effective than psychoeducation in bipolar disorder? *Canadian Journal of Psychiatry, 53*(7), 441–448.

Zaretsky, A. E., Segal, Z. V., & Gemar, M. (1999). Cognitive therapy for bipolar depression: A pilot study. *Canadian Journal of Psychiatry, 44*, 491–494.

# 15

# Cognitive Behavioral Therapy for Bipolar Affective Disorders

## Matthias Schwannauer
### University of Edinburgh, UK

## Introduction

Bipolar disorder is a severe, enduring, and pervasive psychiatric disorder, which affects approximately 2% of the population (Grant et al., 2005; NICE, 2006), and is equally distributed between men and women. The disorder is identified and characterized primarily by shifts in polarity of mood, from depressed to manic. It is these shifts which differentiate bipolar from unipolar disorders, and are crucial in its diagnosis. The mean onset is located in late adolescence and early adulthood, which causes lasting psychosocial difficulties partly due to the impact of the age of onset and the crucial impact on individual development (Ramana & Bebbington, 1995), but also as a result of the high likelihood of repeated episodes within few years in up to 80% of the bipolar population (Goodwin & Jamison, 2007). Following a severe episode, psychosocial and psychological impairments are evident for a number of years (Goldberg & Harrow, 2004; Rosa et al., 2009), and individuals diagnosed with bipolar disorder are likely to report significantly lower physical and mental quality of life (Gutierrez-Rojas et al., 2008), along with experiencing frequent relapse (Judd et al., 2008). One of the tragic manifestations of the complexity and the lasting impairments often caused by the traumatic impact of early and multiple episodes is the high suicide rate in bipolar disorder, with up to half of all individuals with bipolar disorder attempting suicide (Valtonen et al., 2005). As may be expected, both attempts and ideation are associated with depressive aspects of the illness, and hopelessness and severity of depression are key indicators of risk (Valtonen et al., 2007). This places the issue of suicidal risk in the centre of the therapeutic intervention.

The second key challenge for the treatment of bipolar disorder is the high proportion of comorbidity. The disorder is associated with a significant risk of substance abuse, high rates of anxiety disorder (McElroy et al., 2001; Otto et al., 2006), personality disorder (Brieger, Ehrt, & Marneros, 2003), and to a lesser extent eating disorders (McElroy et al., 2001). In an epidemiological study of bipolar outpatients, McElroy et al. (2001) found that at least 65% of their sample met criteria for at least one comorbid axis I disorder. Furthermore, comorbidity was associated with an earlier

*The Wiley-Blackwell Handbook of Mood Disorders*, Second Edition. Edited by Mick Power.
© 2013 John Wiley & Sons, Ltd. Published 2013 by John Wiley & Sons, Ltd.

age of onset and greater illness severity. Other studies show comorbid conditions to be associated with poorer response to treatment (Henry et al., 2003; Schmitz et al., 2002) and an increased risk of suicide attempt (Simon et al., 2007), thus highlighting the need for specific interventions targeting these groups. Psychotic symptoms are commonly observed in bipolar disorder, affecting approximately 75% of manic patients. Studies have shown that patients with a prior history of psychotic symptoms showed poorer outcome and a more severe course of illness.

Cognitive behavioral therapy (CBT) is the most commonly implemented interventions for bipolar disorder. CBT aims to identify and target core beliefs, dysfunctional attitudes, and negative automatic thoughts along with maladaptive behaviors. Widely used and with demonstrated success rates (Miklowitz et al., 2007; Veltro et al., 2008; Zaretsky, Lancee, Miller, Harris, & Parikh, 2008), criticism primarily focus on the inability of CBT to explain the mixed emotional states frequently seen in bipolar disorder.

One of the first challenges faced by the CBT therapist in bipolar disorder is the strong heterogeneity of this disorder group and its various phenomenological manifestations. In comparison with other mood disorders, the emotional, cognitive, and behavioral problems associated with bipolar disorder range from long periods of depression to varying degrees of euphoria, irritability, agitation, and psychotic symptomatology. Most individuals suffering from bipolar disorder experience cyclical symptoms and multiple episodes of both depression and mania over the life span, which creates significant disruptions in the patients' lives as well as lasting psychological and psychosocial difficulties.

CBT has been shown to be a highly effective short-term psychotherapeutic intervention for a wide range of disorder groups, especially recent developments in CBTs for treatment-resistant schizophrenia and severe and enduring depressive disorder, and their increasing positive evidence base initiated the prospect for the development of psychological interventions for bipolar disorders. However, to date, there has been little consistent evidence of the effectiveness of CBT for bipolar disorders; most studies report effectiveness in terms of relapse prevention, a strong overall effect on depression, and small inconsistent effects on mania (Gregory, 2010; Lynch, Laws, & McKenna, 2010; Miklowitz & Scott, 2009).

## The Cognitive Behavioral Model of Bipolar Disorder

Many authors have argued that there is a marked lack of a coherent psychological model of bipolar disorder (Jones, 2001; Power, 2005). Recent research, however, highlighted the role of cognitive and psychosocial factors in the development and course of bipolar disorder, and first treatment manuals were published in recent years delineating the application of CBT principles to bipolar disorders (Basco & Rush, 1996; Newman, Leahy, Beck, Reilly-Harrington, & Gyulai, 2002; Scott, 2001b). A body of research focused on cognitive factors such as attributional styles, information processing (Alloy et al., 2005), and dysfunctional attitudes (Lam, Wright, & Smith, 2004; Goldberg, Wenze, Welker, Steer, & Beck, 2005); perfectionism, deficits in problem-solving skills, and elevated scores of sociotropy and autonomy (Lam et al., 2000); and maladaptive schemata (Young, 1999). The behavioral activation system (BAS) and reward responsiveness play an essential role in the cognitive and behavioral aspects of bipolar disorder. Especially in relation to hypomania and mania, BAS activation is associated with heightened mood states, increased goal-driven behaviors, less perceived need for sleep, and increased anger and impulsivity. Individuals with a bipolar disorder and higher BAS tendencies, therefore, had shorter interepisode intervals in relation to hypomania and mania (Alloy et al., 2008). Further, circadian rhythm instability has long been associated with mood instability; more specifically, daily rhythm disturbances as well as seasonal variations have been repeatedly associated with mood instability in bipolar disorder and its inherent cyclical nature (Jones, 2006).

These factors appear to play a significant role in the interaction of considerable changes in behavior, reactions to and the creation of significant psychosocial stressors, disruptions in chronobiological functioning, and varied responsiveness to psychotropic medications. One of the reasons for the complex pattern of factors influencing phenomenology and course of the disorder for each individual is the huge variability in the spectrum of bipolar disorders ranging from chronic cyclothymic presentations to episodic manifestations of severe depression and mania including psychotic features.

Overall, the cognitive behavioral model aids our clinical understanding of the psychopathology of bipolar disorder and the ways in which specific problems and interactions can be targeted; it does not, however, offer any further etiological clarification of this disorder. Researchers suggested that comparable cognitive structures and biases underlie both unipolar and bipolar depression (Alloy et al., 2005; Lam et al., 2004), particularly in terms of systematic attributional errors and sensitivity to personal failure or interpersonal rejection. Specific to individuals suffering from bipolar disorder is the extreme valence shift in the content of their thinking. A cognitive model of bipolar disorder needs to integrate the variability in the stress responses of individuals. In other words, depending on the type of stressor or circumstance, individuals with bipolar disorder can respond with the development of depressive symptoms or with the development of manic responses; this can vary between individuals or over time. The model also needs to take into account that bipolar individuals display traits like thought processes in the form of long-standing predispositions and state-like responses to environmental triggers and physiological activation. Further, it needs to take into account the specific effects of significant life events and environmental stressors on individuals' affect regulation, in line with a diathesis–stress model of mood disorders (Lam, Jones, Hayward, & Bright, 1999). In particular, the fact is that only certain life events appear to be able to predict mania, while others do not (Johnson, Winett, Meyer, Greenhouse, & Miller, 1999). A clinical working model of bipolar disorder, therefore, needs to encompass biology, individual beliefs, behavioral reactions, interpersonal functioning, environmental triggers and life events, and the individual's idiosyncratic conceptualization of these events.

Beck's (1979) cognitive behavioral model suggests that depressed mood is mediated by particular patterns of thinking that accentuate mood shifts. Individuals who are depressed become more negative in how they perceive themselves, others, and the world in general; as a result, they are prone to systematic cognitive distortions in that they tend to overgeneralize, self-blame, jump to negative conclusions, and tend to view things in black and white terms. The avoidance of social contacts and other safety behaviors often results in an interaction of mood shifts and negative thinking patterns. These cognitive styles of depression are thought to arise out of early learning experiences. Beck suggested in his cognitive model that mania is a mirror image of depression, determined by a hyper-positive triad of self, others, and the future. Scott, Stanton, Garland, and Ferrier (2000) found that individuals with bipolar disorder demonstrated lower levels of self-esteem, overgeneralized memory, poorer problem-solving skills, and higher levels of dysfunctional attitudes, particularly related to the need for social approval and perfectionism. They further found that these vulnerabilities persisted between episodes in patients who were adherent to prophylactic treatment. Beck and colleagues worked on a reformulation of the original linear cognitive model for bipolar disorders (Beck, 1996; Newman et al., 2002). This reconceptualization includes the notion of "modes". Modes are understood as integrated "cognitive affective behavioral networks" of powerful combinations of schemata, overlearned behavior pattern, and intense, difficult to modulate emotions. When schemas and modes are activated by specific life events, chronobiological disruption, or other such triggers, the bipolar individuals' predispositional reactions become expressed by extremities in emotional and behavioral functioning. They argue that individuals' belief systems interact with their inherent perception of current stressors and events. This activation of long-standing beliefs and schemata determines their affect and behavior, and influences their information processing by directing the individual toward information consistent with the schema. In this way, a negatively valenced schema is activated during a depressed phase, directing memory retrieval toward the events of loss and rejection and focusing current attention on the possibility of failure. In a manic phase, a positively valenced schema is activated, and is likely to lead to problematic decision making by selectively ignoring the need for adaptive caution and inhibition.

Clinically, a reliable understanding of the individual's cognitive assumptions and core beliefs that encompass his or her perception of themselves, the world, and the future, helps the therapist to demonstrate an accurate understanding of the individual's experiences and to focus on the assumptions and beliefs that cause most distress and dysfunction. It is, therefore, important to assess individuals' core beliefs independent of their presenting symptom pattern. A grandiose and manic individual might have the same core schema of "unlovability" and "incompetence" as a depressed patient. Bipolar individuals appear to maintain consistent maladaptive core beliefs and schemata that shift polarity in their manifestations. The successful modification of these beliefs through cognitive therapy should result in the reduced amplification of the dysfunctional mood swings of the bipolar client.

Apart from the reformulation of the cognitive model for bipolar disorder by Beck and his colleagues, other alternatives have been formulated to capture the complex interactions between thoughts and emotions. Teasdale and Barnard (1993) differentiated between propositional and implicational "schematic" levels of information processing. They argue that propositional-level cognitions, or direct appraisals of any given information, do not directly activate emotional reactions, but are mediated on a level of implicational meaning by a process of schematic appraisal, in the context of present and past propositional information. Power and Dalgleish (1997, 1999) support this model and add an additional direct or associative route to emotions. This model has several clinical implications by disentangling the rational or schematic processes of change that appear to be primarily focused on by classical cognitive therapy approaches from the associative or direct associations of certain cues and emotional reactions. Jones (2001) utilized this multilevel approach to emotion and cognition to investigate the vulnerability of bipolar individuals to mood changes following disruptions in their circadian rhythms. Following this model in individuals with bipolar disorder, schema change is achieved through associative links through behavior modification and corrective experiences, rather than rational cognitive techniques such as the challenging of automatic thoughts and restructuring. Patients should, therefore, be encouraged to experience subsyndromal mood changes and stimulation utilizing adaptive coping strategies with the subsequent absence of prodromal symptoms.

Key cognitive behavioral conceptualizations relate to increased sensitivity in individuals with bipolar disorder to neuropsychological BASs in relation to goal attainment life events and to the destabilizing impact of circadian rhythm disruptions (Jones, 2001). Separate from these neuropsychological models of mood regulation, authors focused on cognitive styles and cognitive biases in bipolar disorder that influence compensatory behavioral strategies, which are thought to contribute to the development of mania (Leahy, 2005). These models, however, remain very unintegrated and are predominantly tested independent of alternative assumptions.

A study put forward an integrative conceptual model of mood swings in bipolar disorder that aimed to put together the empirical evidence for alternative models of affect in bipolar disorder. They suggest a functional pattern where the interpretation of intrusions and internal mood states leads to paradigmatic response styles in bipolar disorder that are driven and catalyzed by dysfunction in the BAS, a vulnerability to circadian rhythm disruptions, and specific cognitive appraisal processes in the face of perceived mood changes. These self-reinforcing patterns can then quickly spiral into the development of mania and depression through specific "ascent behaviors" (e.g., risk taking, increased alcohol and drug use, etc.) or "descent behaviors" (e.g., social withdrawal, rumination, etc.), which are triggered in the individual as an attempt to control unwanted mood states. The authors emphasize that this describes a model of mood regulation that also applies to similar difficulties in related disorder groups, such as psychosis and schizoaffective disorder, and that it is not specific to bipolar disorder. A key aspect of this model appears to be the misinterpretation of internal states (physiological, emotional, or cognitive) as bearing significant personal meaning and with a number of contradictory appraisals. These appraisals of changes in internal states can include signs of an imminent catastrophe, a personal success, or a personal weakness. These appraisals then trigger immediate efforts at exerting control. The model further proposes that the appraisal of changes in internal states and the associated ascent/descent behavior are influenced by a range of factors such as personal core beliefs regarding self and others and beliefs about affective states. These beliefs are affected by past experiences and current stressors.

## The Application of CBT in the Treatment of Bipolar Disorder

Overall, a cognitive behavioral approach to the treatment of bipolar disorder is aimed at enhancing nonpharmacological coping skills, to enhance elements of self-efficacy and responsibility in the treatment of the condition, to support individuals in recognizing and managing psychosocial stressors and the impact of past episodes, to introduce specific strategies to deal with cognitive and behavioral difficulties, and to modify underlying schemata and core assumptions. An important aspect in this treatment framework is the range of intervention strategies that seek to enhance constructive mood regulation strategies and adaptation to the effects and consequences of bipolar disorder.

All CBT models for bipolar disorder rely on the basic characteristics of the original CBT model for depressed mood. The cognitive behavioral model appears to be most effective when the individuals are full collaborative partners in the treatment process. The therapist educates the individual about the diathesis–stress model of bipolar disorder, socializes the individual into the cognitive model of mood changes, and appraises them of the rationale for particular interventions. An assessment of the individual's core beliefs and underlying schemata are essential in the case formulation of individual vulnerabilities that form an integral part of the treatment plan.

The CBT treatment of bipolar disorder is naturally phase specific. The specific focus of the intervention will vary depending on the individual formulation of treatment goals and the phase of the disorder in which the patient presents. For example, if a patient presents in an acute phase of a bipolar episode the cognitive behavioral strategies will be aimed at crisis intervention, the treatment of acute symptoms, an assessment of risk and factors that are maintaining the episode, and the establishment of a good therapeutic alliance. If a patient presents in the recovery phase following a recent episode or in a phase of stabilization between episodes, the CBT treatment would intend to be insight oriented, to explore the meaning and context of symptoms, interpersonal functioning, preventative cognitive strategies, and self-management skills, to reduce the impact of the psychosocial disorder and to build resilience regarding ongoing stressors.

The following section outlines the four main components of cognitive behavioral psychotherapy for bipolar disorder: psychoeducation; early warning signs and coping with prodromal symptoms; cognitive behavioral strategies for dealing with manic, hypomanic, or depressive symptoms; and finally the targeting of associated difficulties in psychosocial functioning, especially related interpersonal difficulties.

Crucial for the adaptation of a cognitive behavioral intervention to any psychiatric disorder is the individual case formulation. This should be developed in collaboration with the client and it should be based on a developmental and cognitive model of the specific phenomenology of the bipolar disorder. The cognitive formulation is the starting point for the therapeutic intervention and can be used as an alternative explanation of the patient's difficulties and will help to engage the client in a cognitive way of understanding and working with the presenting problems.

## Self-Monitoring and Prodromal Changes

Dealing with manic and hypomanic phases has been described as being the biggest clinical challenge in the treatment of bipolar individuals. Most individuals suffering from bipolar disorder would describe a manic phase as being inescapable, once their mood starts to rise the initial positive reinforcement of experiencing new sources of energy and creativity develops, especially when this happens after long periods of depressed mood it easily develops into a self-reinforcing pattern that seems impossible to stop.

The psychoeducational component of the cognitive behavioral intervention is an important starting point in this stage of problematic mood changes. The individual's awareness of possible consequences and manic episodes developing in a way that they require increased external control and medications seems crucial in preventing the negative impact of full-blown manic episodes. Past episodes provide the best source for information.

The early warning signs paradigm, originally developed for relapse prevention in early-onset psychotic disorders, especially schizophrenia, has been adapted for use with people suffering from bipolar disorders (Lam & Wong, 1997). Patients learn to identify prodromal and early symptoms of relapse and develop a range of behavioral techniques to improve their coping skills in order to counteract early symptoms effectively and to avoid their development into a full-blown episode.

In most cases, the change in mood, cognition, and behavior is a gradual process. This allows time for the clinician and the individual to utilize psychological interventions while he or she is still responsive to cognitive and behavioral techniques. Teaching patients to recognize early symptoms of psychotic relapse and seek early treatment is associated with important clinical improvements (Perry, Tarrier, Morriss, McCarthy, & Limb, 1999). Recent advances in the identification and formulation of individualized early warnings signs (Lam & Wong, 1997) and the prodromal "'relapse signature" (Smith & Tarrier, 1992) allows clinicians to reformulate the process of cycling into mania as an interaction of the individual's life situation, cognitive processing, and their general level of coping skills. We can help patients to develop an individualized profile of prodromal changes and to be sensitized to significant mood changes early enough to curtail vicious cycles. This therapeutic step is influenced by the idiosyncratic beliefs that each patient associates with changes in their mood and that might compromise their coping abilities in the face of prodromal changes. For example, the patient who believes that his or her manic episodes follow a predetermined course, no matter what he or she does, might well be less cautious and responsible in the face of early hypomanic mood changes and, therefore, exacerbate the development of manic symptoms. These maladaptive beliefs underlying the individual's coping strategies and reactions are crucial especially in the prevention of manic episodes. In utilizing cognitive therapy strategies such as cognitive reframing and guided discovery, patients can learn to view new behaviors as an active process in which they execute a choice and that despite the undeniable attraction of hypomanic impulses some degree of control could be established.

One of the difficulties described by many patients is that of developing a hyper-vigilance regarding minor changes in mood and their misinterpretation as onset of a manic episode rather than an accurate reflection of ordinary happiness, which can lead to inappropriate safety behaviors and avoidance. Within a cognitive behavioral framework, this can be avoided by teaching the patient to monitor their mood on an ongoing basis using individualized mood monitoring tools that allow the patient to look out for several specific prodromal signs in connection with actual environmental stressors and events, in order to avoid the generalization of mood changes. Specific and detailed monitoring and rating of daily mood and relating any mood fluctuations to events in their daily schedule can introduce greater sensitivity and understanding of regular mood fluctuations and which particular stressor they react to. Further, we should employ coping strategies in response to prodromal changes that are appropriate to the mood changes observed. These coping strategies include activity schedules, the observation of sleep and dietary routines, the practice of relaxation exercises and graded task assignments, time delay rules and problem-solving techniques in the face of impulsive decision-making, and stimulus control techniques such as the regulation of alcohol and caffeine consumption, and the reduction of risk-seeking behaviors and stimulating activities. Jones argues, in a review discussing the benefits of cognitive behavioral interventions for individuals suffering bipolar disorder, that the indicated mechanisms of change over and above the known benefits of cognitive therapy indicate behavioral techniques such as extended activity scheduling and stabilization of daily routines and sleep cycles that predominantly influence circadian rhythm (Jones, 2001).

Disruption and irregularity in circadian rhythms, social events, and activities have been found to significantly impact on mood and can trigger affective episodes in peo-ple suffering from bipolar disorders. In support of this effect, the regulation of social interactions and balanced sleep–wake cycles have been found to be effective in pre-venting relapse and subsyndromal mood swings in bipolar disorders. Bipolar patients are highly sensitive to disruptions in their biological rhythms (Malkoff-Schwartz et al., 1998). The regularity of daily routines and activities, as well as the regularity of sleep–wake cycles has been identified as a major protective factor (Frank et al., 1999). The psychological factors that influence individuals' ability to maintain stability, such as advance planning, attention to detail, and self-restraint, are the very difficulties that are associated with bipolarity. The therapist must, therefore, be very cautious in intro-ducing these ideas that might easily be perceived as being overly controlling and meet significant resistance from the patient. One way to evaluate whether positive mood changes are indicative of a hypomanic or manic episode is to engage in calming activ-ities and "time out" as a way of self-assessment as to whether it is possible for the patient to remain still and to concentrate for significant periods of time.

The most effective intervention toward the successful coping with prodromal symp-toms and counteracting mood changes is to reevaluate the experience of past episodes and their consequences and to engage in a cost–benefit analysis of letting things take their natural course or to engage in constructive self-monitoring and self-regulating strategies. A useful therapeutic step within that is the acknowledgment of the diffi-culties to resist especially hypomanic mood changes and the initial gratification that goes along with it. In this, we need to bear in mind that both appraisals of current symptoms as well as the memory of past episodes is influenced by mood congruent biases. It is, therefore, valuable to use life-charting techniques and diary keeping to encourage patients to process recent changes in the context of past experience and in interaction with other life changes (Basco & Rush, 1996).

## Cognitive Strategies

The cognitive therapy techniques used for bipolar disorders include strategies aimed at the processing of symptoms and cognitive distortions relating to hypomanic and manic episodes. Further, it aims to address beliefs and attributional biases linked to the psychological effects of long-term impairment through chronic mood-related difficulties and/or residual symptoms. Many of the effective cognitive strategies for dealing with depression are similar to those used with unipolar depressed individuals.

Most patients suffering from bipolar disorders describe mood-related difficulties and their social and interpersonal consequences as dating back to early adolescence. The long-standing nature of many of the associated difficulties and variation in intensity and severity over time makes it difficult for many patients to identify areas of normal functioning or the clear demarcations of the "healthy self." Some schema work can, therefore, prove to be extremely useful in reexamining the value and evidence for old belief systems and the generation of new sets of beliefs adaptive to the current actuality.

Cognitive therapy follows a constructionist view of reality as being created by the individual's idiosyncratic preconceptions, perceptions, and memories. Cognitive therapy strategies, in the face of significant emotional difficulties, take into account the systematic distortions and maladaptation that can significantly influence the individual patient's world view. This approach aims at the correction or reevaluation of these systematic mood congruent biases by reexamination of actual experiences and current interpersonal interactions, including the therapeutic relationship (Newman et al., 2002). In the presence of signs of mania and hypomania, cognitive therapists would aim at helping the patient to reality test and reexamine their extremely positive world view and self-perception taking into consideration their current interactions and environmental stressors. Similar microtechniques and strategies come into play, for example, in the observance of daily thought records. Systematic thinking errors are driven by hyper-positive automatic thought patterns and beliefs not unlike the ones observed in depression but with the opposite valence, such as overgeneralization, mind-reading, and personalization. In the reevaluation of these thought patterns, it is important for the therapist to support patients in the process of rationalizing by emphasizing the maladaptive nature of such styles and consideration of likely consequences of hyper-positive thinking.

Especially for manic or hypomanic patients, these attempts might be perceived as extremely counterintuitive and controlling in the light of their self-perception of enjoying life and their new-found energy. Patients may feel quickly criticized or put down. Mansell and Lam (2006) found that in a small study on advice taking, bipolar participants were significantly more likely to oppose the advice following a positive mood induction than nonbipolar controls. It is, therefore, important for cognitive therapists working with bipolar patients to aim at preserving their sense of autonomy, self-efficacy, and control over their own lives. Techniques that support the self-efficacy and the reevaluation of maladaptive beliefs include behavioral experiments, the feedback of close others, and anticipatory problem-solving.

Patients can be encouraged to test out their assumptions by creating real-life experiments. In hypomanic patients, this technique could lead to some reckless behavior when hyper-positive thoughts are put to the test. In hypomania, therefore, behavioral experiments can be constructed to test the assumed consequences of not following impulses and acting with caution and time delays. To make constructive use of their social support system, bipolar patients often have to meet previous agreements with significant others regarding their intervention and advice, as hypomanic individuals often do not appreciate the influence of others.

One of the main features of manic or hypomanic phases is excessive risk taking. This is accompanied by a set of cognitive biases that leads many bipolar patients to underestimate the potential harm or overestimate the potential benefits of their behaviors (Leahy, 1999). Newman et al. (2002) introduce a version of the cost–benefit sheets often employed in CBT problem-solving techniques to get bipolar patients to balance risk and benefit of actions prospectively; the "productive potential versus destructive risk rating technique." In this technique, patients use a two-column table balancing the "productive potential" and the "destructive potential" with the support of the therapist, which should allow individuals in a hypomanic or manic phase to consider the potentially negative consequences of their actions for others.

Related to these techniques, which attempt to help bipolar patients to reevaluate their hyper-positive thoughts, are the following CBT applications to moderate their impulsivity. One example for this is the "time delay" rule, encompassing contracted agreements to delay the execution of "spontaneous" ideas that might include adventurous activities or large purchases. The CBT technique of scheduling daily activities is commonly used to help depressed patients to master day-to-day activities and to reactivate the enjoyment of favorite pastimes; for bipolar patients this technique can be employed to slow down the vicious cycle of mania driven by excessive activities, poor decision making, and more poorly deliberated and ineffective activities. Anticipatory problem-solving regarding early warning signs of imminent mood swings and in relation to life stressors that might exacerbate symptoms (Johnson & Miller, 1997) appear to be crucial in these two areas where the coping abilities of bipolar patients can be particularly challenged. Therapeutically, the process of anticipatory problem-solving includes the retrospective evaluation of past crises, to identify potential problem areas in major life domains, and using problem-solving techniques to deal with these problem areas and obstacles in advance. Another technique to moderate hypomanic and manic moods is stimulus control. This includes the ability to moderate drug and alcohol use and not to engage in extreme sports and other risk-taking and "exciting" activities; medium- to long-term choices in this connection include the regulation of working patterns that do not include extreme hours and frequent disruptions of sleep cycles. These strategies, especially when viewed medium to long term, might seem very challenging to individuals who are prone to act impulsively and like to engage in activities without much prior consideration and planning. To avoid conflict with the high autonomy of bipolar patients, the therapist needs to aim to take as collaborative a position as possible.

Many bipolar patients argue that, in particular their high moods, euphoria, and heightened irritability, are autonomous from their volition. Therapeutically, it can be extremely challenging to moderate these mood states and to increase the patient's willingness to participate in interventions that are incongruent with their current mood. CBTs that can be applied in that context are relaxation and breathing exercises, cognitive strategies to compare the lasting effects of pleasant affective states versus their intensity, and the appraisal of positive beliefs that are linked to the high feelings themselves.

Individuals with bipolar disorder experience frequent and prolonged periods of depression which over time fosters feelings of hopelessness strongly associated with suicidal thinking and suicide. This is seen as being directly related to the problems created by frequent mood swings and associated behaviors. Bipolar patients frequently have to reassemble their lives after episodes of manic acting out and depressive withdrawal; they find it difficult to trust their euthymic mood and not to worry about the impending relapse. The diagnosis itself, its cyclical episodes, and their treatments are further associated with stigma and shame, which makes it harder for individuals to utilize and maintain their social support network and prolongs their depressogenic beliefs and hence their vulnerability for relapse (Lundin, 1998). In sum, bipolar disorder contains painful and unstable affect, extremes of cognitions and behaviors, interpersonal deficits, and a lasting sense of Sisyphus' despairing exhaustion. As a result, the lifetime suicide rates have been found to be between 15% and 25% (Goodwin & Jamison, 2007). An assessment of risk, therefore, needs to be an ongoing feature in the treatment of individuals suffering from bipolar disorder.

The cognitive behavioral treatment of depression is discussed in detail elsewhere in this volume and at large applies well to the depressed mood states within bipolar disorder. Here I would only like to point to a few specific aspects that might be more specifically relevant to individuals suffering from bipolar disorder.

Many people suffering from bipolar disorders report a long history of several significant illness episodes, the traumatic impact of multiple hospital admissions, and partially successful treatment regimes involving several different psychotropic medications. Individuals in this disorder group often suffer from significant residual symptoms and have experienced short periods of remission followed by frequent relapses. This poses a particular challenge to the clinician, the patient, and their significant others might express increased hopelessness regarding remission and skepticism regarding the model offered by the clinician. Key characteristics of chronic or partially remitted disorders, such as suicidal ideation, hopelessness, low self-esteem and self-efficacy, avoidant coping strategies, and poor problem-solving, are amenable to change utilizing the cognitive behavioral strategies.

In a high-risk population such as patients with bipolar disorder, it is advisable to negotiate an antisuicide agreement, and although such contracts do not prevent suicides they highlight and validate the importance of a safe environment for patients and therapists alike (Kleepsies & Dettmer, 2000; Stanford, Goetz, & Bloom, 1994). In the face of intense suicidal ideation, the therapist aims to reveal the beliefs underlying suicidal thoughts and to engage the patient in the exploration of alternative and life-affirming beliefs. These interventions include the open investigation of the pros and cons of suicide, the gentle challenging of assumptions behind suicidal thoughts (e.g., suicide as solution to all problems), and consideration of the social context and the consequences of such thoughts and actions. As utilized in the cognitive behavioral treatment of unipolar depression, the increase of mastery and pleasure in productive and enjoyable activities can instill hope and encourage self-efficacy. Cognitive factors associated with increased risk of suicidality are "cognitive rigidity," perfectionism, and poor autobiographical recall (Blatt, 1995; Ellis & Ratcliff, 1986; Evans, Williams, O'Loughlin, & Howells, 1992; Scott et al., 2000). Cognitive rigidity refers to depressogenic all or nothing thinking and has a strong link with hopelessness and despair associated with suicidality. This particular thinking style is therefore at the core of cognitive interventions. Likewise, perfectionism describes a set of beliefs that makes individuals vulnerable to depression and hopelessness, and it compromises constructive problem-solving. Zuroff et al. (2000) suggest that perfectionist beliefs are related to self-criticism, perceived stress, increased interpersonal problems, and they can further impede the therapeutic alliance. Poor autobiographical recall has been linked to problem-solving deficits in unipolar and bipolar depressed individuals (Evans et al., 1992; Scott et al., 2000); it compromised the individual's ability to learn from experience and it can thus solidify old dysfunctional beliefs.

Central to the effective treatment of chronic or acute depressive difficulties in bipolar patients is the optimal utilization of their social support network. The consequences and interactional styles of both manic and depressed episodes can easily compromise the individual's relationships. A careful assessment of the individual's social networks and the relationships that survived many mania-induced conflicts and depression-induced estrangements will provide a fruitful starting point for the rebuilding of a stable and supportive social environment. Detailed analysis of specific interactions or situations as well as role-playing and other social skills training techniques might provide crucial assets in the cognitive behavioral intervention.

## Interpersonal Functioning

The third phase of the treatment is targeted toward the interpersonal difficulties that precipitate or resulted from the disorder. This is where cognitive strategies address core beliefs and schemata. The goals for this phase of the treatment include the experience of increased self-efficacy and the rebuilding of a more solid and autonomous sense of self. This takes into account the impact of the illness which often occurs in a developmentally critical time when self-esteem and identity are formed. It further appears that the impact of mania and depression at an early age is significant as they dramatically affect important developmental milestones such as educational achievements, early work experience, and important interpersonal relationships. Essential cognitive structures such as dysfunctional core beliefs will likely become self-perpetuating. Examples of these beliefs include a distorted sense of autonomy or personal capability, vulnerability to harm or illness, and a sense of defectiveness and unlovability. It is important to address the recognition of maladaptive core beliefs that may have been established by the early onset of the disorder or traumatic events as it will help those individuals to understand and cope with the specific psychosocial impairments experienced later in the life course.

These interpersonal vulnerabilities and risk factors can play a major part in the recovery and prevention of relapse of the individual. Therapeutically, some of these processes will consist of the facilitation of successful transitions following major episodes, significant psychosocial changes, and the adjustment to necessary lifestyle changes. Similar to the above mentioned model of the importance of corrective experiences and behavior change in individuals with bipolar disorder, these changes in the cognitive emotional schemata of the bipolar patient are achieved through consistent behavioral adaptations to the vulnerabilities intrinsic to the disorder. In their reformulation of the interpersonal psychotherapy framework (IPT) for bipolar disorder (IP/SRT), Frank et al. (1997) combine the key interpersonal difficulties associated with bipolar disorder with an introduction of the strict monitoring of social routines and circadian rhythms. By addressing the interpersonal problems and the regularity of daily routines, this method addresses both concurrent symptoms and the impact of interpersonally based stressors on the patient's life, and increases his or her resilience to potential vulnerabilities.

The application of these techniques within a CBT framework allows the patient to develop an understanding of how adverse interpersonal experiences create maladaptive schemata about the self, dysfunctional attachment beliefs, and impair the acquisition of effective interpersonal problem-solving strategies. How these might alter the threshold of stress needed to trigger a depressive or manic reaction, and how the generation of these events might be maintained by dysfunctional ways of solving emerging interpersonal difficulties and from conflicts arising from maladaptive expectations about others (Lovejoy & Steuerwald, 1997). The direct therapeutic targeting of these interpersonal vulnerabilities can lead to schema change and the development of stable supportive interactions in the presence of negative life events that aid the prevention of relapse.

## Affect, Meaning, and Relapse

A key aspect of the experience of relapse is the experience of high levels of emotional distress and affective dysregulation in the period before, during, and following an acute episode. There have been a number of psychological conceptualizations of relapse (Birchwood, 1995; Gumley, White, & Power, 1999). All of these models have emphasized how individuals interpret subtle signs (e.g., cognitive perceptual changes) and/or symptoms (e.g., interpersonal sensitivity) as evidence of a forthcoming relapse. Coping strategies adopted by individuals may enable them to reduce their levels of emotional distress or support affective stabilization. For example, being able to talk with a trusted friend or family member, being able to self-soothe, having a kindly, accepting, and compassionate attitude to oneself, being able to decatastrophize relapse, or being able to access appropriate support and assistance available may all positively impact on coping. A study reported on the use of spontaneous cognitive and behavioral coping strategies during prodromal stages, and also the impact that these had on functioning. They reported that the use of behavioral coping strategies had an effect on reducing the likelihood of manic relapse. On the other hand, having few interpersonal resources, living in a highly stressful environment, or being socially isolated may well limit the availability and flexibility of coping strategies or the opportunities for help seeking.

The use of coping strategies such as substance use or medication discontinuation (to reduce side effects) may provide short-term relief but enhance relapse risk in the medium and long term. Social avoidance and withdrawal may enhance interpersonal sensitivity, rumination, and emotional distress leading to feelings of helplessness, hopelessness, and suicidal thinking. Hultman, Wieselgren, and Ohman (1997) found that individuals with a withdrawal-orientated coping style were more likely to relapse than individuals who had a socially orientated coping style. In addition, problematic thought control strategies or avoidance strategies may prevent disconfirmation of excessively negative beliefs about relapse thus maintaining: (a) an elevated sense of threat of relapse and (b) increasing the likelihood of greater relapse acceleration at the appearance of early signs.

Safety behaviors are a kind of coping strategy specifically targeted at attempting to avoid a feared outcome. Not only do these behaviors attempt to avert a feared outcome, but they also prevent the individual from disconfirming unhelpful beliefs, and thus play a role in the maintenance of anxiety and psychological distress.

## Outcomes

Early investigations of CBT techniques in bipolar disorder focused almost solely on the adherence to medical treatments, education on the importance of good sleep and routine, and the detection and good coping strategies of early warning signs. Main examples of this particular CBT application are Benson (1975) and Cochran (1984). Benson (1975) reports a retrospective analysis of 31 bipolar disorder patients who were all in a manic phase at the start of treatment, receiving a combination treatment of lithium and psychotherapy. Comparisons were made between relapse in this group of people with a diagnosis of bipolar disorder and previous reports of relapse rates with lithium alone. He reports that 14% of his patients relapsed compared with reported mean relapse rate of 34% with lithium alone. He suggests that psychotherapy is important to keep the patient motivated to continue lithium, to provide basic therapeutic support, and to monitor patient's mood as a way of early detection of falling serum lithium levels. Cochran's (1984) study is probably the most cited paper in the context of cognitive therapy for bipolar disorders. She evaluated the effectiveness of a preventative treatment adherence intervention with 28 outpatients with a diagnosis of bipolar disorder who have recently started lithium treatment. The intervention consisted of six sessions of a modified cognitive behavioral treatment aimed at cognitions and behavior that seemed to be interfering with treatment adherence. Comparison was drawn with a control group who received standard outpatient follow-up, at the end of treatment and after 6 months follow-up. Neither the patient self-report nor the lithium levels showed an effect of the intervention, solely the psychiatrists' observation showed better perceived adherence in the treatment group after therapy. At

6 months follow-up, patients in the treatment group showed significantly less hospitalizations and affective episodes. The intervention as described does not seem to take into account the symptoms and other manifestations of the disorder, but only pays attention to compliance with pharmacological treatment.

A number of studies since focused predominantly on relapse prevention and the identification of prodromal symptoms and early signs of relapse. Perry et al. (1999) investigated 69 patients with a diagnosis of bipolar disorder who had had a relapse in the previous 12 months. Subjects were randomized into two conditions, 7–12 sessions with a research psychologist plus routine care or routine care alone. The CBT intervention consisted of teaching patients to recognize early symptoms of manic and depressive relapse and producing and rehearsing an action plan. By comparison, the treatment group experienced significantly longer intervals until manic relapse than the control group. They further found significant improvements on measures of social functioning and employment in the treatment group compared with the control group 18 months after the baseline assessment.

Several more comprehensive studies utilizing a CBT framework focused not only on treatment adherence, relapse prevention, and reduction of symptomatic distress but also on psychosocial functioning. Palmer, Williams, and Adams (1995) describe a psychoeducational and CBT program in a group format for people with a diagnosis of bipolar disorder, currently in remission. Four participants attended seventeen weekly group sessions. At the end of treatment, three out of the four participants showed significant improvements in depressive and manic symptoms. Three out of the four participants showed significant improvement in their social adjustment at the end of treatment and two at follow-up. Zaretsky, Zindel, and Gemar (1999) designed a cognitive behavioral intervention focusing on the treatment of acute symptoms rather than relapse prevention. They demonstrated, in a matched case-controlled design, the effectiveness of a 20-session CBT intervention for acute depression in the context of a bipolar disorder compared to the effectiveness in recurrent unipolar depression by comparing both groups in parallel. They found that depressive symptoms in eight bipolar and eight unipolar patients were significantly reduced after CBT intervention. Lam et al. (2000) describe a cognitive therapy approach for a total of 12 bipolar patients. The treatment consisted of 12–20 sessions over 6 months. On a global symptom level (over 12 months), the treatment group had significantly fewer episodes and fewer hospitalizations compared to the control group. The monthly self-report and observer ratings of manic and depressive symptoms confirmed that there was a significantly lower level of manic and depressive symptoms in the treatment group over the course of the 12 months. The therapy group performed significantly better on medication compliance, social functioning, self-controlled behavior, and coping with mania and depression prodromes. Patelis-Siotis and colleagues (2001) reported outcomes of a 14-session adjunctive group CBT treatment for patients suffering from a bipolar disorder. Forty-nine outpatients with a diagnosis of bipolar disorder currently maintained on a stable mood level on medication treatment participated in a CBT group therapy program focusing on psychoeducation and cognitive behavioral intervention strategies. The results indicate no significant changes in mood-related symptoms between baseline and end of treatment, however, they found a significant increase in psychosocial functioning.

Scott (2001a) reports on the outcome of a randomized controlled study that tested the feasibility and potential benefits of cognitive therapy for people with a diagnosis of bipolar disorder. Following assessment, patients were randomly assigned to immediate cognitive therapy or to a 6-month waiting list control condition. Both groups contained 21 subjects. Patients were followed up at 6-monthly intervals for a maximum of 18 months. In comparison with the waiting list control groups, the CBT group showed significant reduction in symptoms and improvement in global functioning. They also found that significantly fewer subjects met criteria for relapse after CBT than before and hospitalization rates were significantly lower in the year after CBT intervention.

These positive findings were not replicated in a larger study. Scott et al. (2006) compared individual CBT with treatment as usual (TAU). This randomized control trial (RCT; $N = 253$) held weekly CBT sessions with patients for 15 weeks, then sessions become less frequent until 26 weeks of treatment. Patients were also given two "booster" sessions to assess progress. Scott did not find an overall effect for CBT with regard to relapse prevention for bipolar disorder. However, this trial established that individual CBT was effective in individuals with less than 12 previous major mood episodes, but less effective with those having experienced more than 12 previous episodes.

Individual CBT has also been successful in improving bipolar symptoms in adolescents (Feeny, Danielson, Schwartz, Youngstrom, & Findling, 2006). The focus of this manualized individual CBT approach was medication adherence, and it incorporated CBT techniques shown to be successful with adults along with psychoeducation. Sixteen patients aged 10–17 years completed 12 weekly sessions with homework. At the end of the trial, the group undergoing CBT were compared to a matched group, and demonstrated significant improvements in symptoms.

Elements of psychoeducation are often incorporated into CBT; Zaretsky et al. (2008) investigated the value of psychoeducation through comparing a psychoeducation intervention only to a joint CBT and psychoeducation approach. Participants diagnosed with bipolar disorder had either seven sessions of individual psychoeducation or seven sessions of psychoeducation followed by 13 individual sessions of CBT. The focus of the intervention included targeting dysfunctional thinking, identifying stressors, sleep, and communication. At the end of the trial, it was concluded that those individuals having the additional CBT experienced fewer depressed mood episodes compared to those who had psychoeducation only.

Other work has focused on evaluating the implementation of group CBT. Veltro et al. (2008) audited 5 years worth of data pertaining to readmissions to hospital for major psychiatric disorders, including bipolar disorder. Data was compared pre and post the implementation of a group CBT intervention, which centered on the vulnerability/stress model and coping. Following the review, a statistically significant reduction was found in the number of readmissions to hospital for bipolar disorder following treatment with group CBT. More recently, further support for group CBT was provided by Gomes et al. (2011). Fifty euthymic bipolar disorder patients were involved in a trial comparing the impact of group CBT and TAU on the recurrence of episodes. Participants received 18 sessions of group CBT, which covered the domains of: information, cognitive and behavioral strategies, a focus on specific problems, and relapse prevention techniques. No difference was observed in the occurrence of episodes between the groups; however, for individuals undergoing group CBT the duration to relapse was significantly longer.

In sum, several reviews have looked at the efficacy of psychotherapy for bipolar disorder (Beynon, Soares-Weiser, Woolacott, Duffy, & Geddes, 2009; Miklowitz & Scott, 2009; Szentagotai & David, 2010), and indicate that CBT for bipolar disorder works better than waiting for treatment (Scott et al. 2001a), is more beneficial than brief psychoeducation (Zaretsky et al., 2008), and has mostly proved to be superior to TAU with respect to functioning and relapse prevention (Ball et al., 2006). Focusing on overall relapse rates from four RCTs in their meta-analysis, Lynch et al. (2010) concluded that CBT is not effective for bipolar disorder.

# Conclusions

In conclusion, it seems that there is increased evidence for the clinical efficacy and effectiveness that CBT can be the most useful mode of psychological intervention for individuals suffering from bipolar disorder. It appears that CBT is acceptable and appeals to patients with bipolar disorder for its structured application, the high level of autonomy, and its potential to integrate past and current experiences in a comprehensive and applicable framework. Further, reformulations and adaptations of the cognitive behavioral model of affective and psychotic disorders allow the integration of developmental and interpersonal facets of bipolar disorder in a most beneficial way. A discussion of the most optimal form of delivery of this psychotherapeutic intervention remains inconclusive. The significant deficits and losses experienced by patients with bipolar disorder in all aspects of their lives support longer and more integrated treatment modalities and calls for the investigation of a comprehensive developmental model of bipolar psychopathology. In particular, the integration of interpersonal and family aspects in the treatment of this complex population merits further clinical and empirical investigation.

# References

Alloy, L. B., Abramson, L. Y., Urosevic, S., Walshaw, P. D., Nusslock, R., & Neeren, A. M. (2005). The psychosocial context of bipolar disorder, environmental, cognitive, and developmental risk factors. *Clinical Psychology Review, 25,* 1043–1075.

Alloy, L. B., Abramson, L. Y., Walshaw, P. D., Cogswell, A., Grandin, L. D., ... Hogan, M. E. (2008). Behavioral Approach System and Behavioral Inhibition System sensitivities and bipolar spectrum disorders: Prospective prediction of bipolar mood episodes. *Bipolar Disorders, 10,* 310–322.

Ball, J. R., Mitchell, P. B., Corry, J. C., Skillecorn, A., Smith, M., & Malhi, G. S. (2006). A randomized controlled trial of cognitive therapy for bipolar disorder: Focus on the long-term change. *Journal of Clinical Psychiatry, 67,* 277–286.

Basco, M. R., & Rush, A. J. (1996). *Cognitive behavioural therapy for bipolar disorder.* New York: Guildford Press.

Beck, A. T. (1979). *Cognitive therapy and the emotional disorders*. New York: International Universities Press.

Beck, A. T. (1996). Beyond belief: A theory of modes, personality and psychopathology. In P. M. Salkovskis (Ed.), *Frontiers of cognitive therapy* (pp. 1–25). New York: Guildford Press.

Benson, R. (1975). The forgotten treatment modality in bipolar illness: Psychotherapy. *Diseases of the Nervous System, 36*, 634–638.

Beynon, S., Soares-Weiser, K., Woolacott, N., Duffy, S., & Geddes, J. (2009). Psychosocial interventions for the prevention of relapse in bipolar disorder: Systematic review of controlled trials. *British Journal of Psychiatry, 192*, 5–11.

Birchwood, M. (1995). Early intervention in psychotic relapse, cognitive approaches to detection and management. *Behaviour Change, 12*(1), 2–19.

Blatt, S. J. (1995). The destructiveness of perfectionism: Implications for the treatment of depression. *American Psychologist, 50*, 1003–1020.

Brieger, P., Ehrt, U., & Marneros, A. (2003). Frequency of comorbid personality disorders in bipolar and unipolar affective disorders. *Comprehensive Psychiatry, 44*(1), 28–34.

Cochran, S. D. (1984). Preventing medical non-compliance in the outpatient treatment of bipolar affective disorder. *Journal of Consulting and Clinical Psychology, 52*, 873–878.

Ellis, T. E., & Ratcliff, K. G. (1986). Cognitive characteristics of suicidal and non-suicidal psychiatric inpatients. *Cognitive Therapy and Research, 10*, 625–634.

Evans, J., Williams, J., O'Loughlin, S., & Howells, K. (1992). Autobiographical memory and problem-solving strategies of parasuicidal patients. *Psychological Medicine, 22*, 399–405.

Feeny, N. C., Danielson, C. K., Schwartz, L., Youngstrom, E. A., & Findling, R. L. (2006). Cognitive-behavioural therapy for bipolar disorders in adolescents: A pilot study. *Bipolar Disorders, 8*, 508–515.

Frank, E., Hlastala, S., Ritenour, A., Houck, P., Tu, X. M., Monk, T. H., … Kupfer, D. J. (1997). Inducing lifestyle regularity in recovering bipolar disorder patients: Results from the maintenance therapies in bipolar disorder protocol. *Biological Psychiatry, 41*, 1165–1173.

Frank, E., Swartz, A. H., Mallinger, A. G., Thase, M. E., Waever, E. V., & Kupfer, D. J. (1999). Adjunctive psychotherapy for bipolar disorder: Effects of changing treatment modality. *Journal of Abnormal Psychology, 108*, 579–587.

Goldberg, J. F., & Harrow, M. (2004). Consistency of remission and outcome in bipolar and unipolar mood disorders: A 10-year prospective follow-up. *Journal of Affective Disorders, 81*, 123–131.

Goldberg, J. F., Wenze, S. J., Welker, T. M., Steer, R. A., & Beck, A. T. (2005). Content-specificity of dysfunctional cognitions for patients with bipolar mania versus unipolar depression: A preliminary study. *Bipolar Disorders, 7*(1), 49–56.

Gomes, B., Abreu, L., Brietzke, E., Caetano, S., Kleinman, A., Nery, F., & Lafer, B. (2011). A randomized controlled trial of cognitive behavioral group therapy for bipolar disorder. *Psychotherapy and Psychosomatics, 80*, 144–150.

Goodwin, F., & Jamison, K. (2007). *Manic-depressive illness: Bipolar disorders and recurrent depression* (2nd ed.). Oxford, UK: Oxford University Press.

Grant, B. F., Stinson, F. S., Hasin, D. S., Dawson, D. A., Chou, S. P., Ruan, W. J., & Huang, B. (2005). Prevalence, correlates, and comorbidity of bipolar I disorder and axis I and II disorders: Results from the National Epidemiologic Survey on Alcohol and Related Conditions. *Journal of Clinical Psychiatry, 66*, 1205–1215.

Gregory, V. (2010). Cognitive-behavioral therapy for mania: A meta-analysis of randomized controlled trials. *Social Work in Mental Health, 8*, 483–494.

Gumley, A., White, C. A., & Power, K. (1999). An interacting cognitive subsystems model of relapse and the course of psychosis. *Clinical Psychology and Psychotherapy, 6,* 261–279.

Gutiérrez-Rojas, L., Gurpegui, M., Ayuso-Mateos, J. L., Gutiérrez-Ariza, J. A., Ruiz-Veguilla, M., & Jurado, D. (2008). Quality of life in bipolar disorder patients: A comparison with a general population sample. *Bipolar Disorders, 10,* 625–634.

Henry, C., Van denBulke, D., Bellivier, F., Etain, B., Rouillon, F., & Leboyer, M., (2003). Anxiety disorders in 318 bipolar patients, prevalence and impact on illness severity and response to mood stabilizer. *Journal of Clinical Psychiatry, 64,* 331–335.

Hultman, C. M., Wieselgren, I., & Ohman, A. (1997). Relationships between social support, social coping and life events in the relapse of schizophrenic patients. *Scandinavian Journal of Psychology, 38*(1) 3–13.

Johnson, S. L., & Miller, I. (1997). Negative life events and time to recovery from episodes of bipolar disorder. *Journal of Abnormal Psychology, 106,* 449–457.

Johnson, S. L., Winett, C., Meyer, B., Greenhouse, W., & Miller, I. (1999). Social support and the course of bipolar disorder. *Journal of Abnormal Psychology, 108,* 558–566.

Jones, S. H. (2001). Circadian rhythms, multilevel models of emotion and bipolar disorder—An initial step towards integration? *Clinical Psychology Review, 21,* 1193–1209.

Jones, S. H. (2006). Circadian rhythms and internal attributions in bipolar disorder. The psychology of bipolar disorder. In S. H. Jones, & R. P. Bentall (Eds.), *The psychology of bipolar disorder: New developments and research strategies.* Oxford, UK: Oxford University Press.

Judd, L. L., Schettler, P. J., Akiskal, H. S., Coryell, W., Leon, A. C., Maser, J. D., & Solomon, D. A. (2008). Residual symptom recovery from major affective episodes in bipolar disorders and rapid episode relapse/recurrence. *Archives of General Psychiatry, 65*(4), 386–394.

Kleepsies, P. M., & Dettmer, E. L. (2000). An evidence-based approach to evaluating and managing suicidal emergencies. *Journal of Clinical Psychology, 56,* 1109–1130.

Lam, D., Wright, K., & Smith, N. (2004). Dysfunctional assumptions in bipolar disorder. *Journal of Affective Disorders 79,* 193–199.

Lam, D. H., Bright, J., Jones, S., Hayward, P., Schuck, N., Chisholm, D., & Sham, P. (2000). Cognitive therapy for bipolar illness. A pilot study of relapse prevention. *Cognitive Therapy and Research, 24,* 503–520.

Lam, D. H., Jones, S. H., Hayward, P., & Bright, J. A. (1999). *Cognitive therapy for bipolar disorder.* Chichester, UK: John Wiley & Sons.

Lam, D. H., & Wong, G. (1997). Prodromes, coping strategies, insight and social functioning in bipolar affective disorder. *Psychological Medicine, 27,* 1091–1100.

Leahy, R. L. (1999). An investment model of depressive resistance. *Journal of Cognitive Psychotherapy, 11,* 3–19.

Leahy, R. L. (2005). Clinical implications of the treatment of mania: Reducing risk behaviors in manic patients. *Cognitive and Behavioral Practice, 12,* 89–98.

Lovejoy, M. C., & Steuerwald, B. L. (1997). Subsyndromal unipolar and bipolar disorders II: Comparisons on daily stress levels. *Cognitive Therapy and Research, 21*(6), 607–618.

Lundin, R. K. (1998). Living with mental illness: A personal experience. *Cognitive and Behavioural Practice, 5,* 223–230.

Lynch, D., Laws, K., & McKenna, P. (2010). Cognitive behavioural therapy for major psychiatric disorder: Does it really work? A meta-analytical review of well-controlled trials. *Psychological Medicine, 40,* 9–24.

Malkoff-Schwartz, S., Frank, E., Anderson, B., Sherrill, J. T., Siegel, L., Patterson, D., & Kupfer, D. J. (1998). Stressful life events and social rhythm disruption in the onset of manic and depressive bipolar episodes: A preliminary investigation. *Archives of General Psychiatry, 55*, 702–707.

Mansell, W., & Lam, D. (2006). "I won't do what you tell me!": Elevated mood and the assessment of advice-taking in euthymic bipolar I disorder. *Behaviour Research and Therapy, 44*, 1787–1801.

McElroy, S. L., Altshuler, L. L., Suppes, T., Keck, P. E., Frye, M. A., Denicoff, K. D., . . . Post, R. M. (2001). Axis I psychiatric comorbidity and its relationship to historical illness variables in 288 patients with bipolar disorder. *American Journal of Psychiatry, 158*, 420–426.

Miklowitz, D., & Scott, J. (2009). Psychosocial treatments for bipolar disorder: Cost-effectiveness, mediating mechanisms, and future directions. *Bipolar Disorders, 11*(Suppl. 2), 110–122.

Miklowitz, D. J., Otto, M. W., Frank, E., Reilly-Harrington, N. A., Wisniewski, S. R., Kogan, J. N., . . . Sachs, G. S. (2007). Psychosocial treatments for bipolar depression: A 1-year randomized trial from the Systematic Treatment Enhancement Program. *Archive of General Psychiatry, 64*(4), 419–426.

National Institute of Health and Clinical Excellence [NICE]—Developed by National Collaborating Centre for Mental Health. (2006). *Bipolar disorder: The management of bipolar disorder in adults, children and adolescents, in primary and secondary care.* (NICE Clinical Guideline 38). London: NICE.

Newman, C. F., Leahy, R. L., Beck, A. T., Reilly-Harrington, N. A., & Gyulai, L. (2002). *Bipolar disorder—A cognitive therapy approach.* Washington, DC: American Psychological Association.

Otto, M. W., Simon, N. M., Wisniewski, S. R., Miklowitz, D. J., Kogan, J. N., Reilly-Harrington, N. A., . . . Pollack, M. H.; STEP-BD Investigators. (2006). Prospective 12-month course of bipolar disorder in out-patients with and without comorbid anxiety disorders. *British Journal of Psychiatry, 189*, 20–25.

Palmer, A. G., Williams, H., & Adams, M. (1995). CBT in a group format for bi-polar affective disorder. *Behavioural and Cognitive Psychotherapy, 23*, 153–168.

Patelis-Siotis, I. (2001). Cognitive-behavioural therapy: Application for the management of bipolar disorder. *Bipolar Disorder, 3*, 1–10.

Perry, A., Tarrier, N., Morriss, R., McCarthy, E., & Limb, K. (1999). Randomised controlled trial of efficacy of teaching patients with bipolar disorder to identify early symptoms of relapse and obtain treatment. *British Medical Journal, 318*, 149–153.

Power, M. J. (2005). Psychological approaches to bipolar disorders: A theoretical critique. *Clinical Psychology Review 25*, 1101–1122.

Power, M. J., & Dalgleish, T. (1997). *Cognition and emotion: From order to disorder.* Hove, UK: Psychology Press.

Power, M. J., & Dalgleish, T. (1999). Two routes to emotion: Some implications of multi-level theories of emotion for therapeutic practice. *Behaviour and Cognitive Psychotherapy, 27*, 129–141.

Ramana, R., & Bebbington, P. (1995). Social influences on bipolar affective disorders. *Social Psychiatry and Psychiatric Epidemiology, 30*, 152–160.

Rosa, A. R., Reinares, M., Franco, C., Comes, M., Torrent, C., Sánchez-Moreno, J., . . . Vieta, E. (2009). Clinical predictors of functional outcome of bipolar patients in remission. *Bipolar Disorders, 11*, 401–409.

Schmitz, J. M., Averill, P., Sayre, S., McCleary, P., Moeller, F. G., & Swann, A. (2002). Cognitive-behavioural treatment of bipolar disorder and substance abuse: A preliminary randomized study. *Addictive Disorders and Their Treatment, 1*, 17–24.

Scott, J. (2001a). Cognitive therapy as an adjunct to medication in bipolar disorder. *British Journal of Psychiatry, 178,* 164–168.

Scott, J. (2001b). *Overcoming mood swings: A self-help guide using cognitive and behavioural techniques.* London: Constable Robinson.

Scott, J., Paykel, E., Morriss, R., Bentall, R., Kinderman, P., Johnson, T., ... Hayhurst, H. (2006). Cognitive-behavioural therapy for severe and recurrent bipolar disorders: Randomised controlled trial. *British Journal of Psychiatry, 188,* 313–320.

Scott, J., Stanton, B., Garland, A., & Ferrier, N. (2000). Cognitive vulnerability to bipolar disorder. *Psychological Medicine, 30,* 467–472.

Simon, N. M., Zalta, A. K., Otto, M. W., Ostacher, M. J., Fischmann, D., Chow, C. W., ... Pollack, M. H. (2007). The association of comorbid anxiety disorders with suicide attempts and suicidal association in outpatients with bipolar disorder. *Journal of Psychiatric Research, 41,* 255–264.

Smith, J. A., & Tarrier, N. (1992). Prodromal symptoms in manic depressive psychosis. *Social Psychiatry and Psychiatric Epidemiology, 27,* 245–248.

Stanford, E., Goetz, R., & Bloom, J. (1994). The no harm contract in the emergency assessment of suicidal risk. *Journal of Clinical Psychiatry, 55,* 344–348.

Szentagotai, A., & David, D. (2010). The efficacy of cognitive-behavioural therapy in bipolar disorder: A quantitative meta-analysis. *Journal of Clinical Psychiatry, 71,* 66–72.

Teasdale, J. D., & Barnard, P. J. B. (1993). *Affect, cognition and change: Re-modelling depressive thought.* Hove, UK: Lawrence Erlbaum Associates.

Valtonen, H., Suominen, K., Mantere, O., Leppämäki, S., Arvilommi, P., & Isometsä, E. (2005). Suicidal ideation and attempts in bipolar I and II disorders. *Journal of Clinical Psychiatry, 66,* 1456–1462.

Valtonen, H. M., Suominen, K., Mantere, O., Leppämäki, S., Arvilommi, P., & Isometsa, E. (2007). Suicidal behaviour during different phases of bipolar disorder. *Journal of Affective Disorders, 97*(1–3), 101–107.

Veltro, F., Vendittelli, N., Oricchio, I., Addona, F., Avino, C., & Figliolia, G. (2008). Effectiveness and efficiency of cognitive-behavioral group therapy for inpatients: 4-year follow-up study. *Journal of Psychiatric Practice 14,* 281–288.

Young, J. E. (1999). *Cognitive therapy for personality disorder: A schema-focused approach* (3rd ed.). Sarasota, FL: Professional Resource Exchange.

Zaretsky, A., Lancee, W., Miller, C., Harris, A., & Parikh, S. (2008). Is cognitive-behavioural therapy more effective than psychoeducation in bipolar disorder? *Canadian Journal of Psychiatry, 53*(7), 441–448.

Zaretsky, A. E., Zindel, V. S., & Gemar, M. (1999). Cognitive therapy for bipolar depression: A pilot study. *Canadian Journal of Psychiatry, 44,* 491–494.

Zuroff, D. C., Blatt, S. J., Sotsky, S. M., Krupnick, J. L., Martin, D. J., Sanislow, C. A., & Simmens, S. (2000). Relation of therapeutic alliance and perfectionism to outcome in brief outpatient treatment of depression. *Journal of Consulting and Clinical Psychology, 68,* 114–124.

# 16

# Self-Management and the "Expert Patient in Bipolar Disorders"

Anne Palmer

Norwich, UK

## Introduction

This chapter focuses on the philosophy and role of self-management programs for people with bipolar disorders (BDs). The term self-management came to prominence in the 1960s and 1970s reflecting the rise of the "self-help" movement. The latter evolved partly as a consequence of dissatisfaction with traditional models of medical care that assumed service users would comply without question with the advice and instructions proffered by health professionals. Many service users found more acceptable approaches to their long-term physical or mental health problems and they took greater control of their lives through sharing experiences and seeking support from their peers instead of relying on organized health care systems. In some instances, this idea was taken to the extreme and individuals sought to cope without any professional input. In other settings, the user-led self-help groups and the professionally led mental health services worked side by side. Although their interactions spanned the spectrum from the truly harmonious to the overtly antagonistic, the ensuing dialogue and negotiation between service users and service providers created an environment in which self-management programs became a reality for many individuals with persistent health problems.

Today, self-management is about people with BD taking charge of their own health and has come to mean any program that enables them to actively manage some or all of the key aspects of their own mental health problem. It can take many forms. Whatever the form, the key defining principle in self-management is that the person with BD actively makes informed choices about the treatments and approaches they wish to pursue to manage their own health and well-being.

There are obvious advantages in an approach that promotes the idea that an individual with a serious health problem can and should be actively involved in the process of managing his or her own mental health problem. However, this chapter will also consider hindrances to self-management such as the impairments in problem solving associated with a suicidal frame of mind and highlight the potential dangers in

---

*The Wiley-Blackwell Handbook of Mood Disorders*, Second Edition. Edited by Mick Power.
© 2013 John Wiley & Sons, Ltd. Published 2013 by John Wiley & Sons, Ltd.

promoting unrealistic expectations of what an individual can control or achieve through their own efforts.

The expertise and experience of both professionals and service users have been pivotal in the development of self-management programs for BD. Before reviewing these programs, an outline of the contemporary literature about individual responsibility for health risks and the associated political context will be discussed.

## Changes in the Concepts of the Individual and the Location of Risks to Health

From her review of contemporary psychological literature, Ogden (1995) argues that, in the twentieth century, there have been fundamental shifts in our view of the individual and his or her relationship to the environment.

In the 1960s, there was a move away from the notion that individuals were passive, without agency, with their behaviors being a response to external circumstances, toward a view of the individual as an interactive being. The revised model proposed that the individual processed and appraised information from the external world and that their behaviors were then shaped by their interactions with their environment. Thus, the nexus of "illness risk" moved, from being identified with factors that were out with the individual (biomedical models) to being the product of interpersonal interactions with external factors (the biopsychosocial model).

In the last decades of the twentieth century, there was a further shift to the view of the individual as being "intra-active." The intra-active individual is still conceptualized as an interactive being, but is also viewed as having a sense of authorship over their actions, thoughts, and emotional experiences, volition and control over his or her behavior, and as being the architect of intentions and plans.

Changing views about individual identity are reflected in contemporary cultural views about the nexus of health risks. Ogden writes that following the paradigm shifts discussed above, current models emphasize that health risks and health-related behaviors are inherent within the individual, who has personal control and responsibility over his or her own (healthy or unhealthy) lifestyle. The application of this model to a person with BD would indicate that the individual has the ability to control his or her own behavior and to manage and master health treatments. In this context, risks to health are viewed as a breakdown in self-control and self-efficacy. Ogden terms this the creation of the "risky self," which is implicit in both the concept of the "expert patient" (Donaldson, 2001) and the definition of "recovery" which are discussed in the following sections.

## The Political Context and Self-Management

The expert patient's programme holds out the promise of thousands of confident and more informed patients and large numbers of lay people involved in evidence based self-management programmes of one kind or another. However, in order to achieve this there will need to be a major shift in cultural attitudes, and this in turn will depend in part on convincing patients and professionals of the value of this approach (Donaldson, 2001).

As the Chief Medical Officer for England and Wales, Liam Donaldson's paper has significantly influenced the dialogue between service users and service providers. The document clearly identifies that the main challenges to the provision of a quality health service are not from acute, but from long-term health problems, because the latter is the predominant disease pattern in the United Kingdom and across most of the developed and developing world.

The paper found that comprehensive health programs have not yet been provided and Donaldson suggests that one reason for this is the failure to use as a resource the knowledge and experiences of the individuals with long-term health problems. He recommends a fundamental shift in the way in which such long-term health problems are managed, and central to this proposal is the active recruitment and involvement of "expert patients."

The expert patient may be defined as someone who has "confidence, skills, input, and knowledge to play a central role in the management of life with chronic disease, and to minimize its impact on their day-to-day living." Essentially, this means the person with a long-term mental health problem takes a central role in decisions about their problems. They must be regarded as experienced partners in the process of health care, instead of as inexperienced recipients of treatment (Lorig, Mazonson, & Holman, 1993). It follows that policies to modernize the design and delivery of services within the NHS must emphasize the role of the person with BD as a partner who shares their expertise with other health care providers.

## The Philosophy of Recovery

Yanos, Primavera, and Knight (2001) write that the focus of recovery in BDs should be on good community adjustment rather than just the alleviation of psychiatric symptoms. Copeland (1994) also challenged the definition of recovery as a mere reduction in symptoms, and strongly argued, from her own and other people's experiences of BD, that a fuller recovery from a severe and enduring health problem is possible.

Following the publication of Anthony's (1993) synthesis of the writings of people with experience of recovery, this perspective (or The Recovery Model, as it has come to be known) has become more widely recognized, and adopted, within service user and professional circles. Evidence for this recognition comes from the growing number of recovery-orientated programs established, and from individuals writing about their recovery.

A recent review of the literature identified involvement in self-managed care and other types of consumer delivered mental health services as one of the main factors in recovery (Yanos, Primavera, & Knight, 2001).

Contemporary philosophic and recovery models see the person with BD as an intra-active individual and inform current thinking about self-management. We work collaboratively with the people with BD so that they have the information and skills to help them actively manage their own health. The expertise and experience of the service user is valued; the person makes their own choices about the treatments and approaches they wish to pursue in managing their own health and well-being.

Self-management is especially important for people with BD because of its well-recorded association with secondary disabilities, all of which can impact on recovery. These include a decline in social status and stigmatization, difficulties encountered in adjusting to variable functioning, dealing with the challenges in maintaining roles and relationships that are important, and relatively poor problem-solving skills (Scott, Garland, & Moorehead, 2001). Impairments in problem-solving skills may explain why interpersonal problems are so common in this group.

The models described above also have implications for health professionals. A collaborative working relationship between client and clinician requires the clinician to acknowledge and work with the clients' perceptions of their problems and an exploration of the clients' representation of illness model. At the same time, the clinician should neither collude with inappropriate models nor be so rigid in their own theoretical stance that they cannot find common territory to form a working alliance. This is a challenge that many clinicians find frustrating. But in reality, for the collaboration to be effective, the clinician and client must first develop a shared and accepted model of what is happening for that individual. Only when that negotiation is complete, can they use this agreed (individualized) formulation to identify and prioritize the treatment or management interventions to be used. For many clinicians, this requires three things. A change in their style of interviewing and interaction, an acceptance of stress-vulnerability models of the health problem being treated and an acceptance that health or well-being is not simply the absence of symptoms but is also about helping the individual to get on with what matters in life to them.

We have talked about contemporary literature, political and recovery models, which inform current thinking about self-management, but in a clinical setting we need to know where the person with BD sits with regard to these models because their beliefs can help or hinder successful self-management.


## Beliefs about Health

The model by Leventhal, Meyer, and Nerenz (1980) about illness beliefs provides a framework for understanding the self-regulation processes that determine health-related behaviors, such as self-management. It is made up of interrelated components.

The first component is the interpretation of the health problem. A person confronted with a health problem, in this case BD, must first get to grips with the health problem itself and what it seems to them to involve. The ways in which a person thinks about (interprets) their health problem creates a representation of that problem. This representation gives personal meaning to the health problem and is organized around five themes:

1.  *What is it?* (identity): the label given to the health problem such as a medical or self diagnosis.
2.  *Why has it happened?* (cause): the perceived cause of the health problem, which can for example, be based on cultural ideas, myths, or medical knowledge.

3. *How long will it last?* (time line): an estimation of how long the health problem or the phase of the health problem will last, and will it recur.
4. *What effects will it have?* (consequences): a prediction about possible effects on the person's life, which can be about finance, relationships, own health and so on, and can be seen as positive or negative and serious or minor.
5. *What can I do to make it go away?* (cure/control): the possibility that the health problem can be cured or ameliorated and perceptions of control over the health problem by self and/or others.

The second component concerns how an individual copes with or manages his or her own health problem. According to Leventhal et al. (1980), beliefs or cognitive representations about health problems described above provide a framework which functions to guide a return to, or maintenance of, a state of good health. Two broad forms of coping have been described. These are Approach Coping (e.g., "take the pills," "joining self-management groups") and Avoidance Coping (e.g., disengagement, venting).

The third component is the individual's appraisal of their coping strategy. The individual evaluates the effectiveness of the coping strategy and decides whether to continue or use a new one. Not everyone will move to this stage, especially where avoidance is a form of coping, and not recognized as such.

Leventhal et al. (1980) postulate that the association between health problem representations and emotional responses, such as fear, can lead to avoidance coping as a protective measure. For example, if self-management is seen as symbolic of having a feared health problem, then nonadherence or changing the identity of the health problem to something more trivial may be a strategy to avoid exposure to threat.

Avoidance coping is also linked to Weinstein's (1982) concept of unrealistic optimism. Individuals vary in their optimism and an individual whose optimism is unrealistically high may, for example, interpret their health problems as: "It isn't serious", "they've got it wrong," and "its normal, other people have highs and lows." They may then not monitor for early warning signs and fail to develop appropriate strategies to avoid or prevent escalation of episodes. In addition, they may feel so safe that they are more likely to engage in dangerous behaviors, such as sleep-disrupting activities. For these reasons, if the individual's optimism is unrealistic, then it is likely to lead to avoidance of self-management.

Just as individuals with BD have beliefs about their health problems, they also have beliefs about their ability to carry out health-related behaviors. These seem to be crucial in the stages of self-regulation of health behaviors.

Bandura (1977) used the term self-efficacy not as a trait, but to describe the individual's beliefs about the extent to which they can control a particular behaviour in a particular situation. Self-efficacy beliefs are associated with feelings of helplessness. In learned helplessness, the individual perceives his/her responses as futile, leading to failure to initiate coping responses.

Self-efficacy is a widely applied construct in models of health behavior and is considered one of the best predictors of health behavior (Conner & Norman, 1995). One of the advantages of learning self-management may be that practicing new coping skills increases self-confidence and a new self-model ("self as able to manage health problem") is formed.

The building up of self-efficacy beliefs or self-confidence is aided by having an expert tutor. Bray, Gyurcsik, Culos-Reed, Dawson, and Martin (2001) found that when people first take responsibility for their own health, an expert tutor is vital. They investigated the role of what they term proxy efficacy, which they define as the belief that another person has the skills and ability to deal with issues on our behalf that, in turn, increases people's confidence to carry out health-enhancing behaviors. It is speculated that having a credible fellow sufferer as a tutor may further enhance the individual's perception of capability and efficiency. A final and important point about Bray et al's work is that it gives a rationale for why self-management might be effective besides being acceptable to people with BD.

## Studies that Illustrate the Importance of Self-Management

There has been little written about self-management for BD and, at the present time, there are few adequate trials that attest to its success or otherwise.

The idea of the person with BD as self-managing their own problems is implicit in cognitive behavioral therapy (CBT) groups for BD (Palmer & Gilbert, 1997; Palmer, Williams, & Adams, 1995). These authors write that participants were helped to recognize and then to challenge their own attitudes and beliefs and to acquire active problem-solving and coping strategies through repeated experiences within therapy and homework practice. The emphasis placed on repeated homework in CBT is important, not just for the individual to practice managing their mental health problem, but to build up modified or new schematic models such as "self as able to manage BD." Thus, use of the strategies learnt in group sessions may be the key to promote changes in the individual's confidence and beliefs that they can be an active agent in their own actions and can reinstate control over their life should the early symptoms of a BD episode reoccur. This further encourages the use of self-management strategies and a virtuous circle is formed.

Bauer (2002) takes up this theme of the person with BD as a comanager when he writes that, in contrast to a paternalistic order-following approach to treatment, a collaborative model expects the clients to be partners in managing their own health problems. He argues that the organization of clinical resources to deliver care to clients who present for treatment can also build on the collaborative approach of CBT (Bauer, 2002; Bauer, McBride, Chase, Sachs, & Shea, 1998). Bauer et al. (1998) provided an "Easy Access Service" where individuals with BD learnt self-management in groups led by two nurses. The participants in the group had access both to information about BD and to opportunities to learn problem-solving skills, compared with those receiving treatment as usual. Results showed that participants in the group did better than those participants receiving "treatment as usual" in terms of reduced symptoms, improved social functioning, and reduced health care costs. Although service by Bauer et al. was initially a "stand-alone" one, it has now been extended so that it is part of an integrated service, which has been evaluated in a very large, longitudinal, multi-center, randomized, controlled trial in the Veterans Affairs Centre system (Bauer, Biswas, & Kilbourne, 2009). Findings from this study showed that learning self-management together with provider support for guideline implementation and facilitated treatment access/continuity can improve treatment guideline concordance over the long term in participants with BD, and even in those with severe impairments.

The above studies are important because the resolution of the acute symptoms of BD is too often regarded as the treatment endpoint in health services. However, current research indicates that individuals with BD experience profound and ongoing functional disabilities even when the acute episode is resolved (Bauer, 2002). It is therefore noteworthy that interventions that help individuals with BD to enhance or acquire problem-solving skills not only provide encouraging evidence for reductions in symptoms but also in restoring social functioning (Scott et al., 2001). The emphasis on functional outcomes is consistent with the philosophy of the Recovery Model. Furthermore, a study identifies self-managed care as one of the main factors in promoting the perception of recovery in an individual.

"User-led," self-management programs, previously known as Expert Patient Programmes (EPP), have developed over the past 20 years for people with chronic physical health problems in areas such as arthritis and asthma. One example is the Chronic Disease Self-Management Programme developed at Stanford where professionally trained instructors with chronic disease train course volunteer tutors with various long-term health problems.

Donaldson's (2001) paper made a strong case for the active recruitment and involvement of "expert patients" in services for people with long-term health problems to minimize their impact on day-to-day living. Its philosophy informed the EPP for people with long-term health problems piloted in the United Kingdom and included mental health.

EPPs have now been incorporated into a Community Interest Company (CIC). A number of PHCs have commissioned the CIC to run courses. These are free and open to adults of any age who are living with chronic health problems including mental health. The course aims to help the person to take control of their health and well-being by learning new skills to manage their condition on a daily basis. It looks at issues such as dealing with pain, tiredness, relaxation, and healthy living.

The Bipolar Disorders Association (previously Manic Depression Fellowship) has played an important role in developing user-led self-management programs. They argue that most individuals with BD have the potential, with optimal treatment, to return to normal social and occupational functioning, so avoiding poor long-term outcomes and becoming a burden on carers and families. However, such an outcome is often not achieved. One reason for people with BD not reaching optimal functioning is that the NHS (National Health Service, UK) is poorly resourced for their care. In our experience, comprehensive treatment programs are far from being routinely provided. This is despite the fact that epidemiological data show that there are an estimated 500,000 people with BD in the United Kingdom (Weissman et al., 1998) and when burden of disease is measured by "disability adjusted life years," mood disorders are at the top of the list in America and third in Europe (World Health Organization, 1999). Another reason may be that we have not regarded people with BD as potential deliverers of health care services.

In the development stage of their program the Bipolar Disorders Association consulted both within their own membership and with professionals working in the field. This meant that, right from the beginning, the skills and expertise of both professional and user were incorporated into the program. However, the program is now organized and delivered entirely by people with BD and the Bipolar Disorders Association, their representative organization, rather than professionals.

The program has been designed to give information about BD and also to enable the participants to take an active role in their own care; improving self-efficacy in dealing with problems when they impact on daily living or undermine self-image. It is comprehensive and it teaches the participants how to identify triggers and warning signs and how to implement strategies to reduce the severity of an episode.

## A Note of Caution about Personal Responsibility

As discussed at the beginning of this chapter, reconfiguring individual identity as "intra-active" and relocating the risks to health to within the individual gives a rationale for the philosophy of self-management. However, in his presidential address at Yale University, Brownell sounds a note of caution about overemphasizing individual personal responsibility and individual control over health.

Brownell (1991) describes U.S. culture as one that places immense emphasis on the power and responsibility of the individual. This description is mirrored in Ogden's views about the concept of personal responsibility for health being deeply ingrained in the individualism and self-reliance of the new right in this country. Brownell postulates that whereas good health was seen as a means of attaining personal goals, it now also symbolizes self-control, hard work, ambition, and success in life. People expect and are expected to control their health, and this has moral nuances. Those individuals who have good health or remain well are judged as having positive qualities (strong and hardworking) compared to those who fall ill or have less than perfect health who are judged as having negative qualities (passive and weak).

The individual who fails to maintain or gain good health is likely to be feeling frightened, overwhelmed, and vulnerable, and may add to their own distress by making harsh judgments about themselves. Ensuing feelings of guilt and shame are likely to further escalate their distress. Moreover, they may be harshly judged and blamed by others, especially by what Brownell terms the "self-righteous healthy." Exposure to people with health problems also makes healthy individuals feel more vulnerable and uncertain. This often leads to rationalizations or coping strategies that focus on the belief that the world is a just and fair place. As such "people get what they deserve and deserve what they get" (Lerner, Miller, & Holmes, 1976; Wortman & Lehman, 1985).

Other writers have also questioned whether, in contemporary western culture, the point has been reached where it is not possible for an individual to become unwell without that person being at fault (Marantz, 1990). Marantz highlights the dangers of characterizing episodes of illness as preventable because this implies that the individual with that health problem becomes responsible for any reoccurrence. He argues that attributing responsibility in this deterministic way happens because we all like to be able to explain why something has happened. However, calculating risk is only meaningful with respect to whole populations and not to individuals and were a risk factor to be correctly identified, it is not an absolute cause of disorder. Marantz goes on to state that there is no known lifestyle (or self-management program) that can ensure an absence of health problems. For these reasons, he concludes that we should encourage people to modify known risk factors while, at the same time, "allowing them the luxury of getting sick without feeling guilty."

Brownell argues that one of the reasons that people are so ready to attribute personal blame to others for health problems is to be found in paradoxical but coexisting beliefs about control. That is, we have control over our health yet at the same time are vulnerable to unpredictable factors. One resolution of this seeming paradox is overstating personal control and responsibility because it enables individuals to cope with the fear of having no or little control. Given the phenomenology of BD, where an individual experiences marked and often unpredictable mood swings, it is vital to accept the limitations of personal responsibility and try to work within the realms of what can or cannot realistically be controlled or managed by any one individual.

In this and the previous section, we have cautioned about the overemphasis on personal responsibility and highlighted the importance of identifying health-related beliefs, which may hinder self-management. We now turn to another particularly difficult challenge to any treatment including self-management: the suicidal frame of mind.

## The Suicidal Frame of Mind

Suicidal ideation and behavior are found across many diagnoses. BD is high on the list of such diagnoses, having the second highest rate of suicide after depression. It has been estimated that between 10% and 15% of people with the diagnosis whose problems are severe enough to have led to a hospital admission eventually die by suicide (Hawton, Sutton, Haw, Sinclair, & Harris, 2005). Suicide is associated with both the depressed and the mixed states of BD.

The risk of getting into a suicidal frame of mind is heightened when external events (such as significant problems or losses in recent day-to-day life) combine with internal events (quite small changes in mood state) compared to periods when life is going relatively well. When these external and internal factors combine, a toxic spiral can begin which ends with a suicidal frame of mind (Williams, 1997).

Typically, the suicidal frame of mind starts with the person feeling worthless and overwhelmed by their problems, which to them appear insuperable, especially those with interpersonal difficulties (Williams, 1997). The person thinks that he or she is unable to get anything right and feels trapped in a situation from which there is no possibility of escape by their own or by others' efforts. It seems to them that they have always felt like this, that it will last forever, and the psychological pain seems unbearable and unendurable. The toxic spiral ends with dying being seen as the only escape from the psychological pain (Williams, 1997).

A key element of self-management is helping the person with BD to learn ways of problem solving so that they can better cope when faced with life's difficulties and crises and not consider suicide as the only option. Underlying the suicidal frame of mind are deficits in cognitive processing, primarily over general memory and low recall of positive memories (Williams, 1997). Once these cognitive processing deficits are established, they have a profound impact on the person's ability to problem solve. Positive memories take longer to come into awareness and the person is unable to access specific details of past successful problem solving (Williams et al., 2008; Scott et al., 2001).

In his handbook, Williams (1996) writes that it is likely to be beneficial if the clinician helps the person to become aware of and then to work on ways of managing these temporary cognitive processing deficits. He sets out a variety of cognitive and behavioral techniques that may be helpful.

He alerts us to the danger of trying to teach and encourage normal problem solving because this may inadvertently make things worse in the following way. The person is trying to solve their current interpersonal problems, trying to reduce the gap between where they are and where they want to be, but is unaware that they are using summary memories that do not contain sufficient detail or hints for successful problem solving. They may ruminate about their lack of success, their ability to imagine the future narrows down, and they feel increasingly hopeless.

This highlights a possible disadvantage of using solely problem solving self-management for some people with BD. The clinician needs to be keenly aware that people with BD who want to self-manage may find themselves struggling to "fix" things, and so becoming preoccupied with their own self-focused critical thoughts. They may ruminate about the past and the future in a way that increases their despair and about their present uncontrollable and hopeless reality compared with what might have been. Rather than struggling to reduce the gap between where they are and where they want to be, some people with BD may find that learning mindfulness as a part of self-management is both relevant and acceptable to them. Mindfulness Based Cognitive Therapy (MBCT) integrates CT with training in mindfulness and is designed for people in recovery rather than an acute state of crisis (Williams et al., 2008).

## Mindfulness Based Cognitive Therapy

MBCT is a promising new approach for people who have had thoughts of suicide in the past (Williams, Dugan, Crane, & Fennell, 2006; Williams et al., 2008). It is a mood regulation strategy in its own right but, unlike traditional CBT, no training is given on changing the content of thoughts and solving problems (Brown & Ryan, 2003; Williams et al., 2008).

Participants are taught in classes rather than attending individual or group therapy sessions. The aim is to teach them to notice mood shifts early and to turn to face their experiences rather than becoming trapped into trying to fix or avoid them. In the class and for homework, participants practice remaining in full contact with their present reality by recognizing and carefully examining and accepting their thoughts, feelings, and physiological sensations without buying into them or altering them, that is, without judgment. They are encouraged not to struggle with these experiences or try to change them and to practice kindly awareness (self-acceptance and compassion). They are encouraged to notice the effects of negative thinking patterns, exploring these with kindness and curiosity and then releasing them or letting them go.

Overall, the emphasis is on developing a different relationship with the thoughts, feelings, and body sensations that would normally escalate mood-activated patterns of unhelpful thinking and form a toxic spiral, deepening hopelessness and the sense of entrapment that opens the way to another suicidal crisis. Participants are encouraged to tolerate of all types of thoughts and memories (pleasant and unpleasant) and to replace their habit of self-judgment and experiential avoidance (affective gating) with allowing things to be as they are, self-acceptance, and compassion. Encouraging tolerance of all types of thoughts and memories (pleasant and unpleasant) may reduce the need for avoidance and striving to fix things (Hayes, Follette, & Lineham, 2004; Williams et al., 2006).

Mindfulness presents people with a very different way of being with unwanted experiences, enabling them to move toward the things they value even when they experience unwanted thoughts and feelings. It has to be borne in mind, however, that while practicing mindfulness as a part of self-management can be an acceptable experience for some service users that may not be the case for others.

## Conclusion

This chapter has discussed the development of self-management approaches to BD. With these approaches, the person with BD is no longer a passive recipient of care but has personal control over their own health care and is a central component of health care delivery for other people with BD. What was a chasm between those who offer therapy and those who have the BD has been reduced, and therapist and the person with BD work together to understand and manage the problems that arise.

We have highlighted the common thread that runs through shifting ideas about individual identity, the recovery model, and government policy. The person with a long-term health problem is now seen as someone with knowledge and expertise to contribute to the management of their own health problem and the services provided.

The individual is seen as someone who has personal control and responsibility for his or her own health. The rise of self-efficacy and personal responsibility models have impacted at the national (expert patients), service (collaborative clinician–client approaches to treatment), and community (user-led, self-management programs) levels.

The above contemporary philosophy is well accepted but self-management is not for the fainthearted. It is accepted that random events and factors limit the degree to which health is under the control of the person and that there is no known lifestyle (or self-management programme) which can ensure absence of health problems.

Common to the self-management programs that we have discussed is that the person with BD chooses how to manage their own health problem and gets on with their lives in a way that matters to them while minimizing any unnecessary and painful struggle in the process.

Since BD is a relapsing condition, it makes sense to talk about the provision of self-management skills within socially supportive systems that people can return to time and again. The huge importance of providing a mutual social support system should never be underestimated.

Finally, although the difficulties of understanding and coping with a long-term health problem such as BD should not be underestimated, as strongly expressed by one of the participants in Pollack's (1996) study: "It is a lot easier for me to take control of my life than to have someone run it for me."

# References

Anthony, W. A. (1993). Recovery from mental illness: The guiding vision of the mental health service system in the 1990s. *Psychosocial Rehabilitation Journal, 16*(4), 11–23.

Bandura, A. (1977). Self-efficacy: Toward a unifying theory of behaviour change. *Psychological Review, 84*, 191–215.

Bauer, M. S. (2002). Psychosocial interventions for bipolar disorder. In M. Maj, J. J. Lopez-Ibor, & N. Sartorius (Eds.), *Bipolar disorder. Evidence & experience in psychiatry* (Vol. 5, pp. 281–313). WPA Series. Chichester, UK: John Wiley & Sons.

Bauer, M. S., Biswas, K., & Kilbourne, A. M. (2009). Enhancing multiyear guideline concordance for bipolar disorder through collaborative care. *American Journal of Psychiatry, 166,* 1244–1250.

Bauer, M. S., McBride, L., Chase, C. V., Sachs, G., & Shea, N. (1998). Manual-based group psychotherapy for bipolar disorder: A feasibility study. *Journal of Clinical Psychiatry, 59,* 449–455.

Bray, S. R., Gyurcsik, N. C., Culos-Reed, S. N., Dawson, K. A., & Martin, K. A. (2001). An exploratory investigation of the relationship between proxy efficacy, self efficacy and exercise attendance. *Journal of Health Psychology, 6*, 425–434.

Brown, K. W., & Ryan, R. M. (2003). The benefits of being present: Mindfulness and its role in psychological well-being. *Journal of Personality and Social Psychology, 84*(4), 822–848.

Brownell, K. D. (1991). Personal responsibility and control over our bodies: When expectation exceeds reality. *Health Psychology, 10*(5), 303–310.

Conner, M., & Norman, P. (Eds.) (1995). *Predicting health behaviour.* Buckingham, UK: Open University Press.

Copeland, M. E. (1994). *Living without depression and manic depression.* New York: New Harbinger Publications, Inc.

Donaldson, L. (2001). *The expert patient: A new approach to chronic disease management for the 21st century.* London: Department of Health.

Hawton, K., Sutton, L., Haw, C., Sinclair, J., & Harris, L. (2005). Suicide and attempted suicide in bipolar disorder: A systematic review of risk factors. *Journal of Clinical Psychiatry, 66,* 693–704.

Hayes, S. C., Follette, V. M., & Linehan, M. M. (2004). *Mindfulness and acceptance: Expanding the cognitive-behavioural tradition.* New York: Guilford Press.

Lerner, M. J., Miller, D. T., & Holmes, J. (1976). Deserving and the emergence of justice. In L. Berkowitz, & E. Walster (Eds.), *Advances in experimental social psychology* (pp. 47–69). New York: Academic Press.

Leventhal, H., Meyer, D., & Nerenz, D. (1980). The common sense representations of illness danger. In S. Rachman (Ed.), *Medical psychology* (Vol. 2, pp. 7–30). New York: Pergamon.

Lorig, K. R., Mazonson, P. D., & Holman, H. R. (1993). Evidence suggesting that health education for self-management in patients with chronic arthritis has sustained health benefits while reducing health care costs. *Arthritis and Rheumatism, 36*(4), 439–446.

Marantz, P. R. (1990). Blaming the victim: The negative consequence of preventative medicine. *American Journal of Public Health, 80,* 1186–1187.

Ogden, J. (1995). Psychosocial theory and the creation of the risky self. *Social Science and Medicine, 40*(3), 409–415.

Palmer, A. G., & Gilbert, P. (1997). Manic depression: What psychologists can do to help. In V. P. Varma (Ed.), *Managing manic depressive disorder* (pp. 42–60). London: Jessica Kingsley Publications.

Palmer, A. G., Williams, H., & Adams, M. (1995). Cognitive behavioural therapy for bipolar affective disorder in a group format. *Behavioural and Cognitive Psychotherapy, 23*(2), 153–168.

Pollack, L. E. (1996). Inpatients with BD: Their quest to understand. *Journal of Psychosocial Nursing & Mental Health, 34*(6), 19–24.

Scott, J., Garland, A., Moorehead, S. (2001). A pilot study of cognitive therapy in bipolar disorders. *Psychological Medicine, 31*, 459–467.

Weinstein, N. (1982). Unrealistic optimism about susceptibility to health problems. *Journal of Behavioural Medicine, 3*, 441–460.

Weissman, M. M., Leaf, P. J., Tischler, G. L., Blaser, D. G., Karno, M., Bruce, M. L., & Florio, L. P. (1998). Affective disorders in five United States communities. *Psychological Medicine, 18*, 141–153.

Williams, J. M. G. (1996). *The psychological treatment of depression*. London: Routledge.

Williams, J. M. G., Alatiq, Y., Crane, C., Barnhofer, T., Fennell, M. J. V., Duggan, D. S., & Goodwin, G. M. (2008). Mindfulness-based Cognitive Therapy (MBCT) in bipolar disorder: Preliminary evaluation of immediate effects on between-episode functioning. *Journal of Affective Disorders, 107*(1–3), 275–279.

Williams, J. M. G., Barnhofer, T., Crane, C. E., Watkins, E., Hermans, D., Raes, F., & Dalgleish, T. (2007). Autobiographical memory specificity and emotional disorder. *Psychological Bulletin, 133*(1), 122–148.

Williams, J. M. G., Dugan, D. S., Crane, C., & Fennell, M. J. (2006). Mindfulness based cognitive therapy for prevention of recurrence of suicidal behaviour. *Journal of Clinical Psychology, 62*(2), 201–210.

Williams, M. (1997). *Cry of pain: Understanding suicide and self-harm*. London: Penguin Books.

World Health Organisation. (1999). *Annual Report*. Geneva: Author.

Wortman, C. B., & Lehman, D. R. (1985). Reactions to victims of life crises: Support attempts that fail. In I. G. Sarson, & B. R. Sarson (Eds.), *Social support: Theory, research and applications* (pp. 463–490). Boston, MA: Martinus Nijhoff.

Yanos, P. T., Primavera, L. H., & Knight, L. E. (2001). Consumer-run service participation, recovery of social functioning, and the mediating role of psychological factors. *Psychiatric Services, 52*(4), 493–500.

# Part III
# General Issues

# 17

# Current Approaches to the Assessment of Depression

## Dave Peck
### Edinburgh, UK

Bebbington (Chapter 1 in this volume) outlined formal methods of diagnosing depression using instruments such as SCAN, SCID, and PSE. This chapter concentrates on the assessment of the level of depression, rather than on diagnostic methods. Some instruments can be used for both purposes, but overlap between the two chapters has been kept to a minimum.

Although some debate exists, it is generally recognized that depression is best construed as a unitary disorder along a continuum of severity. The main exception to this simple classification is bipolar depression, in which periods of depression are interspersed with periods of excitement and mania.

Apart from the traditional questionnaires and rating scales normally used in the measurement of depression, several other approaches have been developed. These alternatives can and perhaps should be used in conjunction with more traditional methods, because they often inquire into aspects of depression *such as slowness* that can be neglected by scales and questionnaires. In this chapter, these alternatives will be termed "behavioral" (lower case b) methods. They will receive more attention than might seem to be justified on the basis of the frequency of their reported use, in the hope that readers will consider using them in their own clinical and research endeavors. All measurements are subject to measurement error; however, the sources of error in behavioral methods are different from those of the traditional scales. A more rounded and comprehensive assessment of depression should result if behavioral measures are included in assessment batteries, despite them being more time-consuming than rating scales and questionnaires.

Numerous measures of depression have been developed for use in particular groups, such as adolescents, older adults, or patients with heart disease. There are so many of such measures that it is not feasible to cover them in this chapter. The focus instead is on more general measures of levels of depression that can be used in a variety of settings.

Most of the rating scales are copyrighted and are only available commercially. However, some are available free on the Internet; for example, the Hamilton Depression Rating Scale (HDRS) can be downloaded from http://healthnet.umassmed.edu/mhealth/HAMD.pdf

*The Wiley-Blackwell Handbook of Mood Disorders*, Second Edition. Edited by Mick Power.
© 2013 John Wiley & Sons, Ltd. Published 2013 by John Wiley & Sons, Ltd.

# Psychometric Measures

It is possible to classify psychometric measures of depression in several ways. One useful way is whether the measure is nomothetic or idiographic. That is, whether the measure is a standard instrument with set questions and a set of norms against which an individual score can be compared (nomothetic); or whether the instrument has a standard format, but with the content entirely determined by the specifics of the individual's problems (idiographic). A second way is whether the instrument is completed by the client (self completed) or by the clinician (observer completed); the latter can be subdivided into instruments based on standard rating scales and those based on structured interviews. A third classification is whether the instrument is designed to assess depression alone, or whether it includes assessments of other mental states (multistate instruments).

These differences are important because the different kinds of instrument often tap different aspects of depression, and may be differentially sensitive to the occurrence and rate of clinical change (Fava et al., 1986). Furthermore, *the scores of* observer- and self-completed scales may not correlate highly. For example, Sayer et al. (1993) found that the correlations between the observer-completed HDRS and the self-completed Beck Depression Inventory (BDI) varied between 0.16 and 0.73, depending on the group under investigation. They suggested that the lower correlations may have arisen from the use of a restricted range of severity in some of the groups.

A comprehensive guide to psychometric measures of depression, including sample copies of some instruments is available in Nezu, Ronan, Meadows, and McClure (2000).

## Nomothetic observer-completed instruments

Ideally, these instruments should be administered by a trained interviewer, but in practice it is unlikely that all clinicians will have received the relevant training. The advantages of observer-completed instruments are several: they are more suitable if the client is very depressed, uncooperative, or distractible; the client can be given the opportunity to elaborate on their responses; and clinicians often have a different but equally valuable and valid perspective on client problems. A disadvantage is that clients may be unwilling to respond openly to certain items if they are face to face with a clinician.

*The Hamilton Depression Rating Scale*    The HDRS comprises 17 items, rated 0–2 or 0–4 and has an emphasis on somatic symptoms. There are several alternative versions of the HDRS, with extra items to cover more psychological symptoms (Klerman, Weissman, & Frank, 1994), but mostly the 17-item version is employed. It focuses on symptoms over the last week or so. Little *published* guidance is available on how to administer the scale, *indicating* that the observer should be an experienced clinician. Specific training is required for its use, and it should only be used as part of a comprehensive assessment, along with information from a variety of other sources; unfortunately such recommendations are widely ignored (Snaith, 1996). Hamilton

**Table 17.1.**
Number of "Hits" in Google Scholar for Papers Whose Title Includes the Name of the Main Measures of Depression

| Depression measure | Google Scholar hits |
| --- | --- |
| Beck Depression Inventory | 176 |
| Hamilton Depression Rating Scale | 60 |
| Patient Health Questionnaire-9 | 53 |
| Montgomery–Asberg Depression Rating Scale | 17 |
| Major Depression Inventory | 17 |
| Inventory of Depressive Symptomatology | 15 |
| Center for Epidemiological Studies-Depression | 5 |
| Zung Self-Rating Depression Scale | 5 |

*Note:* The search used full titles of measures, rather than abbreviations; included *downloads* with at least summaries; and identified papers published from January 2004 only.

(1967) is the key reference. The psychometric properties of HDRS have been extensively investigated. Inter-rater reliability is generally good (O'Hara and Rehm, 1983).

Questions have been raised about the sensitivity of the HDRS to detect differences between drug treatments, and this lack of sensitivity may reduce the statistical power of studies using this scale (Faries et al., 2000). A 6-item version of the HDRS has been developed; O'Sullivan, Fava, Agustin, Bare, and Rosenbaum (1997) reported that this short version was as sensitive to change as the longer versions.

Many researchers have expressed severe reservations about the value of the HDRS (Bagby, Ryder, Schuller, & Marshall, 2004). Nevertheless, it remains one of the most commonly used instruments to measure depression (see Table 17.1).

*Montgomery–Asberg Depression Rating Scale*　This instrument contains 10 items, rated on a 4-point scale; useful descriptions of all the items are provided, along with cues at each rating point. The administration should be preceded by a flexible clinical interview. The Montgomery–Asberg Depression Rating Scale (MADRS) focuses entirely on psychological aspects of depression; this lack of somatic items is said to make it particularly suitable for use in general medical populations because it omits aspects of depression such as poor appetite that could also occur in a physical illness without any features of depression. Interestingly, the MADRS seems to be as useful when administered over the telephone as it is face to face (Hermens et al., 2006)

The Inventory of Depressive Symptomatology (IDS) and the Quick Inventory of Depressive Symptomatology (QIDS) both have observer- and self-completed versions. For details, see section under self-completed instruments.

## Nomothetic self-completed instruments

*Beck Depression Inventory*　The BDI has 21 items, rated on a 4-point scale of severity, focusing mainly on psychological aspects of depression. Items were derived from the authors' clinical experience. The original reference is Beck, Ward, Mendelson, Mock, and Erbaugh (1961). According to Richter, Werner, Heerlein, Kraus, and Sauer

(1998), scores on the BDI tend to be markedly skewed, most scores being in the lower ranges. These authors also note that even in a sample of psychiatric patients, the mean item score on the 3-point scale rarely exceeds 2, suggesting that the BDI scales do not discriminate well between levels of severity; internal consistency is acceptable but test–retest reliability is poor. Some factor analytic studies have reported that the BDI is multifactorial, others found that it measures just one factor. A later version of the BDI (BDI II) has been developed (Beck, Steer, & Brown, 1996). Some of the original items were replaced (e.g., on symptoms of weight loss) and the BDI II is now explicitly linked to DSM-IV criteria, with a common time frame of 2 weeks. The psychometric properties of BDI II are better (Dozois, Dobson, & Ahnberg, 1998; Steer, Brown, Beck, & Sanderson, 2001) and many of the deficiencies of the original version appear to have been rectified. Although the BDI was not designed to detect cases, several studies have *indicated* that it can be usefully employed in this way; for example, after myocardial infarction (Strik, Honig, Lousberg, & Denollet, 2001) and in low back pain (Love, 1987). As shown in Table 17.1, the BDI is a very popular instrument.

*MADRS-S*   This is a self-completed version of the observer-completed MADRS. There are nine items rated on a 0–3 scale, measuring depression over the past week. Svanborg and Asberg (2001) compared it with the BDI and found that the instruments correlated at +0.87 and were equally effective in discriminating between different diagnoses and in assessing sensitivity to change. Fantino and Moore (2009) found high internal reliability ($\alpha = 0.84$), good consistency over time, and high sensitivity to change.

*Zung Self-Rating Depression Scale*   Zung Self-Rating Depression Scale (SDS) comprises 20 items rated on a 4-point scale covering symptoms over the last week (Zung, 1965). Psychological and somatic items have similar weight. It correlates moderately with other scales but there is inconsistent evidence on its sensitivity to change. Becker (1988) has provided a useful short review.

*Center for Epidemiological Studies-Depression Scale*   There are several versions of this self-report instrument, of which the most commonly used is the 20-item Center for Epidemiological Studies-Depression (CES-D 20; Radloff, 1997). Other versions contain 8 or 10 items. It addresses all key aspects of depression, including psychomotor retardation, on a 4-point scale from "none or almost none of the time" to "all or almost all of the time," over the last week. Several studies (Bracke, Levecque, & Van De Velde, 2008) have reported good psychometric properties. It has been widely used in epidemiological studies (Canady, Stommel, & Holzman, 2009), but can also be used to monitor changes in levels of depression.

*The Major Depression Inventory*   This was first described by Bech, Rasmussen, Olsen, Noerholm, and Abildgaard (2001). It was explicitly designed to be consistent with DSM-IV and ICD-10 criteria for major depressive disorder. Hence, it is commonly used as a diagnostic instrument but it can also be used to assess severity. Symptoms over the last 2 weeks are rated on a 0–5 scale, producing a range of 0–50. In a large-scale study of the Dutch version, high levels of internal reliability, concurrent validity, sensitivity, and specificity were reported (Cuijpers, Dekker, Noteboom, Smits, & Peen, 2007).

*The Patient Health Questionnaire-9 (PHQ-9)*    The PHQ-9 is a relatively recent arrival, but it has increased rapidly in popularity. It comprises nine questions specifically linked to DSM-IV. Symptom severity is rated on a 0–3 scale, over the last 2 weeks. It was designed as a brief measure of levels of depression, and of the degree of response to treatment. The internal reliability, factor structure, validity, and sensitivity to change are all good (Cameron, Crawford, Lawton, & Reid, 2008). Gilbody, Richards, Brealey, and Hewitt (2007) also reported good psychometric properties, concluding that it is as useful as longer observer-completed instruments; however, the shorter 2-item version was said to have poor sensitivity.

*IDS and QIDS*    These are also relative newcomers; the original references are Rush et al. (1986, 2003). They were designed to overcome deficiencies noted in other scales, such as items having different weightings, or not corresponding to DSM criteria. IDS has 30 items, and QIDS has 16, assessing symptoms on a 0–3 scale over a 7-day period. They are available in observer- and self-completed formats, and only minimal training is required. The psychometric properties are good, but most of the evaluative studies have been conducted by the same team that devised the measures. However, some independent evaluations of the psychometric properties have been reported (Drieling, Schärer, & Langosch, 2007). Detailed information on psychometric properties can be found at http://www.ids-qids.org/index2.html#ABOUT.

## What are the most commonly used measures?

Table 17.1 shows the frequency of appearances of the titles of the main measures of depression in Google Scholar searches since January 2004. The absolute frequency should not be taken too seriously, because searches will have been performed for a variety of different purposes, and searchers may have used slightly different titles for the measures. Nevertheless, this exercise should give a reasonable indication of the relative levels of interest in the measures. It is clear that the BDI and the HDRS have maintained their predominance since the first edition of this volume (Peck, 2004). The extensive knowledge that has accumulated about these instruments, but also practitioner inertia, may explain their continued popularity.

It should, however, be noted that a relative newcomer, the PHQ-9, also attracted a large number of searches. Another Google product, Insight, provides an indication of changes in frequency of Internet searches *over time*. Since 2004, the BDI has shown a sharp decline, the HDRS has shown a steady but smaller decline, whereas the PHQ-9 has shown a rapid rise. It appears that the predominance of the older measures of depression is under threat; this trend is probably welcome in view of the limitations that have been found in the older measures.

## Multistate Instruments

*The Minnesota Multiphasic Personality Inventory (MMPI)* is a long questionnaire comprising 567 items in a "true/false" format. There are 10 clinical scales including one for depression, plus several other groups of subscales, some of which may also be used for assessing aspects of depression. There are numerous revisions of the MMPI which have been documented by Butcher and Williams (2009).

*The Kellner Symptom Questionnaire* is a 92-item adjective checklist measuring depression, anxiety, hostility, and somatic concern. It is very quick to complete, and reliability, validity, and sensitivity to change are good. British norms are available (Zeffert, Clark, Dobson, Jones, & Peck, 1996).

*The Symptom Checklist (SCL-90)* is a 90-item self-report instrument designed to measure nine different dimensions of mental health problems on a 5-point scale; it measures depression, in addition to phobic anxiety, hostility, and interpersonal sensitivity. Depression items include loss of interest in sex, no interest in things, and feeling hopeless. Global scores (e.g., of overall severity) can also be derived. Normative data are extensive, and reliability and validity are good. A key reference is Derogatis, Limpman, and Covi (1970). The revised version (SCL-90-R) is usually used.

*The Brief Symptom Inventory (BSI)* is a short form of the SCL-90-R. It comprises 53 items rated on a 5-point scale, and takes about 10 minutes to complete. There are nine symptom scales and three global indices (e.g., global severity). British norms are available (Ryan, 2007).

*The General Health Questionnaire (GHQ)* is self-completed, and has four different versions, with 12, 28, 30, or 60 items. It is very widely used and is useful in studies to detect mental health problems "over the last few weeks" in nonpsychiatric settings. It should not be used to arrive at a clinical diagnosis, or to assess long-standing problems. Subjects are asked to rate a series of statements on a 4-point scale assessing change from the "usual"; responses can be scored in four different ways. There are four sets of items measuring depression, anxiety, social dysfunction, and somatic symptoms. A key reference is Goldberg (1972).

*The Brief Psychiatric Rating Scale (BPRS)* is observer completed, and comprises 24 items rated on a 7-point scale from "not present" to "extremely severe." There is one specific item for depression, but other relevant items include "suicidality," "guilt," and "motor retardation." The original reference is Overall and Gorham (1962). Crippa, Sanches, Hallak, Loureiro, and Zuardi (2001) have produced a structured interview guide to accompany the BPRS, which is said to increase inter-rater agreement.

*The Hospital Anxiety and Depression Scale (HADS)* was developed by Zigmond and Snaith (1983). Items concerned with biological aspects of depression are excluded, permitting its use for assessing depression in physically ill populations. There are seven items in each of the two subscales, rated on a 0–3 scale. It is quick to complete and to score. The psychometric properties have been extensively investigated, most impressively in a large study by Mykletun, Stordal, and Dahl (2001) whose findings strongly supported the clinical and research value of the HADS. It is very widely used in European studies; for example, it was the most commonly used instrument in a review of studies of depression in cancer patients by Wasteson et al. (2009), having been used in 76 of 202 studies, compared to only 15 uses of the BDI. However, it features much less frequently in North American publications.

When intercorrelating the various scales within a multistate instrument, strong relationships are often reported, particularly between depression and anxiety. This has led some researchers (Tyrer, 1990) to suggest that anxiety and depression may not be distinct states.

# Recently Developed Approaches

A number of instruments have been developed that appear promising for use in particular circumstances but need further development before they can be recommended for use in routine clinical settings.

In a sentence completion test, subjects were asked to finish incomplete sentences in their own words; responses can be interpreted as indications of depressive thinking, especially of dysfunctional beliefs. Reasonable levels of reliability, validity, and sensitivity to change have been reported (Barton, Morley, Bloxham, Kitson, & Platts, 2005).

Cheung and Power (2012) criticized the lack of attention paid to interpersonal problems in commonly used depression rating scales and reported on the development of a new scale intended to overcome this deficiency. Initial results are promising, with high levels of internal consistency and a correlation of 0.77 with the BDI II.

In an intriguing and potentially invaluable approach, Wichers et al. (2010) asked subjects with a history of major depression to complete the Daily Life Emotional Pattern Scale. Subjects completed a series of 7-point Likert scales, providing information on mood on 10 occasions during the working day for 5 consecutive days; completion was prompted by an electronic beep from a wrist device. Items included, for example, "lonely" and "guilty" (negative affect), and "cheerful" and "energetic" (positive affect). They were also asked to record positive and negative events between bleeps. Future negative affect was strongly predicted by these measures of mood fluctuations during ordinary daily life.

## Idiographic instruments

Idiographic instruments have a standard structure, but a content that is tailored to the requirements of a particular study or individual. They are not used to assess depression exclusively, but they have been used sufficiently often in studies of depression to warrant their inclusion in this chapter.

*Goal Attainment Scale*   The Goal Attainment Scale (GAS) was designed to assess how far goals have been achieved on a 5-point scale. Typically, the scores range from +2 to –2, with 0 as the expected level of attainment. At least two points, preferably more, should be behaviorally "anchored" by descriptors. For example, the expected goal may be "spends at least 6 hrs out of bed"; +2 could be "gets up regularly before 8 a.m. and remains up"; +1 could be "spends most of the day out of bed"; –1 could be "gets up for occasional meals"; and –2 could be "spends nearly all the time in bed." The method was originally devised to monitor broad treatment strategies and intervention programs (Kiresuk & Sherman, 1968), but is now often used to assess individual progress.

*Visual Analog Scale*   This typically consists of a 10 cm line with bipolar adjectives at each end. Subjects are asked to put a cross anywhere on the line that best describes how they are feeling in terms of the adjectives. Scoring is simply the distance from the end of the line to the point of endorsement. It has long been used to measure aspects of mood (Zealley & Aitken, 1969). It is particularly useful when there are no standard scales available to measure a particular construct, or when you wish to rate a concept on many different dimensions but using the same format. It is quick to complete and to score. A recent study measuring anxiety levels reported high levels of validity and rapid sensitivity to change (Williams, Morlock, & Feltner, 2010).

*Semantic Differential*    As its name implies, the Semantic Differential (SD) was orig-inally devised to measure the meanings of particular concepts across different individ-uals (Osgood, Suci, & Tannenbaum, 1957); it could be regarded as a special form of the Visual Analog Scale (VAS). It consists of a concept (e.g., "My mood now") to be rated along lines that are divided into seven boxes, with bipolar adjectives at each end; for example, "sad" to "happy." Subjects are asked to put a cross in the box that most accurately reflects their view or interpretation of the concept. Any number of bipolar scales can be used. It can be used as the framework around which to develop a new measure (Mehmet, 2009)

*Personal Questionnaire Rapid Scoring Technique*    This ingenious method requires subjects to state their problems (up to 10) in their own words, and to rate them from "maximum possible" to "absolutely none" in a series of paired comparisons. It is particularly useful for detailed analyses of an individual's problems, and for tracking them over time. Versions of different lengths are available. A key reference is Mulhall (1976); it has been used in a number of clinical areas, for example, to analyze change in different forms of psychotherapy (Barkham, Shapiro, & Firth-Cozens, 1989), and more recently, to evaluate outcomes in art therapies (Odell-Miller, Hughes, & Westacott, 2006).

## Behavioral Assessment of Depression

Psychomotor abnormalities are common in depression and are of two main types: retardation and agitation. Retardation is characterized by a lack of energy and con-centration, physical and cognitive slowness, slow verbal response times, and lack of facial expressions. Agitation is characterized by an inability to remain seated, pacing, hand wringing, and repeated exclamations of distress. The value of direct behav-ioral observations of motor activity in depressed people was outlined 30 years ago by Lewinsohn and Lee (1981); they noted that simple ratings of ward behavior corre-lated well with the HDRS and with the BDI (about 0.70). Tryon (1991) published a review of the measurement of activity in psychology and in medicine ("actigra-phy"). He reported that actigraphy was useful in examining sleep–wake periods, and in assessing psychomotor agitation and retardation in depression. Activity lev-els (e.g., measured from the wrist) changed markedly from admission to discharge, and immobility was a particularly sensitive indicator of the intensity of depression. Caligiuri and Ellwanger (2000) found that 6% of depressed patients displayed abnor-mal psychomotor activity on a variety of tests, many of the patients showing signs similar to those found in Parkinson's Disease. Changes in actigraphy have been shown to be sufficiently sensitive to detect differential responses to various anti-depressant drugs, especially via early morning recordings (Stanley, Fairweather, & Hindmarch, 1999).

More recently, Berle, Hauge, Oedegaard, Holsten, and Fasmer (2010) compared motor activity in schizophrenia, major depression, and healthy controls. The patient groups' overall activity levels were significantly and substantially lower than those of the controls; they also reported that activity patterns in the schizophrenia group were less complex and more structured than in the other groups.

Sobin and Sackeim (1997) provided a useful early review of psychomotor abnor-malities in depression. They reported that in bipolar patients, activity increases during manic phases and decreases during depressive phases, and that in unipolar patients, 24-hour gross motor activity was higher than in schizophrenic patients and bipo-lar patients, these differences being particularly marked during the night. Depressed patients also manifested more self-touching, less eye contact, less smiling, and less eye-brow movements. Overall reaction times, decision times, and motor response times were all slower in depression. Sobin and Sackeim (1997) concluded that such mea-sures are sufficiently sensitive to warrant consideration as viable objective measures of depressive states. Finally, they stressed that retardation and agitation are not mutu-ally exclusive, and that both should be measured in any comprehensive assessment of psychomotor symptoms in depression.

Recently, Buyukdura, McClintock, and Croarkin (2011) reviewed research on psy-chomotor retardation. They described various ways in which it can be measured (including the use of rating scales such as the motor agitation and retardation scale), and speculated about the neurobiological correlates of psychomotor abnormalities. They concluded that levels of retardation may be useful in predicting response to medication and to electroconvulsive therapy.

As regards speech patterns, Lewinsohn and Lee (1981) described a method of coding and monitoring the interactions of depressed people in their own homes and during group therapy, using time-sampling methodology. Hale, Jansen, Bouhuys, Jenner, and van den Hoofdakker (1997) recorded the interactions of depressed people, especially with their partners. During speech, patients displayed more movements (e.g., self-touching), and less head nods and shakes. However, the value of such measures of verbal interaction in monitoring changes in level of depression remains to be demonstrated.

Measurement of formal speech characteristics appears to be more promising. Vanger, Summerfield, Rosen, and Watson (1992) found that overall speech activ-ity decreased, and silences increased, in line with the level of depression, and with the emotional salience of the discussion topic. Kuny and Stassen (1993) observed speech patterns and measured voice sound characteristics in 30 recovering depressives, on seven occasions throughout their hospital stay. Several of their measures were closely related to the time course of recovery, such as voice timbre, loudness, and variability of loudness. These associations were clear in about two-thirds of their sample, but not in the remaining third (mainly those with poor or variable recovery). Sobin and Sackeim (1997) listed a number of speech and voice characteristics related to depres-sion, including low voice amplitude, decreased monitoring and correction of speech, and reduced speaking time.

Moore, Clements, Peifer, and Weisser (2008) have provided a good technical account of the features of speech most clearly related to depression and how to assess them.

## General guidelines on choosing measures of depression

There are no rigid criteria for deciding which measures to choose; the choices may differ, for example, if you work in a clinical or a research setting. There are however some general principles that may be of assistance in selecting measures.

First, it is good practice to include standard measures, not least because the main psychometric properties are probably well known. Moreover, with a standard measure you should be able to compare your findings with standardization norms, and with the findings of other studies that have used the same measure.

Second, the psychometric properties should be above certain minimum levels. There is debate about these levels, but it has been suggested that reliability coefficients (of all types), for example, should be at least 0.80; similarly, the various indices of validity should be around 0.70 (Kline, 1993). The more types of reliability and validity that have been demonstrated as acceptable in a measure, the more useful that measure is likely to be. Those measures that have survived more advanced psychometric scrutiny such as confirmatory factor analysis or item response theory should also be preferred.

Third, and particularly in research work, more than one type of measure should be employed. Thus, at a minimum, a self-completed and an observer-completed measure should be selected; ideally, these should be accompanied by an idiographic and a behavioral measure. The use of just one measure is unlikely to tap the full range of depressive phenomena.

Fourth, measures should be chosen that are simple and quick to complete because the concentration powers of depressed people are likely to be impaired. Moreover, the scoring system should be straightforward to reduce the possibility of researcher errors.

Fifth, one may wish to measure other states in *addition* to depression, and may therefore consider it simpler to use a multistate instrument rather than a series of single-state measures.

## Summary

Depression is a multifaceted phenomenon, with a variety of psychological and motor aspects. However, in the measurement of depression, clinicians and researchers tend to use a narrow range of scales and questionnaires that relate only to psychological aspects, especially mood. The HDRS and the BDI are by far the most popular psychometric instruments for measuring depression, but there are indications that their predominance may be diminishing. An unfortunate consequence of the typical narrow focus on psychological aspects of depression is that other aspects such as speech patterns and motor abnormalities have been relatively neglected as measures of depression in research studies.

# References

Bagby, R. M., Ryder, A. G., Schuller, D. R., & Marshall, M. B. (2004). The Hamilton Depression Rating Scale: Has the gold standard become a lead weight? *American Journal of Psychiatry, 161,* 2163–2177.

Barkham, M., Shapiro, D. A., & Firth-Cozens, L. (1989). Personal questionnaire changes in prescriptive versus exploratory psychotherapy. *British Journal of Clinical Psychology, 28,* 97–107.

Barton, S., Morley, S., Bloxham, G., Kitson, C., & Platts, S. (2005). Sentence completion test for depression (SCD): An idiographic measure of depressive thinking. *British Journal of Clinical Psychology, 44,* 29–46.

Bech, P., Rasmussen, N., Olsen, L. R., Noerholm, V., & Abildgaard, W. (2001). The sensitivity and specificity of the Major Depression Inventory, using the Present State Examination as the index of diagnostic validity. *Journal of Affective Disorders, 66,* 159–164.

Beck, A. T., Steer, R. A., & Brown, G. K. (1996). *Beck depression inventory manual.* San Antonio, TX: Psychological Corporation.

Beck, A. T, Ward, C. H., Mendelson, M., Mock, J., & Erbaugh, J. (1961) An inventory for measuring depression. *Archives of General Psychiatry, 4,* 561–571.

Becker, R. E. (1988). Zung self-rating depression scale. In M. Hersen, & A. S. Bellack (Eds.), *Dictionary of behavioral assessment techniques.* New York: Pergamon.

Berle, J. O., Hauge, E. R., Oedegaard, K. J., Holsten, F., & Fasmer, O. B. (2010). Actigraphic registration of motor activity reveals a more structured behavioural pattern in schizophrenia than in major depression. *BMC Research Notes, 3,* 149.

Bracke, P., Levecque, K., & Van De Velde, S. (2008). The psychometric properties of the CES-D 8 depression inventory and the estimation of cross-national differences in the true prevalence of depression. Retrieved from http://csdiworkshop.org/v2/index.php/2008-3mc-conference/2008-presentations/

Butcher, J. N., & Williams, C. L. (2009). Personality assessment with the MMPI-2: Historical roots, international adaptations, and current challenges. *Applied Psychology: Health and Well-Being, 1,* 105–135.

Buyukdura, J. S., McClintock, S. M., & Croarkin, P. E. (2011). Psychomotor retardation in depression: Biological underpinnings, measurement, and treatment. *Progress in Neuro-Psychopharmacology and Biological Psychiatry, 35,* 395–409.

Caligiuri, M. P., & Ellwanger, J. (2000). Motor and cognitive aspects of motor retardation in depression. *Journal of Affective Disorders, 57,* 83–93.

Cameron, I. M., Crawford, J. R., Lawton, K., & Reid, I. C. (2008). Psychometric comparison of PHQ-9 and HADS for measuring depression severity in primary care. *British Journal of General Practice, 58,* 32–36.

Canady, R. B., Stommel, M., & Holzman, C. (2009). Measurement properties of the centers for epidemiological studies depression scale (CES-D) in a sample of African-American and non-Hispanic White pregnant women. *Journal of Nursing Measurement, 17,* 91–104.

Cheung, H. N., & Power, M. J. (2012). The development of a new multidimensional depression assessment scale: Preliminary results. *Clinical Psychology and Psychotherapy, 19,* 170–178.

Crippa, J. A., Sanches, R. F., Hallak, J. E., Loureiro, S. R., & Zuardi, A. W. (2001). A structured interview guide increases brief psychiatric rating scale reliability in raters with low clinical experience. *Acta Psychiatrica Scandinavica, 103,* 465–470.

Cuijpers, P., Dekker, J., Noteboom, A., Smits, N., & Peen, J. (2007). Sensitivity and specificity of the Major Depression Inventory in outpatients. *BMC Psychiatry, 7,* 39. Retrieved from http://www.biomedcentral.com/1471-244X/7/39

Derogatis, L. R., Limpman, R., & Covi, L. (1970). SCL-90: An outpatient psychiatric rating scale—Preliminary report. *Psychopharmacology Bulletin, 9*, 13–28.

Dozios, D., Dobson, K. S., & Ahnberg, J. L. (1998). A psychometric evaluation of the Beck Depression Inventory-II. *Psychological Assessment, 10*, 83–89.

Drieling, T., Schärer, L. O., & Langosch, J. M. (2007). The Inventory of Depressive Symptomatology: German translation and psychometric validation. *International Journal of Methods in Psychiatric Research, 16*, 230–236.

Fantino, B., & Moore, N. (2009). The self-reported Montgomery–Asberg depression rating scale is a useful evaluative tool in major depressive disorder. *BMC Psychiatry, 9*, 26. Retrieved from http://www.biomedcentral.com/1471-244X/9/26

Faries, D., Herrera, J., Rayamajhi, J., DeBrota, D., Demitrack, M., & Potter, W. Z. (2000). The responsiveness of the Hamilton Depression Rating Scale. *Journal of Psychiatric Research, 34*, 3–10.

Fava, E. A., Kellner, R., Lisansky, J., Park, J., Perini, G. I., and Zielezny, M. (1986). Rating depression in normals and depressives: Observer vs self-rating scales. *Journal of Affective Disorders, 11*, 29–33.

Gilbody, S., Richards, D., Brealey, S., & Hewitt, C. (2007). Screening for depression in medical settings with the Patient Health Questionnaire (PHQ): A diagnostic meta-analysis. *Journal of General Internal Medicine, 22*, 1596–1602.

Goldberg, D. (1972) *The detection of psychiatric illness by questionnaire* (Maudsley Monograph 21). London: Oxford University Press.

Hale, W. W., III, Jansen, J. H., Bouhuys, A. L., Jenner, J. A., & van den Hoofdakker, R. H. (1997). Non-verbal behavioral interactions of depressed patients with partners and strangers: The role of behavioural social support and involvement in depression persistence. *Journal of Affective Disorders, 44*, 111–122.

Hamilton, M. (1967). Development of a rating scale for primary depressive illness. *British Journal of Social and Clinical Psychology, 6*, 278–296.

Hermens, M. L., Ader, H. J., van Hout, H. P., Terluin, B., van Dyck, R., & de Haan, M. (2006). Administering the MADRS by telephone or face-to-face: A validity study. *Annals of General Psychiatry, 5*, 3.

Kiresuk, T. J., & Sherman, R. E. (1968). Goal attainment scaling: A general method for evaluating comprehensive community mental health programmes. *Community Mental Health Journal, 4*, 443–453.

Klerman, G. L., Weissman, M. M., & Frank, E. (1994). Evaluating drug treatments of depressive disorders. In R. F. Prien, & D. S. Robinson (Eds.), *Clinical evaluation of psychotropic drugs: Principles and guidelines*. New York: Raven Press.

Kline, P. (1993). *The handbook of psychological testing*. London: Routledge.

Kuny, S., & Stassen, H. H. (1993). Speaking behavior and voice sound characteristics in depressive patients during recovery. *Journal of Psychiatric Research, 27*, 289–307.

Lewinsohn, P. M., & Lee, W. (1981). Assessment of affective disorders. In D. H. Barlow (Ed.), *Behavioral assessment of adult disorders*. New York: Guilford Press.

Love, A. W. (1987). Depression in chronic low back pain patients: Diagnostic efficiency of three self-report questionnaires. *Journal of Clinical Psychology, 43*, 84–89.

Mehmet, B. (2009). Developing a cognitive flexibility scale: Validity and reliability studies. *Social Behavior and Personality: An International Journal, 37*, 343–353.

Moore, E., II, Clements, M. A., Peifer, J. W., & Weisser, L. (2008). Critical analysis of the impact of glottal features in the classification of clinical depression in speech. *IEEE Transactions, Biomedical Engineering, 55*, 96–107.

Mulhall, D. (1976). Systematic self-assessment by PQRST (Personal Questionnaire Rapid Scoring Technique). *Psychological Medicine*, *6*, 591–597.

Mykeltun, A., Stordal, E., & Dahl, A. A. (2001). Hospital Anxiety and Depression (HAD) scale: Factor structure, item analyses and internal consistency in a large population. *British Journal of Psychiatry*, *179*, 540–544.

Nezu, A. M., Ronan, G. F., Meadows, E. A., & McClure, K. S. (2000). *Practitioner's guide to empirically based measures of depression*. New York: Plenum.

Odell-Miller, H., Hughes, P., & Westacott, M. (2006). An investigation into the effectiveness of the arts therapies for adults with continuing mental health problems. *Psychotherapy Research*, *16*, 122–139.

O'Hara, M. W., & Rehm, L. P. (1983). Hamilton Rating Scale for Depression: Reliability and validity of judgments of novice raters. *Journal of Consulting and Clinical Psychology*, *51*, 318–319.

Osgood, C. E., Suci, G. J., & Tannenbaum, P. H. (1957). *The measurement of meaning*. Urbana: University of Illinois Press.

O'Sullivan, R. L., Fava, M., Agustin, C., Bare, L., & Rosenbaum, J. F. (1997). Sensitivity of the six-item Hamilton Depression Rating Scale. *Acta Psychiatrica Scandinavica*, *95*, 379–384.

Overall, J. E., & Gorham, D. R. (1962). The brief psychiatric rating scale. *Psychological Reports*, *10*, 799–812.

Peck, D. F. (2004). Current approaches to the assessment of depression. In M. J. Power (Ed.), *Mood disorders: A handbook of science and practice*. Chichester, UK: John Wiley & Sons.

Radloff, L. S. (1997). The CES-D scale: A self-report depression scale for research in the general population. *Applied Psychological Measurement*, *1*, 385–401.

Richter, P., Werner, J., Heerlein, A., Kraus, A., & Sauer, H. (1998). On the validity of the Beck Depression Inventory. A review. *Psychopathology*, *31*, 160–168.

Rush, A. J., Giles, D. E., Schlesser, M. A., Fulton, C. L., Weissenburger, J. E., & Burns, C. T. (1986). The Inventory of Depressive Symptomatology (IDS): Preliminary findings. *Psychiatry Research*, *18*, 65–87.

Rush, A. J., Trivedi, M. H., Ibrahim, H. M., Carmody, T. J., Arnow, B., Klein, D. N., ... Keller, M. B. (2003). The 16-item Quick Inventory of Depressive Symptomatology (QIDS), Clinician Rating (QIDS-C), and Self-Report (QIDS-SR): A psychometric evaluation in patients with chronic major depression. *Biological Psychiatry*, *54*, 573–583.

Ryan, C. (2007). British outpatient norms for the Brief Symptom Inventory. *Psychology and Psychotherapy: Theory, Research and Practice*, *80*, 83–191.

Sayer, N. A., Sackeim, H. A., Moeller, J. R., Prudic, J., Devanand, D. P., Coleman, E. A., & Kiersky, J. E. (1993). The relations between observer-rating and self-report of depressive symptomatology. *Psychological Assessment*, *5*, 350–360.

Snaith, P. (1996). Present use of the Hamilton Depression Rating Scale: Observation on method of assessment in research on depressive disorders. *British Journal of Psychiatry*, *168*, 594–597.

Sobin, C., & Sackeim, H. A. (1997). Psychomotor symptoms of depression. *American Journal of Psychiatry*, *154*, 4–17.

Stanley, N., Fairweather, D. B., & Hindmarch, I. (1999). Effects of fluoxetine and dothiepin on 24-hour activity in depressed patients. *Neuropsychobiology*, *39*, 44–48.

Steer, R. A., Brown, G. K., Beck, A. T., & Sanderson, W. C. (2001). Mean Beck Depression Inventory II scores by severity of major depressive episode. *Psychological Reports*, *88*, 1075–1076.

Strik, J. J., Honig, A., Lousberg, R., & Denollet, J. (2001). Sensitivity and specificity of observer and self-report questionnaires in major and minor depression following myocardial infarction. *Psychosomatics, 42*, 423–428.

Svanborg, P., & Asberg, M. (2001). A comparison between the Beck Depression Inventory (BDI) and the self-rating version of the Montgomery–Asberg Depression Rating Scale (MADRS). *Journal of Affective Disorders, 64*, 203–216.

Tryon, W. W. (1991) *Activity measurement in psychology and medicine.* New York: Plenum.

Tyrer, P. (1990) The division of neurosis: A failed classification. *Journal of the Royal Society of Medicine, 83*, 614–616.

Vanger, P., Summerfield, A. B., Rosen, B. K., & Watson, J. P. (1992). Effects of communication content on speech behaviour of depressives. *Comprehensive Psychiatry, 33*, 39–41.

Wasteson, E., Brenne, E., Higginson, I. J., Hotopf, M., Lloyd-Williams, M., Kaasa, S., & Loge, H.J.; European Palliative Care Research Collaborative (EPCRC). (2009). Depression assessment and classification in palliative cancer patients: a systematic literature review. *Palliative Medicine, 23*, 739. Retrieved from http://pmj.sagepub.com/content/23/8/739

Wichers, M., Peeters, F., Geschwind, N., Jacobs, N., Simons, C. J. P., Derom, C., ... van Os, J. (2010) Unveiling patterns of affective responses in daily life may improve outcome prediction in depression: A momentary assessment study. *Journal of Affective Disorders, 124*, 191–195.

Williams, V. S. L., Morlock, R. J., & Feltner, D. (2010). Psychometric evaluation of a visual analog scale for the assessment of anxiety. *Health and Quality of Life Outcomes, 8*, 57.

Zealley, A. K., & Aitken, R. C. B. (1969). Measurement of mood. *Proceedings of the Royal Society of Medicine, 62*, 993–996.

Zeffert, S., Clark, A., Dobson, C. J., Jones, A., & Peck, D. F. (1996). The Symptom Questionnaire: British standardisation data. *British Journal of Clinical Psychology, 35*, 85–90.

Zigmond, A. S., & Snaith, R. P. (1983). The Hospital Anxiety and Depression Scale. *Acta Psychiatrica Scandinavica, 67*, 361–370.

Zung, W. W. K. (1965). A self-rating depression scale. *Archives of General Psychiatry, 12*, 63–70.

# 18

# Suicide and Attempted Suicide

## Andrew K. MacLeod
### University of London, UK

Suicidal behavior is often assumed to be linked to depression. This chapter addresses some key questions about the relationship between depression and suicidal behavior. First, evidence will be reviewed concerning the prevalence of suicidal behavior in those who are depressed and the rates of depression in those who are suicidal. It will become clear that there is a strong link but that the nonoverlap is much greater than overlap: Many people who complete suicide or attempt suicide are not depressed and the overwhelming majority of depressed people will not attempt or complete suicide. The chapter will then move on to discuss *how* depression might be related to suicidality. Several factors will be discussed that might account for both the overlap and lack of overlap. The final two sections of the chapter will cover evidence on risk assessment and treatment of suicidal behavior. The evidence reviewed is not always specific to depression, as often studies on suicidality do not differentiate between depressed and nondepressed suicidal behavior. However, given the overlap between depression and suicidality, the evidence is very relevant to depressed, suicidal behavior. Before proceeding, it is important to clarify what is meant by suicidal behavior.

## Types of Suicidal Behavior

The concept of suicide is relatively straightforward, as it is defined by a legal judgment where there is clear evidence that the person intended to take his or her own life. Cases where clear evidence is lacking though the suspicion is of suicide are usually recorded in other ways. Nonfatal suicidal behavior is more complicated because of the range of behaviors encompassed and the variety of terms used. The terms usually imply something about the level of intent to die, for example, "attempted suicide" implies a strong intention to die whereas "deliberate self-harm" does not. It is tempting to make judgments about level of intent but difficult to do in practice. People are often unaware of the medical lethality of the overdose they have taken (by far the most common type of self-harm), thus rendering this a poor criterion. Also, when asked, people most commonly say they wanted to escape; they may often not be clear about whether they wanted to die or not (Bancroft et al., 1979; Hawton, Rodham, & Evans, 2006). Finally, individuals with more than one episode of self-harm are quite likely to have a mixture of levels of intent across different episodes (Brown, Comtois, &

*The Wiley-Blackwell Handbook of Mood Disorders*, Second Edition. Edited by Mick Power.
© 2013 John Wiley & Sons, Ltd. Published 2013 by John Wiley & Sons, Ltd.

Linehan, 2002; Sakinofsky, 2000). One solution suggested by Kreitman (1977) was to use the term "parasuicide" as a descriptive term to cover all deliberate but nonfatal acts of self-harm, thus remaining neutral about level of intent to die. As Kerkhof (2000) has pointed out, this term has not really caught on with clinicians, who tend to use attempted suicide or deliberate self-harm. In this chapter, the terms deliberate self-harm and attempted suicide will be used interchangeably to describe a deliberate but nonfatal act of self-harm, whatever the medical lethality or motivation behind the behavior. A final reason for not distinguishing types of parasuicide is that, although some studies have specifically addressed the issue of measuring intent, most have not; therefore, the literature typically groups together all nonlethal suicidal behaviors.

## How Many People Engage in Suicidal Behavior?

Suicide is the 10th leading cause of death worldwide, accounting for 1.5% of all deaths (Windfuhr & Kapur, 2011). Rates do vary across countries. For example, rates in Northern European countries and most, but not all, former Soviet states are high (e.g., Belarus: 37/100,000) and rates in Mediterranean countries tend to be low (e.g., Greece 4/100,000). Suicide is predominantly a male behavior: the aggregate male/female ratio across countries is 3.5:1 (World Health Organisation, 2001). However, as Windfuhr and Kapur (2011) note, data are not typically collected as part of a cross-national study but rather collected within each country independently, making comparisons difficult.

Deliberate self-harm is much more common than suicide, though data tend to be less reliable due to the even more varied ways they are collected as well as different definitions of being used in different places. A World Health Authority (WHO) multicenter study using standardized recording of parasuicides presenting to hospital in centers in 16 European countries found a mean, age-standardized rate per annum of 186/100,000 (Kerkhof, 2000). Rates varied across countries from 69/100,000 in the Spanish center to 462/100,000 in the French center. The UK rates, where Oxford was the center, were the second highest with 384/100,000. Unlike suicide, deliberate self-harm is more common in females—the female to male ratio in the WHO European study was 1.5:1. Kerkhof (2000) estimated that in that WHO study, lifetime prevalence of medically treated suicide attempts was about 2% for males and 3% for females. Estimates have also been made from population surveys rather than hospital presentations. This has the benefit of potentially detecting nonpresenting cases but the reliability of the data is unknown. Prevalence will depend on the exact question asked. Most surveys estimate between 1% and 4% of the population have engaged in parasuicide, though some figures are higher (Kerkhof, 2000). Nock et al. (2008) reporting data from a WHO survey found a 2.7% prevalence for attempts. From a large population survey in the United States, 4.6% reported having made a suicide attempt (Kessler, Borges, & Walters, 1999). About half said it was a serious attempt with at least some intent to die, even if ambivalent, and half said it was a cry for help where they did not want to die. Suicidal thoughts, or ideation, are probably more common again, but very difficult to estimate. Kessler et al. (1999) found that 13.5%

reported having suicide ideation at some point in their lives and Nock et al. (2008) in the WHO survey found 9.2% reported suicide ideation. Again, the exact question asked will have a bearing on the rate found.

Repetition of deliberate self-harm is common and represents a serious clinical problem. In the WHO European study, 54% of attempters had a previous attempt and 30% made another attempt during the 1-year follow-up (Kerkhof, 2000). Approximately 1% of attempters go on to complete suicide within 1 year, and studies with a follow-up period of at least 5 years show rates of between 3% and 13% (Sakinofsky, 2000). The risk is particularly elevated immediately following the attempt and declines thereafter, but still remains significantly higher than average 3 years later (Qin et al., 2009). Between one-third and two-thirds of those who die by suicide will have had a previous attempt (Sakinofsky, 2000).

## Suicidal Behavior in Depression

### Completed suicide

How many depressed people complete suicide? An influential study by Guze and Robins (1970) estimated that the lifetime risk of a depressed person completing suicide was about 15%. This figure has been widely quoted since, but has been questioned. Bostwick and Pankratz (2000) argued that this figure is an overestimate because the studies analyzed by Guze and Robins used only the most severe (i.e., hospitalized) depressed patients and had fairly short follow-up periods. As the risk of suicide is greatest following discharge from hospital (Harris & Barraclough, 1997), projecting rates within a short, postdischarge follow-up to lifetime rates is likely to lead to overestimation. This is particularly the case when the figure is based on proportionate mortality prevalence—the number of deaths by suicide relative to the number of deaths in the sample. Bostwick and Pankratz (2000) reanalyzed the data from the Guze and Robins review as well as newer data using case fatality prevalence (proportion of total sample that died by suicide) rather than proportionate mortality prevalence (proportion of deaths that were suicides). They also divided the new data by severity into cases that were hospitalized because of suicide concerns, and inpatients who were not specifically hospitalized because of suicide risk and outpatients. Their estimates of lifetime prevalence of suicide in affective disorder patients for the newer data were 8.6% for those hospitalized because of suicidal risk, 4.0% for those hospitalized without risk specified, and 2.2% for outpatients. For the nonaffectively ill population, the risk was less than 0.5%. The data used by Guze and Robins reanalyzed in this way yielded a lifetime risk of 4.8%.

Some studies have actually followed up patients and reported suicide rates over a longer period. In a very substantial study, Ostby, Brandt, Correia, Ekbom, and Sparen (2001) followed up over 39,000 unipolar major depression patients and 15,000 bipolar patients who had been inpatients in Sweden between 1973 and 1975. The average follow-up period was 10 years. During the follow-up period, 5.2% of the unipolar group and 4.4% of the bipolar group completed suicide. Both groups had elevated general mortality rates, as indicated by standardized mortality ratios (SMRs). SMR is the number of deaths from a particular cause divided what would be expected in the population from that cause. Thus, an SMR of 2 means that the group had twice the number of deaths from that particular cause than would have been expected. Interestingly, most causes of death, including natural causes, were overrepresented in both patient groups. However, death by suicide was by a long way the most overrepresented. The SMRs for death by suicide were 20 in the unipolar group and 10 in the bipolar group. These SMRs are actually very similar to those reported by Harris and Barraclough (1997) in a meta-analysis of studies that had at least a 2-year follow-up and had lost fewer than 10% of cases at follow-up. These authors found a mean SMR of 20 for major depression, 15 for bipolar disorder, and 12 for dysthymia. In a large prospective European study, Angst, Angst, Gerber-Werder, and Gamma (2005) reported SMRs of 22 for unipolar depression and 12 for bipolar depression. In a clinically useful study, McGirr, Renaud, Seguin, Alda, and Turecki (2008) found that suicide was more likely to occur in the first episode of depression—75% of suicides occurred in within the first episode.

### Attempted suicide and ideation

Rates of attempted suicide are, as would be expected, higher than rates of suicide. Fombonne, Wostear, Cooper, Harrington, and Rutter (2001) reported a 20-year follow-up of a sample of individuals who had been depressed as youths. The suicide risk in the sample was 2.5%, but 44% had attempted suicide at least once. This sample of early-onset depression may represent an unusually high risk of attempts. Most other studies have found lower rates of a history of attempted suicide in depressed patients. For example, Bottlender, Jager, Strauss, and Moller (2000) reported a history of self-harm in 27% of bipolar patients and 18% of unipolar patients. As in the case for suicide in bipolar patients, depression seems to be the key. Lopez et al. (2001) found that 33% of their sample of 169 bipolar I disorder patients in Northern Spain reported one or more previous suicide attempts. Severity of depressive episodes was one factor that distinguished those with and without a history of attempts.

How many of those who are depressed have suicidal ideation? Of course, it depends on what is meant by suicidal ideation, but it is probably accurate to say that more than half of depressed people have suicidal thoughts (Lonnqvist, 2000). For example, Schaffer et al. (2000) retrospectively reviewed 533 patients with major depression and found that 58% had suicidal ideation. There are also high rates of suicidal thoughts in bipolar patients, though it seems to be mainly accounted for by levels of depression rather than mania. Dilsaver, Chen, Swann, Shoaib, and Krajewski (1994) studied a sample of bipolar I patients, some of whom also met criteria for concurrent major depression, which they termed "depressive mania." Of the 49 pure mania patients, only one exhibited suicidal ideation as measured by the SADS suicidality subscale. In contrast, 24 of 44 depressive mania patients showed suicidal thoughts. Strakowski, McElroy, Keck, and West (1996) also found higher rates of suicidal ideation in patients with mixed bipolar disorder than those with manic bipolar disorder. Further analysis showed that depression levels rather than group status (mixed vs. manic) predicted suicide ideation. Oquendo et al. (2000) found that bipolar patients who had a history of suicide attempts had more episodes of depression than did those without a suicidal history.

There is no doubt that the relative risk of suicide, attempted suicide, and suicide ideation is very substantially increased in depression, both unipolar and bipolar. However, estimates do vary, influenced mainly by the particular samples studied and the methods used. A reasonable estimate would be that just over half of depressed patients have suicidal ideation and somewhere between 20% and 33% have a nonfatal attempt. Lifetime suicide risk in unipolar depression is almost certainly lower than the 15% commonly cited. The evidence is that bipolar disorder carries a lower risk than unipolar disorder, and depressive episodes would seem to be the key factor for suicide risk in bipolar disorder.

## Depression in Suicidal Behavior

Estimates vary considerably of how many people who complete suicide were depressed (Lonnqvist, 2000). This is perhaps not surprising, as accurate data are difficult to arrive at and usually rely on a retrospective method of trying to build a picture of the person, called psychological autopsy. For example, Foster, Gillespie, and McClelland (1997) conducted interviews with general practitioners, family, friends, and work colleagues to study the characteristics of 118 people out of 154 who completed suicide in Northern Ireland in 1 year. They estimated that an Axis I disorder was present in 86% of cases but that this was major unipolar depression in only 32% and bipolar depression in 4% of cases. One very large-scale study looked at reported suicides over a 5-year period in the United Kingdom (Department of Health, 2001). The study found that about one-quarter of almost 21,000 suicides over the period were in contact with mental health services and so consultants were able to provide diagnostic information about these individuals. Of those in contact with services, 42% met criteria for major affective disorder and 10% for bipolar disorder. It is reasonable to assume that the rates of depression might be lower in those not in contact with services, so the overall rate may have been lower than 42%.

It does appear that depression is more common in nonfatal self-harm than it is in suicide. This is true even when comparable methods of assessment are used. Beautrais (2001) found that in a sample of 202 suicides in New Zealand, 56% met diagnostic criteria for a mood disorder, according to information supplied by a significant other. She compared this to patients who had made a medically serious but nonfatal suicide attempt, also using a significant other as a source of information for direct comparability. She found that 78% of the attempters met criteria for a mood disorder. Even where data are not restricted to medically serious attempters, there is a high rate of depression in parasuicide. For example, Haw, Hawton, Houston, and Townsend (2001) found that 71% of their unselected sample of 150 self-harm patients presenting at "Accident and Emergency" met diagnostic criteria for major depressive episode (only one patient met criteria for bipolar disorder).

To summarize, depression is common in those who complete suicide and especially in those who attempt suicide. Estimates vary considerably and there is no definitive figure in either case. However, it appears likely that somewhere between one-third and one-half of those who complete suicide are depressed whereas between half and three-quarters of attempters are depressed.


## Reasons for Discordance

Obviously, there will be pathways to suicide other than depression, and many other risk factors have been identified (e.g., Maris, Berman, Maltsberger, & Yufit, 1992). But, why is depression without suicidal behavior so common? Why is there not a higher incidence of suicidal behavior in depression? One possibility is that it is necessary to have additional risk factors that add to the risk that depression carries. Or, it may be that those who are depressed but not at suicidal risk have certain protective factors which offset any depressive risk. A second possibility lies within the nature of the depressive experience itself: Are there certain facets or features of depression that are particularly related to suicidality?


### Additional risk factors

High comorbidity is generally associated with greater risk of suicidal behavior. One particular type of comorbidity that has received attention is comorbid Axis I and Axis II disorders. For example, Foster, Gillespie, McClelland, and Patterson (1999) found in the Northern Ireland study a much higher risk of suicide in those with Axis I–Axis II morbidity than those with Axis I morbidity only. Personality disorder has also been found to be an additional risk factor in the case of suicide attempts. Soloff, Lynch, Kelly, Malone, and Mann (2000) compared the characteristics of suicide attempts in patients who had both borderline personality disorder and major depression with those who had only major depression or only borderline personality disorder. Depressed and borderline patients did not differ from each other in characteristics of suicide attempts (number of attempts, level of lethal intent, medical damage, objective planning, and degree of violence of method), but those with both the disorders had higher levels of objective planning and a greater number of attempts. Comorbid depression and substance misuse are also associated with higher rates of suicidality than is depression alone (Cornelius et al., 1995).

A number of studies have examined psychological variables that differentiate depressed suicidal from depressed nonsuicidal individuals. Roy (1998) found that depressed patients who had attempted suicide were more introverted than depressed patients who had never attempted suicide. Seidlitz, Conwell, Duberstein, Cox, and Denning (2001) measured a range of emotion traits in older (older than 50 years) depressed inpatients who either had a suicide attempt or had never attempted suicide. Attempters were lower in warmth and positive emotions but the groups did not differ on other emotions such as anger, sadness, and guilt. Importantly, the groups did not differ on severity of depression as measured by the Hamilton depression score (excluding the suicide item) ruling out severity of depression as an overriding explanation for both emotions and suicidality. The strategy of comparing suicidal and nonsuicidal depressed patients has also been used to look at problem-solving skills. Schotte and Clum (1987) measured problem-solving skills in depressed inpatients with suicidal ideation and inpatients who were equally depressed but did not have any suicide ideation. The suicidal group performed more poorly than the depressed nonsuicidal group in a number of ways: they thought of fewer relevant steps to solve problems, gave more irrelevant solutions, thought of more drawbacks with their solutions, and said they were less likely to implement their solutions. Williams et al. have linked this difficulty with problem solving to the difficulties that suicidal individuals have recalling specific autobiographical memories (e.g., Williams, 2001), and also suggested that in some individuals small changes in mood may be enough to trigger a spiral of poor problem solving, hopelessness, and suicidal ideation (Hepburn, Barnhofer, & Williams, 2006). Dour, Cha, and Nock (2011) found that a combination of emotional reactivity and poor problem-solving skills predicted the probability of a recent attempt.

As well as additional risk factors, a lack of factors that protect against suicidality in the face of depression might play an important role. Linehan, Goodstein, Neilsen, and Chiles, 1983 developed the Reasons for Living Inventory (RFL) to assess beliefs that inhibit suicidal behavior. The scale has six subscales covering survival and coping beliefs (e.g., I still have many things left to do, I am curious about what will happen in the future), responsibility to family, child-related concerns, fear of suicide, fear of social disapproval, and moral objections to suicide. Those who have attempted suicide endorse fewer reasons for living compared with psychiatric controls or the general population (Linehan, Heard, & Armstrong, 1993). In the context of depression and suicidality, Malone et al. (2000) measured reasons for living in patients with major depression who either had or had not attempted suicide. The attempters and nonattempters had comparable Hamilton depression scores, though the attempters were significantly higher on depression as measured by the Beck Depression Inventory. The attempters had lower scores on the RFL generally and particularly on the subscales of responsibility to family, survival and coping beliefs, fear of social disapproval, and moral objections.

## The nature of the depressive experience—hopelessness

Are certain features or aspects of the experience of depression linked to suicidality? Perhaps the most obvious question is whether severity of depression is related to suicidal behavior. Not surprisingly, the evidence suggests that it is. Simon and Von Korff (1998) in a large follow-up study found that the risk of suicide greatly increased with type of treatment received. The rates in those treated as inpatients were much higher than those treated as outpatients. Assuming that treatment reflects severity, it is reasonable to conclude that rates are related to severity of depression. Alexopoulos, Bruce, Hull, Sirey, and Kakuma (1999) found that suicide ideation and suicide attempts in an elderly depressed sample were predicted by severity of depression, along with low social support and having previous attempts with high intent.

A more interesting question is whether there are particular aspects of depression that link to suicidality. The evidence is very clear that hopelessness about the future is the component of depressive experience that relates to suicidal behavior (see Nimeus,

Traskman-Bendz, & Alsen, 1997). Studies report that hopelessness mediates the relationship between depression and suicidal intent within deliberate self-harm populations (Salter & Platt, 1990; Wetzel, Margulies, Davis, & Karam, 1980). Furthermore, hopelessness has also been found to be related to repetition of deliberate self-harm 6 months later (Petrie, Chamberlain, & Clarke, 1988) and completed suicides up to 10 years later (Beck, Brown, & Steer, 1989; Fawcett et al., 1990).

## Lack of positive future thinking

Studies of suicidal future thinking have generally relied on the Beck Hopelessness Scale (Beck, Weissman, Lester, & Trexler, 1974) as a measure of hopelessness about the future. This is a 20-item true/false self-report measure that assesses global outlook for the future (e.g., "the future seems dark to me"). MacLeod and colleagues (MacLeod, Pankhania, Lee, & Mitchell, 1997; MacLeod, Rose, & Williams, 1993; MacLeod et al., 1998, 2005) examined future-directed thinking in self-harming patients more directly by adapting the standard verbal fluency paradigm. In the standard verbal fluency task, participants are given a time limit and asked to generate as many exemplars of a category as they can, for example, words beginning with a particular letter. In the future thinking task developed by these authors, individuals were asked to think of future positive events (things they were looking forward to) and negative events (things they were not looking forward to), for a range of time periods ranging from the next 24 hour to the next 10 years. Participants were given a time limit, and a fluency measure of the number of different events that they generated for each category was recorded. This method has the advantage of being a direct measure rather than a self-report measure, that is, it provides an objective measure (count) of responses rather than relying on participants saying how many items of each type they could generate if they were asked. The second major advantage is that it provides separate scores for positive and negative future thinking, in-line with a range of theoretical approaches which distinguish between positively valenced and negatively valenced psychological systems (e.g., Ito & Cacciopo, 1998). The results have consistently shown that deliberate self-harm patients are less able than controls to provide events they are looking forward to, but do not differ from controls in the number of events they are not looking forward to (MacLeod et al., 1993, 1997, 1998). It therefore appears that the future thinking of parasuicidal individuals is characterized by a lack of positive anticipation in the absence of any increase in negative anticipation.

The lack of positive anticipation that characterizes suicidal individuals fits well with the research on reasons for living. One of the main ways that reasons for living might inhibit suicidality is by protecting people from hopelessness about the future. In fact, a number of the items on the RFL specifically measure a view of the future that anticipates positive and meaningful experiences. A study by Greene (1989) also indirectly supports this view. She found that depressed women high in hopelessness differed from equally depressed women who were low in hopelessness by having young children. One interpretation is that having young children provides a trajectory into the future that protects the person from hopelessness in the face of depression.

It has been suggested that suicidal behavior is fundamentally about wanting to escape (Shneidman, 1999; Williams, 2001). The person might be trying to escape from depression or from other, different painful states of awareness. Hopelessness about the future is the key element of depression that leads to suicidal behavior. In the case of hopelessness, the escape is not necessarily about escaping stress or negative experiences but can be about trying to get away from the painful state of mind that arises when someone has no positive future to look forward to.

# Risk Assessment

There are two main clinical issues in relation to suicidal behavior: Can it be predicted and can it be prevented? More specifically, in relation to depression, how useful is depression in predicting suicidal behavior and is treating depression an adequate treatment for suicidal behavior? As will be seen, suicidal behavior cannot be predicted accurately using the whole range of known risk factors, let alone depression. Treating suicidal behavior has proved to be equally difficult. As would be expected from the discordance between suicidality and depression, treating depression is not an adequate treatment for suicidality.

## Predicting suicidal behavior

Hopelessness is often cited as a good predictor of suicidality, as touched upon earlier. For example, Beck et al. have found that hopelessness predicts suicide in patients who had been hospitalized because of suicide ideation (Beck, Steer, Kovacs, & Garrison, 1985) and in general psychiatric outpatients (Beck, Brown, Berchick, Stewart, & Steer, 1990). For suicidal inpatients, a score of 10 or more (out of 20) on the Beck Hopelessness Scale successfully identified 10 of 11 patients who completed suicide in a 5- to 10-year follow-up (Beck et al., 1985). In a sample of almost 2,000 outpatients, a score of nine or above correctly identified 16 out of the 17 suicides that occurred in a 3- to 4-year follow-up. As would be expected, hopelessness outperformed depression in prediction. However, the cost of such high sensitivity (not missing those who are at risk) was poor specificity. Specificity refers to the ability to avoid labeling people as being at risk when they are not, that is, the ability to avoid false positives. In both of these studies, the rate of false positives was very high. In the inpatient study, 88% of those identified as being at risk did not complete suicide, and the rate was 98% in the outpatient study.

Other studies have used a much wider range of factors to try to predict suicidal behavior with similar results. There are many ways in which those who complete suicide or attempt suicide differ on average from those who do not. These risk factors include sociodemographic factors, such as gender, class, and employment status; psychological factors, such as poor problem solving and hopelessness; and psychiatric factors, notably depression. Sometimes completers and attempters differ from the general population in the same way and sometimes they diverge. These factors are discussed in more detail by Maris et al. (1992) and Williams (2001). Pokorny (1983) followed almost 4,800 psychiatric inpatients over a 5-year period. Sixty-seven of the group completed suicide, a rate of 1.4%. A predictive model based on a range of known risk factors correctly identified 35 of the 67 as being at high risk. This moderate success on "hits" was offset by over 1,000 false positives. Trying to improve specificity has the effect of reducing sensitivity. For example, Goldstein, Black, Nasrallah, and Winokur (1991) in a similar type of study managed to reduce the false positive rate but at the cost of "missing" all 46 suicides in their sample. The problem is translating group differences into prediction at the individual level. Powell, Geddes, Deeks, Goldacre, and Hawton (2000) compared 112 people who completed suicide while in hospital with a group of randomly selected control patients from the same hospitals. There were many differences between the two groups and a number of the variables were statistically significant risk factors (i.e., clearly differentiated between the groups). However, using these factors to predict at an *individual* level whether someone would complete suicide was of little use: Only 2 of the 112 patients who completed suicide had a predicted risk of suicide above 5% based on these risk factors.

Predicting deliberate self-harm has also been shown to be difficult, though one of the problems that besets suicide prediction—low base rates—is less marked. Kreitman and Foster (1991) identified 11 factors that predicted repetition of parasuicide, including previous parasuicide, having a personality disorder, and having high alcohol consumption. Depression was not one of the identified risk factors in their study. Repetition was linked with the number of risk factors present: those who had three or fewer risk factors showed a 5% repetition rate whereas those with eight or more had a 42% repetition rate. However, as Kreitman and Foster (1991) point out, a large majority of their repeaters were in the midrange of risk scores, which simply reflected the fact that the vast majority of the sample scored in the midrange. If a cutoff of 8 or above was adopted for prediction, 76% of those who repeat would be missed. Adopting a lower cutoff would improve the hit rate but rapidly increases the number of false positives.

Predictive models fail for a number of reasons. Suicidal behavior, especially suicide, is relatively rare, and rare behaviors are inherently difficult to predict. Many of the factors used in these predictive studies do not reflect the psychological state of individuals but instead appear to be quite distant from the actual behavior (MacLeod, Williams, & Linehan, 1992). This can be seen most clearly in sociodemographic variables such as ethnicity, gender, and age, where although there may be a statistical connection between these variables and suicidality, there are clearly going to be many mediating factors that translate these variables into suicidal behavior. More generally, predictive models, or summative checklist approaches to risk, cannot take into account the individuality of the person. Someone may have many risk factors but these can be "trumped" by an overriding protective factor, such as a feeling of duty or responsibility to family or religious beliefs prohibiting suicide. Conversely, someone may have very few risk factors but the few that they do have are very important, for example, a recent major loss, and so they may be at high risk. As Shea (1999) notes:

> people don't kill themselves because statistics suggest that they should. The call to suicide comes from psychological pain. Each person is unique. Statistical power is at its best when applied to large populations, and at its weakest when applied to individuals. But it is the individual who clinicians must assess (p. 11).

## Clinical risk assessment

The arguments outlined above and the failure of prediction to work at the individual level have led to a more or less consensual view that the emphasis should not be about *prediction* but about assessing *risk* (Maris et al., 1992). In other words, the task for the clinician is to gauge whether risk is elevated, not to make a forecast of whether someone will kill themselves/harm themselves or not. The window of increased possibility of suicidal behavior is what Litman (1990) has called the "suicide zone." Someone is in the suicide zone when they are in a state where killing themselves is a possibility, but at the same time perhaps only about 1 or 2 in every 100 who are in that zone of acutely high risk will kill themselves (Litman).

Clinical assessment differs from the predictive research in that it is concerned with immediate or short-term risk. It also differs from the predictive research in focusing more on individual factors rather than "objective" factors. In fact, many of the factors that dominate the predictive models seem to be largely ignored by clinicians. Jobes, Eyman, and Yufit (1997) surveyed practicing clinicians on their methods of assessing suicide risk. They found that their respondents rarely used any formal risk assessment measures, relying much more on a clinical interview covering a broad range of questions. Interestingly, though not suprisingly, the three areas of questioning given the highest utility rating for arriving at an assessment were whether the person had a suicidal plan, had suicidal thoughts, and had a method available. Observations that were considered by clinicians to be most useful in making their assessments were difficulty establishing an alliance with the patient, evidence of alcohol or drug use, and evidence of depressed affect.

In summary, hopelessness or indeed any known combination of variables is not a good predictor of suicidal behavior. The cost of identifying those who will complete or attempt suicide is that many of those who will not are incorrectly labeled as being at risk. Reducing this high number of false positives results in missing those who are at risk. Predictive models perform poorly because suicidal behavior is rare and because they cannot take account of individual variability. The focus has shifted from prediction to risk assessment where the emphasis is on relative risk (is it possible?) rather than absolute risk (will it happen?). Clinical assessment of individuals can take account of individual factors but the accuracy of such assessment is not known, and perhaps, not generally knowable as it will depend on who is doing the assessing. The challenge is to integrate the empirical research base with an individually sensitive approach to clinical assessment.

# Intervention

There are two broad strategies to intervening in suicide. One approach is to treat suicidal behavior indirectly by treating any accompanying psychiatric disorder, of which the main candidate would be depression. The second approach is to develop treatments that focus specifically on tackling suicidal ideation and behavior. Due to the clear discordance between depression and suicidal behavior, even a highly effective treatment for depression is unlikely to be an effective treatment for suicidal behavior. A review by Khan, Warner, and Brown (2000) illustrates the point. These authors reviewed suicide rates in documented trials of new antidepressants over a 10-year period in the United States. Data from almost 20,000 patients were included. The overall rate of suicidal behavior was low—just less than 1% completed suicide and almost 3% attempted suicide. Importantly, for the argument here, the active treatments produced depressive symptom reduction of 41% compared to 31% for placebo but the groups did not differ in rates of suicide. There are some limitations to generalizing from these findings. The trials were very brief—4–8 weeks—and the patients in the trials were not typical in that they were not actively suicidal and not comorbid (Hirschfeld, 2000). However, the data demonstrate that reductions in depression can take place without accompanying reductions in suicidality. Studies of recovery also show that improvements in depression, hopelessness, and psychosocial function can all occur without any reduction in repetition of suicidal behavior (Townsend et al., 2001). One possible exception to this is the use of lithium to treat bipolar disorder in particular. There is evidence from epidemiological studies that patients taking lithium have reduced suicide risk. However, this is mainly based on naturalistic studies of those attending lithium clinics (Verkes & Cowen, 2000). Clearly, there may be selection factors operating in that those motivated and able to adhere to a lithium regime might be at lower risk to start with.

There is a wide range of psychological treatments aimed specifically at reducing suicidal behavior. Treatments tend to focus on preventing repetition of parasuicide, partly because of the near impossibility of demonstrating treatment effectiveness in such a rare behavior as completed suicide. On the whole, treatments do show evidence of some effectiveness, with self-harm rates in those given a specific treatment being lower than those who received treatment as usual (Hawton et al., 1998). One difficulty demonstrating effectiveness of treatment is undoubtedly influenced by the relative rarity of suicidal behavior. An additional major factor, increasingly recognized, is the heterogeneity of those who engage in suicidal behavior. The only thing that these individuals necessarily have in common is a single behavioral act.

Studies have been mixed, with some showing no effects and some showing positive results. There is no really clear pattern to those who show positive effects: they include brief treatments as well as longer-term treatments, and treatments based on psychodynamic principles as well as those on broadly cognitive-behavioral principles. Linehan reported significantly lower rates of self-harm in borderline personality disorder patients given dialectical behavior therapy (DBT; Linehan, Armstrong, Suarez, Allmon, & Heard, 1991). DBT is an intensive intervention, with weekly individual and group session for about 1 year. The group sessions aim to teach skills, such as interpersonal problem-solving skills, strategies for regulating emotions, and ways of tolerating distress, and the individual sessions focus on understanding suicidal episodes and dealing with issues of adherence to treatment. Bateman and Fonagy (1999) also reported a statistically significant reduction in self-harm rates along with other outcome measures in borderline personality disorder patients, this time receiving psychoanalytically oriented partial hospitalization (maximum 18 months), compared to those receiving standard psychiatric treatment. In both of these cases, benefits were maintained at follow-up (Bateman & Fonagy, 2001; Linehan et al., 1993). Brown et al. (2005)

reported lower rates of repetition in attempters given cognitive therapy compared to those receiving treatment as usual.

Brief treatments with unselected samples have also shown evidence of effectiveness. Salkovskis, Atha, and Storer (1990) employed a brief (five sessions) home-based problem-solving approach with patients who had a history of self-harm The sessions covered standard problem-solving training, such as help with identifying problems, generating solutions, and implementing solutions, all applied flexibly to the individual's situation. Compared to a treatment as usual group, those receiving the intervention showed reduced depression, hopelessness, suicide ideation, and also significantly lower repetition rates at 6 months, though at 18-month follow-up, the groups were no longer significantly different on repetition. Guthrie et al. (2001) found that recent attempters given four sessions of home-based, brief psychodynamic interpersonal therapy aimed at resolving interpersonal problems showed lower deliberate self-harm rates at 6-month follow-up than those receiving treatment as usual.

It is difficult to say why some studies have found a positive effect against a background of most showing no difference between a targeted intervention and treatment as usual. The Linehan et al. (1991) and Bateman and Fonagy (1999) studies focus on a particular subset of attempters—those meeting criteria for borderline personality disorder—thus, reducing the heterogeneity of the sample and also targeting a group with higher rates of self-harm. The Salkovskis study may have accommodated heterogeneity as they emphasized the flexible application of the treatment to individual cases. In contrast, a group intervention that included problem solving reported by Rudd et al. (1996) found no significant benefit over and above treatment as usual. The problem-solving intervention in the Rudd et al. (1996) study was implemented in groups of 12–14, thus necessarily limiting the extent to which treatment could be tailored to the individual. These explanations are post-hoc, but it is clear that heterogeneity of patients, as well as low base rates, represents major obstacles to successful intervention. One important factor may be the problem of ensuring a therapeutic dose of the intervention is delivered in a sample of individuals who are often ambivalent about treatment.

## Individualizing treatment

Heterogeneous conditions call for multifaceted treatments that can be delivered flexibly depending on the individual. In a climate of evidence-based, often manualized treatments, this represents a challenge. Davison (1998) points out that empirically supported manualized treatments do not take account of patient variability. Can an evidence base be reconciled with individualized treatment? Over 20 years ago, Liberman (1981) outlined a framework for doing just that. Liberman described a *modular* approach to the treatment of depression where, because of the complexity of the condition, a broad spectrum, multicomponent approach to treatment is needed. Crucially, though many factors are involved in causing and maintaining depression, not all factors will contribute equally to all patients. As not everyone has all factors equally, a broad spectrum approach is "intrusive and encumbers the patient with many interventions, some of which may not be necessary or applicable" (Liberman, 1981,

p. 241). A modular approach consists of an array of treatment strategies that are selected after a careful assessment of the individual patient's needs. The modules for each condition would be specified and determined in advance on the basis of empirical evidence. Some modules may be more primary. For example, Liberman suggests that all depressed patients start with a problem-solving module and move beyond that to modules that match their particular problems, if needed. Interestingly, the same idea of starting with problem solving has been advocated for suicidal behavior (Hawton & van Heeringen, 2000). Treatment for suicidal behavior would have modules for tackling poor problem-solving skills, hopelessness/lack of future positivity, and so on. A similar approach has been described by Evans et al. (1999) though without the explicit feature of selective targeting of different modules for different individuals. The modular approach provides a framework for containing the diversity of interventions needed to approach a heterogeneous population such as suicide attempters.

In fact, though not fully specified by Liberman (1981), a modular approach provides a framework for a full scientist–practitioner program. The initial, research-based steps would consist of establishing characteristics of those with the particular condition. In the case of suicidal behavior, a lot of progress has been made in respect to this. Therapeutic strategies to target those particular deficits would then be developed and evaluated for effectiveness. At the level of clinical application, each patient would be assessed on each characteristic and the module selected based on assessment outcome. Evaluation would include not only the target behavior (suicidal behavior) but also the specific focus of the treatment module that is delivered (e.g., hopelessness/lack of positive future thinking). In the case of suicidal behavior, some of this work has already been done (e.g., Linehan, 1993), but there is a need to develop intervention strategies that specifically target hopelessness/lack of positive future thinking. This may focus on formulating positive goals but is particularly likely to need strategies to help individuals to form plans to achieve positive goals. Vincent, Boddana, and MacLeod (2004) found that deliberate self-harm patients had less difficulty thinking of goals than they had thinking of plans to achieve those goals.

## Summary and Conclusions

There is a strong link between depression and suicidal behavior, but there is also high divergence, shown especially by the fact that the vast majority of depressed people do not complete or attempt suicide. The presence or absence of other factors might help explain this divergence. Factors such as other psychiatric diagnoses, especially personality disorder, protective factors, and other psychological factors such as personality and affective traits, and problem-solving skills have all been shown to distinguish suicidal from nonsuicidal depressed individuals. The relationship between depression and suicidality is mainly dependent on one particular facet of depression—hopelessness about the future. Hopelessness appears to consist mainly of a lack of positive thoughts about the future rather than preoccupation with a negative future. Risk assessment and intervention in suicidal behavior are difficult because of the relatively low base rate of suicidal behavior and the heterogeneity of those who engage in it. Predictive models, whether using depressive hopelessness or a range of factors, are only able to identify those at risk through producing unacceptably high numbers of people incorrectly classified as at risk. Because of predictive inaccuracy, the emphasis has shifted to assessment of relative risk rather than absolute risk. Treatments of depression are never likely to themselves be effective treatments for suicidal behavior. The majority of studies testing specific interventions for suicidal behavior have shown no benefit over treatment as usual, though a number of studies have shown positive results. There is no obvious pattern to the successful interventions in terms of their content, though they do seem either to target a specific subgroup of parasuicides or involve a brief, flexible treatment delivered at home. Both these strategies potentially limit the problem of heterogeneity. A modular approach provides a framework for incorporating a range of treatment strategies derived from the interface between basic and applied research. Developing strategies to tackle depressive hopelessness, particularly lack of positivity about the future, is one of the most needed and promising lines for future research.

# References

Alexopoulos, G. S., Bruce, M. L., Hull, J., Sirey, J. A., & Kakuma, T. (1999). Clinical determinants of suicidal ideation and behaviour in geriatric depression. *Archives of General Psychiatry, 56,* 1048–1053.

Angst, J., Angst, F., Gerber-Werder, R., & Gamma, A. (2005). Suicide in 406 mood-disorder patients with and without long-term medication: A 40 to 44 years' follow-up. *Archives of Suicide Research, 9,* 279–300.

Bancroft, J., Hawton, K., Simkin, S., Kingston, B., Cumming, C., & Whitwell, D. (1979). The reasons people give for taking overdoses. *British Journal of Medical Psychology, 52,* 353–365.

Bateman, A., & Fonagy, P. (1999). Effectiveness of partial hospitalization in the treatment of borderline personality disorder: A randomized controlled trial. *American Journal of Psychiatry, 156,* 1563–1569.

Bateman, A., & Fonagy, P. (2001). Treatment of borderline personality disorder with psychoanalytically oriented partial hospitalization: An 18-month follow-up. *American Journal of Psychiatry, 158,* 36–42.

Beautrais, A. L. (2001). Suicides and serious suicide attempts: Two populations or one? *Psychological Medicine, 31,* 837–845.

Beck, A. T., Brown, G., Berchick, R. J., Stewart, B. L., & Steer, R. A. (1990). Relationship between hopelessness and ultimate suicide: A replication with psychiatric outpatients. *American Journal of Psychiatry, 147,* 190–195

Beck, A. T., Brown, G., & Steer, R. A. (1989). Prediction of eventual suicide in psychiatric inpatients by clinical ratings of hopelessness. *Journal of Consulting and Clinical Psychology, 57,* 309–310.

Beck, A. T., Steer, R. A., Kovacs, M., & Garrison, B. (1985). Hopelessness and eventual suicide: A 10-year prospective study of patients hospitalized with suicidal ideation. *American Journal of Psychiatry, 145,* 559–563.

Beck, A. T., Weissman, A., Lester, D., & Trexler, L. (1974). The measurement of pessimism: The hopelessness scale. *Journal of Consulting and Clinical Psychology, 42,* 861–865.

Bostwick, J. M., & Pankratz, V. S. (2000). Affective disorders and suicide risk: A re-examination. *American Journal of Psychiatry, 157,* 1925–1932.

Bottlender, R., Jager, M., Strauss, A., & Moller, H. J. (2000). Suicidality in bipolar compared to unipolar depressed inpatients. *European Archives of Psychiatry and Clinical Neuroscience*, *250*, 257–261.

Brown, G. K., Ten Have, T., Henriques, G. R., Xie, S. X., Hollander, J. E., & Beck, A. T. (2005). Cognitive therapy for the prevention of suicide attempts. *Journal of the American Medical Association*, *294*, 563–570.

Brown, M., Comtois, K. A., & Linehan, M. M. (2002). Reasons for suicide attempts and nonsuicidal self-injury in women with borderline personality disorder. *Journal of Abnormal Psychology*, *111*, 198–202.

Cornelius, J. R., Salloum, I. M., Mezzich, J., Cornelius, M. D., Fabrega, H., Ehler, J. G., ... Mann, J. J. (1995). Disproportionate suicidality in patients with comorbid major depression and alcoholism. *American Journal of Psychiatry*, *152*, 358–364.

Davison, G. C. (1998). Being bolder with the boulder model: The challenge of education and training in empirically supported treatments. *Journal of Consulting and Clinical Psychology*, *66*, 163–167.

Department of Health (2001). *Safety first: Five-year report of the national confidential inquiry into suicide and homicide by people with mental illness*. London: Author.

Dilsaver, S. C., Chen, Y., Swann, A. C., Shoaib, A. M., & Krajewski, K. J. (1994). Suicidality in patients with pure and depressive mania. *American Journal of Psychiatry*, *151*, 1312–1315.

Dour, H. J., Cha, C. B., & Nock, M. K. (2011). Evidence for an emotion-cognition interaction in the statistical prediction of suicide attempts. *Behaviour Research and Therapy*, *49*, 294–298.

Evans, K., Tyrer, P., Catalan, J., Schmidt, U., Davidson, K., Dent, J., ... Thompson, S. (1999). Manual-assisted cognitive-behaviour therapy (MACT): A randomized controlled trial of a brief intervention with bibliotherapy in the treatment of recurrent deliberate self-harm. *Psychological Medicine*, *29*, 19–25.

Fawcett, J., Scheftner, W. A., Fogg, L., Clark, D. C., Young, M. A., Hedeker, D., & Gibbons, R. (1990). Time-related predictors of suicide in major affective disorder. *American Journal of Psychiatry*, *147*, 1189–1194.

Fombonne, E., Wostear, G., Cooper, V., Harrington, R., & Rutter, M. (2001). The Maudsley long-term follow-up of child and adolescent depression 2. Suicidality, criminality and social dysfunction in adulthood. *British Journal of Psychiatry*, *179*, 218–223.

Foster, T., Gillespie, K., & McClelland, R. (1997). Mental disorders and suicide in Northern Ireland. *British Journal of Psychiatry*, *170*, 447–452.

Foster, T., Gillespie, K., McClelland, R., & Patterson, C. (1999). Risk factors for suicide independent of DSM-III-R axis I disorder—Case-control psychological autopsy study in Northern Ireland. *British Journal of Psychiatry*, *175*, 175–179.

Goldstein, R. B., Black, D. W., Nasrallah, A., & Winokur, G. (1991). The prediction of suicide—Sensitivity, specificity and predictive value of a multivariate model applied to suicide among 1906 patients with affective disorders. *Archives of General Psychiatry*, *48*, 418–422.

Greene, S. M. (1989). The relationship between depression and hopelessness. *British Journal of Psychiatry*, *154*, 650–659.

Guthrie, E., Kapur, N., Mackway-Jones, K., Chew-Graham, C., Moorey, J., Mendel, E., ... Tomenson, B. (2001). Randomised controlled trial of brief psychological intervention after deliberate self-poisoning. *British Medical Journal*, *323*, 1–5.

Guze, S. B., & Robins, E. (1970). Suicide and primary affective disorders. *British Journal of Psychiatry*, *117*, 437–438.

Harris, C. E., & Barraclough, B. M. (1997). Suicide as an outcome for mental disorders. *British Journal of Psychiatry*, *170*, 205–228.

Haw, C., Hawton, K., Houston, K., & Townsend, E. (2001). Psychiatric and personality disorders in deliberate self-harm patients. *British Journal of Psychiatry, 178*, 48–54.

Hawton, K., Arensman, E., Townsend, E., Bremner, S., Feldman, E., Goldney, R., ... Traskman-Bendz, L. (1998). Deliberate self-harm: Systematic review of efficacy of psychosocial and pharmacological treatments in preventing repetition. *British Medical Journal, 317*, 441–447.

Hawton, K., Rodham, K., & Evans, E. (2006) *By their own young hands: Deliberate self-harm and suicidal ideas in adolescents.* London: Jessica Kingsley Publishers.

Hawton, K., & van Heeringen, K. (2000). Future perspectives. In K. Hawton & K. van Heeringen (Eds.), *The international handbook of suicide and attempted suicide* (pp. 713–723). Chichester, UK: Wiley.

Hepburn, S. R., Barnhofer, T., & Williams, J. M. G. (2006). Effects of mood on how future events are generated and perceived. *Personality and Individual Differences, 41*, 801–811.

Hirschfeld, R. M. A. (2000). Suicide and antidepressant treatment. *Archives of General Psychiatry, 57*, 325–326.

Ito, T. A., & Cacciopo, J. T. (1998). Representations of the contours of positive human health. *Psychological Inquiry, 9*, 43–48.

Jobes, D. A., Eyman, J. R., & Yufit, R. I. (1997). How clinicians assess suicide risk in adolescents and adults. *Crisis Intervention and Time Limited Treatment, 2*, 1–12.

Kerkhof, A. J. F. M (2000). Attempted suicide: Patterns and trends. In K. Hawton & K. van Heeringen (Eds.), *The international handbook of suicide and attempted suicide* (pp. 49–64). Chichester, UK: Wiley.

Kessler, R. C., Borges, G., & Walters, E. E. (1999). Prevalence of and risk factors for lifetime suicide attempts in the national comorbidity survey. *Archives of General Psychiatry, 56*, 617–626.

Khan, A., Warner, A., & Brown, W. A. (2000). Symptom reduction and suicide risk in patients treated with placebo in antidepressant clinical trials. *Archives of General Psychiatry, 57*, 311–326.

Kreitman, N. (1977). *Parasuicide.* London: Wiley.

Kreitman, N., & Foster, J. (1991). The construction and selection of predictive scales, with special reference to parasuicide. *British Journal of Psychiatry, 159*, 185–192.

Liberman, R. P. (1981). A model for individualizing treatment. In L. P. Rehm (Ed.), *Behaviour therapy for depression: Present status and future directions.* New York: Academic Press.

Linehan, M. M. (1993). *Skills training manual for treating borderline personality disorder.* New York: Guilford Press.

Linehan, M. M., Armstrong, H. E., Suarez, A., Allmon, D., & Heard, H. L. (1991). Cognitive behavioural treatment of chronically parasuicidal borderline patients. *Archives of General Psychiatry, 48*, 1060–1064.

Linehan, M. M., Goodstein, J. L., Neilsen, S. L., & Chiles, J. A. (1983). Reasons for staying alive when you are thinking of killing yourself: The reasons for living inventory. *Journal of Consulting and Clinical Psychology, 51*, 276–286.

Linehan, M. M., Heard, H. L., & Armstrong, H. E. (1993). Naturalistic follow-up of a behavioural treatment for chronically parasuicidal borderline patients. *Archives of General Psychiatry, 50*, 971–974.

Litman, R. E. (1990). Suicides: What do they have in mind? In D. Jacobs & H. N. Brown (Eds.), *Suicide: Understanding and responding* (pp. 143–156). Madison, CT: International Universities Press.

Lonnqvist, J. K. (2000). Psychiatric aspects of suicidal behaviour: Depression. In K. Hawton & K. van Heeringen (Eds.), *The international handbook of suicide and attempted suicide* (pp. 107–120). Chichester, UK: Wiley.

Lopez, P., Mosquera, F., de Leon, J., Gutierrez, M., Ezcurra, J., Ramirez, F., & Gonzalez-Pinto, A. (2001). Suicide attempts in bipolar patients. *Journal of Clinical Psychiatry, 62,* 963–966.

MacLeod, A. K., Pankhania, B., Lee, M., & Mitchell, D., (1997). Depression, hopelessness and future-directed thinking in parasuicide. *Psychological Medicine, 27,* 973–977.

MacLeod, A. K., Rose, G. S., & Williams, J. M. G. (1993). Components of hopelessness about the future in parasuicide. *Cognitive Therapy and Research, 17,* 441–455.

MacLeod, A. K., Tata, P., Evans, K., Tyrer, P., Schmidt, U., Davidson, K., . . . Catalan, J. (1998). Recovery of positive future thinking with a high-risk parasuicide group: Results from a pilot randomised controlled trial. *British Journal of Clinical Psychology, 37,* 371–379.

MacLeod, A. K., Tata, P., Tyrer, P., Schmidt, U., Davidson, K., & Thompson, S. (2005). Hopelessness and positive and negative future thinking in parasuicide. *British Journal of Clinical Psychology, 44,* 495–504.

MacLeod, A. K., Williams, J. M. G., & Linehan, M. M. (1992). New developments in the understanding and treatment of suicidal behaviour. *Behavioural Psychotherapy, 20,* 193–218.

Malone, K. M., Oquendo, M. A., Haas, G. L., Ellis, S. P., Li, S., & Mann, J. J. (2000). Protective factors against suicidal acts in major depression: Reasons for living. *American Journal of Psychiatry, 157,* 1084–1088.

Maris, R. W., Berman, A. L., Maltsberger, J. T., & Yufit, R. I. (Eds.). (1992). *Assessment and prediction of suicide.* New York: Guilford Press.

McGirr, A., Renaud, J., Seguin, M., Alda, M., & Turecki, G. (2008). Course of major depressive disorder and suicide outcome: A psychological autopsy study. *Journal of Clinical Psychiatry, 69,* 966–970.

Nimeus, A., Traskman-Bendz, L., & Alsen, M. (1997). Hopelessness and suicidal behaviour. *Journal of Affective Disorders, 42,* 137–144.

Nock, M. K., Borges, G., Bromet, E. J., Alonso, J., Angermeyer, M., Beautrais, A., . . . Williams, D. (2008). Cross-national prevalence and risk factors for suicidal ideation, plans and attempts. *British Journal of Psychiatry, 192,* 98–105

Oquendo, M. A., Waternauz, C. Brodsky, B., Parsons, B., Haas, G. L., Malone, K. M., & Mann, J. J. (2000). Suicidal behaviour in bipolar mood disorder: Clinical characteristics of attempters and non-attempters. *Journal of Affective Disorders, 59,* 107–117.

Ostby, U., Brandt, L., Correia, N., Ekbom, A., & Sparen, P. (2001). Excess mortality in bipolar and unipolar disorder in Sweden. *Archives of General Psychiatry, 58,* 844–850.

Petrie, K., Chamberlain, K., & Clarke, D. (1988). Psychological predictors of future suicidal behaviour in hospitalized suicide attempters. *British Journal of Clinical Psychology, 27,* 247–258.

Pokorny, A. D. (1983). Prediction of suicide in psychiatric in-patients—Report of a prospective study. *Archives of General Psychiatry, 40,* 249–257.

Powell, J., Geddes, J., Deeks, J., Goldacre, M., & Hawton, K. (2000). Suicide in psychiatric hospital in-patients: Risk factors and their predictive power. *British Journal of Psychiatry, 176,* 266–272.

Qin, P., Jepsen, P., Norgard, B., Agerbo, E., Mortensen, P. B., Vilstrup, H., & Sørensen, H. T. (2009). Hospital admission for non-fatal poisoning with weak analgesics and risk for subsequent suicide: A population study. *Psychological Medicine, 39,* 867–873.

Roy, A. (1998) Is introversion a risk factor for suicidal behaviour in depression? *Psychological Medicine, 28,* 1457–1461.

Rudd, M. D., Rajab, M. H., Orman, D. T., Stulman, D. A., Joiner, T., & Dixon, W. (1996). Effectiveness of an outpatient intervention targeting suicidal young adults: Preliminary results. *Journal of Consulting and Clinical Psychology, 64,* 179–190.

Sakinofsky, I. (2000). Repetition of suicidal behaviour. In K. Hawton & K. van Heeringen (Eds.), *The international handbook of suicide and attempted suicide* (pp. 385–404). Chichester, UK: John Wiley & Sons.

Salkovskis, P. M., Atha, C., & Storer, D. (1990). Cognitive-behavioural problem solving in the treatment of patients who repeatedly attempt suicide. *British Journal of Psychiatry, 157*, 871–876.

Salter, D., & Platt, S. (1990). Suicidal intent, hopelessness and depression in a parasuicide population: The influence of social desirability and elapsed time. *British Journal of Clinical Psychology, 29*, 361–371.

Schaffer, A., Levitt, A. J., Bagby, R. M., Kennedy, S. H., Levitan, R. D., & Joffe, R. T. (2000). Suicidal ideation in major depression: Sex differences and impact of comorbid anxiety. *Canadian Journal of Psychiatry, 45*, 822–826.

Schotte, D. E., & Clum, G. A. (1987). Problem-solving skills in suicidal psychiatric patients. *Journal of Consulting and Clinical Psychology, 55*, 49–54.

Seidlitz, L., Conwell, Y., Duberstein, P., Cox, C., & Denning, D. (2001). Emotion traits in older suicide attempters and non-attempters. *Journal of Affective Disorders, 66*, 123–131.

Shea, S. C. (1999). *The practical art of suicide assessment: A guide for mental health professionals and substance abuse counsellors.* New York: Wiley.

Shneidman, E. S. (1999). The psychological pain assessment scale. *Suicide and Life Threatening Behavior, 29*, 287–294.

Simon, G. E., & Von Korff, M. (1998). Suicide mortality among patients treated for depression in an insured population. *American Journal of Epidemiology, 147*, 155–160.

Soloff, P. H., Lynch, K. G., Kelly, T. M., Malone, K. M., & Mann, J. J. (2000). Characteristics of suicide attempts of patients with major depressive episode and borderline personality disorder: A comparative study. *American Journal of Psychiatry, 157*, 601–608.

Strakowski, S. M., McElroy, S. L., Keck, P. E., & West, S. A. (1996). Suicidality among patients with mixed and manic bipolar disorder. *American Journal of Psychiatry, 153*, 674–676.

Townsend, E., Hawton, K., Altman, D. G., Arensman, E., Gunnell, D., Hazell, P., . . . van Heeringen, K. (2001). The efficacy of problem-solving treatments after deliberate self-harm: Meta-analysis of randomized controlled trials with respect to depression, hopelessness, and improvements in problems. *Psychological Medicine, 31*, 979–988.

Verkes, R. J., & Cowen, P. J. (2000). Pharmacotherapy of suicidal ideation and behaviour. In K. Hawton & K. van Heeringen (Eds.), *The international handbook of suicide and attempted suicide* (pp. 487–502). Chichester, UK: Wiley.

Vincent, P. J., Boddana, P., & MacLeod, A. K. (2004). Positive life goals and plans in parasuicide. *British Journal of Clinical Psychology, 11*, 90–99.

Wetzel, R. D., Margulies, T., Davis, R., & Karam, E. (1980). Hopelessness, depression, and suicidal intent. *Journal of Clinical Psychiatry, 41*, 159–160

Williams, J. M. G. (2001). *Suicide and attempted suicide.* London: Penguin Books.

Windfuhr, K., & Kapur, N. (2011). International perspective on the epidemiology and aetiology of suicide and self-harm. In R. C. O'Connor, S. Platt, & J. Gordon (Eds.), *International handbook of suicide prevention* (pp. 27–58). Chichester, UK: Wiley.

World Health Organisation (2001). *The world health report.* Geneva, Switzerland: Author.

# 19

# Vulnerability to Depression in Culture, Mind, and Brain

Yulia E. Chentsova-Dutton[1] and
Andrew G. Ryder[2]

[1]Georgetown University, USA
[2]Concordia University, Canada
[2]Sir Mortimer B. Davis—Jewish General Hospital, Canada

Imagine a laboratory mouse that differs from its littermates. Given the opportunity to explore novel environments—a stressful but potentially rewarding scenario for mice—this one instead remains in dark, sheltered areas. It is unusually passive when the researchers further test its response to stress by dangling it upside down or dropping it in water. It does not sleep well or show typical interest in sweet treats. These behaviors appear analogous to human expressions of distress, depression in particular. This connection provides researchers with an animal model for how physiological factors—for example, genetic differences that influence serotonin transporter function (Holmes, Yang, Lesch, Crawley, & Murphy, 2003; Murphy et al., 2001)—leave animals vulnerable to apathy and withdrawal, especially in combination with stress (Willner & Mitchell, 2002).

It is tempting to extend these findings to humans and point to biological vulnerabilities as ultimate explanations of major depression. Not only do such brain-level models allow one to posit low-level causal explanations, but also they lend themselves to empirical study through careful experimentation. We believe this enterprise to be misguided, however, when conducted in isolation. A brain-based vulnerability–stress model cannot be applied to humans without considering the ways in which vulnerability and stress are profoundly shaped by mind and culture. Brain-level models may at times acknowledge that attention to mind and culture helps reveal certain details, but they tend to reduce these higher levels to the brain. Here, the brain provides a coloring book of clearly identifiable images; culture and mind merely shade between the lines.

In our view, by contrast, layers of ceramic glaze provide a better analogy. When a piece of pottery is fired, layers of glaze melt and fuse to reveal and enhance underlying designs or allow new colors and patterns to emerge. It helps to know something about how each coat of glaze is constituted and what it potentially contributes, but it

*The Wiley-Blackwell Handbook of Mood Disorders*, Second Edition. Edited by Mick Power.
© 2013 John Wiley & Sons, Ltd. Published 2013 by John Wiley & Sons, Ltd.

is critical to remember that the effect includes transformations of other coats. Similarly, higher-level layers of mind and culture do not merely "add color," but transform how the brain functions. In contrast to some anthropologists, we also maintain that the reverse is equally true: Human culture, with its vast but not limitless diversity, requires, emerges from, and is shaped by the evolved human brain. The mind is similarly grounded in the brain without being reducible to it, and extends beyond the brain to include frequently used tools and close others (Ryder, Ban, & Chentsova-Dutton, 2011).

Indeed, even though animal models are invaluable for understanding brain mechanisms of mood regulation and designing effective antidepressants, they fail to capture the ways in which the mind is integral to the experience of distress. Humans differ from laboratory mice in many respects, most notably in their capacity for consciousness and meaning-making. The human mind also stands out for its uniquely powerful capacity to infer internal states of others and to communicate with them, allowing us to share (or choose not to share) distressing experiences. Understanding how the human mind responds to the sociocultural environment changes our understanding of what is happening in the brain.

For example, consistent with the animal model, the function of the serotonin transporter gene in humans is linked to individual differences in emotional and social sensitivity (Hariri & Holmes, 2006; Way & Taylor, 2010), and in interacting with stress in shaping depression (Caspi et al., 2003; Karg, Burmeister, Shedden, & Sen, 2011; Uher & McGuffin, 2010; Wilhelm et al., 2006; see Risch et al., 2009). Nonetheless, this and other genes that are associated with depression are slaves with many masters (see Sherman, Kim, & Taylor, 2009). The same allele of the serotonin transporter gene associated with vulnerability to depression is also linked to enhanced sensitivity and to positive interpersonal experiences, such as a nurturing family or effective social support (Kilpatrick et al., 2007; Taylor, Mannie, Norbury, Near, & Cowen, 2011). These seemingly opposed effects suggest that this gene fosters brain functions that support our ability to be sensitive to fortunes as well as misfortunes, yet something important is missing even from this expanded model.

Consider the sizeable cultural group differences found in the prevalence rates for depression. Assuming for the moment that DSM categories can be applied worldwide, the likelihood of meeting the criteria for Major Depressive Disorder within the last year ranges from a low of 1 in about 40 people in some countries (e.g., China and Korea) to a high of 1 in about 12 people in others (e.g., the United States and Canada; Demyttenaere et al., 2007; Kessler et al., 2009; Lin et al., 2008; Ohayon & Hong, 2006; Vasiliadis, Lesage, Adair, Wang, & Kessler, 2007). Although there are outliers that violate this pattern, depression is more common in individualistic than collectivistic cultural contexts (Chiao & Blizinsky, 2010). The next step is to explore the factors that might account for this pattern.

A researcher informed by physiological models of depression may hypothesize that genetic vulnerability to depression varies across cultural contexts. Indeed, it does so— but in the exact opposite direction from the obvious prediction. The short-short allele of the serotonin transporter gene thought to index vulnerability to depression is more, not less, common in collectivistic cultural contexts (Chiao & Blizinsky, 2010, see also Eisenberg & Hayes, 2011). Hence, a population with a higher brain-level vulnerability to depression is at a lower risk for developing major depression and other internalizing disorders. What is going on here?

Chiao and Blizinsky (2010) suggested that the impact of distress in collectivistic cultural contexts is curbed by the close and stable social ties characteristic of these contexts. As a result, what appears to be vulnerability at the brain level is neutralized or even rendered potentially advantageous when mind and culture levels are incorporated into the system (also findings for serotonin 1A receptor gene; Kim et al., 2010). Understanding genetic differences in socioemotional sensitivity is essential, but insufficient, for understanding depression. As we examine depression at the level of gene sequences and neuronal signals, we need to simultaneously attend to thoughts, emotion regulation strategies, pursuit of harmful cultural values, and so on. It is critical for us to consider brain, mind, and culture as fused levels of a single system.

In this chapter, we will rely on the culture-mind-brain framework (Ryder et al., 2011) to interpret recent work on vulnerability to depression and its interaction with stress. We will not offer our readers a comprehensive review of the literature on culture and depression (see instead Chentsova-Dutton & Tsai, 2008). Rather, we will describe a lens for interpreting findings on psychopathology in cultural context, applied to a specific issue and a specific disorder. We will argue that when considering who is vulnerable, none of the levels provide us with sufficient information, neither is it sufficient to add the contributions of each level together. In this regard, the culture-mind-brain framework represents a specific example of the biopsychosocial approach, designed to move beyond three separate domains toward a single, integrated, multilevel system. While exploring the implications of this framework, we will consider the possibility that vulnerability to depression is best understood as an emergent property of the total system, rather than being linked to a specific level. Before we begin, however, we will briefly describe depression and the culture-mind-brain framework in more detail.

## Depression and the Culture-Mind-Brain

### Defining depression

Defining "depression" is complicated even before one introduces cultural variation. The term can be used to describe a mood state, a constellation of symptoms, a discrete episode, a chronic condition, or a disease category with specific inclusion and exclusion criteria. Depressed mood is only one of many potential symptoms of a Major Depressive Episode (MDE) and is not actually necessary for a DSM-IV or ICD-10 diagnosis. Depression instruments assess a wide range of symptoms, only a few of which relate closely to depressed mood (Bagby, Ryder, Schuller, & Marshall, 2004). Several other disorders include depressive mood states, while trait "depressiveness" can be conceptualized as a personality trait; both of these possibilities also confer vulnerability to MDEs (Bagby, Watson, & Ryder, in press; Ryder, Bagby, & Schuller, 2002). MDEs, meanwhile, can be observed in nonpathological bereavement, general medical conditions such as thyroid dysfunction, as part of a broader condition such as Bipolar I Disorder, or as central to Major Depressive Disorder (MDD).

These definitional complexities are only worsened by evidence of cultural variation. If "depression" emerges in response to different stressors, presents with different symptoms, has different social implications, and leads to different treatments, to what extent are we dealing with the same construct? For example, depression in Chinese populations is characterized by an emphasis on somatic symptoms and de-emphasis on psychological symptoms relative to Western populations, with implications for assessment and treatment (Parker, Cheah, & Roy, 2001; Ryder et al., 2008). Is "depression in China" the same thing, a related thing (e.g., neurasthenia; Kleinman, 1982), or a different thing entirely from depression? We have at times used the term "profound distress" to capture a broad range of phenomena recognizable as symptomatic responses to loss without emphasizing a particular symptom and a particular diagnostic manual's conception (e.g., Ryder & Chentsova-Dutton, 2012). As befits the focus of this volume, we will continue to use the term "depression," but will do so with caution.

## The culture-mind-brain framework

Before continuing our discussion of culture and depression, it is necessary first to pause and consider what we mean by "culture" and how this domain fits with others thought central to psychopathology. As explored in more detail elsewhere, we take as our starting point the "cultural psychology" view of culture, with the claim that human culture and psychology "make each other up" (Shweder, 1991). In our efforts to merge cultural psychology with clinical psychology, we have considered both work on culture-mind by cultural psychologists (and anthropologists) and work on mind-brain by clinical psychologists (and psychiatrists). The result is a three-level framework, a single system of culture-mind-brain in which each level is mutually constituted by the other two (Ryder et al., 2011). It is in large part through this idea of mutual constitution that the culture-mind-brain framework represents a specific biopsychosocial approach, rather than merely a mnemonic to remind researchers of the importance of the three levels.

Although not central to traditional perspectives on cultural psychology, recent developments in "cultural neuroscience" confer a much more central role to the brain (Chiao, 2009; Kitayama & Park, 2010; Kitayama & Uskul, 2011). Including the brain along with culture and mind in a mutually constitutive relation underscores that, far from a static organ determining thought and behavior, the human brain is exquisitely attuned to its sociocultural environment. The brain is highly sensitive to cultural inputs, responding to them with marked plasticity, especially early in development (Wexler, 2008). Importantly, however, the range of possible environments is considerable, but not limitless; moreover, plasticity does not mean infinite malleability. Biology shapes and constrains culture, and vice versa (Ryder et al., 2011).

In keeping with a holistic view, nothing happens in the mind that is not reflected in brain activity, but at the same time, there are limits to the brain's explanatory power. The most obvious limit relates to complexity, as relatively simple ideas at the mind-level may be extremely difficult to describe as complex and changing neural patterns. However, we believe we can go beyond the use of "mind" as a higher-order explanatory language without resorting to dualism. A view of the mind as fundamentally tool-using and social allows us to understand mind as extended beyond the brain (Clark & Chalmers, 1998; Hutchins, 1995; Kirmayer, 2012; Vygotsky, 1978). Direction-finding may be greatly facilitated by the hippocampus, but habitual tools such as written directions, maps, smartphone apps, and so on become incorporated into the mind's direction-finding system. Culture helps shape the kind of person you would seek out as a confidante, but the incorporation of a specific other into your emotion regulation system takes place at the mind level.

With these conceptions of brain and mind in place, let us return now to culture. Research in clinical psychology and psychiatry often uses "culture" as a synonym for ethnic group or nationality. There has been a move, however, toward unpacking conceptions of culture, allowing us to ask, specifically, what aspects of culture matter? We emphasize that culture can be situated both "in the head" as meanings (e.g., values, norms, beliefs) and "in the world" as practices (i.e., meaningful behaviors). Differentiating "culture" from "cultural group" underscores how different people within a cultural context think and act in different, even contradictory, ways. Nonetheless, these ways are all culturally meaningful and depend on a shared framework. People do not simply carry cognitive replicas of their cultural context around in their heads, and to proceed as though this is so is to reduce culture to mind (Ryder et al., 2011).

## Depression in the culture-mind-brain

We think of culture-mind-brain as a single system, divided for pragmatic purposes into three levels. One implication is that changes at one level cascade through the whole system. A particular story might be easier to tell at a certain level but will not therefore be limited to that level. At the same time, a "disorder" story at one level does not require disorder at all levels (Ryder et al., 2011). Feedback loops can emerge in which response to a problem exacerbates the problem, even when all lower-level components of the loop are working properly (Kirmayer & Sartorius, 2007). Indeed, loops are a property of human systems where the very awareness that one fits a particular category, such as a psychiatric diagnosis, leads to responses that can modify the characteristics of that category. The belief that depressed people are submissive can contribute to submissiveness when one is labeled "depressed" (Hacking, 1995).

We have previously described possible ways in which people suffering from an onset of depression draw upon culturally available scripts—sequences of meanings and practices—in an effort to understand and cope with the chaos of sensations, thoughts, emotions, and behaviors (Ryder et al., 2011). These scripts include intersubjective beliefs about how others understand what is going on, how public manifestations of symptoms are likely to be interpreted, what can be safely discussed, and so on. The increased attention paid to certain experiences not only identifies culturally meaningful symptoms but also creates a loop in which the symptom itself becomes more salient and perhaps even more severe. If it is safer, for example, to talk about the body during the Cultural Revolution in China, the consequence is not merely a particular stigma-avoiding strategy of symptom presentation, but a different experience altogether (Ryder & Chentsova-Dutton, 2012).

There is evidence that rapid cultural change can increase accessibility of certain scripts, in turn changing patterns of symptom presentation. For example, recent and ongoing processes of modernization and "Westernization" in China have been accompanied by increased endorsement of psychological symptoms and psychosocial explanations of depression (Lee & Kleinman, 2007; Ryder, Ban, & Dere, in press). These changes are of course reflected in brain activity, but they do not imply sudden and pervasive changes in brain functioning. Rather than continuing the futile search for a low-level "core" from which all causal arrows point outward, we are better off focusing on particular levels for pragmatic reasons while maintaining an awareness of the whole. We might choose to enter the system at a given place because doing so helps us to tell a parsimonious story, points to novel research questions, or leads to an effective treatment. Where then do we enter the system when considering vulnerability?

## Vulnerability to Depression in the Culture-Mind-Brain

To date, depression researchers have probed culture, mind, and brain as separate domains with few attempts to bridge them. The most rigorous sustained line of research on vulnerability to depression conducted in a "non-Western" setting (China) has largely focused to date on mind-level phenomena. Cultural explanations are considered, but they are not fully incorporated into the research design or the proposed models (e.g., Abela et al., 2011; Hong et al., 2010; Starrs et al., 2010; for a review, see Ryder, Sun, Zhu, Yao, & Chentsova-Dutton, 2012). Nonetheless, despite the scarcity of integrative work, we aim to demonstrate that adoption of the culture-mind-brain framework allows us to reinterpret existing research and pose novel research questions. As a longer-term goal, we also hope to encourage more research to link these levels together. We will begin by briefly considering what happens when we choose to enter the system at the brain or culture levels. Then, we will turn to the mind level and present research that highlights some of the interactions of mind with brain and with culture. We will conclude by considering how vulnerability could be understood as an emergent property of the whole system.

### Entry at the brain level

Although most studies cannot distinguish between signs of vulnerability and the impact of current or past symptoms, a few have looked at populations at risk, such as children with a family history of depression or healthy twins of people who are clinically depressed. These studies indicate that prior to the occurrence of depression, signs of vulnerability can be identified in the brain, as described in considerable detail elsewhere. For example, vulnerable samples show altered neural responses to affective stimuli (Gotlib et al., 2010; Lévesque et al., 2011; Monk et al., 2008), neurotransmitter activity (Frokjaer et al., 2010; Taylor et al., 2011), and white matter integrity (Huang, Fan, Wiliamson, & Rao, 2010).

Findings such as these provide us with a starting point for delving into the culture-mind-brain system. They are situated in particular social and cultural contexts and, at a minimum, need to be extended to other contexts, not just to confirm biological universals through replication but also to explore better the bidirectionality of brain-culture influences. Brain-level vulnerabilities may be shaped by, and indeed may shape, the cultural context. For example, differences in sensitivity to affective inputs may translate into different preferences for novelty and emotionally evocative information in cultural selection. An integrated program of research would track the ways in which the vulnerable brain shapes modes of thinking, feeling, behaving, communicating, and responding to cultural cues. Mind and culture may weaken, strengthen, or alter the impact of brain-level vulnerabilities, contributing to patterns of group variation in the likelihood of adaptive or maladaptive outcomes.

## Entry at the culture level

What does vulnerability to depression look like at the cultural level? Why is it that some countries, such as the United States, have high and rising prevalence rates of major depression (Klerman & Weissman, 1989; Lewinsohn, Rohde, Seeley, & Fischer, 1993; Wickramaratne, Weissman, Leaf, & Holford, 1989). Mechanisms of cultural selection promote transmission of meanings and practices that evoke salient cultural concerns and schemas, and are memorable and novel (Chentsova-Dutton & Heath, 2009). Although meanings and practices that confer vulnerability may at some point become problematic for successful maintenance of a cultural system, there is no short-term selection mechanism that corrects for them.

Some researchers have argued that "Western" (e.g., European American) cultural contexts are depressogenic (Eckersley, 2006; Eckersley & Dear, 2002; Kasser & Ahuvia, 2002). These individualistic and materialistic contexts may confer vulnerability to depression by broadening discrepancies between realistic outcomes and cultural ideals. Although moderate-size discrepancies may serve as motivational fuel, larger or irreconcilable ones lead to negative self-evaluation, resulting in profound distress. North American cultural contexts foster ideals of personal achievement, self-importance, and happiness. Over time, these cultural ideals have become more pronounced, but in doing so, have also become increasingly unrealistic and unmoored from one's past performance. As cultural selection forces magnify cultural ideals to increase their novelty and distinctiveness, the number of people who fail to attain them increases.

For example, between 1976 and 2000, American high school students increasingly developed unrealistic expectations for educational and professional attainment (Reynolds, Stewart, MacDonald, & Sischo, 2006), leading many to fail to realize these goals. Reminders of such unfulfilled ideals may trigger unfavorable self-evaluation and distress. Indeed, endorsement of materialistic values, a failure to achieve desired lifestyle, and exposure to more successful lifestyles combine to predict depression (see Kasser & Ahuvia, 2002). This line of research identifies a set of cultural characteristics that are linked to tangible individual-level outcomes, such as physical illness and suicide. All the same, we do not yet know how these culture-level vulnerabilities shape and are shaped by the mind and the brain.

Clearly, not everyone in a European American cultural context is vulnerable to depression. Vulnerability emerges in part as a result of the mind's and brain's responses to the salient discrepancies with the cultural ideals. Individual-level meanings and practices constitute, but do not perfectly replicate, culture-level meanings and practices.

The culture-mind-brain framework can point us toward research programs that would examine individual differences in response to the discrepancies and link them to specific cognitive, emotional, and motivational mechanisms. Whether we are entering the system at brain or culture levels, we need to integrate research linking all levels together and interpreting their effects in the context of the others. We now turn to research on mind-level vulnerabilities, which provides us with some initial examples of this integration.

## Entry at the mind level

At the mind level, characteristic patterns of attention, beliefs about the self and the world, social interactions, and ways of appraising stressful events and coping with them can render people vulnerable to depression (see Ingram & Price, 2001). One example comes from the literature on emotion regulation, or, "the activation of a goal to modify the emotion-generative process" (Gross, Sheppes, & Urry, 2011, p. 767). When expressing emotions, we take care to do so in a manner that is sensitive to the situation and to the presence of others. Major depression has been described as the disorder of emotion regulation, characterized by difficulty with effective downregulation of negative emotions and with adjusting emotions to the context (Joormann & Gotlib, 2010; Rottenberg, 2005). Symptoms of depression and emotion regulation likely form a loop: Poor emotion regulation makes one vulnerable to depression, and symptoms of depression further constrict one's regulatory repertoire and attentional resources, thereby impairing regulation.

In the North American cultural context, expressive suppression is an emotion regulation strategy that is associated with the tendency to experience depressive symptoms (Gross & John, 2003; Joormann & Gotlib, 2010). People with anxiety and mood disorders spontaneously suppress their negative emotions more than healthy controls (Campbell-Sills, Barlow, Brown, & Hofmann, 2006). This tendency persists during remission, reflecting a trait-like characteristic (Ehring, Tuschen-Caffier, Schnülle, Fischer, & Gross, 2010). As the mind responds to and shapes interpersonal interactions, understanding of an individual tendency to suppress negative emotions requires an understanding of its interpersonal context, such as conflict in a romantic relationship (Gottman & Levenson, 2002; Richards, Butler, & Gross, 2003). The emotionally flat response of one conversational partner distances the other, generating interpersonal tension that can itself loop around to further worsen the mood.

Expressive suppression has been primarily studied at the level of the mind, with emerging studies bringing increased attention to brain and culture. As can be expected, the brain is recruited to support emotion regulation, with conscious efforts to suppress negative emotions reflected in the prefrontal cortex activation (Goldin, McRae, Ramel, & Gross, 2008; Lévesque et al., 2003).

This activity is not intrinsically dysfunctional, but its chronic and context-insensitive engagement may leave one vulnerable to distress. Over time, ineffective self-regulation, attention to negative stimuli, and increased levels of negative emotions are likely to further tune brain activation, forming a mind–brain loop.

Understanding the brain as one level of a single system that includes mind and culture, we can better describe how neurobiological components of vulnerability can be offset or exacerbated by cultural components. The mind draws from a culturally accessible repertoire of ways to pay attention, think, feel, and communicate. Some patterns of thinking and relating to others tend to be problematic across cultural contexts. For example, low sense of personal control (Auerbach, Eberhart, & Abela, 2010; Steptoe, Tsuda, Tanaka, & Wardle, 2007) and negative automatic thoughts (Calvete & Connor-Smith, 2005) have shown similar patterns of association with depressive symptoms across cultural contexts, albeit in studies limited to college students.

In other cases, understanding the cultural component changes our interpretation of what "vulnerable to depression" means. For instance, the links between suppression and depression are culturally embedded: Emotion regulation is guided by cultural scripts of how one is to experience and express emotions, scripts that vary according to cultural context (Lutz, 1988), for example, Chinese cultural scripts encourage moderation of emotions based on relational demands, whereas European American cultural scripts encourage open or even exaggerated expression of emotions (Russell & Yik, 1996; Wierzbicka, 1999). Indeed, people from East Asian cultural contexts report suppressing their emotions more than those from the European American emotional contexts (Butler, Lee, & Gross, 2007; Gross & John, 2003; Soto, Perez, Kim, Lee, & Minnick, 2011). These differences are particularly pronounced for those who strongly endorse the values of their cultural group (Butler et al., 2007).

Cultural scripts regarding emotion regulation are activated so frequently that they become automatic and rapid, shaping emotional behavior within the first second after an event (Matsumoto, Willingham, & Olide, 2009). For example, and importantly for our argument, the costs of suppression disappear when it is engaged automatically, circumventing deliberate efforts to suppress (Mauss, Cook, & Gross, 2007). In addition, the consequences of suppression depend on the fit with the cultural scripts of experiencing and expressing emotions. These consequences would be expected to differ when comparing a cultural context that values moderated emotional expression with a cultural context that values more open, unrestrained expression.

Indeed, recent studies suggest that the association between self-reported suppression and depressed mood observed in European American cultural contexts is not found in East Asian cultural contexts (Cheung & Park, 2010; Soto et al., 2011). Consistent with self-reports, the pattern of dampened emotional reactivity displayed by depressed European Americans (see Bylsma, Morris, & Rottenberg, 2008) does not hold for depressed Asian Americans who tend to show unchanged or even exaggerated emotional reactivity in the laboratory (Chentsova-Dutton et al., 2007; Chentsova-Dutton, Tsai, & Gotlib, 2010). These studies suggest that, in and of itself, expressive suppression is neither functional nor dysfunctional. Its association with major depression is determined by the extent to which it deviates from culturally normative ways of experiencing and expressing emotions.

## Vulnerability as a system property

In sum, it is at the intersection of culture, mind, and brain that we best understand vulnerability to depression. Dividing vulnerability into its constituent components has only a limited value, as the meaning of each component depends on the entire system. Knowing that a person's amygdala shows exaggerated activity or that a person suppresses negative emotions does not tell us enough about the impact of these patterns on well-being in isolation from knowing the physiological, behavioral, cognitive, emotional, interpersonal, and cultural context of this observation. Understanding vulnerability requires us to consider the system as a whole and consider the possibility of nonadditive effects.

We anticipate that the levels of culture, mind, and brain can interact with one another in various ways. One level may end up balancing out another; for example, resilience at the culture-level may ameliorate the consequences of mind- or brain-level vulnerabilities. Such patterns might emerge when certain meanings and practices serve to promote and maintain group stability over the long term. When rapid cultural change disrupts the balance, more people may be left vulnerable to depression. There may also be some cases where the mutual influence of the layers renders one more vulnerable, with loops linking and amplifying vulnerability. With these ideas we move closer to a unitary vision of culture-mind-brain that transcends the individual levels— vulnerability as an emergent property of the entire system.

One way to illustrate the potential implications of this idea is to show vulnerability in the system without it necessarily being evident at any given level. Consider, for example, neurochemical mechanisms supporting situational or trait-like subordinate behavior in animals and humans (e.g., Baxter, 2003; Kozorovitskiy & Gould, 2004; Kroes, Panksepp, Burgdorf, Otto, & Moskal, 2006; Schneier, Kent, Star, & Hirsch, 2009). These mechanisms offer protective and survival value by reducing aggression and hence stabilizing social groups (MacLean, 1990). Now consider the European American cultural context, which emphasizes values of equality and autonomy and discounts the importance or legitimacy of pre-established social hierarchies (Tsai & Moreno, 2007). Societies with these values report higher levels of well-being (Diener, Diener, & Diener, 1995; Fischer & Boer, 2011), although, as noted earlier, individualistic tendencies also come with their own costs.

So the neurochemical underpinnings of submissiveness confer certain advantages, as do cultural values of equality and autonomy; they are not, in themselves, vulnerabilities. What happens when the two coincide? To begin with, submissiveness is less likely to be accepted, perceived positively, or associated with well-being in the European American cultural contexts as compared with contexts that value and legitimize social hierarchies (e.g., as found in China, India, Japan; Gallois, Barker, Jones, & Callan, 1992; Kitayama, Markus, & Kurokawa, 2000; Rastogi & Wampler, 1999). For example, submissive emotions are unrelated to happiness in the United States but are highly associated with it in Japan (Kitayama et al., 2000).

Indeed, submissiveness is associated with depressive symptoms in Western contexts (O'Connor, Berry, Weiss, & Gilbert, 2002), an association considered so self-evident that submissive behavior is incorporated into animal models of depression (e.g., Malatynska & Knapp, 2005). We contend that neither neurobiological mechanisms of submissiveness nor cultural values regarding hierarchy are inherently dysfunctional. In combination, however, the two may confer vulnerability to depression due to conflict between submissive social position and cultural values that make such a position undesirable. Here, vulnerability can best be understood as an emergent property of culture-mind-brain, rather than clearly emerging at a particular level. Research programs that target multiple levels in a systematic and integrative way will be necessary to uncover these phenomena.

## Conclusions

The biopsychosocial approach to depression has taken us far by encouraging us to consider how factors ranging from brain cells to social norms shape experience and expression of depression and inform treatment. We are reminded to pay attention to all three levels. In practice, however, researchers have tended to generate models that are limited to a given level of analysis. At best, there may be a tacit acknowledgment that something might be happening at other levels, to be captured by other models and pursued by other researchers. The result is that the biopsychosocial approach more often serves as a reminder that biological, psychological, and social are worthy of attention (necessitating a division of labor), rather than as the basis for a single and integrative framework (necessitating interdisciplinary collaboration).

We believe that isolating the layers of the system can be a useful starting point when trying to model emergent processes. To return to our ceramic glaze analogy, a potter may want to know something about chemical properties of the individual layers of glaze in order to envisage the final product. However, such an extensive study of a single layer will only be informative if all other conditions remain identical at each firing. If the composition of the other layers changes, the product will also change in nonlinear ways, producing hard-to-model yet meaningful variability. A potter will be better off with thorough knowledge of how compounds in different layers react with each other under different conditions.

Similarly, cultural-clinical psychology will, no doubt, benefit from integrating findings generated by neuroscientists, psychologists, anthropologists, and other natural and social scientists, but will be better off with models of the entire complex picture of how these observations interact. We encourage researchers to extend this framework beyond vulnerability to other aspects of depression, and, indeed, to other psychological disorders. This research agenda will critically depend on reaching outside of narrowly defined fields, to gain exposure to language, methods, and framework provided by scholars with expertise in approaching depression at different levels of analysis.

One should neither reject nor essentialize findings based on genetically vulnerable mice huddling under the cover of the shelter. We do not believe that, in isolation, these data "uncover the fundamental mechanisms" of human depression. We do believe them to be an important contribution to a multilevel understanding of human depression. Given the complexity of culture-mind-brain, a laboratory mouse offers an excessively coherent and linear model. Not surprisingly, adding mind and culture to the human brain results in a far more complex and embedded system. Although taking this system seriously takes away our ability to resort to straightforward explanations, it offers us the promise of a better accounting for the astonishing diversity in the experience and expression of mental illness.

## Acknowledgments

The authors gratefully acknowledge assistance provided by Sarkis Kavarian and Sylvanna Vargas and the comments provided by Jordan Clemens, Tomas Jurcik, and Sylvanna Vargas on an earlier version of this manuscript.

## References

Abela, J. R. Z., Stolow, D., Mineka, S., Yao, S., Zhu, X. Z, & Hankin, B. L. (2011). Cognitive vulnerabilities to depressive symptoms in adolescents in urban and rural Hunan, China: A multiwave longitudinal study. *Journal of Abnormal Psychology, 120*, 765–778. doi:10.1037/a0025295

Auerbach, R. P., Eberhart, N. K., & Abela, J. R. Z. (2010). Cognitive vulnerability to depression in Canadian and Chinese adolescents. *Journal of Abnormal Child Psychology, 38*, 57–68. doi:10.1007/s10802-009-9344-y

Bagby, R. M., Ryder, A. G., Schuller, D. R., & Marshall, M. B. (2004). The Hamilton Depression Rating Scale: Has the gold standard become a lead weight? *American Journal of Psychiatry, 161*(12), 2163–2177. doi:10.1176/appi.ajp.161.12.2163

Bagby, R. M., Watson, C., & Ryder, A. G. (in press). Depressive personality disorder. In T. Widiger (Ed.), *The Oxford handbook of personality disorders* (pp. 628–647). Oxford, UK: Oxford University Press.

Baxter, L. R. (2003). Basal ganglia systems in ritualistic social displays: Reptiles and humans; function and illness. *Physiology & Behavior, 79*(3), 451–460. doi:10.1016/S0031-9384(03)00164-1

Butler, E. A., Lee, T. L., & Gross, J. J. (2007). Emotion regulation and culture: Are the social consequences of emotion suppression culture-specific? *Emotion, 7*, 30–48. doi:10.1037/1528-3542.7.1.30

Bylsma, L. M., Morris, B. H., & Rottenberg, J. (2008). A meta-analysis of emotional reactivity in major depressive disorder. *Clinical Psychology Review, 28*, 676–691. doi:10.1016/j.cpr.2007.10.001

Calvete, E., & Connor-Smith, J. K. (2005). Automatic thoughts and psychological symptoms: A cross-cultural comparison of American and Spanish students. *Cognitive Therapy and Research, 29*, 201–217. doi:10.1007/s10608-005-3165-2

Campbell-Sills, L., Barlow, D. H., Brown, T. A., & Hofmann, S. G. (2006). Effects of suppression and acceptance on emotional responses of individuals with anxiety and mood disorders. *Behaviour Research and Therapy, 44*(9), 1251–1263. doi:10.1016/j.brat.2005.10.001

Caspi, A., Sugden, K., Moffitt, T. E., Taylor, A., Craig, I. W., Harrington, H.,... Poulton, R. (2003). Influence of life stress on depression: Moderation by a polymorphism in the 5-HTT gene. *Science, 301*(5631), 386–389. doi:10.1126/science.1083968

Chentsova-Dutton, Y., & Heath, C. (2009). Cultural evolution: Why are some cultural variants more successful than others? In M. Schaller, A. Norenzayan, S. Heine, T. Yamagishi, & T. Kameda (Eds.), *Evolution, culture, and the human mind* (pp. 49–70). New York: Psychology Press.

Chentsova-Dutton, Y., & Tsai, J. (2008). Understanding depression across cultures. In I. Gotlib, & C. Hammen (Eds.), *Handbook of depression* (2nd ed., pp. 363–385). New York: Guilford Press.

Chentsova-Dutton, Y. E., Chu, J. P., Tsai, J. L., Rottenberg, J., Gross, J. J., & Gotlib, I. H. (2007). Depression and emotional reactivity: Variation among Asian Americans of East

Asian descent and European Americans. *Journal of Abnormal Psychology, 116*, 776–785. doi:10.1037/0021-843X.116.4.776

Chentsova-Dutton, Y. E., Tsai, J. L., & Gotlib, I. H. (2010). Further evidence for the cultural norm hypothesis: Positive emotion in depressed and control European American and Asian American women. *Cultural Diversity and Ethnic Minority Psychology, 16*, 284–295. doi:10.1037/a0017562

Cheung, R. Y., & Park, I. J. (2010). Anger suppression, interdependent self-construal, and depression among Asian American and European American college students. *Cultural Diversity & Ethnic Minority Psychology, 16*(4), 517–525. doi:10.1037/a0020655

Chiao, J. Y. (2009). Cultural neuroscience: A once and future discipline. *Progress in Brain Research, 178*, 287–304. doi:10.1016/S0079-6123(09)17821-4

Chiao, J. Y., & Blizinsky, K. D. (2010). Culture-gene coevolution of individualism-collectivism and the serotonin transporter gene. *Proceedings of the Royal Society B: Biological Sciences, 277*(1681), 529–537. doi:10.1098/rspb.2009.1650

Clark, A., & Chalmers, D. (1998). The extended mind. *Analysis, 58*, 7–19. doi:10.1111/1467-8284.00096

Demyttenaere, K., Bruffaerts, R., Lee, S., Posada-Villa, J., Kovess, V., Angermeyer, M. C.,... Von Korff, M. (2007). Mental disorders among persons with chronic back or neck pain: Results from the World Mental Health Surveys. *Pain, 129*(3), 332–342. doi:10.1016/j.pain.2007.01.022

Diener, E., Diener, M., & Diener, C. (1995). Factors predicting the subjective well-being of nations. *Journal of Personality and Social Psychology, 69*(5), 851–864. doi:10.1037/0022-3514.69.5.851

Eckersley, R. (2006). Is modern Western culture a health hazard? *International Journal of Epidemiology, 35*(2), 252–258. doi:10.1093/ije/dyi235

Eckersley, R., & Dear, K. (2002). Cultural correlates of youth suicide. *Social Science & Medicine, 55*(11), 1891–1904. doi:10.1016/S0277-9536(01)00319-7

Ehring, T., Tuschen-Caffier, B., Schnülle, J., Fischer, S., & Gross, J. J. (2010). Emotion regulation and vulnerability to depression: Spontaneous versus instructed use of emotion suppression and reappraisal. *Emotion (Washington, DC), 10*(4), 563–572. doi:10.1037/a0019010

Eisenberg, D. T. A., & Hayes, M. G. (2011). Testing the null hypothesis: Comments on "Culture-gene coevolution of individualism-collectivism and the serotonin transporter gene." *Proceedings of the Royal Society B: Biological Sciences, 278*(1704), 329–332. doi:10.1098/rspb.2010.0714

Fischer, R., & Boer, D. (2011). What is more important for national well-being: Money or autonomy? A meta-analysis of well-being, burnout, and anxiety across 63 societies. *Journal of Personality and Social Psychology, 101*, 164–184. doi:10.1037/a0023663

Frokjaer, V. G., Vinberg, M., Erritzoe, D., Baaré, W., Holst, K. K., Mortensen, E. L.,... Knudsen, G. M. (2010). Familial risk for mood disorder and the personality risk factor, neuroticism, interact in their association with frontolimbic serotonin 2A receptor binding. *Neuropsychopharmacology, 35*(5), 1129–1137. doi:10.1038/npp.2009.218

Gallois, C., Barker, M., Jones, E., & Callan, V. J. (1992). Intercultural communication: Evaluations of lecturers and Australian and Chinese students. In S. Iwawaki, Y. Kashima, & K. Leung (Eds.), *Innovations in cross-cultural psychology* (pp. 86–102). Amsterdam, The Netherlands: Swets & Zeitlinger.

Goldin, P. R., McRae, K., Ramel, W., & Gross, J. J. (2008). The neural bases of emotion regulation: Reappraisal and suppression of negative emotion. *Biological Psychiatry, 63*(6), 577–586. doi:10.1016/j.biopsych.2007.05.031

Gotlib, I. H., Hamilton, J. P., Cooney, R. E., Singh, M. K., Henry, M. L., & Joormann, J. (2010). Neural processing of reward and loss in girls at risk for major depression. *Archives of General Psychiatry, 67*(4), 380–387. doi:10.1001/archgenpsychiatry.2010.13

Gottman, J. M., & Levenson, R. W. (2002). A two-factor model for predicting when a couple will divorce: Exploratory analyses using 14-year longitudinal data. *Family Process, 41*(1), 83–96.

Gross, J. J., & John, O. P. (2003). Individual differences in two emotion regulation processes: Implications for affect, relationships, and well-being. *Journal of Personality and Social Psychology, 85*(2), 348–362. doi:10.1037/0022-3514.85.2.348

Gross, J. J., Sheppes, G., & Urry, H. L. (2011). Emotion generation and emotion regulation: A distinction we should make (carefully). *Cognition and Emotion, 25*(5), 765–781. doi:10.1080/02699931.2011.555753

Hacking, I. (1995). The looping effect of human kinds. In D. Sperber, D. Premack, & A. J. Premack (Eds.), *Causal cognition: A multidisciplinary debate* (pp. 351–383). Oxford, UK: Oxford University Press.

Hariri, A. R., & Holmes, A. (2006). Genetics of emotional regulation: The role of the serotonin transporter in neural function. *Trends in Cognitive Sciences, 10*(4), 182–191. doi:10.1016/j.tics.2006.02.011

Holmes, A., Yang, R. J., Lesch, K. P., Crawley, J. N., & Murphy, D. L. (2003). Mice lacking the serotonin transporter exhibit 5-HT(1A) receptor-mediated abnormalities in tests for anxiety-like behavior. *Neuropsychopharmacology, 28*(12), 2077–2088. doi:10.1038/sj.npp.1300266

Hong, W., Abela, J. R. Z., Cohen, J. R., Sheshko, D. M., Shi, X. T., Hamel, A. V., & Starrs, C. (2010). Rumination as a vulnerability factor to depression in adolescents in mainland China: Lifetime history of clinically significant depressive episodes. *Journal of Clinical Child & Adolescent Psychology, 39,* 849–857. doi:10.1080/15374416.2010.517159

Huang, H., Fan, X., Williamson, D. E., & Rao, U. (2010). White matter changes in healthy adolescents at familial risk for unipolar depression: A diffusion tensor imaging study. *Neuropsychopharmacology, 36*(3), 684–691. doi:10.1038/npp.2010.199

Hutchins, E. (1995). *Cognition in the wild.* Cambridge, MA: MIT Press.

Ingram, R. E., & Price, J. (2001). (Eds.). *Vulnerability to psychopathology: Risk across the lifespan.* New York: Guilford Press.

Joormann, J., & Gotlib, I. H. (2010). Emotion regulation in depression: Relation to cognitive inhibition. *Cognition and Emotion, 24*(2), 281–298. doi:10.1080/02699930903407948

Karg, K., Burmeister, M., Shedden, K., & Sen, S. (2011). The serotonin transporter promoter variant (5-HTTLPR), stress, and depression meta-analysis revisited: Evidence of genetic moderation. *Archives of General Psychiatry, 68*(5), 444–454. doi:10.1001/archgenpsychiatry.2010.189

Kasser, T., & Ahuvia, A. (2002). Materialistic values and well-being in business students. *European Journal of Social Psychology, 32*(1), 137–146. doi:10.1002/ejsp.85

Kessler, R. C., Aguilar-Gaxiola, S., Alonso, J., Chatterji, S., Lee, S., Ormel, J., . . . Wang, P. S. (2009). The global burden of mental disorders: An update from the WHO World Mental Health (WMH) surveys. *Epidemiologia E Psichiatria Sociale, 18*(1), 23–33.

Kilpatrick, D. G., Koenen, K. C., Ruggiero, K. J., Acierno, R., Galea, S., Resnick, H. S., . . . Gelernter, J. (2007). The serotonin transporter genotype and social support and moderation of posttraumatic stress disorder and depression in hurricane-exposed adults. *American Journal of Psychiatry, 164*(11), 1693–1699. doi:10.1176/appi.ajp.2007.06122007

Kim, H. S., Sherman, D. K., Taylor, S. E., Sasaki, J. Y., Chu, T. Q., Ryu, C.,... Xu, J. (2010). Culture, serotonin receptor polymorphism and locus of attention. *Social Cognitive and Affective Neuroscience, 5*(2–3), 212–218. doi:10.1093/scan/nsp040

Kirmayer, L. J. (2012). The future of critical neuroscience. In S. Choudhury, & J. Slaby (Eds.), *Critical neuroscience: A handbook of the social and cultural contexts of neuroscience* (pp. 367–383). Oxford, UK: Blackwell.

Kirmayer, L. J., & Sartorius, N. (2007). Cultural models and somatic syndromes. *Psychosomatic Medicine, 69*, 832–840. doi:10.1097/PSY.0b013e31815b002c

Kitayama, S., Markus, H. R., & Kurokawa, M. (2000). Culture, emotion and well-being: Good feelings in Japan and the United States. *Cognition and Emotion, 14*, 93–124. doi:10.1080/026999300379003

Kitayama, S., & Park, J. (2010). Cultural neuroscience of the self: Understanding the social grounding of the brain. *Social Cognitive and Affective Neuroscience, 5*(2–3), 111–129. doi:10.1093/scan/nsq052

Kitayama, S., & Uskul, A. K. (2011). Culture, mind, and the brain: Current evidence and future directions. *Annual Review of Psychology, 62*, 419–449. doi:10.1146/annurev-psych-120709-145357

Kleinman, A. (1982). Neurasthenia and depression: A study of somatization and culture in China. *Culture, Medicine and Psychiatry, 6*(2), 117–190. doi:10.1007/BF00051427

Klerman, G. L., & Weissman, M. M. (1989). Increasing rates of depression. *Journal of the American Medical Association, 261*(15), 2229–2235. doi:10.1001/jama.261.15.2229

Kozorovitskiy, Y., & Gould, E. (2004). Dominance hierarchy influences adult neurogenesis in the dentate gyrus. *Journal of Neuroscience, 24*(30), 6755–6759. doi:10.1523/JNEUROSCI.0345-04.2004

Kroes, R. A., Panksepp, J., Burgdorf, J., Otto, N. J., & Moskal, J. R. (2006). Modeling depression: Social dominance-submission gene expression patterns in rat neocortex. *Neuroscience, 137*(1), 37–49. doi:10.1016/j.neuroscience.2005.08.076

Lee, S., & Kleinman, A. (2007). Are somatoform disorders changing with time? The case of neurasthenia in China. *Psychosomatic Medicine, 69*, 846–849. doi:10.1097/PSY.0b013e31815b0092

Lévesque, J., Eugčne, F., Joanette, Y., Paquette, V., Mensour, B., Beaudoin, G.,... Beauregard, M. (2003). Neural circuitry underlying voluntary suppression of sadness. *Biological Psychiatry, 53*(6), 502–510. doi:10.1016/S0006-3223(02)01817-6

Lévesque, M. L., Beauregard, M., Ottenhof, K. W., Fortier, E., Tremblay, R. E., Brendgen, M.,... Booij, L. (2011). Altered patterns of brain activity during transient sadness in children at familial risk for major depression. *Journal of Affective Disorders, 135*(1–3), 410–413. doi:10.1016/j.jad.2011.08.010

Lewinsohn, P. M., Rohde, P., Seeley, J. R., & Fischer, S. A. (1993). Age-cohort changes in the lifetime occurrence of depression and other mental disorders. *Journal of Abnormal Psychology, 102*(1), 110–120. doi:10.1037/0021-843X.102.1.110

Lin, E. H., Von Korff, M., Alonso, J., Angermeyer, M. C., Anthony, J., Bromet, E.,... Williams, D. (2008). Mental disorders among persons with diabetes—Results from the World Mental Health Surveys. *Journal of Psychosomatic Research, 65*(6), 571–580. doi:10.1016/j.jpsychores.2008.06.007

Lutz, C. (1988). *Unnatural emotions: Everyday sentiments on a micronesian atoll and their challenge to Western theory.* Chicago: University of Chicago Press.

MacLean, P. D. (1990). *The triune brain in evolution: Role in paleocerebral functions.* New York: Plenum Press.

Malatynska, E., & Knapp, R. J. (2005). Dominant-submissive behavior as models of mania and depression. *Neuroscience & Biobehavioral Reviews*, 29(4–5), 715–737. doi:10.1016/j.neubiorev.2005.03.014

Matsumoto, D., Willingham, B., & Olide, A. (2009). Sequential dynamics of culturally moderated facial expressions of emotion. *Psychological Science*, 20(10), 1269–1275. doi:10.1111/j.1467-9280.2009.02438.x

Mauss, I. B., Cook, C. L., & Gross, J. J. (2007). Automatic emotion regulation during anger provocation. *Journal of Experimental Social Psychology*, 43, 698–711. doi:10.1016/j.jesp.2006.07.003

Monk, C. S., Klein, R. G., Telzer, E. H., Schroth, E. A., Mannuzza, S., Moulton, J. L., III, ... Ernst, M. (2008). Amygdala and nucleus accumbens activation to emotional facial expressions in children and adolescents at risk for major depression. *American Journal of Psychiatry*, 165(1), 90–98. doi:10.1176/appi.ajp.2007.06111917

Murphy, D. L., Li, Q., Engel, S., Wichems, C., Andrews, A., Lesch, K. P., & Uhl, G. (2001). Genetic perspectives on the serotonin transporter. *Brain Research Bulletin*, 56(5), 487–494. doi:10.1016/S0361-9230(01)00622-0

O'Connor, L. E., Berry, J. W., Weiss, J., & Gilbert, P. (2002). Guilt, fear, submission, and empathy in depression. *Journal of Affective Disorders*, 71(1–3), 19–27. doi:10.1016/S0165-0327(01)00408-6

Ohayon, M. M., & Hong, S.-C. (2006). Prevalence of major depressive disorder in the general population of South Korea. *Journal of Psychiatric Research*, 40(1), 30–36. doi:10.1016/j.jpsychires.2005.02.003

Parker, G., Cheah, Y. C., & Roy, K. (2001). Do the Chinese somatize depression? A cross-cultural study. *Social Psychiatry and Psychiatric Epidemiology*, 36(6), 287–293. doi:10.1007/s001270170046

Rastogi, M., & Wampler, K. S. (1999). Adult daughters' perceptions of the mother-daughter relationship: A cross-cultural comparison. *Family Relations*, 48, 327–336. doi:10.2307/585643

Reynolds, J., Stewart, M., MacDonald, R., & Sischo, L. (2006). Have adolescents become too ambitious? High school seniors' educational and occupational plans, 1976 to 2000. *Social Problems*, 53(2), 186–206. doi:10.1525/sp.2006.53.2.186

Richards, J. M., Butler, E. A., & Gross, J. J. (2003). Emotion regulation in romantic relationships: The cognitive consequences of concealing feelings. *Journal of Social and Personal Relationships*, 20(5), 599–620. doi:10.1177/02654075030205002

Risch, N., Herrell, R., Lehner, T., Liang, K. Y., Eaves, L., Hoh, J., ... Merikangas, K. R. (2009). Interaction between the serotonin transporter gene (5-HTTLPR), stressful life events, and risk of depression: A meta-analysis. *Journal of the American Medical Association*, 301(23), 2462–2471. doi:10.1001/jama.2009.878

Rottenberg, J. (2005). Mood and emotion in major depression. *Current Directions in Psychological Science*, 14(3), 167–170. doi:10.1111/j.0963-7214.2005.00354.x

Russell, J. A., & Yik, M. (1996). Emotion among the Chinese. In M. H. Bond (Ed.), *The handbook of Chinese psychology* (pp. 166–188). Hong Kong: Oxford University Press.

Ryder, A. G., Bagby, R. M., & Schuller, D. R. (2002). The overlap of depressive personality disorder and dysthymia: A categorical problem with a dimensional solution. *Harvard Review of Psychiatry*, 10(6), 337–352. doi:10.1080/10673220216230

Ryder, A. G., Ban, L. M., & Chentsova-Dutton, Y. E. (2011). Towards a cultural-clinical psychology. *Social and Personality Psychology Compass*, 5, 960–975. doi:10.1111/j.1751-9004.2011.00404.x

Ryder, A. G., Ban, L. M., & Dere, J. (in press). Culture, self, and symptom: Perspectives from cultural psychology. In T. Hansen, P. Berliner, & K. Jensen de Lopez (Eds.), *Culture in self in mind: Conceptual and Applied Approaches.* Aalborg, Denmark: Aalborg University Press.

Ryder, A. G., & Chentsova-Dutton, Y. E. (2012). Depression in cultural context: "Chinese somatization," revisited. *Psychiatric Clinics of North America, 35*(1), 15–36. doi:10.1016/j.psc.2011.11.006

Ryder, A. G., Sun, J., Zhu, X., Yao, S., & Chentsova-Dutton, Y. E. (2012). Depression in China: Integrating developmental psychopathology and cultural-clinical psychology. *Journal of Clinical Child and Adolescent Psychology, 41*(5), 682–694. doi:10.1080/15374416.2012.710163

Ryder, A. G., Yang, J., Zhu, X., Yao, S., Yi, J., Heine, S. J., & Bagby, R. M. (2008). The cultural shaping of depression: Somatic symptoms in China, psychological symptoms in North America? *Journal of Abnormal Psychology, 117*(2), 300–313. doi:10.1037/0021-843X.117.2.300

Schneier, F. R., Kent, J. M., Star, A., & Hirsch, J. (2009). Neural circuitry of submissive behavior in social anxiety disorder: A preliminary study of response to direct eye gaze. *Psychiatry Research, 173*(3), 248–250. doi:10.1016/j.pscychresns.2008.06.004

Sherman, D. K., Kim, H. S., & Taylor, S. E. (2009). Culture and social support: Neural bases and biological impact. *Progress in Brain Research, 178*, 227–237. doi:10.1016/S0079-6123(09)17816-0

Shweder, R. A. (1991). *Thinking through cultures: Expeditions in cultural psychology.* Cambridge, MA: Harvard University Press.

Soto, J. A., Perez, C. R., Kim, Y. H., Lee, E. A., & Minnick, M. R. (2011). Is expressive suppression always associated with poorer psychological functioning? A cross-cultural comparison between European Americans and Hong Kong Chinese. *Emotion, 11*(6), 1450–1455. doi:10.1037/a0023340

Starrs, C. J., Abela, J. R. Z., Shih, J. H., Cohen, J. R., Yao, S., Zhu, X. Z., & Hammen, C. L. (2010). Stress generation and vulnerability in adolescents in mainland China. *International Journal of Cognitive Therapy, 3*, 345–357. doi:10.1521/ijct.2010.3.4.345

Steptoe, A., Tsuda, A., Tanaka, Y., & Wardle, J. (2007). Depressive symptoms, socio-economic background, sense of control, and cultural factors in university students from 23 countries. *International Journal of Behavioral Medicine, 14*(2), 97–107. doi:10.1007/BF03004175

Taylor, M. J., Mannie, Z. N., Norbury, R., Near, J., & Cowen, P. J. (2011). Elevated cortical glutamate in young people at increased familial risk of depression. *International Journal of Neuropsychopharmacology, 14*(2), 255–259. doi:10.1017/S1461145710001094

Tsai, A. Y., & Moreno, D. (2007, May). *Culture and hierarchy: Sitting in the professor's chair.* Poster presented at the 19th Annual Convention for the Association of Psychological Science, Washington, DC.

Uher, R., & McGuffin, P. (2010). The moderation by the serotonin transporter gene of environmental adversity in the etiology of depression: 2009 update. *Molecular Psychiatry, 15*(1), 18–22. doi:10.1038/mp.2009.123

Vasiliadis, H.-M., Lesage, A., Adair, C., Wang, P. S., & Kessler, R. C. (2007). Do Canada and the United States differ in prevalence of depression and utilization of services? *Psychiatric Services, 58*, 63–71. doi:10.1176/appi.ps.58.1.63

Vygotsky, L. S. (1978). *Mind in society: The development of higher psychological processes.* Cambridge, MA: Harvard University Press.

Way, B. M., & Taylor, S. E. (2010). Social influences on health: Is serotonin a critical mediator? *Psychosomatic Medicine, 72*(2), 107–112. doi:10.1097/PSY.0b013e3181ce6a7d

Wexler, B. E. (2008). *Brain and culture: Neurobiology, ideology, and social change.* Cambridge, MA: MIT Press.

Wickramaratne, P. J., Weissman, M. M., Leaf, P. J., & Holford, T. R. (1989). Age, period and cohort effects on the risk of major depression: Results from five United States communities. *Journal of Clinical Epidemiology, 42*(4), 333–343. doi:10.1016/0895-4356(89)90038-3

Wierzbicka, A. (1999). *Emotions across languages and cultures: Diversity and universals.* New York: Cambridge University Press.

Wilhelm, K., Mitchell, P. B., Niven, H., Finch, A., Wedgwood, L., Scimone, A., . . . Schofield, P. R. (2006). Life events, first depression onset and the serotonin transporter gene. *British Journal of Psychiatry, 188*, 210–215. doi:10.1192/bjp.bp.105.009522

Willner, P., & Mitchell, P. J. (2002). The validity of animal models of predisposition to depression. *Behavioural Pharmacology, 13*(3), 169–188. doi:10.1097/00008877-200205000-00001

# 20

# Mood Disorders and Chronic Physical Illness

## Somnath Chatterji and Nicole Bergen
### World Health Organization, Switzerland

Mood disorders are among illnesses that have the largest impact on health and have significant impacts on peoples' lives worldwide. Chronic physical conditions such as diabetes, heart disease, cancer, and obstructive lung disease, often tend to co-occur with common mental disorders such as anxiety and depression. This co-occurrence increases disability and leads to an increased utilization of health services through an interactive relationship. Yet, this relationship is seldom recognized and managed adequately.

The World Health Organization ranked depressive disorders as the number one contributor to disease burden in middle- and high-income countries, and the third most significant burden of disease globally (World Health Organization, 2008). Epidemiological studies have shown that people living with mood disorders, such as depression and bipolar disorder, experience higher rates of chronic physical illness than people without these disorders. Depression was reported to be two to three times higher among patients with chronic illness, compared to age- and gender-matched controls (Katon, 2011), and a greater number of chronic diseases was associated with higher prevalence of depression (Maharaj, Reid, Misir, & Simeon, 2005; Wong, Mercer, Woo, & Leung, 2008). Mood and anxiety disorders were associated with an increased likelihood of chronic pain, cardiovascular conditions, diabetes, and respiratory disease (Levinson, Karger, & Haklai, 2008). This is most likely a bidirectional relationship and mediated through various physical and psychological processes and altered illness behaviors.

Evidence suggests that those with comorbid depression and chronic disease suffer worse health outcomes than those with chronic disease alone (Moussavi et al., 2007), including greater medical symptom burden, disability, and increased risk of morbidity and mortality (Katon, 2011). In addition, comorbid depression is associated with elevated health care costs and poor adherence to self-care treatment (Katon, 2011). People with mental illness are at an increased risk of early death from natural causes as well as cardiovascular, respiratory, and endocrine diseases (Roshanaei-Moghaddam & Katon, 2009). Increasing psychological distress is known to increase the risk of mortality and depression is likely to nearly double the chances of premature death.

*The Wiley-Blackwell Handbook of Mood Disorders*, Second Edition. Edited by Mick Power.
© 2013 John Wiley & Sons, Ltd. Published 2013 by John Wiley & Sons, Ltd.

This chapter offers a descriptive literature review, discussing the current state of knowledge pertaining to: (a) mood disorders as risk factors for chronic disease; (b) determinants of mood disorder comorbidity; (c) health outcomes of comorbid mood disorder and chronic disease; and (d) associations between comorbid mood disorders and adherence to chronic disease interventions (Gale et al., 2012; Russ et al., 2012).

## Mood Disorders as a Risk Factor for Chronic Disease

The relationship between depression and diabetes has been suggested to be bidirectional, each serving as a risk factor for the other; however, there is stronger evidence for depression as a predictor of diabetes (Campayo, Gomez-Biel, & Lobo, 2011; Mezuk, Eaton, Albrecht, & Golden, 2008). A study by Carnethon, Kinder, Fair, Stafford, and Fortmann (2003) investigated this relationship in a cohort of over 6,000 participants. After an average follow-up of 15.6 years, participants with a high number of depressive symptoms were more likely than those with a low number of symptoms to have developed diabetes (relative risk [RR] = 2.52, 95% confidence interval [CI] 1.73–3.67); those with an intermediate number of symptoms were nonsignificantly more likely to develop diabetes (RR = 1.24, 95% CI 0.91–1.70) (Carnethon et al., 2003).

A systematic review and metaregression analysis by Van der Kooy et al. (2007) recovered 28 longitudinal case-control or cohort studies that quantified the relationship between depression and cardiovascular disease among adult populations. Authors pooled data from over 80,000 subjects with an average follow-up time of 10.6 years to estimate the risk associated with depressive symptoms or disorders and the development of various cardiovascular diseases. Overall, depression increased the risk of cardiovascular disease (odds ratio [OR] = 1.46, 95% CI 1.37–1.55), although study heterogeneity was high at 56%. The onset of myocardial infarction had an OR of 1.60 (95% CI 1.34–1.92, heterogeneity 0%), based on pooled data from eight studies (Van der Kooy et al., 2007). Similar results were reported by Brown, Stewart, Stump, and Callahan (2011), who followed 2,728 primary care patients (15.5% of whom had elevated depression symptoms) for 15 years. Depression conferred an elevated risk of incident acute myocardial infarction (RR = 1.55, 95% CI 1.24–1.93, $p = 0.0001$, adjusted for cardiovascular risk factors), as well as other cardiovascular events and death (Brown et al., 2011). A study of 657 middle-aged men found incident myocardial infarction to be elevated in those with a high level of depression as compared to those with no depression, after five years of follow-up (2.26 times higher, $p < 0.05$) and after 10 years of follow-up (RR = 2.4, $p < 0.05$) (Gromova, Gafarov, & Gagulin, 2007).

Evidence to support mood disorders as a risk factor for chronic diseases such as respiratory disease or cancer is less forthcoming. A meta-analysis of eight studies of chronic obstructive pulmonary disease (COPD) and depression reported comorbid depressive symptoms in one in four people with COPD; however, data were cross-sectional, precluding causality inferences. The majority of studies included in the meta-analysis relied on self-reported data from various questionnaires (Zhang, Ho, Cheung, Fu, & Mak, 2011). Prevalence studies variably support an association between cancer and mood disorders, with differences stemming from heterogeneity in conceptualization of mood disorders and cancer type (Boyes, Girgis, D'Este, & Zucca, 2011; Massie, 2004; Wiltink et al., 2011).

## Determinants of Comorbidity

The risk of comorbid mood disorders and chronic physical illness is not equally experienced among populations and may demonstrate variance according to socioeconomic and lifestyle determinants. The odds of comorbid mood disorder and diabetes have been widely reported to be higher in women than in men (Anderson, Freedland, Clouse, & Lustman, 2001; Egede, Zheng, & Simpson, 2002; Fisher et al., 2008; Katon et al., 2004; Manarte, Dias, Gois, & Boavida, 2010; Mier et al., 2008; Tellez-Zenteno & Cardiel, 2002), and diabetic women reported more symptoms of depression (Manarte et al., 2010). These findings mirror general trends of higher mood disorder prevalence among women (Wittchen et al., 2011). Risk factors for depression and diabetes comorbidity also include younger age (Egede et al., 2002; Fisher et al., 2008; Katon et al., 2004) and less education (Katon et al., 2004; Mier et al., 2008), as well as being unmarried (Egede et al., 2002) or widowed (Tellez-Zenteno & Cardiel, 2002). In the United States, a cross-sectional analysis of adults enrolled in managed health care plans found 18% of participants had comorbid depression, with rates two to three times higher among those of low socioeconomic status. Major depression was more often reported by participants with an annual income of less than $15,000 (29%) than those with an annual income of more than $75,000 (9%). Participants with less than a high school education had higher rates of depression (26%) than those with at least a high school education (14%), and depression was more frequently reported by those unemployed due to health reasons (48% vs. 33%) (Waitzfelder et al., 2010).

Gender was a mediating factor in the association between depression or anxiety and incident ischemic heart disease in a case-control study of about 300 patients and 900 controls at a general practice in the United Kingdom. Based on a review of medical records, men with a recorded depression diagnosis were three times more likely to develop ischemic heart disease than nondepressed controls (OR = 3.13, 95% CI 1.27–7.70, $p = 0.01$), whereas depression was not a risk factor for ischemic heart disease in women (OR = 1.34, 95% CI 0.7–2.56, $p = 0.38$) (Hippisley-Cox, Fielding, & Pringle, 1998).

A review by Yohannes (2005) identified female gender as a minor factor in predicting depression in older adults with COPD, based on research conducted in Manchester in the United Kingdom. Females with COPD experienced greater decreases in quality of life than men which, in turn, is an important factor for the onset of depression (Yohannes, 2005). A meta-analysis of eight studies, primarily from Western settings, concluded that gender did not account for differences in the prevalence of comorbid depressive symptoms and COPD in adult populations. Analyses included nearly 40,000 people with COPD and an equal number of controls, the vast majority of whom were recruited from the community settings (Zhang et al., 2011). Likewise, age, smoking status, ethnicity, and forced lung expiration volume were not determinants of depression in people with COPD (Jennings, Digiovine, Obeid, & Frank, 2009; Zhang et al., 2011). A large prospective study by Hanania et al. (2011) reported the following correlates of comorbid depression in patients with COPD: female sex (OR = 1.76, 95% CI 1.38–2.25, $p < 0.001$), currently smoking (OR = 1.41, 95% CI 1.1–1.82, $p = 0.008$), and age (OR = 0.81, 95% CI 0.68–0.96, $p = 0.015$, per 1 year increase). Depression was assessed using a self-administered questionnaire, applying a cutoff point for major depression with sensitivity of 80% and specificity of 70%. The authors acknowledged that the overall explanatory value of the multivariate model is low and suggested that depression may be an independent marker of COPD (Hanania et al., 2011).

In a population study of 1,323 newly diagnosed cancer patients, health behaviors, psychological factors, and social indicators were more important correlates of comorbid depression and cancer than socioeconomic characteristics. These included low positive social interaction (OR = 2.4, 95% CI 1.6–3.7, $p < 0.001$), currently smoking (OR = 2.4, 95% CI 1.2–4.8, $p = 0.044$), and low physical activity (OR = 3.5, 95% CI 2–6.2, $p < 0.001$) (Boyes et al., 2011). Rodin et al. (2009) reported a high disease burden, insecure attachment, low self-esteem, and young age as risk factors for depression among patients with metastatic cancer (Rodin et al., 2009).

## Depression and Chronic Disease Outcomes

A large study including a quarter of a million participants highlighted the major impact of comorbid depression, concluding that, when comorbid with angina, arthritis, asthma, or diabetes, depression resulted in worse health than either depression or any chronic disease alone, or any other combination of comorbid chronic diseases (Moussavi et al., 2007). This was also the case in a Canadian study of more than 45,000 participants aged 15 to 79 years, which suggested that depression had more than an additive effect on disability in people with comorbid chronic conditions (OR = 6.34, 95% CI 5.35–7.51), compared to those with either a chronic condition (OR = 2.12, 95% CI 1.93–2.32) or depression (OR = 2.49, 95% CI 1.91–3.26) (reference group: no chronic condition or depression) (Schmitz, Wang, Malla, & Lesage, 2007). A literature review by Katon, Lin, and Kroenke (2007) reported similar findings, also noting that for diabetes, pulmonary disease, heart disease, and arthritis, physical disease symptoms (such as pain) were at least as strongly associated with depression/anxiety as were physiological measures. This review included over 16,000 patients and 31 studies (18 cross-sectional studies, 11 longitudinal studies, and two randomized control trials) in a mixture of inpatient and outpatient settings (Katon et al., 2007).

There have been mixed findings about the impact of depression on diabetes control and outcomes, stemming from methodological issues such as sample sizes, control groups, measures of depression, and confounding variables (Waitzfelder et al., 2010). In the largest study to date, Waitzfelder et al. (2010) tested the association between depression and glycemic control in a diverse sample of 8,790 participants in the United States, using the eight-item Patient Health Questionnaire to measure depression (sensitivity 88% and specificity 88%, compared to interviews with mental health professionals). Authors reported mean HbA1c values of 7.9 among patients with diabetes with severe depression, compared to 7.7 among patients with diabetes and minimal or no depression ($p = 0.02$). Depression severity was significantly associated with diabetes symptom scores ($p < 0.001$) (Waitzfelder et al., 2010). Comparing groups with comorbid minor or major depression to those with diabetes alone, Heckbert et al. (2010) did not report a difference in long-term management of glycemia, blood pressure, or blood lipids, after adjusting for disease characteristics and cardiovascular disease. The study included 3,762 patients with type 2 diabetes and an indication for medication, tracked for an average 4.8 years (Heckbert et al., 2010). A meta-analysis of 27 cross-sectional studies reported depression to be consistently and significantly linked with diabetes complications ($p < 0.00001$) in type 1 and type 2 diabetes. Sub-analyses revealed significant, positive associations with specific complications, including nephropathy, retinopathy, neuropathy, macrovascular complications, and sexual dysfunction, although heterogeneity was reported in most cases (de Groot, Anderson, Freedland, Clouse, & Lustman, 2001).

Chamberlain et al. (2011) followed 799 participants with cardiovascular disease (myocardial infarction or heart failure) for an average of 6.2 years, comparing hospitalization and death rates among those with or without preexisting mental illnesses. Adjusting for demographic and disease characteristics, depression was nonsignificantly associated with increased hospitalization (hazard ratio [HR] = 1.24, 95% CI 0.98–1.57) and showed borderline significance with all-cause mortality (HR = 1.30, 95% CI 1.00–1.69) (Chamberlain et al., 2011). Depression was not associated with cardiac mortality among 588 myocardial infarction patients, followed for up to eight years ($p = 0.97$) (Dickens et al., 2007).

Depression has been associated with increased exacerbations in COPD patients, which may be attributable to behavioral mechanisms, such as low commitment to treatment plans or reluctance to seek help during emerging exacerbations (Jennings et al., 2009; Norwood, 2006). Among a sample of older Chinese adults with COPD, those with comorbid depression were more likely to report disability in activities of daily living (OR = 2.89, $p = 0.049$) and poor/fair self-rated health (OR = 3.35, $p = 0.004$) (Ng, Niti, Fones, Yap, & Tan, 2009). Comorbid depression in COPD patients was associated with poor performance on a physical walking test ($p < 0.01$) as well as low physical ($p < 0.01$) and mental ($p < 0.001$) quality of life scores in a study of 238 German participants (von Leupoldt, Taube, Lehmann, Fritzsche, & Magnussen, 2011).

In 2009, the impact of depression on cancer progression and mortality was investigated in a meta-analysis of prospective studies. Depressive symptoms were not found to affect cancer progression (unadjusted RR = 1.23, 95% CI 0.85–1.77, $p = 0.28$), based on pooled results of only three studies. However, data from a larger selection of studies ($n = 25$) demonstrated a significant association between depression and mortality (RR = 1.25, 95% CI 1.12–1.40, $p < 0.001$), with mortality rates up to 25% higher in patients with depressive symptoms, and up to 39% higher in patients diagnosed with major or minor depression (Satin, Linden, & Phillips, 2009).

A small-scale study by Starkstein, Mizrahi, and Garau (2005) reported improvements in depressive symptoms after 17 months, among patients with comorbid Alzheimer disease and depression at baseline. Researchers noted significant improvements in several physiological domains, and half of the participants had depression remission at follow-up, independent of antidepressant therapy or apathy score at base-line (Starkstein et al., 2005). Further research to confirm this association is warranted.

## Access and Adherence to Interventions/Treatments

One explanation for why people living with comorbid mood disorders and chronic physical illness may suffer worse health outcomes may be a lack of access and/or low adherence to interventions or treatments. While Ani et al. (2009) reported that the co-occurrence of chronic physical conditions with depression did not significantly affect the treatment or follow-up care of depression (compared to those with depression only) (Ani et al., 2009), others have noted an impaired ability to adhere to self-care regimens, as depression can adversely affect memory, energy, motivation, and executive functions (Katon, 2011). A meta-analysis of 12 studies found depression patients to be three times more likely to be noncompliant with physician recom-mendations than nondepressed patients (OR = 3.03, 95% CI 1.96–4.89). Studies considered adherence to both prevention and/or treatment recommendations, mea-sured by patient self-reports, physician or medical records, pill counts, physiological tests or assays, or electronic medication monitoring. Sample sizes ranged from 20 to 106 participants and included two studies done in children (DiMatteo, Lepper, & Croghan, 2000).

Patients with comorbid depression and diabetes were found to receive fewer mean number of recommended processes of care for diabetes than patients with minimal or no depression ($p < 0.001$) (Waitzfelder et al., 2010), an interesting finding given that comorbid patients have higher rates of health care utilization ($p < 0.01$) and total health care cost ($p < 0.01$) (Boulanger et al., 2009). A possible explanation may be that patients with comorbid depression and diabetes presented with more clinical complexity, and physician time may have been spent discussing depression in lieu of standard diabetes care (Waitzfelder et al., 2010). Compliance with diabetes treatment was studied in 99 diabetic patients at a retinopathy clinic in New Zealand. Compliance decreased with increasing comorbid depression; however, this trend was only evident in self-ratings and not in clinician ratings (Clarke & Goosen, 2005).

For patients with cardiovascular disease, depression has been associated with med-ication nonadherence: Depressed patients were more likely to forget to take medica-tion (OR = 2.4, 95% CI 1.6–3.8, $p < 0.001$) or decide to skip taking medication (OR = 2.2, 95% CI 1.2–4.2, $p = 0.01$) (Gehi, Haas, Pipkin, & Whooley, 2005). Following acute myocardial infarction patients for 4 months, patients with at least mild-to-moderate depression were less likely to adhere to dietary, exercise, social, and stress-reduction lifestyle changes, and those with major depression and/or dysthymia were less likely to take medications as prescribed. Adherence was self-reported in a 10-item telephone survey, which was obtained from 204 of 276 (74%) initial partici-pants (Ziegelstein et al., 2000). Depressed patients with recent myocardial infarction reported higher health service consumption over the following 18 months (Kurdyak, Gnam, Goering, Chong, & Alter, 2008); however, dropout from a cardiac rehabilita-tion program was more common among those with depression, anxiety, low ego, and social introversion (Blumenthal, Williams, Wallace, Williams, & Needles, 1982).

Comorbid depression decreases treatment adherence among people with COPD, as patients may lack motivation or ability to participate in physical rehabilitation or appropriately use oxygen (Norwood & Balkissoon, 2005). For patients with a history of depression, smoking cessation efforts are more likely to fail, and may carry an increased risk for depression reoccurrence (Glassman, Covey, Stetner, & Rivelli, 2001).

In a review of adherence to oral cancer therapy, Partridge, Avorn, Wang, and Winer (2002) cited a history of having mental illness as a factor associated with nonadherence (Partridge et al., 2002). Wang et al. (2002) reported a significant association between depression and noncompliance with oral medication in a sample of 496 hypertensive patients, adjusting for demographic, clinical, and psychosocial variables (OR = 0.93, per increase on a 14-point scale, 95% CI 0.87–0.99) (Wang et al., 2002).

# Conclusion

Mood disorders constitute a considerable health burden, especially when comorbid with chronic physical illness. Populations living with mood disorders may be at an increased risk for developing diabetes or cardiovascular diseases—although these relationships are likely bidirectional—and comorbidity often results in worse disease outcomes. The role of socioeconomic and other determinants of comorbid mood disorders was variable by disease type; future research may help to further characterize at-risk populations. While more research is required to understand better patterns of treatment access and adherence among populations with comorbid mood disorders and chronic disease, there is no doubt that the recognition and adequate management of mood disorders in people with chronic physical conditions is critical. Physical illness often tends to overshadow the diagnosis when such patients come into contact with health services leading to a neglect of their mental health needs. This is especially true in those with multiple chronic conditions and among older adults where these comorbidities are the rule rather than the exception. Improving services in an integrated manner for this population is likely to produce significant gains in population health (Weich et al., 2012).

# References

Anderson, R. J., Freedland, K. E., Clouse, R. E., & Lustman, P. J. (2001). The prevalence of comorbid depression in adults with diabetes: A meta-analysis. *Diabetes Care*, *24*(6), 1069–1078.

Ani, C., Bazargan, M., Hindman, D., Bell, D., Rodriguez, M., & Baker, R. S. (2009). Comorbid chronic illness and the diagnosis and treatment of depression in safety net primary care settings. *Journal of the American Board of Family Medicine*, *22*(2), 123–135.

Blumenthal, J. A., Williams, R. S., Wallace, A. G., Williams, R. B., Jr., & Needles, T. L. (1982). Physiological and psychological variables predict compliance to prescribed exercise therapy in patients recovering from myocardial infarction. *Psychosomatic Medicine*, *44*(6), 519–527.

Boulanger, L., Zhao, Y., Foster, T. S., Fraser, K., Bledsoe, S. L., & Russell, M. W. (2009). Impact of comorbid depression or anxiety on patterns of treatment and economic outcomes among patients with diabetic peripheral neuropathic pain. *Current Medical Research and Opinion, 25*(7), 1763–1773.

Boyes, A. W., Girgis, A., D'Este, C., & Zucca, A. C. (2011). Flourishing or floundering? Prevalence and correlates of anxiety and depression among a population-based sample of adult cancer survivors 6 months after diagnosis. *Journal of Affective Disorders, 135*(1–3), 184–192.

Brown, J. M., Stewart, J. C., Stump, T. E., & Callahan, C. M. (2011). Risk of coronary heart disease events over 15 years among older adults with depressive symptoms. *American Journal of Geriatric Psychiatry, 19*(8), 721–729.

Campayo, A., Gomez-Biel, C. H., & Lobo, A. (2011). Diabetes and depression. *Current Psychiatry Reports, 13*(1), 26–30.

Carnethon, M. R., Kinder, L. S., Fair, J. M., Stafford, R. S., & Fortmann, S. P. (2003). Symptoms of depression as a risk factor for incident diabetes: Findings from the National Health and Nutrition Examination epidemiologic follow-up study, 1971–1992. *American Journal of Epidemiology, 158*(5), 416–423.

Chamberlain, A. M., Vickers, K. S., Colligan, R. C., Weston, S. A., Rummans, T. A., & Roger, V. L. (2011). Associations of preexisting depression and anxiety with hospitalization in patients with cardiovascular disease. *Mayo Clinic Proceedings, 86*(11), 1056–1062.

Clarke, D. & Goosen, T. (2005). Depression and compliance with treatment in a sample of Northland diabetes patients. *New Zealand Medical Journal, 118*(1222), U1657.

de Groot, M., Anderson, R., Freedland, K. E., Clouse, R. E., & Lustman, P. J. (2001). Association of depression and diabetes complications: A meta-analysis. *Psychosomatic Medicine, 63*(4), 619–630.

Dickens, C., McGowan, L., Percival, C., Tomenson, B., Cotter, L., Heagerty, A., … Creed, F. (2007). Depression is a risk factor for mortality after myocardial infarction: Fact or artifact? *Journal of the American College of Cardiology, 49*(18), 1834–1840.

DiMatteo, M. R., Lepper, H. S., & Croghan, T. W. (2000). Depression is a risk factor for non-compliance with medical treatment: Meta-analysis of the effects of anxiety and depression on patient adherence. *Archives of Internal Medicine, 160*(14), 2101–2107.

Egede, L. E., Zheng, D., & Simpson, K. (2002). Comorbid depression is associated with increased health care use and expenditures in individuals with diabetes. *Diabetes Care, 25*(3), 464–470.

Fisher, L., Skaff, M. M., Mullan, J. T., Arean, P., Glasgow, R., & Masharani, U. (2008). A longitudinal study of affective and anxiety disorders, depressive affect and diabetes distress in adults with type 2 diabetes. *Diabetic Medicine, 25*(9), 1096–1101.

Gale, C. R., Batty, G. D., Osborn, D. P., Tynelius, P., Whitley, E., & Rasmussen, F. (2012). Association of mental disorders in early adulthood and later psychiatric hospital admissions and mortality in a cohort study of more than 1 million men. *Archives of General Psychiatry, 69*(8), 823–831.

Gehi, A., Haas, D., Pipkin, S., & Whooley, M. A. (2005). Depression and medication adherence in outpatients with coronary heart disease: Findings from the Heart and Soul Study. *Archives of Internal Medicine, 165*(21), 2508–2513.

Glassman, A. H., Covey, L. S., Stetner, F., & Rivelli, S. (2001). Smoking cessation and the course of major depression: A follow-up study. *Lancet, 357*(9272), 1929–1932.

Gromova, H. A., Gafarov, V. V., & Gagulin, I. V. (2007). Depression and risk of cardiovascular diseases among males aged 25–64 (WHO MONICA–psychosocial). *Alaska Medicine, 49*(2 Suppl.), 255–258.

Hanania, N. A., Mullerova, H., Locantore, N. W., Vestbo, J., Watkins, M. L., Wouters, E. F., … Sharafkhaneh, A. (2011). Determinants of depression in the ECLIPSE chronic obstructive pulmonary disease cohort. *American Journal of Respiratory and Critical Care Medicine, 183*(5), 604–611.

Heckbert, S. R., Rutter, C. M., Oliver, M., Williams, L. H., Ciechanowski, P., Lin, E. H., ... Von, K. M. (2010). Depression in relation to long-term control of glycemia, blood pressure, and lipids in patients with diabetes. *Journal of General Internal Medicine, 25*(6), 524–529.

Hippisley-Cox, J., Fielding, K., & Pringle, M. (1998). Depression as a risk factor for ischaemic heart disease in men: Population based case-control study. *British Medical Journal, 316*(7146), 1714–1719.

Jennings, J. H., Digiovine, B., Obeid, D., & Frank, C. (2009). The association between depressive symptoms and acute exacerbations of COPD. *Lung, 187*(2), 128–135.

Katon, W., Lin, E. H., & Kroenke, K. (2007). The association of depression and anxiety with medical symptom burden in patients with chronic medical illness. *General Hospital Psychiatry, 29*(2), 147–155.

Katon, W., Von, K. M., Ciechanowski, P., Russo, J., Lin, E., Simon, G., ... Young, B. (2004). Behavioral and clinical factors associated with depression among individuals with diabetes. *Diabetes Care, 27*(4), 914–920.

Katon, W. J. (2011). Epidemiology and treatment of depression in patients with chronic medical illness. *Dialogues in Clinical Neuroscience, 13*(1), 7–23.

Kurdyak, P. A., Gnam, W. H., Goering, P., Chong, A., & Alter, D. A. (2008). The relationship between depressive symptoms, health service consumption, and prognosis after acute myocardial infarction: A prospective cohort study. *BMC Health Services Research, 8*, 200.

Levinson, D., Karger, C. J., & Haklai, Z. (2008). Chronic physical conditions and use of health services among persons with mental disorders: Results from the Israel National Health Survey. *General Hospital Psychiatry, 30*(3), 226–232.

Maharaj, R. G., Reid, S. D., Misir, A., & Simeon, D. T. (2005). Depression and its associated factors among patients attending chronic disease clinics in southwest Trinidad. *West Indian Medical Journal, 54*(6), 369–374.

Manarte, L. F., Dias, S., Gois, C., & Boavida, J. M. (2010). Independent factors associated with depression in type 1 diabetes mellitus. *Acta Diabetologica, 47*(3), 201–207.

Massie, M. J. (2004). Prevalence of depression in patients with cancer. *Journal of the National Cancer Institute Monographs, 32*, 57–71.

Mezuk, B., Eaton, W. W., Albrecht, S., & Golden, S. H. (2008). Depression and type 2 diabetes over the lifespan: A meta-analysis. *Diabetes Care, 31*(12), 2383–2390.

Mier, N., Bocanegra-Alonso, A., Zhan, D., Wang, S., Stoltz, S. M., Acosta-Gonzalez, R. I., ... Zuniga, M. A. (2008). Clinical depressive symptoms and diabetes in a binational border population. *Journal of the American Board of Family Medicine, 21*(3), 223–233.

Moussavi, S., Chatterji, S., Verdes, E., Tandon, A., Patel, V., & Ustun, B. (2007). Depression, chronic diseases, and decrements in health: Results from the World Health surveys. *Lancet, 370*(9590), 851–858.

Ng, T. P., Niti, M., Fones, C., Yap, K. B., & Tan, W. C. (2009). Co-morbid association of depression and COPD: A population-based study. *Respiratory Medicine, 103*(6), 895–901.

Norwood, R. (2006). Prevalence and impact of depression in chronic obstructive pulmonary disease patients. *Current Opinion in Pulmonary Medicine, 12*(2), 113–117.

Norwood, R., & Balkissoon, R. (2005). Current perspectives on management of co-morbid depression in COPD. *Chronic Obstructive Pulmonary Disease, 2*(1), 185–193.

Partridge, A. H., Avorn, J., Wang, P. S., & Winer, E. P. (2002). Adherence to therapy with oral antineoplastic agents. *Journal of the National Cancer Institute, 94*(9), 652–661.

Rodin, G., Lo, C., Mikulincer, M., Donner, A., Gagliese, L., & Zimmermann, C. (2009). Pathways to distress: The multiple determinants of depression, hopelessness, and the desire for hastened death in metastatic cancer patients. *Social Science and Medicine, 68*(3), 562–569.

Roshanaei-Moghaddam, B., & Katon, W. (2009). Premature mortality from general medical illnesses among persons with bipolar disorder: A review. *Psychiatric Services, 60*(2), 147–156.

Russ, T. C., Stamatakis, E., Hamer, M., Starr, J. M., Kivimaki, M., & Batty, G. D. (2012). Association between psychological distress and mortality: Individual participant pooled analysis of 10 prospective cohort studies. *British Medical Journal, 345*, e4933.

Satin, J. R., Linden, W., & Phillips, M. J. (2009). Depression as a predictor of disease progression and mortality in cancer patients: A meta-analysis. *Cancer, 115*(22), 5349–5361.

Schmitz, N., Wang, J., Malla, A., & Lesage, A. (2007). Joint effect of depression and chronic conditions on disability: Results from a population-based study. *Psychosomatic Medicine, 69*(4), 332–338.

Starkstein, S. E., Mizrahi, R., & Garau, L. (2005). Specificity of symptoms of depression in Alzheimer disease: A longitudinal analysis. *American Journal of Geriatric Psychiatry, 13*(9), 802–807.

Tellez-Zenteno, J. F., & Cardiel, M. H. (2002). Risk factors associated with depression in patients with type 2 diabetes mellitus. *Archives of Medical Research, 33*(1), 53–60.

Van der Kooy, K., van Hout, H., Marwijk, H., Marten, H., Stehouwer, C., & Beekman, A. (2007). Depression and the risk for cardiovascular diseases: Systematic review and meta analysis. *International Journal of Geriatric Psychiatry, 22*(7), 613–626.

von Leupoldt, A., Taube, K., Lehmann, K., Fritzsche, A., & Magnussen, H. (2011). The impact of anxiety and depression on outcomes of pulmonary rehabilitation in patients with COPD. *Chest, 140*(3), 730–736.

Waitzfelder, B., Gerzoff, R. B., Karter, A. J., Crystal, S., Bair, M. J., Ettner, S. L., . . . Dudley, R. A. (2010). Correlates of depression among people with diabetes: The Translating Research into Action for Diabetes (TRIAD) study. *Primary Care Diabetes, 4*(4), 215–222.

Wang, P. S., Bohn, R. L., Knight, E., Glynn, R. J., Mogun, H., & Avorn, J. (2002). Noncompliance with antihypertensive medications: The impact of depressive symptoms and psychosocial factors. *Journal of General Internal Medicine, 17*(7), 504–511.

Weich, S., Bebbington, P., Rai, D., Stranges, S., McBride, O., Spiers, N., . . . Brugha, T. (2012). The population impact of common mental disorders and long-term physical conditions on disability and hospital admission. *Psychological Medicine, 43*(5), 921–931. doi:10.1017/S0033291712001705

Wiltink, J., Beutel, M. E., Till, Y., Ojeda, F. M., Wild, P. S., Munzel, T., . . . Michal, M. (2011). Prevalence of distress, comorbid conditions and well being in the general population. *Journal of Affective Disorders, 130*(3), 429–437.

Wittchen, H. U., Jacobi, F., Rehm, J., Gustavsson, A., Svensson, M., Jonsson, B., . . . Steinhausen, H. C. (2011). The size and burden of mental disorders and other disorders of the brain in Europe 2010. *European Neuropsychopharmacology, 21*(9), 655–679.

Wong, S. Y., Mercer, S. W., Woo, J., & Leung, J. (2008). The influence of multi-morbidity and self-reported socio-economic standing on the prevalence of depression in an elderly Hong Kong population. *BMC Public Health, 8*, 119.

World Health Organization (2008). *The global burden of disease: 2004 update.* Geneva, Switzerland: Author.

Yohannes, A. M. (2005). Depression and COPD in older people: A review and discussion. *British Journal of Community Nursing, 10*(1), 42–46.

Zhang, M. W., Ho, R. C., Cheung, M. W., Fu, E., & Mak, A. (2011). Prevalence of depressive symptoms in patients with chronic obstructive pulmonary disease: A systematic review, meta-analysis and meta-regression. *General Hospital Psychiatry, 33*(3), 217–223.

Ziegelstein, R. C., Fauerbach, J. A., Stevens, S. S., Romanelli, J., Richter, D. P., & Bush, D. E. (2000). Patients with depression are less likely to follow recommendations to reduce cardiac risk during recovery from a myocardial infarction. *Archives of Internal Medicine, 160*(12), 1818–1823.

# 21

# Depression in Older People
## *Cognitive Behavior Therapy, Evidence and Practice*

### Ken Laidlaw
University of Edinburgh, UK

## Introduction

This chapter provides a brief contemporary review of the science and practice of a model of psychological treatment (cognitive behavior therapy) for depression in older people. As a consequence of the demographic transition taking place globally and the subsequent increase in life expectancy, the need for specialist psychotherapists trained to work with older people will become increasingly important in our aging societies (Knight, Karel, Hinrichsen, Qualls, & Duffy, 2009).

In many cases, clinicians may find it helpful to examine their own expectations about older people and their personal attitudes to aging, as this may influence their own expectation for change when working with depressed older people who themselves may be very negative toward aging and about the possibilities for change.

Chronological age provides limited data by itself, so therapists working with older people need to spend time understanding the appropriate developmental context in which an older person may experience depression. Any clinicians embarking on work with this client group will benefit from knowledge of normal as well as abnormal aging and as such this chapter incorporates relevant information from gerontology that may be useful for clinicians to apprehend when using psychological methods to treat depression in later life. (Gerontology is the scientific study of the aging process as opposed to geriatrics which is the study of health and disease in later life.)

### Demographic changes and the globalization of aging

Global population aging witnessed today is unprecedented in the whole of human history (UN, 2011). Never before has the world witnessed the levels of longevity that people are achieving now with virtually all nations experiencing growth in the number of older people (Kinsella & Wan, 2009). Increasing longevity is a phenomenon affecting the developed and developing world alike, with increases in the number of people aged 60 years and older in the developed regions of the world projected to

*The Wiley-Blackwell Handbook of Mood Disorders*, Second Edition. Edited by Mick Power.
© 2013 John Wiley & Sons, Ltd. Published 2013 by John Wiley & Sons, Ltd.

rise from 274 million in 2011 to 418 million in 2050, peaking at 433 million in 2100 (UN, 2011). In the developing regions of the world, there is an equally rapid increase in the number of people aged 60 years and older, with 510 million in 2011 estimated to increase to 1.6 billion in 2050 and 2.4 billion by 2100 (UN, 2011). Thus, the largest number of older people will be found in the developing regions of the world and it is the developing world that is aging most rapidly (Kinsella & Wan, 2009). In the developed regions of the world, the largest increase in the number of older people occurs between 2011 and 2050 with the United Nations (UN) (2011) estimating that the annual increase in those aged 60 years and older is likely to be 2.4% from 2011 to 2050 and 0.7% from 2050 to 2100.

Linked to increases in longevity is a decline in fertility; thus, in the developed world, many societies have larger populations aged 60 years and older in comparison to those aged 15 years and younger. In the developed regions of the world, over one-fifth of the population is currently aged 60 years and older and this is projected to increase to 32% in 2050 and 33% in 2100 (UN, 2011).

The oldest old section of society shows the largest increase in relative numbers. Overall global projections between 2005 and 2040 estimates a percentage increase in number of people aged 85 years and older of 301%, whereas for those aged 100 years and older, a percentage increase of 746% is estimated (Kinsella & Wan, 2009). In 2011, there were 109 million people aged 80 years and older and by 2050 this is set to increase to 402 million—almost 3.7 times more people aged 80 years and older alive. In 1950, 1% of the population were aged 80 years and older, and by 2050 8% of the global population will be aged 80 years and older. Between 2000 and 2100, life expectancy at birth (global average) has increased from aged 66 to 81 years (UN, 2011). As these global figures make little sense because of great variation across nations, when considering the Europe and North America, life expectancy at birth from 1950 to 2100 increased from age 66 to 87 years for Europe and from age 69 to 88 years for North America as a whole (UN, 2011). Life expectancy at age 75 has also increased with an average life expectancy of between 11 and 12 years in United Kingdom and United States (UN, 2011).

There are many older people alive than in previous generations and people are living longer and healthier than ever before (Laidlaw & Pachana, 2009). As a consequence of demographic changes, many more psychotherapists are going to come in to contact with older people seeking help. In all probability the issues older people bring into therapy will change as longevity of life increases (Laidlaw & Pachana, 2011). Therapists may be ill-prepared to meet the needs of a "graying society" as a recent survey of Clinical Psychologists in US found. Qualls, Segal, Norman, Neiderehe, and Gallagher-Thompson (2002) asked practitioners how much specialist training they had received in working with older people. Although a majority provided psychotherapy to older people only a minority had completed supervised practice in working with this population. Knight et al. (2009) outline specific skills and competences that therapist may wish to consider when working with older people. Therapists knowledgeable about longevity statistics and demographic change will arguably be better equipped to identify and challenge *erroneous* age-related negative cognitions (e.g., growing older is depressing) that could sound understandable and realistic to therapists inexperienced in working with older people (Laidlaw & McAlpine, 2008).

Demographic changes also predict wider societal repercussions for the delivery of health care for older people. Smaller family sizes mean restricted number of informal carers and in dementia care, this may become a significant issue (Laidlaw & Pachana, 2009). Societal changes such as increased rates of divorce, family breakup, and reconstitutions impact on an individual's social capital and hence access to social supports (Gray, 2009), potentially leading people to seek more support from formal care providers such as psychotherapists.

## Prevalence of depression in older people

Depression and anxiety are major causes of mental health problems in later life, but rates of depression and anxiety in later life may be lower than rates reported for younger or middle-aged adults (Blazer, 2010; Jorm, 2000). Data from the Epidemiological Catchment Area Study suggested that rates of major depressive disorder among older adults were lower than those for other age groups (Unutzer, Katon, Sullivan, & Miranda, 1999). Recent evidence suggests that anxiety disorders may also be very common and that depression and anxiety very often overlap in older people although anxiety tends to be neglected and undertreated in primary care (Vink, Aartsen, & Schoevers, 2008).

In a systematic review of community-based studies assessing prevalence of late life depression, Beekman, Copeland, and Prince (1999) calculated an average prevalence rate of 13.5% for clinically relevant depression symptoms. More recently, McDougall et al. (2007) reported findings from a large epidemiological study looking at the prevalence of depression in people aged 65 years and older from across England and Wales. Using a subsample from the larger sample, McDougall et al. (2007) estimated prevalence of depression among older people to be 8.7%, with a prevalence rate for severe depression to be 2.7%. The authors commented that there did not appear to be a relationship between age and prevalence of depression but factors associated with depression were being female, medical comorbidity and disability, and social deprivation. The Centers for Disease Control and Prevention note that contrary to the popular belief, older people experience less frequent occurrence of mental distress with lifetime histories of depression at 10.5% and anxiety at 7.6% that are lower than those reported for depression and anxiety (19.3% and 12.7%, respectively) in adults in midlife (50–64 years).

Medical conditions increase rates of depression in later life, with a greater burden of illness resulting in an increased risk of depression, but most older adults who develop physical problems do not develop depression (Blazer, 2010). Nevertheless medical illnesses complicate the recognition and treatment of depression and anxiety. Depression is also increased in the presence of cognitive impairment and dementia with a consequent impact on treatment responsiveness (Wilkins, Kiosses, & Ravdin, 2010). It is estimated that 80% of older Americans have at least one chronic health problem and up to 50% will have two. As longevity increases among older people, therapists may be confronted with an increase in medical issues with a complexity and chronicity attached to them that is rarely seen currently. Death is also more likely to arise because of noncommunicable diseases such as cancer, heart disease, and stroke rather than due to injury or infections. Thus older people may be more likely to have lived with a number of chronic diseases for many more years before their eventual demise. This again provides a complicating factor that therapists may need to reconcile with new or existing models of psychotherapy.

Depression rates may also be elevated in those populations who reside in institutional settings (Jorm, 2000). In a recent review of the literature on the diagnosis and treatment of depression in long-term care (LTC) facilities in the United States, Thakat and Blazer (2008) quoted rates for depression as high as 35% of residents and noted that depression is very often underrecognized in care home residents. Seitz, Purandare, and Conn (2010) carried out a literature review for the prevalence of psychiatric disorder in LTC and identified 26 studies of depression prevalence in LTC and the report rates from 5% to 25%, with a median prevalence rate of 10% for depression in residents in LTC. Depression symptoms were recorded at a much higher rate ranging from 14% to 82%, with a median prevalence rate of 29% for depressive symptoms in residents in LTC. This suggests that depression may be elevated in residents in LTC, but perhaps arriving at a formal diagnosis of depression is more difficult in the context of an LTC facility. Likewise, providing treatment for depression in an LTC facility can be challenging (Hyer, Carpenter, Bishmann, & Wu, 2005) and as yet there is no real evidence base established for the application of structured psychological therapies for depression in LTC (Thakat & Blazer, 2008). Evidence, such as it is does exist, suggests older people may benefit from a psychosocial approach to emotional distress (Hyer et al., 2005).

In a scholarly review of depression and anxiety in later life, Jorm (2000) notes that when studies assess age differences in depression and anxiety and systematically control for risk factors, depression is shown to reduce with age. Jorm (2000) suggests that depression and anxiety rates reduce with age because of a multitude of factors such as decreased emotional responsiveness with evidence suggesting that levels of neuroticism decrease with age; increased emotional control where older people have developed skills in coping strategies that result in better emotional stability; and psychological immunization where people develop a resilience and resistance to depression through exposure to adverse life events.

Blazer (2010) explains the paradox of low relative rates of depression in the presence of challenges associated with age in terms of three protective factors associated with aging such as mature emotional regulation competence, consistent with the work by Carstensen's theory of socioemotional selectivity theory (Carstensen, Isaacowitz, & Charles, 1999), increased wisdom (Baltes & Smith, 2008), and resilience as older people cope better with stressful events; as Blazer (2010) notes, these are events that are experienced as being "on time" (p. 172), and thus are expected so that an older person may cope with these events better than is anticipated or expected. Echoing this, Sadavoy (2009) notes that rates of depression are surprisingly uncommon when considering the challenges that can be posed by old age. Consistent with this evidence, and contrary to the notion that old age is a stage of life to be feared with depression as an outcome of old age because of losses and challenges, is the aging paradox where older people typically report high levels of life satisfaction at the stage of life mostly associated with cognitive and physical decline (Carstensen & Lockerhoff, 2003). The idea that depression reduces as one ages and this may be because of positive life span development factors where older people are more skillful in emotion regulation is an intriguing one for anyone wishing to work therapeutically with this client group. This proffers the possibility that *older people may make better candidates for psychological therapy.* As if to emphasize this point Knight (2006, p. 24) notes, "The more traditional, largely pessimistic, view has been that adult development and increased experience make people rigid and set in their ways. Yet some clinicians working with the elderly have felt that the effect is quite the reverse: that growth and experience teaches adults to be more flexible, less dogmatic, and more aware that there are different ways of looking at life."

A common finding is that older people underutilize mental health services (Boddington, 2011; Unutzer et al., 1999, 2003) and older people with mental health problems are at enhanced risk of having their needs neglected. Despite the availability of efficacious psychological treatments for depression and anxiety, primary care patients expressing a preference for nonpharmacological treatments are less likely to receive it (Unutzer et al., 2003). This is an intriguing finding that may be explained in part by a lack of awareness among primary care providers about the efficacy of psychological treatment for later life depression and anxiety or a lack of confidence in identifying and diagnosing depression and anxiety in older people. As depression may be complicated by the presence of multiple chronic health conditions, there may also be a fear of opening up a "Pandora's box" of issues that may be difficult to contain and manage by primary care providers (Unutzer et al., 1999, p. 235). Additionally, another barrier may be a mistaken belief that depression in later life results from what Unutzer et al. (1999, p. 235) describe as the "fallacy of good reasons" where providers attribute the onset and maintenance of problems to "old age" and believe there is no point in intervening as they erroneously believe problems to be unchangeable. Burroughs et al. (2006) carried out qualitative interviews with older people and primary care providers about treatment for depression in later life. Both providers and patients endorsed a concept of depression in later life as "justifiable" and "understandable" with consequent low expectations for treatment outcome. Similarly, Sarkisian, Lee-Henderson, and Mangione (2003) found that when depressed older people attributed depression as a result of aging, they were much less likely to seek treatment for depression. Therapeutic nihilism endorsed by depressed older people and accepted as factual by primary care providers is very unfortunate especially as recent research suggests older people hold positive attitudes toward health seeking for mental health problems, and may be even more positive in their attitudes about this than younger adults (MacKenzie, Scott, Mather, & Sareen, 2008). Older people themselves, given a choice, often prefer to receive psychotherapeutic treatments rather than psychotropic medication (Gum et al., 2006). The hope is that increasingly it will become the norm for older people to be offered access to psychological therapies.

## Cognitive behavior therapy with older people

Cognitive behavior therapy (CBT) with older people is an active, directive, time-limited, and structured treatment approach whose primary aim is symptom reduction (Laidlaw, Thompson, Siskin-Dick, & Gallagher-Thompson, 2003). The most common form of CBT used in the United Kingdom is based upon the cognitive model of dysfunctional information processing in emotional disorders developed by Beck, Rush, Shaw, and Emery (1979). In the Beck's stress–diathesis model of psychopathology, cognitions (which can be thoughts or images) are determined by latent maladaptive beliefs (schemata), attitudes, and assumptions. The most basic premise of CBT can be summed up by the writings of Greek philosophers such as Epictetus who wrote, "Men are disturbed not by things, but by the views which they take of them."

CBT can be differentiated from other forms of psychotherapy by its emphasis on the empirical investigation of the patient's thoughts, appraisals, inferences, and assumptions. This aim is achieved through the explicit use of cognitive and behavioral techniques such as activity scheduling, graded task assignments, problem-solving techniques, thought identification and monitoring, and examining and challenging core beliefs about the self, world, and future.

CBT is the most systematically researched psychological treatment approach for depression in later life (Laidlaw & Thompson, 2008) and as such may be considered the treatment of choice for many psychiatric disorders particularly given its availability within NHS health settings. CBT is particularly appropriate as a treatment for the psychological problems and challenges experienced by older adults because it is skill enhancing, present oriented, problem focused, straightforward to use, and effective (Satre, Knight, & David, 2006). Additionally, CBT is empowering of individuals as they learn new ways to cope with what may be old problems that have recurred over many years, and as such it can be effective in increasing positive affect as well as reducing negative affect (Laidlaw, 2010a). Importantly, however, if clinicians wish to be more effective, they need to be knowledgeable about aging and open minded about the possibilities for change at any age.

## Age-appropriate models of CBT with older people

It is frequently asked how is CBT different with older people and whether therapists working with older people need to consider modifications to ensure CBT is maximally effective and applicable with older people. Modifications may be indicated and may be required in order to address normal age-related changes such as the presence of physical frailty or changes to cognitive processing and status (Grant & Casey, 1995). Modifications to a treatment model are intended to enhance treatment outcome but seek to remain consistent with values and core philosophy of the therapy modality (i.e., CBT), whereas adaptations are intended to alert clinicians to the possibility that the treatment model they have chosen may be inadequate for the circumstances or the population they intend to apply this model with (Laidlaw, 2001). While there may be clinical necessity for the former in some instances, the evidence for the latter is still lacking.

In some regard, modifications could be said to be unnecessary as outcome studies of CBT for late life depression have by and large applied standard models of CBT with relatively good outcome (Laidlaw, 2001). One cannot prescribe modifications to an already efficacious treatment approach solely on the basis of chronological age as this does not necessarily provide the best basis of understanding about how "old" an individual behaves or a particularly accurate description of their difficulties or health status. Nonetheless, older people are part of a heterogeneous population that contains up to four different generations and therefore the need for modifications may become more acute as mental health professionals work with much older clients than ever before. This is largely uncharted territory with respect to both biological and nonbiological approaches to psychological distress in later life and certainly to the application of existing psychotherapy treatment models (Laidlaw & Pachana, 2011).

In many respects, older people come into therapy for the same reasons that younger people do such as relationship problems and difficult life transitions (Knight, 2004). Sometimes the complexity of problems that older people bring to therapy can be daunting and overwhelming to novice therapists simply because they are unused to working with older clients and lack knowledge about normal aging (Laidlaw, 2010b). Sadavoy (2009) provides some guidance for therapists working with older people when he suggests that there are five "C's" associated with psychogeriatrics and these are chronicity, complexity, comorbidity, continuity, and context. The suggestions by Sadavoy (2009) acknowledge that working with older people can be challenging.

Current models of CBT may need to take account of demographic changes so as to maximize therapeutic outcomes by augmenting CBT outcome with gerontological theory as this provides for a conceptual approach to enhance age-appropriate CBT treatment models. Possible "candidate" theories from gerontology that may augment CBT with older people and are consistent with the values and orientation of CBT are theories focusing on optimal aging (selection, optimization with compensation; Freund & Baltes, 1998) that advocate an active problem-focused positive approach to meet the challenges of aging. Theories of negative age stereotypes (Stereotype Embodiment Theory; Levy, 2009) that are long-held vulnerabilities that older people may have internalized from a younger age can act much like a stress–diathesis in the development of problems in later life. Finally, when working with older people who have a chronic history of depression, this can result in older people developing a negative narrative of themselves as weak or as failures. The use of wisdom theories (Baltes & Smith, 2008) can help people become more accepting and compassionate toward themselves. Drawing on experience and becoming "wise" by reflecting upon and reframing narratives associated with past experiences may promote growth (Bauer & McAdam, 2004) and hence potentiate the effectiveness of CBT. Readers interested in a more thorough treatment of these issues are referred to Knight and Laidlaw (2009) and Laidlaw (2010a).

The position advocated here is a simple and traditional idea within CBT. In order to enhance possibilities for treatment outcome in CBT, the person does not need to change to fit the model, but the model needs to change to fit the person to ensure maximal effectiveness. CBT theorists have always focused on the development of theory-driven models to aid treatment. What is advocated here is that intervention strategies focused upon a problem-solving, explorative approach to understand problems are retained but the use of these strategies are contextualized in an age-appropriate conceptual frame of reference and in so doing, a wider canvas for considering interventions is drawn on in CBT with older people. Thus, when looking at the individual's level of beliefs and attributions about problems and possibility for change, this may be influenced by the individual's own beliefs about aging. Thus, if persons believe themselves to have a few remaining good years of life, the level of passivity and hopelessness will be increased and a belief in the possibility of change may be reduced. For these reasons, the augmentation of the cognitive theory of CBT with gerontology theories is likely to enhance treatment outcome. Interested readers can see a fuller elaboration of these concepts in Laidlaw (2010a).

Depression in later life may not necessarily be different in symptomatology in comparison to presentations with adults of working age, but in order to work most effectively with older people. Use may need to be made of a contextualization framework or specific formulation mode for CBT with older people (Knight & Laidlaw, 2009). There may be age-specific developmental factors to take account of when working with older people because loss (either through bereavement or loss of health) is a common experience in aging that impacts upon the quality and quantity of social networks. In the experience of therapists working with older people, depression treatment can be complicated by the fact that the client may be the last surviving member of their age cohort (sociocultural context) and have an increased sense of their own mortality simultaneously experiencing increased social isolation because they have diminished social capital older resources available to draw upon (Gray, 2009). Thus, CBT with older people can be different in regard to the types of challenges that people may face as they age. This means that psychotherapists may need to understand a wider knowledge base around aging, longevity, and cognitive and affective development.

The comprehensive conceptualization framework (CCF) (Laidlaw, Thompson, & Gallagher-Thompson, 2004) for CBT with older people helps therapists, particularly those inexperienced in working with older people and provides a way of framing or contextualizing older adults' problems within the standard Beck model of CBT model. The main elements of the CCF are cohort beliefs, transition in role investments, intergenerational linkages, the sociocultural context, and health status. Each element serves to broaden the understanding that a therapist will draw on when working with elders. The CCF model is outlined in much more detail elsewhere (see Laidlaw et al., 2004), therefore, main elements are summarized in Table 21.1.

The CCF provides a means of contextualizing an individual's current set of difficulties within a life span developmental perspective (see Figure 21.1). For example, taking account of cohort beliefs, allows a therapist to acknowledge that different generations have different experiences that shape their values and worldview and as such these may have change across generations. In order for therapist to reflect on the importance of cohort beliefs and values, let us consider the current cohort of older people who are true age pioneers and who in the main tend to live much longer than their parents and grandparents and do so in a healthier state. Consider an 80-year-old woman alive today, born in 1932, her own father born in 1901 when life expectancy at birth in the United Kingdom was 45 for men. Her grandparents were born in the nineteenth century and would likely have been born about 1880. The 80-year-old woman in your clinic therefore has a model for aging from her grandparents that is completely different from her own experience and that of you as the therapist working with her. Thus, the current cohort of older people may be influenced in their values and beliefs by their models of aging that may be very outdated and the therapist needs to be aware of this important contextual factor when engaging in treatment.

**Table 21.1.**
Comprehensive Conceptualization Framework (CCF) for CBT with Older People

| Element of CCF | Description of CCF element | Clinical relevance |
|---|---|---|
| Cohort beliefs | Generational beliefs held by people born in similar years or at similar time periods that may determine values of these individuals across generations. | Cohort beliefs and values provide the context in which beliefs at a wider more societal level can be understood; thus, stigma about depression in older people may be understood at a cohort level. Cohort beliefs of older generations can also sometimes clash with the therapist's beliefs. For example, beliefs about lifestyle choices and gender roles may differ markedly, making therapists feel uncomfortable. |
| Intergenerational linkages | Within families, there are different generations that come into regular contact. The different generations have different needs and outlooks. There may be opportunities for sharing of family values across generations and there may be opportunities for generativity where an older generation may help a younger generation share in wisdom of experience. | Intergenerational relationships may provoke tensions. If older people feel their views are being ignored or they are being marginalized because they are old, this can cause tensions within the family. Likewise, if older people have previously cared for their "elderly relatives" when younger, they may adhere to beliefs of filial care that are not shared by other members of their family. Carers and care recipients may also have intergenerational negative linkages. Older people in receipt of care may experience distress as they feel they are a "burden" for their family. |
| Sociocultural context | Depressed older people may state that their problems are to do with aging. Health care professionals may also be seduced into the "fallacy of good reasons" (Unutzer et al., 1999) believing such statements are factual and realistic appraisals of a difficult time of life. Levy (2009) has developed a theory of negative age stereotypes becoming self-stereotypes that can impact upon an individual in terms of affect, cognition, behavior, and physiology. | Many older people have an implicit assumption (that can be challenged with cognitive restructuring techniques) that old age inevitably means loss and decrepitude. In CBT, internalized negative age stereotypes can be considered to be a latent and maladaptive vulnerability about aging that has been reinforced and often endorsed by themselves and society for decades. Levy (2009) suggests that negative societal attitudes about age are internalized from a very young age and reinforced throughout adulthood by an attentional bias to negative information about aging. Stereotypes internalized during childhood become self-stereotypes that functions as a predisposing vulnerability or diathesis for development of negative attitudes to aging. A possible mechanism |

(continued)

**Table 21.1.**
Continued

| Element of CCF | Description of CCF element | Clinical relevance |
|---|---|---|
| | | for activation of negative age stereotypes predicting and determining attitudes to aging can be found by considering a stress–diathesis interaction. As individuals age, negative age stereotypes operating outside the individual's conscious awareness, become activated by congruent negative experiences attributed to aging. Stated simply, negative events are attributed to the aging process and this explanatory construct reinforces individual negative appraisals congruent with the self-stereotype suggesting an unpleasant experience of aging is the norm. Depressed older people endorse negative attitudes to aging that are plausible, distorted, and unhelpful and may be accepted by the health care professionals they come in contact with. Older people who selectively attend to negative indicators of aging such as loss due to bereavement, or physical health changes such as long-standing, limiting, and non-life-threatening condition may be more prone to activations of the internalized negative age stereotype (the diathesis). The sociocultural context also takes into account the values of the therapist. |
| Transitions in role investments | The transitions in role investment experienced by people are important variables to consider when working with older people. In later life, there may be transitions that an individual needs to navigate in order to adapt successfully to age-related changes. Common transitions that may be challenging are becoming a primary caregiver for a loved one, or transitioning to living alone. For many older people experiencing the bereavement of their partner means they may be experiencing living alone for the first time in many years and for some, this is the first experience of this in their adult lives. | Transitions in role investments commonly seen in later life can become problematic when people attempt to cope with a change in circumstances by rigidly and inflexibly adhering to outmoded coping strategies that in the past served them well. Examples of transitions in role investments with the potential for distress are when an individual loses independence because of a change in physical health status or, when taking on a new role, such as caregiving. The amount of investment one has in the roles that give life personal meaning may be an important determinant in how successfully one adapts to a changed circumstance. |

| Health status | | |
| --- | --- | --- |
| | • Increasing age brings with it an increased likelihood of developing chronic medical conditions. Ill-health can be understood in terms of three components: impairment, disability, and handicap.<br><br>• Impairment refers to the loss or abnormality of body structure, appearance, organ, or system (e.g., infarct in a stroke).<br><br>• Disability is the impact of the impairment (i.e., infarct in a certain part of a person's brain) on the individual's ability to carry out "normal" activities.<br><br>• Handicap can be thought of as the social impact that the impairment or disease has on the individual. Consequences of handicap are visible when a person interacts with his or her environment. Thus, a person who has experienced a stroke may find that other people treat them differently, by excluding him or her from normal communications. | CBT therapists can usefully employ elements of the Baltes model of Selection, Optimization with Compensation (SOC: Freund & Baltes, 1998) approach to optimal aging. Highly valued roles and goals are maintained as older people select alternative means of achieving these goals. Selection (usually "loss-based selection") is a process where highly valued roles and goals are maintained in the face of loss where an individual modifies goal attainment due to a reduction in resources. Optimization requires that an individual focuses resources on achieving goals through practicing or relearning of activities. It must be done in an intentional manner. Compensation requires that an individual engage in alternative means of achieving the highest possible level of functioning, therefore taking account of the reality of a person's capacity and physical integrity. SOC can be incorporated into psychotherapy, especially CBT, as the problem-solving orientation is a good fit with an aim of symptom reduction and achievement of an improvement in functioning. The usefulness of the classification to therapists is that it allows one to consider an individual's impairment or disease simply and to separate out the consequences from the impairment. CBT works at the level of disability and handicap, but not at the level of impairment. |

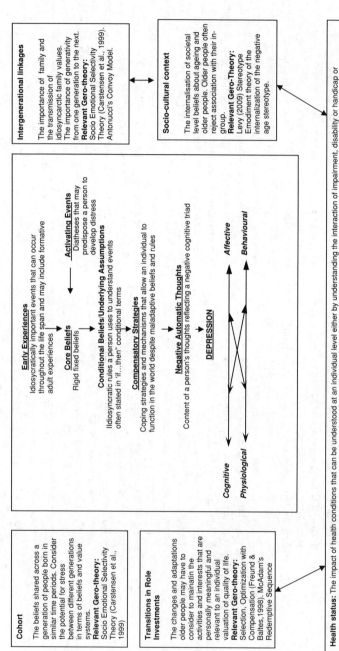

**Intergenerational linkages**

The importance of family and the transmission of idiosyncratic family values.
The importance of generativity from one generation to the next.
**Relevant Gero-theory:**
Socio Emotional Selectivity Theory (Carstensen et al., 1999). Antonucci's Convoy Model.

**Socio-cultural context**

The internalisation of societal level beliefs about ageing and older people. Older people often reject association with their in-group.
**Relevant Gero-Theory:**
Levy (2009) Stereotype Embodiment theory of the internalization of the negative age stereotype.

**Early Experiences**
Idiosyncratically important events that can occur throughout the life span and may include formative adult experiences

**Activating Events**
Diatheses that may predispose a person to develop distress

**Core Beliefs**
Rigid fixed beliefs

**Conditional Beliefs/Underlying Assumptions**
Idiosyncratic rules a person uses to understand events often stated in 'if...then' conditional terms

**Compensatory Strategies**
Coping strategies and mechanisms that allow an individual to function in the world despite maladaptive beliefs and rules

**Negative Automatic Thoughts**
Content of a person's thoughts reflecting a negative cognitive triad

**DEPRESSION**

*Cognitive*  *Affective*  *Physiological*  *Behavioural*

**Cohort**

The beliefs shared across a generation of people born in similar time periods. Consider the potential for stress between different generations in terms of beliefs and value systems.
**Relevant Gero-theory:**
Socio Emotional Selectivity Theory (Carstensen et al., 1999)

**Transitions in Role Investments**

The changes and adaptations older people may have to consider to maintain the activities and interests that are personally meaningful and relevant to an individual valuation of quality of life.
**Relevant Gero-theory:**
Selection, Optimization with Compensation (Freund & Baltes, 1998). McAdam's Redemptive Sequence

**Health status:** The impact of health conditions that can be understood at an individual level either by understanding the interaction of impairment, disability or handicap or by reference to the WHO international classification of functioning, disability and health (ICF) taking account of body factors, societal and individual perspectives and the environment.

The strategies that may assist an individual to effectively manage the impact of a potentially limiting chronic and/or deteriorating condition are summarized by the use of Selection, Optimization with Compensation

**Figure 21.1.** Comprehensive Cognitive Formulation (CCF) for CBT with Older People. Reproduced with permission from Laidlaw et al. (2004)

Likewise, there may be transitions in role investment such as becoming the primary carer for one's spouse who has developed dementia, or alternatively, as one develops disability and loses independence, this can be a painful and difficult transition for individuals to make (Broomfield et al., 2010).

Within the CCF, each individual is considered to be constantly striving to achieve homeostasis throughout his or her life trajectory. People come into therapy because of transitions in circumstance that are proving hard to navigate alone by recourse to habitual strategies and the CCF helps therapists contextualize problems within an age-appropriate frame of reference that retains the treatment focus of a CBT formulation.

## Psychological treatment outcome for late life depression

As the most remarkable increases in the number of older people are in those people termed the oldest old, psychotherapists are likely to treat nonagenarian (aged 90–99 years) and centenarian clients in the coming years. This is largely uncharted territory as most psychological therapy models were developed with younger age groups with primarily unimodal presentations of distress. A psychotherapist working with a depressed 95-year-old may be faced with many more issues of complexity in the implementation of effective psychological treatment interventions. Clinicians turning to the evidence base for guidance on efficacy of psychological therapies with older people will find that the data are more biased toward studies with the youngest old, with many early studies including adults aged 55 years and older (Cuijpers, van Straten, Smit, & Andersson, 2009). Recent studies have started to recruit older participants from primary care settings so that the research data are closer to the experience of clinicians outwith academia. Undoubtedly, there remains a need for more, and better, outcome studies in psychological therapies with older people. There will be a great need for more process-based research that can answer what changes may be necessary in order to enhance treatment outcome in late life depression.

Meta-analyses and systematic reviews suggest that CBT is an effective treatment approach to reduce depression in later life (Laidlaw, 2001; Scogin, Welsh, Hanson, Stump, & Coates, 2005; Wilson, Mottram, & Vassilas, 2008) while others report a statistical advantage for CBT compared to other forms of psychological intervention (Pinquart, Duberstein, & Lyness, 2006; Pinquart & Sorensen, 2001). Overall, a consensus has emerged about CBT as the most efficacious treatment approach with older people.

Table 21.2 summarizes evidence from systematic reviews and meta-analyses over the past 10 years. In the main, there are some general conclusions that can be reached and these are outlined below:

- Evidence for the efficacy of CBT in late life depression is stronger than for other forms of therapy, but there remain insufficient studies of optimal quality to definitively conclude that CBT is superior to other forms of psychological therapy in older people.
- Individual CBT treatment appears to be superior to group CBT interventions.

**Table 21.2.**
Reviews of CBT and Psychotherapy Outcome for Late Life Depression

| Authors | Level of analyses | Results | Conclusions |
|---|---|---|---|
| Laidlaw (2001) | Focused review of eight studies of CBT for late life depression (review of five meta-analyses in addition to outcome studies). | When using the BDI as the outcome measure, CBT showed the largest treatment gains in comparison to other psychological therapies. Many methodological flaws evident in earlier outcome studies. | CBT is an efficacious treatment for late life depression. Evidence supportive of this comes from outcome studies and from meta-analyses and systematic reviews. |
| Pinquart and Sorensen (2001) | 122 psychosocial intervention studies. | CBT and psychodynamic psychotherapy effective on self-rated and clinician-rated measures of depression. Individual therapy more effective than group. | The review considered a number of moderator variables that influence outcome and note that for clinician-rated depression (CRD), longer duration of psychotherapy was more effective. For CRD, there were larger improvements overall. Therapists with specialist training in older adults produced more effective outcomes. |
| Scogin et al. (2005) | 20 studies selected comparing six evidence-based treatments identified as beneficial. Combination studies and maintenance treatments excluded from review. | The following treatments met criteria for evidence-based treatments: CBT, behavior therapy, cognitive bibliotherapy, problem-solving therapy, brief psychodynamic therapy, and reminiscence therapy. | The most notable omission in this review is interpersonal psychotherapy (IPT). Many of the interventions need additional support as the number of studies are still relatively small, and most report data on "young" older people (age 60–75 years). There is also limited evidence when looking at the combination of psychotherapy and pharmacotherapy. |
| | 25 studies, with 17 comparing psychotherapy with control condition. | Psychological therapies effective with older people. Broad inclusive approach to psychosocial interventions with moderate-to-large effect size (0.72) generated overall. No clear differences between different types of psychological therapies emerge. | The quality of studies included in the review was variable. Definitive conclusions for comparisons between medication and psychotherapy were not possible due to insufficient studies, but no overall differences in outcome were identified. There was some |

| | | indication that combination of medication and psychological therapy was more effective than either alone, but the number of studies are small. |
|---|---|---|
| Pinquart et al. (2006) | 89 studies (62 pharmacological; 32 psychological; and 5 combination treatments). Major depressive disorder in 37 studies; 52 studies with mixed diagnoses. | For CRD, 66% of patients receiving pharmacotherapy and 72% receiving psychotherapy showed above average improvement in outcome. For self-rated depression, 65% of patients receiving pharmacotherapy and 69% receiving psychotherapy showed above average improvement in outcome. | CBT more effective for depression in comparison to other medications and psychotherapies. Indications suggest that minor depression or dysthymia responds better to psychotherapy than pharmacotherapy. Few studies (five) compared treatments with a control condition. There is a paucity of studies conducted with the oldest old (aged 75 years and above). |
| Wilson et al. (2008) | Cochrane Review with 82 randomized controlled trials of psychotherapy for late life depression reviewed; nine studies included in analyses. Overall, 12 studies included in the review (three additional papers examined bibliotherapy). CBT was the main treatment reviewed. | Seven CBT studies and two psychodynamic psychotherapy studies were included in the review and analysis. Five studies compared CBT with a waiting control condition. CBT was significantly more effective than waiting list controls with superior outcome for dropout of CBT compared to waiting list controls. Compared to active treatment controls CBT was superior in outcome. There was mix of group and individualized interventions. | Overall, narrowness of review limits definitive conclusions as very few studies met criteria for inclusion. Although there is a paucity of good quality randomized controlled trials, CBT is an effective treatment with older people in comparison to active treatment controls and waiting list controls. |

(*continued*)

**Table 21.2.**
Continued

| Authors | Level of analyses | Results | Conclusions |
|---------|-------------------|---------|-------------|
| Cuijpers et al. (2009) | 112 studies compared psychotherapy outcome between older adults and adults of working. 20 studies involving older adult participants included in analyses. | The effect sizes of both groups did not differ significantly from each other (older adults: $d = 0.74$; younger adults: $d = 0.67$). Older adult and adult outcome studies report comparable effect sizes of 0.62, thus about 73% of psychotherapy patients improved. The older adult studies were more heavily weighted toward complete analysis rather than ITT. In regression analyses, there was no effect for age of participants; thus, outcome in psychotherapy studies between younger and older people are comparable. | There is no significant difference between psychotherapy outcome for adult versus older adult in the research literature. There are gaps in knowledge in terms of outcome of psychotherapy with older adults including severe depression and depression in the oldest old. "Although more research is needed on representative clinical samples, in older old adults, and in more severe forms of depression, our study shows that currently there is no reason not to apply psychotherapy for depression in old age." (Cuijpers et al., 2009, p. 23). |
| | Examined data for group-based psychotherapy interventions for late life depression. Of 360 papers screened, 296 were rejected, 64 were examined in detail and 6 included in review. All six studies were CBT based. | CBT effective with overall significant mean difference at $p < 0.001$. CBT was more efficacious than waiting list conditions but not in comparison to active treatment control conditions. Gains in CBT were maintained at follow-up although length of this was difficult to determine across studies included in review. Attribution between intervention and controls groups appear equal. | As with the Cochrane Review, reported by Wilson et al. (2008) above, the narrowness of this review limits conclusions about group-based CBT efficacy as very few studies met criteria for inclusion. The quality of studies was not optimal as most of the effect size can be attributed to three of the six studies included in review. A number of the studies included young older adults in their trials. |

*Source:* Laidlaw (2010b), updated and revised.

- CBT appears comparable in efficacy to medication, in terms of both treatment outcome and dropout, but the data are very small as this comparison has rarely been undertaken with older people with depression.
- There are limited data examining the effect of combination treatments (i.e., CBT plus medication vs. medication or CBT alone) in late life depression and this is an area that needs further focus.
- CBT is as efficacious with older adults as with younger adults, but the literature on psychotherapy outcome with the oldest old (aged 75 years and above) is insufficient as many of the earlier outcome studies tended to recruit very "young old" participants and with the change in demographics this data may no longer be appropriate.
- Many of the earlier psychotherapy and CBT outcome studies tended to report data on complete samples rather than use intention to treat (ITT) designs and hence results may be less conservative than would be optimal. Recent CBT outcome studies have reported efficacious outcomes when using ITT designs.

Two recent studies, conducted in UK primary care settings and not yet incorporated into any systematic review, merit further discussion. In the first UK evaluation of individual CBT for late life depression in primary care, Laidlaw et al. (2008) randomly allocated participants to one of the two treatment conditions; CBT alone or treatment as usual (TAU). In the TAU condition, older participants received the range of treatments they would ordinarily receive in primary care, without external influence or pressure. Laidlaw et al. (2008) reported benefits in depression outcome for CBT alone and TAU, at the end of treatment and at 6 months followup. However, after taking account of baseline scores between the groups, a significant difference in outcome emerged, with participants in the CBT treatment group recording significantly lower scores on the Beck Hopelessness Scale (which measures optimism and pessimism) at 6 months after the end of treatment, compared with participants in the TAU group. Moreover, significant differences favoring CBT also emerged on evaluation of the number of participants who remained depressed according to Research Diagnostic Categorization (RDC) status (a way of systematically agreeing symptom level measures of depression) at the end of treatment and at 3 months follow-up. Thus, although the study was small and the levels of depression mild, the findings suggest that CBT by itself (participants who received this treatment did not receive medication) is an effective treatment for late life depression. This study remains one of the very few to compare the efficacy of psychological treatment with treatment usually offered in primary care, and one of the very few that has systematically measured the effectiveness of CBT as a treatment in a nonmedicated treatment group.

A more recent study (Serfaty et al., 2009; Serfaty, Csipke, Haworth, Murad, & King, 2011; Serfaty et al., 2009) provides further compelling evidence for CBT as an efficacious treatment for late-life depression in primary care. This study compared CBT plus TAU, a talking control condition plus TAU, and TAU alone. CBT participants on average achieved better treatment outcomes compared with the talking control condition and TAU, with 33% of those receiving CBT recording a 50% or greater reduction in Beck Depression Inventory (BDI) scores, compared to 23% and 21%, respectively, for those receiving TAU and the talking control treatment. Importantly,

Serfaty et al. (2009) conclude that their results discredit the myth that depressed older people are lonely and simply need a listening ear, as those in the talking control group did less well than those in the CBT treatment group. For readers interested in more detail about the talking control condition, Serfaty et al. (2011) provide a very interesting description.

## Conclusions

People are living longer and in many cases healthier than ever before. Thus, when therapists work with older people, it is important that they educate themselves about this new experience of aging and about the new cohort of older people. There is a positive narrative that can be developed about aging that is different from the frame of reference that may be seen when working with depressed older people.

Evidence suggests older people report high levels of life satisfaction, have better emotional stability, and are able to engage in emotional regulation strategies when compared with younger adults; thus, there is a need for more research into cognitive and affective aspects of aging, so that we can improve the psychological treatments aging clients receive and at the same time educate our clinicians about what to expect when they work with the new generation of older people. To that end if there are reasons to adapt CBT in order to augment its effectiveness with older people, this should be approached from a conceptual basis so that practical and effective changes are made to improve the experience of therapy and its outcome. It is no longer acceptable to suggest banal changes to therapy such as slowing sessions down, encouraging repetition of information, and ensuring that interviews take place in a quiet well-ventilated and well-light room (Laidlaw & McAlpine, 2008).

There is a mature evidence base for the effectiveness of psychological treatments for older people; however, many gaps in knowledge remain and there is a need for future research into the effectiveness of psychological treatment for depression in older people in physical conditions with high levels of psychological distress, such as dementia, poststroke depression, and Parkinson's Disease. Many of these conditions are currently at early stages of evaluation of efficacy in terms of psychological and physical treatments for depression.

Overall, there have been important developments in psychological treatments for depression since the first edition of this chapter was published in the first edition and there remains much to be excited about as the field expands and the reach of CBT extends into areas not considered before such as treating people with dementia and working with the oldest old, as well as developing specific CBT models for older people. Working with the new cohorts of older people promises to be a very stimulating and educative process and it is hoped that many more clinicians will see the benefits that come from serving this very interesting population.

## References

Baltes, P. B., & Smith, J. (2008). The fascination of wisdom: Its nature, ontogeny, and function. *Perspectives on Psychological Science, 3*, 56–64.

Bauer, J. J, & McAdam, D. A. (2004). Personal growth in adults' stories of life transitions. *Journal of Personality, 72*, 573–602.

Beck, A. T., Rush, A. J., Shaw, B. F., & Emery, G. (1979). *Cognitive therapy of depression*. New York: Guildford Press.

Beekman, A. T., Copeland, J. R. M., & Prince, M. J. (1999). Review of community prevalence of depression in later life. *British Journal of Psychiatry, 174*, 307–311.

Blazer, D. G. (2010). Protection from depression. *International Psychogeriatrics, 22*, 171–173.

Boddington, S. (2011). Where are all the older people? Equality of access to IAPT services. *PSIGE Newsletter, 113*, 11–14.

Broomfield, N., Laidlaw, K., Hickabottom, E., Murray, M., Pendrey, R., Whittick, J., & Gillespie, D. (2010). Post-stroke depression: The case for augmented cognitive behaviour therapy. *Clinical Psychology & Psychotherapy: An International Journal of Theory & Practice, 18*(3), 202–218.

Burroughs, H., Lovell, K., Morley, M., Baldwin, R., Burns, A., & Chew-Graham, C. (2006). 'Justifiable depression': How primary care professionals and patients view late life depression? A qualitative study. *Family Practice, 23*, 369–377.

Carstensen, L., Isaacowitz, D., & Charles, S. T. (1999). Taking time seriously: A theory of socioemotional selectivity. *American Psychologist, 54*, 165–181.

Carstensen, L., & Lockenhoff, C. E. (2003). Aging, emotion, and evolution: The bigger picture. *Annals of the New York Academy of Sciences, 1000*, 152–179.

Cuijpers, P., van Straten, A., Smit, F., & Andersson, G. (2009). Is psychotherapy for depression equally effective in younger and in older adults? A meta-regression analysis. *International Psychogeriatrics, 21*, 16–24.

Freund, A. M., & Baltes, P. B. (1998). Selection, optimization, and compensation as strategies of life management: Correlations with subjective indicators of successful aging. *Psychology and Aging, 13*, 531–543.

Grant, R. W., & Casey, D. A. (1995). Adapting cognitive behavioral therapy for the frail elderly. *International Psychogeriatrics, 7*, 561–571.

Gray, A. (2009). The social capital of older people. *Aging and Society, 29*, 5–31.

Gum, A., Arean, P., Hunkeler, E., Tang, L., Katon, W., Hitchcock, P., . . . Unutzer, J. (2006). Depression treatment preferences in older primary care patients. *The Gerontologist, 46*, 14–22.

Hyer, L., Carpenter, B., Bishmann, D., & Wu, H.-S. (2005). Depression in long term care. *Clinical Psychology: Science and Practice, 12*, 280–299.

Jorm, A. F. (2000). Does old age reduce the risk of anxiety and depression? A review of epidemiological studies across the life span. *Psychological Medicine, 30*, 11–12.

Kinsella, K., & Wan, H. (2009). *An Aging World: 2008* (U.S. Census Bureau, P95/09-1). Washington, DC: U.S. Government Printing Office.

Knight, B. G. (2004). *Psychotherapy with older adults* (3rd ed.). Thousand Oaks, CA: Sage Publications, Inc.

Knight, B. G. (2006). Unique aspects of psychotherapy with older adults. In S. Quall & B. G. Knight (Eds.), *Psychotherapy for depression in older adults* (pp. 3–28). Hoboken, NJ: John Wiley & Sons, Inc.

Knight, B. G., Karel, M. J., Hinrichsen, G. A., Qualls, S. H., & Duffy, M. (2009). Pikes Peak model for training in professional geropyschology. *American Psychologist, 64*, 205–214.

Knight, B. G., & Laidlaw, K. (2009). Translational theory: A wisdom-based model for psychological interventions to enhance well-being in later life. In V. Bengston, M. Silverstein, N. M. Putney, & D. Gans (Eds.), *Handbook of theories of aging* (2nd ed., pp. 693–706). New York: Springer.

Laidlaw, K. (2001). An empirical review of cognitive therapy for late life depression: Does research evidence suggest adaptations are necessary for cognitive therapy with older adults? *Clinical Psychology & Psychotherapy, 8,* 1–14

Laidlaw, K. (2010a). Are attitudes to ageing and wisdom enhancement legitimate targets for CBT for late life depression? *Nordic Psychology, 62*(2), 27–42.

Laidlaw, K. (2010b). CBT approaches in older adults: What the research tells us. *Healthcare Counselling and Psychotherapy Journal (HCPJ), 10,* 16–21.

Laidlaw, K., Davidson, K. M., Toner, H. L., Jackson, G., Clark, S., Law, J., Howley, M.,... Cross, S. (2008). A randomised controlled trial of cognitive behaviour therapy versus treatment as usual in the treatment of mild to moderate late life depression. *International Journal of Geriatric Psychiatry, 23,* 843–850.

Laidlaw, K., & McAlpine, S. (2008). Cognitive-behaviour therapy: How is it different with older people? *Journal of Rational Emotive Cognitive Behaviour Therapy, 26*(4), 250–262.

Laidlaw, K., & Pachana, N. A. (2009). Aging, mental health and demographic change: Challenges for psychotherapists. *Professional Psychology: Research and Practice, 40*(6), 601–608.

Laidlaw, K., & Pachana, N. A. (2011). CE Corner: Aging with grace. *Monitor on Psychology, 42,* 66–71.

Laidlaw, K., & Thompson, L. W. (2008). Cognitive behaviour therapy with older people. In K. Laidlaw, & B. G. Knight (Eds.), *Handbook of the assessment and treatment of emotional disorders in later life* (pp. 91–115). Oxford, UK: Oxford University Press.

Laidlaw, K., Thompson, L., & Gallagher-Thompson, D. (2004). Comprehensive conceptualisation of cognitive behaviour therapy for late life depression. *Behavioural & Cognitive Psychotherapy, 32,* 1–8.

Laidlaw, K., Thompson, L. W., Siskin-Dick, L., & Gallagher-Thompson, D. (2003). *Cognitive behavioural therapy with older people.* Chichester, UK: John Wiley & Sons, Ltd.

Levy, B. R. (2009). Stereotype embodiment: A psychosocial approach to aging. *Current Directions in Psychological Science, 18,* 332–336.

MacKenzie, C., Scott, T., Mather, A., & Sareen, J. (2008). Older adults' help-seeking attitudes and treatment beliefs concerning mental health problems. *American Journal of Geriatric Psychiatry, 16,* 1010–1019.

McDougall, F. A., Kvaal, K., Matthews, F. E., Paykel, E., Jones, P. B., Dewey, M. E., & Brayne, C. (2007). Prevalence of depression in older people in England and Wales: The MRC CFA study. *Psychological Medicine, 37,* 1787–1795.

Pinquart, M., Duberstein, P. R., & Lyness, J. M. (2006). Treatments for later-life depressive conditions: A meta-analytic comparison of pharmacotherapy and psychotherapy. *American Journal of Psychiatry, 163,* 1493–1501

Pinquart, M., & Sorensen, S. (2001). How effective are psychotherapeutic and other psychosocial interventions with older adults? A meta-analysis. *Journal of Mental Health and Aging, 7,* 207–243

Qualls, S. H., Segal, D., Norman, S., Neiderehe, G., & Gallagher-Thompson, D. (2002). Psychologists in practice with older adults: Current patterns, sources of training and need for further education. *Professional Psychology: Research and Practice, 33,* 435–442.

Sadavoy, J. (2009). An integrated model for defining the scope of psychogeriatrics: The five Cs. *International Psychogeriatrics, 21,* 805–812.

Sarkisian, C. A., Lee-Henderson, M. H., & Mangione, C. M. (2003). Do depressed older adults who attribute depression to "old age" believe it is important to seek care? *Journal of General Internal Medicine, 18,* 1001–1005.

Satre, D., Knight, B. G., & David, S. (2006). Cognitive behavioural interventions with older adults: Integrating clinical and gerontological research. *Professional Psychology: Research and Practice, 37,* 489–498.

Scogin, F., Welsh, D., Hanson, A., Stump, J., & Coates, A. (2005). Evidence-based psychotherapies for depression in older adults. *Clinical Psychology Science and Practice*, *12*, 222–237.

Seitz, D., Purandare, N., & Conn, D. (2010). Prevalence of psychiatric disorders among older adults in long term care homes: A systematic review. *International Psychogeriatrics*, *22*, 1025–1039.

Serfaty, M., Csipke, E., Haworth, D., Murad, S., & King, M. (2011). A talking control for use in evaluating the effectiveness of cognitive-behavioral therapy. *Behaviour Research and Therapy*, *49*, 433–440.

Serfaty, M., Haworth, D., Blanchard, M., Buszewicz, M., Murad, S., & King, M. (2009). Clinical effectiveness of individual cognitive behavioural therapy for depressed older people in primary care. *Archives of General Psychiatry*, *66*, 1332–1340.

Thakat, M., & Blazer, D. G. (2008). Depression in long term care. *Journal of the American Medical Directors*, *9*, 82–87.

UN (United Nations), Department of Economic and Social Affairs, Population Division. (2011). *World population prospects: The 2010 revision, Volume II: Demographic profiles* (ST/ESA/SER.A/317) New York: United Nations.

Unutzer, J., Katon, W., Callahan, C., Williams, J., Hunkeler, H., Harpole, L., . . . Oishi, S. (2003). Depression treatment in a sample of 1,801 depressed older adults in primary care. *Journal of the American Geriatrics Society*, *51*, 505–514.

Unutzer, J., Katon, W., Sullivan, M., & Miranda, J. (1999). Treating depressed older adults in primary care: Narrowing the gap between efficacy and effectiveness. *Milbank Quarterly*, *77*, 225–256.

Vink, D., Aartsen, M. J., & Schoevers, R. A. (2008). Risk factors for anxiety and depression in the elderly: A review. *Journal of Affective Disorders*, *106*, 27–44.

Wilkins, V., Kiosses, D., & Ravdin, L. D. (2010). Late-life depression with comorbid cognitive impairment and disability: Nonpharmacological interventions. *Clinical Interventions in Aging*, *5*, 323–331.

Wilson, K., Mottram, P., & Vassilas, C. (2008) Psychotherapeutic treatments for older depressed people. *Cochrane Database of Systematic Reviews 1* (Art. No.: CD004853). doi:10.1002/14651858.CD0044853.pub2

# 22

# Summary and New Directions

## Mick Power
### University of Edinburgh, UK

## Introduction

The chapters in this book provide a testament to the vibrant state of development in research and in clinical practice in the mood disorders. The juxtaposition of the unipolar and bipolar disorders together provides an opportunity to consider these disorders in a more unified and integrative fashion than is often the case. The view that psychotic phenomena, whether in depression or in other disorders such as schizophrenia, are something qualitatively different from "everyday experience" can reasonably be questioned in the case of the mood disorders; however controversial, this questioning may appear for schizophrenia (e.g., Bentall, 2003). Medicine has advanced through the recognition that the supposed "devils" and "miasmas" of earlier times are in fact a number of disease entities and acute illnesses; this same approach has also benefited psychiatry through, for example, the identification of the organic process in tertiary syphilis, or the identification of the brain's role in the what was earlier thought to be the "noble" disease of epilepsy. In parallel, developments in cell and molecular biology have begun to offer up the actual mechanisms by which our genes provide a starting point for the processes of development. Fractional differences in starting points can manifest themselves in major differences in outcome, as chaos theory tells us (see Chapter 10); thus, even in twins with the same genotype and with one twin affected by a bipolar disorder, there are significant differences in whether or not the second twin will go on to develop a bipolar disorder. The issue of the high genetic contribution to bipolar disorders has for too long led to the use of simplistic approaches to bipolar disorders, when it may be more useful to view the unipolar–bipolar distinction as an heuristic one, but in which there is no clear demarcation between different subtypes of depression. As Cavanagh (see Chapter 11) quotes memorably in his chapter, should we consider depression more like a citrus fruit that divides naturally along certain segments, or like an apple that can be divided along any point or direction? One of the major starting points for mood disorders must be still the question of classification and diagnosis; therefore, pointers in this direction will be considered first. We will then review some of the other key developments including epidemiology, theoretical models, and treatment issues, together with one or two additional points before drawing to a conclusion.

*The Wiley-Blackwell Handbook of Mood Disorders*, Second Edition. Edited by Mick Power.
© 2013 John Wiley & Sons, Ltd. Published 2013 by John Wiley & Sons, Ltd.

# Diagnosis

It is of course very easy and very tempting to take pot shots at classification and diagnosis in psychiatry. From a skeptical viewpoint, it appears to the outside that every few years a bunch of experts sit around and "horse-trade" their favorite, often self-promoting diagnoses. The history of the classification and diagnosis of depression has witnessed, for example, a varying set of categories such as neurotic–endogenous, reactive–endogenous, and neurotic–psychotic. As Bebbington (Chapter 1) summarizes, these and other distinctions appear to reflect a dimension of severity of depression, in which rarer symptoms (e.g., delusions of guilt) only appear in the most extreme variants. The current proposed changes to DSM-V have already caused controversy even before they are finalized with, for example, the resignation of several members of the Personality Disorders committee (Emmelkamp & Power, 2012). In contrast, the proposed changes for the mood disorders (see www.dsm5.org) consist of minor tweaking to the key established distinction between unipolar disorder (labeled as Major Depressive Disorder) and bipolar disorder, with a continuation of the distinction between Bipolar I (which includes a manic episode) and Bipolar II (which includes a hypomanic episode).

The problem for classification and diagnosis in depression in systems such as DSM and ICD, indeed for all psychological disorders, is that there is no *theoretical* basis for the systems in use. Indeed, the classifications such as DSM are deliberately aimed to be atheoretical, which, in practice means that a hodgepodge of bits of different theories get incorporated. Imagine that Mendeleev had approached the Periodic Table for the chemical elements in the same way; well, there are clearly substances that are "shiny silver ones" (e.g., aluminum, silver, iron), while there is another group that are "shiny golden ones" (e.g., copper, gold). Another distinction could be made between "soft, malleable" substances that explode (e.g., potassium, sodium, phosphorus) versus "hard, non-explosive" substances (e.g., zinc, tin, silicon). These distinctions would have some value, at least for a while, but because they are not theoretically based, they will be inconsistent, contradictory, and change with fashion, as can be witnessed with the consensus committee meetings for DSM. Except, that is, when the committee members fall out with each other and cannot reach a consensus, as has just happened with the Personality Disorders committee, as noted above.

So what might be the answer for classification and diagnosis in depression? The first step, and one that many chapters in this handbook argue explicitly for, is that there needs to be a dimensional approach, in which the severity of the disorder ranges from minimal to maximal severity. But how should this dimension be conceptualized? Indeed, should there be only one dimension considered? These two questions are significant, first, because we need to know whether the opposite to "very depressed" on the severity dimension is "not depressed" or whether it is the bipolar opposite of depression "very happy." The traditional approach to the manic state in bipolar disorders might suggest this latter option; namely, that the "opposite" state to depression is a state of elation. However, this traditional account fails to explain why recent empirical studies of the manic and hypomanic states show that elation may not be the most highly characteristic aspect, but that "mixed states" and mood lability may be more accurate conceptualizations (Cassidy, Forest, Murry, & Carroll, 1998; Cavanagh, Schwannauer, Power, & Goodwin, 2009). This issue certainly demands a broader approach to the assessment of depression than the current reliance on self-report and on clinical interviews, as Peck has cogently argued (see Chapter 17).

The second question asks if there is more than one dimension what should these other dimensions be? A starting point may be two possible dimensions, both capturing severity, but one relating to genetic/biological factors and one relating to psychological/social factors. Such factors are of course etiological rather than merely symptom-based, and are generally avoided in DSM type classification systems with the one exception of Post-Traumatic Stress Disorder, in which the stressor is both etiological and nosological. The dimensions have the advantage that they provide a dimensional classification system within which both the unipolar and bipolar disorders can be placed according to their putative etiology, while acknowledging that the majority of depressions have a contribution from both. Such an approach would also allow the incorporation of some of the recent problems highlighted with bipolar disorders, in which the initial diagnosis is almost always wrong if the first episode is a depressed one, given that the diagnostician can only really be certain after further episodes and whether or not these are manic/hypomanic ones. Recently, there have been suggestions that very short periods of "highs" might be predictive of later manic episodes, and that short "highs" in reaction to antidepressant treatment might be similarly indicative (e.g., Perugi et al., 1997), a possibility that is being reviewed for DSM-5.

A two-dimensional approach might provide a starting point for the nosology of depression but it still may not go far enough in overcoming the consensus-driven versus theory-driven approaches. Even the proposal mentioned above that all depressions should be treated as bipolar until proven otherwise, and that there may be further bipolar 1, 2, 3, 4, etc., subtypes may simply amount to further atheoretical descriptive game-playing, however useful the distinctions might be. A more radical approach to depression and its classification might be to get a theory! To return to the periodic table, by analogy the best theory cannot simply be a theory of just the alkaline metals but has to place depression in the context of other psychological disorders, especially given the high rates of comorbidity with other disorders such as anxiety (see Chapter 1). There can be no accusations of modesty for the following speculations, but they are provided as an illustration of how one might go about developing a theoretically based classification rather than being presented as *the* correct one.

The basic emotions approach has a long and distinguished history that includes Descartes and Darwin, and recent exponents such as Ekman, Plutchik, Izzard, and Tomkins. The approach was extended by Oatley and Johnson-Laird (1987) in their functional account of emotion, which assumed that a set of five basic emotions could be used to derive all other more complex emotions. Power and Dalgleish (1997, 2008) further extended this proposal and argued that emotional disorders might also be explainable in such a system with certain additional theoretical assumptions such as the idea of "coupling" or "blending" of emotions (cf. Plutchik, 1980). The preliminary conceptual analysis suggested that from a basic emotions point of view many emotional disorders could be viewed as the coupling of two or more basic emotions, and that many supposedly "unitary" disorders like obsessional compulsive disorders and phobias might be more appropriately derived from different basic emotions. In relation to depression, there are a number of possible combinations of coupled emotions. If sadness is taken as the commonest emotion in depression, then when combined with disgust, especially in the form of self-disgust (i.e., as self-loathing, shame, guilt, which are complex emotions derived from the basic emotion of disgust; see Power & Dalgleish, 2008; Power & Tarsia, 2007), the coupling provides for one subtype of depression together with some inhibition of happiness. However, other combinations are also possible; for example, anxious depression could occur from the coupling of sadness and anxiety, perhaps with some disgust plus some happiness inhibition. Agitated or irritable depression is likely to be a coupling of sadness with anger and again some increased disgust and inhibited happiness. When happiness is increased rather than inhibited, then the mixed states occur, especially in the dysphoric mania category where both increased happiness and increased anxiety occur. Combinations such as sadness and anger, but without increased disgust are more likely to be seen in examples of extreme or "pathological grief," for example, following sudden and unexpected loss of a loved one (see Power, 1999).

Although we are yet to obtain solid and replicated data for the full range of this basic emotions analysis of the emotional disorders, a recent study (Power & Tarsia, 2007) compared basic emotion profiles across groups of normal controls, depressed, anxious, and mixed anxiety depression (not, however, the subclinical category appendixed in DSM-IV, but rather a group of patients who met DSM criteria for both major depression and one of the anxiety disorders such as GAD or phobia and that is being considered in DSM-V). The basic emotion profiles, obtained using the Basic Emotions Scale (Power, 2006) showed no elevation of anger, but that the sadness and the disgust levels were significantly higher in the depressed and the mixed groups than in the anxiety and control groups. The anxiety levels were elevated in all of the clinical groups in comparison to the controls, but the clinical groups did not differ significantly from each other. Whether this reflects the fact that the patients were primarily an outpatient group and will be replicated in larger, more extensive studies remains to be seen. Finally, the happiness levels were highest in the control, intermediate in the anxious, and lowest in the mixed and depressed groups. The study also showed that *shame* was more important than *guilt* as a key emotion in depression. In sum, the Basic Emotions Scale showed that different profiles of basic emotions are found across different emotional disorders, though whether or not such profiles could ever provide a theoretical basis for the classification and diagnosis of the emotional disorders remains to be seen.

We would also note that the key symptoms of depression can be usefully grouped into four categories, that is, cognitive, emotional, somatic, and interpersonal, while also noting that all self-report and clinical interview measures of depression have unbalanced numbers of items from each of these categories, with the interpersonal category being the poorest represented (Cheung & Power, 2012). We have recently developed a New Multidimensional Depression Scale with balanced numbers of items from each category (Cheung & Power, 2012), and are currently collecting further clinical data in order to test the psychometric properties of the scale.

# Epidemiology

The epidemiology of depression remains a mystery, but then how could it be otherwise without a sound theoretically based diagnostic and classification system. The situation is akin to trying to study astronomy with nothing but a dirty milk bottle; nevertheless, despite the considerable inadequacies in the measuring tools, there are still some surprises in the epidemiology that no theory of depression has yet been able to cope with. The lifespan and gender data on depression (see Chapters 1, 5, and 19) seem to show that the approximate 2:1 ratio of women to men for depression appears sometime around puberty and then disappears sometime in later life; children show an approximately equal rate, and this is also true in older adults. In addition, there are clearly cultural effects in that cultures in which women have been traditionally devalued show higher rates of depression in women, but there are also generational cohort effects in that some Western cultures seem to be showing an increase in depression and suicide rates in young men (Chapter 18). The good news for depression research is that no simplistic model can account for the epidemiological data; the bad news is that there is as yet no complex model that can account for it either.

The present and the immediate future for epidemiology are showing increased use of genetic epidemiology methods for studying both unipolar and bipolar depressions through the use of large-scale twin studies (e.g., Kendler & Prescott, 1999) and large-scale family studies that can look at, for example, obligate carriers (e.g., Chapter 12). A study by Sullivan, Neale, and Kendler (2002) found that for unipolar depression there was 37% heritability, no significant shared environment effects, but only individual-specific environmental factors (e.g., specific individual life events or traumas) in their analysis of the presence and absence of depression in a large family study. These genetic epidemiology studies show great promise and can begin to disentangle genetic, gender, age, and cultural effects in their contribution to both unipolar and bipolar disorders in the coming decades. However, large-scale prospective high-risk studies, in which adolescents and young adults who are at increased risk because of affected family members and other factors, also need to be carried out in order to examine exactly how genetic and psychosocial factors interact to produce or protect the individual from depression.

# Theoretical Models

Theories of depression are like other theories that span the biopsychological domain in that either they are of the "mindless brain" variety and focus solely on putative biochemical or brain circuit mechanisms, or they are of the "brainless mind" variety and focus solely on fashionable psychological models that might be impossible to implement in the brain. Western culture does, of course, have a long philosophical tradition that has encouraged this mind–brain dualism, so one should not be harder on theories of depression than on theories in other areas. Many of the chapters in this book have fallen, not surprisingly, into one or other of these categories, but it is hoped that at least some of the chapters have begun to outline what these integrative mind–brain theories might look at in the area of depression and that they have begun to "mind the gap" (e.g., Chapters 4 and 10).

Before a consideration of these theories, however, perhaps we should first point to the means by which advances can be made in such integrated mind–brain theories. That is, what methods in themselves span this false divide, in order to provide progress in our knowledge base for depression? One of these methods was discussed in the last section through the use of genetic epidemiology by means of which some approximations to the genetic and nongenetic contributions can begin to be sketched. Such methods can help to identify candidate genes, and from there an exploration of their biological mechanisms can begin. However, there are also many other methods that span this divide and by means of which empirical progress can be made. One such is that of neuroimaging, which is still in its early days in relation to depression (see Chapters 2 and 12). I have to confess to having been one of the skeptics initially about imaging approaches such as fMRI, because they seemed to be simply the "new phrenology" (though maybe in fact we have been too harsh in our long dismissal of phrenology!). Anyway, methods such as fMRI provide the possibility of a method that immediately integrates the biological and the psychological; carefully designed "subtraction methodologies" can lead to important advances of the underlying substrate and the brain circuits involved in those particular psychological processes. However, although the "subtraction methodology" can provide a very elegant approach, it does have its own pitfalls that are not yet understood. One of the key concerns is the subtraction methodology itself; it amounts to the fundamental question of does "3 minus 2" equal the same as "2 minus 1" with this approach. In fact, the original exponent of the subtraction methodology approach in the nineteenth century, the Danish physiologist F. C. Donders, used the subtraction approach to study reaction times to simple and complex stimuli, the argument being that additional processes were involved, for example, if there were greater numbers of choices between stimuli. Although the method was both elegant and influential, later approaches in cognitive psychology demonstrated that Donders' principles broke down under certain important conditions (e.g., see Neisser, 1967). To give a concrete example for fMRI, let us say that a subtraction study is set up that shows neutral faces and faces showing a specific emotion such as disgust to groups of depressed and control subjects. The argument then is that any remaining differences reflect the unique status of the processing of disgust in depression. But the question of "does $3 - 2 = 2 - 1$?" then applies; for example, if the control group were anxious patients rather than controls would the same findings occur? Or if only female faces were used? Or if the faces were all familiar ones for the individual? Or if the stimuli were short video clips rather than photographs? So even an example as apparently straightforward as the processing of facial stimuli proves to be extremely complex once it is argued that the "equivalent" subtraction has to be achieved in several different ways before some confidence can be gained in the conclusions. Kagan (2012) has also argued that such neuroimaging studies also fail to take account of possible contextual effects on cognitive processing, and provides numerous examples of such contextual effects and how they might impact on fMRI findings.

A further point that can be made briefly concerns the types of neuropsychological tests that can be used in studies such as fMRI, psychological priming, genetic epidemiology, and so on. The tradition in cognitive psychology, and therefore in the development of neuropsychological and related tests, has been to use *emotionally neutral* stimuli; thus, the question "What is the capital of Albania?" is an emotionally neutral knowledge question for most people, in contrast to "When did your father stop beating you?" which is emotionally valenced for everyone. In between these two extremes, there needs to be the development of emotionally valenced tasks that are the equivalent of emotionally neutral tasks currently in use, especially when these can be linked to fMRI type studies. For example, in relation to depression (and other emotional disorders), there are key questions of the role of the frontal cortex in the executive control of emotion and emotion processing that have only begun to be asked. However, in order to study emotional disorders, executive function tasks need to be modified so that they have emotionally valenced versions (see Power, Dalgleish, Claudio, Tata, & Kentish, 2000).

Further developments will also be made in our understanding of the evolutionary role of depression (see Chapter 10), and in our understanding of the animal models that may offer possible testing of human models. The area of anxiety research has clearly benefited from the animal work by LeDoux (1996), which has offered considerable support for multi-level approaches and should provide an impetus for such developments in the area of depression (Power & Dalgleish, 2008). Classic experimental psychology methods such as those based on priming and subliminal activation methods of nonconscious processes should also continue to provide further data for a richer theorizing about depression (e.g., see Chapter 3), but they may now be of greatest use when they are tied into fMRI and other electrophysiological methods so that bridges continue to be made across the mind–brain gap. They will also be of most value when they explore emotionally valenced stimuli rather than the emotionally neutral stimuli that have been used traditionally in experimental psychology. Fast-acting and other nonconscious brain mechanisms have evolved to process "emotional meaning" or the "emotional significance" of events, as noted above in the comments on developing emotionally significant neuropsychological tests.

Before finishing this section, some comments must also be made specifically about theoretical developments in the bipolar disorders. The study of bipolar disorders has suddenly opened up for psychological and social approaches, having long been ignored and left to the medico-biological approach (Power, 2005). Even here, there have been few significant advances in theory and the approach has focused primarily on pharmacotherapy (see Chapters 6 and 12). The promise of the psychological and the social approaches have been raised by Wright (Chapter 13) and by Parikh and Kennedy (Chapter 14). Although the primary focus of these latter two chapters was on treatment (see also next section), the fact that the CBT, IPT, and self-management approaches (Chapters 15 and 16) have an impact on the course of bipolar disorders is in itself of theoretical importance. Wright has highlighted both the role of specific types of dysfunctional beliefs that may be specific to bipolar disorders and has considered an integration of these CBT-based concepts into a conditioning-based model of approach-avoidance. Schwannauer (Chapter 15) and Wright (Chapter 13) have extended proposals made earlier by Goodwin and Jamison (1990) that individuals with bipolar disorders may be especially sensitive to disruption of psychosocial rhythms, a problem that many significant life events (e.g., job loss, birth of a child, retirement) and even more minor events (e.g., vacations, weekends, jet-lag) possess.

## Treatment

The development and adaptation of treatment approaches for both unipolar and bipolar disorders continues to gather pace. In the area of unipolar disorders there are now well-established pharmacotherapeutic treatments that continue to be added to with new generations of antidepressants (see Chapter 6). Psychological treatments such as Cognitive Behavior Therapy and Interpersonal Psychotherapy have been shown to be efficacious in randomized control trials in adults (see Chapters 7 and 8). The main challenge now for psychosocial approaches, and one that Markowitz (Chapter 8) details most clearly, is how these effective psychosocial treatments can be adapted for use with different populations such as adolescents (see Chapter 5), older adults (see Chapter 21), and specific disorder groups such as suicidal patients (see Chapter 18) and medical comorbidity groups (see Chapter 20).

Perhaps in some ways the most exciting area for the development of psychosocial treatments is now occurring in the neglected area of the bipolar disorders. Kay Jamison's writings, both in her own autobiography (Jamison, 1995) and in her accounts of other famous sufferers (Jamison, 1993), have been at the forefront of drawing both lay and scientific attention to the bipolar disorders. The development of psychological treatments is in large part a consequence of her major contributions. In Chapter 15, Schwannauer outlined the recent development of CBT approaches to bipolar disorders, in particular, the work of Newman, Leahy, Beck, Reilly-Harrington, and Gyulai (2001) and Lam, Jones, Hayward, and Bright (1999). Both the CBT and the IPT adaptations have highlighted specific aspects of the disorder to focus on. For the CBT adaptation, the work on early warning signs that has proven fruitful in CBT work with schizophrenia (e.g., Birchwood, 2000) provides an important new clinical tool. When such early warning signs are identifiable, it allows the possibility for sufferers and carers of alternative management strategies (see Chapter 16). The problem arises when such early warning signs do not occur, such as when there is a rapid transition into the disordered state. Perhaps in these cases the adapted IPT approach, IPSRT, with its focus on disrupted circadian rhythms, may provide an additional clinical strategy. However, because these CBT and IPT approaches are at an early stage of development, they are currently being compared against each other, and against pharmacotherapy, in a substantial NIMH-funded RCT. Ultimately though, one suspects that the best psychosocial approaches to the management of these difficult and tragic disorders will require combined treatments that include pharmacotherapy, CBT, IPT, and family approaches (e.g., Miklowitz & Goldstein, 1997) as appropriate (see Chapter 14).

## Conclusions

This crystal-ball gazing into the future of depression has occurred with the help of a cast of leading experts in all of the relevant areas. There is no aspect of depression where any sitting back and resting on laurels can yet be done, but both the science and the practice in this area should see considerable developments in the coming decades. It is hoped that the juxtaposition of the unipolar and bipolar disorders together will provide the possibility of cross-fertilization in the areas of classification and diagnosis, theory, research, and clinical practice. Too often these disorders are considered separately, or the focus on bipolar disorders takes an overly psychosis-based viewpoint. Both unipolar and bipolar disorders can, at the extremes, include psychotic aspects such as the loss of contact with reality and the presence of delusions and hallucinations. The view taken here is that these phenomena can occur at the extremes of dysregulated emotion systems; similar examples from other areas include the extremes of love seen in De Clerambault syndrome, delusional beliefs about contamination or danger to self and others seen in extreme OCD cases, delusional beliefs about body shape and size seen in anorexia, and so on (Power, 2000). In all areas of psychopathology there are cases at the extremes in which delusion and reality become confused. Emotions have evolved to provide heuristic shortcuts under circumstances of great significance to the individual and to the group, but evolutionary systems that provide advantage can also provide disadvantage. The emotional disorders, of which the unipolar and bipolar disorders are one set of examples, show how both the advantages and disadvantages can be apparent even in the same individual. Throughout history, these disorders have made remarkable contributions through remarkable individuals. To quote from one such individual, Winston Churchill, "We are all worms. But I do believe that I am a glow-worm." Churchill's life was a testament to both the tragedy and the greatness that depression can bring. For the great majority of sufferers and carers, however, the experience of these disorders feels only to be an experience of tragedy; the work presented in this volume will, it is hoped, provide some pointers as to how such tragedy can be turned into everyday misery, and even offer the occasional experience of genuine success.

# References

Bentall, R. P. (2003). *Madness explained: Psychosis and human nature*. London: Allen Lane.

Birchwood, M. (2000). The critical period for early intervention. In M. Birchwood, D. Fowler, & C. Jackson (Eds.), *Early intervention in psychosis: A guide to concepts, evidence and interventions* (pp. 28–63). Chichester, UK: John Wiley & Sons.

Cassidy, F., Forest, K., Murry, E., & Carroll, B. J. (1998). A factor analysis of the signs and symptoms of mania. *Archives of General Psychiatry, 55*, 27–32.

Cavanagh, J., Schwannauer, M., Power, M. J., & Goodwin, G. M. (2009). A novel scale for measuring mixed states in bipolar disorder. *Clinical Psychology and Psychotherapy, 16*, 497–509.

Cheung, H. N., & Power, M. J. (2012). The development of a new multidimensional depression assessment scale: Preliminary results. *Clinical Psychology and Psychotherapy, 19*, 170–178.

Emmelkamp, P. M. G., & Power, M. J. (2012). DSM-5 personality disorders: Stop before it is too late. *Clinical Psychology and Psychotherapy, 19*, 363.

Goodwin, F. K., & Jamison, K. R. (1990). *Manic-depressive illness*. New York: Oxford University Press.

Jamison, K. R. (1993). *Touched with fire: Manic-depressive illness and the artistic temperament.* New York: Free Press.

Jamison, K. R. (1995). *An unquiet mind: A memoir of moods and madness.* New York: Knopf.

Kagan, J. (2012). *Psychology's ghosts: The crisis in the profession and the way back.* New Haven, CT: Yale University Press.

Kendler, K. S., & Prescott, C. A. (1999). A population-based twin study of lifetime major depression in men and women. *Archives of General Psychiatry, 56*, 39–44.

Lam, D. H., Jones, S. H., Hayward, P., & Bright, J. A. (1999). *Cognitive therapy for bipolar disorder: A therapist's guide to concepts, methods and practice.* Chichester, UK: John Wiley & Sons.

LeDoux, J. E. (1996). *The emotional brain: The mysterious underpinnings of emotional life.* New York: Simon & Schuster.

Miklowitz, D., & Goldstein, M. J. (1997). *Bipolar disorder: A family-focused treatment approach.* New York: Guilford Press.

Neisser, U. (1967). *Cognitive psychology.* New York: Appleton-Century-Crofts.

Newman, C. F., Leahy, R. L., Beck, A. T., Reilly-Harrington, N. A., & Gyulai, L. (2001). *Bipolar disorder: A cognitive therapy approach.* Washington, DC: American Psychological Association.

Oatley, K., & Johnson-Laird, P. N. (1987). Towards a cognitive theory of emotions. *Cognition and Emotion, 1*, 29–50.

Perugi, G., Akiskal, H. S., Micheli, C., Musetti, L., Paiano, A., Quilici, C., . . . Cassano, G. B. (1997). Clinical subtypes of bipolar mixed states: Validating a broader European definition in 143 cases. *Journal of Affective Disorders, 43*, 169–180.

Plutchik, R. (1980). *Emotion: A psychoevolutionary synthesis.* New York: Harper & Row.

Power, M. J. (1999). Sadness and its disorders. In T. Dalgleish & M. J. Power (Eds.), *Handbook of cognition and emotion* (pp. 497–520). Chichester, UK: John Wiley & Sons.

Power, M. J. (2005). Psychological approaches to bipolar disorders: A theoretical critique. *Clinical Psychology Review, 25*, 1101–1122.

Power, M. J. (2006). The structure of emotion: An empirical comparison of six models. *Cognition and Emotion, 20*, 694–713.

Power, M. J., & Dalgleish, T. (1997). *Cognition and emotion: From order to disorder.* Hove, UK: Psychology Press.

Power, M. J., & Dalgleish, T. (2008). *Cognition and emotion: From order to disorder* (2nd ed.). Hove, UK: Erlbaum.

Power, M. J., Dalgleish, T., Claudio, V., Tata, P., & Kentish, J. (2000). The directed forgetting task: Application to emotionally valent material. *Journal of Affective Disorders, 57*, 147–157.

Power, M. J., & Tarsia, M. (2007). Basic and complex emotions in depression and anxiety. *Clinical Psychology and Psychotherapy, 14*, 19–31.

Sullivan, P. F., Neale, M. C., & Kendler, K. S. (2002). Genetic epidemiology of major depression: Review and meta-analysis. *American Journal of Psychiatry, 157*, 1552–1562.

# Author Index

Aartsen, M.J., 465
Abbott, D.H., 267
Abdollahi, M., 148
Abdul Kadir, N., 98
Abela, J.R., 122, 438, 441
Abe, M., 330
Aber, J.L., 122
Abildgaard, W., 402
Ablon, J.S., 187
Abram, D., 249
Abramson, L.Y., 73, 74, 79, 122, 123, 176, 331
Abwender, D.A., 121
Acitelli, L.K., 218, 223
Adair, C., 434
Adams, M., 375, 388
Addis, M.E., 266, 335
Adler, C.M., 318, 319
Adler, G., 25
Adler, Z., 90, 252
Agras, W.S., 206
Agren, H., 48
Agustin, C., 401
Ahadi, S., 110
Ahnberg, J.L., 402
Ahnert, L., 113
Ahuvia, A., 439
Ainsworth, M.D.S., 93, 110, 111
Aitken, R.C.B., 406
Aizenstein, H.J., 59
Akiskal, H.S., 230, 232, 235, 276, 295, 296, 297, 298, 299, 305
Akiskal, K., 296
Alatiq, Y., 326
Albani, F., 151
Albrecht, S., 452
Albus, K.E., 94

Alda, M., 318, 416
Alexeeenko, L., 144
Alexiou, T., 23
Alexopoulos, G.S., 50, 153, 154, 419
Alford, B.A., 72
Allan, C.L., 156, 157, 158
Allan, S., 256, 257, 258, 260, 270
Allen, J.G., 100, 247
Allen, J.P., 112
Allen, L., 122
Allen, M.H., 151
Allen, N.B., 240, 254
Allmon, D., 424
Alloy, L.B., 73, 74, 122, 123, 176, 326, 331, 349, 362, 363
Almeida, D.M., 218
Aloe, L., 315
Alonso, J., 15
Alsen, M., 420
Alter, D.A., 456
Altshuler, L.L., 44, 150
Alwin, J., 113
Amico, F., 50
Amsterdam, J.D., 53
Anacker, C., 42, 54
Anand, A., 316
Anda, R.F., 26
Anderman, E.M., 121
Anderson, A.K, 52
Anderson, I., 49
Anderson, J.C., 25, 26
Anderson, L.M., 125
Anderson, R.J., 453, 455
Andersson, G., 155, 186, 475
Andrade, L.A., 251
Andrade, P., 158, 159

# Subject Index

acceptance and commitment therapy (ACT), 185
acetylcholine, 48
actigraphy, 406–7
activities Schedule, 179–80
adenosine monophosphate (AMP) 54
adolescence, 94, 96, 107, 115, 119–21, 154, 186, 201–2, 376
age effects, 16, 17–18, 19–20
age stereotypes, 469
agitation, 406
agomelatine, 147
Alzheimer's disease, 455–6
amygdala, 49, 58
anger, 179, 250, 259, 488
anhedonia, 174, 267
anorexia nervosa, 206
anticonvulsants, 150, 151, 152
antidepressants, 44, 48, 50, 52, 53, 54, 143, 147, 150, 152, 200
antiglucocorticoids, 146
antipsychotics, 150, 152
anxiety, 262, 466, 487
appetitive system, 174
arousal, 109, 110
assessment, 177–9
attachment, 93–6, 99, 109–10, 111–12, 117, 194, 255, 268
attachment style interview (ASI), 94
attention deficit hyperactivity disorder (ADHD), 301
attractiveness, 257
attributional style, 122–3
atypical depression, 56–7
augmentation, 44, 143–4, 146, 147, 154
autobiographical memory, 372

automatic processes, 182
automatic thoughts, 70
automatic thoughts questionnaire (ATQ), 72
autonomy, 175, 177
avoidance, 387

*Ba*, 173
basic emotions, 185–186, 487–8
beck depression inventory (BDI), 178, 186, 234, 401–2
beck hopelessness scale (BHS), 420
behavioral activation therapy, 266, 272
behavioural activation system (BAS), 328, 331–3, 363, 365
behavioural assessment, 399, 406–8
behavioural models, 174, 217, 249, 328
behaviourism, 70
benzodiazepines, 151
bereavement, 79, 196
bias, 176–7, 240–41, 246, 370
biological markers, 302
biological model, 433–5
biological vulnerability, 433
biopsychosocial approach, 87, 235–6, 252–3, 269, 384, 435
bipolar disorders, 4, 149–50, 174, 206, 257, 291, 299–300, 343–4, 399, 485, 489, 491–2
Bipolar Disorders Association, 389
bipolar spectrum, 232–3, 294, 295–6
booster sessions, 184
brain-derived neurotrophic factor (BDNF), 40, 50, 156, 315
brief psychiatric rating scale (BPRS), 404
brief symptom inventory (BSI), 404
bulimia, 206